Obsolete Objects in the Literary Imagination

FRANCESCO ORLANDO

Obsolete Objects in the Literary Imagination

RUINS, RELICS, RARITIES, RUBBISH,
UNINHABITED PLACES, AND
HIDDEN TREASURES

*Translated from the Italian by Gabriel Pihas and
Daniel Seidel, with the collaboration of
Alessandra Grego*

Foreword by David Quint

*Yale University Press
New Haven &
London*

Published with assistance from the Louis Stern Memorial Fund.

Set in Sabon type by Keystone Typesetting, Inc. Printed in the United States of America.

Library of Congress Cataloging-in-Publication Data
Orlando, Francesco, 1934–
[Oggetti desueti nelle immagini della letteratura. English]
Obsolete objects in the literary imagination : ruins, relics, rarities, rubbish, uninhabited places, and hidden treasures / Francesco Orlando ; translated from the Italian by Gabriel Pihas and Daniel Seidel, with the collaboration of Alessandra Grego ; foreword by David Quint.
p. cm.
Includes bibliographical references and indexes.
ISBN-13: 978-0-300-10808-8 (alk. paper)
ISBN-10: 0-300-10808-7 (alk. paper)
1. Exoticism in literature. 2. Picturesque, The, in literature. 3. Ruins in literature. 4. Literature, Modern — History and criticism. I. Title.
PN56.E7807513 2006
809′.9332 — dc22
2005027649

A catalogue record for this book is available from the British Library.

The paper in this book meets the guidelines for permanence and durability of the Committee on Production Guidelines for Book Longevity of the Council on Library Resources.

10 9 8 7 6 5 4 3 2 1

Originally published in Italian as *Gli oggetti desueti nelle immagini della letteratura: Rovine, reliquie, rarità, robaccia, luoghi inabitati e tesori nascosti,* © 1993 and 1994 Giulio Einaudi editore s.p.a., Turin. This translation is based on the revised and expanded 1994 edition.

In memory of my parents and their home

Plusieurs vérités séparées, dès qu'elles sont en assez grand nombre, offrent si vivement à l'esprit leurs rapports et leur mutuelle dépendance, qu'il semble qu'après avoir été détachées par une espèce de violence les unes d'avec les autres, elles cherchent naturellement à se réunir.
— Fontenelle, *Préface sur l'utilité des mathématiques*

Contents

Foreword

From the age of nineteen to twenty-three, Francesco Orlando was the literary disciple in Palermo of Giuseppe Tomasi di Lampedusa, who offered him informal courses on English and French writers. To Lampedusa's dictation, Orlando produced the typescript of the bulk of *Il Gattopardo*, and was thus present at the birth of the great novel. He has written a moving, two-part memoir of this formative, if also difficult relationship, as well as an indispensable critical study of Lampedusa's masterpiece: *Ricordo di Lampedusa seguito da Da distanze diverse* (1996); *L'intimità e la storia: Lettura del "Gattopardo"* (1998). In a famous exchange that refers back to the novel itself, Prince Fabrizio, the Leopard of the title, tells the Piedmontese Baron de Chevalley about the artistic and intellectual belatedness of his native Sicily: "novelties attract us only when they are dead, incapable of arousing vital currents." The dictum might already suggest the subject of *Obsolete Objects in the Literary Imagination* (*Gli oggetti desueti nelle immagini della letteratura*), and this Sicily might stand for Literature itself in Orlando's argument: the repository of the outmoded and the historically superseded. But, in fact, Orlando's study reveals, as if refuting Lampedusa's formulation, the uncanny affective afterlife that literature affords to things past.

Now Professor of French Literature at the University of Pisa, Francesco Orlando is one of the world's leading literary theorists and a scholar-critic whose grasp of literary history recalls such masters as Erich Auerbach and Ernst Robert Curtius. As the culmination of his critical studies, *Obsolete Objects in the Literary Imagination* represents both sides of Orlando's achievement.

In his earlier work, available in English as *Towards a Freudian Theory of Literature, with an Analysis of Racine's "Phèdre"* (1978), Orlando found a model for the capacity of the literary text to say two contradictory things at once — the ambiguity so prized by Anglo-American New Criticism — in the concept of Freudian negation. For Orlando, the real lesson of Freud for literary interpreters lies not in detecting psychoanalytically charged motifs in the text (the phallic symbol, the mother's body), nor in reading it as a key to its author's biography. It lies rather in Freud's model of the unconscious as that which the conscious, rational mind represses, but which nonetheless surfaces in the neurotic symptom as the return of the repressed. Orlando distinguishes literature as a communicating language between author and reader from the noncommunicating language of the unconscious; it nonetheless operates by the same logical structure of an incomplete and ambivalent negation. Drawing on the concept of the tendentious joke in *Jokes and Their Relation to the Unconscious*, which he contends is Freud's most direct and productive confrontation with the literary, Orlando asserts that "literature or poetry is the seat of a socially institutionalized return of the repressed." Literary works, that is, give a home and a voice to the desires, values, and ideas that a dominant culture rejects — as these works, too, may officially reject them — and thereby surreptitiously give them what Orlando terms a semipositive valorization. The social function of literature is thus to be a safety valve in which the discontents of civilization can be pleasurably discharged; it is by its nature subversive of cultural orthodoxy, and in this sense Plato was right to banish poetry from his utopian and inhuman republic. Because, moreover, the repressions of the dominant culture change over time, it is possible to historicize this model and to view the literary text as the site of continuing, unresolved social conflict: a model in literary studies for a reconciliation of Freud and Marx.

Orlando does not limit this model to the subject matter — or in Louis Hjelmslev's terms, the "content-purport" — of literature. It applies, too, to its formal elements. Orlando reminds us that the "figures" of classical rhetoric (figures that at the time he wrote were being studied anew by French semioticians) were knowing abuses of logic, designed to persuade and to give pleasure. Such figures complicate an ideally transparent or straightforward communication, and they can perhaps expand to include all devices of fiction-making that, in the terms of the Russian formalists, cause estrangement: they are to be understood, Orlando suggests, as the return of a repressed infantile pleasure in playing with words and meaning. For this reason, as Orlando contends in his brilliant study of Enlightenment literature and thought, *Illuminismo, barocco e retorica freudiana* (1982; 1997), the *lumières* of the late seventeenth and eighteenth century attacked metaphor itself as a regressive mental activity, characteristic of an immature, childish stage of human culture, and aligned it with the superstition of Christianity they sought to dispel. Nonetheless, Orlando, true to his model of literature as "a semiotic compromise-formation which allows one to say yes or no to anything simultaneously," notes a nostalgia even in these Enlightenment polemics for the very religious culture, including the pleasures of its mythopoesis, that the *philosophes* were trying to put behind them. We may recall the plangent remarks by Goethe's Lynceus in *Faust, Part Two* as he watches the church of Philemon and Baucis fall before Faust's land development scheme in an ironic emblem of secular progress: "What pleased the eyes for so many centuries is gone." Romanticism, Orlando observes, would soon enough reclaim this cultural territory and the power of metaphor, and it would do so not least by exploring the world of childhood. The relationship between the Romantic memoir of childhood and nostalgia for the *ancien régime* that Enlightenment and Revolution had swept away is the subject of Orlando's earlier *Infanzia, memoria e storia da Rousseau ai romantici* (1966).

Obsolete Objects in the Literary Imagination returns to and completes this historical trajectory of Orlando's work: from the classicism of Racine's *Phèdre* and Molière's *Misanthrope* to the Enlightenment, from the Enlightenment to Romanticism and to the full ascendancy of the bourgeoisie. For while this book undertakes nothing less than an encyclopedic survey of Western literature from its beginnings in the ancient Near East, and of nearly every genre imaginable (drama, epic, essay, short story, letter, memoir), its center is the nineteenth and twentieth centuries and their characteristic forms: the lyric and, above all, the novel. This book, then, is primarily about modernity, whose "historical turning point" lies just before the French Revolution and in the beginnings of Romanticism: it is after this turning point that images of used-up, outworn, dead, and discarded objects proliferate and increase geometrically in Western literature and take on new ranges of meaning. For from that moment on, Orlando argues, the functional became *the* dominant value of Western culture and society, which, as we have moved "forward," consign the products of the past to a nonfunctional oblivion, whether to a museum or, more usually, to the trash heap.

But these objects return, depicted in literature whose own cultural function is to remind us of what we have lost and are constantly losing in our rush into

the future. They appear frequently in the telltale form of the list, which groups
together disparate items, regardless of their former contexts. They are recuper-
ated with the ambivalence that Orlando sees in all such negations: as the
dilapidated, dirty, haunted ruin that cannot fall down fast enough; as the
buried treasure of memories and older values looked back upon with nostalgia. At the heart of the book, the fourth chapter charts the full range of
affective reactions produced by these images in a branching tree of twelve
categories that also suggests Orlando's debt to structuralism and its binary
oppositions. The ensuing fifth chapter traces through an exhaustive series of
examples the chronological range of each category, where it begins and ends in
literary history: the book's modern focus becomes clear here, as a traditional,
universal sense of *memento mori* is complemented by more socially inflected
feelings and attitudes. This preoccupation with things that rapidly lose their
utility and value testifies to the uncertain social and economic bourgeois world
that has succeeded the continuity of the *ancien régime*, a world of commodities with built-in obsolescence and of decontextualized kitsch, a world where
the fluctuations of the marketplace constantly threaten the self-made man
with déclassement, rich today, poor tomorrow.

Obsolete Objects in the Literary Imagination is one of a kind: already a
classic in the field of comparative literature, its examples and case studies,
analyzed with rare critical intelligence and subtlety, range across nearly every
European language and literary tradition. An incidental pleasure and lesson
for English-speaking readers lies in the book's configuration of literary history
in which France plays at least as important a shaping role as England and
North America, a reflection only in part, I think, of Orlando's professional
vocation. At a time of worldwide English-language hegemony, when the study
of French culture is on the decline in the United States, it is a salutary reminder
that the history of literature looks different when viewed from Europe. The
grand if implicit argument of the book is that literature itself has come to
embody as well as to serve as the abiding home of the nonfunctional or disinterested, in a modern world given over to rapid technological change and to
the shifting fashions of mass culture. But Orlando also insists upon the critical
force of this nonfunctionality, the force of literature as a preserve of the social
unconscious. He views this strength as inseparable from the aesthetic pleasure
of literature: the giving voice to wishes and desires that protest on many fronts
against utilitarian reason, against social morality dictated by the haves to the
have-nots, against the capitalist bottom line, and perhaps against the transience of all human things. As the compromise-formation that Orlando conceives it to be, literature cannot free itself or its society from their reigning

reality principle, nor can it turn into pure rhetorical figure — both would mean literal madness and unreadability. Nevertheless literature gives the pleasure principle its due and takes part in the experience of human liberation. "Poetry makes nothing happen," Orlando might agree with W. H. Auden, but it can "still persuade us to rejoice."

David Quint
Yale University

Acknowledgments

Translating this book was not only a long undertaking, but also, for stylistic reasons, a particularly difficult one. I am therefore grateful to all who played a part in it, in addition to the translators: to Paul Tucker, who advised me during a stage in which the problems seemed almost insurmountable; and to Harvey Sachs, who began the project effectively but was then obliged to interrupt his work early. The ultimate result could not have been achieved had other friends not given so generously of their time and labor. I am thinking of the prolonged and precious contribution, in a late stage, of Simone Marchesi, who had already assumed the burden of bibliographical inquiries that were impossible for me to conduct in Italy. I am thinking of the number of improvements which I owe to the masterly revision of David Quint, a revision so thorough as to persuade me here and there to rewrite, cut from, and add to the original text. And I am thinking of the final intervention of Gavin Lewis, who, going well beyond a copyeditor's official task, constantly succeeded in reconciling two independent and sometimes incompatible requirements, the flow of the English and fidelity to the Italian. I should not forget, in addition, the particular suggestions of Anthony Johnson and Franco Moretti.

Personally, while I was hardly able to assume any responsibility for the flow of the English, nobody could take over my responsibility to guarantee fidelity to the Italian. The necessary checking demanded many hours of attentive and intelligent collaboration: I found it in two young students and friends, first Andrea Vignali, and then Luciano Pellegrini. The latter, in the last year of our work, became a vigilant assistant without whom I do not know how I could have accomplished many demanding tasks, let alone those requiring computer skills.

I will not repeat the acknowledgments I made in the Italian edition of all those who brought texts to my attention. For two of the few texts I have added here, I am indebted to Stefano Perfetti and Fernando Mastropasqua respectively; the former also furnished me with expert bibliographical assistance in the Greco-Latin field; and I would not have been able to appreciate the latter's suggestion, in an even more ancient field, without the kindness of Giovanni Mazzini.

In the very last revision, and in the correction of the proofs, Francesco Ghelli made available to me his exceptional talents as well as his implacable meticulousness.

Note on the Translation

The translation of all quotations in Greek, Latin, Italian, French, Spanish, Portuguese, and German was done by the translators of the body of the text, keeping in mind the author's translations in the notes to the Italian edition — so as to ensure stylistic unity and a degree of literality allowing the reader to follow the author's often very precise verbal analysis.

Titles of works in languages other than English appear in the text in English translation. For all languages listed above with the exception of Greek, the original titles either appear in parentheses on first mention, or are given in a shortly following source note. Quotations and titles from other languages are taken from standard English-language translations identified in the notes.

Obsolete Objects in the Literary Imagination

What This Book Is About

I

The subject, or rather the medley of objects, of the inquiry to be undertaken here may certainly appear bizarre at first sight. And not only at first sight: perhaps even the reader who has reached the end of this book will find it hard to summarize in a few words, just as the author finds it hard at the outset. I am persuaded I have ascertained — at length and analytically — the existence of a unified subject of this inquiry. Yet now, in order to provide a brief glimpse of it to the reader, I can find no better way than to go back twenty years in time. To return, in other words, to the most distant and confused insights concerning that subject, which I came by accidentally in the course of my readings, prompting me to set down certain literary passages in a notebook — before having any idea that it might be worth the trouble to continue my note taking in an increasingly methodical way.

These passages were extremely varied in every respect: not only were they drawn from several different authors, but they also belonged to different literary genres, languages, and periods. I am trying to recall how the constants that I felt I was identifying in the passages matched, leading me to set them side by side despite such diverse and numerous variants. I would say that it was the conjunction of a constant in form — more precisely, in syntax — with two constants in theme, that is, in content, that were themselves linked to each other. The form was that of a *list,* of varying length and emphasis in its entirety and in its constituent parts. The first of the thematic constants was that the lists did not include abstractions: no situations, conditions, valuations, considerations, or emotions, but rather *things* in the material sense of the word — physically concrete things presented on the imaginary plane of reality of the various literary texts. The second thematic constant was the decisive one, and the one most difficult to describe. It consisted in the fact that these things appeared in every instance more or less *useless* or *old* or *unusual* — within that imaginary plane of literature which varied from text to text, and consequently in contrast with the implied and ever varying ideals of usefulness, or newness, or normality.

Interest in forms similar to or identical with the list has certainly not been lacking within the tradition of stylistic and rhetorical studies. But even Leo Spitzer's well-known essay on "enumerative style"[1] did not seem to me to be limited in any way by the condition that the randomly enumerated things had to be physical things, much less decayed or obsolete ones. On the other hand, with respect to theme, only one particular kind of such objects — and on a monumental scale — seemed to have attracted scholars' specific attention. I am referring, of course, to the theme of ruins, Roman and otherwise: a theme that is not at all limited by the verbal form of the list, and that, moreover, is common to the visual arts — an area that I would have been (and am) too ignorant to explore in my search for parallels for this type or for other types of objects. Both as a unified set, and in the case of almost all of its heterogeneous examples, the combination in literature that had begun to interest me seemed, truly, never to have received any attention.

However, the formal constant of the list was soon dropped as an indispensable prerequisite for a passage to be drawn into my collection, although it continued to recur with considerable frequency in the passages that I began to select solely on the basis of their thematic constants. And yet I did not begin by mentioning this formal constant only to be truthful in recounting the genesis of my inquiry, nor even because of the quantity of lists present in the materials that I collected. Rather, posing the question about why the thematic constants I was dealing with were often articulated in lists is itself a good start at defining these constants and understanding the common characteristics they concealed. I have mentioned that what is in question are physical things, and physical things represented as having been, or in the process of being, deprived of or diminished in their functionality; I have added that such characteristics were to be determined on a case-by-case basis, given the historical variability of the ideals of functionality. But in any case a list verbally piles objects on top of each other, next to each other, in immediate alternation with each other, thereby making of all the other objects the sole neighboring context allowed to each of them. Thus it seems to lend itself more to the denial of any relationship of functionality between man and things than to its representation — which, if the relationship be whole and intact, would rather require the evaluation of the things taken one by one.

But if any kind of discovery was in fact beginning to take shape and find confirmation in the growing number of passages being compared, it suggested the exact opposite of a demonstration of the integrated, intact relationship of functionality. Some of the results of independent studies I had made of French literary texts were leading me in the same direction; beyond French literature, the endless vastness of the territory to be explored dissuaded me from undertaking appropriate and well-ordered readings, impossible as they would have been to plan in advance. Already a great number of passages unpremeditatedly encountered had been necessary to awaken in me the impression that the relationship between man and things — functional or otherwise — occupies a far more commanding position in what we call literature than is usually believed. An even greater number would be necessary for me to approach the true discovery, which, like all discoveries worthy of this name, shared with Poe's purloined letter the characteristics of unseen evidentness, of an unobserved obviousness, of common knowledge as yet inarticulate. It meant finally becoming aware of the extraordinary literary fortune of useless or old or unusual things, of the predilection for their literary representation, rather than that of useful, new, or normal things. An indisputable predilection, quantitatively and perhaps also qualitatively, at least from a certain period onward.

2

For the time being, I shall make use of somewhat imprecise terminology in order to indicate my determining thematic constant, and it is too soon even to be at all precise about the chronological distribution of the texts that I was approaching. But one can already see the absolutely excessive proportions of the thematic material that, through extremely limited observations, I had unwittingly brought into play. It involved — through the testimony of literature — the very relationship between human beings and the physical world subjugated by them, as well as the boundaries between culture and nature throughout the process of transformation of this world. The very relationship between human beings and time, which leaves its traces on things, was also at stake, inasmuch as it projected onto things the limits of both the metahistorical human condition as well as the historical duration of civilizations. In short, all these issues, and the deterrent effect of their scattered immensity, would have too easily discouraged the carrying out of a study within the canons of ortho-dox historicism. On the other hand, they would have too easily encouraged the writing of an essay proceeding with impunity under the sign of metahistory rather than of history, of nonsense rather than meaning; possibly even, as many would have done gladly, under the symbol of death. For opposite, though perhaps complementary reasons, neither of these two options could tempt me.

I mention this second option only because the signs of metahistory or death, together with the more lugubrious one of nonsense, were in the ascendant around the mid–1970s; and it was during the 1974–75 academic year that I deemed my inquiry ripe to be presented as a university course, and in February 1975 that I casually announced and gave a brief account of it in a later pub-lished text. Who in the world could have sacrificed a more formidable mass of imaginary objects, in a more deadly orgy of dehistoricizations and designifica-tions, than the one presented by the innumerable derelict things put side by side in my research? These derelict things would invariably have suffered the ideological fate of things during the second half of the 1970s, namely, to evaporate into signs — signs that were all the purer (or rather, signifiers with a signified all the more absent) the more they were defunctionalized by *l'écri-ture*. In fact, however strong my interest had remained in two dimensions at that time on trial or out of fashion — that is, history and meaning — the nour-ishment provided for this interest by the first organized results of my inquiry was even stronger. I could not be tempted by any metaphysical elimination of those literarily physical objects; nor could I be tempted to renounce, in the name of the canons of historicist orthodoxy, an experiment which appeared to me so promising exactly from a historical point of view. And this would be the case even if the final result could not but be an essay based on selected mate-rials (which, indeed, is what this book is), rather than a study based on exhaus-tive materials.[2]

Earlier, I made use of the expression "literary testimony," regarding my final thematic constant. This term provides a clue as to how I, too, had in some way taken advantage of the crisis in historicist orthodoxy. Behind it lies a convic-tion that has little to do with accredited literary sociology, although it scoffs at the idea — current in the 1970s and '80s — of literature's subject being either itself or nothing, or else absolute alterity. It is, rather, the conviction that literature, precisely as a testimony to the past, possesses an irreplaceable qual-ity that cannot be controlled by the authority of professional nonliterary histo-rians, something that cannot be compared with any other kind of document that these historians work with, because it is both something more and some-thing less than those other documents. I am well aware, of course, that an account of the history of the relationship between man and things solely through literary documents would be absurd; and even worse since it would be wholly impossible to bring together such documentation in a way that would be appropriate and well ordered, let alone exhaustive. But it is also true that, for me, the so-called masterpieces are the most profound testimonies of the historical past, and that not even the relative fortuity of the selected texts can avoid giving pride of place, in the long run, to these so-called masterpieces. Nor am I forgetting the conditioning proper to the series of texts themselves, which is passed on from one to the other with variations, and which forbids our conceiving them as existing in an unmediated relationship with extra- and preliterary reality: that is, the literary codes. But even literary codes and their variations, as the inevitable mediators between the historic past and the texts, cannot avoid functioning as testimonies to what they are mediating; moreover, my research provided information on them, too.

3

The fact that literature, both through its texts and through its codes, is irreplaceable as a testimony of the past, is only the consequence of a more general postulate, of Freudian derivation, that I myself was developing during the 1970s in a cycle of books.[3] The reader of the present book can be spared the elaborate conceptual burden of the entire cycle, but it is necessary to specify a few of the theoretical implications that the present book has inherited. Although this general postulate does not lose sight of literature's official or even conformist sides, it also shows it to be the imaginary site of a return of the repressed.[4] In other words, it assumes that literature is either openly or secretly concessive, indulgent, partial, favorable, or complicit toward everything that encounters distancing, diffidence, repugnance, refusal, or condemnation outside of the field of fiction. If this is the case, literature possesses the permanent value of a photographic negative of the positive cultural reality from which it emanates, and as a historic archive it is unequaled by the sum of all the other, more fortuitous and less organic documents that can bear witness to past rebellions, infractions, and frustrations. But what must now interest us is how the general scope of a concept like the return of the repressed in literature, and of a correlative concept of repression, becomes specific through various transgressions that contradict various imperatives.

We can most readily suppose that the transgressions that literature is most inclined to represent will contradict a moral or practical imperative—one that dictates law to desire itself, of every kind, erotic or political (in the broad sense), even before restricting actions. Nevertheless, in Freud's work, beyond anything he says about literature, there is a no less important, readily distinguishable imperative that can, rather, be defined as *rational*. Transgressions of this imperative are, above all, logical and linguistic concessions to the appeal of the irrational; they are primitive mental and verbal liberties. They are the vehicle for the actual return, in dreams or parapraxis, of what has been repressed, whereas in jokes they become an end in themselves, and they overcome repression through communication. It was starting from these transgressions of such a rational imperative in logical and linguistic forms (and only secondarily starting from transgressions of moral and practical imperatives in the imaginative content of the texts), that a Freudian theory of literature seemed to me deducible, beyond the work of Freud himself. But also, even transgressions of the rational imperative, when they restore credit to all those elements of archaic or infantile fantasy that have been overcome, can take their place within the texts' fictional contents, and not merely characterize their forms.

I have related how the origins of this book were more gradual and involuntary than those of its predecessors, and much less directly connected with Freudian-stimulated experimentation and speculation. Yet no one who has read that cycle of books would fail to notice a vaguely familiar feel common to the transgressive textual contents (not belonging to the physical order, but morally or rationally rejected) that they dealt with, and to the images of physical things that in the course of this study so far I have labeled as useless, old, unusual, decayed, obsolete, or derelict. Of course, such adjectives would be ill-applied to the majority of those transgressive textual contents: criminal and tragic passions, sympathies with the maniacal and the comic, critically subversive hopes, and regressively credulous nostalgia. And it may seem strange, at first glance, that images of merely physical things are related to imaginary moral or rational transgressions. But carrying out the opposite experiment would suffice to confirm the relationship — that is, to attribute to things some adjectives carrying the emotional charge of human rejection directed against them. It will be seen that I am not taking undue advantage of the relatively approximate nature of the language with which, for the time being, I characterize things, if, for example, I should speak of them as accursed, abject, foul, squalid, shady, dreadful, pitiable, moving, extravagant, or ridiculous. It is as if the return of the repressed, which elsewhere would not be of a material nature, had become incarnate and incorporated in things. Then, one would have to ask: in spite of what sort of repression? I see no problem in conceiving another imperative, distinguishable not only from the moral one but also from the rational one, and in calling it a *functional* imperative; no problem, for two reasons.

The first reason is formal: the original Freudian model for repression and return of the repressed is a logical or antilogical model that *a priori* lacks definite contents. I have had to claim repeatedly, in defending my previous books, and I shall repeat here, that there is nothing to stop one from refilling the model with new contents when necessary, so long as they can reproduce among themselves the logical or antilogical relationship of the original terms.[5] The second reason concerns these new contents: the needs and ideals of functionality in question, however historically variable they may be with respect to a corpus of so many heterogeneous literary texts, are nothing other than the application of abstract needs and ideals of Western rationality to the physical world. The Freudian "reality principle" takes its historic shape and its modern, capitalistic version in the "performance principle" — to borrow Marcuse's justly well-received term. Our functional imperative does nothing but specialize, materialize, and make executive the rational imperative itself, with the same tendency to increase its own demands, ceaselessly. If the representation of nonfunctional things is favored by literature, this is a not negligible confirmation of the fact that literature, in its imaginary space, is inclined to contradict the real order of things.

4

In this way, the obligation of presenting this book through a preliminary definition of its subject, hard to summarize as this may be, could be considered achieved. My resorting to my previous Freudian studies — which would have complicated things if I had done it less schematically — simplified them instead, and this book's subject may now be described as perhaps too well defined, because schematically so. Just as literature welcomes an immoral return of the repressed, by which a moral repression is contradicted, and an irrational return of the repressed, by which a rational repression is contradicted, so we may suppose that it welcomes (and here we specify the last two terms set opposite each other) a return of the *antifunctional* repressed, by which a functional repression is contradicted. Any more precise determinations of this book's subject coincides with more concrete definitions of these last two terms, both of which — the negative no less than the positive — vary historically, as I have said. For such determinations and definitions, I need only refer the reader to the specific cases discussed in the textual quotations and analyses that follow. Perhaps I should also confirm the reader's expectation that a study of a presumable return of the antifunctional repressed in literature will deal predominantly, although not exclusively, with the literature of the last two centuries. Nevertheless, it would not be suitable for me to close this introduction without having first tried to forestall the reader's legitimate doubts by some highly generalized reflections on the concept of nonfunctionality itself.

The issue to be addressed is not the historic relativity of nonfunctionality but rather its inward ambivalence, which, through numerous variants, is sufficient to provide a far from illusory impression of a metahistorical constant, almost a logical one. This is the ambivalence which appears any time a positive element necessarily presupposes a negative one, or any time a thing may be derived exclusively from its opposite. There are in fact situations in which the functional must postulate the nonfunctional and can only spring from it, and there are literary images that assume the double face of such situations. These images would seem to overstep our discussion's limits, inasmuch as the things demonstrate undeniable connotations of functionality; on the contrary, they are pertinent because this actually present functionality presupposes another that has been lost — thus recouping and lending value to the nonfunctional. As there will be a great many concrete examples, I shall keep this demonstration short. For the time being I will use some abstract examples that we can imagine independent of any actual literary texts. Nevertheless, I shall of course enumerate them in accordance with matchings and groupings that I intend to propose in connection with the real literary texts that the reader will come upon later. Furthermore, I shall use intentionally conventional examples, one by one, as if they were so many illustrations codified by the collective imagination before or after having been codified by literature. The series will perhaps seem extremely heterogeneous: monumental ruins, deconsecrated churches, dried flowers, necromantic relics, buried treasures, and antiquarian furnishings.

As the goal of pilgrimages, as memorials to the past, and as occasions for meditation, monumental ruins seem to be anything but deprived of function. They are visited and venerated and constitute items of cultural use. Nevertheless, they are the remnants, fragmentary in varying degrees, of buildings that in their day were constructed to be lived in, and that have been absolutely uninhabitable for centuries or millennia. Their objective defunctionalization may certainly seem secondary and may almost pass unnoticed, given the recuperation and revaluation they have undergone. But recuperation and revaluation are grafted directly onto the previous defunctionalization: in turning to chronological succession and causal necessity, rather than to the current ranking of function and nonfunction, the loss of function is what appears to be of primary importance. More exceptionally in our history: if a church has become deconsecrated as a result of revolutionary devastation, nothing will serve the cause of religious and, for that matter, political restoration so eloquently as the sight and scandal of the church's profanation. But this does not alter the fact that it is impossible to celebrate mass or otherwise to carry out religious services in it; if decay is at its worst, one could not pray in it without being drenched by rain. The violent interruption of all normal functionality is the effective condition of a silent reproof and mournful propaganda.

The dried flower hasn't been preserved by chance among the yellowed leaves of a book, if it serves from time to time as a moving memento of a person who has passed away and of a bygone day. But only a little vegetal cadaver, liable to crumble between one's fingers, can bear this commemorative function; the flower cannot do this so long as it retains its color and perfume, not only because of the inadequacy of short intervals of time to the distance of memory but by virtue of its very freshness. Entering into the homeopathic or metonymic logic of black magic, necromantic relics are those parts of dead human or nonhuman bodies that are technically necessary for calling up the incorporeal whole that is called a ghost. But as long as magic were willing to be content with chopped-off parts of living bodies, we would stay on the margins of the abstract exemplification suitable for our purposes; on the other hand, I won't waste words on the negativity par excellence of the cadaver in comparison with the function of all functions—the vital function.

Buried treasure, more than any of the previous examples, forces us to admit to a salvaging of functionality, as long as it is imagined as salvageable—that is, provided that its existence is known or hoped for and the adventure of hunting for it has been undertaken. But whether the treasure consists of coins or jewels or a combination thereof—whether, in other words, its possible new function tends to coincide more or less with its monetary value, this value will not limit itself to the one it had prior to its disappearance and recovery. It will have earned interest, in a manner of speaking—interest that matured in a greedy imagination, not in a bank, but during a long intermediate stay deep in the earth or at sea. Finally, antiques are common enough merchandise, and high-priced merchandise at that, so much so as to make their annexation to the realm of the nonfunctional seem contradictory, if it is true that functionality in its pure state is quantified by the social value of merchandise. In this case, physical defunctionalization is proportional to the very length of datable and perceptible time that has elapsed, and upon which value is calculated; and yet, assuming that it is not excessive, it is the indispensable premise for any non-fraudulent form of commercialization. It is clear that more recently produced but less prestigious and costly furnishings would be more functional, inasmuch as they are more practical, solid, or durable.

5

From this point on we shall describe as *primary* the nonfunctionality that I have indicated six times in this series of examples, because that is what it is chronologically and causally; and we shall describe as *secondary* their added-on functionality, however showy it may be. The examples in this series are enumerated according to the results of future matchings and groupings, and they correspond ideally to half of our materials. But inasmuch as they stand ambivalently between the nonfunctional and the functional, they might seem only half-pertinent to our material. And it is not difficult to contrast them now with simple examples that correspond to wholly pertinent materials. Such will be all examples (and they might appear to be the only ones) in which the lack of any secondary functionality whatsoever concedes no redemption at all to the nonfunctional — excepting only the one that we take for granted in every case: the pure, formal quality of literary discourse, in which the images of nonfunctional things appear. (It goes without saying that the reader will not for a moment confuse what I am talking about now with what I am not talking about at all: first, the denial of a sort of functionality that we understand to be an attribute of some specific imaginary contents of the texts; second, the denial of the literary functionality of the texts, understood here as their formal quality. More simply put, in the first case we deny functionality if we say that a text discusses old stuff, and we would deny it in the second case if we were to say that we don't like a text).

Let me, then, cite other examples, which in turn synthesize another ideal half of our field. I shall take equally conventional examples, one by one, thereby composing an equally heterogeneous series and continuing to imagine them outside of actual literary texts. I shall now say just a few words about each of them, since in this case I will not be going back to them in order to stress ambivalences, as I did with the previous ones. Let us contemplate, in succession: a shabby or patched-up suit, regardless of whether it is worn by a miser, a poor man, or a picaroon, with respectively a comical, pitiful, or picturesque effect; the rundown interior of a home, regardless of whether its faded upholstery, worm-eaten woodwork, and rusty tools point to lower-class residents or impoverished ones; a birthplace or family home in which one grew up or at least spent one's childhood, now ruined, or demolished and replaced by new constructions; a ghostly castle, in whose terrifying abandoned rooms the past lingers with the threat of a visible return; a city swallowed up by the desert, in which the menace that creeps into human dwellings with every cobweb on the walls or nettle between the flagstones is fulfilled; a banal souvenir that allows the authenticity of a profile to be cheapened and belied, depriving it of its proper ballast of time and its proper background of space. Not one of these six images would appear other than absolutely unpleasant outside the field of literature. And if, on the contrary, lingering on such images in literature is quite capable of providing pleasure—as anyone who instinctively remembers appropriate texts will concede—this is simply a particular aspect of one of the most ancient issues in aesthetics: the redemption through artistic euphoria of the painful or the ugly.

To put the matter in more modern terms, let us again borrow from Freud a concept that is irreplaceable both for its logical strangeness and, alas, for the frequency with which it should be applied: compromise-formation. In other words, let us allow that a single linguistic manifestation can express two contrasting or even incompatible requirements. If the antifunctional return of the repressed is ugly or painful, and if the only thing that makes images such as the six given above tolerable or downright enjoyable is their acceptability in literature, we must refer to a purely literary compromise-formation. Whereas in the case of such images as the six I formerly presented, we have seen underlying the properly literary compromise-formation a compromise with the functional in the situations themselves—at what we may call a preliterary level: an ambivalence through which the return of the antifunctional repressed is redeemed or mitigated. It is worth underlining this ambivalence for a deeper preliminary understanding of the concept of nonfunctionality at this point. It is typical of complex (or partially positive) examples, existing within them; but, as we shall see, these examples often maintain relationships characterized by alternation, interference, mixing, or reversibility with simple (or solely negative) examples. As a result of ambivalence or other similar relationships between the nonfunctional and the functional, the latent unity of the whole field—and hence of the very subject of this inquiry—is at stake.

6

The fact is that beyond this subject in itself, what is called into question is an ambivalence intrinsic to the relationship—for human beings—between things and time. Time uses up and destroys things, breaks them and reduces them to uselessness, renders them unfashionable and makes people abandon them; time makes things become cherished by force of habit and ease of handling, endows them with tenderness as memories and with authority as models, marks them with the virtue of rarity and the prestige of age. The scale that weighs a positive quality here and a negative one there is unstable and unpredictable, and it also shifts according to what one might call quantitative doses. Time wears things out *or* lends them dignity; it wears things out *and* lends them dignity. And in fact a thing may be either *too* worn-out, or *not* worn-out *enough* by time, to be dignified by it. Let us recall a historic oscillation — the one that accompanied the great rise of the European bourgeoisie, once the notion of the privilege of birth came to be disputed — that is, a nobility conferred by time, genealogically, upon the previous ruling class. On the one hand, the need to devalue such a form of nobility could not be renounced, in order to affirm effectively the notion of individual merit; on the other, the temptation to usurp it through the expedient of belated, retrospective, or alternative (for example Napoleonic) ennobling, was ineradicable. Nineteenth-century fiction, which bears incomparable witness to this oscillation, reflected it profusely in literary images of things.

This reference to such an exemplary instance of time's ideological ambivalence in history does not contradict the impression of having to do with a metahistorical and almost logical constant, as I said above. We shall see the image of the cadaver appear frequently (as if it were a permanent, secret, symbolic referent) in the textual quotations, naturally attracted to the metaphorical regions that abut on our subject. And ambivalence of the relationship to time is not the only ambivalence in the image of the cadaver. At the same time, what is at stake is the ambivalence that places man and his things on a scale that is just as unstable and unpredictable, between culture and nature: nature makes a cadaver into an indifferent, precarious, pestilential wreck to be eliminated as quickly as possible, an object of refuse par excellence; culture consecrates it as something to be venerated and ideally preserved forever, as an object of worship par excellence. No halfway measures here, between an extreme physical non-value (that of primary nonfunctionality) and supreme moral value (that of secondary functionality). But it is not through symbolic references to cadavers that we will arrive at the fundamental problem in this preliminary section, let alone confirm the latent unity of the subject of our inquiry. (If this were the case, I would have ended up by literally setting the symbol of death over this inquiry — which is exactly what I have said I do not want to do.) First, for me, no symbolic referent would sufficiently guarantee the unity of the subject in question. That unity will be uninterruptedly demonstrated through the texts, by conjunctions, convergences, conversions, and associations — the less predictable the more significant — among all of what I take to be parts of the subject of inquiry itself.

Besides, to the extent that symbolic referents and metahistorical or logical constants are of interest here, the cadaver image is most obviously part of a universal human experience — but not necessarily of childhood experience, which is of primary importance for a Freudian. The oldest form of ambivalence, with respect to the individual, is, rather, that revealed by Freud in the early childhood relationship with excrement, and it begins at birth. Theses that were considered incredible and scandalous at the beginning of the twentieth century are only too well known today. As feces are the first thing produced by one's own body, for a very small child they represent a first, symbolic gift to adults — the first occasion for being considered worthy or unworthy, for social exchange or ransom. Initially important, attractive, and fragrant to the child, the feces are destined to become equally shameful, repugnant, and stinking as its upbringing proceeds. Here too the polarization becomes extreme, but, contrary to the case of the cadaver, there is a split — once repression has taken place — between contempt, which lies entirely in the realm of disciplined consciousness, and persevering esteem, which lies only in the unconscious. What is a worthless piece of trash for the conscious mind will, in the unconscious, be tantamount to gold as the substance of supreme splendor, and to money as overall mediator of value. One may even say that there are two ambivalences concerning these unformed, primordial "things" called feces: the one between pleasure and disgust, the other between gift and refuse. In the former, nature and culture are set in opposition to each other, and both reverse with the passage of time.

If we had reached the ultimate depth even with this last form of ambivalence, still, as students of literature it is the Freudian logical or antilogical model that interests us more than the anthropological or psychological contents with which that model is filled. And the model, taken in its less narrow meaning — here we must refer to return of the repressed in a much broader sense than its technical and psychic one — is filled with content very closely connected to literature in Freud's brilliant comparison between the psychic realm of imagination and reserves or parks for the protection of nature. The latter are spaces dedicated to the preservation of the original state of nature, he says, "in places where the requirements of agriculture, communications and industry threaten to bring about sudden changes on the original face of the earth that will make it unrecognizable." And he adds: "Everything, including what is useless and even what is noxious, can grow and proliferate there as it pleases."[6] Thus by means of a comparison the functional imperative of Western rationality — with its coercive effects on the physical world — is called into question. But the comparison may also be extended to a form of imagination that has already been transformed into a language, that is, into literature (or art) as an institution. In an exemplary way, it suits literature as the site of an antifunctional return of the repressed. A space that is devoted even to the useless or the actually noxious is, no longer metaphorically, nothing else than the space of a purely literary compromise-formation — in the language of which, images that are only negative find a redemption that is only formal.

Whereas the more or less universal anthropological or psychological ambivalences represented by time, the cadaver, and feces seem rather to be reflected by the literary ambivalence of partially positive images — into which, as we know, a preliterary compromise flows between the antifunctional and the functional.

7

Freud's richly intuitive comparison, with its significantly modern terms of reference, helps us to set the subject of our inquiry in a large-scale historical perspective. Of course, it helps us to do so starting with what is most typical: negative or simple examples. But the extension of the discussion to complex examples and to partially positive images will now be continuously implied, given the ambivalence that dominates the whole. Most of the texts in which our thematic constants are to be found belong to the literature of the last two centuries, as I have already indicated. An immense historical leap may in fact be noted in the frequency, development, and number of constants such as these, and it can be dated, roughly, from the late eighteenth and early nineteenth centuries. It coincides with the period in which industrial revolution in England and political revolution in France were forcing upon the world well-matured models of secular rationalization that had begun two centuries earlier and that, in two more centuries, would change the face of the earth beyond recognition. The great ideological moment of that rationalization was what we call the Enlightenment; Marx and Engels have spoken of how the Enlightenment's criticism of tradition was able to elicit intransigent, grandiose claims of rational universality, although it was set in motion by bourgeois class interests and led by a utilitarian requirement — what was to become the performance principle, which is our functional imperative.

When we read, in Engels, that "everything must justify its existence before the tribunal of reason or give up existence," that "every old traditional notion was flung into the lumber-room as irrational,"[7] it is clear that literature is also concerned, because the texts of the trial in question were often very great pieces of literature. But before long, the alliance between literature and Enlightenment rationality (the subject of the last book in my cycle, of which this book thus represents the conceptual sequel) was soon subverted in the Romantic rebellion; literature once again showed its preference for many ancient, traditional conceptions that had previously been rejected, thus turning itself into the site of an irrational return of the repressed. And Engels' passage is once again a metaphorical point of departure — albeit a much more tenuous one than Freud's — for evoking our constants and, almost, for suggesting their literary-historical position. It would seem legitimate to say that at that time literature, by welcoming our constants in such an increased measure, was heading toward a preference for lumber that had been flung away — if we take the image literally; it made its very self into a lumber room, as the site of an antifunctional return of the repressed.

In the meantime, the economic aspect of the bourgeois rationalization of the world was what we call capitalism. The most famous book ever written on the subject begins — taking up the first sentence of a previous book by Marx — with this statement: "The wealth of those societies in which the capitalist mode of production prevails, presents itself [at first sight] as 'an immense accumulation of commodities.' "[8] Here literature is certainly not spoken of, and the notion of immensity or monstrosity is not metaphorical, although it lends visual concreteness and connotations of excess or waste to an abstract concept; nor does it go in an antifunctional direction, but rather in a hyper-functional one. And yet, if we wished to transpose the sentence — on the grounds of the postulate that literature contradicts and subverts the real order of things — we would only have to replace one word and invert another, to come up with this: "The *literature* of those societies in which the capitalist mode of production prevails, presents itself at first sight as 'an immense ac-cumulation of *anticommodities*.' " In looking at the massive presence of our constants in texts that date from a certain period on, this statement would be nothing more than an overstatement of truth by metonymy, antonomasia, and hyperbole. Like commodities in a real situation, well ordered by a functional imperative, so our constants, in a literature that has become the site of an irrational return of the repressed, are parts taken for wholes, summarize ex-ceptional qualities, and stimulate exaggeration.

Let us look again at symbolic referents — but not metahistorical ones, this time. To speak of anticommodities means to consider even commodity fetish-ism as in some way ambivalent — if not outside literature at least in the ways in which literature reflects it. But in whatever imaginary situation ambivalence is attributed to commodities — adults' main fetish — one attributes its principal modern historical materialization to none other than the ambivalence of all ambivalences, that is, to the one which is first infantile and then unconscious: feces. To describe as anticommodities the literary images of useless or noxious things means referring them virtually, again, to excrement — to that which is least commercializable among discarded articles. If the repressed value of excrement is overturned in the conscious devaluing of it, so likewise in litera-ture's predilection for anticommodities the social apotheosis of commodities is, strictly speaking, inverted, together with its exchange value and its use value. And this, too, can be extended to the images of things whose function has been lost and changed, images that are only partially negative. This is the case even in the extreme example, examined above, of antiques — where the regaining of a function has actually made them into commodities, of a special type.

Thus, the ambivalence together with which our constants are historicized is that from which the logical or antilogical Freudian model itself draws its most complicated and most remote origins. As proof, it allows us to change the model's contents yet again; I am thinking of another passage, in which Freud accomplishes something that is both more and less than a comparison. He finds, on repeated relationships, a link (achieved thanks to an intermediate element, the removal of olfactory stimuli) between disgust for the feces that were originally esteemed, and denial of divinities that have been culturally surpassed and transformed into demons.[9] From this are drawn the four terms of an implicit proportion, whereby demons bear the same relationship to bygone gods as the disgusting feces bear to the feces once considered precious. Consequently, excrement and the demon are considered equivalent, as objects of rejection. If literature is for us the site of the immoral return of the repressed, and hence could be said to be a space reserved for the demon (which to some extent is also the site for the irrational return of the repressed), then, similarly, insofar as it is the site of an antifunctional return of the repressed it will also be seen as a space granted to excrement. This space is more deeply ambiguous not only than the lumber room, but also than the immense or monstrous accumulation of anticommodities or than the preserve for wild flora and fauna. Sometimes, it is an imaginary receptacle of gold that once was shit; at other times, an imaginary depository for shit that once was gold.

II

First, Confused Examples

The time has come to let the texts speak for themselves; but which texts, out of so many possible ones? Their selection and arrangement in a certain order will follow from my intention to begin to demonstrate, in concrete terms, that unity of the subject of inquiry which I have discussed in the abstract in the first chapter. However, it is important to keep always in mind that each of these examples was initially *stumbled upon* in that accidental, involuntary, and gradual way I have described (I, 1). In consequence the selection and organization of the examples will somehow mimic the comings and goings of chance, following a variety of literary associations that do not always or as yet do not entirely lend themselves to rationalization. Thus, it seems to me that the most fitting text to initiate the series is by an author far less celebrated than many others: the French poet Charles Cros (1842–88). Cros' posthumous and relatively recent rise in fortune is due to the surrealists' esteem for him and to his prose monologues for the theater, but our purpose here is better served by the octosyllabic sonnet that he placed as a preface, in 1879, to his verse collection *The Sandalwood Chest* (*Le Coffret de santal*):

> Knick-knacks of uncertain use,
> Dead flowers upon almahs' breasts,

> Hair, gifts from delighted virgins,
> Locks quickly torn from strumpets,
>
> Somber pictures and distant blues,
> Faded pastels, hard cameos,
> Phials still smelling of perfume,
> Jewelry, rags, rattles, puppets,
>
> What a great clutter in this chest!
> All for sale. Accept my offer,
> Reader. Perhaps these old things
>
> Will move you to tears or laughter.
> You'll have to pay, and as for me,
> I shall buy some nice fresh roses.[1]

The first eight lines are, of course, a list. One may wonder whether the first one, with its immediate questioning of the functionality of the objects — knick-knacks "of uncertain use" — constitutes a component on a par with those that follow, or whether it is rather an initial synthesis of the list, casting a predicate of dubious functionality over all the items that follow. In any case, the list intensifies the primary defunctionalization of the things that have been named, quickening the rhythm at the end and piling four useless items into the eighth line. The exclamation about the "clutter" — the final synthesis — introduces the tercets and the surprise they contain: the items named were not bundled together at a level of imaginary reality, but rather metaphorically, with direct reference to the nonimaginary reality of the literary marketplace. In other words, they exemplify the contents of the same "chest" that appears in the title of the collection, and this is why container and contents are being offered for sale. The fact that the poet intends to buy himself "fresh roses" — a conclusive counterpart to the "dead flowers" of the second line — in exchange for his earnings, seems to mean that the sale of his literature will make lived experiences possible for him. Perhaps these experiences will not be convertible into new literature, owing precisely to their freshness.

The subsequent collection of poems is thus identified exclusively with artificial, gratuitous, or withered objects: paintings, gewgaws, remnants of bourgeois décor, the fetishes of erotic memory. But, thanks to an inevitable metonymic extension from the parts to the whole, such an identification implicates all literature, far beyond Cros' collection. Reciprocally (and this is still more interesting, for our purposes), the mass of objects of this sort *stands for* literature, be it as a single, present piece of it, be it as an institutional whole. The paradox of the commercialization of useless things is implicit, inasmuch as the poems likened to such things actually do go on the market. And the paradox perfectly illustrates what I suggested to be the ambivalence between commodities and anticommodities (I, 7), based on the Freudian ambivalence toward feces but reflected by literary images: the little sonnet's objects, anticommodities at the immediate level where they represent themselves, represent literature when, at the metaphoric level, they become commodities. Poetic discourse cannot confirm theoretical discourse unless it exaggerates it figuratively. In the previous chapter I spoke of literature as the site of an antifunctional return of the repressed (I, 3–4), but only by freely altering a sentence by Marx did I dare to do so with so absolute an identification — by way of metonymy plus antonomasia and hyperbole — between container and the things contained.

2

Given Cros' position in literary history, and the importance as a model already acquired by *The Flowers of Evil* (*Les Fleurs du mal,* 1857) when Cros' little sonnet was composed, there is little risk of being mistaken in tracing in it certain reminiscences of one of Charles Baudelaire's (1821–67) most famous poems. Thus, prudently, our first transition from one text to another closely approaches the most traditional forms of literary history with regard to the relationship between a text and its "source." I am referring to the following lines from the second of the four poems entitled *Spleen:*

> I've more memories than if I were a thousand years old.
>
> A large chest of drawers encumbered with balance sheets,
> Poems, love letters, lawsuits, and romance scores,
> With heavy hair rolled up in receipts,
> Hides fewer secrets than my sad brain.
>
> . . . .
>
> I am an old boudoir full of wilted roses,
> Where antiquated fashions lie in a mess,
> Where plaintive pastels and pale Bouchers,
> Alone, exude the smell of an uncorked flask.[2]
>
> . . . .

There is the list, the clutter and the mess, the mixture of domesticity and worldliness in the junk, the chest of drawers replacing Cros' chest as a container, the secondary erotic memory-function of its contents, the wilted flowers and the hair, the paintings with their faded colors, and the flask with its smell. There is even the fact that all these things have a metaphorical status, although in this case they are not at all a metaphor of literature, either for the text that hosts them or for the institution, but rather — as the personal pronouns and possessive adjectives reveal — a metaphor of the individual corresponding to the "I" of the speaker and of its relationship to its own past. The originality of Cros' composition, however, is left intact, thanks above all to an essential difference in tone. Its series of objects, as it goes by, is caressed by melancholic irony as well as by tender satisfaction, whereas Baudelaire's emanates an almost sinister depression (further dramatized by the context, which has not been quoted), as if remnants of the past inspired repugnance rather than complacence. Bureaucratic balance sheets, lawsuits, and receipts are combined with literary and amorous relics, either without irony or with the gray irony of chance and reciprocal alienation. On the one hand, once the poem's speaking subject has entered a metaphorical relationship, he wholly absorbs the objects, but on the other, he lets them stand out, "alone," as he says about the paintings in the boudoir. It is the first time in the history of poetry that objects make up a microcosm of so great a symbolic range and take on so closed and complete an affective relationship between self and world.

3

Let us now jump forward in time rather than backward, to Jorge Luis Borges (1899–1986), who as a poet prolonged well into the eighties of both his and the century's age the peculiarity of a non-"obscure" language — neither in a symbolist, nor in a surrealist or in an expressionist sense. As far as early French symbolism is concerned, broadly considered as originating with Baudelaire, it is impossible to affirm positively but all the more impossible to deny — in referring to a poet to such an extent nourished by literary culture — the existence of particular echoes of Baudelaire himself; or even, in this case, of Cros. And yet the fact remains that the aged Borges left no less than four poems entirely consisting of lists, and of lists of things; that in all of these the generic reminiscence of the atmosphere of early French symbolism is unmistakable; and that two out of four are simply entitled *The Things* (*Las cosas*) and *Things* (*Cosas*). Let us read the first of them, which is to be found in the collection *Eulogy of Shadow* (*Elogio de la sombra*), dated 1969:

> The cane, the coins, the key-chain,
> The docile lock, the late notes
> That won't be read by the few days
> Left to me, the papers and the chessboard,
> A book and in its pages the wilted
> Violet, monument to an undoubtedly
> Unforgettable and already forgotten evening,
> The red occidental mirror in which an illusory

Dawn is burning. How many things,
Files, thresholds, atlases, goblets, nails,
Serve us like silent slaves,
Things blind and strangely secret!
They will last longer than our oblivion;
They will never know that we have left.[3]

In this sonnet as in that of Cros, the list occupies two quatrains and invades the third with the ending of the nominal sentence of which it consists. Then, in the ninth line—again, as in Cros' sonnet—an exclamatory phrase takes off from a retrospective synthesis of the list ("How many things"), but here, in the next line, in the form of an apposition, an entire second, compact list made up of five items is added. These objects, however, unlike those of either Cros or Baudelaire, are neither obsolete nor worn out, with the sole exception of the wilted violet in the book. Nor are they gratuitous; on the contrary, they are objects meant to be used, objects that "serve us," literally, like slaves. The atmosphere of obsolescence or worn-out-ness or gratuitousness that nonetheless enfolds them perfectly exemplifies, on the one hand, the defunctionalizing effect that the list of things has on the things themselves, as I said in the first chapter (I, 1). On the other hand, it derives from what this time, too, is a metaphorical valence, not so much of the objects in themselves as of human relationship to them. And "human" is to be taken in a metahistorical and metaphysical sense, as declared in the passage from the feeling of privacy of the first person singular that appears in the fourth line to the gravity of the first person plural that is repeated in the last lines. The mystery of the certainty of transience and death and of the uncertainty of a beyond dictates expressions like "few days," "unforgettable and already forgotten," "occidental mirror," and "illusory dawn." But a highly discreet animistic displacement ends by making the objects alone into an unsuitable, long-lasting, and negative subject. It is not said that we ourselves will never be aware of having passed on, forgetful of things: rather that the things will ignore the fact—just as their obliging silence prefigures.

4

One quotation—a predictable one, for Italian readers—is situated much closer, chronologically, to the atmosphere of the early greatness of French symbolism. I am alluding to the very well-known opening lines of *Grandma Speranza's Friend* (*L'amica di nonna Speranza*) by Guido Gozzano (1883–1916), first published in 1907 in *The Road to the Shelter* (*La via del rifugio*):

Loreto in straw and the bust of Alfieri, of Napoleon,
Flowers in frames (good things in bad taste),

The somewhat gloomy fireplace, boxes without comfits,
Marble pieces of fruit protected by glass bells,

A few unusual toys, chests made of valves,
Objects with the warning *hail, remembrance,* coconuts,

Venice portrayed in mosaics, slightly dull watercolors,
Prints, coffers, albums decorated with archaic anemones,

Massimo d'Azeglio's canvases, miniatures,
Daguerreotypes: figures dreaming in perplexity,

The grand old chandelier hanging in the middle of the parlor,
Whose quartz shows a thousandfold the good things in bad taste,

The cuckoo clock that sings the hour, chairs adorned with crimson
Damask . . . I'm reborn, I'm reborn in eighteen fifty![4]

This list, the longest so far, is developed over more than thirteen lines; here, too, it forms a nominal sentence in which the things function, so to speak, as their own predicates. Immediately thereafter, the first of the poem's five sections is closed in less than a line, but in the meantime a poetic "I" has emerged for an instant, together with a date. The "I" will not reappear until the fifth section, when, finally becoming explicit, it will attribute to itself skeptical nostalgia for a past that is spread over the whole text. In that last section (as in the poem's epigraph), the date will be specified down to the month and day, and the importance of the dating fits in with the other main novelty with respect to our previous texts: the presence of narration in the verses. Thus the list operates also as a description, such as might open a prose short story. Contrary to Borges' everyday things, rendered absolute in a metaphysical and metahistorical sense, here we have dated or historicized everyday things: chosen because of their typicality in relation to a period in the collective past. I would say that the choice of grandma's day was not made at random. Fifty or sixty years — the space of two generations — are as far back as an individual can go to summon up a still concrete image through family memories.

Gozzano's text plays upon intergenerational detachment accentuated by the evolution of the bourgeoisie, and in this detachment it mixes irony with regret. This ambivalence is what dictates the description, "good things in bad taste," which in Italy has achieved the status of a proverb. But from the grandmother's point of view — that is, from the point of view of the people included in the narration — such things, all of which are after all highly fitting appurtenances of an haut-bourgeois interior, are in no way in bad taste, thus not *good* either—in other words, not made lovable by their ingenuousness. The judgment about value or taste is the author's judgment, set in opposition to what is presumably the characters' judgment. To us, it suggests for the first time the modern problem (which does not go back earlier than the mid–1800s) of so-called bad taste or, to use a more specialized term, kitsch. A problem that at first would appear unrelated to an inquiry concerned with the literary images of nonfunctional things: and not for its extraliterary quality, but because the decorative function of the objects in that parlor is undoubted. Nevertheless, how could one not take notice of the evident relationship between this list and the three previous ones, which neither mentioned nor induced us to mention anything about the bad taste of their components?

5

Let us then, for the first time, risk making a transition from one text to another which is not supported by any specific literary-historical relationship. The difference between poetry and prose is only one of the many that distance the previous excerpt from the one that I draw from a novel by Joseph Roth (1894–1939), *Flight without End: A Chronicle* (*Die Flucht ohne Ende: Ein Bericht*), published in 1927. Franz Tunda, a former officer in the Austrian army who has been taken prisoner in Russia during the First World War and has stayed on because of a love affair, does not manage to fit into the new revolutionary society. But this does not make his condition as an outsider less desperate upon his belated return to the West. He has just arrived at the home of his brother, an orchestral conductor, in the Rhineland, and the veteran's detachment from good bourgeois life compounds the estrangement that has always separated the two brothers:

> Years earlier, the conductor had bought a silver samovar from Russian refugees, as a curiosity. In honor of his brother, who must have become a sort of Russian, the item was brought in, by the liveried servant, on a small table with wheels. The servant wore white gloves and, in order to warm up the samovar, picked up little cubes of coal with a pair of silver sugar tongs.
> It raised a stench of the kind made by a narrow-gauge locomotive.
> At this point, Franz had to demonstrate how to deal with a samovar. He had never used one in Russia, but he didn't admit this; instead, he trusted to his intuition.
> In the meantime, he saw many Jewish objects in the room: candelabras, cups, Torah scrolls.
> "Have you converted to Judaism?" he asked.

It turned out that in this city, in which the oldest impoverished Jewish families lived, one could get "almost for nothing" many precious items of artistic value. Moreover, in the other rooms there were also some Buddhas, although no Buddhists lived on either side of the Rhine, and there were also old manuscripts by Hutten, a Lutheran Bible, Catholic ritual objects, ebony Madonnas, and Russian icons.

That's how conductors live.[5]

At first sight, not even the rough, preliterary content could be described as identical between this prose and Gozzano's verses. In both cases, the subject is the decor — extravagant, to a certain extent, as a result of excessive and gratuitous ornamentation — of an haut-bourgeois interior, but in Roth there is no question of bad taste; on the contrary, cultivated refinement is suggested. And although in both cases the formal elaboration of the material can only make one think of irony, one could hardly imagine more different forms of irony. In the poem, the irony is easy to see and affectionately backward-looking; in the story, it is presented both caustically and dryly. Let us attempt to replace the idea of a pure difference, and the risk of its presenting us with nothing interesting, with the ever-interesting idea of an opposition. The respective ironies project two opposing attitudes toward the values of a good bourgeois conscience onto the ornaments in question. The pre–First World War poet relegated them to the past and indulged in their as yet intact innocence. The postwar prose writer reduces them to a feeling of security that has already been put on the defensive, and through the eyes of his protagonist, who is neither Russian nor Western, neither a communist nor a bourgeois, he subjects them to literal alienation.

The effect might recall the great eighteenth-century tradition of Enlightenment irony (rather than that of Brecht), all the more so when — elsewhere in the novel — technical devices or practical conveniences are portrayed as no less superfluous than the luxury objects mentioned here.[6] But the estrangement of these objects strips naked all that was veiled in Gozzano. This is the latent absurdity in every secondary functionality of the ornamental type — to use a previously established term (I, 5) — at least every time that the loss of primary functionality implies the removal of objects from their authentic first context. The Jewish, Protestant, Catholic, Orthodox, and even Buddhist ecclesiastical objects and fittings are doubly decontextualized — spatially, inasmuch as they are a mixture of localized traditions, and temporally, thanks to the antiquity of their deactivated religious purposes. The fact that the conductor's parlor is not characterized by bad taste or kitsch, that in other words the objects are assumed to be well recontextualized, must not distract us from seeking understanding in the direction of decontextualization. The profanation of the objects came about in consequence of bargain sales, the result of exploiting the situations of Russian fugitives and impoverished Jewish families. Franz Tunda, for his part, must "have become *a sort of* Russian"; when he is forced to deal with the samovar, an emblem, he politely simulates the experience with it that he never acquired. But is not the whole ornamental exhibition intended elegantly to simulate experiences never undergone by either the hosts or their guests, through conventional approximation and minimum-cost appropriation?

6

Without having to change language, we can take a few steps backward to German Romanticism, and specifically to 1812 and the lengthy story *Isabelle of Egypt: Emperor Charles the Fifth's First Love* (*Isabella von Ägypten: Kaiser Karl des Fünften erste Jugendliebe*), by Achim von Arnim (1781–1831). Arnim's name is linked above all to the famous collection of reworked popular poetry, *The Youth's Magic Horn* (*Des Knaben Wunderhorn*), published by him together with Brentano; but his own fame, too, was renewed in the twentieth century thanks to the surrealists (who, through their praise or attacks, exercised in the area of literary taste what was perhaps their most long-lasting influence on literature as such). But whereas in Cros' case the phenomenon could be better explained by texts other than the sonnet that I quoted, in the present case one would do well to bet on Breton's predilection for the very excerpt that I am about to quote. A group made up of the protagonist, a young gypsy girl, an old gypsy woman who is something of a witch, and two supernatural characters — a living dead person and a living mandrake — is traveling in Flanders; to get new clothes, they all stop in at the home of a friend of the old woman's who deals in used and occasionally stolen goods:

> Meanwhile, the mandrake was so astonished by all the ridiculous stuff in the room — where, lying in separated heaps, there were old braids, rags, kitchenware, and bed linen — that he couldn't stop gawking; everything was new to him, but he quickly learned all about everything. Frau Nietken, a junk dealer with quite extensive business dealings, collected the most singular stock of old stuff of every sort; thus, not even the smallest household objects matched or were appropriate to the house, as is the case everywhere else; but by a very natural choice on the part of people who, in their purchases, had always taken away what was usable, she was left with only what was most bizarre, with what had been created on the whim of some bygone time or of some rich man, for some special occasion. The chairs in the attic, for instance, were supported by wooden Moors with multicolored umbrellas over their heads; they came from the garden of a rich merchant from Ghent who had done much business

in Africa. In the middle of the room there hung a strange, twisted brass crown that had once illuminated the suppressed synagogue in Ghent; now, mounted above it, there was a twisted, colorful wax candle in honor of the Mother of God. The altar was actually a gaming table that had abdicated its former function, from which the leather pockets for money had been torn and replaced with what had been a salt cellar, now filled with holy water. On the walls hung woven tapestries that represented tournaments of old; the knights and their iron armor hung down in shreds.[7]

We notice once again after quoting Roth's text that, as I already mentioned (I, 4, 7), imaginary commodities may very well take their place among the literary images that I have placed beneath the sign of anticommodities. In other words, there is no incompatibility between the presentation of some objects as objects for buying and selling and the connotations of the nonfunctional—not only because of the time lapse that is part of the very definition of antique items, but just as much thanks to an unpredictable game of primary defunctionalizations and secondary refunctionalizations. The merchandise had already been sold, in Roth's text, and its nobility, which contrasted with the cheapness of the purchase, was conserved through its decorative usage. Here, we are looking (through a mandrake's eyes!) at the interior of what is both home and shop to the junk dealer, and we see old stuff piled up as commodities for sale. We would see nothing other than this if the woman didn't assign domestic functions to all the "bizarre" things that other people's natural choice in taking "the usable" had left her—twice-discarded things, in other words. The reuse she makes of them requires no recontextualization, and it remains unconcerned with the paradoxes of decontextualization, because it is either practical or pious, but it has no decorative purpose. Thus the chairs supported by wooden Moors with their multicolored umbrellas—the result of the whims of wealth and of African commerce—serve no purpose, it seems, other than that of everyday sitting.

The candelabra that comes from Jewish worship (here, too), is reconsecrated to Catholic practice, whereas an object of as little devotional use as a gaming table has moved from the secular to the sacred realm—a fate that is the reverse of the comparable items in Roth's text. It has been transformed into the altar before which the group found Frau Nietken kneeling, and to which a former salt cellar has been attached as a holy water stoup. My assumption that the surrealists' admiration could have centered on this piece of writing was made precisely because of the eccentricity of decontextualizations of this sort, because of their disguising of chance in dreamlike creativity, and because of their contemporary effect as complacently counterfeit kitsch. I said contemporary effect, but I doubt that this effect is produced without in some way stretching the text's original meaning, without approaching it through a code common to more recent texts and distancing it from the code that it would have shared with earlier texts. In simpler terms, I think it is probable that the original meaning provided for a grotesque effect less distant from the really and truly comic. If, further along, a series of comparable passages will confirm this, our inquiry will have accidentally appropriated a semantic-philological competence; it will have helped restore to a text the literal and not indeterminate signified that may become corrupted over time, like the well-defined letter of the signifier.

7

After having concentrated on four verse compositions and two prose excerpts — one of them earlier and one later — it is now time to turn to the great realistic novels of the nineteenth century, and we will begin with their most mature phase. I have chosen a passage from *A Simple Heart* (*Un Coeur simple*) by Gustave Flaubert (1821–80), published in 1877 as the first of the *Three Tales* (*Trois Contes*). In the industrious, rough, humble, and generous life of the servant Félicité, and after a long series of devoted self-sacrifices — to a youthful love, to her mistress's children, to a ship-boy nephew, and to an old, excommunicated man — all of them unfortunate, she has concentrated her adoration on an American parrot that was given her as a gift. When the bird dies, the woman, who is now old and in poor health, has it stuffed and gives it a place of honor in her own room; and it is only now, toward the end of the story, that the room itself is described to us:

> This place, into which she allowed few to enter, looked like both a chapel and a bazaar, containing as it did so many religious objects and miscellaneous things.
>
> A large wardrobe made opening the door difficult. Opposite the window above the garden, a bull's eye looked out at the courtyard; a table, near the cot, held up a water pitcher, two combs, and a cube of blue soap in a chipped dish. Against the walls there were to be seen: rosaries, medals, several Blessed Virgins, a holy water stoup made of coconut; on the commode, covered by a sheet, like an altar, a box made of seashells that Victor had given her; then, a watering-can and a ball, some notebooks, geographical prints, a pair of ankle-boots; and on the nail meant for the mirror, hanging by its ribbons, the little fur hat! Félicité pushed this kind of respect so far that she even kept one of the master's frock coats. All the old stuff that Mme. Aubain no longer wanted she took for her room. This was why there were artificial flowers at the edge of the commode and a portrait of the Count of Artois in the recess of the dormer window.[8]

Félicité's life, almost entirely given over to the functionality of work, is quite the opposite of the description of her room, which gives only two or three lines to the objects that she needs for sleeping and washing; almost all the space is left to an affective reliquary of defunctionalized things, as a result of which the place feels like both a bazaar and a chapel. The pairing is identical to the one indicated in Arnim's text — Frau Nietken's merchandise and her altar. But here, nothing is for sale, and perhaps the Madonnas and other "religious objects" in the strict sense are not the most venerated ones; the real religion that the woman mixes with or substitutes for the confessional one are the devotions of memory. Victor, the nephew who died overseas and who had given her the box, is named, whereas only an exclamation point reminds the reader that a hat had belonged to the young mistress who had died prematurely: it had been found, eaten up by insects, among the child's clothes and toys, and Félicité had claimed it for herself.[9] The pity for the rejected things is almost a displacement of the self-pity that the old servant barely allows herself, and it ingenuously goes beyond personal memory, embracing with a collector's love "all the old stuff" that the mistress had thrown away. Since it is connected to her respect for her betters, it extends to a suit that belonged to her mistress's husband, whom Félicité never knew, and even to the portrait of the Count of Artois, a political relic: much time has passed since Charles X ascended the throne and was then driven out, together with his dynasty. About to take its place is a popular illustration in which Félicité can admire in advance the amalgamation of parrot and Holy Spirit that she will imagine in her death agony, in the tale's famous last sentence.[10]

The compounding of the Bourbon portrait with artificial flowers is a final touch of ironic decontextualization of objects, as was, en passant, the coconut holy water stoup; this is consonant with the premise that the place feels like both a chapel and a bazaar. Félicité's "miscellaneous things" are less bizarre than those of Frau Nietken, but even if they are bizarre there is no reason to suspect that they are not to be taken seriously, not to say sorrowfully. The passage is certainly part — even typical — of Flaubert's dissolving and disillusioned view of the modern world as kitsch — in other words, as, precisely, a decontextualization of everything. Yet, as in Gozzano, this value or taste judgment is an author's judgment and is unrelated to the character, whose tenderness makes each fetish respectable and lends subjective homogeneity to the whole picture. Through the medium of a character rather than directly, thanks to a lyrical "I," we again find the constant of our first, verse examples in full-blown fictional realism — an emotional investment in otherwise unusable trash. And here the pity for rejected things, as an antifunctional return of the repressed, is really reabsorbed in that other return of the repressed that is the act of taking on such a character as a protagonist, with respect to an established social and moral order.

8

Not to be able to check original texts is compromising, but the impossibility of ignoring nineteenth-century Russian fiction is too specifically confirmed by our inquiry to allow us to give up certain texts that I know only in translation. I can only deal with a translation as a text in itself, and resign myself to the fact that not only everything about the original's signifiers but also a great many of its signifieds remain unreachable for me. Let us go back to the first flowering of the Romantic-realistic period in that language — to 1842, the year in which Nikolai V. Gogol (1809–52) published as Volume I of his novel *Dead Souls* the only part he was to complete. The title has two meanings: the moral-metaphorical one alludes to the aridity and greed of Chichikov, the protagonist; the literal one refers to his bureaucratically imaginative plan of fraud, which provides the novel with both its plot and the layout of its episodes. He goes into the Russian provinces and buys the peasants' "souls," in order to speculate in them at the end; that is, he buys the names of the serfs who had died during the five years between one census and the next, since, as far as the national treasury was concerned, they were considered alive until the end of that period. I shall excerpt two fragments, located a few lines apart, from the point at which Chichikov enters the home of Plyushkin, the fifth of the landowners whom he tricks. Plyushkin's peasant village has already been described with various references to decrepitude, abandon, mildew, and increasing wildness; and likewise the house's façade and surroundings:

> It looked as if they were washing the floors in the house, and all the furniture had for the time being been piled up there. On one table there even stood a broken chair, and next to it a clock with a stopped pendulum to which a spider had already attached its web. Near it, leaning its side against the wall, stood a cupboard with old silver, decanters, and Chinese porcelain. On the bureau, inlaid with mother-of-pearl mosaic, which in places had fallen out and left only yellow grooves filled with glue, lay a various multitude of things: a stack of papers written all over in a small hand, covered by a marble paperweight, gone green, with a little egg on top of it, some ancient book in a leather binding with red edges, a completely dried-up lemon no bigger than a hazelnut, the broken-off arm of an armchair, a glass with some sort of liquid and three flies in it, covered by a letter, a little piece of sealing-wax, a little piece of rag picked up somewhere, two ink-stained pens, dried up as if with consumption, a toothpick, turned completely yellow, with which the master

had probably picked his teeth even before the invasion of Moscow by the French.

    From the middle of the ceiling hung a chandelier in a hempen sack, which the dust made to resemble a silk cocoon with a worm sitting inside it. On the floor in the corner of the room was heaped a pile of whatever was more crude and unworthy of lying on the tables. Precisely what was in this pile it was hard to tell, for there was such an abundance of dust on it that the hands of anyone who touched it resembled gloves; most conspicuously, there stuck out from it a broken-off piece of a wooden shovel and an old boot sole. One would never have known that the room was inhabited by a living being, were its presence not announced by an old, worn nightcap lying on the table.[11]

It is a surprising spectacle as seen through Chichikov's eyes—which are ours, here—and so is the sight of the proprietor himself, who is dressed so indecorously that one can hardly tell his sex. The author's voice will soon intervene, explaining and recounting what Chichikov has learned from a fragment of malicious gossip about Plyushkin's greed, its slow beginnings and its compulsive development. And in this tale, more objects of a kind that concerns us will be listed because Plyushkin habitually gathers and piles them up,[12] with a fetishism or collector's mania which is caricatured compared to Félicité's. Like Flaubert's servant, Gogol's landowner is aged and has become locked in a maniacal relationship with objects. In the former, however, the disinterestedness that aspires to salvage memories is related to order, cleanliness, and a cult for objects chosen one by one. In the latter, the selfish goal of saving up provisions pays no heed to disorder, doesn't worry about filth, and won't be held back by the uselessness or vileness of anything. The first fragment includes a long list that is introduced by the synthesis, "a various multitude of things," and is extraordinary for the inventiveness of groupings in the sphere of the domestic and degraded. But the list in the second fragment, which seems to be summarized in advance by the words "whatever was more crude and unworthy of lying on the tables," is literally lost in a trail of dust, and two foul items can barely be distinguished.

    This is the first time that we find objects with such base connotations in our series of texts. We become aware of how these connotations are less dependent on everyday humbleness or modesty of economic value than on slovenly upkeep: as if the result of this latter, filth, implicitly shifted its coloring from the physical sphere into the moral sphere. And this is even more true of avarice than it could ever be of poverty. Plyushkin is in fact very rich, although only the cupboard full of silver and chinaware show it here, and he is far from being the only miserly character in mainstream nineteenth-century realistic fiction.

We shall return later to the reasons behind the recurrence of this type of character. For now, let us rather propose three connected observations, with respect to realistic fiction. First: the clarity and indeed the verisimilitude of the description quoted above are not incompatible with frequent drifting into the comparative-metaphorical region. Second: every figure of this type is also hyperbolic — a fact that, in the abstract, is more dangerous to verisimilitude. Third: more than one of these hyperbolic comparisons establishes a slightly joking tone, which is harmless to verisimilitude only if the dose is minimal, but which in turn is not incompatible with the tragic essence that is generally attributed to the character of Plyushkin.

By way of example of an opposite case, here are a few lines in which the attention to detail, to microscopic humbleness, does not call for comparison, exaggeration, or amusement: "mother-of-pearl mosaic, which in places had fallen out and left only yellow grooves filled with glue." Conversely, here is the actual opening of the description: "*It looked as if* they were washing the floors. . . ." And, using the idea of a general cleaning as a prelude to a spectacle of general dirtiness, metaphor and hyperbole are jokingly complicated by antiphrasis or irony. Here are all the other passages with the rhetorical character that I have indicated: a lemon "*no bigger than* a hazelnut"; two pens "dried up *as if* with consumption"; a chandelier "which the dust *made to resemble* a silk cocoon"; the dusty hands "*resembled* gloves." Let us add a dubitative formulation, whose "zero degree" is comparative: "a toothpick, turned completely yellow, with which the master *had probably* picked his teeth [= yellow *as if* the master *had picked* his teeth with it] even before the invasion of Moscow."

Of course, Erich Auerbach's brilliant literary-historical thesis regarding the whole field of the "representation of reality" sheds light also onto our limited area of concern. That is, that the achievement of certain authors of the 1830s and '40s consisted less in the freedom to introduce in literature "everyday triviality, practical preoccupations, ugliness and vulgarity" of life — previously considered indecent or insignificant — than in the possibility of taking these aspects of life entirely "seriously and even tragically" instead of, as was the case before, chastising and redeeming their lack of dignity through a comical or satirical distancing effect.[13] Thus the figuratively joking passages in this Gogol text simply enrich, and certainly do not call into question, the meticulous, unsqueamish seriousness of the new representational code. But, without mistaking them for foreign bodies in the aesthetic sense, we may still single them out for what they are in historical perspective: the by-products of a relatively recent transition and the still valid legacies of an abrogated literary code.

9

It was Alexander Sergeevich Pushkin (1799–1837) who, shortly before Gogol's time, inaugurated the new code of concrete representation in Russian literature. I use the word "concrete" in both the descriptive-sensorial sense and the other, historical-environmental one, with which we may endow it following Auerbach.[14] Throughout European fiction, even the most ancient imaginary demands of the supernatural had to come to terms with this code. The result was that genre of compromise between the real and the unreal, between criticism of the supernatural as not verisimilar and the credit that we surreptitiously grant to it, that is studied today under the rubric of the fantastic. And it is legitimate to include the Pushkin story of which I would now like to examine an excerpt, *The Queen of Spades* (1834), in that category. A young officer tells his friends of his grandmother, an eighty-seven-year-old Russian countess: sixty years earlier, at the court of Versailles — and thanks to Saint-Germain, a prodigious adventurer — she is said to have made use of an infallible secret for winning three times in a row at cards. Hermann, one of the friends, greedy for money, finds a way of entering the old woman's palace in the evening; he wants to surprise her in the middle of the night and drag the secret out of her. This is what we make out indistinctly, in the half-dark interior:

> Hermann ran up the stairs, opened the door of the anteroom, and saw a servant asleep in an ancient soiled armchair under a lamp. Hermann walked past him with a light but firm step. The reception hall and the drawing room were dark, with only a feeble light falling on them from the lamp in the anteroom. Hermann entered the bedroom. A gold sanctuary lamp burned in front of an icon-case filled with ancient icons. Armchairs with faded damask upholstery and down-cushioned sofas, their gilt coating worn, stood in melancholy symmetry along the walls, which were covered with Chinese silk. Two portraits, painted in Paris by Mme. Lebrun, hung on the wall. One of them showed a man about forty years old, red-faced and portly, wearing a light green coat with a star; the other a beautiful young woman with an aquiline nose, with her hair combed back over her temples, and with a rose in her powdered locks. Every nook and corner was crowded with china shepherdesses, table clocks made by the famous Leroy, little boxes, bandalores, fans, and diverse other ladies' toys invented at the end of the last century, along with Montgolfier's balloon and Mesmer's magnetism.[15]

The facts that the armchair is "ancient" and "soiled," or that the upholstery on the other armchairs is "faded," or that the gilt coating on the sofas is "worn," do not lack a motive: the countess, too, is rich but miserly in her senility.[16] But as with so many other passages in nineteenth-century fiction, one must ask oneself whether the moment of lingering before the objects — a moment that entails such adjectives and predicates — is not also an end in itself, to some extent. In other words: Does it not have a literary function directly proportional to the reduction of functionality that has been attributed to the objects? Here, functionality is ornamental dignity, diminished by wear and tear, albeit much more nobly than in the Gogol text. But connotations of lowness that are neither grotesque nor ridiculous but rather are taken seriously — in keeping, once again, with Auerbach's conception of literary-historical evolution — are connotations of reality par excellence: they *constitute reality* in and of themselves. Verification of this point lies in the improbability that, all things being equal, or apart only from the fact of miserliness, the narrator would have stopped to describe furnishings had they been perfectly preserved or brand new. Connotations of optimum decorative functionality would not have constituted reality, or at least not to the same extent, simply because in any prior literary period it was possible seriously to attribute such connotations to things, possibly in order to glorify or idealize people and places.

More than holy images would have done — as in Félicité's case — here the list of little objects makes the bedroom into a sort of sanctuary for an old person's favorite memories. Instead of Félicité's humble, miscellaneous things, here we have high-class knick-knacks and furnishings that are not so much worn out as antiquated, and that, together with the two portraits, make everyone think back to the same period: the late eighteenth century and the *ancien régime* in France. It is a sort of second temporal background — a specific and localized one — that lends its historical weight to the tale and that the decor itself proposes as an unchangeable model of good taste from the point of view of the character who owns it. Mme. Vigée-Lebrun, the painter, had done a portrait of Marie Antoinette; the "famous Leroy" had been the first to make chronometers, which gives his name the same implicit meaning as the references to the much more famous Montgolfier and Mesmer. The technical and scientific innovations of a whole period, its highest peaks of functionality and rationality — real or presumed — wind up, after six decades, as so much junk alongside the most frivolous products of that same age.

This six-decade backward glance is what I called grandma's day in reference to Gozzano's text (and there, too, an outmoded technical innovation — "the daguerreotypes," or early photography — was included).[17] In the present case, however, the decrepit, mysterious grandmother is still alive; Hermann, who makes her die of fright, will then believe that she winks at him from her coffin, and subsequently that she visits him at the witching hour to give him the names of the three winning cards. The supernatural doubt that runs through the episode and obscures its epilogue in no way interferes with the realistic concreteness — in the descriptive sense as well as the historicizing one — that the defunctionalization of the objects helps along. On the contrary, this is the paradox of "fantastic" fiction: the same connotations attaching to objects may, through compromise-formation, constitute reality and uncannily set up the unreal. Everything antiquated or worn out that the palace displays by night, although it includes true-to-life motives and chronological references, is no less qualified to leave the door half-open to the indeterminable spaces and times of fear, and to suggest its incomprehensible causalities.

10

Toward the middle of the hundred years that "fantastic" fiction lasted, from the late eighteenth to the late nineteenth century, the size of an aristocratic town residence was perfectly sufficient to contain supernatural doubt, although the most propitious settings for this purpose were and remained castles, owing to their vastness and age. In the 1927 novel by Virginia Woolf (1882–1941) *To the Lighthouse,* a spectral, nocturnal visitation of an entirely different sort may run through the rooms of a rundown middle-class vacation home. The house is on one of the Hebrides Islands, and has been regularly rented for the summer by a philosophy professor and his educated family. But throughout most of the second part of the novel ("Time Passes"), which covers a period of many years including the First World War, the house is empty and shut up. In an especially original interlude, the things in the house are endowed with human traits and adopt the same preeminence attributed to them in the Borges sonnet named after them, as well as the same metaphysical meaningfulness, which in this case, however, is connected to their gradual disintegration. In darkness and silence, abandoned rooms and objects become, in their own way, the subjects of the narrative from which human characters are absent: brief news about the latter is occasionally provided in square brackets, and three times the news is of a death. The theme of worn-out furnishings and of the unstoppable deterioration of the house has already been presented in the first part. Mrs. Ramsay, the protagonist, fretted over it, and this was how her innate solicitude for others, enterprising yet discreet, and especially her wifely and motherly concern, manifested themselves in her unfolding thoughts:

> and saw the room, saw the chairs, thought them fearfully shabby. Their entrails, as Andrew said the other day, were all over the floor; but then what was the point, she asked herself, of buying good chairs to let them spoil up here all through the winter when the house, with only one old woman to see to it, positively dripped with wet? Never mind: the rent was precisely twopence halfpenny; the children loved it; it did her husband good to be three thousand,

or if she must be accurate, three hundred miles from his library and his lectures and his disciples; and there was room for visitors. Mats, camp beds, crazy ghosts of chairs and tables whose London life of service was done — they did well enough there; and a photograph or two, and books.

At a certain moment, she supposed, the house would become so shabby that something must be done. If they could be taught to wipe their feet and not bring the beach in with them — that would be something. Crabs, she had to allow, if Andrew really wished to dissect them, or if Jasper believed that one could make soup from seaweed, one could not prevent it; or Rose's objects — shells, reeds, stones; for they were gifted, her children, but all in quite different ways. And the result of it was, she sighed, taking in the whole room from floor to ceiling, as she held the stocking against James's leg, that things got shabbier and got shabbier summer after summer. The mat was fading; the wall-paper was flapping. You couldn't tell any more that those were roses on it.[18]

The figurative hints in the little list of exhausted furniture — "crazy *ghosts* of chairs and tables whose London *life of service* was done" — have none of the playfulness of those in Gogol. It is rather as if Mrs. Ramsay suffered from feeling the unavoidability of retaliation — at least within the relatively decent means of her family — for the advantages offered by the holiday (distancing her husband from his professional environment, her children taking an interest in the fauna, flora, and marine minerals). The retaliation consists in the decay of things produced precisely by the nearness of the sea: in winter the house "positively dripped with wet," in the summer the children brought "the beach in with them."[19] In short, as if nature's invasiveness were the price exacted for the relief or vital stimulus it provides in alternative to culture. And even before this we had understood that the invasiveness of nature becomes a menacing symbol complementary to human frailty: when the sudden ceasing of the hum of voices exposes to Mrs. Ramsay's hearing the sound of the sea on the beach, and the terror of a foreboding of the island's destruction and sinking.[20] Now, in the long interlude of the second part, already during the first night, gusts or bits or fragments of wind move about the still lived-in house; they are personified and questioning. They have been able to enter through the doors — which are corroded by rust and warped by humidity — and it is to the decaying objects that they address mysterious questions; insisting on being told how long these objects would last, and sounding impatient because of the objects' extended resistance:

Nothing stirred in the drawing-room or in the dining-room or on the staircase. Only through the rusty hinges and swollen sea-moistened woodwork certain airs, detached from the body of the wind (the house was ramshackle after all) crept round corners and ventured indoors. Almost one might imagine them, as they entered the drawing-room, questioning and wondering, toying with the flap of hanging wall-paper, asking, would it hang much longer, when would it fall? Then smoothly brushing the walls, they passed on musingly as if asking the red and yellow roses on the wall-paper whether they would fade, and questioning (gently, for there was time at their disposal) the torn letters in the waste-paper basket, the flowers, the books, all of which were now open to them and asking: Were they allies? Were they enemies? How long would they endure?[21]

Questions of the same sort recur two chapters further along, when the same airy anthropomorphizations storm through the deserted house.[22] There are not many texts of such length that are so uninterruptedly pertinent from our point of view. I shall even refrain from quoting from the chapter in which Mrs. McNab, who is too old to carry out the heavy task of opening and cleaning the house once in a while, weaves thoughts about its disastrous state into memories of Mrs. Ramsay, who has long been dead; this comes after the echoes and reflections of the now long-past war.[23] In the following chapter, the house and garden are again made livable — thanks to the efforts of two more people — for the arrival, imminent at last, of one of the guests of former times. The radical picture of the irruption of nature — atmospheric, vegetable, and animal — into the human dwelling at the beginning of the chapter is thus all the more hyperbolic; this precedes the hypothesis of collapse and burial beneath wild plants, which remains in the future conditional but raises the discourse to a level of solemnity reminiscent of psalms and prophecies, and the fate of the modest abode to that of a Babylon buried beneath the sand:

> The house was left; the house was deserted. It was left like a shell on a sandhill to fill with dry salt grains now that life had left it. The long night seemed to have set in; the trifling airs, nibbling, the clammy breaths, fumbling, seemed to have triumphed. The saucepan had rusted and the mat decayed. Toads had nosed their way in. Idly, aimlessly, the swaying shawl swung to and fro. A thistle thrust itself between the tiles in the larder. The swallows nested in the drawing-room; the floor was strewn with straw; the plaster fell in shovelfuls; rafters were laid bare; rats carried off this and that to gnat behind the wainscots. Tortoise-shell butterflies burst from the chrysalis and pattered their life out on the window-pane. Poppies sowed themselves among the dahlias; the lawn waved with long grass; giant artichokes towered among roses; a fringed carnation flowered among the cabbages; while the gentle tapping of a weed at the window had become, on winter's nights, a drumming from sturdy trees and thorned briars which made the whole room green in summer.[24]
>
> For now had come that moment, that hesitation when dawn trembles and night pauses, when if a feather alight in the scale it will be weighed down. One

feather, and the house, sinking, falling, would have turned and pitched down-
wards to the depths of darkness. In the ruined room, picnickers would have lit
their kettles; lovers sought shelter there, lying on the bare boards; and the
shepherd stored his dinner on the bricks, and the tramp slept with his coat
round him to ward off the cold. Then the roof would have fallen; briars and
hemlocks would have blotted out path, step, and window; would have grown,
unequally but lustily over the mound, until some trespasser, losing his way,
could have told only by a red-hot poker among the nettles, or a scrap of china
in the hemlock, that here once someone had lived; there had been a house.[25]

11

If any of my readers are beginning to find the thematic constants sufficiently reliable to render the sudden shifts caused by variations of period,
language, and literary genre tolerable, I hope they will now accept all three
variations at once. Let us return to poetry, to French, and to the nineteenth
century — specifically, to 1853, when the exiled Victor Hugo (1802–85) published the singular collection entitled *Chastisements* (*Châtiments*). The poems
are so many pieces of invective against usurpation, abuse of power, and the
corruption of a statesman and his reactionary regime — of Napoleon III and
the Second Empire. But so great was Hugo's metaphorical and hyperbolic
creativity that all that we lose because of the lack of political concreteness we
regain in visionary violence or satirical truculence; and one man and one
regime summarize all the social ills inherent in the entire course of history.
Thus it is sufficient to allude to the man and regime, surprisingly and very late,
only in the final half-line of a poem that is nearly a hundred lines long: *The
Sewer of Rome* (*L'Égout de Rome*). I shall quote a segment from the middle,
and from the ending:

> The hideous dungeon spreads in all directions;
> In places it opens its infected, sow-breathed holes
> Beneath the feet of passersby;
> This sewer turns into a river during the rainy season;
> Toward noon, all about the bright red openings,
> The hard iron bars cut up the sun,
> And the wall looks like zebras' backs;
> All the rest is miasma, darkness, shadows.
> Here and there the paving stones seem bloody,
> As in assassins' homes: the stone sweats terrifyingly;
> Oblivion, plague, and night do their work here.
> The rat running collides with the mole; grass snakes
> Slither along the wall like black lightning bolts;

Shards, rags, green-footed columns,
Reptiles that leave traces of saliva,
The spider's web hanging from the beams,
Puddles in the corners, fearful mirrors
Where unknown slow, black beings swim,
Make a dreadful bustle among the shadows.

. . . .

At the back, you can make out, in a shadow where
No reflection of day, no breath of wind can reach,
Something fearful that was once alive,
Jaws, eyes, bellies, viscera,
Carcasses that make spots on the great walls;
You approach, and your eye will long remain fixed
On this monstrous pile, sunk in the mud,
Flung down there through a hole feared by drunkards,
Without being able to distinguish whether the remains
Of the doleful carrion still have a visible form,
And are dogs that have croaked or rotten caesars.[26]

The tendency to polarize extremes, giving value both to what is sublime and to what is low, inspires Hugo's literary poetics as well as his ideological Manicheism and predestined him to descend to the depths of such a theme. He did it again, in prose and at greater length, in the celebrated chapters on the Paris sewers in his novel *Les Misérables,* but the ancient, imperial Rome of the poem is also shown as a modern-style capital of immense proportions. The sewer appears as a sort of equally immense reverse image of it or backdrop to it, and acts as a photographic negative of the monstrous variety of shops, waste, and vices. It is in itself a monumental, subterranean artifact, and it receives the residue of other artifacts, such as the shards and rags in the list in the first quotation; but it mixes them together with the natural corporeal condition of live, repellent animals such as rats, moles, and grass snakes (followed later by bats and toads), or by traces of them, like (from the same list) reptiles' saliva and spiders' webs. Although there are a few too many animals, in keeping with the hyperbole, they are at home in the place. There is a contamination of culture by nature, but not the usurpation found in the interior described by Virginia Woolf, by toads and mice but also by swallows and butterflies.

The sewer is in fact, institutionally, culture's rendering of accounts to nature; it has the regular function of absorbing antifunctional matter, dispersing it, and making it disappear — not only the matter that hasn't been assimilated into the human body (this is where excrement moves from its status as a secret, symbolic referent of a number of themes [I, 6–7], to the status of theme, or nearly so, in a text), but everything thrown away or decomposed that has begun to return to dust or, in other words, to become part of nature again. If dust made the objects that were virtually listed in Gogol's text indistinct in full light, in the shadowy hallucination of Hugo's text the list in the first quotation leads into much more rotten and horrible indistinctness. As to the second quotation, it merely articulates, confusedly, its own list within the shapelessness of putrefaction and, in a double sense, it touches upon the borderline between the human and things. It touches upon it inasmuch as the corporality of the human cadaver (at this point another of our symbolic referents [I, 6] emerges) may be located at the same borderline, and all the more so when all honors are denied it. But this is so also because we cannot even distinguish between the carrion of dogs and that of emperors: and this is where the ferocious imprecation against Napoleon III — a caesar unworthy of a capital C — was lying in ambush.

12

In keeping to the same thematic constants, we are now attracted towards another French text, this time from the twentieth century. It defies definition within traditional literary genres, inasmuch as surrealism — as an ideology, first and foremost, and also as a poetics — forbids us to talk of fiction in the sense of the word which implies fictitiousness. Nor does the quality of sincerity that it prescribes allow reference to autobiography in the sense of the word which implies narrative. Or rather, the criterion of selection of truthful facts to be narrated has changed, as *Mad Love* (*L'Amour fou*), a piece of prose by André Breton (1896–1967) that was published in 1937, shows throughout, and specifically in the brief episode that I shall quote. In Brittany, on 20 July 1936, the writer and the woman with whom he is living the relationship referred to in the title get off a bus, at random, near a little beach that they had already visited a few days earlier:

> Very quickly bored, that first time, by contemplating a gloomy expanse of sand and pebbles, we had had no other imaginative recourse than to set ourselves looking for minute and by no means numerous bits of wreckage that might have been scattered over it. Besides, they were not lacking in charm, once they had been brought together: many very small-sized electric light bulbs, pieces of floating blue wood, a champagne cork, the last two centimeters of a pink candle, a cuttlefish bone no less pink than the candle, a little round metallic candy-box engraved with the word "violet," a minuscule crab skeleton — a marvelously intact skeleton, and of such a chalky white that it made me think it was the thrush of the sun, which was invisible that day, in

Cancer. All of these elements could have converged in forming one of those talismanic objects of which surrealism is so enamored. But, on 20 July, the question of resuming that pastime hardly existed, because the sea, which had not receded as far, had manifestly not left behind anything that might have been a bit unexpected. It was the oppressive repetition, after too few days had passed, of a place that was particularly banal and hostile because of the banality itself, like all places that leave the capacity for attention totally vacant.[27]

In the first surrealist manifesto (1924), in accusing realistic descriptions in fiction—including the greatest—of flatness, Breton had written: "My notion of life's continuity is too unstable to make my minutes of depression, of weakness, equal the best"; "I don't take into account the moments of nothingness in my life."[28] Given such a hierarchy of moments, which is also incompatible with a continuous or steady autobiographical tale, the visit on 20 July would as little deserve to be recalled as any other object of flat realistic description. The location is "a gloomy expanse of sand and pebbles" where nature becomes hostile, not as a result of its unhealthiness, as in Hugo's and Woolf's texts, but for moral or aesthetic reasons—as a result of tedious, frustrating banality. On the occasion of the first visit, however, the imagination had nonetheless drawn resources from the sea's scattered legacies on the shore, striking a glimmer of preciousness or magic in every piece of debris that at least had the merit of being unexpected. The list that we read is the first of our series to have been actively composed, so to speak; that is, it was made by the story's characters, who have looked for things and put them together before the story put them together in words.

The appreciation of such things seems to implicate their reduction to perfect uselessness, and the sorting out, according to the workings of pure chance, be it of natural or of cultural debris. The pieces of floating blue wood, the pinkish cuttlefish bone, and the very white crab skeleton seem to have been cleaned and polished by the water, while the light bulbs, cork, candle end, and candy box have been decontextualized by their sojourn in it, in a way that is the opposite of the decontextualization that generates kitsch—by removing them from the area of culture, instead of adding up and tampering with more than one of them. Moreover, the surrealists delighted in a taste for simulated kitsch, as I mentioned apropos of the Arnim excerpt; thus highly disparate elements could converge to form one of its typical talismanic objects. Through such a pastime paradoxical, if not caricatural, refunctionalization would be acquired —one that would base itself on the very negation of all functionality, and on the voluntary production of anticommodities, not in literature but in reality. In the case at hand, the charm of the antifunctional is already guaranteed or strengthened by reabsorption and restitution on nature's part; these make the episode into a highly mediated and very modern variant of the theme of sunken treasures that the sea has flung ashore.

13

As a fiction writer, Prosper Mérimée (1803–70) shared the descriptive inclinations of his time to the least possible degree, remaining relatively faithful to a pre-nineteenth-century literary code. I shall excerpt from his prose two lists, each too short to be tantamount to a description in itself. In the historical novel of 1829, *Chronicle of the Reign of Charles IX* (*Chronique du règne de Charles IX*), the young Protestant protagonist learns that his love for a lady of the Catholic court is reciprocated, when, unseen, he comes upon a nocturnal scene of "white" magic:

> The table was covered with strange things that he could barely make out. They seemed to be arranged in a certain bizarre order, and he thought he could distinguish pieces of fruit, some bones, and shreds of bloody cloth. A figurine of a man, not more than a foot high and, it seemed, made of wax, was placed over these disgusting cloths.[29]

In *Carmen* (1845), when the archaeologist who is the initial narrator makes the acquaintance of the beautiful gypsy witch who gives the novella its title, he cannot resist the temptation, between the exotic and the occult, to have her tell his fortune:

> As soon as we were alone, the gypsy took from her case some cards that seemed to have done a good deal of service, a magnet, a dried chameleon, and some other objects needed for her art. She then told me to make the sign of the cross in my left hand with a coin, and the magic ceremonies began.[30]

Speaking, as I did earlier (I, 1), of solidarity between the list's formal structure and its contents consisting of nonfunctional things, I neglected the most obvious probable exception: a list of instruments or ingredients that make up precisely what is needed for carrying out a practical operation. Naturally, the exception is only valid if it involves working on a material object with material means. If on the contrary the means or the end, or both, are supernatural yet nevertheless are not satisfied by words only but require objects as well, magic's figurative and symbolic logic will flee from physical or chemical functionality; and its choices will appear (rightfully so, I would say) strange as far as secular rationality is concerned. This is why it is not only in the historical sense that the list of magical objects may be called the prototype or archetype of all the various lists of strange things — inasmuch as figurative and symbolic logic are more intrinsic to the phenomenon of literature than the logic proper to science and the functional. The two fragments from Mérimée are late, concise echoes of a most ancient and abundant literary-historical topic, and they lend themselves well, at the formal level, to exemplifying two contrary successions that are possible with every list, between the possible synthetic designation of listable elements and their real, true analytical listing.

In the first text, synthesis precedes analysis: first, *strange things* are referred to, then *pieces of fruit, some bones, shreds of bloody cloth* . . . ; in the second text, the inverse is the case: first *cards, a magnet,* and *a dried chameleon* are mentioned, then *some other objects needed* . . . Expressing this in abstract formulas, we would have the following order in the first case: $x / a, b, c$ . . . ; in the second, the order: a, b, c . . . $/ x$. We have encountered the first order in Gogol, for instance: first, *a various multitude of things* was referred to, and then thirteen elements followed one another in various syntactical relations to each other. The second order was found in Borges: first, there were ten elements, and then *How many things* . . . (but five more elements in the following line); and the same in Cros: first, thirteen elements, and then *What clutter* . . . (but perhaps the first element was already a synthesis). The combination of the two possibilities yields the formula, $x / a, b, c$ . . . $/ x$. Such a combination was recognizable in the last part of Hugo's text and in that of Breton, but less clearly than in Flaubert's text, where we first read *so many objects . . . and miscellaneous things* . . . , and then, after a few lines, a list of eleven elements, and finally, further below, *all the old stuff* . . . The list's structure is comparable to a fan that can be not only open or closed, as circumstances require, but also partly open and partly closed, depending on the desired amount of folding or opening of its numerous ribs.

14

Our confusing survey cannot end without a couple of examples in which, at last, this formal constant — the list — is *not* present; it may have seemed to more than one reader that it was the sole really undeniable constant throughout all the preceding examples. Let us make a transition to the long story, *The Strange Case of Dr. Jekyll and Mr. Hyde,* by Robert Louis Stevenson (1850–94), which belongs simultaneously to two separate genres: fantastic fiction and science fiction. It dates from 1886, and during that fin de siècle era the first of the two genres was nearly exhausted, whereas the second was approaching a long period of fertility. What the story holds in common with science fiction is the futuristic justification of the incredible, the rational up-

dating of magic; what it holds in common with the fantastic is the unaware-
ness at the beginning — and uncertainty to the end — of both the person who is
observing and the reader. What is interesting for us is that the first disquieting
sign at the beginning of the tale, the first tear in the material of efficient
everyday normality, is the description of a building that is absurd in appearance, unusable, rundown, and dirty:

> Two doors from one corner, on the left hand going east, the line was broken
> by the entry of a court; and just at that point, a certain sinister block of
> building thrust forward its gable on the street. It was two stories high; showed
> no window, nothing but a door on the lower storey and a blind forehead of
> discoloured wall on the upper; and bore in every feature the marks of pro-
> longed and sordid negligence. The door, which was equipped with neither bell
> nor knocker, was blistered and distained. Tramps slouched into the recess and
> struck matches on the panels; children kept shop upon the steps; the school-
> boy had tried his knife on the mouldings; and for close on a generation no one
> had appeared to drive away these random visitors or to repair their ravages.[31]

The building appears to be the only point at which the squalid surrounding
area looks out upon an important, active, and prosperous London street, amid
houses and shops with gaily gleaming paint and brasses. This street was mentioned in the lines immediately preceding the quotation, so that a lingering to
describe the functional (confirming the reasons, briefly mentioned with respect
to the Russians, that make it relatively unusual in realistic fiction) is motivated
by an effect of contrast and is useful precisely for introducing the antifunctional. The strangeness of the façade with its "blind forehead," windowless
above the "blistered" door and its ravaged recess, will gradually be explained
— as will all the other, stranger things. It is not part of a house, but rather of
what was once a theater for anatomical dissections, next to which Dr. Jekyll,
who has bought it and let it go to ruin, has set himself up in a respectable,
comfortable apartment.[32] Whereas the degree of abandonment and disorder
attributed to the inside of the theater (when it is in turn described) does not
exceed the limits of verisimilitude, there is never an adequate realistic explanation of why the exterior has been left in such sordid condition.

On the other hand, the respective metaphoric values are of a clarity that is
all the more impressive for being impossible to grasp in a first reading until one
is very far along. Thus, the rundown laboratory of official science makes
visible the presumed, bold surpassing of it by scientific magic: science fiction
vindicates the discredited aspirations of real magic of the past and mimics the
periodic aging (of which I spoke in commenting on Pushkin) of rational,
functional progress. As to the building's double façades and entrances, they

simply correspond, materially, to the duality of the sole protagonist in his opposite personalities. Of course, it would have been more verisimilar if the access reserved for Dr. Jekyll's negative double had camouflaged itself in an ordinary outward appearance, but the need for verisimilitude is not as strong as the compromise-formation proper to the fantastic, which (as could be glimpsed in the Pushkin excerpt) makes antifunctional things constitute reality in order to give credence to the unreal. The description that we have read of the lurid side of the building, into which the bestial Mr. Hyde disappears like a dangerous animal entering its den, anticipates the repulsiveness of evil that will be laid bare in his body. It is a supernatural repulsiveness, and neither the vastness of castles or palaces nor nocturnal darkness and isolation are needed to call it up; for, on the contrary, in the heart of London, the character or half-character can hide it only by going through a door, and the building's face can show it off permanently with sinister shamelessness.

15

Extra-European maritime imperialism, of which London was the heart, also possessed its own supernatural legend of accursed powers. One of the only three myths of modern — rather than ancient or medieval — genesis, it ran parallel to the myths of immoderate pleasure and immoderate knowledge, respectively represented by Don Juan and Faust. One cannot avoid noticing a disguised version of this legend in the story entitled *MS. Found in a Bottle* (1833) by Edgar Allan Poe (1809–49). At least superficially, the element of transgression is missing here; the character (shortly to become famous thanks to Heine and Wagner) of the Flying Dutchman whose arrogance leads him to sail around a forbidden cape, thereby challenging the devil or God, is absent. This makes the image of the ghost ship — which is condemned to sail for centuries in remote oceans, with its many-centuries-old crew and captain — gain all the more in importance and take on human characteristics. These decrepit seamen — tottering, talking softly to themselves in an incomprehensible language, absorbed in impenetrable meditations and activities, and blind to the presence of the narrator, who has ended up on board as the result of a collision that sunk his own ship — are not ghosts; on the contrary, they fit in with the most original of the compulsive paths taken by Poe's imagination: they are real, true, living corpses. We do not yet know whether their corporality, which is human despite their being half-cadavers, will in itself demand our attention.

But the no less exceptional corporality of the old ship — putrid and worm-eaten, yet expandable or *growing* — surprisingly resembles the crumbled stone in the intact masonry of the House of Usher, in the author's best-known story;[33] and this match is sufficient to remove all hesitation about the possibility of interpreting the gigantic black vessel itself as a great coffin or, better, as a huge, living cadaver. At first sight, we would certainly say that its excessive, undefined antiquity is what makes it sinister. Undefined, but not undefinable: the signs that denote this antiquity are highly suggestive in terms of both chronology and history: they refer us, approximately, to the fifteenth and sixteenth centuries, with their transoceanic navigations and intercontinental discoveries. The captain, his head bent, examines a document signed by a monarch, and near him and the sailors are scientific devices that have been outdated for centuries — rather than for decades, as in Pushkin, or only with respect to a fantastic hypothesis, as in Stevenson. Here, however, the mysterious permanence in the use of such devices gives them a distorting, supplementary distance, and the nautical instruments, maps, and folio volumes with their iron clasps are repeatedly, and with varying wording, endowed with connotations of a strangeness beyond obsolescence:

> . . . and groped in a corner among a pile of singular-looking instruments, and decayed charts of navigation.

> Around them, on every part of the deck, lay scattered mathematical instruments of the most quaint and obsolete construction . . .

> The cabin floor was thickly strewn with strange, iron-clasped folios, and moldering instruments of science, and obsolete long-forgotten charts.[34]

The narrator is an antique dealer by profession, as we learn later on, and his very soul has become as much of a ruin as an oriental city; and yet he has never experienced this sort of antiquity. Its secret cannot be guessed, because it is marvelously expressed immediately after the denial of the possibility of expressing it. Here are the lines that linger over the ship's form, her masts and sails, and on the inward reactions awakened by looking at them carefully:

> What she *is not,* I can easily perceive; what she *is,* I fear it is impossible to say. I know not how it is, but in scrutinising her strange model and singular cast of spars, her huge side and overgrown suits of canvas, her severely simple bow and antiquated stern, there will occasionally flash across my mind a sensation of familiar things, and there is always mixed up with such indistinct shadows of recollection, an unaccountable memory of old foreign chronicles and ages long ago. . . .[35]

Perhaps no other writer has come so close to recognizing, in the sensation or emotion of the uncanny, the unrecognizable return of things that were "familiar," as Freud was to do much later. In Poe's sentence, their familiarity is only apparently in contrast to the fact that a memory of old, foreign chronicles of long ago is mixed together; the memory only seems to be "unaccountable." Only the centuries-long time lapses marked off by collective history can translate, for the author and adult readers, the time lapses that individual childhoods mark off in the incommensurability of their own days, hours, and minutes. And so we close our survey with this example, in which, through things, the supernatural adds historic cultural obsolescence to natural physical decay, but prolongs both the use of manmade articles and the life of material things in its childlike and measureless time.

III

Making Decisions in Order to Proceed

I

If, with the examples of the previous chapter, I proceeded by imitating *a posteriori* disorder — the disorder of an inquiry that is still in question — I must now simulate *a priori* order if I am to proceed. I refer to a type of order that displays, one after another, the postulates that underlie the subject of inquiry, and the options or restrictions that give direction to the plan — having reconsidered them retrospectively. Is there a risk of being out of date, which should be justified before carried through to the end, in confronting my subject and my project using a systematic approach? I could cite the age of this inquiry, which developed at a time when a similar attitude found its clearest (although perhaps not its most important) endorsement in so-called structuralism — or I could invoke some individual characteristics of this inquiry in particular. I would be hard put to express these characteristics better than Fontenelle did in the passage that I used as an epigraph at the beginning of this book: "Once their number is sufficiently large, many disparate truths demonstrate to the mind their relationships and their interdependence in so lively a way that they make it seem as if, after having been detached from each other with a sort of violence, they naturally seek to join together again."[1] I would say, in fact, that the book must embrace too disparate and too numerous truths to be realizable by unsystematically exploring here and there only some of their relationships and interdependencies. Freeing oneself from the duty of joining *all of them* together, thus reinforcing what seems to be their natural tendency, would mean leaving *all of them* in that state of detachment from whose violence they seem to have suffered, and to be silent about them.

And yet it is not true that this would be the only way to make a book out of them; it is likely that others in my place would prefer to hurl lightning flashes at the darkness of that bundle of truths and interrelations. The intermittence of those blinding flashes exalts what it isolates but does not deal with the before or after, or with whatever has remained in the shade. Better the pale and flickering but also constant and movable light of a candle, I say, if it is held by a patient hand. Allow me to set aside the metaphor and admit to prejudices that extend beyond the circumstances of this book's existence: I actually doubt that any unsystematic way of thinking *exists,* with the exception of that which is left only partially explained. And I doubt that the motives for defining it as unsystematic can ever be other than *interested,* in both the good and the bad rhetorical sense — as a benefit, privilege, or enchantment of expression, or as a feint, allurement, or abuse of persuasion. It does not seem incomprehensible, even to me, that the system — with its claim to responsibility for finding the greatest possible number of relationships, with its anticipation of external control by controlling itself through a number of obligatory connections — turns out to be constricting and falsely reassuring. But it is the lesser evil: if there is more of sudden intimation and more of promising profundity in the unconnected and irresponsible flash of truth, for that very reason there is also — contrary to what is often said — too much intellectual arrogance. And there is less courage in the face of the latent burden of consequences, and less curiosity with respect to the whole field that is potentially open to exploration.

2

For these reasons I shall proceed with all due speed to a clarification of what is methodologically implicit, on pain of repeating — if not enlarging — the same theoretical proposition to which I referred in the first chapter (I, 3). How many and what sort of decisions must be made, in order to proceed from the first and minimal one, which says yes to the question of *whether* to undertake the research, to the last of those that will have to determine in the highest degree *how* to carry it out? The first decision may be formulated thus:

I. *There exist certain textual constants worthy of attention.*

One might be tempted to consider this not merely minimal but downright superfluous. Most discussions in the area of literary studies presuppose that attention is to be devoted to one or another constant, to something that *keeps coming back,* either within a single text or between one text and other texts. This is obvious with respect to discussions whose orientation is either literary-historical or alternatively rhetorical-formalistic — in short, all discussions whose workings are analytical. The constants in question will be of extremely diverse kinds in each case, and no doubt many more of them could be established in the abstract than those that are worthy of attention or interesting to study. Often, following a law of inverse proportions between probability and information, the less one would suspect these constants of being interesting to study, the more they turn out to be so. I would like this to prove to be the case with our constants, the existence of which is presumed to be at the intersection of many texts that are not only very numerous but also highly varied with respect to author, period, language, and literary genre; this is so to such an extent that in the second chapter, in making transitions from one example to another, I exploited in an almost provocative way some constants of subject matter usually held to be accidental and meaningless. It would be well worth taking the above-mentioned decision, if only because of the suspicions of excess, of impertinence in the literal sense that the concept of constants in general causes to fall upon *our* constants (when does it ever happen that an *a priori* criterion determines which constants are pertinent?).

In any case, this decision is not to be taken for granted with respect to other types of discussion about literature; this is most obvious regarding those types of discussions whose main goal is to pronounce aesthetic judgments — to fulfill, as Croce said, "the task of discerning the beautiful and the ugly":[2] criticism, in the strict sense. The exception carries a great deal of weight, and I do not think that it must be made only with regard to Italian Croceanism. Nor do I believe, moreover, that the fate of Croceanism is to remain something tossed aside, as it seems to have been for the last thirty years; nor, above all, that the overcoming of it in Italy — which in its day took place quickly and furtively, silently and indisputably — was an authentic, profound occurrence. Aesthetic criticism rarely deigned to turn its attention to constants, excepting the wholly theoretical one of the quality of the texts to be judged. The lack of interest in or disdain for the existence of points of contact, formal as well as material, within one text or among various texts, of constants not of value but of fact, was simply, one might say, the other side of an exclusive interest in, or cult of, variants — of the incomparable individuality of each textual moment. If by definition every comparison leads to the recognition of constants and variants, to deny any importance to the former in order to confer it all on the latter meant that the very need to understand and acquire knowledge through comparison, rather than through direct intuition, was being resisted. Either all of this has never entirely ceased, or it has begun to concern us again.

3

As soon as it has been decided, however, that constants exist and that they matter, and before deciding—also in order to decide—what to do with them as an object of study, we must pose a question such as: Why do they exist and where do they come from? And inasmuch as literature does not come from nowhere and can only originate either in an earlier reality or in earlier literature, let us consider these two hypotheses in relation to our constants. Let us consider them by comparing them, rather than by treating them separately, and let us establish a preliminary balance to try to stop the regular seesawing of opinion due to ideological biases which put them in opposition to each other, thereby making them incompatible. Let us at once make two complementary decisions regarding our constants, with the following formulations:

II. *To see them as referring directly to real facts is inadequate.*

III. *To attribute them purely to literary tradition is inadequate.*

Possibly only in one case can the presence of thematic constants in the texts be explained through direct reference to real facts—that is, unmediated by literary codes—without seeming to be an overly crude procedure: when the constants belong to the work of an individual author and the real facts belong to the life story of an individual person. Such a case would not concern our research, which covers works of a great many authors. But it is also only an apparent exception. Not even with respect to general linguistic communication does the social aspect in the concept of the code exclude the possibility that individual usage may submit to a code. In literature it would be even less of a contradiction in terms to speak of codes that belong to an individual's works, through which a single person's experience is filtered and organized. Furthermore, we hardly ever become interested in a work without taking for granted that it has had or could have readers, success, and literary fortune—thus, that it could modify the common code of its successors, and thus, that its constants are transferable from the circuit that runs between literature and reality to the circuit that runs between literature and literature. And it is not difficult to reduce to absurdity every attempt to make the first of these into a closed circuit with respect to the second, if the direct reference is to real data of collective, rather than individual, experience.

During the first chapter's approaches to the unity of the subject of inquiry (I, 6), I began by abstractly contemplating the most constant possible aspects of our constants, and I did not balk at referring them back to the most collective possible experiences of the human race. Culture versus nature, time's ambivalence, the ambivalence of the cadaver and of excrement . . . The abstraction that sacrifices millions of concrete variants between the most varied texts to such high constants of constants, simultaneously steps over literary codes — abstractions of lesser length and historic mediators of any constants whatsoever. And the pertinence, undeniable at bottom, of the most universal referents does not make up for their absolute inability to explain the problems posed by our constants' chronological distribution: the distribution which I amply indicated in the first chapter (I, 7), and which I took into account in the second, by arranging the examples at rather regular intervals between the accidental beginning and ending dates of 1812 and 1969, and not earlier. As a whole, our constants were certainly not born on or around the earlier of these dates, but from that point on they become much more frequent or intense than before. Who would wish to claim that from then on, certain constants in Western literature originate directly in the most unchangeable aspects of the human condition, and that their coincidence with an ever growing, or rather ever culminating, secular rationalization of the world is simply irrelevant?

On the other hand, we are exposed to a no less flagrant reductio ad absurdum, starting with the chronological distribution of the constants, if we keep to the hypothesis of direct reference to collective experience and limit ourselves to subverting the type of real facts from which we can expect explanatory power. That is, if we replace the great, fixed anthropological referents with the referents of cultural, social, political, and economic history of a time when ideas and the very face of the earth changed at the same rate of speed. It is in fact true that an accelerated rate of innovation, by accelerating the rate at which things become obsolete, also increases the number of things that have been set aside — a process that we have already seen reflected in literary images (II, 9, 14). And yet, who would admit that in the real world between 1812 and 1969 anticommodities prevailed over commodities, and that useless or old or unusual objects were more numerous, more notable, and more important than before in comparison with useful or new or normal things? In the first chapter, I maintained that literature is an irreplaceable testimony to the past (I, 2–3). But I defined as an antifunctional return of the repressed the phenomenon that, in literature, increases within the period from which I took my examples in the second chapter. This is why a positive answer to my last rhetorical question would be even less admissible than a positive answer to the previous one. In this case, there is, between literary constants and real facts, a relationship to which the contrasting, inverse structure of a return of the repressed seems applicable; and the impossibility of referring them to each other *directly* is a result of such a relationship.

Direct reference, then, does not mean being naïve only with regard to, and because of, a lack of mediation from a code. "Direct" draws a pejorative sense also from the false immediacy of a mirroring that does not invert itself — in other words, from the lack of contradiction. Anyone who has read attentively this book's first chapter (even without knowing my previous cycle of books) will sense the whole theoretical weight of the reservation in question. It is already transporting us from the second of the decisions made toward the third, but it would be useful for it to bring us back again from historical to universal referents. Our inquiry is about the relationship between referents and thematic constants, and it is well known that precisely the term "thematic criticism" was attributed to a trend of the *nouvelle critique* in France during the 1950s and '60s. There is no space here for doing justice to individual scholars; the interesting point is that they interposed — between the universal referents that they assumed existed and the thematic constants of the texts that they were dealing with — an individual or collective imaginary that was different from the literary code and yet was preconstituted and articulated, and therefore not unlike a code in itself. Only indirectly, here, do my reservations concern the archetypal immobility of the universal referents of such an imaginary, inspired by Jung, and by that which most separates him from Freud.

In the first place, my reservations coincide with the objection that was quickly applied to thematic criticism from the structuralist point of view, namely, that its shapings of the imaginary lacked the necessary high level of abstraction and were amorphous enumerations of too concrete matters.[3] It is truly easy to conceive of a book — in French, around 1960 — made up of our constants, and in which theme after theme would have been brought together with sensual delight, always at such low levels of abstraction as to border on the things themselves. To stay with the examples given in the second chapter: the theme of the private reliquary would have been mentioned, and so would the deconsecrated furnishings, the piled-up trash, the invasive flora and fauna, the sea wrecks, the archaic tools, and even, no doubt, the theme of the chest and of the chest of drawers, the hair and dead flowers, the objets d'art and the old armchairs, the sewer and mice and toads, the shards, and the rotten door. So long as analysis confines its collection of thematic constants to images of things, functional or not, it will be of little relevance whether its levels of abstraction oscillate and are more or less high. The level of abstraction of an analysis will be neither sufficient nor coherent until it brings into relief the logical or antilogical relationships that alone can give form and meaning to concrete textual materials — relationships that exist between real facts and their assumption into literary constants, but that also belong literally and definitely to the constants themselves.

4

Let us move on from the hypothesis of a coded imaginary to that of a code specific to literature, which has thus far always been indicated by treating the words "code" and "tradition" as synonyms. However much naïveté was attributed to the direct realistic reference, to trace literary constants back to a literary tradition does not run the risk of appearing a naïve operation; a fact ensured even by a vague affinity between this procedure and the least naïve conceivable system of reasoning, that is, the least risky — tautology: literature is literature. Most times, this procedure will have to be accepted as being pertinent and shrewd, and on rare occasions it might lend itself to the suspicion of being shrewd only as part of an evasive tactic, inasmuch as the homogeneity that is not guaranteed between literature and reality is guaranteed between literature and other, previous literature. Nevertheless, thematic constants remain the most problematic, by definition, within this kind of homogeneity. They do not allow themselves to be wholly reduced to it, as metrical, syntactical, rhetorical, or narratological constants do. Every time the specificity of literature has congealed into a preconception of autonomy, thematic constants have offered only the minor embarrassment of having to choose between emptying them of all substance, considering them as mere ingredients of the compositional process — which was the tendency of early Russian formalism — or else of pretending, as far as possible, that they do not exist, as usually happened with structuralism. At this point, an elementary and summary distinction must be made with respect to the concepts of tradition or code in twentieth-century literary studies (at the price of having to call, for the sake of conciseness, upon many other words ending in *-ism*).

During the first two decades of the century, the renewal of literary studies in the principal European languages had as a common — but not a lowest common — denominator an inversion of the tendencies toward direct realistic reference that had been in their time one of the nineteenth century's achievements: historicism, biographism, and sociologism, all Romantic at first and then later positivist. On the other hand, in French culture, in which nineteenth-century methods persisted unperturbed in the accepted doctrine of the universities, the specificity of literature was early on, and perhaps most clearly, asserted by writers, rather than professors, critics, or philosophers. But literature's specificity, and even its autonomy, may be affirmed on the basis of two opposed attitudes towards the temporal and historical dimension: either by taking it into account and distributing specific or autonomous connections and developments across it, or, on the other hand, by actually obliterating this dimension and perhaps projecting, over and above it, the ideal contemporaneity of everything. Through the alternation or interweaving of these two attitudes, throughout the century, the concepts of literary tradition or code have varied greatly. The first attitude was more typical of German and Italian neo-idealism — despite Croce's theoretical extremism — and it easily came to terms with positivism's erudite legacy. This made possible a sort of literary historiography whose authority is firmly based on the sense of tradition that characterizes it. The second attitude was at first more typical of Russian formalism, but also of the formalism that may be ascribed to great English- and French-language poets. Along with Saussure's semiotic conception, it has merged into structuralism, dominated as it is by the idea of code, and it can be traced down to structuralism's recent aftereffects.

For the sake of clarity, but certainly not with historical propriety, we may speak of literary tradition when a code is seen to develop diachronically, and of literary code when a tradition is seen to project itself synchronically or panchronically. Interest in thematic constants has been anything but equal under the headings of tradition or of code, respectively, that is, in positivistic-idealistic studies of literary history, and in formalistic-structuralistic studies of literary theory. I have already mentioned the lack of interest shown by these last; this is all the more unfortunate inasmuch as it might have been hoped that they could have codified thematic constants that are not limited to documentable historic relationships between one text and another, as is required by concepts such as source, favor, taste, fashion, model, and *locus communis* or topos. In fact, in those studies in which a theoretical space transcends these concepts' requirements, such a space has been opened — sometimes with outstanding results — only to codes of rhetorical or narratological or in any case formal constants. At the opposite extreme, studies whose space is concentrated within historical tradition have produced more than just a few masterpieces, including some masterpieces of general literary studies, by paying attention to thematic constants. Setting aside what is, for our purposes, the most important such study — Auerbach's *Mimesis,* to which I have already referred, and which is in any case arranged not by themes but by authors and periods — two famous books must be mentioned because of the coincidence between their chronological areas and this book's division into periods.

The overlap with Ernst Robert Curtius's *European Literature and the Latin Middle Ages*[4] is primarily negative: that study documents the continuity of a great number of topoi, from Greco-Latin antiquity to the very end of the Renaissance, indeed to the eighteenth century — up to a Romanticism that is mainly excluded, despite a few quotations toward the end. It is interesting that the lower, final limit of the classical, millenary heritage of constants reaches our constants' upper limit of distribution, in the already mentioned sense —

not of their birth as a whole but of a maximum level of their growth and renewal. It is no less interesting that, in this sense, our constants have approximately the same upper limit (which may be set at any desired point during the second half of the eighteenth century) as the modern ones documented by Mario Praz in *The Romantic Agony*.[5] I am referring to perverse constants in the erotic, affective, and moral order, as ours are in the functional and physical order; thus they are in some way complementary and in fact contemporaneous through the whole nineteenth century, with no precise lower limit down to the present day. Nevertheless, these books, differing as they do in the treatment of their documentation — formidable in both cases for learning and historical reliability — allow an unproblematized hiatus to remain between literary tradition and real facts.

The distancing from real facts and from the problems that they pose is to some degree a necessary evil in any study that traces literature back to previous literature. It results from the division of intellectual labor, even leaving aside the gusto that not infrequently accompanies this procedure within Italian culture, where a dash of mandarinism or specialist narcissism is somewhat hereditary. But tautology's shadow, which serves as a guarantee of the procedure's shrewdness, does not in every sense eliminate the risk of naïveté, at least where thematic constants are concerned. The direct reference to real facts seemed naïve, besides being unmediated by code or tradition, because it is unmediated by contradiction; in turn, the tracing back of thematic constants to *pure* literary tradition eludes (owing to the false immediacy of the homogeneity between literature and literature) those logical or antilogical tensions that presuppose a relationship with real facts. Through a kind of vicious circle — the individual work refers back to the corpus of preexisting works, the preexisting corpus is to be split into individual works — the historicism of studies in the literary tradition can at most set that tradition apart from history or push it back beyond history. In other words, it has no real answers to certain questions, be they innocent or mischievous. Why do codes last? Why do thematic constants continue to interest new authors and readers? When does the parthenogenesis of literary tradition date from? — somewhere between the Bible and Homer, who historically founded it for us, and the prehistoric passage from the ape to man, with the origin of language, or of labor, or of sexual taboo?

5

In the act of making the second and third decisions, I spoke of preliminary balance between the two juxtaposed hypotheses. This balance will have consisted in the attempt, repeated several times, to reduce them both to the absurd. But it has several times become clear that the balance cannot consist in either hitting the right empirical mean, nor in merely compensating for the inadequacy of each hypothesis by combining it with the other. It is not simply a matter of mediating realistic references through literary tradition, thereby making the one indirect and the other impure. It is above all a matter of mediating both of them through the logic of compromise-formation. The contradiction between constants and real facts that this kind of logic presupposes must be presupposed not only to be literarily introduced into each individual text but also to be institutionalized within a tradition, since we are discussing constants between one text and another. Reciprocally, what happens to our constants between the late eighteenth and early nineteenth centuries (coinciding approximately with the decline of the topoi studied by Curtius, and with the coming of the themes studied by Praz) must be conceived as the start of one or more traditions — without excluding at all our presupposition of a contradiction with reality.

We would do well to look back at the most clamorous of the preceding examples of reductio ad absurdum, in order to formulate further decisions that have virtually been made already. Let us consider the following aberrant proposition: "In a century and a half of literature there has been an increase in the images of nonfunctional objects, because an increase of such objects has prevailed in the real world." A true statement is combined with a false one by a causal conjunction — *because* — which implies a positive mirroring process between literature and reality. If we limit ourselves to correcting the false statement, we will replace — in accordance with good logic — the causal conjunction with the concessive one; but this leaves things unexplicated: "There are more nonfunctional objects in literature *although* there are more functional objects in the real world." But if we recall (to keep to the metaphor) that every mirror — even nondistorting ones — reverses images, we replace the mirage of a positive mirroring with the model of a negative one. In a transition familiar to the bad logic of the compromise-formation, which recurs in the cycle of my Freudian books,[6] we will turn the concessive around and make it become causal, in accordance with truth: "There are more nonfunctional objects in literature *because* there are more functional objects in the real world." The collection of imaginary anticommodities would not have become immense or monstrous if the collection of tangible commodities derived from society's wealth had not preceded it in becoming such. As for real nonfunctional objects: at that same time, certain selected types of them began to be preserved in public museums and private collections. These are extraliterary compromises, and they are institutional, as is literature. But in verbal art the dominant tendency of the world would come to be opposed with a much broader, unforeseeable, and immaterial freedom.

There is one fact that may appear as an obvious objection to these conclusions: that numerous series of isolated occurrences, as well as whole parts of the totality of our constants, date from before the historical turning point under discussion. But it is not being claimed that an enormous transformation of reality, with all of its provocative power, actually founds a contestatory discourse of literature. If this discourse as such becomes more evident beginning from a certain date, both more and less than this is being claimed: that it is founded in a contradiction of and opposition to reality, in due proportion, even before that date. In relation to the phenomenon we are concerned with here, the historical turning point is a moment of truth, not of genesis. And in that story of the relationship between man and things, which cannot adequately be documented by literature (I, 2), it is a unique turning point—if we trust a passage of Lévi-Strauss—since the other one is prehistoric and since the process unleashed by "a multiplicity of inventions aimed in the same direction" has been repeated "twice, and only twice, in the history of humanity." Regarding the modern scientific and industrial revolution, "in its breadth, its universality and in the importance of its consequences, only the Neolithic revolution represented, at the time, an equivalent."

In the same passage, one reads that Western civilization (in the days when it might have been located between the Middle East and Greece) increased its "initial Neolithic capital" by an alphabet, arithmetic, and geometry; but that this was followed by "stagnation" for two thousand or twenty-five hundred years, "from the first millennium before the Christian era until about the eighteenth century."[7] The fact that such a long period of relatively stable civilization, according to Lévi-Strauss, coincides with the length of the topical tradition we can mark off in literary studies, in accordance with Curtius's book, can only make one stop and think. An immense periodization seems to emerge from it; if both of these time periods *end* approximately during the eighteenth century, then the twilight of the topical literary tradition is also to be connected with the revolution—scientific and industrial as well as ideological and political—that took place in and around that century. But besides this, if both of these time periods *begin* after a prehistoric revolution whose period of adjustment was much longer and much more widely dispersed, then the origins of topical literary tradition must also be connected to an (archaic) rationalization of the world. From a certain moment onward, the tradition in question includes the most ancient constants in our whole; they, in turn, may be presumed to be codified compromise-formations, offered again and again for millennia. One may sometimes detect in them the traces of equally ancient preliterary compromises.

We may now verify what was predictable as early as the end of the first chapter: two decisions proceeding from points of view that are usually as separate and contrasting as theory and history, are practically one and the same in this case. The typically historical decision to interpret our constants' chronological distribution; the typically theoretical decision to interpret our constants in accordance with the Freudian logical or antilogical model. This time, we virtually have one decision in two, rather than two decisions in one. Let us formulate them thus, with respect to our constants:

> IV. *A historical turning point may be interpreted within their distribution.*

> V. *They may be theoretically interpreted as compromise-formations.*

6

We have reached this point using the word "constants" in the plural, with the margins of indeterminateness that it maintained in the first chapter's preliminaries as well as in the second chapter's samples. All that remains to be done is to dispute such an indeterminate plural, by asking questions that move us towards final procedural decisions. Which constants, precisely? And, if the question becomes legitimate, how many of them? According to those who, in their impatience with systematic ways of thinking, consider the classifying of phenomena — literary ones, at least — the height of indelicacy, these questions ought not to be asked. And yet, classifying is not so very different, substantially, from speaking, although it is certainly less immediate and more arbitrary; language itself never stops imposing classifications of phenomena, more or less systematically. In cases in which the alternative to speaking is either to submit to being spoken for by the extant language and suffer its constraints and inappropriateness, or to remain silent and resign oneself to that language's lacunae, classifying only means trying to improve its resources. If ancient, medieval, and modern codifications of literary constants had not done this with success, we would not be speaking about literature, inasmuch as we would not even have such words as "metaphor," "sonnet," or "novel" at our disposal. Sobriety in the coining of neologisms is to be recommended as working to the advantage of the procedure's linguistic success, even more than to the advantage of delicacy. It will be objected, however, that I have recognized the fact that better codified or classified literary constants are in any case of a formal kind. By what criterion — possessed of a certain rigor — are we to differentiate between such full-bodied thematic constants as ours are?

In fact, each of the last four of the five decisions that have already been made contained a criterion worth being considered with a view toward that end — albeit one that has already been rejected in the case of the second and third decisions, through criticism of, respectively, direct realistic reference and pure literary tradition. In absolute terms, it is undeniable that our constants could be organized according to real referents or subject matters, as also according to literary genres and national languages (had we not to comply respectively with the second and third decision). The constants could even be organized according to periods or chronological distribution (if we wished to amplify the criterion that is implicit in the fourth decision); and according to types of compromise-formations or contradictory situations (if we wished to articulate the criterion suggested by the fifth). Not one, among all these criteria, seemed to me up to the task of single-handedly setting the classifying procedure in motion and keeping it going. And yet we cannot ignore with impunity the specific demands of even one of them, in elaborating the distinctions that hold up and are productive on the decisive proving ground, namely that of the texts. It will immediately be clear that of the two related criteria — our constants' belonging to literary genres and linguistic levels, and their succession in periods or dates — both would, in and of themselves, yield extremely poor results in terms of information. And yet, it is equally clear that any arrangement or subdivision that had no connection to the mainstreams of literary tradition would be unsatisfactory, as would be any one of them that did not in some way demonstrate an awareness of the historical turning point to which we have referred.

As to the reality criterion: of its three previous reductions ad absurdum (III, 3), let us return for the moment to the one that I have derived (in criticizing so-called thematic criticism) from excessive adherence to things. It would be entertaining to trace this adherence by using the first chapter's conventionally invented examples, instead of the second chapter's textual ones, in order to show how broadly things are themselves interchangeable. By making things up in a less conventional way and by imitating the textual examples' unpredictability, nothing could prevent one from attributing a comic effect to the ghostly castle or a terrifying one to the worn-out suit, or a secondary propagandistic function to the antiques and a function as a commodity to the deconsecrated church. But the game is too easy — so much so that before long it would become difficult, not only and not so much because the interchangeability of things would end by revealing its finiteness, even in fictitious examples, but above all because the images of concrete things would not turn out to be variable, except within those abstract relationships that I refer to as, precisely, our constants. No one of our possible predicates of nonfunctionality can be predicated at will to any and every noun; within the classification resulting from language, just as every concrete thing corresponds to a conceptual class, so the abstract relationships that qualify these things reflect, in themselves, real facts and contain remnants of things that are binding. Compromise-formation, which in our case lends its name to such relationships, is an extremely abstract concept and an "empty model." But even if it is schematized and reduced to a formula as "x although y," it maintains a reference to factual situations: to some incompatibilities between one demand, whatever it may be, and another.

Thus, while one repeats the move from real facts to compromise-formations, one can already begin to see why not even the latter are sufficient to provide in their turn the required criterion. The most theoretical of my cycle of Freudian books ended with a typology of compromise-formations in literature's differing contents; these compromise-formations depicted ways and levels of a return of the repressed as it is immediately exemplified through transgressions against a moral or practical imperative.[8] In the present book's first chapter, after having distinguished the less obvious form of return of the repressed represented by transgression against a *rational* imperative, with its literary ambivalence between form and content, I spoke for the first time about return of the repressed as transgression against a *functional* imperative (I, 3). In all three cases, literature's differing contents become the site of imaginary transgressions against an extraliterary imperative, but the degree of the concepts' abstraction is not identical in the three cases. It seems to me that it must vary according to the degree to which the imaginary transgressions correspond or do not correspond to possible transgressions that are themselves extraliterary, real. If this is so, it is much more likely that categories derived from extratextual deduction will be seen to be pertinent to the analysis of concrete texts, while, in the absence of any extraliterary connection, only the induction that draws them, by abstraction, from the texts themselves can guarantee pertinent categories.

In the case of transgressions against moral or practical imperatives, which literature can represent with greater or lesser complicity, their universal preexistence with respect to any literary representation whatsoever is evident. This is why a typology of compromise-formations was possible at a high level of abstraction for a relative return of the repressed, in seeming, provisional independence from the texts. On the other hand, nothing before and outside of literature corresponds to the transgression against a functional imperative that literature produces while taking pleasure in representing objects connoted in a specific way. It is a transgressive representation, but it is not the representation of a transgression: on the imaginary plane where objects are limited to being there, a transgressor-subject is not provided. In the sense in which we are speaking, not even the character (if by chance someone of the sort exists) who is the agent responsible for defunctionalization, as a result of his negligence, violence, etc., counts as such a subject. The imaginary responsibility for taking pleasure in the contradiction of the functional imperative belongs entirely to either the author or the reader — or, better, to the text. It is established by the literary word, just as by those verbs that linguists call performative — "I swear," "I declare," and so on — an action is enunciated that is completed through the very act of stating it.

Moreover, even in the case of transgressions against a rational imperative there is no transgressor-subject except the author, reader, or text, no matter whether one is dealing with figurative forms or supernatural contents; and yet this is not why one can say, in such a case, that nothing corresponds to transgression before and outside of literature. If we limit the discussion to supernatural contents and to belief in them, they not only existed before written literature, in myth or oral folklore, but they also existed before all these in archaic or infantile fantasy. Such an intermediate status of the irrational return of the repressed, I think, would make neither impossible nor futile a relative typology of compromise-formation like the previous one (the one deducible from an equally high level of abstraction). On the other hand, in the case of the antifunctional return of the repressed, the analogous hypothesis has never ceased to seem to me impracticable, throughout the long gestation of this inquiry. Here it will be useful to speak of individual or codified compromise-formations only on a case-by-case basis — that is, through single texts, or through text categorized according to further criteria. And only the distinction — which was introduced in the first chapter — between purely literary compromise-formations and those participating in preliterary compromise (I, 4–5) is general enough to be taken up again in a classifying operation.

7

It is now clear why only the inductive (or at least the inductive sooner than the deductive) criterion is adequate for the operation in question. The specific contents of the texts collected in this volume will be all the more irreplaceable in stating similarities and contradictions, the less their similarities and oppositions, and their specific transgressive qualities, could have been surmised in extraliterary ways before the texts had been collected. Certainly, in this book too I am interested in "the content's forms and substances"

— to use the semiological terms of Hjelmslev that I used in my earlier typology; and this to the same extent to which I take an interest in texts the content of which, within their concrete linguistic existence, is by definition a substance carved out by a form. But had I not, at the same time, taken an interest in one or more of what Hjelmslev would term the corresponding "content purports" — abstract ones, and by definition not carved by a form — the texts would never have been gathered together and the book would never have been conceived. "Content purport" is Hjelmslev's technical term for what I have called — and will call later in this book, for clarity's sake — "subject matter" (following a hint from French and Italian translators, who speak of *matière, materia* of content). On that previous occasion I had already expressed doubt as to whether the "content purport," which, according to the semiologist, lacks a linguistic existence, is for that reason absolutely nonexistent and is truly something that cannot be talked about.

I had maintained that the very reasoning by which Hjelmslev arrives at his concept belies this nonexistence or ineffability,[9] and I would like to add that the beautiful metaphors that he relies upon belie it by themselves. "It is like one and the same handful of sand that is formed in quite different patterns, or like the cloud in the heavens that changes shape in Hamlet's view from minute to minute"; "the form's being projected on to the purport, just as an open net casts its shadow down on an undivided surface."[10] However unfailing and inescapable the difference of patterns, the change in shape, and the shadow of the net may be, nothing would assume different patterns if *one and the same* handful of sand did not exist, nothing would change in shape if *the* cloud did not exist, and there would be no shadow of the net to divide anything if there were not *a* surface. Sand, cloud, and surface possess a recognizable consistency through the forms that they assume or that are projected on them, and the unruly metaphors show themselves to be more materialist than the thoughts that they have been charged with materializing. In fact, the semiologist *talks* about a subject matter ("content purport"), extracting it from various linguistic formulations that he compares with each other. Thus it has been possible for me to extract one or more of them and discuss them, thereby comparing a variety of literary texts on the basis of thematic constants; in fact, it is only this common subject matter, postulated by and at the same time emerging from the comparison, that has allowed me to discuss those texts and their forms and substances from a new point of view.

The area given to the classifying operation will be that which exists between a pure datum of subject matter — a sort of semantic lowest common denominator — and the series of texts to which it is common. Let us imagine abstract matter as a nearly incorporeal point, located high up, and concrete literature, down below, as a straight line made up of many segments, each of which corresponds to the linear syntagma of a text. The empty space in between corresponds to a lack of well-defined terms for our constants — better defined than those we have used heretofore — if classification is nothing other than a search for words that are good by approximation. It will be a question of allotting words at intermediate levels: levels that become more and more concrete than the lowest common denominator — the range of which they gradually specify and subdivide–and more and more abstract than the texts — the characteristics of which they gradually put into an order and a hierarchy. Through these lévels, definitions of categories will be obtained by means of successive oppositions, that is, of contrary or contradictory relationships from which variants will be thrown into relief against constants and differences against similarities (such as emerged from all the examples in the second chapter). From top to bottom, we will set an ever increasing number of words; the more we ascend toward the lowest common denominator, the more parts the complete definitions will have in common; and the more contrasting parts they have, the more we descend toward the texts. The lowest common denominator will be the only one that belongs to all the definitions, and each definition will halt only at words that do not form part of any of the others.

I had spoken of a criterion that was more inductive than deductive; nevertheless, the clear and reasoned movement of the operation from level to level will be deductive or descending. But at every level it will collide with a latent, foreseeable inverse movement that will be inductive or ascending. And this will have decisive authority in forestalling and circumscribing the choices that the former exacts: just as the lowest common denominator emerges from the texts through comparison, so our determining all inferior abstractions, for the sake of convenience, depends on our familiarity with the texts. A movement as double-edged and convergent as this one, enlivened by the initiatives of inductive information and directed by the rules of the deductive game, must of course be arbitrary. But certainly not in the sense of being gratuitous, not because I am tempted to take liberties in understanding or connecting the texts; arbitrary rather in the strategic sense, inasmuch as respect for the texts leaves room for the demands of clarity, economy, and elegance, beyond that of the consistency of the operation. Even the halting of definitions at the level of terminal oppositions will be strategically arbitrary inasmuch as it is an abstention from a possible descent to further oppositions. I do not know whether it would ever be possible to descend to categories so precise that they could define one single text: even if such categories could remain more abstract than a description or paraphrase or recitation of that text, they would lack the utility of categories, which lies in offering a word for a plurality of things.

Finally, even the use of its results that the operation foresees will be arbitrary and strategic, because it aims at nuanced, mutually interfering, or polar categories rather than at closed, alternative ones.

So we have made the last two decisions — once again as a pair, and this time as a result of their strict consequentiality; let us formulate them thus, again with respect to our constants:

> VI. *They deserve definitions that are in part equal and in part different.*

> VII. *They allow for strategic arbitrariness in every part of the definition.*

8

In order to proceed with defining our constants as categories, let us therefore define the lowest common denominator, our constant in the singular. At the beginning of the book I spoke of useless, old, or unusual things; in the title, I spoke of obsolete objects, thereby displaying an adjective that is in a way synonymous with all the other three; subsequent adjective-making was variegated and more or less concrete. The vocabulary that must now be taken on will be the more respectful, *a priori*, of the texts, the more it is abstract. To designate the materiality of physical things in the content purports (or subject matters) of the texts, let us choose the most abstract noun possible; and to designate the connotations of these things, let us choose the most abstract of the negative predicates that have already been used. Let us speak of (images of) NONFUNCTIONAL CORPORALITY, providing each of these two terms in succession with some explanation.

The abstract character of the noun would be excessive were we not to begin introducing pertinent oppositions in order to define it. It could be a question of human or nonhuman, living or nonliving CORPORALITY. Combining the oppositions: (1) living human, (2) nonliving human, (3) living nonhuman, and (4) nonliving nonhuman. The reader knows that it is the fourth hypothesis that interests us — inanimate things, both natural and manufactured by culture. And yet, awareness of the texts teaches us that it would be inconvenient and pedantic to ignore the second and third hypotheses, if they are mixed in with the hypothesis that interests us. There is the cadaver's corporality and that of live animals, especially certain animals. Within the limits of the possible — that is, of what can be textually distinguished — it is rather the first hypothesis that we must exclude from consideration. It is true that the living human body can take on connotations of weakness, decrepitude, infirmity, and deformity, and that it can also appear as mortuary, bestial, or inanimate. Yet awareness of the texts teaches us that to take such images into consideration would too greatly alter, and would broaden beyond all bounds, a subject of research that is well-defined although already boundless.

The reader will perhaps not be unduly surprised if I refuse to make any real preliminary specifications regarding the negated predicate, FUNCTIONAL — the very idea of functionality, which is so essential to this inquiry. In this case, it is historical prudence, rather than empirical adaptability, that advises against a rigorous definition, once and for all, of the adjective, and even against delimiting the area of its current meaning. Its meaning must be left open to specifications, or to implications, that will be amply variable on a case-by-case basis, in view of a body of texts that is so exceptionally heterogeneous with respect to the periods and locations of their cultural provenance. Functional will mean that which answers to a manifest or latent idea of functionality within each text and in relation to the culture to which that text belongs. This relationship can be or not be contradictory, if one looks at authorial intentions and ideology; but it is always objectively and textually contradictory, at least to the extent to which, by hypothesis, functionality is negated. And even the prefix NON-, the negation of the predicate, may be understood in more ways than one; hence other variations in the terminology already used. It may be understood, that is, in a literal and general sense, as mere deprivation of the predicate of functionality; but also in a stronger or more conflictual sense, as disturbance, damage, or subversion of it — from which comes the recourse to an adjective like *anti*functional. The temporal implication of the loss of a previous function may give the sense of *no longer* functional to the negation of the predicate. The loss may be diminution as it is happening, and the negation may have a protracted sense, such as *less and less* functional.

Thus we have the three terms of the lowest common denominator, and it is time to close this methodological chapter with them; but I preceded the enunciation of them with the parenthetical *images of . . .* It is a premise that will always be implied, from now on, since it remains beyond doubt that we are speaking only of literature. Nevertheless, one cannot escape this question: Between the degree of literary substance that makes us speak of an image or else of a description, a theme, or at least a hint, and on the other hand the simple, fleeting mention in a text of some nonfunctional corporality, at which point do we begin to pay attention? The answer cannot be empirically quantitative, and it cannot stop with a word count or line count. It requires a vast number of examples, like the classifying operation; it is only when this is behind us, and with the help of its results, that we will be able to attempt to give the answer. The area of simple, fleeting mentions of nonfunctional corporality would be contiguous by default, in a manner of speaking, to the semantic space that has just been defined.

But contiguity by opposition also exists: if we subject both the lowest common denominator's noun and its adjective to contradictory oppositions, two combined oppositions again create four hypotheses. There can be literary representations of (1) functional corporality, (2) nonfunctional corporality, (3) functional noncorporality, and (4) nonfunctional noncorporality. The hypothesis that we are studying is the second of these; let us admit that the fourth corresponds to the constants studied by Praz — constants that I have described as perverse in the erotic, affective, and moral order, just as ours are perverse in the physical order. The third — the opposite of what interests us not in one way but in two — will then correspond to representations of good feelings, proper opinions, and correct behavior. In both of these hypotheses, contiguity exists by opposition, but the opposition regards the noun itself more than, or without, the adjectival predicate. It is too general to encourage incursions, unless they be occasional. There remains the first hypothesis — the images of functional corporality — which will delineate a future area of complementary interest to us, into which we shall advance, at least toward the end. It is, moreover, a field that has been more investigated than ours by literary scholars; although ours was, on the other hand, far more investigated by literature or by its authors, as we shall now set out to prove.

IV

A Tree Neither Genealogical Nor Botanical

In 45 B.C. Servius Sulpicius Rufus, the Roman governor of Greece, wrote from Athens to his friend Cicero, whom he knew to be broken-hearted over the death of his daughter Tullia. Here as also in later periods, particularly important letters shared in the formality of a literary genre without thereby losing either their intimate quality or their originality. This was the case with the letters of condolence, known as letters of consolation precisely because of the task which their argument was required to assume. In order to shake Cicero out of his private grief, Sulpicius eloquently reminds him of current public calamities, of the universality of mortality, and of the responsibility that Cicero bears, as an extremely famous man, to set an example to others. Belonging to the second of these lines of argument is the following passage, a text destined to a long-enduring fortune:

> I want to tell you something which has brought me no little consolation, in the hope that it might diminish your sorrow. In returning from Asia, as I sailed from Aegina to Megara, I looked at the surrounding areas: Aegina was behind me, Megara before me, on my right was the Piraeus, on my left Corinth, cities once flourishing, that now lie prostrate and ruined before our eyes. I began to think to myself thus: "What! We tiny men are indignant if only one of us dies

67

or is killed, although by necessity our life is brief, when in one little space so many corpses of cities lie thrown down? Do you not want, Servius, to rule yourself and to remember that you were born a man?" Believe me, this reflection much revived me; try, if you will, to raise before your eyes the same spectacle.[1]

In comparison with the nineteenth- and twentieth-century examples in chapter II, the reader will find this first ancient Latin text truly poor in images of nonfunctional corporality. Here, the images properly speaking seem to boil down to, first, a pair of past participles that give a zero degree description of the current state of the "prostrate and ruined" Greek cities; and, second, a metaphor for the same thing, in Latin only three words: *oppidum cadavera proiecta,* "thrown-down corpses of cities." The brief account grows out of the solemnly consoling admonition that functions without the slightest descriptive emphasis and with a measured evocative effect. Yet such sobriety obviously does not constitute a limitation, either aesthetically or in its interest for us. The plurality of names of places gazed at simultaneously and symmetrically, the distant perspective from a boat in the center of the sea that renders it verisimilar, the opposition between the famous names of the cities and the spectacle of decadence, and, finally, the spontaneous transition to reflection — together create a vague vision of grandiose, luminous sadness.

At the end of the previous chapter I raised the question of the degree of literary substance of the images (III, 8), and here, right away, is an occasion for overcoming any post-nineteenth-century prejudice that tends to conceive of images as necessarily descriptive or, at any rate, as a question merely of the number of words. There can be more than sufficient literary substance without an emphasis on description, without lengthy lingering aside from the narrative or logical thread, and in a very small number of words. Moreover, in confronting any text, including this passage, we will avoid taking the imagery that interests us out of its context, in this case a line of reasoning. Here the argument about the universality of the mortal condition inspires the metaphor of cities as cadavers. It anthropomorphizes the inanimate so as to associate it with the death of the human animal. The cadaver referent present in the whole issue we are considering (I, 6) is exhibited by this first, and prototypical, ancient example. But the essential conceptual premises of images previously adduced coincide with Sulpicius's universalizing argument, which makes me consider this example an excellent starting point for our task of classification.

A first premise is made clear by the opposition between temporal adverbs: the cities flourished "once," but "now" they are seen to lie in ruins. Let us say that the nonfunctional situation is connected here to a *passage of time.* A second premise is taken for granted regarding the cities' mortality, namely, that a society's destiny only realizes itself over a very long passage of time; it is left to the letter's recipient to compare this to the shortness of human life, thereby transcending his mourning through the collective dimension that opens with the first person plural, "we tiny men" and "if only one of us"; or with the second person addressed by the writer to himself, "remember that you were born a man." Let us say that here the passage of time is *collectively perceived*, or socially, rather than individually or subjectively. A third premise seems to me no less clear although notable only in the writer's omission: it lies in his silence regarding whatever might have caused, dated, or characterized the transformation of flourishing cities into ruined ones. No doubt the relevant historical facts would have been well known to Cicero, as to any cultured person of the time. Yet within the expressive economy of the text, all that matters is simply that such a transformation did in fact happen; it is unnecessary to recall why, when, or how. Let us say that here the passage of time — of which not only the length is indeterminate — *is of nonpertinent determination*.

Not one of the semantic elements to be found in this text, as outlined by these three conceptual premises, is essential to our lowest common denominator. An imaginary object may be defined by nonfunctional corporality without its nonfunctionality being connected to a passage of time at all. And if it does in fact connect to it, the passage of time may very well be *individually perceived* rather than collectively, and its *determination* may well be *pertinent* rather than nonpertinent. Now, oppositions among the elements present in or absent from the text are precisely what we must worry about, if we wish to proceed from commenting on the passage in Sulpicius to beginning our classifications. If the example has been chosen well, the oppositions in the abstract between how it is constructed and how it could have been constructed will be equivalent to the concrete oppositions between this and other actual, similar texts. The oppositions will be concrete, it should be understood, only by comparison, only in a sense external to the individual text (thus, for example, with respect to the passage of time, what matters is the opposition between the real presence of the semantic element and its possible absence, not the internal opposition between the two temporal adverbs). We have so far provided ourselves with three useful oppositions; we established in the previous chapter that we would set them one by one under the lowest common denominator, using them as parts of the definitions of categories to be arrived at (III, 7).

From this point on, we will call what we are in process of constructing or outlining a "semantic tree." Increasing numbers of lines and words will branch off from a single trunk — the lowest common denominator — as in a real tree, while, on the other hand, their layout should preferably be read from top to bottom — from the abstract to the concrete — as in a family tree or a philological stemma. Unlike these other trees, however, ours will never have more than one bifurcation at each branch; in other words, it will consist only of binary oppositions. Here is the small piece of the tree that we have already outlined so far:

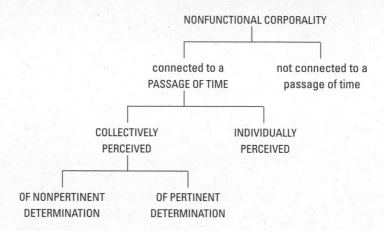

The images of nonfunctional corporality in Sulpicius's text begin to be defined if one reads from top to bottom and at each level on the left side. I say "begin to be defined" not only because the succession of vertical levels does not end here, nor does the definition, but also because of the absence, so far, of parallel oppositions on the right-hand side of our tree; each individual definition's grip on the texts will be proportional to the number of such oppositions, and will depend on them as a whole. Yet at this point one can already make most of the necessary observations regarding the procedure we are undertaking. At the first level, I took the lowest common denominator as the point of departure, excluding from the tree the preliminary oppositions developed at the end of the previous chapter that limited the sphere of the noun, that is, that defined the contiguous and contradictory areas around it (III, 8). It is logical that the initial opposition involving the passage of time must necessarily be set visually above the other two oppositions, since the other two are its predicates or specifications. However, the predicates, as such, should both be of equal status; the fact that one is above another is a first example of a strategically arbitrary decision suggested in advance by knowledge of the corpus of texts (III, 7). And it is superfluous to mention how merely arbitrary and strategic are the verbal choices we have made in giving names to each element. The very knowledge of the corpus that prompts our choices makes their precision difficult and suspect, if the belated structuralist exercise is to be taken seriously, and not simply as fortuitous and playful . . . Fortunately, the most critical moment of truth for the present inquiry is not at stake in such precision.

For instance: at the third level, I have written the adverbs *collectively* and *individually*—the most concise ones. But in commenting on Sulpicius, I had given the first adverb as an alternative to "socially," which is also a contrary to the second. In turn, I had given the second adverb as an alternative to "subjectively," whose usual contrary ("objectively") would be out of place. A language's words are not algebraic or logical symbols, and contraries and synonyms excluded from the tree can return to make themselves rightfully felt in the analysis of the texts. Furthermore, in speaking of contraries it must be stressed that they are not the only genre of opposition used. The opposition between contraries such as white and black alternates with the opposition between contradictories such as white and nonwhite; the oppositions applied to the lowest common denominator's terms at the end of the previous chapter were of the second kind. The distinction is important because (according to Aristotelian and scholastic logic), when there are two contradictories, both of them cannot be false and both of them cannot be true. Less radically, even contraries cannot both be true, whereas both can be false. Consequently, contraries offer equal information on either side, while between contradictory terms the positive pole offers more than the negative. In the current, provisional state of the tree, with one opposition between contraries and two between contradictory terms, the negative pole with respect to the passage of time remains generally nebulous; no other opposition has yet been placed beneath it. Let us leave it hanging and concern ourselves instead with documenting how far the particular determinations of a passage of time—a collectively perceived one—can become pertinent to the images of a text.

2

In 1802, at the same time as the concordat between Napoleon and the Church of Rome, François-René de Chateaubriand (1768–1848) published *The Genius of Christianity, or Beauties of the Christian Religion* (*Le Génie du Christianisme, ou Beautés de la religion chrétienne*). It is an apologia for religion of a new kind, as also were the circumstances under which it was conceived. For a decade, Catholicism had been denied and persecuted in France, as a result, not of another revealed religion's intolerance, but because of a state's antireligious tendency. Throughout a whole century, intellectuals had successfully worked at discrediting not only the truth of religion but also its cultural prestige. Thus, in Chateaubriand's book, at the dawn of a restoration, the defense of the truth of faith matters far less than the illustration of a thesis in itself mundane: Christianity, over the centuries, far from being incompatible with the values of civilization, culture, and art, had been their greatest life giver. The book is an uninterrupted vindication of the past and, as often as possible, of the surviving material artifacts that testify to its values. In general, it would be difficult to find a more abundant catalogue, combined with literary excellence, of the images that concern us — were it not for the writer's entire oeuvre, given its thematic tendency and stylistic temperament (his dates of birth and of death could delimit our historical turning point within an eighty-year period). In the part dedicated to worship and tombs, a chapter on the basilica of Saint-Denis — formerly the venerated burial site of the kings of France, from the Merovingians to the penultimate Bourbon — was indispensable. But, to the majestic melancholy of the royal necropolis (in itself so well suited to Chateaubriand's prose), had been recently added more violent and more rapid causes of desolation than the millenary passage of time; and from this piece of prose — of which I quote the last paragraph — it is not so easy to guess which ones:

> But where is the description of these tombs, which have already been erased from the face of the earth, carrying us? They exist no longer, these sepulchers! Little children have made sport with the bones of mighty monarchs: Saint-Denis is deserted; birds have used it as a place of passage, grass grows over its shattered altars; and instead of the dirge that used to echo beneath its domes, there is no longer anything to be heard but the raindrops that fall through its uncovered roof, the falling of some stone that comes loose from its ruined walls, or the sound of its clock resonating among the empty tombs and the devastated underground passages.[2]

Here as throughout the brief chapter, the references are to events that took place at the height of 1793. Out of hatred for the monarchy and, at the same time, in the republic's hunt for lead, the tombs were violated and partially destroyed by official order, and the kings' remains uncovered and thrown into a common grave — a supreme national oedipal gesture, more than sufficiently notorious to readers nine years later. Moreover, the tone of the allusion is most reverent and compassionate toward the ideal objects of sacrilege — as is proper to the high stylistic register. Already in the opening paragraph, the allusions were indirect insofar as they had the flavor of a psalm or a biblical prophecy[3] — the same atmosphere that the phrase about the bones becoming things of amusement for children suggests here. The original text's most direct allusion (part of an apostrophe to Louis XIV, in which his ashes are described as the "object of the fury of this people whom you made into all that they are") was part of the only sentence that the censors removed.[4] And the allusive sublimation of facts goes together with a more substantial attempt to dehistoricize them, through the transferal of their causes to the supernatural level. It was

God in His wrath who had sworn to castigate France, and the desecrators can be alluded to, paradoxically, as "sent by divine justice."[5] Nevertheless, such a dehistoricization can only be attempted by taking historic evidence of the facts themselves as a point of departure; it is *a posteriori*, so to speak, and not *a priori*, like our previous example.

To return to the semantic tree's terms: here, Chateaubriand is still speaking the language of a tradition — scriptural or classical — that customarily solemnized the effects of a nonpertinent determination of the passage of time. But in itself, the rhetorical function of the allusion — which, on the surface, conceals this determination — in the end makes it fully pertinent; it postulates the understanding of continuous implicit meanings with respect to the why, the when, and the how, and certainly not only to the fact of the basilica's decay in itself. As Auerbach masterfully demonstrated regarding a passage in Stendhal,[6] this passage, too, would be incomprehensible without a precise amount of historic information. Even in the sentence that concludes a metahistorical meditation on death, what contributes virtually to determine "bygone times" is the intensity of sensorial evocativeness, employed by Chateaubriand in a way that was quite new in his day: "Everything declares that we have descended into the realm of ruins; and it seems to us, from an indefinable odor of antiquity that has spread beneath these funereal arches, that we are so to speak breathing the dust of bygone times."[7] One finds an even more intense sensorial evocation — less visual than auditory, this time — at the stupendous end of the paragraph quoted above. The juxtaposition of the imperfect "used to echo" with the present "there is no longer anything to be heard but," circumscribes the passage of time which we know has been relatively brief; this is certainly not individually perceived, even if the majority of readers at the time would have been able to remember earlier times through individual memory. The readers are exhorted to deplore it as a collective trauma, through the faithfulness of mourning and the regression of nostalgia.

3

I have said that the succession of vertical oppositions did not end with the small part of the semantic tree that we have drawn so far. Before adding in any possible parallel horizontal opposition to the right, we ought to follow the succession to the left, where less need be added so as to reach the first complete definitions of our categories of texts. I shall take a particularly hybrid example that will provide us with a singular kind of transition. It has two precedents, in different languages: in the early sixteenth century, Baldassar Castiglione had taken up the theme of the ruins of Rome in a famous sonnet, varying it, in the last tercet, by applying the law of all-consuming time to the relief of his own love sorrows. Approximately a century later, Lope de Vega parodied Castiglione's sonnet, consoling himself — in the final tercet — with the fact that even his overcoat had been defeated by all-consuming time. Lope's parody would be perfectly instructive for us, but I prefer to quote a later imitation by Paul Scarron (1610–60) — the master of the French genre called *burlesque* — in a sonnet published in 1650:

> Superb monuments to human pride,
> Pyramids, tombs, whose vain structure
> Has shown that art, through the craft of hands
> And assiduous work, can conquer nature,
>
> Old ruined palaces, the Romans' masterpieces
> And the greatest efforts of their architecture,
> Coliseum, where often those inhuman peoples
> Strove in contests to kill each other,
>
> By the ravages of time you have been abolished,
> Or at least for the most part you've been demolished;
> There is no cement that time does not dissolve.
>
> If your marble so hard has felt its power,
> Should I be upset that a nasty black doublet
> That's lasted two years is worn out at the elbow?[8]

Scarron did not improve his sonnet by moving the satirical tone up into the quatrains in a variant later edition;[9] as I have reproduced it from the first edition, it depends on a surprise held back until the penultimate line. And the surprise would be less witty if the first twelve lines did not keep to the lofty seriousness that the theme of ruins traditionally demanded. The first quatrain vainly declares that art conquers nature; the first tercet, its maxim contained in a beautiful, solemn line, answers that time conquers art. Then, the symmetry that has slyly been set up collapses in the comparison that ought to have completed it (perhaps also because Baroque modernism was happier with a commonplace about a victory for art than with one about a victory for time). The disparity in level of dignity between decayed Roman monuments and the hole in the elbow of a doublet is too great not to produce a comic effect — through degradation or unmasking. Among the examples in chapter II, in the texts of Arnim and Gogol respectively (II, 6, 8), we came upon images of nonfunctional corporality whose oddness or baseness were meant to produce grotesque or playful effects. The opposition that is now about to add to the tree's growth will be between the presentation of images seriously, to the point of solemnity, and the presentation of them nonseriously, to the point of comicality. How are they to be situated with respect to the oppositions placed above them?

Clearly the state of both the monuments and the piece of clothing depends on time. But the fact of the doublet's belonging to the versifying "I" might make us claim that the passage of time is individually perceived, and the specification of two years that its determination is pertinent. We would be wrong, because, on the one hand, one sole law triumphs over and above the leap from the monumental to the domestic, and it is a law perceived as collective. Moreover, while the triumph of the law over marble justified a degree of astonishment, its reiterated triumph over cloth is all the cheaper, inasmuch as the doublet was "nasty": the poor quality is the only motive for measuring — almost with a sense of satisfaction — the duration of its resistance to wear and tear. Thus the new opposition is to be placed on the tree's left side, but not without having observed that we have drawn it from Scarron's text using a different procedure with respect to the three located above it, taken from Sulpicius's text. That is to say that we have not set elements that are present in the text in opposition to elements that are absent from it, but rather have opposed two elements both present in the same text; more precisely, one present before to one present after, insofar as there is a succession of opposed thematic categories within the same text. We are dealing with a phenomenon that is after all exceptional, and as we shall see, not limited to burlesque or comic cases. From now on, we shall refer to this as *commutation*.

I can immediately take another example of commutation that goes, however, in the opposite direction; it is to be found in the episode of Astolfo on the moon in *Orlando Furioso* by Ludovico Ariosto (1474–1533). Things that have been lost in this lower world and that can be found in the world above take on the form of other things that symbolize them, and more than one of these symbolizing things are expressly defunctionalized — as are, hypothetically, all of those that are symbolized. They are defunctionalized on one occasion in a respectable form ("ruins of cities and castles") and various times in an extravagant or lower form ("tumid bladders," "burst cicadas," "broken jugs," "spilled soup," "a great mountain . . . of various flowers . . . that once smelled good, now stink powerfully." As John the Apostle explains these symbolizing things to Astolfo, they are wittily converted into their respective symbolized things, one after another. But in the octave in which this happens to the first of the images in the series that I have quoted, the dominant playful, grotesque tone is inverted for a few lines into the elevated, grave tone with which one speaks of human transience:

> He saw a mountain of tumid bladders
> That seemed to have tumult and shouts inside them;
> And he learned that these were the ancient crowns
> Of the Assyrians and of the Lydians' land,
> And of Persians and Greeks who once were so glorious,
> And whose very names are now almost obscure.[10]

Human transience expressed by certain images — a shifty point of departure in Scarron's text and an ephemeral point of arrival in Ariosto's — was a steadily serious theme in that of Sulpicius. Let us now document the other pole of the new opposition, beyond this special case of commutation, through a wholly suitable example.

4

From the first text from Latin antiquity we learned, among other things, the lesson that images can have sufficient literary substance with a minimum of words. In a text from a century and a half later, we find a greater literary substance in images with a greater number of words, although this does not justify greater expectations regarding the seriousness of the description: I am referring to an epigram by Marcus Valerius Martial (c. A.D. 40–104) — the thirty-second in Book XII, written shortly before the poet's death. The victim being apostrophized is one Vacerra, a penniless man who has been thrown out of his home, and whose removal we are made to imagine through a series of mocking invectives. His wife, mother, and sister carry his things through the streets, and Vacerra follows them:

> A three-legged camp bed and a two-legged table passed
> And with a lantern and a corniol vase
> A broken chamber pot cracked on the short side leaked;
> The neck of an amphora was under a brazier covered with verdigris;
> That there were anchovies or rotten sardines
> One would suppose by the fetid smell of an urn,
> Worse than the air of a sea hatchery.
> Nor was a slice of Tolosan cheese missing,
> Nor a crown of mint blackened in four years
> And the shorn garlic and onion strings,
> Nor the pan full with the obscene resin of your mother,
> Which the Summenian women use to depilate.[11]

Here, once again through the formal constant of the list, the very objects of the parade, rather than the eyes and mind of the onlooker, seem to be moving, as conjunctions follow upon one another: "and . . . and . . ." (in the two Latin forms, *et, -que*), "with . . . ," then to the negative "nor was missing . . . nor . . . nor . . ." If the vileness of such objects and the inevitable avarice that they imply are looked at completely pitilessly — that is, if they are made to seem ridiculous — the cause is above all the long-winded hyperbole, whose aggressiveness pushes them to the limit. A table that is left with only two legs is more unlikely to be kept than a camp bed that at any rate still has three; and it is still less likely that a chamber pot would be leaking liquid while being transported or that a wreath of mint should have survived fully four years. The hyperbole is then grafted onto a comparison, when the stink of fish is declared to be stronger than the fumes of a sea hatchery. The reader will recall already having encountered in this book the triple combination of hyperbole, of comparison or metaphor, and comic effect: it is precisely the combination that I observed in Gogol's text (II, 8). There, however, it did not seem right to compromise the substantial seriousness of the presentation — the seriousness that was one of the two ways in which I, following Auerbach, allowed "realistic concreteness" to be spoken of, that is, as a literary-historical antithesis to a previous refusal to take seriously things with low connotations.

But this Latin epigram literally would not exist without such a refusal. The ancient code governing the separation of high or low genres and styles — which, through modern classicisms, will manage to leave residues even in a Gogol — is fully in force here; within it, the necessity for some sort of relationship between comic distancing and deforming figurativeness becomes understandable. And how better to keep one's distance from a lowly object than by exaggerating its baseness? This is the direction taken by hyperbole. But how better to exaggerate or at least accentuate the lowness of an object than by blending it with others even lower or at least as low? This is the metaphor's direction, and it is much more important for the general category of texts to be defined here than this single text by Martial might suggest. In the lines that precede the ones that have been quoted, the three women are already indicated as caricatures, and Vacerra is compared to his things through a hyperbolical comparison: "more yellowed than a far from recent box-tree branch."[12] The following, final lines clearly allude to a certain dishonesty in the character. Through the ridiculousness that hyperbole and metaphor have helped along, moral and social contempt take pleasure in venting themselves through insult. In this sense, the Roman epigram presented an ideal terrain, although within the same hierarchical code other genres — such as comedy or satire — were able to take in images as vile and funny as Vacerra's shabby things.

The prejudicial, post-nineteenth-century association of the humbleness of represented objects with realism — generically understood as the adherence of representation to truth — must in part be adjusted and in part overturned here.

Martial certainly had every right to claim that real life was to a great extent recognizable in his epigrams and to take pride in his own poetics, in contrast to the pompous outdatedness of epic and tragic themes or that of the mythical tall tales, which he counters with his famous: "our page has the flavor of man."[13] But the undeniable truthfulness of such a flavor of man is above all of a psychological, or rather, of a moralistic nature, in the sense of a critical representation of custom. None of its realistic implications can automatically be extended to the images that we are studying—if by realism we mean the seriousness or historicity of representation. In this epigram, the caricatural deformation is proportional to the objects' humbleness. The more hyperbolic and metaphorical it is and the more it moves one to smile or laugh, the more it leans toward results that are all the less realistic, if not grotesquely fantastic. This same deformation can only exclude—to use the terms of the semantic tree—all pertinence to the determination of a passage of time. More verisimilar circumstances surrounding Vacerra's poverty would have restrained the exaggeration and attenuated its mockery; the passage of time in itself, nullified by the negative moral universality of the satiric picture, is no less collectively perceived than in the positive moral universality of the reflection on human transience.

I will now give a picture of the part of the tree that has grown by an opposition:

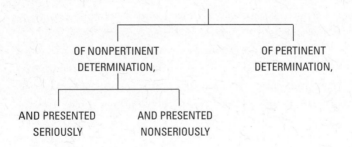

The penultimate opposition's two elements are, as we know, predicates of the superior element, *passage of time,* while the new one's two elements refer back to the supreme element, *corporality.* This second opposition is our first terminal opposition, and a bottom-to-top reading is now possible for two whole definitions. We shall not descend below this fifth level; we know from the previous chapter (III, 7) that such a stopping point is arbitrary in the strategic sense, precisely insofar as we abstain from a possible descent to further oppositions. It means only that we are familiar with sufficiently homogeneous and sufficiently numerous texts regarding which we shall say that those images that recur are images of: *nonfunctional corporality* connected with a *collectively perceived passage of time of nonpertinent determination, and presented seriously.* Or, in the case of texts that are also sufficiently homogeneous and numerous, . . . *and presented nonseriously.*

The text we read by Sulpicius is an example of the first category, Martial's of the second. Scarron's and Ariosto's texts go back and forth between the one category and the other, thereby exemplifying between the one and the other the phenomenon that I have called commutation; the identity of the two definitions, excluding the terminal opposition, functions as a basis for the phenomenon. All at once, two categories interchange by virtue of their many common semantic elements, but because of one sole opposition the succession excludes their mixing together. The mixing of all of them with all of the categories, even among those that have only minimal parts of the definitions in common, is, however, much more frequent — interferences, shadings, oscillations, or inclinations toward several semantic poles at the same time. Let us use the term *contamination* for such phenomena, in which the process of classifying finds a goal and not an obstacle, and that has a strategic value in its eventual applications as well. We shall speak of *pure* and *impure* examples, depending on whether the contamination tends toward minimal or maximal levels. It would be discourteous to the reader not to choose pure examples so long as the construction of the tree is in progress; it would be improper thereafter not to stress the impure examples — which is what many of those in the second chapter were, implicitly. An example that allows a terminal opposition to be placed below the other pole of the penultimate opposition as well is needed immediately. The definition of a category that includes the Chateaubriand text we looked at will be completed by it, and so will that of another category that has elements in common with it excluding the final one.

5

In French, the modern capacity for sensorial evocation was already ripe but still new in Chateaubriand's early prose; at the time of Balzac's later works it had already penetrated the code of European fictional realism. Of course it is a capacity that makes up an important part of the usual, general meaning of the word "realism" — so wrongly applicable to Martial's ancient text. This time, however, if speaking of realism can be of use with respect to Balzac, it will be above all in one of the two precise senses in which Auerbach does so — not so much in that of seriousness in representing low things, as has been the case until now, as in that of the inseparability of the representation from its own historic points of reference. In fact, as in Chateaubriand's case, we have to document the relevance of the full determination of a passage of time — again collectively perceived — in a text's images. Two excerpts from *Cousin Bette* (*La Cousine Bette*), one of the last novels of Honoré de Balzac (1799–1850), will suffice: it takes place under the July Monarchy — between 1838, the date with which the text's first sentence opens, and 1846, the date with which its penultimate paragraph closes[14] and the very year of its publication.

In the first excerpt, Crevel, the former perfume salesman, now a well-to-do stock owner, dressed in a National Guard captain's uniform, is about to be received in private by Baron Hulot's still beautiful but virtuous wife. Baron Hulot, older than Crevel, shone as a soldier under the Empire and was ennobled by Napoleon; his economic situation has now become precarious, and the other man is counting on the disparity of wealth in his hope of seducing the baroness. But in the second excerpt, his visit is about to end in failure:

> . . . the National Guardsman studied the furnishings of the salon where he found himself. Seeing the once red silk curtains, faded to purple by the sun's action and with its folds worn through long use, a rug whose colors had disappeared, furniture that had lost its gilding and whose silk, marbled with stains, was worn out in stripes, expressions of disdain, happiness, and hope naïvely followed each other on the parvenu merchant's flat face. He was looking at himself in the mirror above an old Empire grandfather clock, parading himself for his own inspection, when the swishing of a silk dress told him of the baroness's arrival. And he immediately got back into position.
>
> Having flung herself onto a little sofa that must surely have been very pretty around 1809, the baroness — pointing Crevel to an armchair whose arms ended in bronzed sphinx heads, the paint of which was flaking off, thus allowing the wood to be seen — made a sign for him to be seated.[15]

> The baroness rose to force the captain to retreat, and she pushed him back into the great salon.
>
> "Must the beautiful Madame Hulot live amid such rags?" he said.
>
> And he indicated an old lamp, a candelabra lacking its gilding, the rug's threads, in short, the tatters of opulence that made this great white, red, and gold salon into a cadaver of imperial festivities.[16]

Even in Balzac's longest descriptions, every physical detail is a clue to something; in the present case, the descriptive passages flit quickly before the eyes, or actually the gestures, of a person who is interested in taking advantage of the situation and of what it indicates. The emphasis on the worn-out decor certainly serves this end before serving that of constituting reality. But an eighteenth-century fiction writer would have summarized this with a few abstract words, only for psychological and practical effect; here, physically concrete specifications — to which well-preserved or new objects would probably not have lent themselves so well—constitute reality. A material's transition from a certain color to another is specified, and the sun's action is mentioned as the cause; the disappearance of colors (a topos, as we shall see, of nineteenth-century descriptive realism) is instead attributed to the rug; the objects' threadbare state is pointed out through folds or stains or stripes or flakes. In the second excerpt metaphorical figurativeness occurs twice: "tatters of opulence," "cadaver of festivities"—the latter being another appearance of a general symbolic referent that we already know. Here, too, we might be tempted to see remnants of the figurativeness that disguised low things in the old code. In any case we would find no trace of the tendency toward the comical that used to accompany and to motivate it, as I have shown, and no lowering of the serious tone.

Far from resembling the metahistorical seriousness of the first example on the tree, this one is tightly conjoined with the historicity of representation. The great age of a piece of furniture is even dated to the precise year—not with the month and day, as is the case of the dates that open and close the novel (or as in Gozzano's poem: II, 4), but through an approximation that makes the need for it still more significant: the sofa had been very pretty *around* 1809." The erotic and economic rivalry among characters like Hulot and Crevel is itself dated, inasmuch as it suggests a turnover from one epoch to another, since each of the two characters typifies one or the other of these eras. As a wonderful expression in another Balzac novel (quoted by Auerbach) declares: "Epochs rub off on the men who pass through them."[17] Crevel is a perfect man of the July Monarchy, just as Hulot remains a man of the Empire, and his not having updated his salons' luxuriousness betrays his failure to attach himself to subsequent regimes. It is in this sense that we encounter a difference worthy of taking its place on the semantic tree as an opposition—between the presentations of a historic determination pertinent and forceful both with respect to things and men, in Chateaubriand's and Balzac's texts respectively.

The imperial baron is in a state of decay as a result of his faults and vices, because he is a ladies' man and a squanderer. The decay has no counterpoise in any ideal values that might attach to his house and his furniture, for, let's say, stylistic and aesthetic reasons, and much less for political or ideological ones. The basilica of Saint-Denis's size, antiquity, beauty, fame, or weight of history —none of these are necessary in order that such ideal values should compensate, for any reason, for the material decline of the things, so that the passage of time could become an ennobling factor. Among the texts in chapter II we already touched upon an example that can approach that of Chateaubriand, although its dimensions and claims are much smaller: the eighteenth-century knick-knacks belonging to Pushkin's aged countess (II, 9). Antiquated rather than worn out, they appeared to us to have been historicized in a rather positively exemplary way, as relics of a regime and an era of taste. But Pushkin's text was, on the whole, an impure example, and the bad condition of the aged countess's sofas and armchairs seems instead to approach, rather, that of Hulot's house, which is socially inappropriate with no way of redeeming this fact's negativity — excepting, of course (and as I was saying earlier), from the purely literary function of constituting reality.

The adjectives that I have just employed seem to me fit to be incorporated into the tree's second terminal opposition: *exemplary,* on the one hand; *inappropriate,* on the other. This time, we do not have two contradictory terms, but rather two contraries:

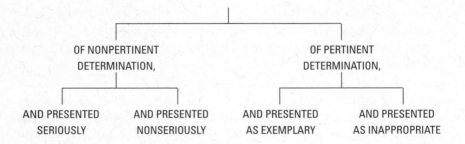

OF NONPERTINENT DETERMINATION,

OF PERTINENT DETERMINATION,

AND PRESENTED SERIOUSLY

AND PRESENTED NONSERIOUSLY

AND PRESENTED AS EXEMPLARY

AND PRESENTED AS INAPPROPRIATE

Readers may now go over for themselves the complete definitions of four categories, from top to bottom; there is, however, an objection that they would be right to make. The opposition between serious and nonserious presentations only distinguishes the latter category from the former, while, in keeping with previous texts and lines of reasoning, the serious presentation could also make us contrast the third — and, more significantly, the fourth — with the second. It is an incongruity by default that derives from the hierarchic and economical criterion that I am following — hierarchic inasmuch as it sets the oppositions above or beneath each other, economical inasmuch as it avoids repeating them at several points on the tree and chooses the setting that is strategically preferable for each.

The other possible criterion, which would cause the oppositions to intersect each other (as I did in III, 8, for the lowest common denominator and its attributes) instead of ranking them, would offer less arbitrariness but absolutely no economy. The results would be unusable if, in wishing to extend the reach of the first terminal opposition, we were to try to make it intersect with the one above it, but to economize with the second terminal opposition: except for the first two categories under a transformed definition (let us say, for the sake of brevity, *nonhistoricized serious, nonhistoricized nonserious*), not only would the third and fourth be confused with each other (*historicized serious*), but furthermore a category not easy to document with texts known to me would appear (*historicized nonserious*). The least arbitrary criterion possible would consist in investigating each text according to all the oppositions considered pertinent, in succession, releasing them from all rankings that cannot be reduced to a logical subordination. But with so prudent a procedure — leaving aside its tedium — the classificatory rigor would end up creating an effect equivalent to that of its contrary — *a priori* distrust of classification. Meticulousness in recognizing the constants would revert to the exclusive cult of the variants of which I have spoken (III, 2), of past or present idealistic flavor. For our purposes, as much rigor as helps us recognize the real constants within groups of texts is sufficient, and the imperfection to which I am resigned with respect to the tree is symptomatic of a complication that has to do with the relations among these first four categories. No classification would have been satisfactory, I said (III, 6), without somehow taking into account what I have called a historical turning point.

This phenomenon, which has been indicated as an increase in frequency, development, and number of constants between the late eighteenth and the early nineteenth century (I, 7; III, 3, 5), concerns them as a whole and thus the entire tree; it can be noted along the chronological succession of texts in some categories, whereas in others it marks the upper limit of the distribution of texts. Direct effects of the historical turning point and symmetrical coincidences with it are revealed only in comparisons among the first four categories. One may say that it marks the lower chronological limit — the prevailing one, at least — of only the first two of them, which in turn coincides, not accidentally, with the upper limit of the other two, thereby suggesting something like a metamorphosis, a continuation through change. The categories in which the passage of time is of nonpertinent determination — and that have so far been documented by ancient examples, but can otherwise be documented up to the eighteenth century — seem to have abandoned the field in the nineteenth century in favor of the categories in which it is of pertinent determination. Those with a metahistorical core have withdrawn, and those with a historical core have taken their place; and one and the same adjective with three distinct meanings circulates in this discussion: historical, the determination of the passage of time in images; historical, that is, literary-historical, the turning point in the frequency or intensity of distribution of the constants; also literary-historical, the extra, diachronic dimension that enters here to complicate the tree's synchronic or panchronic flatness. We shall refer to such a relationship, where one category withdraws and another takes its place, as *transformation*.

It is transformation, with its succession of times, that brings me to save the *serious/nonserious* opposition for the earlier literary-historical period, in which the two possibilities coexisted in synchrony. In the later period, the serious presentation is almost taken for granted, and if it is again set against the nonserious one it is, rather, in diachrony. At the turning point, one may suppose that there are parallel transformations between, respectively, the first and third of the four categories and between the second and the fourth — that is, between, respectively, those in which either the partial positivity (of an occasion for high, serious meditation, of an investing of exemplary value, bound together with certain images) or the sole negativity (of a baseness that causes a smile or laughter, of degradation that proclaims itself to be inappropriate) is evident. The reader will have recognized the distinction illustrated in chapter I by conventional examples and then judged to be general enough to be taken up again in the classificatory operation (III, 6). The distinction, namely, between images in which primary nonfunctionality is redeemed by recovering secondary functionality and images in which it is not redeemed by anything aside from literature's formal quality. The regular alternation of partially positive — or, as I shall call them, semipositive — categories with negative ones will continue throughout the tree. It is authorized by the equal frequency of these two types of images in the texts, and derives from the very adoption of binary terminal oppositions; the contradictory or contrary pole in them will, on a case-by-case basis, be negative not only logically but in various concrete ways, from the ideological to the moral, aesthetic, practical, economic, hedonistic, and emotional.

It is urgent that we propose names for the categories we have defined, if it is true that we are classifying because we sense a need for words (just as Père Ubu invented pataphysics, "the need for which was universally making itself felt").[18] Short names, easier to handle than definitions, are required, but no mere one-word attribute would suffice for summarizing and distinguishing; the smallest form in which they can be coined is that of the substantivized double adjective (however rarely used in English), and I am taking them from the most memorable lexical cues among those that have been deployed in the course of the discussion of the examples. Furthermore, I shall begin to use + and − signs to underline the alternation of semipositive and negative categories. To complete this part of the tree once and for all, I shall add two clarifying terms, in parentheses, beneath the poles of the penultimate opposition, and a contrary given as a limit beneath the contradictory pole of the first terminal opposition — starting with the *passage of time*:

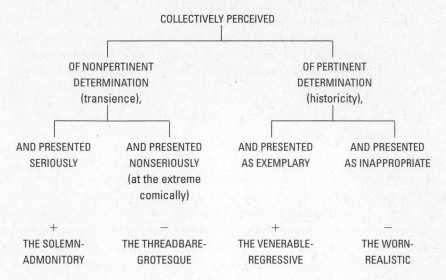

COLLECTIVELY PERCEIVED

OF NONPERTINENT DETERMINATION (transience),

OF PERTINENT DETERMINATION (historicity),

AND PRESENTED SERIOUSLY

AND PRESENTED NONSERIOUSLY (at the extreme comically)

AND PRESENTED AS EXEMPLARY

AND PRESENTED AS INAPPROPRIATE

+ THE SOLEMN-ADMONITORY

− THE THREADBARE-GROTESQUE

+ THE VENERABLE-REGRESSIVE

− THE WORN-REALISTIC

6

Before we move the tree toward new categories, let us go back to other examples of the defined and denominated categories. For each of them, let us consider three more texts. For the solemn-admonitory I shall look all the way back to the first book of *Of the Changeability of Fortune* (*De varietate fortunae*) by Poggio Bracciolini (1380–1459), probably written shortly after 1431 and published together with the other three books in 1448. In the separate printed edition of 1511, the title continued as follows: *. . . of the City of Rome, and Description of the Ruin of the Same* (*. . . urbis Romae, et de ruina ejusdem descriptio*). Poggio and the humanist diplomat Antonio Loschi, curial officials of a dying pope, take advantage of their leisure by visiting "the city's deserted sites." Once they have dismounted from their horses, they sit amid the ruins of the Tarpeian Rock; the panorama contemplated from above moves Antonio to open the dialogue, sighing and marveling. He thinks of Marius at Carthage, who doubted whether there could be "a grander spectacle" than that city's misfortune. But the misfortune of the city before Antonio's eyes seems to him comparable to no other, natural or human, among the many that history remembers:

> What is most wonderful to tell and most sorrowful to see, is that the cruelty of fortune has to such an extent changed her aspect and beauty, that now deprived of all her glory, she lies prostrate like a gigantic putrescent corpse, eaten away on all sides: it is truly deplorable that this city which at one time teemed with illustrious men and leaders, was nurse to so many generals of

war, so many excellent princes, and mother to so many and so great virtues, progenitor of so many good qualities, from which descended military discipline, the sanctity of customs and life, the sanctions of law, the examples of all virtues and the rules of good life, once the ruler of the world, should now, through the iniquity of fortune which overthrows all things, be not only divested of her sovereignty and majesty, but condemned to vile servitude, disfigured, dishonored, so that only by ruin she reveals her past dignity and magnitude.[19]

At this point the distinction or comparison introduced in the very first lines is being developed, between the crumbling of the ancient buildings that disfigure Rome's present aspect and the destruction of the empire of which Rome was the center. We would not expect that the latter of the two would be considered the less extraordinary and deplorable. It took place, in fact, in the order of things — the political or military one — in which fortune gives and takes away "as if by right": it is said that "kingdoms are changed, empires succeed each other, nations crumble," etc., with solemnly normalizing verbs in the atemporal present tense. Within the capital's walls, on the other hand, fortune has raged with more unpredictable, capricious, and cruel arbitrariness. Considering Rome's many monuments to be "above fortune" or "beyond fate," the founders did not presume too much, and their descendants' astonishment shows them to have been right.[20]

It is a loss of architectural beauty that illustrates the scandal, even if the real justification for the Romans' attempt at immortality cannot be comprehensively described by supreme aesthetic worth. This is proclaimed by the fluent double (anaphoric and asyndetic) list — echoed further on in a list of monuments: that of the cultural values (moral, military, and juridical, besides the artistic ones) of which Rome was progenitor. But the meditation does not concern past greatness — displayed, at this point, "only by ruin" — but rather the fact of the fall and the deploring of it, or, in more abstract terms, primary defunctionalization and secondary refunctionalization. Of course, even in this second example of the solemn-admonitory, the literary substance of images boils down to a spare emphasis on adjectives and participles involving ruin, and on a powerful metaphor. "Like a gigantic putrescent corpse, eaten away on all sides": there can be no doubt that the noun comes from Sulpicius, and we realize that the shift from a casual visit to famous places to a meditation inspired by them also comes from that source, with the difference that here the visit is intentional rather than accidental. Furthermore, by inventing gigantic proportions Poggio expresses the emblematic inseparability of greatness and decadence, also inseparable from Rome's uniqueness, a quality which Sulpicius did not attribute to the Greek cities. And this uniqueness consists in a primacy of excellence — not, for instance, in the historical circumstances first of the unification of the so-called civilized world and then of its breakdown. Here, too, what is pertinent about decadence is the fact in itself, not the why, the when, or the how. In Poggio's reply, the dialogue continues concerning his archaeological and epigraphic activities — he has transcribed inscriptions "hidden amid bushes and brambles" — but it ends with a discussion of the definition of fortune, which is led back from the accidental to divine will.[21]

As in the dedicatory proem, here the eulogy of written history returns. Events that otherwise "antiquity usually obliterates" are made by writing to "seem recent"; the lack of it consigns truly recent events to oblivion.[22] It is as if writing, for all its physical perishability, were more resistant than the materials of which monuments are made; therefore the powers of philology are greater than those of archaeology. In the famous epistle in which Poggio had given the news of his having rediscovered Quintilian, the precious codex appeared "still safe and unharmed" despite a metaphorical, centuries-long "imprisonment" deep in a monastery tower, and despite the nonmetaphorical "mold and dust" that covered it.[23] It is by the impotence of similar human remedies, in the face of the spectacle of Rome, that the space of the solemn-admonitory is opened. It is a lesson in human transience, proffered, however, by a profane historical event, with the impressiveness of its unrestorable remains. This relative secularization of the medieval Christian sense of transience is precisely what makes certain concrete images possible. A few years after Poggio's death, the two great revivals of the *ubi sunt* theme — Villon's in French and Manrique's in Spanish — would take, respectively, "last year's snows" and "the meadows' dew" as symbols;[24] soon, nothing is left of them — the contrary of hard, enduring stone. It is true that in the *Roman de la Rose* the house of Fortune had a side that gleamed with gold and silver, and another, made of mud and straw, that was dirty and falling apart because of thousands of cracks.[25] But it was a symbol of inconstancy and transience themselves, not an image of any reality whatever, much less historical reality. In the omnipresent symbolic signification of things, which is a tendency of medieval literature, we can see, fleetingly, the main reason for its absence from this book.

Nevertheless, the religious implications that the theme of ruins — and, with it, solemn-admonitory images — preserve throughout the fifteenth and sixteenth centuries must not be underestimated. From humanistic Latin, let us move on to an example in the vernacular, whose good fortune in Europe testifies to the wide diffusion of the theme during the Renaissance. It is the sonnet we mentioned earlier by Baldassar Castiglione (1478–1529); Du Bellay freely translated it into French among the sonnets of *Les Antiquités de Rome,* well before Lope de Vega parodied it in Spanish. The variation on the theme, which comes in the last tercet (its amorous meaning is even clearer when read in the context of the other sonnets), includes neither images of any sort nor commutation from the serious to the nonserious. This hardly detracts from the example's purity:

> Proud hills, and you sacred ruins,
> Who only the name of Rome still keep,
> Ah, what miserable relics you hold
> Of so many exalted, extraordinary souls!
>
> Colossi, arches, theaters, divine works,
> Triumphal pomp, glorious and happy,
> You have turned into a bit of ash
> And finally become a cheap fable for the vulgar.
>
> Thus, if for a time the famous works
> Make war on time, slow-paced time
> Enviously brings down both works and names.
>
> So I shall live happily among my martyrs:
> For if time brings an end to what is on earth,
> It may yet bring an end to my torment.[26]

An explicit ideological or argumentative element is once again confirmed as typical of the solemn-admonitory, which is matched by the scarcity of images. As I said not far back, this category is for the most part anterior to the historical turning point, and thus also to the modern capacity for sensorial evocation, among other things. Here the images are limited to growing out of the series of vocatives that open both of the quatrains, and that first specify the "sacred ruins" as "colossi, arches, theaters" — which almost form a list — and then qualify them as "divine works" and "triumphal pomp." The first quatrain bemoans the decay of people, and only the second that of things properly speaking. Out of this, a moral involving universal symmetry is drawn in the first tercet, through syntax that overturns it and a play on words that compresses it: time is first defeated but then defeats; it is defeated for short periods and defeats over long periods. Although there is nothing exclusively Christian in this, if we compare it with the first ancient example — nor is there conflict with the admiration for pagan culture, which the sonnet has in common with Poggio's prose — the religious basis of this sense of transience is more recognizable here than in the former. There are echoes of Petrarch between the lines; the most obvious among them is adapted to the ruins of Rome, which have "become a cheap fable for the vulgar," but the original, in the first sonnet of the *Canzoniere* ("To the people all / I was long a fable"), is too close to a famous ending for the reader not to be at least reminded of it ("that everything the world likes is a brief dream"). In the preceding line by Castiglione the monuments appear as having turned "into a bit of ash," as the beauty of Petrarch's Laura is turned into "a bit of dust," or into "scattered ash," according to two other and no less celebrated passages in that most imitated of poetic collections.[27] In these same echoes, the cadaver metaphor — which calls the remains of inanimate things ash, using a word that is consecrated to the cult of the dead — is latent; the universality of the end given by time to what is "on earth" does not prejudice, but rather postulates, an eternity elsewhere.

7

On the other hand, implied religious certainties have entered a state of crisis — as is only to be expected — in the diffuse revival of the solemn-admonitory that is the well-known eighteenth-century fondness for the theme of ruins. In the example of it that I am choosing, ruins appear to be mediated by the language of painting, inasmuch as we are dealing with art criticism — the first *Salons,* created by a great writer. Denis Diderot (1713–84) describes and discusses the paintings exhibited in 1767 by the young Hubert Robert, who has just returned from Italy. And the critic is convinced that he knows even better than the painter that the genre of images of ruins has its own poetics, and what it is:

> The effect of these compositions, be they good or bad, is to leave you in sweet melancholy. We fix our gaze on the remains of a triumphal arch, a portico, a pyramid, a temple, a palace, and we plunge into meditation. We anticipate the ravages of time, and our imagination scatters over the earth the very buildings in which we live. All at once, solitude and silence reign around us. We alone remain, of an entire nation that no longer exists; and this is the ABC of the poetics of ruins.[28]

There follows a description of the painting entitled *Ruin of a Triumphal Arch and Other Monuments;* according to Diderot, it contravenes the poetics in question because too many human figures appear, with the monuments as background. The same critique and its respective motivations are so amply developed with regard to another painting, *Grand Gallery, Lit from the Back,* as to permit me no more than a fragmentary quotation:

> Do you not feel that there are too many figures here, that three-quarters of them should be erased? Only those that add something to the solitude and silence should be preserved. [. . .] Monsieur Robert, you do not yet know why ruins give so much pleasure, independently of the variety of mishaps that they show; and I am going to tell you about them whatever immediately springs to my mind.

The ideas that ruins awaken in me are great ones. Everything turns to nothingness, everything perishes, everything passes. Only the world remains. Only time endures. How old this world is! I walk between two eternities. Wherever I cast my glance, the objects that surround me announce an end and make me resign myself to what awaits me. What is my ephemeral existence in comparison with that of this sunken rock, of this hollowed-out valley, of this swaying forest, of these rocky masses suspended and quaking over my head? I see the marble of tombs crumble into dust, and I do not want to die! And I want to exempt a weak tissue of fibers and flesh from a universal law that is executed upon bronze! A torrent drags nations, one upon another, to the bottom of a common abyss; I, I alone claim the right to stop at the edge and to fend off the surge that flows beside me![29]

Solitude and silence, in the presence of the greatest symbols of our transience, would certainly have been propitious also for a religious meditation, and perhaps even for introductions to prayer. But then the meditation would not have spiritually isolated the believer from a community of believers; moreover, the more humble and sorrowful it was, the more salutary it would have turned out to be. For the Encyclopedist critic, instead, the inward-turning effect induced by the ruins is emotionally ambivalent: it consists of "sweet melancholy," and it is actually a matter of knowing "why ruins give so much pleasure." The reason for this pleasure is to be sought in the same pre-Romantic individualism — which was by this time fully in existence — that confers necessity and absoluteness on the contemplator's isolation. The "great ideas" in the last paragraph quoted may be summarized by the resignation of the "I" to its annihilation, imposed on it by the overwhelming confrontation with the precariousness of everything in nature, over and above the impermanence of marble, of bronze, and of nations. But if the argument is the same as that of Sulpicius, instead of the plural "we tiny men" (IV, 1), the emphatic singular of "I, I alone" stands out. In the following paragraphs resignation is persistently translated into an original, sentimental, and materialistic sort of carpe diem. I quote another fragment:

In this deserted, solitary, vast refuge, I hear nothing; I have broken with all of life's incumbrances. No one demands anything of me and listens to me. I can speak out loud, torment myself, unrestrainedly pour out my tears.

Under these dark arcades, modesty would be less strong in an honest woman; a tender, timid lover's initiative more lively and more courageous.

Alone among the ruins, the "I" will abandon itself, with no societal checks, to its most spontaneous affective and even sensual life.[30] What is left for the individual is the development of individualism, in those places where, par excellence, it must recognize its perishability, no longer with illusions of an afterlife. Nevertheless, nothing individual is as yet coming into view in the way of a personalized memory; in other words, nothing is calling into question the passage of time, as always, collectively perceived. Not even this becomes of pertinent determination — although it is getting close to becoming so — as long as the feeling that one is the only survivor "of an entire nation that no longer exists" remains a fantasy and the prefigured "ravages of time" remain imaginary.

8

Parallel to the chronological distribution of the solemn-admonitory, that of the threadbare-grotesque is also for the most part prior to the historical turning point and therefore to the modern capacity for sensorial evocation. If, despite this, the texts presented as pure examples of the threadbare-grotesque do not seem analogously poor in images, we know what this is owing to: to the frequent intervention of a figurative inventiveness that, through hyperbole and metaphor, even when its ends are comically deforming, presents concrete objects. As with the solemn-admonitory, I shall set forth an early sixteenth-century Italian example that fortune smiled upon all over Europe, along with the genre or manner that made an adjective (*bernesco*) out of the surname of Francesco Berni (1498–1535). Berni's best-known text is surely the *Chapter of the Priest from Povigliano* (*Capitolo del prete da Povigliano*, 1532), which tells the story of a night's hospitality — as presumptuous as it was sordid — to which a provincial curate subjected the poet together with the humanist Adamo Fumano. Here is their arrival at the wrongly vaunted lodgings, their entrance, and their first views of the inside:

> I thought I would find a palace
> With walls of diamonds and turquoise,
> Having heard so much racket being made:
>
> When God willed, we finally got there:
> We entered through a postern gate,
> Buried in nettles and briars.
>
> There 'twas best to leave the beaten track,
> And go up a certain staircase,
> Where even the nimblest would have broken his neck.
>
> At the top we found ourselves in a hall
> That was not bricked in, thank God,
> For the smoke blew in from below.
>
> I was like a man who thinks over and considers
> What he has done, and what is to be done,
> Since he has been ripped off.

— We misunderstood, Adamo, I said:
This is the home of an Ogre:
We were stark, raving mad!

While I'm scratching my head and twisting,
I see across a dinner table
A rug of pig's wool:

It was not a fresco, but painted in oil;
Some sages say that it had been
A cover for some racehorse;

Then served as a coat for at least three gypsy women,
Then was a hooded cloak, and maybe also a chair cover,
Until it was finally reduced to being a tablecloth.[31]

The expectation of a palace made of precious stones is joking hyperbole inverted positively, and it is immediately straightened into the negative while remaining hyperbole set in metaphor. We may say that the door of the house was *actually like* a fortress's secret entrance ("postern gate"), *actually as if* buried in nettles and briars. The same diagnosis of the rhetoric holds good for the "pig's wool" of which the tablecloth is said to be made, and it holds good for several passages that come after those quoted. When the poet asks for something to drink, in a famous tercet the nonfigurative predicates — that is, that the glass was greasy and clouded and had a broken stem — are elliptically replaced by hyperbole-metaphors:

And lo, immediately there appeared a glass
That had just that moment been confirmed:
It was all sweaty, and it couldn't sit down. . . .[32]

Coming back to the quoted verses and to the tablecloth, the play on words tells us in painterly terms how greasy the cloth was. The incredible series of its metamorphoses, uses, and former proprietors — from racing stable hands to at least three gypsy women, from an overcoat to a chair cover — is the prototype of a topos that will be enormously extended during the Baroque period. I have said that the fading of color from a piece of material would in turn become a topos of nineteenth-century description (IV, 5) — a good occasion for a comparison of the definition of the threadbare-grotesque with that of the worn-realistic, precisely at the point of bifurcation that separates them in the tree. In the more modern topos, the determination of a passage of time, be it dated or not, virtually combines with a chemical process and its optical result. In the topos that typifies the threadbare-grotesque, information about the metamorphoses of the material actually pretends to determine such a passage, but

the more exaggeratedly numerous they are, the more they leave it indeterminate in its inverisimilitude. In the rest of the text, the uses to which the room is
put that the priest offers his guests are no less varied. Granary and bedroom,
pantry and toilet:[33] it is as if the type of series that was at first projected in
astonishing diachrony were contracting — albeit without a list — into stingy,
repulsive synchrony. Let us give our attention, finally, to the parodistic Dant-
esque sound of the fifth tercet quoted, which breaks on the jargonistic word
incanata (rip-off) and implies that the priest's residence is *actually like* hell.
The *capitolo* as a whole contains another parody of Dante, two passages
reminiscent of Petrarch, an invocation of the Muses, and half a dozen other
classical and Christian references[34] — enough to show us how language with
threadbare-grotesque comical tendencies is metaliterary and cultivated. Even
when it is at the first level imitative, it often lives explicitly, and always implicitly, at the expense of the types of serious language that it overturns and
desecrates.

Among the texts from a later period and another language in which the influence of this *capitolo* by Berni is recognizable, there is Satire 11 of Mathurin
Régnier (1573–1613). It is the last but one of a collection published in 1608,
and its narrative grows out of that of the previous satire: the poet, who has fled
from a brawl that interrupted a ridiculous banquet, accidentally enters a
brothel in the darkness of a rainy night. Thus, in the room that he is obliged to
go up to — with no erotic intentions — disfunction and disorder are less surprising than in a priest's dwelling. The ascent of the staircase and the making of the
bed recall Berni,[35] but not without Baroque amplification, on account of which
the poet's inspection of the room or attic swells to enormous length before the
whore arrives on the scene. This room, too, has at least one other use — as a
storage room, which is the equivalent of a chaotic array of uses:

> I enter this pretty place, worthier of note
> Than a proud Monarch's opulent Palace.
> There, I rummage in the most hidden recesses,
> Where the good Lord willed that, for my old sins,
> I should learn of the contempt that drives the soul mad,
> When, for excess of curiosity or distress,
> Wandering all about and roaming high and low,
> It makes us find what we are not looking for.
> Now, the first item I come upon at my feet
> Is a chipped caldron, a watch's cover,
> Four boxes of unguents, one of burnt alum,
> Two unmatched gloves, a worn-out muff;
> Three vials of blue-water, also called second-water,

The little syringe, a sponge, a tube,
Some white powder, a bit of rouge, a rag of a collar,
A broom to burn in going to a witches' sabbath;
An old lantern, a straw-covered stool
That had survived the battle on three legs;
A barrel without a bottom, two bottles on their asses,
That were saying, neckless: "We have lived too long";
A little bag full of Mercury powder,
A greasy old hood, badly dyed,
And in a little chest that opens only with effort,
I find embers of a St. John's fire,
Salt, holy wafers, some ferns, a candle,
Three dead-man's teeth wrapped in virgin parchment;
A Bat, a Magpie's carcass,
Wolf-fat and May-butter.[36]

In its fanciful abundance, this Baroque list surpasses both Martial's ancient one and all the modern ones in our second chapter. In twenty lines it displays more than thirty elements, singular or plural, and if they are not all on the same level it is not because there are synthetic designations of the kind that has already been noted (II, 13), at either the beginning or the end. It is a result of a procedure related to the *mise en abîme* so dear to early seventeenth-century painting, or to the play-within-a-play dear to the theater of the same period. A whole second list is contained within one sole element of the first—the little chest that opens only with effort (and that may make us think of Cros' chest in II, 1, more for the contrast than for the resemblance). The activity of rummaging "in the most hidden recesses" that is attributed to the poet as soon as he has entered seems all the more to prepare the list and explain its existence, the more so since his motives lack factual explanations. And his soul knows the annoyance of finding "what we are not looking for"—useless things, in any case; but here, the common denominator of uselessness mixes worn-out, degraded, and base things with bizarre, eccentric, and rare ones—a frequent mixture with the threadbare-grotesque. Things that belong to the first species come closer to the limit of the comical, as can be seen in the comic personifications of the stool lacking a leg and the bottles lacking necks. Other things have rather been defunctionalized by their status as a confusion of remnants, otherwise they would have been useful ingredients in various arts that would likely be practiced in a pimp's place of residence: perfumes, cosmetics, laundry, pharmaceuticals. Still other things are strange in the sense of being uncanny, like the witch's broom, the dead man's teeth wrapped in parchment, and the bat (which had appeared in Berni, but alive and conventional).[37] I have mentioned the value of a magic list as a prototype or archetype (II, 13); here, it is as a result of an understandable historic contamination that an example of one category touches upon another that has not yet been defined, and that certain ingredients of a threadbare-grotesque list would in any case fall beyond the limits of natural functionality.

9

The bizarre once again gives way to poverty in the array of threadbare-grotesque images, if we move from one to the other of these most propitious literary genres — from the *bernesco* to the picaresque: to the *Story of the Life of a Knave, called Don Pablo; Exemplar of Vagabonds and Mirror of Rogues* (*Historia de la vida del Buscón, llamado don Pablos; exemplo de Vagamundos y espejo de Tacaños*) by Francisco de Quevedo (1580–1645). If it is true that it was written two decades before its publication in 1626, then it came at the beginning of the flowering of this genre in Spanish literature, from the last years of the sixteenth century to the middle of the seventeenth. Three characteristics have been observed in it, on account of either their absence or their excess in comparison with other picaresque novels: abstention from the normally widespread moralizing interventions on the author's part; cold extremism in the choice of both morally and physically base subjects; the most inspired rhetorical elaboration, to the point of making recognizable, within the prose writer Quevedo, the verse-writing poet — Baroque in the variant known at the time as *conceptismo,* the style of witty, even outlandish conceits. The last of these three features is more than ever a good reason for banishing every notion of realism as serious, as opposed to deforming, representation. But the absence of comments also cuts to the bone the critical representation of customs, in the sense that has already been ascribed to Martial (IV, 4); nothing is left but the choice of content to attach the representation to the lower depths of the real — continuing to erase the determination of the passage of time within the universality of human need. The increasing cruelty of the caricature is proportional to the increment in foulness. It is as if the practice of a genre that recounts the lives of socially alienated people were a paradox for a nationalistic, absolutist writer obsessed with the "impurity" of blood and faith — as if it dictated the repression of sympathetic feelings that the tale sets in motion. Thus, in particular, its use of the threadbare-grotesque, which even today can make people laugh, is comical in the strongest sense, that is, pitiless.

The picaroon's parents are a barber-thief and a procuress-witch of non-Christian origin; the high points of cynical and macabre humor will be reached when they end at the gallows and the stake, respectively, with the appearance of an executioner uncle and a banquet party of human jackals in his house.[38] In the beginning, Pablos goes to school, attaches himself to a nobleman's son, and follows him when his father puts him in a boarding school. They both suffer—the servant only a little worse—through an indescribable experience of meanness and undernourishment; this is the novel's most celebrated episode, with Cabra the priest-preceptor, a character who comes to life precisely through the combination (with which we are familiar) of deforming hyperbolic, metaphoric figurativeness and of distancing comical effect (II, 8; IV, 4). In the physical portrait, this figurativeness already seems to motivate the description more than vice versa, and I shall give only one example: Cabra's beard has turned pale with fear of the neighboring mouth, which, out of hunger, threatens to eat it up. Even the depiction of avarice transcends the usual repertoire of anecdotes on this theme, forcing it in the direction of hyperbole, if not letting it slide into that of metaphor. There are no toilets in the house because there is never anything to defecate, and Pablos, in order to husband his strength, doesn't dare to expel what little he should. Only the remarks of Cabra himself, all full of hypocritical optimism about the food he hands out, remain as dryly verisimilar as perfect theatrical lines. Hunger and death: a schoolboy's death from hunger brings the episode to an end,[39] and later, when Pablos learns that Cabra has died, he does not doubt that the cause was hunger.[40]

One of the excerpts that I am quoting informs us of this character's clothing and apartment; the other of the kitchen, which is entrusted to his seventy-year-old aunt:

> On sunny days he wore a gnawed-up beret with a thousand holes and a garnishing of grease; it was made of something that was cloth, with dandruff at its base. According to some, his cassock was miraculous, because no one knew what color it was. Some, seeing that it so lacked hair, claimed that it was of frog's hide; others said that this was an illusion: close up it looked black and from afar nearly blue. He wore it without a belt; he wore no collar or cuffs. With his long hair and his miserable, short cassock, he looked like death's lackey. Each shoe could have been a Philistine's tomb. As for his apartment, there weren't even any spiders in it. He kept the rats away for fear that they might chew up some of the bread crusts that he preserved. He made his bed on the floor and always slept on one side, so as not to wrinkle the sheets. All in all, he was an arch-pauper and proto-miserable.[41]

> God only knows what we went through with the old lady. She was completely deaf; she understood by signs; she was blind, and so attached to the rosary that one day it fell off her over the pot and she brought it to us in the most devout broth that I have ever eaten. Some said: "Black chickpeas! They are

surely from Ethiopia." Others said: "Chickpeas in mourning! Who died?" My master was the first to swallow a bead, and in chewing it he broke a tooth. On Fridays she used to send eggs that had enough beard, made of her white hairs, that they could have aspired to be mayors or lawyers. Then, to replace the ladle with a shovel and to send out a bowl of petrified broth was an ordinary thing. A thousand times I found insects, pieces of wood, and flax for spinning in the pot, and she put everything in so that it would make some padding in our guts and fill them out.[42]

Here, too, it is true that the threadbare-grotesque is filled with images by figurative inventiveness; the cut-down nonfunctional corporality pertains more to its point of departure than to its point of arrival. Although the Baroque topos of the metamorphoses of a piece of cloth will recur further on in the *Buscón* (regarding the clothing stratagems of penniless courtiers),[43] here we encounter the fading of colors, a future nineteenth-century topos, as I have earlier pointed out; it is said to be not a chemical or optical phenomenon but a miracle or illusion, unless Cabra's cassock was made of frog's skin. Such varied opinions are so many figurative outcomes, delegated to a variety of voices: "some . . . others . . ." The same process makes the old woman's rosary beads become either black chickpeas or chickpeas in mourning, thereby transfiguring real facts, believable in themselves, in both passages. It is not at all unlikely that Cabra's shoes were enormously broad, but what is said of them bursts the bounds of rhetorical codification in three words. The association of ideas that leads from enormity to a Philistine, instead of limiting itself to attributing the shoes to him, puts him to bed in them and makes them his tomb: the hyperbole protracts its meaning until it becomes a nearly senseless metaphor. Nor is it unlikely that the hairs that have fallen off the old woman have made the eggs white, and they are not the most nauseating of the foreign bodies in the food. But instead of stopping at the white hairs of a mayor or a lawyer, the association with them goes on to suppose that the eggs themselves are seeking to achieve those positions; the metaphor elides its way beneath a nearly impassable piece of hyperbole. It would be no less complicated to describe, in denominated figures, such finds as "death's lackey" or "arch-pauper and protomiserable." There are no metaliterary allusions such as I pointed out in Berni: such an intense degree of literariness at the level of the word cannot but do without them.

10

I have maintained that the other two categories that have been defined found their upper, rather than lower, limit of distribution in the historical turning point, and that they alternated with the first two (IV, 5). Nevertheless, it is obvious that such limits and transitions can be traced only in an intricate and approximate way. If I wish to go back to the most ancient important example of the venerable-regressive known to me, I find myself more or less in a period coinciding with that of the last example used for the solemn-admonitory: Diderot's *Salons* ran from 1759 to 1781, and the short poems attributed to the third-century Scottish bard Ossian by his presumed translator, James Macpherson (1736–96), were published between 1760 and 1773. In the eighteenth century, the partial imposture of this attribution was both prompted by the Romantic myths of the original and of the primitive, and, thanks to them, covered up and crowned with immense European success. Later on, this imposture contributed as an anecdote both to ensuring that the work's fame lasted and that it fell back into the ranks of the dated and unreadable. But is our taste really so much better than that of Goethe, Chateaubriand, Leopardi, and Pushkin? Furthermore this injustice clashes today with the myth of auto-imitative, intertextual literariness, which is the opposite of the Romantic myth of originality — the more so inasmuch as Macpherson was imitating not only traditional Gaelic poetry but also, as was his duty, and as soon came to be held against him, the classics and the Bible. The short poems' rhapsodic form, in harmony with their thematic uniformity, leads me to quote several very brief passages:

> I have seen the walls of Balclutha, but they were desolate. The fire had resounded in the halls: and the voice of the people is heard no more. The stream of Clutha was removed from its place by the fall of the walls. The thistle shook, there, its lonely head: the moss whistled to the wind. The fox looked out, from the windows, the rank grass of the wall waved round its head. Desolate is the dwelling of Moina, silence is in the house of her fathers. (*Carthon*)[44]

> . . . when he came to Dunlathmon's towers. The gates were open and dark. The winds were blustering in the hall. The trees strowed the threshold with leaves; the murmur of night was abroad. (*Oithona*)[45]

> They saw the fallen walls of their fathers; they saw the green thorn in the hall. Their tears rushed forth in secret. (*Calthon and Colmal*)[46]

> They sleep together: their ancient halls moulder away. Ghosts are seen there at noon: the valley is silent, and the people shun the place of Lamor. (*The War of Caros*)[47]

The intrusion, amid walls, towers, and halls, of plants and animals incompatible with human dwellings (thistles, moss, rank grass, green thorn, and the fox) is an invasion by nature. It recalls to an extent the grass growing and the bird passing through the basilica of Saint-Denis (IV, 2), and, to an extent,

Berni's door "buried in nettles and briars" (IV, 8), but above all the examples encountered in the second chapter (II, 10, 11). And it restates the case for some sort of contamination with a category that is still to be defined. We might have encountered the same contamination in an example of the solemn-admonitory much earlier, historically, than in a venerable-regressive one; if this new category is replacing the old one here, it is still close to it even in other respects. Ossianic passages like the apostrophes to the evening star and to the moon — taken up by Goethe and Leopardi, respectively — express (without images that are of concern to us) perennial, impersonal melancholy over the transitoriness of everything.[48] In the passages that I have cited, however, decadence and abandon are not perceived as a gradual outcome of time running on without pause, but rather as a traumatic consequence of certain events; these are alluded to rather than recounted through clear, unitary narratives, yet they have a character that is specifiable even if not yet specified, that is historical even if not merely remote but even nebulous. Time is split in two by these events, and only comparison with the past as a glorious exemplar lends emotional meaning to present desolation. Not to be taken generically is the formula that opens the first short poem quoted above, half of which is repeated at the beginning and end of another (*Cath-Loda*): "A tale of the times of old! The deeds of days of other years!"[49]

In this last short poem and in yet another (*Oina-Morul*), Ossian's very inspiration, or his harp's task, is identified with the power to "relight," "reach," "regrasp," and "recall" an age characterized by warrior heroism[50] — an age that, although it is supposedly set in the third century, I do not hesitate to call feudal, as an antithesis to the present unwarlike state in which the images of decadence are to be situated when they are made concrete: "Here rise the red beams of war! There, silent, dwells a feeble race! They mark no years with their deeds, as slow they pass along."[51] Macpherson's success preceded the French Revolution, but it irradiated from England in the decades of the maturing Industrial Revolution, in which — previous to and no less importantly than in the French one — the rhythms of both class change and Oedipal-generational change would be accelerated. It is well known that Ossian's writings are full of Nordic clouds and fog, and these are the customary "seat" or "chariot" of ghosts,[52] which sometimes actually blend together: "the grey watry forms of ghosts" (*The Death of Cuthullin*); "the forms of the dead were blended with the clouds" (*Temora* VI).[53] Forms mixed together with the gray, wet sky, but visible even at midday as in the fourth quotation, are too omnipresent to strike terror; they are nothing other than the ghosts, par excellence, of unforgettable fathers. This is why certain final sentences will find so unmistakable an echo in those of Chateaubriand (we read one of them a short while back), not excluding the nostalgia of faint auditory impressions. In the extremely beautiful ending of the first canto of *Fingal,* which was Ossian's first work, the dead are at the same time near and far — like the past of which they are phantasms even more often than are ruined buildings: "The ghosts of the lately dead were near, and swam on the gloomy clouds: and far distant, in the dark silence of Lena, the feeble voices of death were faintly heard."[54]

11

Thus it is legitimate to speak of the venerable-regressive when faced with certain images, even if the level of determination of the values they represent is much vaguer than in the first, exceptional example of Saint-Denis. I would not otherwise dare to link our thematic thread to some lines from *Faust,* Part I, by Johann Wolfgang von Goethe (1749–1832) — lines whose interpretation is as complex and debated as that of the whole masterpiece of which they are among the most famous. From our particular point of view, however, they are pertinent to the highest degree, and this justifies a partial interpretation of them. They develop the brief, and no less famous, stage direction that precedes them; almost like a germ cell of the whole work's gestation, it opened the *Urfaust* of the 1770s and the version published in 1790, and it remained unchanged in the definitive version of 1808: *In a high-vaulted, narrow Gothic room, Faust restless on a chair at his desk.*[55] This is the background against which the character begins by declaring all his knowledge to be useless, a museum of defunctionalized doctrines. Whatever may be the causes of his intellectual bankruptcy and of his consequent turning to magic, and whether we take literally the sixteenth-century setting of the legend, or have in mind the author's era between the Enlightenment and Romanticism, a symbolic relationship is beyond doubt: Faust's room is as narrow and Gothic as his culture. It does not take long for the monologue to fully specify this relationship:

> Alas! shall I yet stick to my prison?
> Accursed, musty hole in the wall,
> Where heaven's dear light itself
> Dimly pierces through painted glass!
> Encumbered by this pile of books
> That worms gnaw at, that dust covers,
> And that up to the high vault above
> Is deep covered with smoky papers;
> Hemmed in by glassware and phials,
> Crammed full of instruments,
> Stuffed with ancestors' household goods —
> This is thy world! this is called a world![56]

The narrowness and clutter are underlined by terms like "prison," "hole," "encumbered," "pile," "deep covered," "hemmed in by," "crammed full," and "stuffed." The must and even the stained-glass windows that cloud the natural light reek of antiquity, as do the worm-eaten, dusty books, smoky papers, glassware, phials, and instruments, as well as the household goods that represent his ancestors' culture in a more humble sense. Seven lines down, animal and human skeletons, all around, are added, amid "smoke and mold."[57] If the room is as packed as a small chest — in its function as a container of useless, old, and unusual objects — not only is their former value and its enduring exemplariness implied, but even the endowing of them, in a way, with the secondary functionality that characterizes our semipositive categories is not wanting. It is of an ideological order, as the venerable-regressive definition demands, and we must not underrate it because this time it implies an occasion for refusal rather than for acceptance. For Faust, the room and objects are a "world," and his new identity can reveal itself only in their presence, since he can assert himself only through the act of rejecting the continuity of tradition that they propose. Following the magic evocations and the pedantic disciple's interruption, the monologue that starts up again (in the final version) returns to the identical type of images of the room, with the identical symbolic meaning:

> What makes this high wall with its hundred compartments
> Narrow around me — is it not dust?
> Junk, that with its thousands of trinkets,
> Weighs upon me in this world of moths?[58]

A few lines further on, the instruments themselves are apostrophized along with the derelict functionality of their parts; their listing, however, makes us imagine them as being complicated rather than rudimentary. In them, it is science itself, rather than an outdated state of science (as in the nineteenth-century cases of Pushkin, Poe, and Stevenson, II, 9, 15, 14), that appears unequal to the task of penetrating nature's mystery:

> You instruments are surely mocking me
> With wheel and cogs, cylinder and clamps
>
> . . . .
>
> And what she [nature] did not reveal to your spirit,
> You will not extort from her with levers and screws.[59]

In the following lines the objects' exemplariness ends up defining itself as an inheritance from a father or from previous generations. It is at one with the accretions of his personal past as a scholar, deposited in soot:

> You old implements that I haven't used,
> You are here only because my father used you.

> You ancient scrolls, you have become smoky
> For so long the dim lamp on this desk has smoldered.[60]

The repetition of a first verb, "to use" (*brauchen*), from the semantic sphere of the functional, refers not to his use, but to his father's; and it prepares the way for proclamations, in the universalizing form of a maxim, repeating another verb, "to serve" (*nützen*), from the same sphere:

> What you have inherited from your ancestors
> You must merit, if you would possess it.
> What serves no purpose is a heavy weight;
> Only what the moment creates can serve its needs.[61]

What is used, what is needed, what serves a purpose, what is useful: these are the contraries of those things whose images we are studying in this book. Here a new individualism, proto-bourgeois in a still heroic sense, achieves a pitiless, complete identification of the former sphere with the present — with the very moment. It immediately and completely relegates the past to the sphere of the antifunctional — "a heavy weight" — no longer allowing for hereditary mediations that had always passed down cultural values. As for the bookish values so dear to his disciple, in the dialogue between the two quoted monologues, they are refused by Faust with the worst of antonomastic images: "A trash-bin and a junk-room."[62] In the name venerable-regressive, which I have given to this category, I would in general like the second adjective to be taken literally, with no pejorative connotations; in this case, however, such a connotation is impatiently dictated by the character and the author. And it is important to me that the arbitrariness of our stopping each definition at a terminal contrary, beneath which further contraries could always be ranged (III, 7), be detected at work. In the case of the venerable-regressive, nonfunctional corporality, presented as exemplary, may in fact be accepted or refused; in the text, I mean, and not in readers' opinions or sympathies. However, it seems to me that, for historical reasons typical of the period that I speak of as the historical turning point, exemplariness remains the best final term of definition. As a constant element, it is stronger even than the variants of acceptance or refusal: if, on the one hand, the renovating impulse must be measured against the weight of a continuity that has to be broken, on the other, an awareness of the ineluctability of decline is rarely missing beneath conservative regret.

Now I will present a case which, rather than accepting or refusing exemplary values from the past, expresses ambivalence between the one and the other. It seems that a real incident inspired the little poem *Rolla*, published in 1833 by Alfred de Musset (1810–57). Jacques Rolla is a twenty-year-old libertine who is spending his last night of love with Marie, a fifteen-year-old prostitute. He had said that once he is completely ruined he will commit suicide, and at dawn he keeps his word. Musset is not at his best here: emphatic without detachment, his rhetorical inventiveness is far from the ironic grace of his prose masterpieces for the theater. As often with his model, Byron, too many comparisons and apostrophes try to revivify the tired formula of the verse tale by interrupting it. They move from mythological, historical, or literary characters to Poverty, from the wild mare to the black people of Santo Domingo, and they become numerous between Rolla's arrival and the dawn, as if to cover up a narrative ellipsis of the night of love.[63] Among others, the author presents an apostrophe to a figure who was still supremely symbolic more than half a century after his death — the same figure to whom a song that became proverbial during the Restoration gave "the blame" for everything:

> Do you sleep happily, Voltaire, and does your hideous smile
> Still flutter over your fleshless bones?
> It is said that your century was too young to read you;
> Ours must make you happy, and your men are born.
> The immense construction that you undermined day and night
> With your broad hands, has fallen upon us.
> Death must have awaited you impatiently,
> During the eighty years that you were courting it;
> You must make hellish love, you two.
> Do you ever leave the nuptial bower
> Where you embrace each other among the worms of the tomb,
> And go walking all alone, your forehead pale,
> In a deserted cloister or an ancient castle?
> What do all those great bodies deprived of life
> Tell you, then, those silent walls, those desolate altars
> That your breath has unpeopled for eternity?
> What do the crosses tell you? What does the Messiah tell you?
> Oh! does he still bleed when, to unnail him
> From his trembling tree, like a wilted flower,
> Your ghost comes back in the night to shake him?
> Do you believe your mission worthily accomplished,
> And, like the Eternal One at the creation,
> Do you find that it is well, and that your work is good?[64]

If this invective is stronger and more significant than others, it may well be the case that it gains something from being an isolated quotation. In any case, it is less randomly inserted into its context: in the same Section IV, the erotic ardor of the young couple makes for apostrophes to cloisters, monasteries, and monks, by way of contrast; the imminent suicide's unbelief makes him challenge "old Arouet" (and, in a more general but equally repetitive way, the "stupid demolishers") two more times.[65] Above all, the theme of the beginning of the poem is taken up again. There, the objects of the repeated question "Do you regret . . . ?" are situations where religious belief is still uncompromised: that of the ancient world, "Where four thousand gods knew not a single atheist," and that of Christianity, so long as "all our monuments and all our beliefs" were intact. The question is rhetorical and the regret undeniable, even though the author's "I" confesses to being an unbeliever. The vision of Christ's cadaver, now barely held up by the nails of Golgotha or fallen to dust,[66] foreshadows the lines that I have quoted; but, more important, foreshadows the parallelism between monuments and beliefs. The "immense construction" undermined by Voltaire and fallen "upon us" — that is, upon the generations of the new century — is truly an archetypal image of the venerable-regressive. A materialization of certainties once assumed to be indestructible, it is historically determined in castles and monasteries — the two seats of the *ancien régime*'s privileged "estates," which the Third Estate had been instigated to destroy.

At bottom, the romantic rancor or orphans' nostalgia behind the apostrophe is not wrong to simplify the politico-ideological situation to such an extent. The moment for even a material restoration of the buildings is ignored; Enlightenment criticism and revolutionary violence are identified with each other; and Voltaire's responsibility is extended beyond the monasteries to the castles. Great inanimate bodies, silent, desolate, depopulated, they appear today as uncanny (in a Freudian sense) as they were familiar for a long time before.[67] And a strange, posthumous reprisal is inflicted on the intellectual instigator by pulling him into the very uncanniness of whose devastating effects he is accused. The equivocation between the universal apparent smile of all skulls and the individual, sarcastically "hideous" smile of the living Voltaire floats over his skeleton. Then he is imagined leaving his tomb for a walk around the scenes of his crime, as a sort of vampire, "all alone" and "pale," a specter still obstinately sacrilegious. More than in the case of Ossian's specters (IV, 10), here the venerable-regressive slides toward contamination by an apposite category that has not yet been defined. Acceptance and refusal of values are shared out here with such perfect ambivalence between the emotional and the intellectual, that the contradictions may pass unnoticed. If the religious certainties were fallacious, why was Voltaire at fault for wanting to overturn them? If they were true, how is it humanly possible that he has succeeded forever, thereby earning, in the last rhetorical question, a negative equivalence with God the creator?

12

As in the first example of the venerable-regressive, so in the first example of the corresponding negative category the degree of determination of the passage of time was exceptional. It will be legitimate to apply the worn-realistic category to images that neither bear dates nor refer to a regime with the precision of Balzac's images, whether the narrative to which they belong is assumed to have taken place shortly or long before the date of publication — the minimum, as in Balzac's case, or the maximum, as one would assume for the literary genre of the historical novel. The latter was a product of the very historicism that transformed the determination of time from nonpertinent to pertinent in the categories in question, within our period of transformations. Yet in this literary genre we do not find the venerable-regressive or the worn-realistic with great frequency; it must present things as recent or new, in a distant past, that today would appear, or do in fact appear, to be old. The more so if these things are large in size or typical or famous — but the less so if they have the dimensions of household objects or items of apparel, whether one is dealing with interiors or even exteriors, both commonplace and unknown. In *The Betrothed* (*I Promessi Sposi;* first edition published in 1825–27, final edition in 1840–42) by Alessandro Manzoni (1787–1873), descriptions of interiors are neither abundant nor wordy. There is an exception for the study of the quibbling Dr. Pettifogger (*Azzecca-garbugli*):

> This was a large room over three of whose walls portraits of the twelve Caesars were distributed; the fourth was covered with a large case of old, dusty books; in the middle of the room, there was a table laden with allegations, supplications, briefs, and edicts, with three or four chairs around it, and on one side a large armchair with a high, square back that ended, in the corners, in two wooden ornaments rising in the shape of horns. It was covered in cowhide, with large upholsterer's nails, some of which had long since fallen out, thus loosening the corners of the cover, which was crumpled here and there. The advocate was in his dressing gown; in other words, he was covered by a worn-out gown that he had used for his harangues many years back, when he used to go to Milan for some important case on days of high pomp.[68]

Much further on, we shall read of Cardinal Borromeo, the novel's most positive character, that "an exquisite cleanliness" was united in him with a frugality so great that he would "not be done with a piece of clothing so long as it was not completely worn out" — rare qualities, it is commented, "in that filthy, magnificent era"[69] of the Spanish-dominated seventeenth century. In the above quotation, the Caesars' portraits stand for magnificence, the dust on the books stands for filth and perhaps for ignorance. The table is "laden" with current cases and recent legislation that are of use to the captious, corrupt advocate, and with the "confusion of papers" into which (it is later said) he digs his hands, rummaging and searching,[70] and that in turn stands for incurable social and legal disorder. But regarding the armchair and its back, we can enjoy a few lines of gratuitous lingering, without any of the threadbare-grotesque's figurative and joking qualities. It is a persistent syntactic string of implicit and explicit complements and relatives; it is prolonged as if the lingering were being forced to restrain itself within the limits of a single sentence. If "long since" is a vague indicator for the upholsterer's nails that have fallen out, we learn that the worn-out gown not only served him "many years back" but also on which specific occasions of forensic pomp. In the time determination, however, a motivation for the fact that much time has passed is not included *a priori*; to put it more simply, there is no reason why Renzo could not have happened into the advocate's house shortly after the latter had bought a new gown or armchair. Neither here nor further on is there any word or sign of the character's economic difficulties, or of his avarice. We shall see him among Don Rodrigo's table guests and courtiers, dressed "in a black cloak" — garb certainly equal to the honor of sitting at that table and in that court.[71]

In the term "worn-realistic," the second adjective has been borrowed (and this is the only such case) from literary history's metalanguage. I indicated the reason in advance (II, 9): in the nineteenth century, base connotations in objects treated seriously constitute reality in proportion to the novelty of the procedure. It is likely that Don Abbondio, a village curate, would live more modestly than a lawyer who enjoys the favor of the squire. This does not mean that it would be unlikely — to put it in simple terms — for him, too, to have refurbished his household goods or his wardrobe shortly before the adventurous night during which an attempt is made to surprise him in his home; predictably, however, this is not at all the case. "Don Abbondio sat . . . upon an old chair; he was wrapped up in an old overcoat, with an old skullcap on his head . . ."[72] A new chair, overcoat, and skullcap might well strengthen and underline a peaceful domestic intimacy in any real-life situation, but this would be difficult in a literary narration that presents itself as its mimesis. Two minuscule examples — significant because they have to do with Don Rodrigo — lead again in the same direction. This man is noble, powerful, and rich in his provincial backwater, and no description of the interior of his *palazzotto* (little palace) is needed to confirm this. The trifle of description of its exterior, with the two nailed-on vultures (one of them "featherless and half-corroded by time"), would be sufficient to indicate that his habits are crude and violent.

The fact that the shutters are "loosened and worn out by the years" (actually "falling off from age," in the 1825 version)[73] seems less motivated, in this description; and further on, when the master is awaiting his bravos' return in a "nasty, unlived-in room on the top floor," he occasionally looks out "through the worm-eaten cracks in the shutters."[74] Now, when Renzo, in going toward the Adda River, takes refuge in a hut to go to sleep, he opens a "big ugly entrance door, *worm-eaten and loosened.*"[75] The same adjectives are used at a great distance from each other for a luxurious, inhabited residence and an abandoned peasant shed; this coincidence, neither calculated nor accidental, says a great deal about preconceptions of the worn-realistic. I must add that the semipositive category—the venerable-regressive à la Chateaubriand—is excluded from the Jansenist Catholic Manzoni's novel. Sedition, famine, plunder, and plague follow on each others' heels; for a writer of his generation, such public upheavals can only have evoked, from a distance, the worst of the French Revolution (there is only one explicit comparison).[76] But the fairly traumatic disasters do not make him think of imposing images that would not be appropriate to the humbleness of his characters. It is Don Abbondio and Perpetua who return, after various vicissitudes, to the house, where amid "the filth" on the floor are listed only "remains and fragments";[77] it is Renzo who gives his overgrown vineyard the "looking-over" out of which the novel's longest description is developed.[78]

13

As I have said, even when a story's setting is contemporary, the worn-realistic may have to do without very precise temporal determinations. This is generally so in the fiction of a country like England, which did not have stormy political history with many vicissitudes like France's between 1789 and 1830 and beyond. The more peaceful and gradual development of English narrative realism, of which Auerbach speaks,[79] is confirmed within our limited area by a subtler passage from the threadbare-grotesque to the worn-realistic. In a literary temperament with such strong humorous or comic propensities as that of Charles Dickens (1812–70), faithfulness to the threadbare-grotesque was at the outset as pronounced as it was creative, and it never completely died out. Nevertheless, it has practically no importance in the excerpt that I am taking from a masterpiece published about halfway through his career: *The Personal History of David Copperfield* (1849–50). The unwitting protagonist is guided through London to find poor Emily, who disappeared after her flight with the seductive and spoiled Steerforth, and at the entrance there is a description of a building, or, better, of its staircase:

. . . and hurried me on to one of the sombre streets, of which there are several in that part, where the houses were once fair dwellings in the occupation of single families, but have, and had, long degenerated into poor lodgings let off in rooms. Entering at the open door of one of these, and releasing my arm, she beckoned me to follow her up the common staircase, which was like a tributary channel to the street.

The house swarmed with inmates. As we went up, doors of rooms were opened and people's heads put out; and we passed other people on the stairs, who were coming down. In glancing up from the outside, before we entered, I had seen women and children lolling at the windows over flower-pots; and we seemed to have attracted their curiosity, for these were principally the observers who looked out of their doors. It was a broad panelled staircase, with massive balustrades of some dark wood; cornices above the doors, ornamented with carved fruit and flowers; and broad seats in the windows. But all these tokens of past grandeur were miserably decayed and dirty; rot, damp, and age, had weakened the flooring, which in many places was unsound and even unsafe. Some attempts had been made, I noticed, to infuse new blood into this dwindling frame, by repairing the costly old wood-work here and there with common deal; but it was like the marriage of a reduced old noble to a plebeian pauper, and each party to the ill-assorted union shrunk away from the other. Several of the back windows on the staircase had been darkened or wholly blocked up. In those that remained, there was scarcely any glass; and, through the crumbling frames by which the bad air seemed always to come in, and never to go out, I saw, through other glassless windows, into other houses in a similar condition, and looked giddily down into a wretched yard, which was the common dust-heap of the mansion.[80]

As a motivation for the state of the individual house and of others in the neighborhood, it is sufficient to know that they were "once" fair, single-family dwellings and had then "degenerated" into poor, rented-out lodgings with one family per room. Whether "fair" means aristocratic or haut-bourgeois, and whether "poor" means petit-bourgeois or proletarian, the description's subject is déclassement, and not in its first stage (as it was in Baron Hulot's home, a private person's failure to keep up with luxury). Here, the grand staircase's degraded magnificence is neither an honor nor a dishonor to any of the various groups of new inhabitants. From a level of defunctionalization that degrades the remnants of that magnificence, we reach one that actually undermines safety in the places where the floor is giving way; the windows' function — eliminated when they are condemned or walled up — is perverted into the antifunctional when they become only empty vehicles for bad air. The notion that the air seems always to go in and never to go out allows us to note a humorous point of style — in other words, a residue of the threadbare-grotesque. But the previous comparison, which goes a little further in the same direction, is integrated into the seriousness of the whole description with its thematic congruence; it actually translates the repair of old wood with new into terms of déclassement, of a marriage between a noble and a plebeian. The still earlier comparison of the staircase with a tributary channel (with respect to the street) connects immediately with a picture of uncontrolled overcrowding, intrusive contiguity, and loss of private dignity. Although they have no glass, the windows are nonetheless a reflection of other windows, inasmuch as they reveal houses similar to this one, in which the urban masses are multiplying all around, and the description ends with its basest component — the courtyard that serves as a common rubbish heap.

Furthermore, déclassement may be seen as thematic throughout the novel, if we turn, rather than to the impossible marriage of Emily and Steerforth, to the lives of the protagonist and other characters (possibly even comparing them with the well-known vicissitudes of Dickens' youth, as the autobiographical basis of the novel authorizes us to do). Yet while déclassement functions as a threat avoided in David Copperfield's story (as in the author's life), it has actually happened to the unnamed proprietors of the houses in question. It is the realization of a nightmare that is no less congenial to the unstable dominion of the bourgeois than is the competitive dream of ascent whose opposite side it represents. I believe that in various authors' works this nightmare is expressed through worn-realistic images, and that it can incubate in even the blandest of them. I have repeatedly given a certain justification for the category's name, with its metalinguistic adjective, and that justification has been based entirely on literature's internal historical evolution (II, 9; IV, 12). But it is not at all incompatible with the general assumption of an extraliterary reference. The images in this category constitute reality also because the advent and overturning, the mobility and precariousness of the newly dominant class are translated par excellence into the conflict between the traces of time and social appropriateness. In the same way, the permanence of values, expressed in venerable-regressive images, that was by contrast typical of the previous order, is reified retrospectively inasmuch as it has lost its authority. However, the squalor of the worn-realistic's images is intensified not only along the scale that descends from luxury or comfort to discomfort or poverty. The opposition between this scale's extremes may intersect with another, namely, an opposition between private and public: between private dwellings and buildings that are publicly frequented — not only public buildings in the literal sense, as we shall see, but also those intended by private people for the public — if, of course, the latter has not been strictly selected by class privilege.

On the one hand, there is the house, be it rich or poor; on the other, there is not only the office, school, or prison but also the boarding house, shop, or law office. Literature seems to bear witness to the fact that bourgeois individualism, to the same extent in which it cares for and cultivates its social identity and family intimacy in its private place of use, is also inclined to disregard, to the point of indecency, the anonymity of any location not intended as its own private place of use. In this sense, one citizen treats other citizens as the secular state treats the unprivileged multitude, and this state's collective prestige is displayed much more by its works than by its pomp. In the Dickens excerpt, the crowding takes away families' identity and intimacy, and yet the windows are decorated with vases of flowers. But where déclassement reaches the point of marginalizing, the state takes the place of the family, and with programmatic neglect. The worn-realistic may become even more tragic than in descriptions of private proletarian interiors. Here is the beginning of *Ward Number Six,* a long novella published in 1892 by Anton Chekhov (1860–1904):

> In the hospital courtyard stands a small building surrounded by a jungle of burdock, nettle and wild hemp. The roof is rusty, the chimney half collapsed. The porch steps have rotted and are overgrown with grass, and only a few traces of plaster are left. The front faces the hospital and the rear looks into open country, cut off from it by a grey hospital fence with nails on top. Those nails with spikes uppermost, the fence, the hut itself . . . all have the melancholy, doomed air peculiar to hospital and prison buildings.
>
> Unless you are afraid of nettle stings, let us take the narrow path to this shack and see what goes on inside. Opening the first door we enter the lobby, where great stacks of hospital rubbish are piled by walls and stove. Mattresses, tattered old smocks, trousers, blue striped shirts and useless, dilapidated footwear . . . all this junk is dumped around any old how, moldering and giving off an acrid stench.
>
> On the rubbish, a pipe always clenched between his teeth, lies the warder Nikita. [. . .]
>
> Next you enter a large, capacious room which is all the hut consists of, apart from the lobby. Its walls are daubed with dirty blue paint, the ceiling is caked with soot as in a chimneyless peasant hut, and you can tell that these stoves smoke and fill the place with fumes in winter. The windows are disfigured by iron bars on the inside, the floor is grey and splintery, and there is such a stink of sour cabbage, burnt wicks, bedbugs and ammonia that your first impression is of entering a zoo.
>
> The room contains beds which are screwed to the floor. Sitting or lying on them are people in navy-blue hospital smocks and old-fashioned nightcaps: the lunatics.[81]

At the level of the category's lowest circles, the list of rubbish in the vestibule may be compared with the list of Gogol's miser's various objects (II, 8). Here, the state's negligence has the same effect that the proprietor's mania for saving had there: to pile up "great stacks" of things that ought instead to be eliminated. The things in question are less outlandish, indeed predictable for their bygone functionality, and taken one by one they are beyond being considered inappropriate. What is inappropriate is the highly visible place where they have accumulated, and the odor that emanates from them is the only characteristic that makes them more disgusting than Gogol's things: the odor proclaims decomposition, that is, the return from culture to nature, as if a sewer's recycling task took place in the open air. Almost as disgusting is the menagerie-like odor of the inside room, and it makes us think back to nature, likening human beings to animals. The invasion of plant life, which, thick as "a jungle," surrounds the pavilion, is the first lines' subject — a subject that brings us back to examples from the second chapter (II, 10, 11), in some way contaminating the worn-realistic with the same not-yet-defined category with which I said (IV, 10) others can be contaminated. It is the story's presumable contemporaneity, this time, that helps to avoid any explicit determination of a passage of time. The time it has taken the plant life to grow, the building to become run down, and the clothing to wear out is of an average length that the reader's sense of reality easily grasps: it is indeterminable precisely inasmuch as it is verisimilar — the contrary of the threadbare-grotesque situation.

No remnant of threadbare-grotesque figurativeness smiles down from the flat darkness of this fin de siècle description. The figure that mixes the levels of narration and narrated (metalepsis, in narratological jargon)[82] — "unless you are afraid of nettle stings" — seems to say to the reader, in the second paragraph: "unless you're put off by so squalid a subject." And of the two comparative elements, one takes the nearer term ("as in a chimneyless peasant hut"), whereas the other is projected onto the visitor's experience ("your first impression is of entering a zoo"). But the description that abstains from metaphor assumes, in its totality, a symbolic meaning that did not appear in the passages from either Balzac or Dickens. Symbolism has been mentioned in relation to Chekhov, and the novella's opening images, set before the revealing little sentence with which I have ended the quotation and contrasting with the title's bureaucratic euphemism, make a situation of human outcastness concrete. The sentence about the "melancholy, doomed air peculiar to hospital and prison buildings" says this without being figurative. And the images are all more metonymic than metaphoric: they are internal to, contiguous with, typical of the condition of the mad (to such an extent that the fear-inspiring caretaker stretches himself out on the rubbish); to the same extent to which they become real, they become symbols. While in such a late text the literary novelty of constituting reality requires strong doses, the nightmare of déclassement reaches its peak as well. The only member of the nobility among the madmen is one of the two protagonists, although the institution's scandalous state is justified in town "by saying that only lower-class townsfolk and peasants went to the hospital."[83] To the other protagonist, marginalization in the depths of provincial Russia appears to be the progress-resisting precondition of "an abomination like Ward Number Six."[84] It is the doctor himself who will end up in the isolation ward, with those who are triply marginalized — by civic geography and the layout of the clinic, before as well as after their marginalization in terms of social status.

14

Having provided conceptual substance for the first four categories by using four examples for each, I shall now return to the plan of the semantic tree. Here, too, I shall set about carrying it forward from the point at which least is lacking in order to arrive at new full definitions of text categories; the reader is requested to go back to the first, partial visualization of the tree (IV, 1). Of the two poles of the same number of oppositions that had been left dangling, the one that speaks of an *individually perceived* passage of time is set further to the left and lower than the one that contradicts the connection to a general *passage of time*. And from the examples we have seen up to now, I have never been moved to call the general connection into question — whereas on several occasions I have been moved to deny that the passage of time was individually rather than *collectively* perceived. With a strategic arbitrary act I had placed another opposition under the first pole of this last mentioned one, and in turn the poles of the new opposition branched out into the first two terminal oppositions (IV, 5). This is the opposition between *nonpertinent* and *pertinent determination* (of the passage of time, as always). Would it be appropriate now to repeat it under the suspended, remaining pole of the opposition? Should knowledge of the texts lead me to answer in the affirmative, the economical as well as hierarchic criterion I have mentioned (IV, 5), averse to repeating the same opposition in several parts of the tree, would here be inapplicable.

In fact, none of the texts known to me creates exceptions to the dictates of a banal extraliterary truth; no human being thinks back to moments in the past without reference to times and experiences that are in some way determined, whether or not those moments are occasioned by specific images. Within the precincts of an individual memory or sensibility, with references circumscribed by the length of a lifetime, temporal and circumstantial determinations have a different type of pertinence than in collectively perceived periods of centuries or millennia. Their pertinence may be greater or lesser, simultaneously; much better motivated or developed but much more predictable or less variable; in any case, it is not sufficiently characteristic as to induce us to divide certain images into two categories. We can respect at no great cost the economical criterion regarding the avoidance of repetition. However the opposition under discussion must not be ignored; inasmuch as abstract symmetry demands it and it yields little in concrete terms, let us say that it will be *neutralized* in the following way:

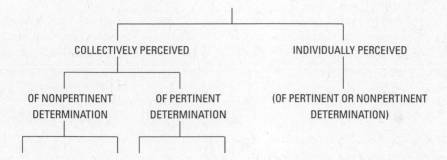

The fact that the first and most significant example of the new category seems to me a passage from an author, Chateaubriand, whose work we have already dipped into is neither an accident nor a difficulty. I had already taken the first example of the venerable-regressive from the *Genius of Christianity* (IV, 2), and *René* is a short novel whose text in the 1802 edition was part of the same great religious apologia; it was not published separately until 1805. The confession of the young protagonist, lonely, wandering, lacking self-knowledge because he is unwittingly the participating object of his sister's incestuous love, follows the chapter entitled *Of Vague Passions* (*Du Vague des Passions*).[85] Before ending up in America, René carries his melancholy all over France and Europe, amid autumnal forests, lonely churches, the graveyards of ancient abbeys, classical ruins, Italian cathedrals, and Scottish moors à la Ossian;[86] these images, which lend weight to the character, are always in tune with a venerable-regressive that is still close to the solemn-admonitory. But in the episode about his visit to the sold-off, uninhabited castle of his childhood and adolescence, the tone falls back into a less culturally mediated emotion:

> The soil where I had been bred was on my road. When I perceived the woods where I had spent the only happy moments of my life, I could not hold back my tears, and it was impossible for me to resist the temptation to bid them a final adieu.
>
> My elder brother had sold our paternal inheritance, and the new owner did

not live there. I arrived at the castle by the long avenue of firs; I crossed the deserted courtyards on foot; I stopped to look at the closed or half-broken windows, the thistles growing at the base of the walls, the leaves strewn over the thresholds of the doors, and the lone flight of stairs where I had so often seen my father and his faithful servants. The steps were already covered with moss; the yellow wallflowers were growing between their loosened and shaking stones. An unfamiliar guardian brusquely opened the doors for me. I hesitated to cross the threshold [. . .].

Covering my eyes with my handkerchief for a moment, I entered under my ancestors' roof. I went through the echoing apartments, where only the noise of my steps was heard. The rooms were barely illuminated by the weak light that entered through the closed shutters: I visited the one where my mother had lost her life in bringing me into the world, the one where my father took his rest, the one where I had slept in my cradle, and finally the one where friendship had received my first vows in a sister's breast. All of the rooms were curtainless, and spiders wove their webs in the abandoned alcoves. I precipitously left the place, I walked quickly away from it, without daring to turn my head.[87]

Later, in his autobiographical tale *Memoirs from Beyond the Tomb,* Chateaubriand told in a few lines of his return to his father's castle at Combourg, and of the sudden illness that stopped him from approaching it, when he saw the spectacle of desolation: it was 1791, and the spectacle signified the Revolution in progress.[88] But *René* is an invented tale; even before the *Genius of Christianity,* it had been part of a prose epic named after a North American Indian tribe, *The Natchez,* and it shares its setting in time: 1725.[89] As a cause of the castle's condition, in the text quoted above, economic (in addition to genealogical) expropriation replaces the Revolution, with which the author but not his character was contemporaneous. Excepting the "half-broken" windows, all the other signs point to prolonged abandonment, and not to violence that has already occurred. Three verb tenses alternate, and they correspond to the two extreme points of a not immemorial length of time. In the visitor's experience, the simple pasts correspond to the story's present moment: "I perceived" or "I entered" or "I walked away from it"; the imperfects correspond to the state of the castle: "growing" (in French: *that were growing*), "were growing," "were" (thrice), etc., and so do the adjectives: from "deserted courtyards" on. The pluperfects — pathetically preceded by the relative adverb "where," which localizes in so many spaces times familiar to the memory as the former are found again together with the latter — correspond to the story's resuscitated past. "The soil where I had been bred" embraces all of the spaces from the outside; the series of rooms — an internal point of arrival — assigns its *where* to the most moving remembrance of each member of the family, respectively, including himself.

Only in the "echoing apartments, *where* . . ." the same relative adverb accompanies the moment of the visit, with the power of acoustic sensory evocation that we have already admired in this writer. The two forms assumed a few decades earlier by the pre-Romantic discovery (thanks to both Rousseau and Goethe) of a dimension of individual memory converge: the memory of childhood or adolescence and the memory of love. The incest theme is concealed beneath the euphemistic reference to the sister, and in the lines that I have omitted one learns of a visit that she had made to the castle before that of René. The measure of the defunctionalization of places and objects is shown by the theme of the invasion of plant life and animal life (spiders' webs), which contaminates the new category with another, not yet defined one, as in more than one previous case (IV, 10, 13). The text has thistles and moss in common with Ossian's, but the very concrete yellow wallflowers are its own. The primary loss, however, is redeemed (in accordance with the alternation of semi-positive categories with negative ones posited above; IV, 5) by a recouping of secondary functionality. And this is not actuated on an ideological level, as in the cases of the venerable-regressive and the solemn-admonitory — with which the text does however demonstrate contiguity or contamination (especially in the exclamatory maxims on the family's precariousness that come immediately after the quoted lines). The recouping is actuated on an affective level, with a bittersweet compromise. Betaking himself to the *where* of the past is an irresistible temptation for René, who stops to look and enters the rooms, one by one, but who has two separate bouts of weeping, hesitates on the threshold, and in the end flees without turning to look back. For the individual, the past's sweetness can only be something lost, even if its ability to be remembered as sweetness has not been lost.

15

Individual memory is better than collective memory at going back through time with closed eyes — in other words, in the absence of physical objects that occasion recollection in the present; and it can make its way to objects from that past that are physically intact in their distance. In such a case images will either be missing, or immune to our categories. This is why in the case of the category that I am about to define, even more than in that of the venerable-regressive, the surviving presence of an object from bygone times would seem necessary; and why visits to sites are so common and so typical. Yet the past's sites or spaces present a sort of intermediate concept between the presence and the absence of objects, with the abstract identity and recognizability that they maintain regardless of any change whatsoever in their tangible aspect. This is demonstrated by the passage that we can turn to as a prototype of Chateaubriand's — given the pan-European success, less than thirty years earlier, of Goethe's *The Sorrows of Young Werther* (*Die Leiden des jungen Werthers*, 1774). Towards the middle of this transgressive love story, the protagonist's visit to his hometown introduces the memory of childhood and adolescence — in all its literary-historical novelty — as a thematic oasis:

> I undertook the homeward pilgrimage with all the devotion of a pilgrim, and many an unanticipated feeling moved me. I had the post coach stop at the great linden tree that stands a quarter of an hour before the city on the road to S.; I got out, and I let the driver proceed, so that I, on foot, could savor each wholly new, life-filled memory to my heart's content. Thus I stood under the linden that once, when I was a boy, had been the destination and boundary of my walks. How different it was! Then, I had longed with blissful ignorance to go out into the unknown world, where I hoped to find so much nourishment, so much pleasure for my heart, to fill and satisfy my striving, longing breast. Now, I am returning from the wide world — oh, my friend, with how many failed hopes, with how many ruined plans! [. . .] I approached the town; I greeted all the old, familiar cottages with their gardens, the new ones displeased me, as did all the other changes that had been made. I entered at the gate and at once I found everything was really just the same as before. My dear friend, I don't want to go into detail; it would become as monotonous in the telling as it was enchanting for me. I had decided to live at the marketplace, just next to our old house. In going there, I noticed that the schoolroom into which a worthy old woman had crammed our childhood had been turned into a general store. I remembered the restlessness, the tears, the dullness of spirit, the anguish of heart that I had put up with in that hole. No step that I took was unremarkable. A pilgrim in the Holy Land does not meet with so many places of religious memory, and it would be hard for his soul to be as full of holy feelings.[90]

Here, too, as we have learned immediately before, the birthplace's nearness has presented itself to the protagonist along the road,[91] at a turning point in his story. The choice to visit it, however, is made much more willingly and with more expectation of joyful emotion in Werther's case than in that of René; in the category's compromise between pleasure and pain, excited and nostalgic pleasure prevails here, relatively speaking. Werther prefers to go ahead on foot, not, like René, inside the former property, but from as far away as a quarter-hour's walk on the road to town, in order to "savor each wholly new, life-filled memory to my heart's content." The objective degree of literary substance of such memories, and thus also of the images, be they present or past, is much less explicit in the recounting than are subjective reflection and emotion; this is a result of the very exuberance of the latter, but also of eighteenth-century reticence vis-à-vis the physical world—hence the assertion that the writer fears the monotonous effect of giving details. On the other hand, there is no hesitation before hyperbolic comparisons that transfer the vocabulary of the holy pilgrimage—in the first and last sentences of the quotation—to what we can call, from now on, the sentimental pilgrimage. They must have seemed audacious when the novel appeared, and they confirm, historically, a seemingly competitive relationship between the secular pathos of childhood memories and the hierarchy of states of mind provided by Christian tradition.[92] In attributing "devotion" and "holy feelings" to the visitor who is doing the remembering, and in giving him the advantage in a comparison with the "places of religious memory" in the Holy Land, it is as if the new category were borrowing the exemplariness of the venerable-regressive or the supreme seriousness of the solemn-admonitory for its private, nonreligious territory.

But is it legitimate to speak of a new category in which, whatever literary substance images may have, no object from bygone times turns out to have been aged by time? The linden (like the mountain, in the omitted lines) remains part of unchangeable nature; the exclamation "How different it was!" is not about the sites but rather about the heart; only youthful plans have been "ruined," just as hopes have failed. The qualification of *old* for the cottages with their gardens and for the character's own house does not refer to decadence so much as it contrasts them with new constructions. And Werther looks upon the latter with displeasure, just as he looks at all other kinds of changes that have taken place and, implicitly, at the transformation of his childhood schoolroom into a store. The renovation is more fundamental and alienating than any sort of decadence in contradicting the sites' identity; it overturns affective reactions and precludes interest in physical evocations. It constitutes the sole, true form of defunctionalization of things, pushed to the point of disappearance and beyond—in this text which, on the threshold of the historical turning point, initiates the category and gives a name to sentimental pilgrimage. A little further on in the novel, fetishism for memory's objects and parsimony in the evocation of their condition also meet—where the object's proportions are smaller than those of buildings or towns. Werther has decided, with difficulty, to put away the worn-out frock coat that he was wearing when he first danced with Lotte, and he has had one made that is the same, with matching vest and trousers. His new suit, however, doesn't satisfy him, but he hopes that "in time" it, too, will become dear to him[93]—as if he were saying that the attempt to mediate between aging and renovation is pretension, that things wear out and are ennobled, become more tattered and more tender *at the same time*.

Within the new category, debased identity cannot easily be replaced by

renovated resemblance. And better than the partially disappeared objects belonging to a subject like Werther, it is the contrary that can become part of the
category: objects that have lasted, that reappear, almost without reference to a
subject. We see this exemplified in a novel from the middle of the following
century, where the proportions of a very rich businessman's London house can
be imagined as halfway between René's noble residence and Werther's petit-
bourgeois, provincial dwellings. I am speaking of *Vanity Fair,* published in
1847–48 by William Makepeace Thackeray (1811–63). George Osborne, a
young officer, has fallen at Waterloo after having been disinherited by his
ambitiously arriviste and proudly loving father, whom he had disappointed by
marrying the daughter of a failed merchant. After more than ten years, the
elder Osborne takes his grandson into his home, attaches the same feelings to
him, and even gives him the bedroom that had belonged to the son:

> It was George's room. It had not been opened for more than ten years. Some
> of his clothes, papers, handkerchiefs, whips and caps, fishing-rods and sport-
> ing gear, were still there. An Army List of 1814, with his name written on the
> cover; a little dictionary he was wont to use in writing: and the Bible his
> mother had given him, were on the mantelpiece; with a pair of spurs, and a
> dried inkstand covered with the dust of ten years. Ah! since that ink was wet,
> what days and people had passed away! The writing-book still on the table,
> was blotted with his hand.
>
> Miss Osborne was much affected when she first entered this room with the
> servants under her. She sank quite pale on the little bed.[94]

To what subject do the eyes belong through which we are looking at the
objects the list of which, in the author's voice, functions as a description of the
reopened bedroom? The former occupant is dead, the new one has not yet
arrived and is a child; the person who enters ahead of the servants is the
spinster daughter who has stayed in the house with the old man. The only
character present, she is too secondary a figure to have the emotion that was
first suggested to the reader as identifiable with the emotion that is later attributed to her. Two other characters count, and both are absent for the same
reason—a reason that refers back to patrimonial rather than sentimental
property, namely, the earlier disinheriting of George by his father. Since then,
the house has been forbidden to Amelia, George's sweet and still ingenuously
faithful wife. Old Osborne is in a double sense responsible for the long closure
and current state of the room, which has something of both consecration and
repression about it—of fetishistic mourning and of abandon and oblivion.
Like a pilgrimage in reverse, in the midst of a lived-in house, however vast it
may be, it is a space from the past *where one does not enter* instead of a space

from the past *where one goes*. Furthermore, the context of the novel dis-
courages the search among the characters under discussion for a subject endowed with disinterested memory and affections. It is only Amelia's candor
that saves her from the sorcery of the "vanity fair" of the novel's title; and she
alone is spared Thackeray's psychological pitilessness, his ironic penetration
of the agglomeration of phenomena known even today (thanks to a term that
he launched, but in a generally more restrictive sense) as snobbery. George
himself is an anything but idealized character, although not without good
qualities. The pathos of his dusty little posthumous museum, uplifted toward
the solemn-admonitory by the exclamation inspired by the inkstand, could
seem impersonal were it not for the fact that within the work's unity, the
quoted passage is closely connected to another, more than a hundred pages
further on, which is also worth quoting.

    With the death of Osborne, "the gloomy old mansion" is abandoned by the
heirs and emptied. In the list of heavily sumptuous objects about to be carried
off and in the images of the barren interior, a profound relationship that surely
characterizes the new category returns to make itself felt: the relationship
between material property and the continuity of memory, and thus between
the expropriation and alienation of memory. However, this imagery differs
too markedly from the preceding, in the variety of pathos proceeding from it,
for us to avoid turning now rather to the corresponding negative category.
And yet the circumstances at last make a sentimental pilgrimage possible —
with a delay owing to others' prejudice and stubbornness. In this pilgrimage
the two, inseparable parts of the theme — the place and the visit — reconnect,
and desolation is answered by tenderness. The appropriate subject, Amelia,
holding the hand of her little son, who bears his father's name, goes all the way
to the room that belonged first to the one and then to the other:

> The house was dismantled; the rich furniture and effects, the awful chan-
> deliers and dreary blank mirrors packed away and hidden, the rich rosewood
> drawing-room suite was muffled in straw, the carpets were rolled up and
> corded, the small select library of well-bound books was stowed into two
> wine-chests, and the whole paraphernalia rolled away in several enormous
> vans to the Pantechnicon, where they were to lie until George's majority. And
> the great heavy dark plate-chests went off to Messrs. Stumpy & Rowdy, to lie
> in the cellars of those eminent bankers until the same period should arrive.
>
>   One day Emmy, with George in her hand and clad in deep sables, went to
> visit the deserted mansion which she had not entered since she was a girl. The
> place in front was littered with straw where the vans had been laded and
> rolled off. They went into the great blank stone staircases into the upper
> rooms, into that where grandpapa died, as George said in a whisper, and then

higher still into George's own room. The boy was still clinging by her side, but she thought of another besides him. She knew that it had been his father's room as well as his own.[95]

16

Between objects and rooms that sadly preserve the intimacy of distant personal possession, and objects and rooms that still more sadly undergo the desecration of family possession that has been cut short, the difference — as I have said — may be contained within the opposition between the new, semipositive category and its negative counterpart. Nevertheless, it is a difference that in this book should not seem wholly new to the reader: I had already underlined an analogous one in the second chapter, between our very first two examples (II, 1, 2). By way of contrast to the melancholy *complacence* with which the contents of Cros' chest are listed, I had counterpoised the depression emanating from the contents of Baudelaire's chest of drawers and little drawing-room, implying at the utmost a whiff of *repugnance* for the past. The example from Borges that followed, with its enumeration of things, could also be taken into consideration, inasmuch as ego, property, and the past are projected onto them (II, 3); but it has now become possible to say that we were dealing with a very fine impure example. The new semipositive category is contaminated with, and is in fact subordinated to, an original modern version of the solemn-admonitory, which is as abundant in concrete nouns as the traditional versions were poor in images. We have now seen three consecutive examples of the not yet defined semipositive category in question; at least one example of the corresponding negative category is needed in order to achieve a terminal opposition — two whole definitions, in other words. I shall go back to Baudelaire to find it, in the poem called *The Little Bottle* (*Le Flacon*). It, too, is probably a "source" of Cros' sonnet for a little chest (which in turn was undoubtedly echoing the one we met with in Mathurin Régnier, IV, 8); while a closet, an alternative container, is lugubriously related to the chest of drawers of Baudelaire himself:

> There are strong perfumes for which every substance
> Is porous. One could say that they penetrate glass.
> In opening a chest that has come from the Orient,
> Whose shouting lock creaks and grumbles,
>
> Or some wardrobe full of the ages' acrid smell,
> Powdery and black, in a deserted house,

One sometimes finds a little old bottle that remembers,
From which a returning soul gushes out all alive.

A thousand thoughts sleep, funereal chrysalises,
Sweetly trembling in the heavy shadows,
That release their wings and soar away,
Dyed in azure, glazed in pink, brocaded in gold.

Here is the inebriating memory that flutters
In the clouded air; the eyes close; Vertigo
Seizes the defeated soul and with both hands pushes it
Toward an abyss blurred by human miasmas;

It lands it on the edge of an age-old abyss,
Where, strong-smelling Lazarus tearing his shroud,
The spectral cadaver of a rancid, attractive,
And sepulchral old love moves as it awakens.

Thus, when I shall be lost to the memory
Of men, in the corner of a sinister closet,
When they have thrown me away, a desolate little old bottle,
Decrepit, dusty, dirty, abject, viscous, damaged,

I shall be your coffin, lovable pestilence!
The witness to your power and your virulence,
Dear poison prepared by the angels! liqueur
That gnaws at me, oh life and death of my heart![96]

This time, the little bottle is the only item contained in the chest or the closet; and in turn it contains potentially a piece of the past, whose vehicle is a trace of perfume. Sweetness and inebriation, a euphoric flutter of flight and a brilliant variety of colors, are bestowed upon the resurrection of these memories. But the poem's vocabulary insists on betraying a deadly distance, an alienating putrescence, from the past; these are prefigured by the chest's strident resistance to being opened, as by the acrid smell of the ages that is attributed to the wardrobe. The memories' point of arrival is revealed to be an "old love" whose only positive quality is the adjective "attractive," efficacious by way of contrast to the negative images and qualifications with which it has already been overloaded. With the emergence of a metaphoric structure that reabsorbs the whole composition, the little bottle is taken up again, as a comparative for the "I" — just like the chest of drawers and the little drawing-room in the second *Spleen* poem; and it is piled up with seven shamelessly, perversely antifunctional adjectives, six of which form a line of their own. As may be seen, however, such an accentuated perversion of the relationship to the past is not the only considerable difference between this example and the three previous ones. Here, the poetic discourse is almost exclusively taken up with the memory's processes instead of its objects, physical or otherwise, as was previously the case. Nor does present love count as an exception, being also an object—alongside the "I" itself—lost to the future memory of others. The sole exception and sole object would apparently be precisely that old love which remains relegated to the indefinable familiarity of half-unconscious childhood memories (such as a love fixed on a mother). Another difference appears to follow from this: both the objects and the processes of memory are no longer in force as much with respect to the real facts of the past as within a network of metaphorical or symbolic relationships that involve the "I," as in the second *Spleen* poem.

Let us compare these three differences with a view to the semantic tree and the strategy behind it. Not only is the difference between prevalently euphoric or dysphoric memory more important than the last two, it also overlaps with them, through broad coincidences. In the combinatorial analysis of the texts known to me, it is by no means impossible that a discourse should euphorically connote the processes of memory, much less unlikely that it should dysphorically connote its objects. But the evocation of memory's processes— unlike that of its objects—is nearly impossible without making use of metaphor; and a euphoric connotation of the images that become part of a metaphor is hard to make compatible with a connotation of nonfunctionality on their part. All the more reason why euphoric images will lie beyond the boundaries of our categories, if they set aside both memory's objects and its processes in order to contract a direct metaphoric or symbolic relationship—literally unprecedented—with the subject. Thus, in the combinations in the texts, these three poles of difference tend to converge, with respect to the examples of the semipositive category: memories that are more dysphoric than euphoric, processes more than objects of memory, and metaphorical rather than memory-related involvements. And thus in particular, in the negative category—unlike the semipositive one—an individually perceived passage of time will not always call memory into question. I had underlined at the time how arbitrary and strategic the verbal choices for the tree are; the adverb *individually* and its contrary were precisely what provided the occasion. In alternation with the first of them, the passage of time might have been said to have been "subjectively perceived" (IV, 1). Now, the rejected synonym can be understood as well, along with the selected one; it is perhaps more easily extended to the symbolic exploitation, in the negative category, of physical objects that are not objects of memory.

Below this specification, which we leave unwritten, we know which terminal opposition is most suitable for completing the two new definitions:

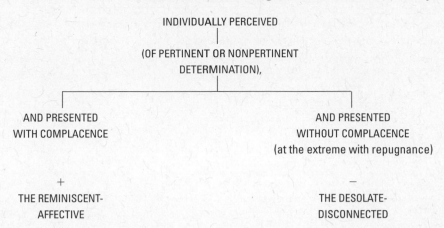

INDIVIDUALLY PERCEIVED

(OF PERTINENT OR NONPERTINENT DETERMINATION),

AND PRESENTED WITH COMPLACENCE

AND PRESENTED WITHOUT COMPLACENCE (at the extreme with repugnance)

+

THE REMINISCENT-AFFECTIVE

−

THE DESOLATE-DISCONNECTED

On the negative side, I prefer the more comprehensive contradictory term, but I am giving the contrary term in parentheses, as a limit. In the name that I am assigning to the semipositive category, both adjectives are predictable, drawn from repeated lexical hints. In the name of the negative category, one of them opens the series of antifunctional adjectives in the last text; the other, anticipating further texts, betrays breakup of the subject as projected onto both memory-related and metaphorical objects.

17

Between the reminiscent-affective and the desolate-disconnected one cannot speak of a transformation as previously defined (IV, 5). In the twentieth century, the first category survived alongside the second. But whereas the former had pre-Romantic origins, on the verge of the historical turning point, the latter seems to me barely noticeable before Baudelaire. Let us choose, in twentieth-century literature, examples of the desolate-disconnected that are freer than the previous one of contamination by the reminiscent-affective — that is, more purely negative — and that better correspond to the category's name. In *Rhapsody on a Windy Night,* a text published in 1917 by T. S. Eliot (1888–1965), we come up against the difficulty of the language of modern poetry for the first time in this book. My task is not to interpret it; I shall only quote a little less than half of the text in three separate fragments:

> Twelve o'clock.
> Along the reaches of the street
> Held in a lunar synthesis,
> Whispering lunar incantations
> Dissolve the floors of memory

And all its clear relations,
Its divisions and precisions,
Every street lamp that I pass
Beats like a fatalistic drum,
And through the spaces of the dark
Midnight shakes the memory
As a madman shakes a dead geranium.

. . . .

The memory throws up high and dry
A crowd of twisted things,
A twisted branch upon the beach
Eaten smooth, and polished
As if the world gave up
The secret of its skeleton,
Stiff and white.
A broken spring in a factory yard,
Rust that clings to the form that the strength has left
Hard and curled and ready to snap.

. . . .

["]The moon has lost her memory.
A washed-out smallpox cracks her face,
Her hand twists a paper rose,
That smells of dust and eau de Cologne,
She is alone
With all the old nocturnal smells
That cross and cross across her brain."
The reminiscence comes
Of sunless dry geraniums
And dust in crevices,
Smells of chestnuts in the streets,
And female smells in shuttered rooms,
And cigarettes in corridors
And cocktail smells in bars.[97]

. . . .

   In the succession of hours that run through the text — beginning with midnight in the first line — on the street along which the narrator walks past the street lamps that speak to him every hour, a concrete, albeit unsteady, factual plane is recognizable. It is, however, indistinguishable from a metaphoric plane of equal generality: recourse to metaphor, as I have said (IV, 16), lends itself almost necessarily to the evocation of the processes of memory rather than its objects. The nocturnal walk equals symbolic movement in time and, unlike the sentimental pilgrimage, an accidental-associative discovery of memories — up to a point of arrival (in the last lines, not quoted here), where the objects of memory that have been reached do not belong to the past, but rather to a mechanical daily present. All four previous occurrences of the word "memory" create specific metaphors — of processes, not objects: the memory has floors that dissolve; it is shaken by a madman's gesture; it throws up things "high and dry"; it has been lost by the moon. But the branch — one of the remembered things — has also been polished "as if . . ." Remembered things of this sort present themselves factually in a wholly disconnected way; they do not occupy available places in a personal story; they do not reveal affective motivations for having appeared. All of the text's images — which are rhapsodic, as the title declares, and dissociated from memory's clear relations, divisions, and specifications — come together only via analogies; the recurrence as a leitmotiv of the root *to twist* is the most hidden example of insistent dysphoric connotations. The unpleasant memory asserts itself as a brief alienation and a fleeting nightmare rather than an occasion for recognition and regret. A single perfume was a euphoric point of departure for Baudelaire; here, before the various "old nocturnal smells" are specified in reminiscences, the moon, which has become a subject, is alone with them; they cross her brain like an incorporeal series of obsessive objects.

Although the things of memory tend to be mixed together with the metaphorical in these lines by Eliot, memory is called all the more into question inasmuch as its objects are immersed in its processes. But the objects of memory are not coextensive with the two last categories — for two opposed reasons. Remembered, physically intact things, which I described as "immune" to our categories (IV, 15), fall beyond the boundaries of the reminiscent-affective. Nonfunctional things that are not at all equivalent to memories are part of the desolate-disconnected, as I have discussed: we could find numerous examples in *The Waste Land* and in all the early poetry of Eliot, obscurely and sordidly metaphorical ones, halfway between hallucination and myth.[98] To come to images of this sort, let us take some from *Nausea* (*La Nausée*), a novel in the form of a fictitious diary, published in 1938 by Jean-Paul Sartre (1905–80). Although the protagonist, Antoine Roquentin, resolves to set down in writing his lively interest in objects of a strange sort, he does it as an act of hatred toward the cult of psychology: "I do not want secrets, or moods, or the inexpressible." Yet it seems undeniable that he feels the degradation of objects of this sort individually or subjectively:

> I am very fond of gathering chestnuts, old rags, and especially papers. I enjoy picking them up, closing my hand over them; I would almost like to bring them to my mouth, as children do. Anny became furious when, holding

them by a corner, I picked up some papers that were heavy and sumptuous but probably soiled with shit. In the gardens, in the summer or early fall, you find little pieces of newspaper, baked by the sun, as dry and fragile as dead leaves, and so yellowed that one might think they had been doused in picric acid. In the winter, other sheets of paper are trampled, ground up, stained; they return to the earth. Others, completely new and even shiny, all white, palpitating, are posed like swans, but the earth is already pulling them down from below. They twist, they tear themselves away from the mud, but only to go flatten themselves out for good a little further off. All of this is good for picking up. Sometimes I simply touch them, looking at them close up; at other times I tear them in order to hear their long crackle, or, if they are very damp, I even set them on fire, not without difficulty; then I dry my mud-covered palms on a wall or a tree-trunk.[99]

All memory-related meanings have disappeared here, and even the metaphorical meaning, if there is one, remains undecipherable. A psychopathological dimension in which both the one meaning and the other could be found is excluded from the character's consciousness (as from that of the author); it is important to us that shit be named, not with reference to this dimension but only because the excremental symbolic referent underlies our whole theme (I, 6–7). What do rags and papers represent to Roquentin? The text is not constructed in a way that gives an answer to the question; and it is constructed this way despite its precise, copious language — figurative to the point of anthropomorphism. Even in the following paragraph, which I am not quoting, a muddy page on the ground appears "covered with bubbles and swellings, like a burned hand."[100] It is the same language whose characteristic applications to the abstract of certain extreme forms of the concrete — from the material to the intellectual — establish a relationship between Sartre the thinker and essayist and Sartre the fiction writer. In Roquentin's predilection for paper, can one not at least recognize a morbid, degraded projection of precisely the material with which an intellectual has par excellence to deal? As such, the character undergoes or chooses a double alienation: the first, which gives the novel its title and has philosophical implications, comes to him as the result of a lonely "metaphysical" crisis in his relationship to the physical world. The fact that he has not been able to pick up that muddy page, as he had wished, is one of the first symptoms. The other alienation has implications that cannot be called political but that separate him through resentment and irony, contempt and envy, from the class of his origins — the dominant bourgeois class.

It is with all these components of a reasoned detachment — not excluding envy — that Roquentin looks at the preservation of materials from the past, secured for the bourgeois by their houses and their things:

They live amid legacies, gifts, and each of their pieces of furniture is a memory. Miniature clocks, medals, portraits, seashells, paperweights, screens, shawls. They have closets full of bottles, pieces of cloth, old clothes, newspapers; they have kept everything. The past is a property owner's luxury.

Where, then, shall I preserve mine? One does not put one's past in one's pocket; one must have a house to arrange it in.[101]

We could not find a clearer critical formulation—fed by so true-to-life a list of useless things—of the frequent relationship between the reminiscent-affective and property, of which I have spoken (IV, 15). Let us take note that the reminiscent-affective too—inasmuch as it involves nonfunctional corporality presented with complacence although more or less mixed with pain—can be accepted or refused, as we saw with the venerable-regressive (IV, 11) and as could be true of each of the semipositive categories—and of course (I repeat) in the text, not in the reader's opinions or sympathies. One hardly needs to say that in itself, the refused presence of a semipositive category in a text is a phenomenon that is absolutely distinct from the presence of the corresponding negative category. In Roquentin's case, however, constants and variants between two separate passages stand out: the protest against certain reminiscent-affective images and the cherishing of certain desolate-disconnected images become reciprocally interpretable.

He who handles dirty papers and would gladly raise them to his mouth seems to have perversely transferred to them the role that more fortunate and more conformist people invest in household trifles—the role, that is, of a gratuitous alternative to functional, normal objects, whose neutrality Roquentin himself defines shortly after the first passage quoted: "One uses them, one puts them back in place, one lives amid them: they are useful, nothing more."[102] Another occasion for the desolate-disconnected in the novel is presented by an avenue on the outskirts of the town of Bouville, and it, too, can be contrasted with a street made central by bourgeois town planning and bourgeois frequentation. This time, the contrast is between outdated and persistent forms of the desolate-disconnected. A century ago, rue Tournebride was "a black, stinking gut, with a gutter that transported fish heads and entrails amid the paving stones"; a year ago, even the last old, indecent shop, much loved by Roquentin, was removed from the street's new commercial elegance.[103] The boulevard Noir, on the other hand, has remained an excluded, uninhabitable area toward which buildings turn their doorless and windowless backsides—its floors made of stones and mud, facing into a glacial wind, and with puddles that do not dry for more than a month each year. One could certainly think of the worn-realistic, or of the undefined category that provides for nature's resistance to culture (IV, 10, 13, 14). But the diarist lingers above all over the bits of posters still sticking to some half-destroyed wooden fence, torn paper with nearly illegible marks on it — like the page in the earlier episode. And his stopping in this place that is "precisely an opposite," that is "inhuman," brings him relief: "I no longer feel myself; I am filled with the purity of my surroundings."[104]

18

The complementarity between the desolate-disconnected and the refusal of the reminiscent-affective in Sartre's novel represents only one outcome of the evolution of the two related categories. In the twentieth century they have tended to approach and mix with each other, but not in equal measure: the advantage has lain entirely with the negative category and the disadvantage with the euphoric component of the semipositive category that Werther in his time could enjoy without limit (IV, 15). We shall consider, as the fourth example of the reminiscent-affective, a formally modern but thematically unmistakable version of the sentimental pilgrimage. The French-language Lithuanian poet Milosz (Oscar Vladislas de Lubicz-Milosz, 1877–1939) first appeared in the late symbolist period; he achieved his most original creations in and around the years of the First World War. The composition entitled *The Coach Stopped in the Night* (*La Berline arrêtée dans la nuit*) is to be found in his last collection (1922), and it is so beautiful that one is sorry to have to leave out the fourteen middle lines:

> While awaiting the keys
> — He is undoubtedly looking for them
> Amid the clothes
> Of Thècle who died thirty years ago —
> Listen, Madame, listen to the old, the deaf nocturnal
> Murmur in the lane . . .
> I'll carry you, so small and so weak, wrapped around twice in my overcoat,
> Through the brambles and the nettles of the ruins up to the high black door
> Of the castle.
> This is how the ancestor, long ago, returned
> From Vercelli with the dead woman.
> What a mute and diffident and black house
> For my child!
> As you already know, Madame, it is a sad story.
> They sleep scattered over distant lands.
> For a hundred years
> Their place has awaited them
> In the heart of the hill.
> With me their race is extinguished.

Oh Lady of these ruins!
We are going to see childhood's pretty room: there,
The supernatural depth of the silence
Is the voice of the dark portraits.
Gathered on my lying-place, at night,
I heard as if in the hollow of a suit of armor,
In the noise of the thaw behind the wall,
The beating of their heart.
What a savage fatherland for my fearful child!

. . . .

No, Madame, I hear nothing.
He is very old,
His mind is deranged.
I'll bet that he has gone drinking.
Such a black house for my timorous child!
In the depths, in the depths of the Lithuanian countryside.
No, Madame, I hear nothing.
Black, black house.
Rusted locks,
Dead vine-shoot,
Locked doors,
Closed shutters,
Leaves upon leaves in the lanes for a hundred years.
All the servants are dead.
As for me, I've lost my memory.
Such a black house for a trusting child!
I no longer remember anything but the orangery
Of my great-great-grandfather and the theater:
The owl's young ate from my hand there.
The moon gazed across the jasmine.
It was a long time ago.
I hear a footstep at the end of the lane,
Shadow. Here is Witold with the keys.[105]

On rereading the poem, one sees that a factual level can be constructed with much less difficulty than in the case of Eliot's slightly earlier composition. The "I" character, accompanied by a woman, returns to a castle in Lithuania where he spent his childhood and to which he is sole heir; at night, his coach stops before a gate or a great entrance door to the lane in the park, until the old surviving gatekeeper finds the keys. The text lasts exactly as long as the wait for the keys, which is declared in the first line and ends with their arrival in the last line. We are not observing the "I"'s gradual entrance into the place of memory, as in René's completed pilgrimage; the reminiscent-affective seems able to speak only on its threshold. The symbolic stop that provides the title but above all *entitles* the discourse, that prolongs the inaccessibility of the objects of a "lost" memory to the last moment and for a moment, makes the discourse oscillate between objects and processes, if not between the memory-related and the metaphorical. Witold is a character who emerges from the real past and at the same time is a symbol of memory, because of his having outlived all the dead servants, and because of his delay, his search through the clothes of a Thècle "who died thirty years ago," and his advanced age and deranged mind. The spatial distance of the castle "in the depths of the Lithuanian countryside" and the historic distance of its feudal characteristics become in turn a symbol of temporal distance, although of course from a Western perspective. And the Western perspective is not so much the one that the proprietor has acquired, through which a race of ancestors who "sleep scattered over distant lands" is "extinguished" (one of them had come back from Vercelli in Italy): the woman who accompanies him is certainly foreign to the place and its characteristics. In this case, too, childhood memory and a love story meet, but a nonsolitary pilgrimage lies outside the thematic tradition.

The woman is sometimes addressed with *vous* and called Madame, sometimes with the more tender, familiar *tu*—perhaps sometimes aloud and sometimes silently. Her relationship to the place is expressed in the present tense when the "I" addresses her with *vous* (with only one exception, in the lines not quoted), but when the "I" addresses her with *tu* the same relationship may be expressed either in the present or in the future—a strange future that, imaginary as it is for her, comes to coincide with the "I"'s childhood past. Thus there is a continuous vacillation of verb tenses, conjugated or implied, that creates effects of dreamlike condensation or of an overlapping cinematic dissolve. Regret for the beauty of his own childhood can be converted into love's hope, and vice versa. But above all, sorrow over his own impressions and fears of long ago is hidden below his compassion for her on account of the sojourn that awaits her in this foreign place. The woman—recipient of the whole declaration and intermittent counterpart of the "I" as a child—embodies the boundary of complacence in the memories; beyond that boundary, unpleasant images would turn in the direction of the desolate-disconnected. This takes place through four exclamations, whose periodic recurrence, however varied it is each time, cannot pass unnoticed in a rereading. A "mute and diffident and black" house, a "savage fatherland" for a "fearful" or "timorous" or, on the contrary, "trusting" child. The same contrast inspires the proposal to carry her—small and weak—protectively "through the brambles and the nettles of the ruins," and it is concealed in the other exclamation—almost an optative— that he would like her to be the lady of these ruins. Not only effects of time, such as rust and the accumulation of leaves—a hundred years old like the wait for burial "in the heart of the hill" — are to be found in the six striking lines without verbs, shortly after the ellipsis. Gloom and solitude appear, in perspective, inherent to the place; the imperiously dominant color that comes back to describe the house, as also the high door and the "dark" portraits, is black.

19

The desolate-disconnected balance sheet shows meager results, and that of the reminiscent-affective shows none at all, in the poetry of Eugenio Montale (1896–1981), up to the change in diction that characterizes the works written in his old age. In the poetry — in the strong sense — of the three great collections written before he was sixty, everything is memory-related yet nothing is specifically so, because everything is metaphorical:[106] the high-level figurativeness sublimates and depersonalizes all personal dimensions — ideological as well as autobiographical — to the point of making them mysterious. With the diaristic and epigrammatic tone of his later output, up to the age of eighty-four, his general attitude toward his persona has changed. On the one hand, his persona is implicitly exhibited everywhere as that of a man who is so important and famous that he can allow himself to put everything into verse, be it his memories or his opinions. On the other hand, his persona is again and again explicitly devalued, taking its private experience as insignificant and transient — just as the ideological baggage is pessimistic and antimagisterial, made of metahistorical fear of change and metaphysical indifference. "I was five percent alive": so he says in one of two poems — almost minuscule and temperamental echoes of Proust's *Against Sainte-Beuve* (*Contre Sainte-Beuve*) — that deride or exorcise literary historians' posthumous indiscretion about writers' lives.[107] In a third, *The Paperweights* (*I pressepapiers*), Montale approaches the critique of memory's external fetishes that exists in Proust — or that which we encountered in Sartre a short while ago (IV, 17). True memory consists of lightning flashes, he says, or it is a candle wick: "As to keepsakes in the literal sense / I possess very few of them. I have no leaning towers / In miniature, minigondolas, or other such / Junky trifles."[108] The anonymous paltriness of such counterexamples contaminates the refused reminiscent-affective with a not yet defined category.[109] Elsewhere, the ideology's pessimism draws repugnant metaphors from a non-memory-related occurrence of the desolate-disconnected: "Truth is in the gnawings / Of the moths and the mice / In the dust that comes out of musty chests of drawers / And in the crusts of aged Parmesan cheeses."[110]

Still elsewhere, a general metaphor of memory's processes is depressing and touristic: "The repertory / Of memory is worn out: a leather suitcase / That has borne the labels of many hotels."[111] Yet in *Xenia II 3* the author confesses to having "long regretted" an object lost in a grand hotel, a "little rusted tin horn" that served as a shoehorn. It was indecent to have brought "such a horror" there, and it is impossible to have someone search for "that nasty bit of tin":[112] we are given to understand that it must have been — to quote a further poem — one of those "Objects that seemed to us / A nonperishable part of ourselves."[113] A part, or actually the whole thing? And what are the objects in question? Their humbleness, or their traumatic debasement, is a precondition for identifying them with an "I" whom glory can in no way exempt from believing itself to be humiliated and from fearing itself to be cowardly. In the forms of the negative category and of the negation of the semipositive one, such an identification may be explicit, the identity may be even projected onto the objects — as happened in a Borges sonnet (II, 3) — thereby making them into the guarantors and organizers of that certainty or awareness which is lacking in the subject. This is the case in *The Hiding Places* (*I nascondigli*, 1971), in which the list of them is steeped in beloved memories, yet which ends up despising them in general as trinkets. Modesty and an everyday quality make up for the signs of time gone by; perhaps they imply them, since it is a matter of things that perpetually run the risk of becoming trash and are saved from it — things that the "I" would like to get rid of and, apparently inexplicably, does not dare to do:

> When I am not certain of being alive
> The certainty is two steps away but it is bothersome
> To find the objects, a pipe, my wife's
> Little wooden dog, her brother's
> Obituary, three or four pairs of eyeglasses
> Hers again! a bottle cork
> That hit her forehead in a long-ago
> New Year's cotillion at Sils Maria
> And other trinkets. They change their dwellings,
> Enter the most hidden holes, at all times
> Have run the risk of the trash bin.
> Plotting among themselves they have organized themselves
> To keep me going, they know better than I
> The thread that ties them to him who would like
> But does not dare to get rid of them. [. . .][114]

In *Xenia II 14* (1966), a comparative equalization of the subject with the suffering personification of the objects is added in — in four terms. The same relation exists between real events and the "I," as between the all-absorbing filth of the Florence flood and everything that was housed in the basement invaded by it. The identity that can be ascribed to certain objects has been traumatically removed even from them: the identification is all the more elaborate the more mortifying it is. Gifts and tokens from famous friends are shown off just like pieces of junk, the former like the latter having been relegated to below ground level and the other side of a double lock. Thanks to their long, common suffering one may well ask whether they are not less repudiated now than they were formerly:

> The flood has submerged the pack of furniture,
> Of papers, of paintings that crammed
> A basement closed with a double lock.
> Perhaps the red morocco leathers have fought
> Blindly, Du Bos' endless dedications,
> The wax seal with Ezra's beard,
> Alain's Valéry, the original
> Of the *Canti Orfici* — and then some shaving
> Brushes, a thousand pieces of junk and all
> Of your brother Silvio's music.
> Ten, twelve days under the naphtha and dung's
> Atrocious etching. They certainly suffered
> A lot before losing their identity.
> I too am encrusted up to my neck if my
> Civil status was doubtful from the start.
> It's not peat that has besieged me, but the events
> Of an unbelievable and never believed reality.
> . . . .[115]

20

At this point, six categories of images of nonfunctional corporality have been defined and documented with four examples each. Thus all the semantic space that in the first partial visualization of the tree had been opened on the left side — that is, under the positive pole with respect to passage of time in general (IV, 1) — has been filled from top to bottom, as far as the terminal oppositions. But the formulation of this positive pole itself, and even more so of the negative one, was at that time minimal and merely provisional. To further specify it now will be the equivalent, on the left side, of retrospectively perfecting the six definitions via the part they all share in common, the top part; while on the right side, it will be the equivalent of starting a plan for a new half of the tree. Previously we had summarily established an opposition between nonfunctionality connected to, or not connected to, a passage of time. Through the examples of the reminiscent-affective and the desolate-disconnected, the relationship of objects to time has raised complications that are not summarized in the last terminal opposition: distinctions between the memory-related and the metaphorical, between memory objects and memory processes, and between objects that are absent or present, intact or decayed, permanent or renovated, and — if renovated — that resemble or do not resemble the former . . . But the solemn-admonitory, the threadbare-grotesque, the venerable-regressive, and the worn-realistic also define objects whose effect bestrides several temporal levels. It is an *imaginary effect* (since such objects are located in the images of literature), which, by definition, reverts to a past, and which, also by definition, functions in the present, so that there may be a past. The reverting to the past counts only through its impact on the present; the impact on the present consists only in the reverting to the past; and this is the element that is common to all six categories.

In an apparently deductive movement (since this time it does not start with a text — in reality always inferred from the awareness of a corpus of texts), we will thus transform what I had provisionally formulated as an opposition among contradictories (passage of time or no) into an opposition among contraries. The reverting to the past may subsist without wholly exhausting the impact on the present moment; in turn, the impact on the present may completely do without reverting to the past; thus the reversion to the past becomes optional from now on, and the impact on the present a free element of a definition. We shall not exclude from the new categories all the images whose effect entails the perception of a passage of time, but only those images to whose effect such a perception is essential, as in the previous categories. *Perception of a passage of time* and *impact on present time* would in themselves furnish two contraries as a result of the opposition between past and present. But since the present is never incompatible with the past in the images' effect, and since the past always makes itself felt in the present, it would not be good strategy to raise to the status of contraries anything but *what predominates,* respectively, in the one or the other; and the major bifurcation of the semantic tree will have to be finally rewritten thus:

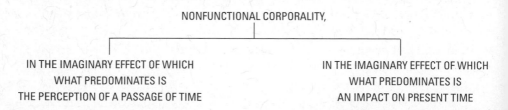

NONFUNCTIONAL CORPORALITY,

IN THE IMAGINARY EFFECT OF WHICH WHAT PREDOMINATES IS THE PERCEPTION OF A PASSAGE OF TIME

IN THE IMAGINARY EFFECT OF WHICH WHAT PREDOMINATES IS AN IMPACT ON PRESENT TIME

Rather than comparing the six definitions on the basis of my transcribing them one after another, the reader will prefer to go over them from top to bottom within the completed half of the tree — which sets in clear relation their shared and differing parts:

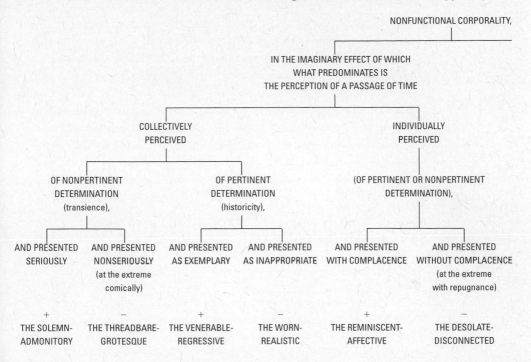

In Book VI of the *Civil War* (*Bellum civile*), more commonly called *Pharsalia* — the poem begun by Marcus Annaeus Lucan (39–65 A.D.) at little more than twenty years of age and left unfinished by him — Pompey's son consults a sorceress on the eve of the battle of Pharsalia in order "to know in advance the course of destiny."[116] Both characters are negative, morally: Sextus Pompey, "unworthy son" of his father, is "moved by fear";[117] Erichtho, after seventy-two astounding lines on the witches of Thessaly, is presented in sixty-two lines as the most sacrilegious and savage of them all.[118] But this does not mean that the former's curiosity about divination seems an illusion or the latter's necromantic ability an imposture. The magical practices in question are relegated to the clandestine character of unpeopled places: Erichtho "lives in deserted tombs"; Sextus comes towards her "across deserted fields."[119] And the practices are considered hateful in that they really and truly do violence to the gods;[120] they create disorder in nature.[121] But they are considered vain practices only because they are unable to alter the future:[122] they would not be spoken of with such execration if their supernatural efficacy were in doubt. The questions that the poet nevertheless poses, as an outsider, or the uncertainties to which he admits, have to do only with the mysterious causes and effects of an unquestioned power.[123] Although no more prodigious feats can be imagined than those of the witches of Thessaly, and "their art is everything incredible,"[124] Erichtho surpasses the others even in technical boldness: she invents new rituals and unknown magic formulae.[125]

The allusion to this prerogative of hers returns very effectively at the culminating moment of the necromancy scene. She has dragged the body of a man who died recently from his last battlefield to a cave that is a "lugubrious border between the hidden world / And ours";[126] in order to let the soul reenter the corpse, she pours a complex philter into it through fresh wounds:

> Here all that nature generated in a sinister birth
> Is mixed. Neither the foamy slobber of the dogs which fear water,
> Nor the bowels of lynxes, nor the hard spine of the hyena
> Were missing, nor the marrow of a deer which has fed on snakes,
> Nor the remora that holds the stern of the ship although the southeastern wind
> Swells the sails, nor the eyes of dragons, nor the warmed stones
> Which resound under the nesting eagle;
> Nor the flying snake of the Arabs and the viper born
> In the Red Sea, guardian of precious shells,
> Nor the skin of a still living Libyan horned viper,
> Nor the ashes of the phoenix deposited on the eastern altar.
> After having mixed the pestilent things most vile and
> Renowned, she added leaves imbued with nefarious words
> And herbs on which she spat at their birth with her horrible mouth
> And all the poisons she herself had given the world.[127]

This is as inventive and surprising a list—albeit not as long—as Régnier's threadbare-grotesque one (IV, 8); and it is incomparably more so than Mérimée's two very short nineteenth-century magic lists (II, 13). It adequately exemplifies the topical richness of magic lists of the sort that flourished from a period of antiquity certainly much more remote than that of Lucan until a little over a century before our historical turning point, with a value (as I have said) that is not only historic as prototype or archetype. Formally most of the list is in the negative, as Martial's threadbare-grotesque list (IV, 4) was in part: "Neither . . . nor . . . nor . . . was missing"; and it would be in keeping with the order *x / a, b, c . . . / x* (II, 13), if it were not complicated, between the first analytical listing and the final synthetic designation, by a further alternation of synthetic and analytical expressions. It is set out, in any case, between two uses of *quicquid* ("all that," "all the . . ."), of which the first comprises things born of nature in a sinister way, and the last comprises poisonous things excogitated by the witch herself. In terms of the major bifurcation of the semantic tree, it is undeniable that what predominates within the imaginary effect of such things is an impact on present time — that is, on the imminent future: the expectation of the prophecy to be wrung from the corpse. In the same terms, the contrary — made up of the perception of a passage of time in the effect of things — is not secondary but is instead lacking. We become aware that the poles of this opposition seem almost to coincide, provisionally, with the poles of another, between nature and culture. In the first example of the new half of the tree, things marked by a passage of time and artifacts turn out to be simultaneously absent; things that make an impact on the present and natural things are the only ones included.

In the previous account of Erichtho's desecrating activities in places of burial — halfway between sadism and necrophilia — in proportion to the presence of cadaveric corporality there are few artifacts: bits of a tomb bed, clothes falling apart, hanged men's ropes, and crucifix nails.[128] In the list quoted, leaves and herbs are natural, albeit imbued with a sacrilegious spell and soaked in her saliva, and the same applies to the poisons that are part of the final *quicquid*, although they were chosen or meted out by her. And all eleven of the ingredients through which the initial *quicquid* is articulated are natural, of an animal nature, whether the animals are rare or exotic or even mythical, such as the remora, dragon, flying snake, and phoenix, or whether part or all of their bodies must go into the mixture; whether the part requires the animal to be dead or leaves it alive, such as the horned viper's transformed skin; and whether it appears possible to procure and preserve, or rather unlikely, such as the saliva of a rabid dog. The ingredients are natural but strange, as if the connotations of strangeness were in some way part of the obsolescence created elsewhere by time. Yet even here, the right to speak of obsolete things, despite the fact that the things in the list have a use, does not depend mainly on such connotations; nor does it depend on the unequivocally literary rethinking, on the poet's part, of such magic, much less on my or the reader's lack of belief in any kind of magic. Strictly speaking, it depends only on the process of defunctionalization and refunctionalization common to all our semipositive categories. That which such a process claims to redeem in the case at hand — with an accursed aim but not in vain — is the repulsive uselessness of dead animals' corporality and, sometimes, the fact that they are not to be found owing to their weird or fabulous nature.

Furthermore, the fact that the purpose that the things are made to serve, their impact on present time, is of a supernatural order, amply transcends the unreality of some of the animals or of the singular characteristics attributed to them. That is, the occasionally supernatural character of the means must not be confused with the institutional one of the end; it is rather with respect to another word that a distinction has become even more important. The word *nature* is now involved in two different, heterogeneous oppositions, with culture and its artifacts, on the one hand, and with the supernatural, precisely, on the other. Both oppositions deserve to become part of the semantic tree, and our economical criterion in any case makes it desirable to establish a hierarchy among them (IV, 5). This time, however, the hierarchy must not be created by a strategic choice, because it is clear that they are not equal in logic. A body of laws—temporal-spatial, etc.—may simply be identified with the concept of nature that contrasts with the supernatural, which in fact consists only of imaginary exceptions to the laws themselves, and may also refer back to entities set above them. This concept of nature is more comprehensive than that which sets nature in contrast to culture, which in turn may simply and respectively be identified with real facts, resulting or not from human intervention. Everything that we call culture is of course also placed beneath the body of laws of the first concept; culture, then, is itself also part of nature, in the sense that corresponds to that concept. On the tree, the opposition between nature and culture can only be placed lower than the one between supernatural and natural, or, better, between *supernatural order* and *natural order*.

But on the natural order side, the interest in the lower opposition is obvious, whereas from the supernatural perspective the difference between nature's products and human artifacts, between *raw* and *wrought* nature—whether or not the former be dominant, as in Lucan—counts very little. It does not provide sufficient characterization to induce us to distribute certain images into two categories—just as, on the right side of the other half of the tree, the pertinence of the temporal and circumstantial determinations was insufficient (IV, 14). Here, too, it is not much trouble for us to apply the criterion of economy and to avoid repetition by neutralizing the superfluous opposition. A new portion of the semantic tree has thus been defined and may in turn be made visible:

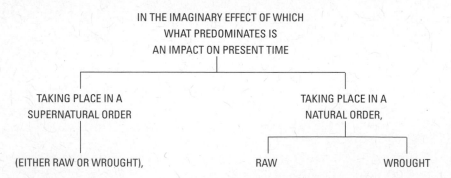

The participle expressing the upper opposition, *taking place in . . .* , refers to the *impact*; while the two adjectives that impose themselves in the lower opposition refer back to the tree's lowest common denominator, that is, to "nonfunctional corporality" at its topmost level.

22

In Lucan's Book VI, author and reader possess only slightly more knowledge than the little gathered or witnessed by the character of Sextus Pompey. The story is here told from the point of view of someone who is ignorant, narratologically speaking: that of the nonexpert, supposing that magic is a science or an art. Nevertheless, for our analytical, thematic, and nonnarratological abstraction, the preeminence in the story of a character like Erichtho counts more than the point of view. One may presume that the sorceress fully knows what she can do and what she is doing; woe — in literature — to the type of supernatural of whose motivations the reader knows as much as a sorceress . . . Under the same supernatural conditions, on the other hand, but given the lack of a protagonist who acts upon them, and in the presence of a protagonist who can only undergo them, the only thing that can happen is that the reader knows as much as the protagonist, or rather as little. Let us move on from the semipositive category to its corresponding negative, drawing examples from what was, in 1794, the most successful Gothic or black novel: *The Mysteries of Udolpho* by Ann Radcliffe (1764–1823). Through it, the long-lived lexicalization of the old castle as a spectral background was consecrated. In other words, in certain imagery we will be aware of the predominance, even in fragmentary quotations, of an impact on the present or a supernatural expectation; and at the same time we will identify, upon artifacts that consist of enormous buildings, the signs of a passage of time — optional to, but not excluded from the examples of the tree's new half (IV, 20). Antiquity and dilapidation — in addition to abandonment and isolation — can give off a death-fume around things, awaken fear, and favor credulity.

It is the sinister appeal of such atmospheres that justifies passages of descriptive lingering over interiors — among the most precocious in European literature, relatively spare and synthetic though they are. Radcliffe's novels require this all the more inasmuch as the mysteries end up being given a rational explanation (unlike those in other Gothic authors' works), after the suspense has been protracted for hundreds of pages. The three following passages are located at great distances from each other in the text:

> . . . she was not less surprised, on observing the half-furnished and forlorn appearance of the apartments she passed in the way to her chamber, whither she went through long suites of noble rooms, that seemed, from their desolate aspect, to have been inoccupied for many years. On the walls of some were the

faded remains of tapestry; from others, painted in fresco, the damps had almost withdrawn both colour and design. At length she reached her own chamber, spacious, desolate, and lofty, like the rest. . . .[129]

It opened into a suite of spacious and ancient apartments, some of which were hung with tapestry, and others wainscoted with cedar and black larchwood. What furniture there was, seemed to be almost as old as the rooms, and retained an appearance of grandeur, though covered with dust, and dropping to pieces with the damps, and with age.[130]

. . . she entered upon a long suite of chambers, whose walls were either hung with tapestry, or wainscoted with cedar, the furniture of which looked almost as antient as the rooms themselves; the spacious fireplaces, where no mark of social cheer remained, presented an image of cold desolation; and the whole suite had so much the air of neglect and desertion, that it seemed as if the venerable persons, whose portraits hung upon the walls, had been the last to inhabit them.[131]

In the first quotation, it is only the palace owned by Montoni, on the Grand Canal, that is being described; a stopping place where nothing disquieting is foretold, except for the gloomy Italian's economic difficulties.[132] Yet the description is similar to the other two, the first of which refers to the Apennine castle of Udolpho itself, and the second to Château-le-Blanc in Languedoc, both theaters of persistent terror. Venice is the first stop on a trip toward the south; it is well known that this geographical direction, from a northern, Protestant point of view, is also a culturally regressive symbolic direction — and in this sense other Gothic authors are not different from Radcliffe. Moreover, the economic causes of deterioration are the same for all three residences. Montoni is also the owner of Udolpho, where he is welcomed with a report of crumbled towers, roofs, and walls; Château-le-Blanc, passing from one owner to another, has been left to fall apart for years.[133] Just as the terrifying supernatural opens a dimension of unreality at the edge of the real, so the category of images that I am about to define insinuates itself parasitically above other categories that are anchored in the real. This was not the case with Poe's ghost ship, among the examples in the second chapter (II, 15), but we saw the so-called "fantastic" gain credit through the worn-realistic in both Pushkin and Stevenson (II, 9, 14); in the former, it also accompanied the venerable-regressive. Now, we could speak again of the worn-realistic, as a result of the loss of social position, or of a refused venerable-regressive — especially if we compare the quotations with those I have taken from Ossian (IV, 10).

The Gothic novel coincides with the venerable-regressive in its predilection for old feudal or ecclesiastical buildings. Except for the fact these seats of the two privileged estates (IV, 11) of the French *ancien régime* now lack exemplarity: we look upon them with the alienation — to put it mildly — of readers from the Third Estate, and this is so even though Emily, the protagonist, is a noblewoman (the fact that the author belonged to the English bourgeoisie is not in itself a decisive factor). It is significant that the adjective *spacious* recurs in all three quotations, and that *lofty,* with its vertically analogous meaning, is present in the first one and in a similar description that has not been quoted (and which lands in the category of the solemn-admonitory).[134] The spatial vastness that the old ruling class granted itself still carries majestic connotations but is already felt as antifunctional excess, as ostentatious waste and scattered solitude, as a custom that contrasts with the new class's ideals of family snugness. In the episode in which Emily ventures into the castle's innermost depths and even reaches a torture chamber,[135] there is no lack of images of overgrown plants and unhealthy dampness; even the new, negative category is contaminated with that (encountered so many times) of the invasion of nature (IV, 10, 13, 14, 17). But under the sign of the pre-Romantic supernatural, the realms of culture and nature flow into each other, assimilate each other, and neutralize each other in a more disconcerting way. Within uninhabitable habitats, the space is no less strewn with false signals, surprises, and dangers than if it were a forest or a desert — a dehumanized human desert, more modern that that of Lucan's tombs and fields.

The antifunctionality of the vast and the empty tends almost to eliminate the corporality of objects properly speaking, and to make space into the very object of this category's images. It matters little that Udolpho's secret passageways are given historical explanations as medieval safety measures in time of war;[136] in the castle's hyperbolic labyrinths, Emily and the faithful Annette are perpetually in danger of getting lost, as we learn from their dialogue on the very evening of their arrival. Annette, who is less enlightened than Emily, reports as a rumor heard from others that "these dismal galleries and halls are fit for nothing but ghosts to live in." And immediately after the second of the previous quotations: " 'How cold these rooms are, ma'amselle!' said Annette: 'nobody has lived in them for many, many years, they say. Do let us go.' "[137] Once the suspicion of criminal — even if not of ghostly — horror has been set forth, the mere mention of numerous turns and doors suffices to suggest broad, mobile backdrops; perhaps with a moan coming from an uncertain location, but with no further literary substance in the imagery.[138] And whether horror is criminal or ghostly is not very important, where the anxiety of the unknown goes back to the absolute quality of children's fear.[139] No matter that Emily is such a reasonable and courageous creature; the Gothic novel inherited from earlier narrative the sex and age of the pursued maiden, but it gives her the attributes of passivity par excellence — of an involuntary and unknowing expectation of the supernatural.

This is the contrary of an expectation that one may consider active, voluntary, and conscious. What is needed in order to proceed with the semantic tree — the terminal opposition most suited to completing the definitions of the new categories — may be pinpointed in the opposition between *active* and *passive expectation*:

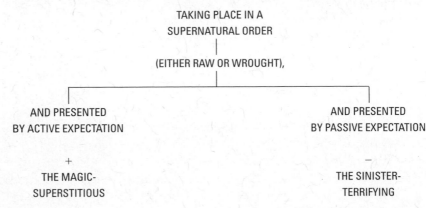

TAKING PLACE IN A
SUPERNATURAL ORDER

(EITHER RAW OR WROUGHT),

AND PRESENTED
BY ACTIVE EXPECTATION

AND PRESENTED
BY PASSIVE EXPECTATION

+
THE MAGIC-
SUPERSTITIOUS

−
THE SINISTER-
TERRIFYING

In the name that I am assigning to the semipositive category, the second adjective will not remain vaguely repetitive with respect to the first, as may seem to be the case: it will, rather, reveal itself to be an alternative to it, even taking into account a group of texts that is more than scanty — indeed, virtual. In the name of the negative category, an increasing gradation is established between the two adjectives. Most of the images fit in with the less intense term, within which the other remains as if impending.

23

In order to document each category of the tree's new half with four examples, let us consider other instances of the magic-superstitious. One is certainly the most famous list of a nefarious miscellany in Western literature: that recited by the three witches in *Macbeth* (datable to 1606) by William Shakespeare (1564–1616). It remains uncertain, in the tragedy, whether the witches are human beings so familiar with the supernatural that they can fly and vanish into thin air, or supernatural beings themselves.[140] Like Lucan's Erichtho, they meet in desert places, moor- or cave-like ones, but they are less formidable than Erichtho and more animal-like and grotesque. In the first scene, well before Macbeth insults them as "filthy hags,"[141] they enjoy hovering "through the fog and filthy air." They say it in rhyme, in the line that is by itself a poetics, that could serve as an epigraph to more than one category of this book's images, and that identifies the beautiful not so much with the ugly as with the dirty or fetid: "Fair is foul, and foul is fair."[142] Thanks to this poetics, in the fourth act's spell-chanting, Shakespeare's sovereign inventiveness achieves an unpredictable balance of irony between horror and the fairytale. There is a contrast between meaning and meter, between the excessive number of horrific words and the childish rhythm of a nursery rhyme, lullaby, or litany:

> *First Witch.* Round about the cauldron go;
>   In the poison'd entrails throw.
>   Toad, that under cold stone
>   Days and nights hast thirty-one
>   Swelter'd venom sleeping got,
>   Boil thou first i' the charmed pot.
> *All.* Double, double toil and trouble;
>   Fire burn and cauldron bubble.
> *Second Witch.* Fillet of a fenny snake,
>   In the cauldron boil and bake;
>   Eye of newt, and toe of frog,
>   Wool of bat, and tongue of dog,
>   Adder's fork, and blind-worm's sting,
>   Lizard's leg, and howlet's wing,
>   For a charm of powerful trouble,
>   Like a hell-broth boil and bubble.
> *All.* Double, double . . . etc.
> *Third Witch.* Scale of dragon, tooth of wolf,
>   Witches' mummy, maw and gulf
>   Of the ravin'd salt-sea shark,
>   Root of hemlock digg'd i' the dark,
>   Liver of blaspheming Jew,
>   Gall of goat, and slips of yew
>   Sliver'd in the moon's eclipse,
>   Nose of Turk, and Tartar's lips,
>   Finger of birth-strangled babe
>   Ditch-deliver'd by a drab,
>   Make the gruel thick and slab:
>   Add thereto a tiger's chaudron,
>   For the ingredients of our cauldron.
> *All.* Double, double . . . etc.
> *Second Witch.* Cool it with a baboon's blood,
>   Then the charm is firm and good.[143]

After Macbeth's entrance, and his choosing to listen to an answer not through the witches' mouths but through their occult "masters," magic makes necessary a few supplementary lines, with a return to the same meter:

> Pour in sow's blood, that hath eaten
> Her nine farrow; grease, that's sweaten
> From the murderer's gibbet throw
> Into the flame.[144]

The list's form, of a monotonous simplicity, fits in with the strophic one: the first witch lingers over a single item, the other two enumerate nine and twelve in a growing number of lines; a three-voice refrain follows the two verses. A final item serves as a conclusion, and two others are added later. "Hell-broth" at the end of the second verse and "ingredients" at the end of the third are synthesizing elements; but in their way, the cauldron (which literally contains the mixture) mentioned at the beginning and in the refrains, and the refrains themselves (which seal it verbally), serve to synthesize it. As in Lucan, no sign of a passage of time in the objects — among which there are no artifacts — counterbalances the actual, active expectation of prophecy. They are duly de- and refunctionalized objects because they all consist of dead animal and human, or vegetal, corporality; their dominant connotation of strangeness is not the exotic one of the tiger, the baboon, or the two oriental people mentioned, nor even the unreal one of the dragon or the witches' "mummy" as a magical cadaveric preparation; the supernatural element as an instrument is to be found rather in the subjects, in the living witches. What is strange above all is the jumble, more impracticable and literarily thought-out than ever. Here, unlike in Lucan, are presented not permanent predicates of certain objects (the remora stops ships, the deer feeds on snakes, etc.), but rather the circumstances of their origin — more like opportunities taken than prescriptions followed (the toad spent thirty-one days under a cold stone and was surprised in its sleep, the strangled newborn babe was born in a ditch, the hemlock dug up in the dark, and the yew cut during a lunar eclipse).

But the very connotation of the strange gives way to the more precisely antifunctional one of the noxious. If the frog, dog, lizard, and goat are inoffensive animals (or have only symbolic connotations of the mortuary or the demonic), the snake, newt, bat, blindworm, and owl are repugnant inasmuch as they slither or are nocturnal; the toad gives off mythical poison, and the adder, wolf, shark, tiger, and baboon symbolize fatal aggressiveness, to which that of the progeny-killing sow is added. As poisonous as hemlock, the yew was metonymous with the archers' bows made from its wood. Religious racism makes infidel Jews, Turks, and Tartars the equivalent of beasts and plants, as well as the whore who has killed her child like the sow, and in addition the hanged murderer. Only the toad is thrown whole into the bewitched pot. In every other case, a part is used to represent the whole, and several times it is the aggressive part par excellence: the forked tongue, stinger, tooth, jaw and maw, gall, carnivore's guts . . . Given their wild substantiality, the witches — who, with their crime-provoking prophecies, are essential to the plot — cannot be reduced to phantoms produced by Macbeth's mind. Yet they belong, by elemental vocation, to the disorder of moral transgression, and they project its murderous bestiality onto what they call "a deed without a name,"[145] no less for the antifunctional quality of the means than for the supernatural quality of the ends.

And now we turn to an example in which expectation of the supernatural, starting with things, is raised by a character as full of humanity as Shakespeare's witches tend toward the inhuman — the character who ended up giving her name to the anonymous *Celestina,* attributed to Fernando de Rojas (14??–1541); it was entitled *Comedy* in the first known edition (1499), and then *Tragicomedy of Calisto and Melibea* (*Tragicomedia de Calisto y Melibea*) in that of 1502, which raised the number of acts from sixteen to twenty-one. Old Celestina is described as a witch the first time she is mentioned.[146] But shortly after her first appearance, in the interminable, astonishing description of her made by the boy Parmeno, this profession of hers turns out to be the last of a series of professions, and indeed the only one that is played down:

> At the city limits, near the tannery, on the riverbank, this good woman has an isolated house, half falling apart, with few furnishings and even fewer provisions. She had six professions, that is to say: washerwoman, perfume-maker, mistress of cosmetics and of restoring virginity, procuress, and a bit of witchery. The first profession was a cover for the others. . . .[147]

The adjectives describing the house bow toward the threadbare-grotesque, whose picaresque future is more clearly announced in other parts of the text, as for instance when Calisto, enjoying the procuress's tale, exclaims that he would have liked to be hidden under her cloak, and she sighs that he would have been visible through thirty holes.[148] Of the six professions, only the disguising one is innocuous; the others are increasingly transgressive. The little list anticipates what would be the most exorbitant orgy of lists of objects, prior to the historical turning point, that I quote in this book — were it not for the fact that the objects related to the professions of perfume-maker and of mistress of cosmetics and of restoring virginity must be considered almost entirely functional for practical activities (II, 13).

It is not because we are dealing with irreverent or forbidden activities, that we cannot define them as functional without leaving something left over. It is because of the obsessive abundance of nouns, the specialized precision of which soon takes on strange characteristics and is subverted into unlikeliness

— a highly elaborate variant of the verbally defunctionalizing effect of lists (I, 1). I shall restrict myself to quoting as a sample the list of containers, as if it were synthetic in itself:

> She had a room full of alembics, measuring flasks, little casks of clay, of glass, of copper, of tin, in a thousand different shapes.[149]

But just as the old woman's cosmetic arts merge downward into those of the procuress, so the latter are inevitably mixed together with the sorceress's doings, which are the most reprehensible; these are practiced using suitable objects, which are the last to be listed:

> She had bones from a deer's heart, a viper's tongue, quails' heads, donkeys' brains, horse membrane, baby's excrement, a Moorish bean, sea pebbles, a hanged man's rope, an ivy flower, a hedgehog's needle, a badger's paw, fern seeds, the stone from an eagle's nest, and a thousand other things.[150]

The formula for synthesis that ends the list by making it longer — using the same hyperbolic numeral of one thousand that is applied to the containers' shapes — had already been employed for ointments and lyes, and it will be applied again to terrifying figments of magic.[151] Although it is perfectly blended into its context, the list is nonetheless a tributary of a tradition known to us. The eagle's nest, if not also the hanged man's rope, remind us precisely of Lucan; the latter is the only artifact among mineral, vegetable, and animal corporalities, not excluding a baby's excrement, without any indication of a passage of time. We know that this lack, and this proportion between culture and de- and refunctionalized nature, are characteristic of the magic-superstitious. They recur two acts later, in a passage that interests us more, owing to its singularity, and that has a more animated form than that of the list.

Here, images that elsewhere are usually remote in their horror, are dramatized in dialogue and made familiar — "quotidianized," so to speak. It is the active dimension of a profession: Celestina instructs one of the young prostitutes she protects and exploits to bring down from the attic everything needed for a diabolical spell. Interrupted and reproached by the young woman, she counters with senile humility. Over half a dozen evil objects are indicated as on the verge of being put into service or in relation to recent acquisitions and tasks:

> *Celestina.* Now go quickly to the high attic on the terrace and bring down the jar of serpent oil that you will find tied to the piece of rope that I took to the field the other night, when it was raining and dark, and open the chest with the fabrics, and toward the right you will find a paper written with bat's blood under the dragon's wing that we tore the nails off yesterday. Be careful not to pour the May-water that they brought me to make up.

> *Elicia.* Mother, it's not where you say it is; you never remember the things you save.
>
> *Celestina.* Don't mortify me on account of my age, in the name of God; don't mistreat me, Elicia. [. . .] Go into the room with the unguents, and in the black cat's skin, where I told you to put the she-wolf's eyes, you will find it, and bring the billy goat's blood, and a bit of the beard that you cut off him.[152]

The familiar-quotidian's compatibility with the macabre is no less extraordinary in the passage in which the old woman shows Parmeno keepsakes of his dead mother. She was her low-life companion, and she praises and mourns her with an emphasis that simultaneously shows opportunism and affection for, among other things, her boldness in going from cemetery to cemetery at midnight, "looking for material for our profession":

> I shall tell you but one thing, so that you will see what sort of a mother you have lost, although it should not be mentioned, but with you everything is all right. She pulled seven teeth out of a hanged man using eyebrow tweezers, while I took off his boots.[153]

I would be doing an injustice to the tragicomedy's admirable variety of style if I did not add that immediately after the above-quoted dialogue with Elicia, the tone of Celestina's spell is rhetorically high-flown and ornate: the bat becomes a "nocturnal bird" and the writing with its blood "vermilion letters."[154]

The spell's solemnity would not have been necessary to make us certain that Celestina believes in supernatural help; the dialogue's practical character would be sufficient. In introducing her, Parmeno has only grasped half of the truth when he says of her magic, "And it was all trickery and lies."[155] She believes in it in an everyday and familiar way, and certainly not exclusively. During and after her services as procuress at Melibea's, she attributes the undertaking's fortunes and misfortunes to the exorcized devil;[156] she knows very well, however, that the devil's real place of action—much more than the bewitched yarn that she sells—is her own infallible, unstoppable, irresistible tongue. The trick that saves her from Melibea's indignation is to replace Calisto's love-ache with a presumed toothache, and the asked-for favor of Melibea's receiving him with the favor of sending him a thaumaturgic prayer and rope: thus the hoped-for, surreptitious efficacy of black magic is exchanged for the exhibited, lied-about efficacy of white magic, as if there were a shift from the first to the second adjective in the term magic-superstitious. Melibea's rope, "which is reputed to have touched all the relics that there are in Rome and in Jerusalem,"[157] has no literary substance as an image, nor is it a relic itself. But its value lies in what ought to be alternatives par excellence to the magical images within this category (IV, 22): partial remains of human corporality, be they real or false, defunctionalized by death and refunctionalized by superstition.

24

In its luxuriant form, which vies with its Latin models, the topos of the magic list ought to have declined together with Baroque style, about half a century after the date of *Macbeth*. Shakespeare was the same age as Galileo, and Bacon and Descartes belong to the same generations as the poets of that style. The new science and technology had begun to ensure entirely different active expectations than the ones that came into play through the supernatural. After the first half of the eighteenth century, the supernatural in literature has already become the stuff of a "return of the surmounted,"[158] and not only in the Gothic novel. As such, it no longer animates magic-superstitious images but rather sinister-terrifying ones; were it not for the century-long interval, I would describe this as a transformation between the opposed categories. Fear of the unknown and its claims to existence survive only obscurely as passive expectation, hidden behind secular certitudes of only recent acquisition. And it is to the flowering of the Gothic (and often as its finest product) that *Melmoth the Wanderer* by Charles Robert Maturin (1780–1824) is usually ascribed, although it was published in 1820. The novel's structure of stories set within a wider narrative contains only the protagonist's vain efforts, during his two-century-long life, to find another victim to take his place in his pact with the devil. The prevalent setting is southern-regressive, as with Radcliffe: all of the tales deal with religious intolerance and fanaticism, and in four out of five cases at the expense of Catholic Spain. In the fifth, however, and in part of the first, that role is filled by Protestant sectarianism, and potentially, in the end, by the persecuting tendency of all revealed religions. This becomes explicit in the critical temptations that Melmoth aims at the innocent Immalee, without sparing political injustice, and attesting — in their clear echoing of Voltaire — to the Enlightenment paternity of the Gothic novel.

Yet the author, who, in a note, dissociates himself from the character,[159] was not a Deist but rather an Anglican curate whose sense of evil has an authentic theological flavor. He was not the first to introduce into this literary genre mystery without Radcliffe's final rational explanations, but he may have produced the genre's masterpiece because, to a much greater extent than others, he simultaneously called the religious problem into question and took it seriously. The literary fascination with a criminal past, a return of the surmounted, cannot be distinguished here from an unsurmounted, continuing obsession with sin. The ambivalence proceeds from the incredulous to the incredible, especially with respect to the theme of magic. What I have chosen in the novel is not a second example of the sinister-terrifying — despite the high quality of the many examples it offers — but rather a fourth, singular case of the magic-superstitious. The arts of the Irish folk sorceress Biddy Brannigan are discredited in the first few pages with a contempt that is not without horror.[160] Yet a few pages later this character is the one who must transmit information about the remote magical events out of which the plot develops, and in which one must not cease to believe — information that is taken up again only toward the end, after hundreds of pages.[161] Meanwhile, the prior of the monastery among whose ruins Isidora is married to Melmoth by the icy hand of a dead priest had a reputation for sorcery.[162] Earlier still, about half-way through the text, the young Monçada [*sic*], who has fled from taking vows in a monastery of ex-Jesuits, as well as from the Inquisition's condemna-tion, enters a subterranean space — one of those that lie beneath the homes of Jews in Madrid. A light through the cracks in a door attracts him, and he is able to look into an unsuspected room:

> In the centre of the room stood a table covered with black cloth; it supported an iron lamp of an antique and singular form, by whose light I had been directed, and was now enabled to descry furniture that appeared sufficiently extraordinary. There were, amid maps and globes, several instruments, of which my ignorance did not permit me then to know the use, — some, I have since learned, were anatomical; there was an electrifying machine, and a curious *model of a rack* in ivory; there were few books, but several scrolls of parchment, inscribed with large characters in red and ochre-coloured ink; and around the room were placed *four* skeletons, not in cases, but in a kind of upright coffin, that gave their bony emptiness a kind of ghastly and imperative prominence, as if they were the real and rightful tenants of that singular apartment. Interspersed between them were the stuffed figures of animals I knew not then the names of, — an alligator, — some gigantic bones, which I took for those of Sampson, but which turned out to be fragments of those of the Mammoth, — and antlers, which in my terror I believed to be those of the devil, but afterwards learned to be those of an Elk. Then I saw figures smaller, but not less horrible, — human and brute abortions, in all their states of anom-alous and deformed construction, not preserved in spirits, but standing in the ghastly nakedness of their white diminutive bones; these I conceived to be the attendant imps of some infernal ceremony, which the grand wizard, who now burst on my sight, was to preside over.[163]

This catacomb, in which a Jew has passed sixty of his one hundred seven years, reminds one — and certainly not by chance — of Faust's room. But Faust transcended inadequate science in the direction of symbolic magic; Adonijah, whom Monçada, even after this quote, believes to be a great sorcerer, pro-fesses to be a clandestine surgeon surrounded by his "ordinary utensils." He describes them as innocuous horrors in comparison with the Inquisition's bloody ones, and his patriarchal majesty and wisdom stand out among the contradictions of the religious problem in the novel.[164] Yet in his youth he had leaned toward the diabolical temptation embodied by Melmoth; he had been punished for it, and had made a vow to record the other's deeds in the manuscript in which we, together with Monçada, will read them throughout the rest of the text.[165] He may not be a figure of the author himself, but he personifies the author's narrative craft in this central part of the novel. Of the four skeletons in vertical coffins, one belongs to his wife and another to his son; he promises to tell the stories of the other two, but in the end we learn only that they were still more grim than those that were narrated, inasmuch as they were the Tempter's victims who wished to be able to see into their futures.[166] In the passage quoted above, the widespread sinister-terrifying within the narrative context seems to create an aura around the opposed category — that is, around images whose apparent form is the magic list. What is singular is that the narrating character on many occasions is already demystifying this appearance within the sentences that create it, turning, in brief prolepses, that which he believes into that which is: instruments whose purpose he does not know but that are really anatomical; gigantic bones that are not Samson's but those of a mammoth; antlers that do not belong to the devil but to an elk. In the case of the abortions, what they are is declared even before the fact that they were believed to be "imps of some infernal ceremony." Magic is rationalized into science; science borrows the antiquated face of magic. On the other hand, the listing or description of real magical instruments elsewhere in the novel, where the corresponding active expectations find elliptic confirmation, would be unthinkable.

25

The second example of the sinister-terrifying category will appear to be dictated by European literary history, if we now turn from the English Gothic novel to the short story by Ernst Theodor Amadeus Hoffmann (1776–1822) that initiated his fantasy genre. The title, *Gluck the Knight (Ritter Gluck)*, anticipates the two last words of the text and the surprise they produce, while the subtitle sets the date of the story as contemporary to its composition: *A Reminiscence of the Year 1809 (Eine Erinnerung aus dem Jahre 1809)*. The great operatic composer (knight of a papal order) had died in 1787, having imposed his reform in Vienna, with librettos in Italian, and in Paris, with librettos in French, without ever setting a German libretto to music. By 1809, from a Romantic and national point of view, Gluck possessed all the qualities to be proclaimed the symbolic representative of the genius ignored in his native land, particularly in Berlin, but also, more generally, by the profane public — to whom he had "revealed the sacred."[167] Mysteriously he is punished for this by surviving incognito amongst the profane and suffering the lasting torture of seeing his art misunderstood — the blame apparently falling from the public back onto the artist. Hoffmann's originality is revealed through the transposition of the theme of the genius, of his inspiration and his destiny, into a fantastic narration, a narration very distant from any explicit symbolism, but even more distant from any traditional spectral quality. Concerning the imagery, of the two terms of the category sinister-terrifying, only the first, here more than in any other case, is appropriate.

The setting, rather than an isolated castle, is Berlin on a lively and warm evening in autumn; the survivor is said to be doomed to wander "as a dead spirit in a deserted space," because for him the town is empty of related spirits.[168] The realistic liveliness of the first sentences anticipates a counterbalancing element of the incredible, which here appears for the first time in literary history, but without the imagery that concerns us (as in II, 9 and 14). A few lines down the page the "I" of a witness character emerges, speaking of how in the midst of the crowd he allows the play of his fancy to run loose, talking with imagined friendly figures that won't go away. This is a preliminary suggestion of a symbolic key to the story, but it is so discreet that the reader cannot but immediately forget it. The apparition of a stranger is presented as real to the senses, and the expectations of the first-person character are little by little depicted as passive, not on account of his qualities or situation, but through the continuous connections between the supernatural and the normal; this mode of presentation might make us think of Kafka rather than the Gothic novel. The stranger *is already there* when he is perceived: "There is murmuring around me [. . .] — I look up and only now perceive that a man, unnoticed by me, has taken a place at the same table. . . ."[169] And when he is out of sight, in an instant he has "disappeared."[170] His speeches and behavior are more obviously alarming signs, even more so the secret of his clothing: under a modern coat he conceals eighteenth-century dress and a sword, which are briefly revealed as he sits down.

This costume is shown immediately before the final revelation;[171] it is a disconcerting announcement of the passage of time, although it bears no sign of decay, and is disconcerting for exactly that reason. But before this the stranger has led the first-person character to his own house:

> . . . until he finally stopped before an insignificant building. He knocked discreetly for some time before at length the door was opened. Walking tentatively in the dark, we reached the stairs and a room on the first floor, the door of which was carefully closed by my guide. I heard another door open; shortly

after, he entered with a lighted candle, and the sight of the strangely decorated room surprised me not a little. Chairs richly adorned in old-fashioned style, a clock with a golden case, and a large heavy mirror created the dismal atmosphere of antiquated pomp. In the middle stood a small harpsichord, on top there was a large porcelain inkstand, and next to it lay a few sheets of music paper. Looking more carefully at these implements of composition I was persuaded, however, that nothing could have been written for a long time, since the paper was yellow and a thick cobweb covered the inkstand.[172]

The insignificant exterior of the house is the last dissimulation of the supernatural within the normal world; the interior, on the other hand, is the right setting for the stranger to play and sing Gluck's music, reading scores with empty staves, and creating masterful variations. Owing to the descriptive lingering in an environment of obsolete objects, the contradiction between verisimilitude and inverisimilitude reaches its climax, or short-circuits itself. It is certainly not verisimilar that a man dead for twenty-two years should still have an apartment in Berlin, as if outside of time; yet it is quite verisimilar that such a room should possess "the dismal atmosphere of antiquated pomp," and furthermore that the composer's implements should reveal their age and disuse. Here again the sinister-terrifying dominates over what could be considered either worn-realistic or venerable-regressive, where the effect of time would be paramount, rather than precisely its suspension. However, the abrupt ending, "*I am Gluck the Knight,*" suspends the time of narration. In the moment in which it provides a supernatural answer to prolonged curiosity, it eludes any further curiosity concerning a narration of which the supernatural itself forbids the continuation.[173]

26

It is again literary history that dictates an example of the sinister-terrifying, when we take the most popular of Henry James' (1843–1916) tales, *The Turn of the Screw*. It was published in 1898: with the century a series of supernatural literary genres came to an end, having begun shortly before its beginning. A later preface, and the title itself, are proof of the author's intention to innovate on what had by that time become conventional aspects of ghost stories.[174] A "turn of the screw" in terror is provided by the fact that the apparitions are directed at two children of ten and eight years of age; and by the fact that they do not mention them to the adults, becoming the accomplices of the deceased, who when still alive had begun corrupting them. The first-person narrator, a barely twenty-year-old governess who struggles to redeem them, is a very distant version of the pursued maiden. She has promised the absent guardian of the children to handle every situation alone: that is, she has taken upon herself the male, paternal duty of rational responsibility. Her forced passivity towards the ghosts doesn't impede her most active desire to make them cease to appear. Her heroism lies less in the difficulty of knowing, than in making the children tell all they know. No less a novelty is the fact that the ghosts are those of a former governess and of a servant: their social déclassement is bound up with the obscenity of the mystery, maximizing the contrast with the angelically refined appeal of the children. Contemporary with Freud's discoveries, the story casts the Victorian horror of infantile sexuality, of the "polymorphous perverse disposition," within a supernatural environment.[175] Consequently the truly Freudian interpretation of this story is not, I believe, one which considers the supernatural as illusory,[176] limiting it to a neurotic subjectivity, and ascribing to the children an entirely unproblematic innocence. More properly it is that interpretation which focuses on the compromise-formation between the supremely irrational and the feminine rationality that must painfully recognize and also interpret it, confronting the silent conspiracy attempting to deny and tolerate it.

The setting is described through the alienation, here, too, both enticed and intimidated, which results from a class difference; already the guardian's house in London had impressed the governess, who comes from a rural parsonage, "as vast and imposing."[177] On the second day after her arrival at Bly, she is given a tour of the house by little Flora:

> Young as she was, I was struck, throughout our little tour, with her confidence and courage, with the way, in empty chambers and dull corridors, on crooked staircases that made me pause and even on the summit of an old machicolated square tower that made me dizzy, her morning music, her disposition to tell me so many more things than she asked, rang out and led me on. I have not seen Bly since the day I left it, and I dare say that to my older and more informed eyes it would now appear sufficiently contracted. But as my little conductress, with her hair of gold and her frock of blue, danced before me round corners and pattered down passages, I had the view of a castle of romance inhabited by a rosy sprite, such a place as would somehow, for diversion of the young idea, take all colour out of storybooks and fairy tales. Wasn't it just a story-book over which I had fallen a-doze and a-dream? No; it was a big, ugly, antique but convenient house, embodying a few features of a building still older, half-replaced and half-utilized, in which I had the fancy of our being almost as lost as a handful of passengers in a great drifting ship. Well, I was, strangely, at the helm![178]

The proprietary self-confidence of the little girl conceals the very first hint of a less explicable daring, in the vastness of the building, a vastness which the metaphor of ship and helm translates for the woman into a sense of responsibility. But it is only in the idealization of the twenty-year-old that Bly appears as a typical castle. Looking back when writing years later, it is simply an edifice — no matter whether aristocratic or haut-bourgeois — made of two different layers, where the more modern utilizes or supplants the older; here the worn-realistic is no longer necessary to support the sinister-terrifying.

The passage of time fades only the manuscript of the story — "old faded ink," "the faded red cover of a thin, old-fashioned, gilt-edged album."[179] And we may properly speak of lingering description almost solely in the case of the background of the first apparition: the governess is daydreaming of meeting again the seductive and extravagant man in whose service she is employed, when she sees another man, of whose very existence she is ignorant — as well as of his death:

> He did stand there! — but high up, beyond the lawn and at the very top of the tower to which, on that first morning, little Flora had conducted me. This tower was one of a pair — square, incongruous, crenelated structures — that were distinguished, for some reason, though I could see little difference, as the new and the old. They flanked opposite ends of the house and were probably architectural absurdities, redeemed in a measure indeed by not being wholly disengaged nor of a height too pretentious, dating, in their ginger-bread antiquity, from a Romantic revival that was already a respectable past. I admired them, had fancies about them, for we could all profit in a degree, especially when they loomed through the dusk, by the grandeur of their actual battlements. . . .[180]

There is a thematic contrast between the apparition and its background which cannot be fully appreciated on a first reading. Further on we will learn that the deceased Peter Quint has appeared wearing the usurped clothes of his master; just as in his lifetime he had usurped the intimacy of the deceased Miss Jessel, who, as governess, was his superior, and the familiarity of little Miles. The heartfelt visionary moralism of the story is no less horrified by social degradation than by sexual depravity. And yet the imagery of the building appears to legitimate something analogous, namely, the periodic class renewal of the nineteenth century, the turnover of estates, possessions, and privileges. Although the antiquity of the towers is false and their architecture an absurdity, their proportions redeem them, their monumentality makes them admirable, and *that* past from which they do truly date is already respectable.

Devoid of immemorial or medieval prestige or decay, the dimensions of the house of Bly are sufficient for space itself to become the object of images, just as was the case at Udolpho, the mysteries of which are mentioned soon after the last passage quoted.[181] The third and only quotation that must be added has the "old" tower in common with the previous two:

> There were empty rooms at Bly, and it was only a question of choosing the right one. The right one suddenly presented itself to me as the lower one — though high above the gardens — in the solid corner of the house that I have spoken of as the old tower. This was a large, square chamber, arranged with some state as a bedroom, the extravagant size of which made it so inconvenient that it had not for years, though kept by Mrs. Grose in exemplary order, been occupied. I had often admired it and I knew my way about in it; I had only, after just faltering at the first chill gloom of its disuse, to pass across it. . . .[182]

By chance the rooms described in my first quotation from Radcliffe as "inoccupied for many years" are here evoked literally; not carelessness, but simply disuse because of the inconvenient, excessive size, entails a chill of nocturnal fear. To be sure, if the story contained no passages such as the three quoted here, space would not be the implied object of images everywhere else in the text. No more than implied, but as if always fraught with a special expectation: "They're [the ghosts] seen only across, as it were, and beyond — in strange places and on high places, the top of towers, the roof of houses, the outside of windows, the further edge of pools; but there's a deep design, on either side, to shorten the distance and overcome the obstacle. . . ."[183] The domestic distances of those final years of the nineteenth century to which the literary genre updates itself still display waste and solitude, if we measure by them the distances between children and the dead, the slow threat of an approaching ghost.

An original relationship between the supernatural and physical place appeared in a novel of the previous year (1897) — a novel unjustly, if only for this originality, ignored by histories of English literature as a mere commercial success. This novel is *Dracula* by Bram Stoker (1847–1912), which is styled as a compilation of reports from diaries, letters, newspaper articles, telegraph messages, and phonograph recordings. The modernity of this style already contrasts with the legend of the vampire and its extreme archaism. This archaism is not only cultural, but dates back to the oral phase of individual experience, to the desire and fear of sucking or devouring and of being sucked or devoured — adding to this the slightly less archaic idea of the return of the dead, bringing doom to the living. Count Dracula had reached fame at the time of the wars against the Turks, when he had dealings with the Evil One in Transylvania. This country, in the tradition that sets supernatural locations onto a centrifugal map, is more distant than Bly and even than Udolpho.

Literally meaning "beyond the forest," it is on the boundaries of civilization, and believed to be full of geological and chemical oddities.[184] We are transported to this country in the first episode, with the arrival of the guest and his gradual discovery that only a single person appears and disappears in the ruined and empty castle, a person who is not living.[185] But the guest is a lawyer whom the Count has called from London to discuss a property he has bought; "from a ruined tomb in a forgotten land," alone for centuries, it took him centuries to succeed in his plan of moving to the city "where the life of man teems."[186] In him, the Undead personify the survival of a past whose abjectness itself becomes a tendency to attack the progressive present. A late supplement to the Gothic novel's Enlightenment origins, the centripetal movement of the Count will ultimately penetrate to where "it is nineteenth century up-to-date with a vengeance," as the guest in Transylvania foresees.[187]

The problem for the vampire is that he also participates in the positive side of the ambivalence regarding the cadaver-referent: "it is not the least of its terrors that this evil thing is rooted deep in all good," and can lie only in ancient and consecrated ground.[188] This creates the most piquant paradoxes: the Count has to be transported to London along with fifty crates of earth dug up from his burial chapel, and ultimately must send the last of these back; to store these crates he is forced to buy large, long-abandoned houses — the scattered dead spaces remaining in the metropolis. The two faces of this ambivalence, something like the worn-realistic and the venerable-regressive transformed into the sinister-terrifying, are already apparent in the lawyer's report and in the Count's answer:

> "At Purfleet, on a by-road, I came across just such a place as seemed to be required, and where was displayed a dilapidated notice that the place was for sale. It is surrounded by a high wall, of ancient structure, built of heavy stones, and has not been repaired for a large number of years. The closed gates were of heavy old oak and iron, all eaten with rust.
> [. . .] The house is very large and of all periods back, I should say, to mediaeval times, for one part is of stone immensely thick, with only a few windows high up and heavily barred with iron. It looks like part of a keep, and is close to an old chapel or church. [. . .]"
> When I had finished, he said: —
> "I am glad that it is old and big. I myself am of an old family, and to live in a new house would kill me. A house cannot be made habitable in a day; and, after all, how few days go to make up a century. I rejoice also that there is a chapel of old times. We Transylvanian nobles love not to think that our bones may be amongst the common dead. I seek not gaiety nor mirth. . . ."[189]

All nobility will be lost in the successive houses, or rather dens, of the Count in Carfax and Piccadilly — much worse than the dwelling of Stevenson's Mr.

Hyde (II, 14). From the description of the first of these, pervaded by the nauseating smell of blood and putrefaction, and swarming with rats, one sentence will be sufficient: "The walls were fluffy and heavy with dust, and in the corners were masses of spider's webs, whereon the dust had gathered till they looked like old tattered rags as the weight had torn them partly down."[190] And a further exploration of the ignominy of the setting would reveal its inadequacy, instead of its suitability, for supernatural purposes: "It was hard to believe that amongst so prosaic surroundings of neglect and dust and decay there was any ground for such fear. . . ."[191] The ancient family tomb of the vampirized young girl, described soon after her burial, bears a "miserable and sordid" aspect, "unutterably mean-looking."[192]

Dracula believes he will escape observation in the London traffic; and his greatest asset may prove to be the skepticism of an enlightened age.[193] But Van Helsing, the pious scientist to whom those threatened by Dracula delegate authority, resembles both Sherlock Holmes and Freud. The latter could have spoken the following words: "I have learned not to think little of any one's belief, no matter how strange it be."[194] While admitting that all he has to go by are traditions and superstitions,[195] the professor considers them as a positivist would. He employs the crucifix, garlic, and the host,[196] which produce an effect on the crates of earth that is described with the verb "to sterilize."[197] Here, as for example in the ambushes at the loading on board and the return of the last case of soil, the method and execution of the plans bring the suspense of horror close to that of a detective story. On the other hand, railways, stenography, typewriting, the telegraph, and the phonograph all work against the vampire; his fierce astuteness is opposed by a solemn private coalition for good that substitutes for the role of the State. Victorian optimism revolts against that transmission of evil through the appetite for blood which lends depth to the legend, and both the women bitten in the neck still preserve their altruistic morality. "This London was no place for him," it is said towards the end of the novel;[198] but in fact, on a literary level it was the only place where the macabre "foulness"[199] could supply itself with new blood and be brought up to date over the length of an entire novel. The character of the vampire, by the name of Nosferatu, will enter the expressionist and surrealist movements, through the film by Murnau (1922) and the analysis of a dream by Breton.[200] If there is any black humor in Stoker it is unintentional, for instance the Count's adroitness with money and business ("he would have made a wonderful solicitor"):[201] in his abandoned house, title deeds and share certificates are found, as well as a washbasin full of bloody water[202] — while in Transylvania, where buried treasures exhale bluish flames, all that is found in his empty room is gold that is at least three hundred years old.[203]

27

Let us return to the semantic tree now that we have defined and documented, with four examples each, the first two categories of its second half, in
which the images have an impact on present time that takes place in a supernatural order. On the side where we presuppose that the impact occurs in a
natural order, we had reached the opposition between raw nature, or nature
simply, and wrought nature, or the artifacts of culture (IV, 21). In order to
place an object within this opposition, our strategy will be to look at the
physical context, natural or cultural, in which it is plunged or included, rather
than at the natural or cultural origin of the object itself. We will place artifacts
on the side of raw corporality, if they have been removed from their human-
governed cultural environment even for a short while, and reabsorbed in an
environment of emerging and overpowering — or even uncontaminated and
wild — nature, thus becoming nonfunctional. Let us consider that if we did not
proceed in this way with the two next categories, primary nonfunctionality
would not be understood strictly in the same way as it has been in the previous
categories; just as often the retrieval of secondary functionality will not be
understood in the same way in the semipositive category. I mean that in both
categories the object accepted as raw nature may have been such originally,
and thus may have preserved itself free of any function for humans, rather
than have lost a previously held function. Also in the semipositive category, the
object may remain forever in a state of raw nature: its image offering only the
positivity of a yearning for a potential, rather than of an actual recovery of
function. Because it is only in the mind and free from consequences — within
the imaginary reality of the text — this latter mode of imaginary functionality
is not to be mistaken for the absence of functionality or for the purely literary
compromise-formation which defines the negative categories (I, 5).

However, the positive recovery may be confined to a yearning for a potential, without any actual recovery or unearthing or recapturing, even in those
instances where the loss of primary functionality has been catastrophic: mis-
carriage, abandon, concealment, burial, drowning. If 1592–93 is the correct
dating for Shakespeare's *Tragedy of King Richard the Third,* then four or five
years earlier the Invincible Armada had been worsted in the Channel, and the
English pirate war against Spanish ships had been raging for over twenty years
at the time the play was being composed. In the first act, the Duke of Clarence,
imprisoned by his brother Edward IV, is murdered by order of a third brother,
the treacherous Duke of Gloucester, who will be the fifteenth-century king
named in the title. Before the entrance of the murderers, who will drown him
in a tub of malmsey, Clarence tells the Lieutenant of the Tower his terrifying

prophetic dream. While sailing towards France, Gloucester, stumbling, thrusts him overboard into the sea; fear of the suffocating waters becomes the nightmare of a hell populated by avenging spirits voicing Clarence's remorse. However, between these two stages of his dream the following verses create an interval that is difficult to qualify emotionally:

> Methought I saw a thousand fearful wrecks;
> A thousand men that fishes gnaw'd upon;
> Wedges of gold, great anchors, heaps of pearl,
> Inestimable stones, unvalu'd jewels,
> All scatter'd at the bottom of the sea.
> Some lay in dead men's skulls; and in those holes
> As 'twere in scorn of eyes, reflecting gems,
> That woo'd the slimy bottom of the deep,
> And mock'd the dead bones that lay scatter'd by.
> — Had you such leisure in the time of death
> To gaze upon these secrets of the deep?
> — Methought I had . . .[204]

It would be impossible to present in a more surreal poetic light certain constants of the national imagery of English-speaking countries: maritime, imperial, adventurous, and exotic (cf. II, 15). In their context of fear and nightmare these verses are an enduring surprise — pointed out by the lieutenant's question — and almost an accidental gift to the reader. The arbitrariness of the dream images, which escape any verisimilitude, at the end of this undersea vision particularly justifies the audacious and enigmatic Baroque relationships that appear, and in turn it is expressed by them: for example, that the jewels in the skulls have taken the place of eyes "in scorn" of them, that they "woo" the depth of the abyss, that they "mock" the scattered bones. Is this the basest mortification or the last transfiguration of the human body, previously devoured by fish? Certainly these remains, in which the cadaver-referent is deposited, seem to have been sublimated thanks to things, thanks to the proximity of so many precious stones, purified by the sea like Breton's cuttlefish bone and crab skeleton (II, 12). Consequently they scarcely count as natural objects, while all other objects in the brief list are cultural objects: not only the anchors, but also the gold (which is in ingots), the pearls (which are in heaps), the stones and jewels that may only be called inestimable and priceless after they have been worked on by man. Such a collection can only be the lost fruit of a hyperbolic number of shipwrecks.

With respect to the semantic tree, as I have already said, artifacts so situated will fall on the side of raw corporality. It is worth our while to put a further distinction ahead of this last predicate, as we insert it into our tree: *still* or *once again* raw. This distinction will not coincide with the terminal opposition that must be established between the semipositive category we have now illustrated and the corresponding negative category; instead, it will intersect it. For both categories, still raw corporality will mean that it has always been such, intact nature; and this is not the case in Clarence's vision. However, both when it has always been raw and when nature has reappropriated it, it may — as I have said — appear to be destined in the texts to remain forever raw. And this is the case in Shakespeare's lines, where the immensity of the underwater treasures enjoys no other retrieval than what I have called the yearning for the potential: astonished and fascinated contemplation by the character, and by the reader with him — a contemplation in whose dreamy ambiguity a high level of euphoria would be undeniable, were it not for the contrast with what precedes and follows. No other than this is the impact of the imagery in present time, and certainly it does not take place in a supernatural order, although the dream does continue in hell. Concerning the signs of a passage of time, or, in this case, of a traumatic moment in time like a shipwreck, they are hidden only in the single word, "fearful," used to describe the wrecks. None of the objects listed in the plural appears deteriorated. The sea that has swallowed them keeps them as a wasted resource, inaccessible to the extent that even in the imagination they may be seen only with the eyes of the dying.

Reminiscent of the verses from *Richard III*, the second example in the new semipositive category will be easily anticipated by those readers familiar with English literature. It is a quatrain, quoted together with those preceding and following it, from the *Elegy Written in a Country Churchyard*, completed in 1750 by Thomas Gray (1716–71). It brings us to the threshold of our historical turning point, to that pre-Romantic incubation period in the middle of the eighteenth century, in which I documented a transformation from the solemn-admonitory to the venerable-regressive with extracts from Diderot and Ossian (IV, 7, 10). It was from themes such as night, ruins, and sepulchers that, during the second half of the century, at least the reminiscent-affective and the sinister-terrifying, in addition to the venerable-regressive, became distinguishable and developed into a wider variety of imagery. These are the very themes of the beautiful opening of Gray's *Elegy*: where the evening substitutes the night and the modest, familiar variant of the rural landscape makes its appearance. However, it is too soon — if I may say so — for the imagery of our categories to become established, excepting the sober instance of the ivy-covered tower (third quatrain) with its "moping owl."[205] The meditation inspired by the cemetery initially appears to conform, without the relevant imagery, to the religious feeling for transience in the solemn-admonitory: peasants and farmers must die just like the great and the powerful, and in vain the latter pride themselves on their funeral pomp. However, the former, excluded in their lifetime from every glory of power and genius, of art and of science, deserve to be mourned as if in death they had disappeared more humbly, more irretrievably, and more completely.

This is stated in the lines quoted below, which follow the earlier quatrains of the poem not without a certain amount of ellipsis; the universal tone typical of the solemn-admonitory here is relativized and partially refuted, through the deploring of a social difference whose injustice is also or mostly hypothetical:

> Perhaps in this neglected spot is laid
> Some heart once pregnant with celestial fire;
> Hands, that the rod of empire might have sway'd,
> Or wak'd to extasy the living lyre.
>
> But knowledge to their eyes her ample page
> Rich with the spoils of time did ne'er unroll;
> Chill penury repress'd their noble rage,
> And froze the genial current of the soul.
>
> Full many a gem of purest ray serene
> The dark unfathom'd caves of ocean bear:
> Full many a flower is born to blush unseen,
> And waste its sweetness on the desert air.
>
> Some village Hampden, that, with dauntless breast,
> The little tyrant of his fields withstood,
> Some mute inglorious Milton here may rest,
> Some Cromwell guiltless of his country's blood.[206]

While in the previous example the imagery relevant for us was mediated by the dream that contained it, here it is mediated and contained by the space of a double metaphor in a separate stanza. Though not grammatically connected, the compared correspondences do not violate the boundaries of the rationality belonging to a still classical taste; and they possess an implicit, perfect precision. On the level of the human comparison, the potential is either abortive ("might have," "repress'd," "froze," "mute," "guiltless") or else limited to a provincial environment (a dauntless "village Hampden"). In parallel, on the level of the natural comparison, the ray of the gem has a purely ideal existence, since the caves of the ocean are "unfathom'd" and "dark"; while the scent of the "unseen" flower is wasted in the "desert" air.

For Gray as well as for Shakespeare, only metaphoric and oneiric space appears sufficiently imaginary to play host to images of resources forever inaccessible. And the dead too are forever dead: in Gray's text a "no more" is repeatedly tolled for them (fifth and sixth quatrains). The stanzas following those quoted concentrate, not on what these silent lives were, but on what they could have been, for better or worse. But in contrast with Shakespeare, here the comparison is also to natural resources always ignored: the mental contemplation of these is even more unlikely and remote from an actual contemplation, and consequently more nostalgic, more euphoric and pathetic at the same time. If there was something emotionally unintelligible in Clarence's blinding, close-up vision, the remoteness of these gems and flowers conveys an unequivocal, though ambivalent, sentimental message. To remain unexpressed or unrecognized is sad, but sweet. The marginal destiny of those lying in this cemetery not only benefits from pity and regret, and the posthumous retrieval they offer, but also from our melancholy envy of their renunciation. We will leave implicit, as the text does, the nevertheless eloquent insinuations about social class. It is the individual "I," who, towards the end of the text, will reveal himself with an unexpected effect, and apply a similar message to himself in death: identifying himself as the author, and entrusting a local old man with the remembrance of his person, a solitary passerby with the final reading of his own epitaph.[207]

28

Turning now to examples pertaining to the corresponding negative category, we know in advance that here too we will find imagery of a corporality definable as either still or once again raw. We will call once again raw those artifacts that a still raw nature is assimilating — or rather a nature unassimilable by man: nonfunctional objects that are no longer or ever less functional, with no chance of redemption. Finally that category will be named, and its definition completed, which we have so often glimpsed without defining, in contamination with other categories. I have already discussed the intrusion or invasion of wild vegetation or animals, in connection with texts quoted as examples of the venerable-regressive (IV, 10), the worn-realistic (IV, 13), the reminiscent-affective (IV, 14), and the sinister-terrifying (IV, 22). In referring to an example of the desolate-disconnected I spoke about the resistance opposed by nature against culture (IV, 17). I noted that historically, that category became contaminated with the solemn-admonitory centuries before it was contaminated with the venerable-regressive, and remained so for centuries (IV, 10); on the same occasion I pointed out its fleeting contamination also with an example of the threadbare-grotesque. In fact, little by little it has been contaminated with almost every category defined so far. And with all six of those composing the first half of the semantic tree: although in the imagery of the new category the impact on present time predominates, there is no revenge of nature against culture in which we may not perceive the passage of time, nor is there a perception of the passage of time without the revenge of nature against culture.

In the second chapter, Victor Hugo's sewer provided a quite pure example of the category in question (II, 11). Examples drawn from an entire section of a novel by Virginia Woolf, exceptionally pertinent over all its length (II, 10), were, on the other hand, the most intensely impure of those quoted in the chapter. Here, we can now say, there was an especially complex contamination: the solemn-admonitory above all, the worn-realistic and the desolate-disconnected also, and even somewhat of the sinister-terrifying were all contaminated with each other, and all with that dominant category. Following an extreme irruption of atmospheric nature in the penultimate quotation of Woolf, as well as of vegetable and animal nature, I referred to the threat of an almost biblical collapse in the final passage quoted, and to prophetic or psalmist reminiscences. These references were not accidental (all the less so in an author from a Protestant culture): I was aware that it would be necessary for us, in order to retrace the path from the imagery of this category back to its original and consecrated model, to return to the prophetic books of the Old Testament. I will have to consider a translation of these books as if it constituted an independent text, just as I have done with passages from Russian authors. In this case, however, I will do so not only because the original Hebrew is inaccessible for me: if I choose the most authoritative ancient translation with the longest-lasting diffusion in the West, the Latin Vulgate of St. Jerome, whatever is not identical to the original can only be of greater interest for us.

Semitic texts before the middle of the first millennium B.C., although they are anything but exotic for us, are too archaic, in the context of the present volume, to make a need for a direct understanding primary. Rather, those texts concern us and often appear familiar to us through their influence on the European literature of our age, beginning with the Fathers of the Church and the blending of the Greco-Latin and Judeo-Christian traditions. I will briefly recall that the writings of the so-called prophets appeared during those centuries when the independence of the two Hebrew kingdoms had undergone the assault of expanding empires, first the Assyrian, then the Babylonian. First the kingdom of Israel was destroyed forever, then the reign of Judah was destroyed for fifty years through mass deportations and exiles: in this was foreshadowed the future destiny of the people who invented monotheism, and with it suffering as punishment from their God, as well as faithfulness to their God while in exile. Isaiah, the first of the major prophets, had performed his ministry towards the beginning of this period, between 740 and 701 B.C., but in the book that bears his name many later passages have been included. The "oracles against pagan nations," of various or uncertain dates, were added because they belong to a literary genre: and the literary genre requires a particular topos. With a retaliatory gesture as defensive as it is offensive, the prophet hurls against the foreigner the threat that it will disappear as a nation settled in a particular place, returning literally into the desert.

Thus for example in Is. XIII:19–22 Babylon is cursed with ruin, and therefore the passage must date after Isaiah; it contains almost every thematic element whose enduring fortunes in the West my inquiry confirms.[208] However, in the most complete example I can find, dated at the end of the sixth century B.C. since it hails the liberation from exile, the curse falls on the hostile nation of Edom that had sided with Babylon (Is. XXXIV:10–11, 13–15):

> From generation to generation it will remain abandoned,
> From age to age no one will pass through.
> And the pelican and hedgehog will possess it;
> The raven and the ibis will dwell there;
>
> . . . .
>
> And in its palaces thorns and nettles shall grow,
> And in its fortresses brambles;
> And it shall be the nest of snakes,
> And the pasture of ostriches.
> And demons will meet donkey-centaurs,
> And hairy monsters will call to each other;
> The ghost of the night will lie there,
> And find its rest.
> There will the hedgehog have her burrow, and feed her little ones,
> And will bury and hatch them under her shadow;
> There will the vultures meet each another.[209]

Compared to the intrusions of nature in human dwellings encountered up to now in texts of more recent periods, more than one difference is immediately striking. And these differences refer us to a specifically ancient and Eastern relationship between nature and culture: the former, desert-like and threatening, the latter, pre-urban and relatively precarious. First, all the verbs employed are in the future tense, or in a Latin remote past tense which is equivalent to the future. This is not a time already elapsed in which a gradual decadence has come to pass, nor is it the traumatic time of a disaster that has taken place. This is the time of the curse, a future tense similar to a confident, implacable, and visionary optative mood of malediction. Furthermore, here the evils of plant and beast do not find their way into palaces and fortresses so as to contend with man for his belongings, imposing on him a form of cohabitation, however intolerable. Here instead the imagined usurpation knows no half-measures, the abolition of man is definitive and catastrophic as befits the execution of the omnipotent will of God in His wrath. If we speak of once again and forever raw nature, and if the latter adverb is dictated by the lack of retrieval or redemption in our negative categories, in this case it is bedecked with grandiose expressions such as "from generation to generation" or "from age to age." One further noteworthy characteristic is that here the names of animals are more dreadful, and more fantastically numerous, than those of plants.

The Western tradition that will draw on similar imagery transfers it from the prophetic future of the curse to the present or past tense of real obsoleteness. It will invert the proportions in number and frequency of plants and animals; it will eliminate divine agency as well as the suffering enemy, and the destruction will be reduced in dimensions from totality to larger or smaller parts. In the biblical texts, on the other hand, with the regularity of a commonplace, this imagery appears totalizing, even in many much briefer passages than the one quoted. The minimal form of this topos is a negation of water and greenery; culture is annihilated by the aridity and sterility of nature.[210] Its most frequent form combines the permanent negation of human presence and habitability with the presence of at least one race of wild, if not also noxious, animals. From the oracles against the nations of Jeremiah, the second major prophet, who witnessed the fall of Jerusalem under siege by Nebuchadnezzar, here is an example impressive for the laconicism of its double apposition in the second line I quote: "And Babylon will be heaps of ruins, / The dwelling of snakes, an astonishment and a hissing, / Because there will be no inhabitants." (Jer. LI:37).[211] The idea of punishment intrinsic to this imagery (as at times the comparison with Sodom and Gomorrah confirms)[212] means it may be turned, together with the wrath of the Eternal, against the guilt of the Chosen People themselves. The topos is two-sided: the same language employed to threaten Babylon may be used by the prophet to make the Eternal threaten Jerusalem.[213]

In the chapter by pseudo-Isaiah following that against Edom, the reversibility consists rather in a symmetrical deliverance of Jerusalem from the evil with which Edom is cursed. Water and verdure will return; the evil beasts, the names of which are synonymous with the absence of man, will disappear.[214] The names alone, essential to the topos from our point of view, provide some literary substance to the imagery. In the quoted passage the topos develops alongside their multiplication, around three plant names, thorns, nettles, and brambles; above all in the Vulgate, leaving aside other translations, not all the referents exist in nature. Pelican and hedgehog, serpent and ostrich, ibis, raven, and vulture all mingle with demons, centaurs that are half-donkeys, satyrs (the "hairy monsters" of the desert), lamias — that is, specters that prey on children by night. And yet the supernatural hardly contaminates the new category with the sinister-terrifying: what is symbolically important here is the animals' behavior, analogous to that of representatives of a verisimilar or a fantastic zoology. And this behavior of the animals is all the more exclusive of man to the extent to which, in counterfeiting him, their manners are familial or social.

Thus they create, beyond their names, a nefarious imagery: in the place of man these creatures meet and call to one another, are provided with pasture and a bed where they find rest, dig burrows where they hatch and feed their young.[215]

29

Now we need an example that offers imagery, not of once again, but of still raw nature for the negative category, just as examples of both kinds were provided for the semipositive one. We say it has always been raw, while admitting in both categories the anomaly I mentioned regarding the others: the possibility that primary nonfunctionality, rather than being a loss of function, would be properly original (IV, 27). The negative category, then, will deal with a nature both intact and inhospitable to man. If there has been a literary tradition of this kind of natural imagery, it did not issue from the Bible. It goes back above all to the ancient and Renaissance elaborations of classical mythology. I will refer to a relatively late period, proud of its belatedness, at once epigonic and modernist, namely, the Baroque. In the *Adonis* (*Adone*) by Giovan Battista Marino (1569–1625), published in 1623, the beautiful young protagonist of the poem dies hunting, killed by a boar as in the myth. The principal innovation on the myth, although not first introduced by Marino, is here conceived and developed according to his tendency to surprise and outdoing (a figure we will dwell upon later [VII, 4]). Adonis is not the victim of the animal's offensive or defensive violence, but of the involuntary violence that occurs when the boar falls monstrously in love with the youth's beauty.[216] Hyperbole and oxymoron adopt the thematic form of a passive, somewhat homosexual zoophilia, which in turn abounds in appropriate stylistic figures, in verbal surprises and outdoings.

The physical setting of this culminating episode of the poem's plot is not that of ignored nature, as in Gray's poem, but of nature forbidden because of its danger. Venus owns a "closed and secret," "protected and secluded" park in Cyprus, where Diana alone is allowed to hunt, and into which Venus is only reluctantly convinced to admit her lover.[217] Here are the three octaves that describe the landscape surrounding the watery den of the boar, a most terrifying beast:

> In between two hills that give their backs to the sun
> Dense with thickets and of flowers bare,
> In the dark hollow of a deep valley
> Lies a ravine in the form of a swamp;
> And but for a single narrow path
> All around is closed by scaly flint.
> That circling rock mountainous and steep
> Allows but one narrow opening.

Here in the middle of the valley, by dismal leaf
Shaded all round, lies a stagnant pool,
That with putrid waves of viscous liquid
Soaks the ever sterile and foul rock.
Nor around the thorny shores,
Too steep, is there much land,
But one may discern a small path,
Surrounded by crags and caves.

Never did set foot on the dreadful shore
A herd, though hungry and thirsty,
Fearing to taste and drink these fetid,
Noxious grasses and waters.
Not only do nymph and faun shun it,
Not only does the sun abhor it and the wind hate it,
But far from that abominable and forbidden strand
Even wolf and owl flee.[218]

In relation to some of the texts used in the construction of the semantic tree, certain issues concerning sources have already arisen, but rarely and incidentally. In this case the question is relevant exactly because room for the category's imagery is created by the distance between ancient and modern sources, by their amplification and exaggeration. In Ovid's *Metamorphoses*, there is no description of the landscape when the death of Adonis is related; when Meleager faces the boar of Calydonia, there is only a steep valley at the bottom of which harmless marsh plants grow, all described in four lines.[219] The fourth and first lines of the Marino quoted here certainly recall very well-known lines from *Orlando Furioso:* "There lies in Araby a pleasant dale, / [. . .] / That in the shade of two mountains . . ."[220] But Ariosto's landscape is remote, shady, and fabulous, with nothing threatening or unwholesome. A more immediate source, not surprisingly, is Tasso, who rendered somewhat harsher his earlier description of the enchanted forest in *Jerusalem Delivered* (*Gerusalemme liberata*), while lengthening the description of the Dead Sea (Sodom and Gomorrah again!) in *Jerusalem Conquered* (*Gerusalemme conquistata*): "Of that foul liquid never does / The tired and weary pilgrim drink, / Nor does herd nor beast . . ."[221] By setting his anonymous pagan swamp on the same level as an accursed place in sacred history, by aiming at a surprising unnatural, rather than supernatural atmosphere, Marino multiplies, in a crescendo of outdoing, the beings that avoid the shores of the lake. That man should avoid it goes without saying, since even such natural divinities like the nymph and the faun stay clear of it, as well as natural phenomena such as the sun and wind. Even animals whose very names signify the uninhabitability of nature for man avoid it, such as the wolf and the owl.

We have previously identified the biblical origins of the symbolic negative value of these animals. Here, not their presence, but their very absence suggests the horror of this place. It is not a desert, and is more mountainous than marshy. The discovery of mountains as not exclusively places of horror occurred in literature only in the pre-Romantic eighteenth century — almost at the time of our historical turning point. In the meantime it was typical of the Baroque poetics of Marino, and of Tasso before him, while continuing to see creation as a hierarchy with a religious base, not to avoid representing its lower extremes; drawing from this in fact a certain satisfaction — secular and gratuitous in Marino's playful literary craftsmanship. This satisfaction is revealed in the work of both authors by the proliferation of adjectives to which expression is largely entrusted. While already in *Jerusalem Delivered* the Dead Sea was a "turbid" or "sterile" lake, in *Jerusalem Conquered* it is not simply described as "fetid liquid" or "abominable . . . waters": adjectives analogous to and not less numerous than those used by Marino are distributed over six octaves.[222] It is in the concentration of adjectives that *Adonis* surpasses its source. In the space of three octaves, some ten adjectives describing the mountain insist on extremes of physical repulsiveness; in the description of the lake, a series such as "viscous," "putrid," "sterile and foul," "fetid," and "noxious." Four more adjectives describe a moral rather than a physical negativity, "dismal," "dreadful," "abominable and forbidden." It would be possible to trace other sources, perhaps no less direct, and certain descriptions of landscapes would confirm an ancient connection with forbidden entry, beyond the connection with death. If it is possible to speak of a traditional Latin topos, the *locus horridus* in contrast with the *locus amoenus:* the infernal landscape was its archetype, first in the sober lines of Virgil, then in the taut verses of Seneca.[223]

In the plan of the semantic tree we can now set the new terminal opposition under the pole of raw corporality; we know also that we are to prefix a distinction. *Resource* and *threat* are the two positive and negative terms that we have already employed, and which must be opposed to each other:

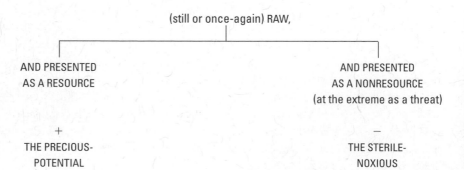

(still or once-again) RAW,

AND PRESENTED
AS A RESOURCE

AND PRESENTED
AS A NONRESOURCE
(at the extreme as a threat)

+
THE PRECIOUS-
POTENTIAL

−
THE STERILE-
NOXIOUS

The positive term does not give rise to any doubts, nor need we await other examples on account of the peculiarity found in the two quotations already given, namely, that the secondary functionality be limited to a yearning of potential. The contrary negative term does not appear forced if we consider the first two respective examples. But until I provide further examples, following the same procedure as with previous terminal oppositions, I will use the contradictory term, more comprehensive than the contraries, and place the latter as a limit in parentheses. The first adjective in the definition of the semipositive category is as foreseeable as the second. In the definition of the negative category, both adjectives are drawn from the exuberant series offered by Marino, combined with my own lexical hints; they are once more set in order of increasing degree.

The reader can now look over the complete definitions of four categories in the second half of the semantic tree, if I sketch out the part that we have worked through so far. We have almost completed the whole tree, only two definitions are missing. Once we have read the next two examples of the precious-potential and sterile-noxious that I promised, there will be only one terminal opposition left to establish, beneath the suspended pole of the upper opposition:

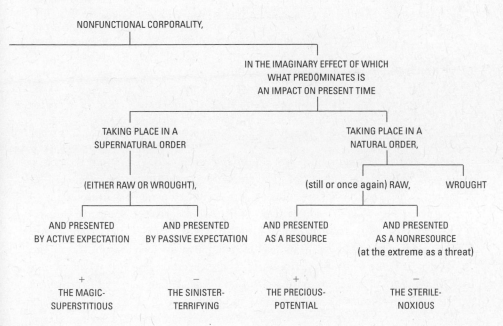

30

The island conceals no treasure when the shipwrecked sailor lands on it, there to remain for more than twenty-eight years. And yet the Caribbean island setting of *The Life and Strange Surprising Adventures of Robinson Crusoe of York, Mariner,* first novel of Daniel Defoe (1660–1731), published in 1719, is the archetype of future treasure islands. Robinson survives because his patient, ingenious capacity for work is supplemented from the start by numerous functional objects, the products of previous collective work. With time and effort he saves these things from his own ship and later from another wreck on the coast, and he provides lists upon lists of them: nonperishable items of food and drink, clothing, arms and powder, nautical instruments, writing implements and books, carpentry tools and pieces of various materials —these latter being useful to him for building other objects.[224] Any piece of wreckage he carries onshore, he soon concludes, will serve him on some occasion.[225] There is one exception, represented by that metal which is deprived of any use-value because in normal social circumstances it materializes all exchange value: the coin. Robinson knows its uselessness in advance, since he declares that the carpenter's work box is "much more valuable than a ship loading of gold would have been at that time."[226] And yet he does find money in his twelfth, though by no means his last, search of the wreck:

> in another drawer I found about thirty six pounds' value in money, some European coin, some Brazil, some pieces of eight, some gold, some silver.
> I smil'd to my self at the sight of this money. "O drug!" said I aloud, "what are thou good for? Thou art not worth to me, no, not the taking off of the ground; one of those knives is worth all this heap; I have no manner of use for thee, e'en remain where thou art, and go to the bottom as a creature whose life is not worth saving." However, upon second thoughts, I took it away. . . .[227]

His second thoughts are as if automatic (today this has almost a comic effect), and remain unjustified. The smile of scorn is instead commented on aloud, with the bitterness of solitude, and an undercurrent religious feeling of precariousness. These feelings find confirmation further on when Robinson again mentions the money, celebrating his fourth anniversary on the island after every attempt to escape by sea has failed. By now he feels cut off from the world, he is the lord of a small world where the abundance of things of use-value is more than sufficient for individual needs; the superfluity of everything else is a moral lesson, however forced and painful is the absence of his fellow-man and of exchange-value. And the coins, which cannot buy him goods or tools, already bear the signs of time in the form of mold. Of course, in the cave which Robinson has enlarged with his hands to use as a cellar, neither four nor twenty-eight years would be sufficient to make the gold once again raw; and when he later discovers a natural cave free from dampness, the walls of which are either diamond or gold, he doesn't bother to move the money there as he does the weapons and gunpowder.[228] Mainly insofar as it is useless, reduced by fortuitous devaluation to an insignificant corporality, the treasure of the island falls under the definition of precious-potential. Neither beneath the earth nor at the bottom of the sea, but outside of and far from society, not irretrievable in the space of a dream or metaphor, but a lengthy wait for retrieval in the most practical space of adventure:

> I had, as I hinted before, a parcel of money, as well gold as silver, about thirty six pounds sterling. Alas! Here the nasty sorry useless stuff lay; I had no manner of business for it; and I often thought with my self that I would have given a handful of it for a gross of tobacco-pipes, or for a hand-mill to grind my corn; nay, I would have given it all for six-pennyworth of turnip and carrot seed out of England or for a handful of pease and beans, and a bottle of ink. As it was, I had not the least advantage by it, or benefit from it; but there it lay in a drawer, and grew mouldy with the damp of the cave in the wet season; and if I had had the drawer full of diamonds, it had been the same case; and they had been of no manner of value to me, because of no use.[229]

Of the three adjectives that disqualify the money, the first calls it "nasty": the Puritan Defoe didn't need to invent the expression, derived from St. Paul,[230] which extends over long periods of our cultural tradition the symbolic relationship with the ambivalence of feces (I, 6–7). The cadaver-referent figures in the novel because of the cannibals, in short horrific lists,[231] while the excrement-referent reappears with the money, but on both occasions the scornful comparison remains ambiguous. Does it condemn its inherent vileness, or does it only attack its temporary uselessness? The second wreck that Robinson finds had carried, bound perhaps for Spain from somewhere south of Brazil, a great treasure: "but of no use at the time to any body." And yet he counts the sacks of coins and their contents, the golden doubloons wrapped in paper, and guesses the weight of the ingots. Further along, the reasons to despise these riches have not altered: " 'twas to me as the dirt under my feet; and I would have given it all for three or four pair of English shoes and stockings." And yet it was a great pity that the poop of the ship was destroyed, "for I am satisfy'd I might have loaded my canoe several times over with money."[232] One page later he compares the vanity of his riches to the most notorious case in history of precious-potential recovered still raw: "I had no more use for it than the Indians of Peru had before the Spaniards came there."[233] The potential is realized when Robinson is freed from the island. He carries the money together with other "reliques" of the reminiscent-affective kind: the goatskin cap, the umbrella, the parrot. The passage of time has left its mark on the small treasure, "which had lain by me so long useless, that it was grown rusty, or tarnish'd, and could hardly pass for silver till it had been a little rubb'd and handled."[234] Robinson in the end is rich; the moralizing of the solitary meditations on the superfluous is quickly transformed into moralizing upon the troubles created by money. It must now be deposited in a place other than a cave, since it must be protected from dangers other than of becoming "mouldy and tarnish'd."[235]

31

"This island is a very singular one. It consists of little else than the sea sand [. . .]. It is separated from the mainland by a scarcely perceptible creek, oozing its way through a wilderness of reeds and slime, a favorite resort of the marsh-hen. The vegetation, as might be supposed, is scant, or at least dwarf-ish."[236] These are the opening lines of a description of Sullivan Island off the coast of South Carolina, with its subtropical and desert climate. We read it toward the beginning of *The Gold-Bug* by Poe, published in 1843, which tells of the search for treasure following difficult clues, deciphered by a combination of genius and luck. When Legrand guides his unwitting companions on shore, the three of them pass "through a tract of country excessively wild and desolate, where no trace of a human footstep was to be seen"; they advance in "a region infinitely more dreary than any yet seen," the description of which also follows.[237] Such imagery, and one of the most renowned treasures in literature, may lead the reader to wonder whether we are not about to find a new example of the sterile-noxious category, rather than a final and quite proper example of the precious-potential. And in fact, in this story, that phenomenon of exchange, which earlier I named "commutation" (a phenomenon by definition possible only between two opposed categories), does take place between the two (IV, 3, 4). And not within the space of a few verses, as in the sonnet by Scarron or in Ariosto's octave, but over the whole span of a much longer text. The hidden valuables not only lie in a narrow and invisible subterranean space, they are lost in a vast and inhospitable, repellent space — but neither still lost nor forever lost, for here there is a complete loss of primary functionality, and an effective retrieval of secondary functionality. The negative category will be transposed into the semipositive category when someone will find what had been hidden in order to be found again.

The yearning for the potential takes the initial and active form of hope: Legrand thirsts to become rich again. The fact that the gold-bug has scales which appear to be of burnished gold, and that the black man believes it to be made of solid gold, has kindled his imagination[238] — an imagination which reasons, even on the basis of the "innumerable Southern superstitions about money buried." The treasure must still be there, he thinks, because so many tales circulate about the search for it, while there are none about its discovery.[239] At the moment when this reasoning is rewarded, the telling of the extent of its worth is simultaneous with that of the discovery, and precedes the fantastic explosion of blinding light in the night:

> In an instant, a treasure of incalculable value lay gleaming before us. As the rays of the lanterns fell within the pit, there flashed upwards from a confused heap of gold and of jewels, a glow and a glare that absolutely dazzled our eyes.[240]

But not all the situations and instruments of this adventure anticipate this light as the gold-bug's color does. While the precious-potential is achieved by commutation with the sterile-noxious, one can hardly speak of a contamination with the sinister-terrifying; and yet the cadaver-referent emerges as a theme, or rather as an inexhaustible guiding thread, leading through the whole intellectual and material progress towards the treasure. Let us reconstruct the narrative order, which Legrand's reserve inverts for the benefit of *suspense*. The starting point is a death's head, which literally resurfaces on the parchment; by turns this head becomes the emblem of piracy, the countersign of the cryptogram, a visible sign from a single distant viewpoint, an actual skull nailed to a branch.[241] The latter is a *dead* branch, the extent of its decay is the object of figurative emphasis on the part of the black man and of anxious questioning by his master.[242] Above the treasure is unearthed decayed wool reduced to dust, mixed with a mass of bones belonging to two skeletons; the container is a wooden chest, oblong in shape (like the parchment) — which may be associated with a coffin even by anyone ignorant of a famous psychoanalytic interpretation of Poe's life, and of the most obsessive constants in his work.[243]

The signs of a passage of time, which, regarding the second half of the semantic tree, we have so far only found in examples of the sinister-terrifying and in Defoe, here appear in other facts preceding the unearthing. They are less than images: the segment of parchment is covered in dirt; it was half buried in the sand next to the unrecognizable remains of an ancient shipwreck; the cryptogram refers to a family that had owned a manor house from time immemorial.[244] These signs are also borne in part by the contents of the chest, that is, by the very images of the precious-potential:

> The chest had been full to the brim, and we spent the whole day, and the greater part of the next night, in a scrutiny of its contents. There had been nothing like order or arrangement. Everything had been heaped in promis-

cuously. Having assorted all with care, we found ourselves possessed of even vaster wealth than we had at first supposed. In coin there was rather more than four hundred and fifty thousand dollars—estimating the value of the pieces, as accurately as we could, by the tables of the period. There was not a particle of silver. All was gold of antique date and of great variety—French, Spanish, and German money, with a few English guineas, and some counters, of which we had never seen specimens before. There were several very large and heavy coins, so worn that we could make nothing of their inscriptions. There was no American money. The value of the jewels we found more difficult in estimating. There were diamonds—some of them exceedingly large and fine—a hundred and ten in all, and not one of them small; eighteen rubies of remarkable brilliancy;—three hundred and ten emeralds, all very beautiful: and twenty-one sapphires, with an opal. These stones had all been broken from their settings and thrown loose in the chest. The settings themselves, which we picked out from among the other gold, appeared to have been beaten up with hammers, as if to prevent identification. Besides all this, there was a vast quantity of solid gold ornaments; nearly two hundred massive finger and ear-rings;—rich chains—thirty of these, if I remember; eighty-three very large and heavy crucifixes;—five gold censers of great value;—a prodigious golden punch-bowl, ornamented with richly chased vineleaves and Bacchanalian figures; with two sword-handles exquisitely embossed, and many other smaller articles which I cannot recollect. The weight of these valuables exceeded three hundred and fifty pounds avoirdupois; and in this estimate I have not included one hundred and ninety-seven superb gold watches; three of the number being worth each five hundred dollars, if one. Many of them were very old, and as timekeepers valueless; the works having suffered, more or less, from corrosion—but all were richly jewelled and in cases of great worth. We estimated the entire contents of the chest, that night, at a million and a half of dollars; and, upon the subsequent disposal of the trinkets and jewels (a few being retained for our own use), it was found that we had greatly undervalued the treasure.[245]

Wear and tear or corrosion make the coins illegible and the watches unserviceable. The fact that the latter have stopped working is also metaphorical: these are the natural effects of time passed mostly underground. On the other hand the jewels broken from their settings and hammered suggest a traumatic interruption of time as well as the unlawfulness of their appropriation and of the piratical hiding-place. The narration ends with the conjecture that the skeletons are those of helpers in the burial of the hoard who were murdered because they knew too much;[246] also the disorder of the heap suggests guilty haste, while in contrast the form of the list follows a laboriously established order. First coins, then jewels, then golden objects (continuation in summary form: "and many other smaller articles"), plus the watches. The extensive catalogue is given movement by the intoxicatingly large numbers used to count the objects and estimate their value or weight, which are summarized in a grand total. But both at the beginning and at the end, after having established an order and after having completed the sale, the value is found to be greater than had been supposed or estimated. What at first had been potential becomes realized: gold, time, and burial have yielded interest in the true financial sense, in which all the prestige of adventure or antiquity is dissolved. Despite the exotic age of the entirely European coins, and the beauty of the stones and artifacts, little is kept for personal use. All is converted into ready money, and thus the secondary functionality is either different or greater than the primary functionality; but the excrement-referent remains only implicit in the story, in this differing from Defoe, and from the cadaver-referent. This is a good opportunity for separating psychoanalytical symbolism from literary textual interpretation. It is too indirect to say that the dung-beetle is the "coprophilic animal par excellence";[247] or, if you will, that the treasure contains not a single particle of silver, but only gold—the light of which is warm and brown. I would rather refer to the commutation between sterile-noxious and precious-potential, an example of the singular reversibility of these two categories, logically modeled on what I had called the ambivalence of ambivalences (I, 6–7).

32

The possible commutation of the sterile-noxious into the precious-potential is only one of the many facets of this volume's unified subject of inquiry—whether this unity be still presumed or by now appears as proven. The sterile-noxious, as still and always having been raw nature, though not necessarily forever so, may also figure in the imagery of modern literature as subject to another reversal—the result of which, however, lies beyond the semantic space we are here concerned with, falling in that field I had identified as contiguous by opposition, under the sign of functionality (III, 8). The epoch of our historical turning point realized, with awareness of confronting a grandiose novelty, that human progress was capable of making the sterile fertile, of suppressing the noxious, of appropriating inhospitable nature. The greatest poet of the age acted in exactly the opposite way to the biblical prophet who invoked the desert in inhabited places. In the final episode of his dramatic poem, he invented an augury of inhabited places in the desert. I am referring again to Goethe's *Faust*. I was already so bold as to isolate some lines from the first part, from the opening monologue of the protagonist (IV, 11); now I would like to draw from the second part, not quite from the concluding monologue, but from the scene which directly introduces it. The moment of Faust's death is so memorable as to make us forget that his redemptive choice is already virtually accomplished in the first scene of the previous act, the fourth (written in 1831), certainly one of the acts that are less often read. The setting is in the mountains, with "steep and cragged rocky peaks"; Faust lands in "the deepest of solitudes." Mephistopheles is scornful on finding him in the midst of the horror of "ravines fearfully agape," and reveals to him that this landscape had once been the very bottom of hell.[248] There the insatiable protagonist announces that "something great" has attracted him, that there is still "room for great enterprises" within the earthly sphere: and in vain does he try to provoke his diabolic interlocutor to guess what he is referring to.[249]

What he then explains does not anticipate the positive vision which will enlighten him at the time of his death, except insofar as in its pure negativity it constitutes the very denial of that vision. His eyes have been captured by the sea, by how it swells and towers before assaulting the flat expanse of the shore, and it halts and retreats to repeat the game. This spectacle has "irritated" him, a surprising irritation expressed in ethical terms. And yet in a hundred thousand years this is nothing new, Mephistopheles sneers *ad spectatores*. Faust continues, as the stage direction specifies, with passion:

> She [the wave] creeps forward, on a thousand shores,
> Herself infertile, spreading infertility;
> Now she swells and grows and rolls and covers
> The repulsive stretch of the deserted strand.
> There wave upon wave rules thrilled with power,
> She pulls back, and nothing is accomplished,
> Such a thing could cause me anguish to the point of desperation:
> Useless power of uncontrolled elements!
> Then my spirit dares to rise above itself;
> It is here I wish to fight, it is this I wish to conquer![250]

We have witnessed the character while he refuses, with no less passion, the moldy venerable-regressive of his narrow chamber; now he rejects, at the other end of the action, the vast uselessness of nature. It drives him to desperation that the water expends its force without purpose, that nothing has been *geleistet,* "accomplished." The verb belongs to the same area as those pointed out in the first monologue (*to need, to use* [*brauchen, nützen*]): the area of the "principle of performance," of a functional imperative (1, 3), which in the heroic bourgeois phase appears eminently as the principle or imperative of liberation. The water of the sea is looked on exclusively at its border with cultivable land. Not only is it infertile, it spreads infertility along thousands of shores: to use the terms of the semantic tree, it is sterilizing or noxious, as well as sterile, both a nonresource and a threat. In Faust's previous and in his following speeches, his language personifies water, seeing it as arrogant, supercilious, and overbearing. It is fitting to anthropomorphize nature when man is worthy of fighting her and beating her: the desert strand is *widerlich,* "repulsive, unpleasant" — just as, a little earlier, the essence of Mephistopheles was *widrig,* "unfavorable, adverse."[251] Mephistopheles assures him that it will be no great effort to obtain from the emperor a vast strand as a fief. In fact Faust is granted a stretch of earth which is actually under water, which must be reclaimed through hard work;[252] much more than a feudal tenant, he becomes a kind of colonizer and contractor. The fact that Mephistopheles becomes the manager of worldwide piracy, that he burns and murders in order to satisfy his master with further property,[253] proves how little the poetic utopia here leans on ideological illusions. In the last of the old, blind Faust's visions — where the devil loses his wager with him and God — the antifunctional has declined from sea to swamp, or "rotten marsh"; without further literary substance in the imagery. What he envisions is the perpetual turning of this landscape into its opposite by means of human activity, freedom every day reconquered, uninterrupted danger and salvation.[254]

Eighty years after Goethe's death, in 1912, Thomas Mann's (1875–1955) *Death in Venice* (*Der Tod in Venedig*) was published. Venice in this story again contrasts the dream of the deliverance of a city from a swamp with the threat of the assimilation of the city into a swamp. Less clearly, here to a certain extent the relationship between human work (not manual) and nature is thematic. But the creative positive quality of the former is initially upset by the too high costs of repression; while the negativity of destructive nature will be tragically interiorized. Gustav von Aschenbach owes his fame as a writer and spiritual guide to the austere daily work, and to the measured and dignified official demeanor, to which he has trained himself ever since adolescence. The story begins with his yielding to an almost deathly fatigue; and the nature that jostles within him, instead of becoming identified with sanity or normality, is radically disjoined from them. Thus the first imagery of external nature, where a sudden desire to travel realizes itself almost as an hallucination, rushes suddenly to the most inaccessible and irreconcilable sterile-noxious. I will only quote the beginning and end of the luxuriant sentence — some elements of which will recur later on:

> he saw, saw a landscape, a tropical swamp under a sky thick with dust; damp, luxuriant and monstrous, a kind of primeval wilderness made of islands, marshes, and slime-bearing streams [. . .] through the knotty stems of the bamboo thicket he saw the eyes of a crouching tiger shine — and felt his heart beating with horror and enigmatic desire.[255]

If this is the desire, the actual summer journey he plans can only be much more moderate: "Not so far away, not quite as far as the tigers"; "an exotic place with no associations, which should be nonetheless easy to reach."[256] Only after he has been disappointed by an island of the Adriatic does Aschenbach identify Venice as his only plausible destination. The Lido beach satisfies him as — here again — a boundary between culture and nature: "This sight of thoughtless, sensual voluptuous culture on the edge of the element."[257] And since he has experienced the danger of the unhealthy lagoon in summer,[258] the unexpected arises not from external, but from internal nature. The texts in which Freud attributed to male homosexuality both a natural and a morbid genesis dated only one or two years before Mann's story. Freud claims the universality of homosexuality in the infantile "polymorphous-perverse disposition," in its persistence in adults, at least unconsciously; he denounces the regressive fixation of the subject on the mother, the narcissistic role exchange between the two which becomes the foundation of the search for love objects.[259] In his intuitive representation of a similar narcissism Mann literally reaches an extreme depth. Aschenbach and Tadzio do not exchange a single word, even when there is an opportunity; the former's pederastic passion always appears to be chastely visual, even when he loses all modesty in his behavior. In order to adore in the other the idealization of oneself as a young man, the other must remain an image and must not become too much of a person. The smile that Tadzio exceptionally bestows on him is less Narcissus's smile than its reversal. It is certainly not the adolescent in the fifty-year-old man, but the fifty-year-old man that hopelessly admires his *own* beauty in the adolescent.[260]

That smile introduces the last stage in the story, and its construction connects the interior phases to the background of the physical environment. In the first aesthetic yearning, curious and discreet, for the Polish youth, the perverse revenge of nature was being prepared; in the euphoria of the beach and in the charm of the city the cholera epidemic had already spread, disguising its signs. The fact that most of these signs involve the sense of smell counterbalances the sparseness of the imagery. A slightly putrid odor is often mentioned as a characteristic of the lagoon;[261] the pure description immediately afterwards of sultriness, multiplicity of odors, perfumes, and stagnant fumes takes up twice the amount of lines necessary to evoke the place: "In a silent square, one of those forgotten places with an enchanted aspect that may be found in the interior of Venice, on the edge of a fountain."[262] This is the moment when the decision to leave is made, in vain. There then follows the first of only three passages where the Venetian landscape acquires a degree of literary substance; no reader, I believe, easily notices that these moments are so rare:

> At the next gondola stand he boarded a vessel and, through the turbid laby-
> rinth of canals, under graceful marble balconies, flanked by the images of
> lions, round slippery corners of walls, before mournful palace façades with
> signboards of businesses mirrored in the water that rocked the garbage on its
> surface, he was taken to San Marco.[263]

Already on the Italian ship Aschenbach had taken to reach Venice the worn-
realistic had preceded the sterile-noxious; alleyways and foundations are repeatedly described as "dirty," and on the final autumn beach the sand is no
longer clean.[264] But disease and death are announced only when a medicinal
odor becomes distinct from the other smells, and in turn is mentioned more
than once.[265]

The "wicked secret" of Venice, which was disinfected too late, blends with
that of the protagonist; his complicity with the cynicism of the city authorities,
in not warning Tadzio's mother of what he has learned, is by now a nauseated
aversion to any form of temperance, effort, and morality.[266] The last visual
description of Venice[267] occurs during his unwitting return to a place in the
heart of the "diseased town" — where garbage, like the phenolic acid in the air,
has become a symptom:

> A small square, forgotten, of enchanted aspect, opened before him, he recog-
> nized it, it had been here that a few weeks earlier he had conceived the failed
> project of escape. On the steps of the cistern, at the center of the place, he let
> himself sink to the ground and leaned his head on the stone circle. There was
> silence, the grass grew among the cobblestones, garbage lay around. Among
> the surrounding weather-beaten houses, of irregular height, one resembled a
> palace, with ogival windows behind which emptiness reigned, and balconies
> with lions. On the ground floor of another building there was a pharmacy.
> Warm bursts of wind occasionally carried whiffs of phenolic acid.[268]

In the meantime the tropical hallucination has been repeated word for word,
including the swamps and the tiger. An English employee of a tourist agency is
giving information; the report is made using the same authorial voice that
censored any detail concerning Aschenbach's erotic desire, and that here, retracing his initial desire to travel, displays the stylized preciosity of Aschenbach the writer:

> For many years already the Indian cholera had shown an ever stronger in-
> clination to increase and spread. Generated in the hot swamps of the delta of
> the Ganges, fostered by the mephitic breeze of that wild primeval wilderness
> of islands, luxuriant and unhealthy, avoided by man, in the bamboo thickets
> where the tiger crouches. . . .[269]

33

Let us now proceed to finish the picture of the semantic tree, completing the last two definitions with the yet to be decided terminal opposition (IV, 29). Let us read through the consecutive parts common to both definitions, excluding the elements that create distinctions: *nonfunctional corporality, in the imaginary effect of which what predominates is an impact on present time, taking place in a natural order, wrought . . .* In order to divide the semantic space which opens under this last element, and to distinguish a semipositive and a negative category within it, what could be the most strategically promising opposition? Already through the general considerations in the first chapter, and the sampling in the second from the texts by Arnim, Flaubert, Gozzano, and Roth, we had discovered problems and devised solutions that now come in handy: in the first place, that the imagery of nonfunctional corporality may very well be imagery of commodities, for sale or sold (I, 4, 7; II, 5, 6). In the case of antiques, the hypothesis is of a primary defunctionalizing and a secondary refunctionalizing in the practical-economic dimension. Within this dimension there would be nothing that would give rise to a negative category, should it not be based on the oversimplified requirements of a low price, or sale at a loss, or unsellableness. A failed, lacking, or bankrupt refunctionalizing is more conceivable within a symbolic-aesthetic dimension. Contrasting this with a successful refunctionalizing in aesthetic terms, or rather in terms of taste, would appear possible and convincing; it would be sufficient to use, as a terminal opposition:

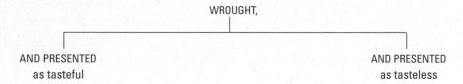

WROUGHT,

AND PRESENTED
as tasteful

AND PRESENTED
as tasteless

And yet, knowledge of the texts does not suggest our choosing an opposition of taste, nor one of price — even if we were only to take into consideration the case of antiques. This problem has already occurred: de- and refunctionalizing involve a cultural de- and recontextualization, both in time and space. If it were not so, independent of the issue under consideration, artifacts neither necessarily nor predominantly affected by the passage of time would be difficult to think of as nonfunctional. In the second chapter, I had switched from the definition "bad taste" to the by now international German word "kitsch" (II, 4, 5, 6, 7, 12), a term which is untranslatable, ill defined, and irreplaceable. Both terms undoubtedly imply an aesthetic dimension. But the term "kitsch" implies connotations that arose no earlier than in mid-nineteenth-century bourgeois culture, meanings which also involve a third dimension difficult to qualify more precisely than as cultural-historical. As we only glimpsed earlier, it is indeed a matter of the authenticity or inauthenticity of the cultural experiences connected to objects, beginning with their spatial and temporal decontextualization. And it is consequently a matter of the intellectual cost of their recontextualization, which a need for rigor might see as somehow moral — something quite different from their cost in money. I would think that this complex dimension, rather than the purely aesthetic dimension, must produce the most penetrating opposition to be verified in the texts. In the meantime, we may accept as confirmed some constants equivalent to the idea of kitsch — in our case, the kitsch of objects: the inauthenticity, or the suspension of proof of authenticity, of experience; and the low intellectual, if not moral, cost of recontextualization. These are circumstances in which a nonexperience is made out to be, with credulous or presumptuous ease, an experience.

The adoption of much more abstract conceptual constants will ensure that the categories of imagery which we are about to define will not be connected to overdetermined subject matter, that is, to antiques, commodities. If I follow the thread of such material constants, as I have already often done in the second chapter, it will be only briefly. In that chapter Arnim's text led me to refer to a kitsch effect of unsold and reused antiques; but the suspicion of anachronism which I mentioned has been confirmed. The junk dealer buys and sells, and in the meantime she makes the best use she can of the most unserviceable commodities. The results of this, though comically random, are not really attempts at decoration, and do not express false cultural urges. Such a phenomenon could not have been represented in literature at that date, and in Arnim's text — independent of a retrospective effect I attempted to suggest — I would not see more than a late and very original instance of the threadbare-grotesque. The antiquarianism referred to by the title of a novel published four years later, in 1816, does not entail the sale of objects for profit but acquisitions guided by the passion of a collector. This is Walter Scott's (1771–1832) third historical novel set in Scotland, *The Antiquary* (1816): the cult of local antiquities that the epithet attributes to the protagonist Oldbuck must be understood in its widest sense. Starting from a collection of books and other objects, this cult moves on to the identification of Romano-Caledonian battlefields and the remains of fortifications, the dating of ruins, the deciphering of inscriptions, and the transcription of popular ballads.

Even though Oldbuck is of German bourgeois descent and is loyal to the reigning dynasty, his erudition is more profound than that of the friend, much more than him a dilettante, with whom he usually argues: Sir Arthur, who in contrast is of an ancient line, and is still loyal, at the end of the eighteenth century, to the Stuarts. Loquacious but caustic, pedantic but critical, ego-centric and misogynist but upright and at bottom well-meaning, Oldbuck is one of the most richly endowed with verbal life of Scott's characters. Towards the opening of the novel, the apartment filled by his collection is described as follows:

> One end was entirely occupied by book-shelves, greatly too limited in space for the number of volumes placed upon them, which were, therefore, drawn up in ranks of two or three files deep, while numberless others littered the floor and the tables, amid a chaos of maps, engravings, scraps of parchment, bundles of papers, pieces of old armour, swords, dirks, helmets, and Highland targets. Behind Mr Oldbuck's seat (which was an ancient leathern-covered easy-chair, worn smooth by constant use), was a huge oaken cabinet, deco-rated at each corner with Dutch cherubs, having their little duck-wings dis-played, and great jolter-headed visages placed between them. The top of this cabinet was covered with busts, and Roman lamps and paterae, intermingled with one or two bronze-figures. [. . .] A large old-fashioned oaken table was covered with a profusion of papers, parchments, books, and nondescript trinkets and gew-gaws, which seemed to have little to recommend them, besides rust and the antiquity which it indicates. In the midst of this wreck of ancient books and utensils, with a gravity equal to Marius among the ruins of Carthage, sat a large black cat, which, to a superstitious eye, might have presented the *genius loci,* the tutelar demon of the apartment. The floor, as well as the table and chairs, was overflowed with the same *mare magnum* of miscellaneous trumpery, where it would have been as impossible to find any individual article wanted, as to put it to any use when discovered.[270]

Four synonymous expressions, referring to the fragmentary abundance of scattered objects, equate the tables and chairs to the floor, and vice versa: "a chaos of . . . ," "a profusion of . . . ," "this wreck of . . . ," "the same *mare magnum* of. . . ." The further details given in each case order their series of items in gradations descending from the distinct to the indistinct, and from what is of interest to what lacks interest. First there is a list with nine named items, papers and weapons which, taken by themselves, are without connota-tions of the threadbare-grotesque; further down, a short list that runs into the unclassifiable, with no other feature but rust; then a list consisting of only two items. Lastly, the organized list gives way to a jumble, where we are assured with humorous objectivity that the unfindable and the unserviceable coincide — as we are assured, a very few lines after the passage quoted here, that it is difficult to sit down without either causing or suffering some kind of damage. In the lines that I have omitted, some charmless Arthurian figures in a tapestry are made fun of, while there is no ridicule in the description of family portraits or paintings of Scottish history. The cherubs decorating the cabinet have "great jolter-headed visages" placed between "little duck-wings"; but the Roman statues and implements are certainly the most valuable things. The threadbare-grotesque triumphs, at the expense of a parodied solemn-admonitory — perhaps that of Poggio Bracciolini (IV, 6)? — in the comparison of the cat with Marius, and consequently of the surrounding relics with the ruins of Carthage. However, that Oldbuck's seat is "worn smooth by constant use" is said with the neutrality of the worn-realistic; and the character is, as it were, mirrored throughout the whole description. There is an analogous relationship on the one hand between the valid core of the collection and the excessive redundancy of the clutter, and, on the other hand, between the competence of the antiquary and his manic verbosity, which never forgoes an association of superfluous ideas and cannot always avoid daring conjectures.

It is obvious what antiquarianism represents thematically: the very literary genre of the historical novel, and its poetics. The scrupulous and nostalgic interest in the past that typifies that poetics, and Scott's novels, is moderated here by affectionate self-irony. Oldbuck is amusing from his first appearance, and it is a humorous sentence that introduces his and other people's learned occupations:[271] he is compared to Don Quixote as the first of bibliomaniacs.[272] With such a protagonist it is unlikely that the novel would be dominated by imagery of the venerable-regressive category.[273] Imagery of the magic-superstitious and of the precious-potential do appear: but the person listing macabre ingredients for spells is a charlatan, and the digging-up of a treasure at the bottom of a tomb is either an imposture or camouflaged charity.[274] And the sinister-terrifying is not even touched on when one character spends the night in a supposedly haunted chamber and dreams of seeing its ghost.[275] The novel is moderate in relation to all of our categories — thus suggesting that the complex of these categories should be considered as a whole. I would consider the description in the quotation as an example half-way between the threadbare-grotesque and the worn-realistic: the former — differing in this from Arnim's text, and opposite to Gogol's (II, 8) — tending to turn into the latter, through the verisimilitude and precision of the passage. Is there anything here to justify the introduction of new categories? The objects are treasured, and yet presented without being appreciated in the way a semi-positive category would require; while they are not decontextualized enough for their devaluation to suggest a new negative category. Oldbuck is scandalized with good reason, later in the novel, by incongruous modern combinations: "A monument of a knight-templar on each side of a Grecian porch, and a Madonna on the top of it!"[276]

34

The scandal produced by similar combinations is exploited in the narrative of one of the earliest of Balzac's original novels, *The Wild Ass's Skin* (*La Peau de chagrin*), published in 1831. The young Raphaël de Valentin, having lost his last sou in a gambling den, has resolved to throw himself into the Seine that night. In order to pass the time he enters the shop of an antique dealer. Here he will be given a talisman, the wild ass's skin that can fulfill any wish, but only while shrinking and shortening the possessor's life in proportion. The description of the shop is very long and passes through various stages: Raphaël gradually loses all sense of reality as the vision of the ancient and exotic wares turns into a hallucination. I will quote from the first phase, the first glimpse of the intricate imagery:

> At first glance, the storerooms offered him a confused picture, wherein all human and divine works jostled against each other. Stuffed crocodiles, monkeys, and boas seemed to smile on stained glass windows from churches, seemingly wanting to bite at busts, chase after lacquered furniture, or clamber up chandeliers. A Sèvres vase, on which Madame Jacotot had painted Napoleon, stood next to a sphinx dedicated to Sesostris. The beginning of the world was paired in grotesque fellowship with yesterday's events. A roasting-spit lay atop a monstrance, a Republican saber upon a medieval arquebus. Madame Dubarry portrayed in pastels by Latour, a star on her head, nude and on a cloud, appeared to be lustfully contemplating an Indian pipe, while trying to guess the use of the spirals winding towards her. Implements of death, poniards, curious pistols, trick weapons, were thrown together pell-mell with implements of life: porcelain soup bowls, Dresden dishes, diaphanous cups from China, ancient salt cellars, feudal comfit boxes. An ivory vessel navigated full sail upon the back of a motionless tortoise. A pneumatic machine put out one of Emperor Augustus's eyes, who remained majestically impassive. Various portraits of French aldermen, of Dutch burgomasters, indifferent now just as they had been in their lifetimes, were elevated above this chaos of antiquities, regarding it with a pale and cold look. Every country in the world seemed to have contributed some fragment of its science, some specimen of its art. It was a kind of philosophical dunghill where nothing was missing, neither the savage's peace pipe, nor the green and golden slipper of the seraglio, nor the Moor's yataghan, nor the Tartar's idol. There was even a soldier's tobacco pouch, even a priest's pyx, even the plumes from a throne.[277]

In this case it is not private and provincial obsession that crowds objects together, but urban and cosmopolitan commodification. No less than by their temporal and spatial heterogeneity, the exasperated decontextualization is produced by their present cramped jumble: there is no room for the cultural aura of any object, because all the other objects leave it no space. The ensemble of the other objects is the sole neighboring context allowed to each — just as happens verbally in a list of things, as I said at the beginning of this book (I, 1). Contiguity in fact, here and there in the quoted text, creates lists, either by making itself explicit: "stood next to," "lay atop," "were thrown together pell-mell"; or by stressing its contrasting group effects: "jostled against each other," "was paired." This same contiguity produces unwonted figures that animate the things, creating random connections amongst themselves, and absurd attitudes. The stuffed animals "seemed to" smile or to threaten to attack the furniture, Mme Dubarry "appeared" lustfully to observe an Indian pipe; without any verb of appearance, the ivory vessel "navigated full sail" upon the tortoise, the pneumatic machine "put out" the eye of Augustus. This kind of figure is worlds apart from the threadbare-grotesque of Scott's description. In the fantastic tone to which they contribute lies a certain amount of astonishment, if not of admiration: could this be the right moment to verify a new negative category, or a semipositive one? That authentic experiences are mediated by these objects is what further phases of Raphaël's contemplation will try to suggest.

In a second phase, it seems to his feverish eyes that the whole of Egypt rises from a single mummy, Greece from a statue, Indian religions from an idol, cavalry from a piece of Milanese armor, etc. In a third phase, staring at the objects, he personifies himself as a savage, a corsair, a monk, and so on.[278] Each object is metonymically or antonomastically evocative: a part capable on its own of furnishing the imagination with the relative historical and geographical whole — which, in its turn, can only be imagined if divided into selected parts, metonymies or antonomasies in the plural rather than in the singular. The mental journey through cheap recontextualizations, through false experiences generated by objects, is more arbitrary and make-believe, but not fundamentally different. And the distinction I made at the outset between nonfunctionality as the attribute of certain imagery in a text, and denial of the functionality of a text as a judgment of value on it (I, 5), may be applied to the concept of kitsch. If in the first phase Balzac intentionally represents objectified kitsch imagery, does he later unintentionally write bad kitsch literature? His unruly genius puts to the test the obviousness and rigor of the distinction, which however must be considered more indispensable than ever if we are to ensure coherent employment of the negative category. The beginning of the quoted passage admirably reveals the virtual contradictions of any display of decontextualized objects, with their offer of unwonted experiences. Immediately after, it is as if the very understanding of the phenomenon favored the involuntary production of such experiences; they are taken seriously in brief, intense doses, but through means that are all the more conventional.

While waiting for the appearance à la Hoffmann of the old shopkeeper, after a last stage of visual delirium on the part of Raphaël, the presumptive suicide,[279] the author prepares us for the arrival of the supernatural. But Balzac is no Hoffmann; and he is not wrong in declaring that such an arrival "must have been impossible" in Paris, on the quai Voltaire, in the nineteenth century — when "we believe only in the curlicued signatures of notaries."[280] I do not intend to doubt the literary status of the supernatural in the many masterpieces which will figure among the *Philosophical Studies* (*Études philosophiques*). But *The Wild Ass's Skin* is not a mature masterpiece, and neither the sinister-terrifying nor the magic-superstitious element dominates in the extraordinary impure example I have quoted. What is truly a wonder in it is the modern world, with its spatially and temporally all-encompassing imperialism and historicism: objects from around the globe and from every epoch are found in the wares on sale in the shop. Not one of the objects, stripped of its aura, is a worthy medium for the venerable-regressive model. I would rather say that, of the categories defined so far, the one with which the new categories are most contaminated is a secularized solemn-admonitory. Everything ends by being metahistorically annulled, in the sum of objects described as "a kind of philosophical dunghill where nothing was missing." And in the last sentence of the paragraph before the quoted passage, it is said that Raphaël "was about to see in advance the bones of twenty worlds";[281] the cadaver- and excrement-referents mark the configuration of all these commodities as anticommodities. Balzac has nonetheless been very helpful to us, and not indirectly as Scott was, in completing the definitions of the new categories, though not in documenting them. For this we will have to turn to a period that comes sometime after our historical turning point.

35

The four novels of Anatole France's (1844–1924) series, *Contemporary History* (*Histoire contemporaine*), were published from 1897 to 1901 — by no means an unworthy conclusion of the century and its narrative tradition. The unity of the first three novels is ensured, both by the unforgettable character of Bergeret, as well as by a relaxed pace reminiscent of a provincial chronicle of current events; the closest thing to a plot is the scheming that leads, at the end of the third novel, to the ascension to the bishopric of the Abbé Guitrel. In *The Elm-Tree on the Mall* (*L'Orme du mail*), the first of the series, the contrast between this astute, unctuous, and likeable priest and his uncompromising superior, Lantaigne, turns into a competition to establish the most comical and even the most sympathetic of the two characters. One of the most indignant accusations Lantaigne hurls at Guitrel has to do with the latter's semi-clandestine acquaintance with the prefect, a Jew, freethinker, and mason. In a detailed political background, on the eve of the Dreyfus affair, the ambitions of the priest and of the functionary of the Republic converge in a hard-won spirit of conciliation, aided by the social and psychological background of the prefect and his wife. In his intimate friendship with a French cleric, Worms-Clavelin "was himself gallicized, naturalized, stripped of the heavy remnants of his Germany and his Asia"; it is for him both vindicating and flattering.[282] And for his wife, who comes from poor Jewish origins, Guitrel's kindness is her great opportunity to satisfy a longing for a certain category of objects which has lasted since her youth:

> She confided to him that she had a passion for curios, that she ran mad for brocades, printed velvets, ornamental vestments, embroidery, and lace. She admitted to a covetousness which had accumulated in her soul since the time when she lingered in her youthful poverty before the shop windows of the second-hand dealers, in the Bréda neighborhood. She told him that she dreamed of a drawing-room with old copes and old chasubles, and that she was also on the lookout for antique jewelry.
>
> He answered that priestly vestments indeed offered precious models for artists, and that was proof that the Church was not the enemy of the arts.
>
> From this day, M. Guitrel hunted down sumptuous antiques in rural sacristies, and a week never passed without him bringing to Rondonneau the younger, under his padded overcoat, some chasuble or cope adroitly carried off from an innocent curate. M. Guitrel was however very careful in restoring to the despoiled vestries the hundred-sou coins with which the prefect paid for the silk, the brocade, the velvet, and the lace.
>
> In six months, Madame Worms-Clavelin's drawing-room became like a cathedral treasury, and a slow-moving odor of incense lingered there.[283]

In answering that the Church is not the enemy of the arts, Guitrel may be unaware that he is reducing to a litotes—a full century later—Chateaubriand's thesis in the *Genius of Christianity* (IV, 2). But the "sumptuous antiques" which he hunts down certainly are not imagery of the venerable-regressive, they are not worthy exemplars for religious or conservative propaganda. Otherwise the abbé would not be practicing a modern, moderate form of simony as he does, despite his scrupulously paying back the small amount of money — and despite the clerical intolerance that he disguises until the about-face of his first pastoral letter, in which among other matters he threatens with excommunication anyone who buys or sells sacred objects.[284] The exemplarity of these antiques is no longer ideological or compelling: it perpetuates itself only in the apparent harmlessness of the ornamental. As such the passage of time to which they have been subjected makes them incomparably suitable for the task of distinguishing and dignifying a drawing-room of the newly arrived. The measure of this is the passionate language in which the obsession of the prefect's wife, neé Noémi Coblentz, is expressed; and in the last sentence quoted, the comparison with a cathedral treasury and the odor of incense, hyperbolic and ironic, provide the measure of her little triumph. The terrible abbé Lantaigne had proven his naïveté by writing to the archbishop that the lady collected sacred objects, "although Jewish."[285] It would have been more correct to write, "*because* Jewish." Her preference for sacred rather than profane antiques depends on this, and in the two following novels we will see her in ecstasy because her daughter is to be educated in Paris by the Ladies of the Precious Blood.[286] If by the end of the century the bourgeois was still yesterday's outcast, and felt that its present privileges were precarious in a society stripped of any hereditary assurances, the Jew was, in a sense, the bourgeois par excellence: more of an outcast yesterday, more precarious today.

The formidable inventiveness of the bourgeoisie in the fields of science, technology, and practical functionality over the two or three centuries of its rise is well known. But this praise does not apply, once the rise was completed, to the field of symbolic prestige and aesthetic ornamentation — exactly the field in which the objects of the two categories which still remain to be defined aspire to refunctionalize themselves as best they can. Why does Mme Worms-Clavelin, all things considered, appear to be successful in her attempt? In the field under discussion, the nineteenth-century bourgeoisie had been essentially imitative. It did not even try to provide itself with new models, insisting on keeping to historical models borrowed from the two privileged estates of the *ancien régime*, the nobility and the clergy. Authentically belonging to this latter model, coming straight from rural vestries under a priest's overcoat, the acquisitions of the prefect's wife are homogeneous and are decontextualized only once. One of the examples in the second chapter allows us a multiple comparison, the acquisitions of Roth's orchestra conductor (II, 5). These too were ecclesiastical, but drawn from many different religions, and thus provoking a proportionately greater irony. They too had been acquired at a very low price; and yet, they served an equally successful decorative purpose. Searching for the best opposition between a semipositive category and a negative one, the positivity of the result cannot but appear even more relevant than the singularity or plurality of decontextualization. Let us put the constants between the two texts before the variants; only one other constant seems to me important enough to justify this first one: success. Both the Worms-Clavelins with the help of Guitrel, and the brother and sister-in-law of Franz Tunda, in decorating their houses, seem to have known completely what they were doing. Whether one or more than one, the decontextualizations of objects are equally intelligible for the characters as for the author and reader: here, despite the irony, there is no disparity between levels of awareness within the two texts.

36

Conversely, I perceived precisely such a disparity in two other examples quoted in the second chapter, Gozzano's poem and Flaubert's story, and had distinguished the character's point of view from that of the author (II, 4, 7). The negative judgment of value or taste passed on certain objects, I said then, is the judgment of the author in contrast to the presumable judgment of the characters. The tenderness with which those objects are charged by the poetical "I" of Gozzano and the protagonist maid of Flaubert, we are now in a position to say, contaminates the as yet undefined negative category, in both instances, with the reminiscent-affective. It will, then, be worthwhile to look for purer examples again in Flaubert, if it is true that his work views the modern world as the irremediable decontextualization of everything. Even when it is set in the ancient world: in *The Temptation of St. Anthony* (*La Tentation de Saint Antoine*), the chaotic cultural syncretism of the late Roman Empire is the most legitimate projection of an all-encompassing colonialism and historicism, and of the consequent devaluation of any authentic uniqueness. And in *Madame Bovary* (1856), at the time of Emma's wedding, a similar devaluation dealing with the dimensions of the known world and of the transmission of the past is projected within the dimensions of a wedding-cake, even a three-layer one:

> They had been to Yvetot to find a confectioner for the cakes and nougats. Since this was his debut in the town, he had taken care of things; and for the dessert course he himself brought in, a layered cake that fetched cries of applause. At the base, first of all, there was a blue square of cardboard reproducing a temple with porticoes, colonnades, and stucco statues all around in niches surrounded by golden paper stars; on the second layer there was a castle tower of Savoy cake, surrounded by minute fortifications in angelica, almonds, raisins, orange quarters; and finally, on the uppermost platform, which was a green meadow with rocks and lakes of jam and nutshell boats, there was a cupid swinging on a chocolate swing, the two poles of which were surmounted by two natural, ball-shaped rose-buds.[287]

In their detailed description, these confectionery images must doubtlessly belong to a negative category. This is due to the vague cultural allusions they display, mixed with the gluttonous appeal of the cake. The most ephemeral of decontextualizations, the edible one, eclipses the heterogeneity of references contained on each layer of the cake. The cardboard temple with its porticoes,

colonnades, and statuettes has a Greek flavor; but the golden stars are somewhat reminiscent of the Three Wise Men. The tower, with its delicious fortifications, smacks of the medieval. The landscape with rocks and jam lakes has an
alpine and pre-Romantic flavor (cf. IV, 29), but the cupid, although on a swing,
seems Greek. An instance of decontextualization is in a way measurable if we
count the number of cultures it includes, and establish how compatible they are
with each other, how compatible with the context into which they are set, and
how conventional are the elements that represent them. I mentioned colonialism, as well as historicism: the references of the cake, disparate and banal by all
the above-mentioned criteria, are all European. A few pages later in the novel,
the retrospective chapter on Emma's education opens with the colonial dream
of the loves of Paul and Virginie, which she read before the age of thirteen. Later
on come the evening readings in the convent — where on Sundays, "for recre-
ation," passages from the *Genius of Christianity* were read aloud. The reactions of the pupil to the book in which the apology for eternal truths had
become an apology for the past, history as melancholy, are expressed in a
musical sentence à la Chateaubriand. After the first popular novels, she is
captured by Walter Scott, and becomes enamored of "things historical."

Not really of material things so much as of characters, eminently decontextualized: a few illustrious or unfortunate women who "detached themselves
like comets from the dark immensity of history, in which here and there also
stood out, but more lost in shadow and without any relationship between
them," a few preeminent males, august or cruel.[288] In their effigies, St. Louis is
not lacking his oak, nor Henry IV his plumes. But, compared to what we were
led to believe of Balzac's Raphaël de Valentin, Emma is far too little educated to
fall as he did into an illusion, albeit presumably a facile one: the illusion of retracing a cultural whole from an evocative attribute, a part. Heroes and hero-
ines shine out, completely unrelated, in the darkness of an ignorance as immense as history. From the lack of context to the false context it is but a step:
and the scrapbooks of her school friends are decorated with tissue-covered engravings that the author's voice dwells on, transcribing the imagery into words.
Those that actually deserve to be personified and addressed, in the long last
sentence of the next quotation, are, first, the conventional features of an Orient
fashionable in the 1820s; then the landscapes of countries that an adjective such
as "dithyrambic" projects towards and away from every possible context:

> And you were there too, sultans with long pipes, enraptured in your bowers in
> the arms of temple dancers, giaours, Turkish sabers, Greek caps, and espe-
> cially you, pallid landscapes of dithyrambic countries, that often show us all
> at once palms and fir trees, tigers to the right, a lion on the left, Tartar
> minarets on the horizon, in the foreground Roman ruins and then some
> crouching camels; all framed by a well-cleaned virgin forest, and with a great

perpendicular ray of sun glittering in the water, on which stand out like white scratches on a steel-gray background, more or less distant, gliding swans.[289]

And yet these depictions are of sophisticated urban provenance in the eyes of Emma, who will become something of a provincial intellectual *manquée*. Flaubert does not greatly distinguish between the provinces and Paris when it comes to the effective diffusion of the phenomenon later known as kitsch, as *A Sentimental Education* (*L'Éducation sentimentale*) attests. It is in her subjective acceptance, in the tendency to take the pretentious literally and to flatter herself with the fictitious, that the provincial woman appears most alone and defenseless. The irony of the quoted sentence implies her point of view. She is the first one not to notice that a landscape cannot contain palms and fir trees, Tartar minarets and Roman ruins, framed by a virgin forest with tigers, lions, and camels all at once. The contiguity of heterogeneous objects, incompatible in space and time, was casual and verisimilar in Balzac's antique store. Here it is as artificial as the cake; and it feeds a sentimentality greedy not for sweets, but for naïve suggestions equivalent to promises. Emma has understood all her education as a series of promises of general happiness. Luxury in which social elevation should be disguised as Romanticism come true seems to her the indispensable background of love.[290] When she is certain of being about to escape with her first lover, the travels and sojourns she fantasizes about repeat the evanescence and the miscellaneousness of her early models.[291] Around her, on the other hand, only the meek and contented mediocrity of her husband, along with all that is most retrograde and resigned in provincial life, succeeds in keeping itself below or this side of kitsch. Rodolphe dilutes a measure of the vulgar reminiscent-affective with kitsch, when he is about to abandon Emma, with his letters and pledges of love crammed into an old cookie can;[292] Homais experiments with it through his cultural ambitions, when he takes charge of the plan for her tomb, which he successively comes to conceive as a temple of Vesta and then a mass of ruins.[293] As for her, she has died of it.

With her trustfulness that is not innocent, with her appeal for sympathy as a tragic character, Madame Bovary is a borderline case — one that may help us dispel residual doubts concerning our opposition between the imagery of valuable and worthless artefacts, between valid and counterfeit connections, between authentic and imposed impressions. Her destiny and her trap is precisely the fact that these impressions lack authenticity. This is not altered by the fact that her desire and her disillusionment are authentic and deeply felt. To establish *a priori* a connection between these two facts it is sufficient that she be passive and unprepared in relation to these impressions. The reader is expected to forgive her because she knows not what she does, in the words of the Gospel. There is no need to forgive the prefect's wife of Anatole France — a much less prominent character—for her social climbing, which delights us; but the tragic or comic quality of the character to whom the artifacts are destined does not determine the presentation of these artifacts. It is a coincidence or divergence between two points of view, a unity of, or disparity between two levels of cultural and aesthetic awareness—where the character appears, either as an equal or as a nonequal, subordinate to the author. And this to the point that the character is not theoretically indispensable, though indispensable—or nearly so—in practice, in order to create divergence and disparity, that is, in order that the points of view and levels of awareness be double. If the wedding cake is not set in direct relation to Emma, there is the whole table of country guests that welcomes the cake with cries of admiration, there is the confectioner who wants to do his best for his town debut. Of course the measure of decontextualization must be taken into account: the more excessive it is, the less the chance that the author will assent to it. What is exceptional in the impure example drawn from Balzac is that the author does assent to it, not at all that a contamination between the opposite categories derives from it (rather than a commutation). The irony of the examples drawn from Anatole France, and even more of those from Roth, although in fact it is at the expense of the characters and not of the objects in themselves, contaminates to some extent the semipositive category with the negative: purer examples of the former may be found.

In the last terminal opposition of the semantic tree, I will write *chosen evocations* at one end and *naïve evocations* at the other. The two adjectives can be taken to mean not simply the awareness or lack of awareness of a character. They may also signify the possible imaginary success or lack of it that the objects achieve. In the names I give to the categories, all four adjectives come from a tested vocabulary:

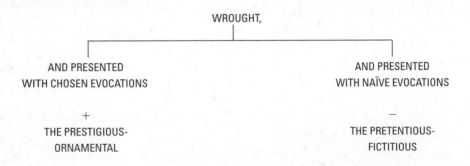

Any reader desiring to peruse the whole of the semantic tree just now completed will find it at the end of this chapter. This information is given only as a formality: it is unlikely that any readers will have waited till now to look at the diagram of the semantic tree — if they have taken an interest in the classifying operation, and have taken half-seriously and half-jokingly the precision of this belated structuralist exercise. It is no less likely that others have instead followed me up to this point in spite of a certain boredom — being interested only in the subject of the inquiry, and in the multiple game of the anthology of texts.

37

Two more examples of the prestigious-ornamental and two of the pretentious-fictitious will be presented alternately, rather than successively as their predecessors were. We know that these categories contain one further and more concrete constant beyond the feature of wrought corporality which is their last shared element in the semantic tree. This is constituted by the phenomenon of de- and recontextualization of objects and complicated by issues that are not exclusively literary, so much so that I almost despaired, in making my way through these complications, of reaching a merely thematic opposition of categories as we found for the other instances. To find the right opposition in accord with the impressions derived from my reading, and to protect it from perpetual contaminations, I therefore directed my search towards a distinction closer to formal narratological categories than the others. The equal degree of awareness in a character and its author concerning the choice of objects and connected impressions defines the prestigious-ornamental. It finds its definitive version, valid for all fin de siècle literature, in 1884 in a paradigmatic and almost encyclopedic text. I am speaking, as one might expect, of the novel by Joris-Karl Huysmans (1848–1907) *Against Nature* (*À rebours*). The young Duke of Floressas, des Esseintes, in the first place an aristocrat but also an intellectual, would have been able to save himself the trouble of choosing his ideas and his objects, by doing almost the reverse, namely inheriting them. Instead he despises his class as reactionary and reduced to imbecility, sells his castle with no regrets, and also "rids himself" of his antique furniture. He buys a "hovel" on the outskirts of Paris, in a secluded location;[294] he has decided to retire there all alone, camouflaging the servants that he cannot do without. This will be the freely chosen shelter, the theater without an audience, for the experiences of an absolute individualist aestheticism. The requisite furniture, rather than be a mere background congenial to the originality of such experiences, will be a part of it. These experiences will be continually formed, from room to room, by the furniture itself.

Of course, even more than in des Esseintes' contempt for the aristocracy, it is in his scorn for the bourgeoisie that the abusive rhetoric typical of right-wing

French authors ever since is most lavishly deployed.[295] And yet his decision to choose instead of inherit is nothing but a repetition from on high of bourgeois practice of borrowing feudal and clerical models: as if in drawing from these with the hand of a connoisseur, but never at first hand—he who could easily have done so—he were imitating imitation, presuming to outdo them by attaining the incomparable. Or as if, with respect to other imported models, as well as to the very functional inventiveness of the new class, he were appropriating the spirit of appropriation and reinventing the spirit of invention. The neurotic aesthete, who shuns the oriental carpets by now accessible to the nouveaux riches,[296] appears to foresee that paradox of modern democracy that squanders all prestige in a descending spiral. The more a model has the appearance of rarity, the more distinguished it appears, but at the same time the more attractive it will be, and hence the more in danger of losing its rarity. Whoever tries to overcome the paradox by raising the level of artifice is mistaken, not in thinking he is the first, but in thinking he will be the last to do so. Baudelaire had inverted the positive and negative ideological signs in favor of artifice and to the disadvantage of nature. His disciple goes further and rejects even tradition, ascribing it to nature—which "has had its day" and is by now reproducible at will. Just as there are no natural landscapes in the novel, there is also no imagery of the venerable-regressive, and the prestigious-ornamental imagery is always part of the exaltation of artifice. It goes from false flowers imitating real ones, and real ones imitating false ones, to the famous "mouth organ" which mixes liquors and flavors like musical timbres; or, trespassing into the most advanced functionality, it makes idols of speedy and powerful locomotives.[297]

The novel's division into chapters makes each one coincide with one or more distinct experiences. That is, it follows the method that Zola, the progressive founder of Naturalism, adopted in his novels: documentary and specialized, it pays tribute in its form to a strict social division of labor. Excepting the vicissitudes of his illness, in which nature comes back into her own and which determine the ending, nothing *happens* to des Esseintes. All that he lives through is either planned or caused by him—with an unresting experimentalism that does little to favor static descriptions. The most literarily evident imagery is of studied effects, of objects that the character has had made. First of all is his own study, at the end of the first chapter:

> Regarding furniture, des Esseintes did not have to make long searches, since the only luxuries in this apartment were to consist of books and rare flowers; he confined himself—intending at a later date to decorate the bare walls with a few drawings or paintings—to setting up ebony shelves and bookcases along the greater part of the walls, covering the floors with skins of wild beasts and furs of blue fox, installing, next to a massive fifteenth-century

money changer's desk, deep armchairs with headrests and an old chapel desk, in wrought iron, one of those antique lecterns on which the deacon once used to place his antiphoner and which now supported one of the heavy folios of Du Cange's *Glossarium mediae et infimae latinitatis.*

The cracked, bluish glass of the windows, studded with bottle-ends with gold-speckled protuberances, blocked the view of the countryside and allowed only a faint light to penetrate. The windows themselves were covered with curtains cut from old stoles, the dark and almost smoky gold of which was smothered by the almost deathly reddish-brown texture.

Finally, on the fireplace, which was itself covered by the sumptuous fabric of a Florentine dalmatic, between two Byzantine monstrances from the ancient Abbaye-au-Bois of Bièvre in gilded copper, was a wonderful triptych divided into separate compartments, wrought like lacework, that held under the glass of its frame, copied on real parchment in marvelous missal letters with splendid illuminations, three poems by Baudelaire. . . .[298]

The clerical component dominates, but the reason that it is more decontextualized with respect to the prefect's drawing room in Anatole France's novel is not simply that it has in its vicinity a money changer's desk, or because it has been turned into a container for profane poetry. It has been tampered with: curtains cut out of stoles, a fireplace covering out of a dalmatic. The controlled practice of decontextualization takes the form of one selection after the other; the vocabulary reflects this, and elsewhere—for instance in the catalogue of kinds of type founts, the quality of the paper and the binding materials of the library[299]—it can be technically much richer. But the implied relationship with Catholicism as an institution is familiar, almost that of a master to one of his household, rather than foreign and that of a despoiling conqueror. This is the only inheritance which des Esseintes is reluctant to repudiate; on the other hand, religion itself, as a sum of sublimations, may contain much that is artificial. In a chapter devoted to it, among memories of faith instilled by the Jesuits and learned questions of theology, he will praise the Church as preserver of exquisitely formed objects over the centuries—without mentioning Chateaubriand. He will ask himself whether to privately own such objects is to commit a sacrilege, but finds pleasure in the idea that it might be so.[300] The bookstand holds the greatest glossary of late Latinity, the triptych holds the most admired modern author. These are anticipations of chapter III, and of chapters XII and XIV: the former devoted to his predilection for the artificiality of the so-called decadence of Latin literature, the latter to his preferences among French authors which have in common a frequently precocious anticonformism. The glass of the windows blocks out the exterior, sealing off that ultimately incredible thing, namely, an interior ordered "for his own personal enjoyment and not to impress others."[301] As alone in his house as Robinson on his island or Aschenbach in Venice (if not as Dracula in his coffin), like the first des Esseintes will finally escape, but under compulsion and in despair; and like the second he will finally succumb to his own contradictions, but without dying at the right time. The tortoise he had armored with gold and precious stones has died in his place, unable to sustain the exorbitant, glittering weight of artifice.[302]

A house that continuously celebrates the idealization of an ego may be directed as a message, not to the ego itself as its mirror, nor even to others in general, but to a single special recipient. This is what marks the difference between des Esseintes and *The Great Gatsby,* hero of the novel published by Francis Scott Fitzgerald (1896–1940) in 1925 — apart from all the other differences consequent to the crossing of an ocean and the experience of a world war. America does not have, except indirectly, an aristocratic and Catholic past: the imitation of old social classes by the new class is translated into the imitation of the old continent on the soil of the new one. The first-person narrator, the young stockbroker Nick, doesn't know Gatsby personally at the beginning of the book. He is his neighbor on Long Island; and Gatsby's residence appears to him as "a colossal affair by any standard — it was a factual imitation of some Hôtel de Ville in Normandy, with a tower on one side, spanking new under a thin beard of raw ivy. . . ."[303] On one occasion, halfway through the novel, the narrator can do nothing but stare at the house for a full half-hour, and he relates its origin. An excess of the antiquarian mania of ten years earlier, the "feudal silhouette" of the house was the focus of a mimetic and anachronistic dream that is more than architectural: it had been built by a brewer, who had offered to pay five years' taxes for all his neighbors if they would let the roofs of their houses be thatched.[304] When the narrator, at the end of the novel, takes a third and last glimpse of the edifice, defining it as "that huge incoherent failure of a house,"[305] he is well acquainted with its interior and its owner. The latter keeps open house day and night for anyone, with or without invitation, for whoever will offer "the subtle tribute of knowing nothing whatever about him."[306] The sumptuousness of the buffet, bar, and orchestra at his receptions is astounding, just like the parade of well-known actors, sports stars, and jazz musicians.

On his first visit, the narrator is accompanied by the golf player Jordan Baker who will introduce him to the owner of the house:

> On a chance we tried an important-looking door, and walked into a high Gothic library, panelled with carved English Oak, and probably transported complete from some ruin overseas.
>
> A stout, middle-aged man, with enormous owl-eyed spectacles, was sitting

somewhat drunk on the edge of a great table, staring with unsteady concentration at the shelves of books. As we entered he wheeled excitedly around and examined Jordan from head to foot.

"What do you think?" he demanded impetuously.

"About what?"

He waved his hand toward the book-shelves.

"About that. As a matter of fact you needn't bother to ascertain. I ascertained. They're real."

"The books?"

He nodded.

"Absolutely real—have pages and everything. I thought they'd be a nice durable cardboard. Matter of fact, they're absolutely real. Pages and—Here! Lemme show you."

Taking our scepticism for granted, he rushed to the bookcases and returned with Volume One of the *Stoddard Lectures*.

"See!" he cried triumphantly. "It's a bona-fide piece of printed matter. It fooled me. This fella's a regular Belasco. It's a triumph. What thoroughness! What realism! Knew when to stop, too—didn't cut the pages. But what do you want? What do you expect?"

He snatched the book from me and replaced it hastily on its shelf, muttering that if one book was removed the whole library was liable to collapse.[307]

Gratitude is not common among Gatsby's too numerous guests: the bespectacled man, later called Owl-eyes, who has been drunk for a week, has a curious way of showing his own. He is insistently admiring, and provides firsthand proof of the authenticity of what, before assuring himself of it, he had considered false. A reversible judgment: the library, with its real—not cardboard—books by American authors, makes the smooth inauthenticity of a millionaire's acquisition authentic. It has been "transported *complete* from some ruin overseas" (from "Merton College" as Gatsby will say),[308] and the adjective which ensures an imposing recontextualization stresses the immensity of the decontextualization. Gatsby's awareness of this is certainly inferior to the narrator's, and still more inferior to the author's. Possibly inferior also to that of Owl-eyes, whose enthusiasm could be suspected of irony if he were not drunk—and who treats as untouchable, because he believes it to be fragile, the compactness of the whole structure. In any case, the issue of authenticity he raises appears to me to have a latent symbolic relationship with the protagonist; and with the moral subject of the novel. The past of the thirty-year-old who has risen from nothing, about whom his guests exchange fanciful calumnies, includes a childhood regulated by a self-discipline à la Benjamin Franklin[309] and a long involvement in the higher spheres of criminality. For his aged father, the house is less real than an old photograph of it, dirtied by much handling.[310] For Gatsby himself, it is an irreplaceable means to an end pursued for five years. Daisy was the first high-class girl he had met, and had possessed. He had never entered a house as beautiful as hers: she made it mysterious, and fragrant "of this year's shining motor-cars and of dances whose flowers were scarcely withered." Even before leaving for the war, and before Daisy married a man of her own class, she had appeared to vanish above him "into her rich house."[311]

"He wants her to see his house":[312] this is his desire, now that his house is the most magnificent, and that frustration and faithfulness may be rewarded at the same time. He inspects it and turns on the lights in the whole building, from the tower to the cellar, before Daisy's visit. He can finally ask her, "Do you like it?"; he can guide her "through Marie Antoinette music-rooms and Restoration Salons"; watch her combing her hair with a golden brush, and see her burst into tears before the magnificence of a pile of men's shirts; he can reevaluate everything on the basis of her eyes' response.[313] The reception in which Daisy participates is therefore the last one. All that is left is "a desolate path of fruits and rinds and discarded favors and crushed flowers."[314] The night of the disaster, the house appears larger than ever to the narrator, and inexplicably dusty and deteriorated.[315] Here the pretentious-fictitious is the ephemeral product of a will to seduce that stems from humble origins, from an insecure class identity. There is no trace of this category in the house where Daisy lives with her husband Tom—a character who stands out with his athlete's arrogance and his shameless respectability;[316] Gatsby should not have discovered so late that her voice sounds "full of money."[317] And in Gatsby's murder, to which another indirect victim of Daisy and Tom is driven, the joint responsibility of husband and wife forms a tangle of reticence and intentions that cannot be punished. Their moneyed and criminal lack of substance is made retroactive along a chain of proxies that descends all the way to them from the author, who leaves the story to the narrator, who is fascinated by Gatsby, who is drawn towards Daisy. If the narrator is not wrong in shouting to Gatsby, at parting, that he is the best of them, he is wrong nonetheless in giving Gatsby credit, in his "corruption," for an "incorruptible dream."[318] In the general absence of mourners at Gatsby's funeral, the only other grateful presence is the unexpected Owl-eyes;[319] and in the far more gigantic spectacles of an oculist's billboard dominating the freeway and the wilderness, inauthentic eyes without a face appear to Gatsby's imminent murderer to be the authentic eyes of God.[320]

38

Also in the case of a work much greater in size than any other mentioned so far, the protagonist is introduced to the reader through his place of residence, in *The Man Without Qualities* (*Der Mann ohne Eigenschaften*) by Robert Musil (1880–1942). In the first part of this great unfinished novel, published in 1930, all the short chapters from the second through the fifth are devoted to this subject; the title of the second is *House and Home of the Man Without Qualities.* After a few sentences, as in the grammatical order of the title, the building precedes its dweller in the description of the exterior:

> It was a partially preserved garden of the eighteenth or even the seventeenth century, and as one passed before the wrought-iron gate, one glimpsed through the trees, on a carefully mown lawn, something like a small mansion with two short wings, a love nest or hunting lodge in past times. To be precise, the main structure dated to the seventeenth century, the park and the top floor had an eighteenth-century look, the façade was renovated and slightly ruined in the nineteenth century, altogether it had a slightly disconnected appearance, as of images photographed one on top of the other. And yet it was of such a kind that inevitably one stopped short before it, and said, "Ah!" And when the windows of the white, charming, beautiful edifice were open, one glimpsed the genteel peace of a scholar's residence, its walls lined with books.
> This house and this home belonged to the man without qualities.[321]

What the metaphor of the superimposed photographs both fixes and agitates is the mutual decontextualization taking place between three layers of architecture — but all three of them local styles, in temporal and linear diachrony, despite some deterioration in the last layer. The composite effect is extravagant and fascinating. It may symbolically refer less to the character of Ulrich than to his country: that imperial-royal and Austro-Hungarian *Kakanien*, whose mild contradictions and conciliatory estrangements will be nostalgically enumerated in the following chapter.[322] Later in the novel Count Leinsdorf, promoter of the "Parallel Action" which was intended to celebrate in 1918 the seventy years of Francis Joseph's reign, will be introduced to us in his family palace. A famous palace, as we are told with another metaphor, because it "stretches the skin" of a small country mansion over the framework of a bourgeois townhouse[323] — while the Prussian, Jewish, and cosmopolitan capitalist Arnheim owns here an ultramodern villa and there a dilapidated castle.[324] The wisdom taken as characteristic of the former Austrian Empire does indeed include a sense of reality, but a reality which is seen as less necessary, or is tolerated as more accidental than elsewhere. Therefore it also includes its contrary, which in the only nonnarrative chapter of this initial series is revealed as "the sense of possibilities."[325] And it is this that will create a contrast between Ulrich and his father, precisely regarding the house. The aged jurist, loyal and beloved counselor of the nobility, is horrified that his son should take possession of "an edifice which, albeit in the diminutive, cannot be called other than a mansion."[326] This is what he has spent his life avoiding— an attempted leap into the upper class; while he is right in positive, nineteenth-century terms, he misunderstands a choice where very little is positive.

Exiled in his youth for having put his patriotism in question in a writing exercise, Ulrich returns in his thirties to ascertain skeptically whether his fatherland makes thought "firm in its roots and true to its soil."[327] "Only out of arrogance and because he abhorred common dwellings" has he rented the castle, not as a historically layered space, but as having been excluded from history: having lost its function as a summer residence, overtaken by urban growth, it has remained neglected, devalued, and uninhabited. The difficulty is in connecting it to present needs,[328] and not simply financially or practically. Ulrich "had placed himself in the pleasant position of having to rearrange his neglected little property from the bottom up to his own liking."[329] This is the year 1913, and the freedom that encumbers him is not simply that of an individual both wealthy and single. It is an incomparably more extended cultural freedom than that practiced by des Esseintes thirty years earlier. "From faithful reproduction to absolute license," "from the Assyrians to Cubism," by now "all" principles and styles are conceivable and available; of all trustworthy conventions none survives. "What should he choose?" The excess of history is equal to a total lack: a tabula rasa opens before the question mark. That it becomes an issue of identity is revealed to Ulrich by a variant of a well-known proverb he reads in art journals, "tell me where you live in and I will tell you who you are." Words which sound to his ears like threats, where the pleasure of choice becomes the disquiet of "responsibility." It is his "good fortune" that three different styles preexist one on top of the other in the mansion, creating a limit to enterprise. In the space of a few lines his surrender is already taken for granted, with his decision to take into his own hands the "building of his personality" by planning by himself the future furnishing of the dwelling. Each concrete proposal he makes can be perfectly substituted by another: "and he started to dream, instead of making decisions."

It is the "disconnection of ideas and their spreading without a central nucleus" which defines "the present."[330] But such a result had been prepared throughout the nineteenth century; we have seen in the imagery of objects how Balzac had intuited it, how Flaubert had known it. At the end of the century it had been critically emphasized by Ulrich's and Musil's master, Nietzsche (although the blame was attributed by him to democracy and the mixture of races).[331] Ulrich rediscovers a wisdom which his father would have expressed by taking the excess of liberty as his point of departure for predicting an inevitable confusion; while he, on the contrary, as his point of departure admits the need for convention, by opposing which one can arrive at something worthwhile. So he ends by entrusting the furnishing of his residence to fashionable decorators. The very tasteful, aristocratic, and official result doesn't appear to concern him and leaves the issue of identity suspended: "He had returned from the moon and had immediately settled down again as if on the moon."[332] The subjective excess of awareness, adapted to the objective excess of history, makes the relinquishing of choice the only possible choice—and random actualities the only history. At this high degree of awareness, the equality between character and author is of a new kind. It is customary to compare Musil's enlargement of the literary genre, the integration of novel and essay, to Proust's: but in the first person employed by Proust, time and experience separate the first-person character from the first-person narrator. I will quote a single example—from chapter 34—to prove how much more the thinker Musil is concordant with his third-person character. Here a momentary metaphysical blurring of the lines composing the furniture of the residence, in the eyes of Ulrich—"I am merely fortuitous—sneers Necessity"—sets off a four-page essay on chance, modernity, and the generations, taking the form of meditations during his walk.[333]

We will include Ulrich's mansion in the prestigious-ornamental category, because the character is equal to a dominating authorial voice. As I have already mentioned, the presence of a character is not properly necessary in the pretentious-fictitious, but only a divergence of points of view and a disparity of levels (IV, 36). Consequently a dominating authorial voice like Musil's will be sufficient, if it be ironically composite rather than seriously unitary. This is the case of the narrative language of Carlo Emilio Gadda (1893–1973); *Acquainted with Grief* (*La cognizione del dolore*) is also an incomplete novel, published in decreasingly fragmentary form in 1938–41, in 1963, and in 1970. The premise of the almost continuous pluralism of the language is the avowed duality of the setting. The burlesqued South American Maradagál region is an extended figure allusive of the Brianza region, of Italy, and of a detailed autobiography; thus Spanish, more than all the languages and dialects of Italy, rightly intervenes in the discourse as well as in the names. Pirobutirro Villa has been only fleetingly mentioned when we read in the first chapter:

> With villas, with villas! with villettas, eight rooms double bath-rooms; with princely villas, forty rooms wide terrace on the lakes panoramic view of Serruchón—garden, orchard, garage, porter's lodge, tennis court, drinking

water, cesspool capacity over seven hundred hectoliters: [. . .]; with villas! with villulas! with large stuffed villas, with small isolated villas, with double villas, with villaesque houses, with rustic villas, with rustic villa outhouses, the Pastrufacian architects had bejeweled little by little almost all the graceful and placid hills of the pre-Andean slopes [. . .]. We will content ourselves [. . .] with pointing out how certain of the most noticeable of those poly-technical products, with a roof all eaves, and each eave all pointed, in the shape of ugly northern and glacial triangles, as if claiming the pretence of being a Swiss chalet, though continuing to roast in the vastness of the Ameri-can mid-August: [. . .] Other villulas, with their angles more outwardly projecting, rose straight, pretty oh so pretty, in a pseudo-Sienese or Pastrufa-cianally Norman turret, with a long black pole on top for the lightning-rod and the flag. Others still decorated with little cupolas and various pinnacles of the Russian type or almost, resembling upturned radishes or onions, with pantiled roofs and quite often polychrome, that is, scales of a carnivalesque reptile, half yellow and half sky-blue. So they had something of the pagoda and of the spinning mill, and were also halfway between the Alhambra and the Kremlin.

Because everything, everything!, had passed though the minds of the Pas-trufacian architects, possibly excepting the marks of Good Taste. Through there all styles had passed: the Humbert and the William and the neoclassic and the neo-neoclassic and the Empire and the Second Empire; Liberty, flow-ery, Corinthian, Pompeian, Anjou, Egyptian-Sommaruga and Coppedè-Alessi; and the candied chalk casinos of Biarritz and Ostend, the PLM and Fagnano Olona, Monte Carlo, Indianopolis, the Middle Ages, that is an easy-going Philip Maria arm in arm with the Caliph; and also Queen Victoria (of England), although she is slumped on a Turkish ottoman. And now the func-tional twentieth century was working on it. . . .[334]

Nothing warns us on first reading this page, with its enjoyably comical pitilessness, that the theme is in more than one place connected to the novel's latent tragic one. One of the villas is the residence of Don Gonzalo Pirobutirro and of his aged mother, to whom the bachelor is linked by a jealous, obstinate, choleric rancor which does not spare the memory of his father the marquis. The rancor reaches the point that the disproportion between violence and its apparent causes implies in particular the Freudian concept of displacement, and in general the likelihood of oedipal elements at work, as unconscious for the character as they are conscious for the author. Only the mother, when she is alone, is entitled to a language anything but comical, and the chapter begins: "She wandered, alone, in the house"; thus, when the son tells of a dream that has terrified him, this takes place in "our deserted house"[335] — as if *house* were the tragic variant of *villa*. The lonely mother, who absurdly "barricaded her-

self in the house every evening," with "the most varied and unexpected furnishings," which are listed more than once,[336] is found murdered in the end.
This denouement is announced from the start by the insistence on the unde-
fended position of the villa, which also has aspects of decay and physical
deficiency: the gate "with wooden bars, half rotten," the wall "crooked, all
lumps," "dwarfish and donkey-like."[337] But these also possess moral aspects,
symbolizing in turn the rupture between parents and son. It is because of his
"faith in the people," whom the son hates, that the father did not worry about
bolts and the wall; the greatest reproach to his mother is that she keeps the
villa open for the first-comer, on whom to "fawn with goodness." If she is
willing to do "anything, so long as it is for others," her son has reasons more
than legal for furiously claiming "possession: the sacrosanct private superpri-
vate mine, mine!"[338] The comparison he makes is not casual, between himself
as the "poor effect" of his male ancestry and an "unexpected curbstone":
which "is, among the surviving walls, a residue of forgotten motives."[339]

On the only occasion when the two are alone together, the mother must
prepare his dinner "as proof of the functional validity of the villa." Or else the
villa itself would be damned with curses, together with his father the builder,
and with "all the infinite villas of Serruchón." Conversely, ever since her youth
and for forty years, the "idea of the villa, a Matrix idea," had been her pride
and comfort "consubstantial with her guts," even before the "objective
villa."[340] The word "villa" tends to be periodically repeated as a scarcely
varied leitmotiv (reiterated as at the beginning of the quoted page), and from
everyone's point of view,[341] thus also from that of the author. The antipathy of
the character for the building and for others similar to it could have very well
been justified aesthetically or culturally, since he is an engineer with a background in the humanities which allows him to read Plato and to write difficult
prose — just like Gadda himself. In reality his motives are always of a different
nature, too darkly violent to allow us to ascribe to him a conscious superiority
to the bourgeois ideals in which his mother shares. The authenticity of her
suffering character, on the other hand, is not diminished beyond the extent to
which the pretentious-fictitious in Flaubert diminishes Félicité's (II, 7). It is
impossible to say that in the quoted page the diverging points of view, the
disparity between levels which exposes them to bilious scorn, coincide with
and anticipate those of the son and the mother. The author is confronted with
no other characters than the architects — through whose heads (just as potentially through Ulrich's) "everything, everything!" has passed. Better still, what
is decisive is the game of pluralism of language, within which the decontextualization is shaped by the most disparate intertextuality.

Each of the many cultural references and linguistic and stylistic levels which are decontextualized by each other implicitly contains a point of view, set at a distance or ridiculed; and the pluralism of the language is mirrored in the plurality of architectural references, the content repeats its form. Both express a decentralized and mixed vision of modernity, in which there seems to be an updated version, almost a caricature, of Flaubert's. A note to one of the partial editions informs us that "the Kremlin-Alhambra-spinning-mill-pagoda exists in actual reality" in the province of Novara; and yet it could easily be drawn from *A Sentimental Education* — where a ballroom named the Alhambra has Moorish galleries, a Gothic cloister, a Chinese roof, Venetian lanterns, Hebes, and cupids.[342] What is typical of Gadda is that the polyglot and metaliterary tendency, through a deeper corrosion, precipitates the pretentious-fictitious into continuous contaminations with the threadbare-grotesque (cf. IV, 8). In one passage omitted in the quotation there are a mention of Catullus and two anonymous parodies in quotation marks.[343] There is pure threadbare-grotesque, just before the final tragedy, in an end of a city street where the list of components concludes with "various shits of different consistency and color, and one or two threadbare toothbrushes, abandoned to the destiny of threadbare things. . . ."[344] But the language of real-estate advertisements used in the opening lines of the quotation portends the direction the comic aggression will take from the end of the quotation onwards. Without avoiding the excrement-referent, resulting from the particular defects of the toilets in Maradagál, it involves as well the field of images of the functional, contiguous to ours by contrast (III, 8): it makes their efficiency appear no less pretentious nor less fictitious than the naïve evocations of the negative category — the last of the twelve to be defined, named, and documented.

Here, then, is the semantic tree. The reader will notice in it general symmetries which may have been invisible in the course of construction: on the fourth level, the parallel of the two neutralizations in the center between the two bifurcations at the sides; on the fifth level, in the series of terminal oppositions, the regular alternation of the contradictories — with the contraries set as utmost limits — and of contraries. In the one case as in the other, it was not intentional, and I do not make any suggestion for possible meanings of this eurhythmy of abstractions made of words and lines.

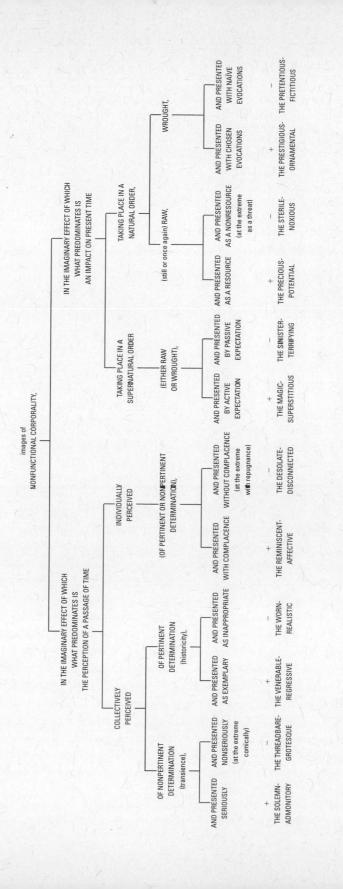

images of
NONFUNCTIONAL CORPORALITY,

IN THE IMAGINARY EFFECT OF WHICH WHAT PREDOMINATES IS THE PERCEPTION OF A PASSAGE OF TIME

- COLLECTIVELY PERCEIVED
  - OF NONPERTINENT DETERMINATION (transience),
    - AND PRESENTED SERIOUSLY
      - (+) THE SOLEMN-ADMONITORY
    - AND PRESENTED NONSERIOUSLY (at the extreme comically)
      - (−) THE THREADBARE-GROTESQUE
  - OF PERTINENT DETERMINATION (historicity),
    - AND PRESENTED AS EXEMPLARY
      - (+) THE VENERABLE-REGRESSIVE
    - AND PRESENTED AS INAPPROPRIATE
      - THE WORN-REALISTIC
- INDIVIDUALLY PERCEIVED
  - (OF PERTINENT OR NONPERTINENT DETERMINATION),
    - AND PRESENTED WITH COMPLACENCE
      - (+) THE REMINISCENT-AFFECTIVE
    - AND PRESENTED WITHOUT COMPLACENCE (at the extreme with repugnance)
      - (−) THE DESOLATE-DISCONNECTED

IN THE IMAGINARY EFFECT OF WHICH WHAT PREDOMINATES IS AN IMPACT ON PRESENT TIME

- TAKING PLACE IN A SUPERNATURAL ORDER (EITHER RAW OR WROUGHT),
  - AND PRESENTED BY ACTIVE EXPECTATION
    - THE MAGIC-SUPERSTITIOUS
  - AND PRESENTED BY PASSIVE EXPECTATION
    - (−) THE SINISTER-TERRIFYING
- TAKING PLACE IN A NATURAL ORDER,
  - (still or once again) RAW,
    - AND PRESENTED AS A RESOURCE
      - (+) THE PRECIOUS-POTENTIAL
    - AND PRESENTED AS A NONRESOURCE (at the extreme as a threat)
      - (−) THE STERILE-NOXIOUS
  - WROUGHT,
    - AND PRESENTED WITH CHOSEN EVOCATIONS
      - (+) THE PRESTIGIOUS-ORNAMENTAL
    - AND PRESENTED WITH NAÏVE EVOCATIONS
      - (−) THE PRETENTIOUS-FICTITIOUS

V

Twelve Categories Not to Be
Too *Sharply Distinguished*

I

The semantic tree allows us, in the first place, to suggest an answer to the question we posed in chapter III (8) about the literary substance of our images. None of the twelve definitions of the categories of images takes determinate physical objects into account; all of them, rather, attribute an "imaginary effect" to the various objects from text to text — that is to say, an interpretation of those objects embedded within the texts, which alone give form and concrete substance to abstract subject matters. In short, the images that interest us consist of certain representations *plus* their interpretation according to the semantic tree. Thus, in using the tree readers must be on their guard against the easy temptation of severing the interpretations from their corresponding representations, thereby reifying the categories *without things* — that is, reifying the moral or ideological or emotional etc. terms of their definitions. We have made our classifications because we needed the right words (III, 6–7); still, it would be incorrect to use the phrase "solemn-admonitory" for a text in which there may be a sense of transience, but not, for example, any ruins; or "reminiscent-affective" if a sentimental memory is stirred up without the presence of any relics; or "sinister-terrifying" if there is a supernatural fear in the absence of any vision of spaces; or "pretentious-fictitious" if there is an inauthentic experience without the appropriate kitsch objects, and likewise for every category. Of the fifty examples we considered in the previous chapter, an instance of the reminiscent-affective from *Werther* (IV, 15) involves the greatest disproportion between the intensity of the interpretation and the thinness of representation: "No step that I took was unremarkable" reads the penultimate line of the quotation, and Leopardi seems to have drawn from and expanded it in these verses of *The Remembrances* (*Le Ricordanze*):

> There is no thing here
> That I see or feel, whence an inner image
> Does not return, nor sweet remembrance rise.[1]

Let us treat this as a counterexample that will serve as a limit case for any other such text. In these verses, things and images are spoken of directly, and in accordance with the definition of our category. And yet it would be incorrect to use the phrase "reminiscent-affective" to describe them, because no things and no images are represented (or else, in the context which follows, they are not connoted in a way that concerns us).

But the point is that we also may well see — and often do see — the opposite split: a representation, however minimal, without a possible interpretation according to the semantic tree. Those who allow that the eleven hierarchical oppositions of the tree are, if not the *only ones* relevant, at least *the most* relevant to the texts we are considering, must also allow that where the tree cannot be applied is precisely where, from our point of view, the substance of the texts is insufficient (a formulation that almost reaches tautology). Let us examine a first series of passages which are, in varying degrees, inadequate. In *Orlando Furioso,* Dalinda secretly receives her lover Polinesso:

> He was perceived to climb by no one;
> Since that part of the palace
> Looks on some broken houses,
> Where none ever pass by day or night.[2]

In one of the tales of the *Decameron,* the Duke of Athens stabs the Prince of Morea and throws him from the window where he has surprised him:

> The palace rose very high above the sea, and the window where the prince then was overlooked certain houses which the force of the sea had caused to fall, where rarely or never did man go: so that it happened, as the duke had beforehand seen, that the fall of the prince's body was not seen or heard by anyone.[3]

In the second part of *Don Quixote,* Sancho Panza, traveling on his donkey, decides to spend the summer night out in the open:

And his defective and unlucky fate willed that while looking for the best place to settle, he and the gray donkey fell into a deep and very dark ravine which opened between certain ancient buildings. . . .[4]

In Corneille's *The Theatrical Illusion* (*L'Illusion comique*), a jailer has arranged for the escape and flight of the prisoner Clindor, along with both of their lovers:

> Some horses are held for us, on the edges of town, by safe hands,
> And I know of an old wall crumbling more each day:
> We could easily escape through its ruins.[5]

In *Jerusalem Delivered,* Ismeno the wizard guides Solimano to the palace within the besieged city through a secret underground passage:

> A hollow cave opened into the hard rock,
> Made a very long time before;
> But being disused, now the passage was blocked
> Again with the thorns and the grass which hid it.[6]

In the poem, tale, novel, comedy, and epic, we see five moments from as many narratives. I have arranged them in a plausible order on a sliding scale: from the text where the greatest verbal economy is used in providing us with information, to the text where the greatest amount of lingering occurs in the representation of objects. If we were only concerned with narrative texts, the substance of the images could be measured precisely by the unnecessary amount of lingering in relation to the necessity of the information to be conveyed: almost, that is, by an inverse proportion, in the verbal space, between narrative functionality and the nonfunctional imaginary. In our five passages, the appearance of some kind of nonfunctional corporality, more or less simple and fleeting, is somehow useful to the characters, or in any case advances the narrative in some way. Boccaccio can have two corpses lie among the ruins for an entire day, and then have them be discovered in an adventurous way; Cervantes gives Sancho, stuck in the ravine, a tragicomic monologue and a surprising means of reuniting with his master. Ariosto's lovers need a deserted neighborhood for their tryst, Corneille's lovers need a narrow passage to escape from Bordeaux, and Tasso's pagans need a tunnel to pass through the ranks of the besieging Christians. With regard to these images, none of the first four passages meets the threshold of substance above which our examples of chapters II and IV were safely settled, and the last passage almost touches this threshold. We may well think that they reflect the parsimony of sensory evocation of the periods preceding the historical turning point; or we may well indulge ourselves by imagining the elaborations which Walter Scott or Victor

Hugo, given the same situations, would have made on these images. This is not entirely fair, however, since there are analogous cases of economy in the middle of the nineteenth century and the twentieth century. In Browning's *The Ring and the Book,* the young priest Caponsacchi distrusts the letter inviting him to a meeting with Count Franceschini's wife:

> Going that night to such a side o' the house
> Where the small terrace overhangs a street
> Blind and deserted, not the street in front. . . .[7]

In Italo Svevo's *The Confessions of Zeno* (*La coscienza di Zeno*), the street which the protagonist walks along in search of his future father-in-law is well suited to the rush he is in to find him:

> High old houses that darken a road so close to the shore of the sea, little frequented at sunset, where I could advance rapidly.[8]

Let us dwell upon the first four passages we quoted earlier. And let us test, by way of a comparison to the semantic tree, the lack of substance of the images which cannot be explained exclusively by their narrative function, or by their date of composition. The first opposition of the tree at once appears to be scarcely applicable. It is not that these passages lack *the perception of a passage of time,* which is implied in Ariosto and Boccaccio, and underlined in Cervantes and Corneille. Nor is it that they lack *an impact on present time,* which practically coincides with narrative functionality itself. But *the imaginary effect* is too slight for us to determine whether either the perception of the passage of time or the impact on present time *predominates* in it, or whether that perception or that impact even takes place, thereby opening a semantic space further divisible according to our subordinate oppositions. The passage of time merely motivates certain situations, and the impact on present time merely prepares for their modifications; both are merely causes and effects working at the behest of the story's movement. As a result, the subordinate oppositions are inapplicable in their hierarchical succession; at most, they might be applicable one by one — using that criterion which I had hypothesized as the less arbitrary one, but which I rejected as too cautious to allow the recognition of any constants (IV, 5). It is undeniable that all these half-images involve a natural rather than a supernatural order, that they represent man-made buildings rather than raw nature, that they are presented in a serious rather than a nonserious way, and that they are portrayed as inappropriate rather than exemplary. But the tree feeds on the vertical solidarity and horizontal oppositions of the parts of definitions which are readable from top to bottom: no superior opposition can be used to classify an image apart from a subordinate opposition, and vice versa. Only in Tasso can an imaginary effect, somewhere between the magical and the sinister, be read through to the relative terminal opposition, although it is left undecided. This is confirmed in the octaves which follow in the episode by expressions like "narrow path," "furtive alley," "dark road," "obscure cavity," "disused steps," and especially "solitary and dark way." So many expressions were certainly not required by narrative functionality.[9]

2

Aside from narrative texts, I know of only one other kind of text in which to linger on certain images might be seen as detracting from a functionality or economy or logic belonging to these texts themselves: the argumentative text. Recall the relationship between reasoning and images in Sulpicius's letter which I chose as the first example of the semantic tree, recognizing an argumentative element to be typical of the solemn-admonitory (IV, 1, 6). While narrative properly belongs to literary genres (including the theater) in a strict or strong sense, only ideological writing of an indirect or weak literariness will be purely argumentative; and yet both these poles can appear in more or less protracted form in every genre of writing. It is when both are lacking that it makes no sense to speak of a lingering on images, and hence it is only through consulting the semantic tree that the lack of substance of the images can be confirmed. This happens above all in those genres or moments — less well defined by recent studies than narrative genres and moments — which I can only designate, using the current terminology, as lyrical. In approaching them, I trust I have established that the inapplicability of the tree in these cases becomes even more radical.

Let us begin with some passages from a quite peculiar narrative genre, such as the fable that features speaking animals. In La Fontaine's *The Eagle and the Owl* (*L'Aigle et le Hibou*), one night the eagle notices the owl's brood of little monsters:

> In the nooks of a hard rock,
> Or in the holes of a hovel
> (I don't know which of the two). . . .[10]

In *The Cat and the Rat* (*Le Chat et le Rat*), the cat, the mouse, the owl, and the weasel

> Inhabited the rotten trunk of an old wild pine-tree.[11]

In *The Mice and the Screech-Owl* (*Les Souris et le Chat-huant*)

pine-tree was felled for its age,
The old palace of an owl, sad and somber retreat
Of the bird chosen by Atropos as his interpreter.
In its cavernous and timeworn trunk. . . .[12]

Once again I have arranged these passages on a sliding scale. In the animal perspective, which La Fontaine assumes poetically so much better than Aesop or Phaedrus, stone nooks or hovel holes are no different: "I don't know which" — nor would we know which category to use in this case. From the human perspective, old pine-trunks are certainly not very functional dwellings. But the fable indeed suspends or overturns such a perspective. What is more, the fable makes it impossible to apply even the opposition between nonfunctional and functional corporality: ruled out at the start (cf. IV, 1) as one that lies at a higher level than the tree itself and its first opposition, concerning the imaginary effect — which is undeniably intense in all three passages. What for man is mildly sterile-noxious, with or without the sinister-terrifying, is for the owl and the other little creatures a suitable residence or "palace": the fanciful and playful collision of the two perspectives, which would not even exclude the threadbare-grotesque, makes the categories and even the idea of their contamination unsatisfactory.

In the following opening lines from Leopardi, deciding if the familiarity of an old building is portrayed from a human or from an animal perspective would also be pointless, though for quite different reasons:

From the top of the ancient tower,
Lonely sparrow, to the country
You go singing until the day's death.[13]

Many lines later, the day's death will seem to express the ephemerality of youth — without, however, any solemn-admonitory images. The "ancient tower" is not solemn-admonitory, nor is it reminiscent-affective or venerable-regressive — nor does it belong to any of the negative categories. And this is so not only because it discloses itself in only two words (we have passed into the realm of lyric poetry, where not only the lack of narrativity but the density of the words themselves puts the idea of lingering into question). Rather, it is thanks to the intrinsic assimilation of the "I" by its explicit term of comparison — *The Solitary Sparrow (Il passero solitario)* of the title, isolated contemplator and singer just like the poet himself. As the top of the tower is literally the proper seat for the one, so it becomes metaphorically the proper seat for the other. In compromising identities and weakening the verisimilar connotations tied to those identities, the metaphorical system in which the minimal representation is caught up neutralizes its potential nonfunctionality. However, the

Italian Leopardi, given his literary culture, although a contemporary of the great Romantic poets of other languages, does not partake of their revolutionary liberation of metaphor.

In Shelley's *Ode to the West Wind,* the autumnal wind, to which the poetic "I" addresses himself, and with which he aspires to identify himself, "wakens from his summer dreams" the Mediterranean Sea, which lay idly, gently rocked by its own currents:

> And saw in sleep old palaces and towers
> Quivering within the wave's intenser day,
> All overgrown with azure moss and flowers. . . .[14]

"Old palaces and towers" are not seen reflected in the sea; on the contrary, it is the southern sea itself that sees them in its sleep. If they quiver, it is because of the intensity of the marine light, and the moss which covers them is azure. Here the anthropomorphic animation of the inanimate overturns not only the physical human perspective but also the connotations attached to the adjective "human." We can only read in this the same radiant euphoria of the entire poem: what would be the point of wondering about our categories? In Keats's *Ode to a Nightingale,* the poetic "I" imagines that the nightingale's song may be the very one which has many times

> Charm'd magic casements, opening on the foam
> Of perilous seas, in faery lands forlorn.[15]

Although we are in "faery lands," we cannot determine precisely why the adjective "magic" should be used to modify "casements," or whether the seas are "perilous" for the inhabitants of these lands, or only for those who consider them "forlorn." In faery lands, to be sure, our criterion of functionality is abrogated or alienated. Although the nightingale's song is the subject of the verb which lends these lines their enchantment, "charmed," the perspective adopted here is not the bird's. It makes sense here to speak of the supernatural — but not, however, of our two supernatural categories for the "casements," or of the sterile-noxious for the seas. The opposition between functional and nonfunctional may well be in play in a dream, but when the high figurativeness of literary language transcends it, literature accomplishes what elsewhere can be accomplished by dreams. I will merely add here one instance of a waking dream referred to in literature — in the clairvoyant madness of Gérard de Nerval's *Aurelia.* In the house of a maternal uncle who has been dead for more than a century, relatives of different eras come alive and live together:

> One of these relatives came towards me and embraced me tenderly. He wore
> an ancient costume the colors of which appeared faded, and his smiling face,
> under his powdered hair, somewhat resembled my own.[16]

We would be hard pressed to analyze the obsolescence of this ancient, pallid dress: the roots of our semantic tree exist in a time and space where the principle of identity is still able to guarantee recognizable connotations, and does not metaphorically — or in the extreme case, oneirically — go adrift.

3

The brevity of these examples drawn from lyric poetry is part of the reason why we cannot apply the semantic tree. But brevity in itself is neither a necessary nor a sufficient condition for this inapplicability — in other cases simply a line of poetry is enough to allow us to apply an entire definition of a category from the tree. And as final confirmation that the substance of images cannot be decided in quantitative terms, let us consider an example. In Book II of the *Aeneid,* Aeneas, as he recounts the fall of Troy and discovers that his words and tears cannot fully evoke the night of slaughter, cries out:

> An ancient city falls, for many years a ruler. . . .[17]

A sublime line that towers over the present, past, and future: in the vision of the city as it falls into ruin, the memory of its untarnished majesty collides with the intimation of the ruins that will be its only remains. The passage of time that evokes pride and astonishment is not the future antiquity of the remains, but rather that of a long dominion now past. It has no force as a historical determination, but only as a contrast with the fact of the fall itself: the noun "city"'s attributes of duration ("ancient") and power ("for many years a ruler"), filling almost the entire hexameter, are set against the catastrophic verb ("falls"), and carry the implicit concessive sense of an "although." It is therefore markedly solemn-admonitory, without any trace of the venerable-regressive that was yet to come. In two single lines of Racine's *Andromaque,* we have the opposite case, thanks to the context, which is not a pure meditative argument, but a circumstantial, political, and doubly interested one. Along with the improbable detail that the Scamander is still dyed with blood, we are given a brief vision of Troy's landscape after the war:

> I see nothing but towers covered with ashes,
> A river dyed with blood, desert countryside.[18]

In the modern age, on the other hand, it is precisely within the venerable-regressive that various allusive contaminations will occur in brief verbal spaces: phenomena which are possible only within the territory covered by the tree, and hence distinct from those cases where it cannot be applied at all. And yet by proceeding along this road, and through the effect of brevity, we arrive at an indecidability among the categories which now prompts us to review briefly a few more dubious cases.

In Maturin's *Melmoth the Wanderer,* which we have already considered (IV, 24), we come across a peculiar double comparison: recently formed streams of water rumble "like a crowd of proud and noisy upstarts" around a dismal mountain path; while the beds of the older streams

> Now stood gaping and ghostly like the deserted abodes of ruined nobility.[19]

And in three novels of the twentieth century (two of which I shall consider at length further on), we read of

> the visioned empty ghost-whistling castles in Sutherland (Lowry, *Under the Volcano*).[20]

> He had a castle in the Hebrides, but it was ruined, he told her. Gannets feasted in the banqueting hall (Woolf, *Orlando*).[21]

> he dreamed of . . . ancient cities, of whose past greatness there only remained cats amidst the rubble (García Márquez, *One Hundred Years of Solitude* [*Cien años de soledad*]).[22]

In a surrealist text:

> Solomon's temple has passed into the metaphors where he shelters swallow's nests and pallid lizards (Aragon, *The Paris Peasant* [*Le Paysan de Paris*]).[23]

With regard to Maturin's comparison, coming not long after the historical turning point, we may very well speak of the venerable-regressive opening up to the sinister-terrifying. But more than a century later, in the line from Lowry's novel, it is not enough to acknowledge that the second category has overtaken the first: the originality of the expression — "ghost-whistling castles" — diverges from the worn-out stereotypes of both categories, and from their contamination. The gannets' feast in Woolf and the domesticity of the cats in Márquez introduce variations, in opposite ways, on the long tradition typical of sterile-noxious animals among the ruins. But intermingling with what other categories — the solemn-admonitory, the venerable-regressive, the worn-realistic? And why not, in Márquez, with the threadbare-grotesque (where the preceding context is pretentious-fictitious)? In the fragment from Aragon, if the venerable-regressive seems to be refused, it is thanks to a lexical convention which expresses cultural decay through the traditional symbols of physical decay. The images in all four twentieth-century fragments seem to be symbols and ciphers, implicit quotations from unidentifiable sources; their conventionality is redeemed by the very literariness which denounces it. That we cannot establish clear categories here does not mean that our tree will be chopped into pieces, as occurred in that other series of examples. On the contrary, our irresolution makes the trunk and the branches stand out more than the leaves: it confirms, at a much later stage, some remote historical nuclei of the unified subject of this book.

For some passages which come before the historical turning point — or better yet, on account of the effect they are capable of producing today — we should speak of deficient or phantom-like cases rather than dubious ones. The contemporary reader's imagination, with its engrained familiarity with more recent literary codes, will react negatively to a dearth of images; a reaction triggered when the categories of this age — the solemn-admonitory and the threadbare-grotesque — remain below the average threshold of literary substance (IV, 1, 6; 4, 8, 9), which is itself relatively low. When President de Brosses is traveling through Italy in 1740 and stops in Modena, he finds that the cathedral has preserved the wooden bucket which supposedly inspired Tassoni's *The Rape of the Bucket* (*La secchia rapita*):

> There was much eagerness to bring us to see it: I was not curious, and easily imagined an old bucket of rotten and worm-eaten wood.[24]

Revolving around an object that is scorned rather than comic, an object that is unseen in the text because predictably banal, this passage briefly brushes up against the threadbare-grotesque. In *Tom Jones,* on the other hand, when the innkeeper prepares a meal for the hero in a room which she calls "The Sun," the threshold is not met: it is no more than a playful antiphrasis on the name ("it was truly named, as *lucus a non lucendo;* for it was an apartment into which the sun had scarce ever looked"), a judgment ("it was indeed the worst room in the house"), and a hyperbole ("having been shown into a dungeon").[25] Today's reader may vaguely think of this as a lost opportunity for an amusing description. And even if the reader is aware that in its eighteenth-century context it could not have been anything but amusing — that is to say, threadbare-grotesque — he can sense something missing only because so many extended and serious descriptions — that is, worn-realistic ones — have intervened between Fielding's day and our own. A few pages earlier I raised the possibility of imagining how nineteenth-century authors would have expanded these same images in similar narrative circumstances, against the background of previous examples, which seemed intrinsically ascetic in their descriptions of objects (V, 1). In some cases it is not easy to refrain from similar comparisons, which are imaginary in more than one sense: when the narrative situations or thematic concerns lend themselves so well to them.

In 1721, the Duke of Saint-Simon was the ambassador of the French regent to the King of Spain, and visited, among other places, the Escorial. He composed his *Mémoires* sometime between 1746 and 1749 — well before Schiller's drama and Verdi's opera. Nevertheless, the legend of the bleak, dark fate of the infante Don Carlos already existed, and it is through this legend that the Duke's enlightened faith clashes with Spanish bigotry. This bigotry is embodied by a "large monk" who serves as the Duke's guide, and who becomes furious while defending Philip II and the absolute authority of the Pope: "such is the fanaticism of the countries of the Inquisition . . ."[26] What about the images used here to describe the place? Auerbach has shown convincingly how, in the great and exceedingly private memoirist, the concrete sense of an overlapping of the physical and the moral spheres is so exceptional that it seems anachronistic for the first half of the eighteenth century.[27] In fact, with all of its mysterious and gloomy suggestions, the post-Romantic reader must be satisfied here by the single sentence: "The Pantheon scared me with a kind of horror and majesty." No one has entered Philip II's apartment since his death — with the exception of the current king, who forced his way in — and the refusal to open it up is unyielding. But Saint-Simon's comment is: "I understood nothing of this kind of superstition"; on the other hand, someone had explained to the Duke that "the whole did not contain more than five or six dark chambers," without upholstery or furniture, "so that I did not lose much in not entering it."[28] There follows an extremely detailed description — with regard to space, objects, and functions — of the putrefaction room (*pourrissoir*) of the royal family. Thanks to the atmospheric connotations which it is Saint-Simon's gift not to withhold from us, the macabre is purified into the cleansed, the luminous, and the odorless: the niches envelop the corpses "without it becoming apparent that the wall, which is everywhere glossy and of dazzling whiteness, has been touched, and the place is very light"; the adjoining room, a sepulcher made from niches and compared to a library, "has nothing funereal about it"; and "although this place is so confined, there is no smell."[29] The historical turning point separates Saint-Simon from the traveler who, returning from Jerusalem, visited the Escorial in 1807, and published his *Travels to Jerusalem and the Holy Land* (*Itinéraire de Paris à Jérusalem*) in 1811 — Chateaubriand. With him there is no danger of any missed opportunity. Since there has been no revolution in Spain, Chateaubriand's funereal metaphorical irony retreats from the venerable-regressive to fall back upon the solemn-admonitory:

> . . . the kings of Spain are buried in identical tombs, ordered by degrees: so that all this dust is labeled and arranged in order, like the curiosities in a museum.[30]

Let us now leave the limbo of images that might have been there but are not, in order to conclude our discussion of peripheral cases with that class of images which are less unreal — those which by all accounts seem not to be there but which nevertheless are there. I am referring to a phenomenon whose premises are certainly documented, in the second and fourth chapters, by the majority of examples drawn from narrative contexts — where the scope of the images is implicitly extended. That is, where we do not limit ourselves to *regarding* them, in the mind's eye, at the moment in which they present themselves to us. Rather, we continue to *see* them, or resume seeing them, in subsequent passages; and without our remembering them, or only barely remembering them. Sometimes it is enough if the images are barely evoked when we first encounter them, in order for them to resonate in our minds or to reemerge afterwards as an unforgettable and indistinct background. This is a phenomenon belonging to literature of all ages, and it can marvelously amplify the sobriety of images which precede the historical turning point. In Tirso de Molina's *The Trickster of Seville* (*El Burlador de Sevilla*), the first Don Juan of European drama goes to the church where the Statue reciprocates the dinner invitation. With Don Juan is his frightened servant, who tries to dissuade him from entering:

> The church is already closed.[31]

Putting aside the stage setting of ca. 1620–30, as well as the fact that Catalinon's fear mixes the comic and the terrible, the evocation of the atmosphere depends verbally on his fear: nightfall outside, darkness and immensity within. In the lines preceding and following the one in which they enter the church, the sinister-terrifying effect is as laconic and indirect as it is lasting:

> How dark is the church,
>
> . . . .
>
> Sir, and it is so vast![32]

In a novel of the late nineteenth century like Fontane's *Effi Briest,* a slight disproportion is also significant — between the importance which Effi's fear will later assume in the story (brought on by the ghost-like sounds coming from the uninhabited floor above her bedroom), and the brevity of the one description we are given of this uninhabited floor.[33] But this phenomenon is not limited to the reticences which the sinister-terrifying demands — however complicitous it may be with them. It is true that among the examples in previous chapters, James's ghost story (IV, 26) was one of the two cases in which the descriptive lingering was the sparest. The other, however, was Mann's story — the more surprising for the scarcity of images of Venice which the reader's memory might believe to have been abundant (IV, 32). Both are examples of a transition between the nineteenth and twentieth centuries and, like the contaminations in the twentieth-century fragments we quoted earlier, they involve a crisis of the nineteenth-century system of categories. In our century, Faulkner was a master of this phenomenon (to such an extent that we are tempted to attribute it to his entire oeuvre). The whole decadent South of his imaginary Yoknapatawpha County (after the novel which introduced it, *Sartoris*)[34] coalesces into images far less frequent and of far smaller length than the reader's memory — or expectation — might afterwards believe. Great buildings, isolated and abandoned, places of tragedy in the action or in the backstory of Faulkner's masterpieces are glimpsed for pages and pages, while their actual descriptions would hardly fill a page: the house that will burn after the murder of its solitary dweller, Miss Bunder, in *Light in August;* the vainglo-rious house of Colonel Sutpen, in front of which one of his sons commits fratricide, in *Absalom, Absalom!*[35] If the question of what category of images we are dealing with here remains an open one, it is thanks to a contamination and not as a result of their implicit extension. This phenomenon passes beyond the confines of our argument: in the sense that, in order to study it properly, we would have to balance our attention to thematic constants with rhetorical and narratological analysis.

4

Our task is now to reconsider the twelve categories one by one. Perhaps it would not be worth the trouble if our only aim were to investigate the chronological distribution of each category and to establish a periodization: I declared at the outset the origin and limits of my documentation (I, 1, 2), and I believe I have shown that it would be impossible — for only one person — to establish a sufficiently exhaustive one. I ask the reader to consider the follow-ing periodizations — which I will apply in case after case to new texts and other ideas — as valid only as provisional perspectives, as conjectural frames. Such periodizations are thrown into question by the very distinction between litera-ture's origins in past reality and its origins in past literature (III, 3–4) — hence the distinction between isolated occurrences and codified recurrences of a certain kind of subject matter. We may conjecture the edges of a frame only on the basis of codified recurrences, since it is always possible that isolated occur-rences are either precocious exceptions or posthumous echoes. In the previous chapter, we discovered that there were four categories which could be docu-mented as nonexceptional in classical — or biblical — antiquity: the solemn-admonitory, the threadbare-grotesque, the magic-superstitious, and the sterile-noxious. And the first and most important of my confessions of igno-rance or doubt — which I need not reiterate at every step of the way — has to do precisely with an upper limit common to all these periodizations, and to an

ideal all-encompassing periodization. Why does it seem as if we were concerned exclusively with post-Alexandrian and Roman antiquity, with Latin
rather than Greek? As a nonspecialist, in fact, I have no greater familiarity
with Latin than with Greek literature, or than with medieval literature in all of
its various languages — the medieval period constituting the other major gap
within the periodizations of most of our categories. I have already had occasion to offer one possible reason for this intervening lacuna (IV, 6), but it was
with slightly less doubt than I now feel as I pose the following question about
ancient origins: Is it possible that the ripening of literary constants, tied to the
relationships among things, man, and time, and between culture and nature,
presupposes a world unified in one empire, with all its abrogations and strat-
ifications of times and cultures?

In any case, in order to sketch out a periodization for the solemn-admonitory
— or better yet, for its codified recurrences — we need only bring together all of
the scattered hints: origins in classical antiquity (IV, I), with the upper limit just
mentioned; lacuna in the medieval period, thanks to the predominance of the
more powerful Christian and Biblical *memento mori* or *quia pulvis es;* revival
in the humanist, Renaissance, and Baroque era between the fourteenth and the
seventeenth centuries (IV, 6); pre-Romantic revival in the eighteenth century
(IV, 7); and lower limit between the eighteenth and nineteenth centuries, thanks
to its transformation into the venerable-regressive. With regard to the upper
limit, the exceptions which prove the rule (for anyone who, like myself, would
find it difficult to trace them in the Egyptian and Near Eastern cultures)[36] are a
few fleeting and wonderful verses from Greek tragedy — akin in theme and
intensity to the line from Virgil (V, 3) on which I have already commented. In
Aeschylus's *Agamemnon*, the title character boasts about the fall of Troy: "the
conquered city may now be recognized by the smoke"; "from the dying cinders
/ raised the fat vapors of her opulence."[37] Euripides' *Trojan Women* unfolds
while the city is burning. "O crushed great splendor / Of our forefathers, you
were as nothing," Hecuba cries at the beginning, and at the end she apostrophizes: "o temples of the gods, o dearest city!" and the chorus of prisoners
responds: "Soon crumbling to the dear earth you will be nameless"; "The name
of the country will soon disappear."[38]

The first regular examples I am aware of, then, are in Greek epigrams on the
ruins of famous cities. Today we read them in Book IX of the *Palatine Anthology* (collected by the Byzantine Cephalas ca. A.D. 900). The uncertainty of
their date and authorship revolves around the "garlands" of the older epigrams, which date back to the first century B.C. They transport us, like Sulpicius's letter to Cicero, to an illustrious Greece in decline. Mycene and Argos
are reduced to "stables of lowing herds": the former city is "like a goat's path,"

has become "oxen meadow, sheep pasture," and "derelict dust"; there remains "not a single trace" of Corinth. And yet through the glorious comparison with Troy, a city celebrated in the past and now "by the ashes of ages consumed," even the cities which fought her survive thanks to the poetry of Homer.[39] Such a poetic rescue, which we do not see in all of the epigrams, was to reappear in the subsequent history of the category: it is something other and more than the secondary meditative functionality of the solemn-admonitory. The consolation and pride of art are alternatives to, although not irreconcilable with, an essentially religious humility in the face of human transience.

Another way of understanding this transience was not to be taken up before the texts of the materialistic eighteenth century (the very age of Diderot): it is typical of a poem like that of Lucretius's *On the Nature of Things* (*De rerum natura*), where it provides the first examples I have discovered in Latin literature. Given this poem's powerful literary originality, we must speak of a solemn-admonitory with a scientific, rather than a philosophical, underpinning. The Epicurean theory of the deterioration of material compounds and of the aging of worlds gives rise to images of walls more majestic than the walls of a city; it also leads to the comparison of those cosmic walls and of elemental rocks, in their undoing, to the most sublime human monuments. Here the nonpertinence of every temporal determination amounts to a universal law of nature:

> Thus also the walls enclosing the vast universe
> Will fall, conquered, into rotting ruins.
>
> Nor does he understand how gradually all things wear out
> And approach their grave, exhausted by the long stretch of life.
>
> Do you not see also the stones conquered by time,
> The tall towers collapse and the rocks decay
> And the cracked statues and temples of the gods crumble. . . .[40]

The Roman conquest would have incorporated many cities in a state of decline into the eastern and southern provinces of the empire — cities which the Romans themselves had sometimes destroyed. Much later, one of Propertius's elegies commemorates the Etruscan city of Veii, within whose walls the shepherd plays his tune, while the fields covering its bone-like remains are harvested. But in this context, which evokes pride rather than lamentation, Rome's victory eclipses the precariousness of all things.[41] This precariousness was said to have brought Marius, in his disgrace, to compare himself to the most feared of hostile cities (cf. IV, 6, 33). In Plutarch, this episode has an eloquence no less concise than the substance of the image itself:

When the officer asked him what should be related to the praetor, he answered with a great sigh: "So tell him that you have seen Gaius Marius, a runaway, seated on the ruins of Carthage," not mistakenly likening by way of example that famous town's fate and his own change of fortune.[42]

It was Troy, however, which, thanks to Homer and Virgil, remained the quintessential city of the solemn-admonitory — before Rome itself would take its place. In Book IX of Lucan (cf. IV, 21), Caesar, having won the day at Pharsalus, goes on a pilgrimage in the Troad plain "as an admirer of renowned things"; there he visits places which evoke a mythical and poetic memory rather than an individual one. Places where, nevertheless, myth and poetry arouse memories at every step, as will later happen for Werther or for Leopardi's "I" (IV, 15; V, 2). "There is no stone without a name": the great visitor had not noticed that the stream he was crossing was the Xanthus, or that he was stepping on Hector's grave. This is a decisive moment in the history of this category. Here the solemn-admonitory is contaminated by a vegetal sterile-noxious far harsher than the herds and flocks of the Greek epigrams: under its crushing weight, the end of the ruins themselves — theme within the theme — unfolds. On the other hand, thanks to the lines which immediately follow those I have quoted and summarized, Caesar is ensured a share of the immortality of what he admires:

> He walks in the places which bear the memorable name of burnt Troy
> And searches for the great vestiges of Phoebus's walls.
> By now sterile woods and rotten trunks of oaks
> Weigh on Assaracus's palace and the temples of the god
> Are clutched by tired roots, while bushes cover
> All the Pergamon: even the ruins have perished.[43]

In 417 Rutilius Namatianus, high official of the empire, composed a poem about his return to his native Gaul, where the Visigoths and Vandals were creating a "long series of ruins." Not long before, Rome herself had been sacked; but in the grateful eulogy that the former prefect offers her — with a belated pathos well aware of her impending doom — the magnificence of the city's temples and aqueducts seems indestructible.[44] On his journey Rutilius also comes across ruins which predate the barbarian invasions. It is significant that he returns to reflect upon them three times, each time offering us hints of images for a line or two, and in one case devoting two lines to Sulpicius's argument on the death of cities.[45] This argument is quoted verbatim by Saint Ambrose as well in a letter of consolation, in which he substitutes Bologna, Modena, Piacenza, and the Apennines for the Greek place names.[46] It was an argument easy to Christianize; considering its subsequent history is the best way of showing how the writers of the old and new faiths, confronted with the historical convulsions of the age and the realization of their material consequences, were to draw from them only a metahistorical lesson. In a poem written by Venantius Fortunatus, the burning of a German ducal palace by a Merovingian king is introduced by maxims on the sudden collapses of dynasties and is followed by a parallel between Thuringia and Troy.[47]

The classical tradition of the solemn-admonitory does not disappear even when we may cross over, linguistically, onto the barbarian side — with the Anglo-Saxon poetry of the seventh and eighth centuries. Among the most beautiful texts of this literature is the fragment on the ruins of the Roman baths at Bath, whose fifty lines or so would be worth quoting in full.[48] If there are too many lines to quote, this is because of a prolonged insistence on the theme which is saturated with specific images: ice on the doorless towers; tileless roofs; "*this* wall, grey with moss and stained with red . . ." More than high medieval Celtic poetry, it is Anglo-Saxon poetry that today reverberates with Ossianic tones. In our semantic tree, it would bring us close to the venerable-regressive; but here the number of a hundred generations after the builders is abstract, and it is the pure melancholy of death which evokes by contrast the past crowd of joyous and richly dressed men. That "powerful" destiny (the law of revolution, *Wyrdh*)[49] which has overturned them cannot be reduced to violence or to time. Moreover, it is with the implied concessive of an "although" — as in Virgil's line — that the crumbling buildings are called "the work of giants" — and they must have appeared as such to a nonurban culture. We encounter this expression in *Beowulf* as well — an epic poem that is also not lacking in Ossianic tones[50] — where it is used as a figure of admiration.[51] The treasure guarded by a dragon furnishes the solemn-admonitory with metallic materials: there is no one left to polish and burnish the arms and golden vases of dead heroes, and the breastplate falls to pieces along with the warrior.[52]

In 1100 Bishop Hildebert de Lavardin's journey to Rome inspired him to compose two Latin elegies. The difference between the two clears a new space for the solemn-admonitory which is not strictly religious: in one elegy, the city prefers being the dilapidated capital of Christianity rather than the former magnificent center of paganism;[53] while in the other elegy, as the poet contemplates the ruin of the city — in spite of which it remains without equal — he makes no mention of any celestial reward:

> Nothing, Rome, equals you, although you are mostly in ruins;
> How great you were in your integrity, in your dilapidation you teach us.

The list of cultural values which follows anticipates Poggio by more than three centuries. Materially, the remains that cannot be equaled and the damages that cannot be repaired achieve a painful, semipositive balance:

So much still remains, so much has fallen into ruin, that neither
The standing part may be equaled, nor the destroyed repaired.[54]

In Dante's *Purgatorio,* the divinely made bas-reliefs representing the punishment of pride are a solemn warning against that sin. After three series of
examples of people, Dante gives us only one antonomastic name of a city —
Troy:

I saw Troy in ashes and in cavernous pits:
Oh Ilion, how base and vile did the carving
Visible there depict you![55]

Starting with its humanistic, relatively secular rediscovery, the solemn-
admonitory images par excellence would become identified with the monuments and civilization of Rome.

But this is not yet the case in Petrarch: in his Latin epistle of 1341, what stimulate "the discourse and the emotion" at every step along his walk are the innumerable historical reminiscences and never the city in its present state;[56] in the
canzone *Gentle Spirit (Spirto gentil)*, the seven-line periphrasis used to describe
the city consecrates all that is contained in a single ruin exclusively to love and
reverential fear.[57] But that supreme culture in history — whose thousand-year
decline would soon lead writers to draw from it a metahistorical lesson — also
handed down its topoi: thereafter, it was simply a matter of applying these
topoi to this culture. The tendential contamination of the solemn-admonitory
by the sterile-noxious allowed for a rapprochement between the biblical and
the classical traditions: when Aeneas Silvius Piccolomini recounts his papal
tour of Tivoli in 1461, he is not content with observing that "the stables of oxen
are opened" and "grass grows" in the ruins of a city gate. To justify a lapidary
maxim on mutability, the substitutive intrusion of animals and vegetables (not,
however, exotic ones) in Hadrian's half-ruined villa perhaps draws its color
from more Eastern sources (IV, 28):

Age has altered everything, the walls which were once covered with painted
carpets and gold-woven drapes, are now dressed with ivy. Where the purple-
clad tribunes used to sit, thorns and berries grow, and snakes inhabit the
chambers of the queens, so transitory is the nature of mortal things.[58]

And in Sannazzaro's Latin elegy on the ruins of Cumae, the same topos with its
vegetation and animals flows into the topos originating with Sulpicius, and
ends on a variation of both which derives a prophecy from the maxim: one day
Rome, Venice, and Naples will be destroyed as well.[59]

The aestheticization of ruins, the admiration of a monument not in spite of
its corrosion and mutilation but because of them — these are scarcely compatible with the solemn-admonitory. They would seem, rather, to be a very dis-

tant premonition of the prestigious-ornamental. Yet the variations do exhibit this tendency in a text like Francesco Colonna's *Hypnerotomachia Poliphili* (that is, *Poliphilus's Strife of Love in a Dream*), of 1499 — a singular text both for its extremely elaborate archaeological fantasy and for its highly artificial language. It is enough to point to the dozens of pages of learned description devoted to an only partially collapsed pyramid-obelisk, to note that another "edifice collapsed into the damp earth by hungry time and putrid antiquity and by negligence" should be "the worthy monument of the great things [. . .] left for posterity" — in the original, terms such as *putre, collapso, relicte* are Latin-ate vernacular.[60] The topos that Rome would never succumb to any enemy, but only to time, already appears in Petrarch's *Africa.*[61] In the Latin epigram (1552) of Janus Vitalis, a humanist born in Palermo, Rome emerges as her own conqueror, defeated only by herself. This epigram, translated by Du Bellay into French and by Quevedo into Spanish, enjoyed such great fortune in Europe that it soon passed from French into English via Spenser.[62] But in the sonnets of *Rome's Antiquities* (*Les Antiquités de Rome*) — from which I choose to quote — we frequently discover a species of the solemn-admonitory directly opposed in meaning to aestheticization: what I would call the solemn-admonitory of disappointment. We can see this phenomenon especially in the first two lines (a faithful translation from the Latin), in the very repetitions of the name that juxtapose the Rome of the present with the Rome of the past:

> Newcomer, who search for Rome in Rome
> And in Rome of Rome discover nothing,
> Those old palaces, those old arches which you see,
> And those old walls, are what is called Rome.
> See now what pride, what ruin: and how
> She who set the world under her laws,
> To master all, has at one time mastered herself,
> And has become the victim of all-consuming time.
> Rome is Rome's only monument,
> And only Rome Rome defeated.[63]

As a literary legislator, Du Bellay, along with Horace, had identified "the fatal discourse of worldly things" as one of the subjects of lyric poetry.[64] Spenser prefaces the collection in which Du Bellay's sonnets are translated with his poem *The Ruines of Time*: a mournful woman, Verlame, personifying Verulamium, an ancient Roman city in Britain, weeps over her own ruin and anticipates the mourning of the recent deaths of famous men. Poetic immortality is the only redemption. The most timeless of our categories is also the most highly codified and the most highly channeled into grandiose commonplaces; claiming that the beginning of Spenser's short poem is a compendium of this tradition, we merely praise his perfect verses all the more.[65] Similarly, in Tasso's *Jerusalem Delivered,* the topos originating with Sulpicius receives perhaps its finest formulation:

> High Carthage lies: barely the signs
> Of her tall ruin the shore retains.
> Cities die, and kingdoms die,
> Sand and grass cover the splendor and the pomp,
> And it seems that man disdains his mortality:
> Oh, our covetous and arrogant minds![66]

The topos is even recognizable, contaminated by the sinister-terrifying, in one of the most morbid masterpieces of the Elizabethan-Jacobean theater: Webster's *The Duchess of Malfi.* In the last act, the duchess is buried near the ruins of an ancient abbey, and her husband, unaware that she has been murdered, is destined to share her fate in the following scene. He likes the place because one cannot take a step without coming "upon some reverend history"; the spectral echo one hears there repeats the words of death — beginning with words which constitute a literary echo: "Churches and cities, which have diseases like to men, / Must have like death that we have."[67]

Between the sixteenth and seventeenth centuries, the tendency towards disappointment — of which I have suggested Du Bellay as a precursor — would prevail, and the significant passages come from other French travelers to Rome. These writers do not question the cultural inheritance or the lesson of decline, but rather the appropriateness of seeking them among the ruins, on this very spot — that very ostentation of grandeur of the one single ruin which so moved Poggio; a skeptical rationalism towards the material fetish and the aura of the city makes its first headway. Montaigne's secretary writes in 1581: "He said that one saw nothing of Rome other than the sky under which she had lain and the plan of his lodging; [. . .]; that those who said that one saw there at least the ruins of Rome said too much: [. . .] that it was likely that these remaining disfigured limbs were the less deserving . . ." (to select just a few lines from the page).[68] In 1623, in a letter to his patron, Guez de Balzac goes even farther. He suggests that if this patron would come to Rome and contemplate its beautiful ruins and stroll "through histories and fables," he would end up convinced that this was a modest occupation for a powerful man, and that the repose and tranquility of Rome "are two things which should be left to the night and the cemeteries."[69]

We shall see more clearly, when we consider the threadbare-grotesque, the reasons why it may be possible to say that during the seventeenth and early eighteenth centuries the solemn-admonitory was destined to be silenced. Bossuet's magnificent sentence on the great empires of antiquity is an example of the absence or metaphorical evanescence of the category's representations, together with the presence of the very interpretation which defines it:

> . . . when you see the ancient and new Assyrians, the Medes, the Persians, the Greeks, the Romans, present themselves before you in succession, and falling, so to speak, one on top of the other: this terrifying clamor makes you feel that there is nothing solid among men, and that inconsistency and agitation are the proper lot of human things.[70]

One of Voltaire's *contes philosophiques, The Princess of Babylon,* stands at the opposite end of the ideological and stylistic spectrum, where the category has just enough time to turn into the threadbare-grotesque. The oddities of the "city of the seven mountains," which are shown to the young oriental foreigner, are "ramshackle huts where a muleteer would not want to spend the night, but which at one time had been the worthy monuments of the greatness of a sovereign people." The pride taken in preserving masterworks of painting which are hundreds of years old, and masterworks of sculpture which are thousands of years old, is mocked by the words of one of the cicerones: "we are something like second-hand dealers who draw our glory from old clothes that have remained in our storehouses."[71]

I find the first examples of a pre-Romantic revival in the letters of another French traveler to Rome, the President de Brosses, himself hardly pre-Romantic. But if his use of adjectives is as solemn as the objects demand, the warning is not expressed except as a subjective emotion in a modest litotes: "it is difficult to find oneself for the first time in the middle of these august solitudes of the Colosseum and the Antonine Baths, without feeling some little pang within the soul at the sight of the ancient majesty of their revered and abandoned antique masses."[72] Do you see "that poor little carriage-gate round and low?" It was the very one Cicero used to pass through with a large escort, "and it is no more than the wretched atrium of some vine-grower. What will become of us? It makes one afraid."[73] Two or three years later, an entirely different tone, but at bottom an equivalent secularization, appears in the long-sustained poem of an Anglican minister, who was as influential then and out of fashion now as Ossian: Young's *Night Thoughts* (1742–44). The religiosity of the meditation on death does not preclude a sense of the cycles and metamorphoses of matter, a sense which recalls Lucretius and may even tempt us to speak of a solemn-admonitory with a scientific basis:

> What is the world itself? Thy world — a grave.
> Where is the dust that has not been alive?

> The spade, the plough, disturb our ancestors;
> From human mould we reap our daily bread.
> The globe around earth's hollow surface shakes,
> And is the ceiling of her sleeping sons.
> O'er devastation we blind revels keep;
> Whole buried towns support the dancer's heel.[74]

Closer to the end of the century, in Goethe's poem *The Wanderer* (*Der Wanderer*), the Mediterranean vegetation near Cumae nearly blots out "the remains of a sacred past" — the ruins of a temple on which, and with which, the poor have built their huts. It is no longer God but Nature that is responsible for the precariousness of the towering monuments of culture — a precariousness that is first felt as a scandal, then as an eternal, life-giving, maternal exchange. It is the first of these two reactions that provokes something like the refusal of the solemn-admonitory:

> Thus, Nature, do you value
> The masterpiece of your masterpiece?
> Indifferently do you destroy
> Your sanctuary?
> Do you sow thistles in it?[75]

We have now arrived at the historical turning point, and in the last codified recurrence of the solemn-admonitory which I will mention, the imminence of the transformation into the venerable-regressive is apparent. Volney's *The Ruins, or Meditation on the Revolutions of Empires* (*Les Ruines, ou Méditation sur les révolutions des empires*), published once the French Revolution had begun, is an ideological treatise which begins with a journey into the memorable and ravaged provinces of the Ottoman Empire. No less original than the idea that ruins attest to the dogma of equality[76] is Volney's concrete ability to describe those of Palmyra, to evoke the oriental landscape in a sunset over the Valley of the Sepulchers: "monotonous and grayish" land, the silence of the desert, the howls of the jackals. In the meditation that follows, the imagined hustle and bustle of some former time, and even the thought of civilizations spread over a thousand remote years, are concretely realized through tangible references. Only their universality preserves the supremacy of the great topoi: the skeleton of the city, beasts and reptiles in courts and sanctuaries, exclamatory maxims about transience, the intimation of a future silence falling on the Seine and the Thames.[77] Sulpicius's legacy (unspared by Sterne's parody in *Tristram Shandy*)[78] finally reached Romanticism through Chateaubriand's prose imitation in *The Martyrs* (*Les Martyrs*),[79] and through Byron's quotation of it in *Childe Harold's Pilgrimage*.[80]

To speak of isolated occurrences of the category after its lower chronological limit is, in each case, to presuppose a new authorial understanding: a choice made out of inventiveness instead of a resort to tradition, even when the inventiveness consists in the very unpredictability of such a resort. There is little room left for erratic examples after such a long peregrination. In Hugo's *The Legend of the Centuries* (*La Légende des siècles*), *Zim-Zizimi* is a theme with variations on the death of powerful men: the ten marble sphinxes on the throne of the Egyptian sultan predict his death one by one, as do the cup and lamp of his solitary feast. I quote the seventh sphinx:

> The tomb where Baal was lain is crumbling in the desert;
> A ruin, it has lost its green granite wall,
> And its dome, sister of the sky, splendid and round;
> The shepherd goes there to pick the stones for his sling;
> And he who in the evening passes by this dismal field
> Hears the sound of the jackal chewing;
> In this place shadows accumulate and the night is complete;
> The traveler, feeling the vault with his stick,
> Calls out in vain: "Is it here that the god Baal used to be?"
> The sepulcher is so old that it no longer remembers.[81]

In Flaubert's *Sentimental Education,* on the day before the barricades of June 1848, Frederick and Rosanette have left Paris for Fontainebleau, and there they visit the palace:

> Royal residences have in themselves a peculiar melancholy which doubtlessly belongs to their dimensions, too considerable for the small number of their guests, to the silence one is surprised to find there after all the fanfares, to their motionless luxury proving by its age the fleetingness of dynasties, the eternal misery of everything—and this exhalation of centuries, benumbing and funereal like the scent of a mummy, is also felt by the naïve.[82]

We discover Troy again in a great American novel of 1920, Edith Wharton's *The Age of Innocence.* The lovers, who renounce one another and submit to the respectability of New York high society, can only escape for their last meeting to a solitary wing of a museum, where "the recovered fragments of Ilium" are a multitude of "small broken objects" frequently in "time-blurred substances" and scarcely recognizable as domestic or personal objects:

> "It seems cruel," she said, "that after a while nothing matters . . . any more than these little things, that used to be necessary and important to forgotten people, and now have to be guessed at under a magnifying glass and labelled: 'Use unknown.' "[83]

As for the forms of the solemn-admonitory in twentieth-century lyric, we are familiar with one example in Borges, where it is contaminated with the reminiscent-affective (II, 3; IV, 16). Borges' other poems which consist almost entirely of lists of things, and two times out of three of many singular nominal sentences, are *Things*, which includes some unreal and impossible ones; *Inventory (Inventario)*, which tends towards the desolate-disconnected; and, though less pertinently for us than the others, *Talismans (Talismanes)*.[84] In the same period, in his *The Chiming Clock (La pendola a carillon)*, Montale's tone is neither diaristic nor epigrammatic (IV, 19). The old, faint object ends up transcending the memory, family, and home of the "I" and emerging in another dimension as it begins to address him:

> I alone at dawn
> Regularly sleepless overheard the vocal
> Ectoplasm, the breath of the *toriada*,
> But for barely an instant. Then the voice
> Of the box was not extinguished but became word
> Scarcely audible and said there is no spring or wind
> That one day won't run you down. I who was
> Time abandon it. And to you who are my only
> Listener I say, try to live
> In Out-of-time, which no one
> Can measure. Then the voice quieted
> And the clock for many more years
> Stayed hanging on the wall. Probably
> There is still its trace on the plaster.[85]

5

The periodization of the threadbare-grotesque — running parallel to that of the solemn-admonitory — will also be obtained almost exclusively by collecting scattered hints (examples IV, 4, 8, 9; cf. II, 6, 8; IV, 3). An Attic Greek text — and a complete exception — is the first one I am able to trace. That we are dealing with a parodic text is certainly significant for the future of the category, even though we must always keep in mind the limited and provisional nature of our documentation. In his tragedy *Telephos* — now lost — Euripides made a daring innovation by having a king wear beggar's rags. Aristophanes mocks this in his oldest surviving comedy, *The Acharnians,* in which the citizen Diceopolis concludes a private peace with the Spartan enemy. Forced to justify himself before the war-mongers who make up the chorus, and hoping to inspire their pity with his clothes, he goes to Euripides' house to ask for some rags.

From among the various degrading tragic costumes, Diceopolis chooses to borrow the rags of Telephos (he also seeks a scorched basket to fill with old rinds, a cracked bowl, etc.).[86] We are in the age which created the classical models destined to last for thousands of years, and, through its parody, comedy punishes any deviation from the dignity which excluded all base things from tragedy. We can quickly document the figurative tendency to laugh at such objects as we pass from the first great Greek comedian to the first great Latin comedian. In Plautus's *Aulularia* (*Comedy of the Pot*), the miser watches over the treasure he has unearthed — a treasure devoid of any precious-potential images. His old servant, exasperated, complains that his home is "full of emptiness and cobwebs." Euclio answers this oxymoron and hyperbole by a literalistic caricature: "I wish these cobwebs to be preserved."[87]

Within the code of high or low genres and styles, in the Ovidian episode of Philemon and Baucis, pastoral idealization managed to preserve a table — one of whose legs is too short and must be balanced with a cracked pot — from being comic.[88] But in Petronius's *Satyricon*, low objects are an integral part of the novelistic parody, and of the atmosphere of licentious hooliganism and superstitious priapism: the "lurid cloth" worn by the rheumy old woman; her "mismatched wooden sandals"; "the cup broken by age" which the sorceress Enotea repairs with pitch, tearing out and reattaching the nail on which it hangs on the "smoky walls"; the "rotten stool" which buckles under her weight, throwing her to the ground and multiplying a series of disasters, "not without the laughter" of the narrator.[89] When a heavily made-up pervert sweats during his violent and obscene courtship of Encolpius, we can see that an image of the threadbare-grotesque can arise at the second level, on a comparative basis: "and in between the lines of his cheeks there was so much make-up paste, that it reminded you of a decrepit, weather-beaten wall."[90] If I now turn again to Martial, it is because of a transition to the tone — not the images — of the solemn-admonitory: a quasi-commutation, the exact opposite of the commutations we saw in the sonnets of Lope de Vega and Scarron (IV, 3), but nonetheless a plausible, distant source for them. The toga given to the poet by an intimate friend of the emperor, splendid and pristine in the days when it was worn, is now so old that a shivering beggar would scarcely accept it. Among some jocular plays on words, a maxim resounds in the form of a question:

> What do not the long days, what do not the years consume?[91]

Although constituting almost the lone alternative to the solemn-admonitory up to the historical turning point — the almost inevitable literary result of certain kinds of subject matters — the threadbare-grotesque was inclined to transcend the imaginary reality that constitutes the foreground of a text. It did so not only through parodic reference, or on a metaphoric or hyperbolic level, but also through symbolic, emblematic, and allegorical forms. We may say in passing that this would make it *a priori* less foreign to medieval literature than the other categories. The House of Fortune in *The Romance of the Rose* (*Le Roman de la Rose*), which we already mentioned (IV, 6), may be regarded as threadbare-grotesque rather than solemn-admonitory precisely insofar as the opposition between the serious and the nonserious is neutralized in the unreality of the symbol.[92] I will merely add here two late examples, from Villon's work. In *Testament,* the poet bequeaths a certain Tower of Billy, with the provision that his heir must repair the doors and windows which are either collapsed or missing altogether: the tower existed as an actual ruin, but the mocking legacy is purely symbolic. And the "envious tongues" are even more symbolic in the famous ballade which gives the recipe for frying them. The grotesque feeds on magical lists: on the fantasy of bestial and deadly, scatological and nauseating ingredients.[93] We need to go back to the Italian fourteenth century, namely to Boccaccio, to find already a lighthearted figurative exaltation of low realities, as concretely presented as in the examples from antiquity. Friar Cipolla's servant, Guccio Pig, whose deadly faults reach the number of nine, promises that he will provide the servant girl he courts with better garments "without considering" his own, that is:

> his hood, on which there was enough grease to season the huge cauldron in Altopascio, his doublet, all torn and patched up and gilded with grime around the neck and under the armpits — with more spots and more colors than Tartar or Indian fabrics ever displayed — and his shoes, all battered, and his rent hose.[94]

But the tendency of the threadbare-grotesque to be incorporated by abstractions and to play with emblems, exploiting and supporting the improbable, continued into the sixteenth century. In Folengo's *Baldus,* the most relevant images are not to be found in the boorish provincial background of the first half of the poem, but rather in the last book, where the fabulous adventures of the second half hit rock bottom. This is the House of Hell, which we know to be metaliterary (if the macaronic Latin were not enough to convince us) from the sheer amount of hyperbolic putrescence:

> The house all over perspires dampness through the peeling walls,
> And from the worm-eaten ceiling drops musty
> Dregs, such as I saw in caves deprived of all light.
>
> The hall is large and spacious, square in shape:
> All around there are rotten wooden seats;

> Like the coffins of the dead which after long time
> Are drawn from the bowels of the earth.

In this hall, a council of mythological and allegorical monsters is held. Ambition makes a speech in which she boasts of the corruption of the Church, translating this corruption in turn into the hyperboles of an allegory — whose undignified images strangle the venerable-regressive in its cradle:

> The dusty hay grows up to one's knees,
> And from the cracked roofs the tall ceilings pour rain.
> Long-legged spiders decorate the walls
> With their sheets. The arms of the crucifix are missing
> And in his head either a bat or a mouse has a nest
> And delivers its young, and gnaws at the legs of so worthy a figure.
> The holy host, made with old rotten flour, gives birth
> To little worms. . . .[95]

In *Gargantua,* the implausible genealogy of the gigantic hero ironically asserts the authority and the antiquity of a book. Rabelais pretends that it was found in a "large, fat, big, gray, pretty, little, moldy booklet, more, but no better, smelling than roses"; it is written in letters "so consumed by age that scarcely three in a line could be recognized."[96]

With Berni, I would say that the points of departure of the threadbare-grotesque become verisimilar once more in themselves, while its end-points remain figurative or metaliterary. His relatives, who outdo the antiquities of Rome — the very subject matter of the solemn-admonitory — in decrepitude, are neither monsters nor giants; the broken chamber pot, whose mortal fragility is reasserted by a Petrarchan quatrain in another sonnet, is not an allegory.[97] However, in the first, anonymous picaresque masterpiece, *Lazarillo de Tormes* (1554), the renewal of the category achieves a perfect economy of balance between the few images of nonfunctional corporality and narrative functionality. The boy's second master, a miserly priest, keeps the communion wafers locked up and inventoried in an old chest; its decrepit condition (as important to Lazarillo's attempts to satisfy his hunger as his possession of the key which opens it) gives him hope that the damage he inflicts can be blamed on mice. In the course of this episode, the figurative embroidery constitutes the bare minimum of residual lingering beyond what is required by the story. After the priest has covered up the holes in the chest with wooden shards and nails, we are told of how Lazarillo reopens a breach:

> I went to the sad chest, and where I had seen it oppose less resistance I attacked it with a knife, which I used like an auger. And since I found the very ancient chest, because of its many years, without strength or heart, in fact very

exhausted and worm-eaten, it immediately surrendered to me and yielded a good-sized hole in its side for my use. Having done this, I slowly open the wounded chest.[98]

His priestly antagonist repeats the same countermeasure, and Lazarillo redoubles his offensive campaign — "we seemed to have signed a contract for Penelope's web, because as much as he wove in the day, I undid at night" — with the result that whoever wished to describe the trunk accurately "would rather have called it an 'old cuirass of another age' than 'chest,' so many nails and tacks did it have on it."[99] Lazarillo's third master is a squire who conceals his own hunger with kindness and haughtiness. The threadbare-grotesque might here be mistaken for the sinister — historically speaking, an error — in the silences and emptiness of his house, whose "dark and melancholy" entrance hall is frightening:

> . . . and not hear above or below the steps of living people around the house. All that I had seen were walls, without seeing a small chair, or a bench, or a seat, or a table, nor even a chest like the other one. In fact, it seemed like an enchanted house.[100]

But the squire himself laughs at the boy's belief that a funeral is about to be held in the house: in fact, Lazarillo has heard the widow lamenting that the dead man would be brought "to the melancholy and dark house, to the house where nothing is eaten or drunk."[101]

As the genre inaugurated by Lazarillo spread for more than two centuries throughout Europe, well beyond Spain, the threadbare-grotesque was to remain one of its recognizable features throughout each of its convergences with other genres. This convergence will rarely be as complex as in Grimmelshausen's great novel, *The Adventures of Simplicius Simplicissimus* (*Der abenteuerliche Simplizissimus*, 1668). And yet, in the first chapter, nothing could be more typical of the category than the "palace" of the peasant, the alleged father of Simplicius. The apologia of this palace is given in a passage of prolonged Baroque figurative subversion. It privileges the countervalues of poverty and nature over the values of wealth and culture, according to conceptions of time, work, and value which, as if it were a hoax *avant la lettre,* resemble those of Marx:

> His chamber, hall and rooms he had allowed to become quite black with smoke within, only because this is the most lasting color in the world, and because a similar tincture takes more time to be perfect than a painter requires for his most excellent works; his tapestries were of the most delicate texture on earth, since they had been made by her who in ancient times dared to weave in competition with Minerva herself; his windows were devoted to St.

Nicolas for no other reason than that such a material, counting from the hemp or linen seed until it reaches its complete development, costs much more time and work than the best and most transparent glass from Murano; his condition made him easily believe that all which is obtained through great effort is also valuable and all the more precious.[102]

Further on, the sordid inn run by a usurious shyster lawyer competes with and outdoes Quevedo's college.[103] In the added-on sixth part, we hear the voice of a personified sheet of paper (building upon the image of paper in the above passage) which lists all of its metamorphoses; it resembles a macrocosmic amplification of the passage in *Buscón* detailing the metamorphoses of a piece of cloth: from hempseed to the page of a book with which Simplicius is about to wipe his ass.[104]

In the meantime, at the beginning of the new century, images of the armor of earlier ages had descended, so to speak, from the metaphorical level of the sentence in *Lazarillo* to a literal one: in an example of the threadbare-grotesque that is among the briefest, and is the most renowned, of Western literature. An "ancient shield" figures among the iconographic attributes used to introduce the hero at the beginning of *Don Quixote*.[105] But only the rust and the mold on his ancestors' armor declare how great a regression in time his decision to become a knight-errant represents. To Quixote, the logical first step is to restore it to use:

> And the first thing he did was to clean some armor which had belonged to his ancestors, and which, taken over by rust and full of mold, had been lying for long centuries stored and forgotten in a corner.

The first contradictions of his fictitious experience follow from this project of rearmament: since the lower part of the visor is missing, he replaces it with cardboard; and since this falls to pieces when he first attempts a thrust at it, he reinforces it but does not attempt to test its strength again.[106] There is no figurative decoration here; madness alone is enough to endow the tale with a comic eccentricity. The Baroque age invented a threadbare-grotesque with an emphasis on the second adjective rather than the first: a threadbare-grotesque of bizarre and rare things, contiguous but not identical with that of poor and base things. That even the new rationality could avail itself of this style, in opposition to the resurgence of the irrational in the literary taste of the age, is proven when Galileo himself criticizes the first master of that taste, in his *Considerations on Tasso* (*Considerazioni al Tasso*). He expresses his reaction to the characters and actions of *Jerusalem Delivered* with the following comparison (preceding a comparison opposed to it, filled with magnificent settings and objects, on his experience of *Orlando Furioso*):

it seems to me as if I were entering a tiny sanctum of some curious little man, who has amused himself by decorating it with things that have, either for their antiquity or for their rarity or for some other reason, something singular about them, but which are in fact small things indeed; since there are, how can I put it, a petrified crab, a dried chameleon, a fly and a spider in jelly within a piece of amber, some of the clay puppets which they say are to be found in the ancient tombs of Egypt.[107]

The bizarre, in its turn, was liable to be contaminated by the magical, or only with the pharmaceutical. This contamination brings seven lines of Shakespeare closer to the category; however, the terminal element of its definition does not apply. In Romeo's description of the apothecary's store, the man desperate enough to sell him the poison, misery and impending catastrophe all lend a compulsory seriousness to the presentation of the objects. And yet there is a genial variation on how typically nonserious their extravagant squalor *could* be:

> And in his needy shop a tortoise hung,
> An alligator stuff'd, and other skins
> Of ill-shap'd fishes; and about his shelves
> A beggarly account of empty boxes,
> Green earthen pots, bladders, and musty seeds,
> Remnants of packthread, and old cakes of roses,
> Were thinly scatter'd, to make up a show.[108]

We find the opposite case in Basile's *The Tale of Tales* (*Lo cunto de li cunti*). The symbolic iconography of the house of Time would be typically serious and solemn-admonitory, were it not lightened by its passage through the Neapolitan dialect and witty fantasy of the fairytale writer:

> on the top of that mountain's peak you will find a house so tattered that no one remembers when it was built: the walls are cracked and the foundations rotten, the doors worm-eaten, the furniture moldy and in sum everything is consumed and destroyed: here you see broken columns, there fractured statues [. . .]. As soon as you have entered you will see on the floor unsharpened files, saws, scythes and sickles and hundreds and hundreds of ash pots, with names written on them, like the jars of an apothecary, which read: *Corinth, Saguntum, Carthage, Troy*, and a thousand other soured cities, which he keeps to remind him of his enterprises.[109]

In a feature of the customs of a nation remote in space, what is exotic and surprising sounds bizarre rather than comical. Father Bartoli, historian of the Jesuit missions, describes the honor in which antiquity is held by the Chinese; and he moves from the great reverence shown towards the elderly to their belief in the added worth things acquire with the passage of time — without, or in contrast with, aesthetic logic:

> And the great pride they take in their possessing old stuff, and in searching for it, and in providing the great with it, and paying very dear for it, may be reduced to this: they have no eyes for statues or medals, for learning about them or judging of their beauty, is not something their eyes are capable of, but for pottery of any material or shape, taking small interest in any masterful execution compared to the interest in their antiquity: in fact, the more eaten and consumed by time they are, the more they are judged to be noble; and the number of grains of rust which were removed in cleaning them, would be equal to the same number of carats of preciousness and finery lost.[110]

The regressive implications of the Baroque taste were inseparable from an element of modernism;[111] and although the *Querelle des Anciens et des Modernes* took place in France only at the end of the seventeenth century, long before this a prejudice against the ancients had been declared, which could be extended from people to things. The threadbare-grotesque expressed, impertinently or unsympathetically, the impoverishment of the reverence due to the past, or else an oedipal impatience with it. Saint-Amant entitles a poetic "caprice" *Ridiculous Rome (Rome ridicule,* 1643); the disappointment felt at the sight of the eternal city grows into a buffoonish insult. The Tiber is a "pool for toads, muddy stream, / A torrent made of ox piss, / Canal fluid with rot," etc. Why not raze to the ground the criminal ruins of the "sorry and barbarous Coliseum, / Execrable remains of the Goths, / Nest for lizards and snails"? And the transition from monumental to contemporary Rome occurs in the following line: "That's enough talking about dead things."[112] Twenty years later, the turn towards classicism restored authority to antiquity, but that very same taste restricted the possibility of a serious lingering on images to a bare minimum. Thus the prolonged silence of the solemn-admonitory can be explained. On the other hand, a system of genres — more rigid than ever — assigned a place to the negative category in the so-called *comique* narrative, or in comedy, satire, and mock-heroic poetry.

The first example is from Antoine Furetière's *The Bourgeois Novel (Le Roman bourgeois,* 1666), whose title was already a playful oxymoron. A boorish magistrate, who cannot write love poetry and cannot afford to pay for it, wants to copy it from the most ancient authors, just to be safe. Ignorant of centuries, names, and styles, he goes in search of "the most spoiled books, whose covers were most torn, which were most dog-eared, and these books were those he believed to be of the greatest antiquity." A wonderful confusion between cultural and material antiquity, which will leave him astonished when he is caught out — when the lines he has copied from a very tattered book turn out to be those of a contemporary author.[113] In the realm of comedy it is enough to recall Molière's *L'Avare*, and the inventory of "gadgets, fittings, and jewels" which Harpagon makes use of as collateral for an exorbitantly usurious loan: among these objects are an alembic for distillation, a lute missing its strings, a giant stuffed lizard, etc.[114] Boileau also indulges in images justified either by the theme of avarice, in a moralistic sense, or by the theme of bookishness, in a specialistic sense. In twenty lines of Satire X he portrays a miserly magistrate and his wife; in six lines of *The Lectern* (*Le Lutrin*), he represents a volume of Gothic law as massive as it is shaky.[115]

In similar environments the category survived, in rarefied form, throughout almost the entire eighteenth century. In one of the *Persian Letters* (*Lettres persanes*), Montesquieu ridicules the delusory oddities of the erudite fetishism of antiquity;[116] in Diderot, Rameau's nephew is taunted for the poverty of the torn and patched-up clothes he once wore, and for the coarse, outdated clothes he now wears.[117] In Goldoni's *The Rustics* (*I Rusteghi*), avarice lurks behind the faded muff and the necklace with broken pearls which the stepmother lends to the bride.[118] In *The Antiquarian's Family* (*La famiglia dell'antiquario*), it is an ignorant count who is possessed by the same mania ridiculed by Montesquieu: he doesn't buy threadbare things so much as farcically spurious ones, *adynata* of archaeological credulity.[119] However, the richest example of the century, I presume, is a text exceptional in every way: Jonathan Swift's poem *The Lady's Dressing Room*. The "inventory" of images abounds, in the indiscreet lover's inspection of her empty dressing room. The dirty shirt stained under the armpits, the towels slimy with sweat and ear wax, the handkerchiefs covered in snuff and snot, etc. — all accuse the female person of a nauseating corporality. Thus he describes her toiletries: the combs "Fill'd up with Dirt so closely fixt, / No brush could force a way betwixt. / A Paste of Composition rare, / Sweat, Dandriff, Powder, Lead and Hair." The basin into which she spits and vomits is a "nasty Compound of all Hues"; ironic comparisons prolong the lingering on the ill-concealed latrine. And the stench finally becomes associated, for the lover, with all women; the author's concluding disavowal sounds intentionally false.[120] An extreme version of the category, no doubt, owing to the extent and violence of the misanthropic — not merely misogynist — scorn. We know that Fielding, one of the latest heirs of the picaresque genre, does not seize any opportunities for the threadbare-grotesque (V, 3); while, in the following century, we recognized a curious variant of this category in Arnim (II, 6; IV, 33).

We also know that, for the threadbare-grotesque, the historical turning point marked a transformation into the worn-realistic. This transformation was particularly gradual in English literature: we saw it in a well-balanced example from Scott (IV, 33), and I pointed out the same phenomenon in a later author like Dickens (IV, 13). With regard to Scott, I will add the originality of an instance where the tradition of the threadbare-grotesque remains tangential, so to speak, to the field of the images. In *The Bride of Lammermoor* the images of the tower, the only remnant of the inheritance of the aristocratic, dispossessed Ravenswood, belong to the worn-realistic or venerable-regressive; but there is, however, the old servant Caleb Balderstone, who, in his quixotic loyalty to the family's reputation, furiously tries to hide their poverty. He claims that a sumptuous dinner prepared for the guests has been destroyed by lightning; he steals a spit-full of ducks from the house of the artisan who has refused to continue paying the feudal dues; and he simulates a fire to keep away illustrious guests. He thus unintentionally provokes what his young master bitterly defines, in accordance with the semantic tree, as "the ridicule that everywhere attaches itself to poverty."[121] As for Dickens, precisely because it no longer occurs everywhere, the distribution of his persistent use of the threadbare-grotesque deserves to be studied. As a comic masterpiece, and his first one, *The Pickwick Papers* contains many excellent examples;[122] here I will give a purely anthological preference to Todgers's boarding house in *Martin Chuzzlewit*. I quote only one brief extract, but ideally we would need both the entire beginning of this paragraph and the three or four pages describing the surrounding neighborhood that shortly follow it:

> The parlour was wainscoted, and communicated to strangers a magnetic and instinctive consciousness of rats and mice. The staircase was very gloomy and very broad, with balustrades so thick and heavy that they would have served for a bridge. In a sombre corner on the first landing stood a gruff old giant of a clock, with a preposterous coronet of three brass balls on his head; whom few had ever seen — none ever looked in the face — and who seemed to continue his heavy tick for no other reason than to warn heedless people from running into him accidentally. It had not been papered or painted, hadn't Todgers's, within the memory of man. It was very black, begrimed and mouldy. And, at the top of the staircase, was an old, disjointed, rickety, ill-favoured skylight, parched and mended in all kinds of ways, which looked distrustfully down at everything that passed below, and covered Todgers's up as if it were a sort of human cucumber frame, and only people of a peculiar growth were reared there.[123]

As for Russian literature, at the very least we must mention *The Overcoat*, in which the derisory pathos of the garment makes the worn-realistic a tributary of the old category[124] — a transformation no less apparent in that text by Gogol which allowed me to introduce both categories (II, 8).

I hypothesize that such recurrences, in which we grasp the passage into the new category in the first half of the nineteenth century, are the last codified ones. Those recurrences mediated by the sympathy of the French Romantics for the age of Louis XIII — or, as we would say today, for the Baroque — are no longer codified, unless in a second degree. In this sense, Theophile Gautier, with his rediscovery of the portraits of poets, *Grotesques* (*Les Grotesques,* 1844), was laying the ground for a historical novel like *Captain Fracasse,* which he finished in 1863. Starting from the long initial description of the "castle of misery," deep in the Gascon province, the seventeenth-century use of metaphor and the more recent one re-created by Victor Hugo achieve a half-playful union. Here are a few fragments:

> all this [the chiaroscuro along the walls of a stairway] so vague, so faded, so destroyed, so disappearing that it was rather the specter of a painting than a real one, and which one should talk about with the specter of words, since ordinary terms are too substantial for it.

> Sometimes the plank of a piece of furniture would unexpectedly crack, as if bored solitude were stretching its joints . . .

> it was the corpse of the past which slowly dissolved into dust in these halls where the present never set foot, it was the sleeping years which cradled themselves in the grey cloths in the corners as if they were hammocks.[125]

An inverted mirror of social hierarchies throughout its history (and a refutation of what Bakhtin quite wrongly took to be the spontaneity of the carnivalesque), the threadbare-grotesque ceases to be obvious in the democratic age. Its isolated occurrences after the lower limit of the category emerge especially in peripheral literary regions, as if, in the central zones, to play with images of the nonfunctional had become impractical, one hundred and fifty years since. In a sonnet of Trilussa (Carlo Alberto Salustri, 1871–1950), *The Antiquarian* (*L'antiquario*) uses the Roman dialect to persuade his client:

> And what do you think of this Baroque sofa?
> Look at the gilding! The brocade!
> There're a few stains? So what, we'll get it clean.

> And then they're antique stains: increased value!
> They're period smudges, do you see?
> Filthinesses from the last century![126]

And in his pluralistic, largely metadialectal style in *That Awful Mess on Via Merulana* (*Quer pasticciaccio brutto de via Merulana*), Gadda describes a cabinet:

It looked as if it contained a collection of those futilities, those knots of yarn, those odd buttons, those oblong rags, of which the good women from the plain and from everywhere else in the fatal peninsula are extremely cautious gatherers, very fastidious keepers against the unlikely event of a future devoid of yarn or string, since there will be nothing to tie up.[127]

Finally, in a libretto written by W. H. Auden for Stravinsky's opera *The Rake's Progress,* the already Baroque list of strange rarities appears on stage (and is summarized in a stage direction). In the next act, all covered with dust and cobwebs, they will be auctioned off.[128] In the twentieth century, the properly comic inheritance of the threadbare-grotesque is handed down, rather, to a more modern category: the pretentious-fictitious.

6

If we move on to the venerable-regressive, the temporal succession of codified recurrences and isolated occurrences is inverted. As we know, its codified recurrences did not appear until the historical turning point, which is characterized by the venerable-regressive more than by any other category; its isolated occurrences, more than following these codified recurrences, preceded them by thousands of years. Already in the *Odyssey,* the rules and functions suspended in Ulysses' absence, and which are to be vindicated upon his return, make the state in which he finds his weapons at home exemplary. Just before the massacre of the suitors, as he handles his bow, Ulysses tries to determine whether the "worms had bored through the horn, while the master was absent"; the traitorous goatherd tries to bring to the suitors a dusty shield that once belonged to Laertes: "and already for a long time had it been in disuse, the leather straps had all become undone."[129] In Aeschylus's *The Libation Bearers,* just after Orestes the matricide has avenged his father Agamemnon, he brings forward in his defense the robe Agamemnon wore when he was murdered. The stain of violence worsens the natural discoloration of the garment: "See this robe dyed red / From the work of Aegistheus's sword. There is my evidence. / Yes, it is blood, blood whose stains have joined with time / To fade and corrode the colors of this patterned stuff."[130] In several Latin passages, certain images reveal the historical values of the Roman fatherland in connection with great civil or frontier wars. For instance, we have the rusty weapons which the plowman will unearth on the battlefield of Philippi, as Virgil prophesizes;[131] the towns of Latium reduced to dust and the countryside emptied, which lead Lucan to predict discord as he narrates the history of Pharsalus;[132] the broken arrows and scattered bones of men and horses, found in the Teutonic forest six years after the defeat of Varus, as Tacitus relates.[133]

Or again, in Tacitus, Germanicus seems to visit Actium or Athens or Ilium and Egypt in search of determinate cultural memories, not mythically universal ones.[134] And, in Lucan, the opposition between an uninterrupted decline and a traumatic one is epigraphic: "It was not voracious time which corroded and left to dissolution / The monuments of the past; it is a civil crime we see / In so many empty cities."[135]

In the end, time was no longer divided in two by political and military clashes, or by the irruption of the barbarians, but by the ideological revolution brought about by Christianity. If, for Propertius, the cobwebs and weeds growing in the deserted temples seemed to reflect the corruption of manners,[136] the very same images elate Saint Jerome in 403 as a kind of refused venerable-regressive: the defeat of one religion is the triumph of another. For us, a thousand-year cycle turned upside down, since among the first images we considered were those of deconsecrated churches:

> The golden Capitol lies in squalor, all the temples in Rome are covered by dust and cobwebs . . .
> Paganism suffers neglect even in the heart of the city. Those who were once the gods of the people have remained with owls and bats in the solitary domes.[137]

The most prescient verses are biblical, in which an outburst of mourning is the prelude to a restoration. In 167 B.C., Antiochus IV Epiphanes, launching an assault against Judaism, profaned the temple of Jerusalem; the Maccabees, reentering it three years later, purify and reconsecrate it: "And they saw the deserted sanctuary and the profaned altar and the burnt doors, and the bushes grown in the portico of the temple just as in a forest or on a mountain, and the apartments of the priests destroyed. And they tore their clothes, and wept greatly."[138]

El Cid Campeador, sent into exile, weeps at the sight of his emptied palaces and vanished hunting equipment. Chance, having mutilated the copy of the poem which has come down to us, decrees that Spanish literature should begin — between the twelfth and thirteenth centuries — with that lamentation and that desolate sight:

> From his eyes   so greatly weeping,
> He turned his head   and looked at them,
> He saw open doors   and entrances without locks,
> Empty hangers   without skins or cloaks
> And without falcons   or molting goshawks.[139]

But in the plays of Lope de Vega, the Spanish aristocracy seems so firmly entrenched in power that it fears no economic decline, and sees no distant historical turning points on the horizon. In *The Best Judge the King* (*El mejor alcalde, el rey*), the father and lover of the young woman kidnapped on the eve of her wedding are considered hidalgos no less because they are farmers: the one "Still has insignias / On the deteriorated escutcheon / Of his portal, and with it, / Of the same period, some spears"; the other keeps "a rusty sword with a broken sheath."[140] It is the pride of Galicia, or of the other northern provinces where the Christian Visigoths resisted the Moors.[141] In the extraordinary and little known *The Batuecas of the Duke of Alba* (*Las Batuecas del Duque de Alba*), a whole community descended from the Visigoths has reverted to barbarism over the course of seven hundred years—living in the mountainous Batuecas region, ignorant of the world.[142] They suspect the existence of a wider world when they discover "an old and very rusty sword" and a skeleton holding weapons in his hands, even before they encounter their contemporaries who can explain these mysteries.[143] The present draws its main evidence from the past, and the evidence points to nobility; the skeleton belongs to a nephew of the last king Rodrigo, whose arms, presented to the duke, consist of: "this rusty spear and this shield." "Merciful God, of what great antiquity!" exclaims the duke.[144]

The passage we quoted from the Book of Maccabees may have been remembered by James Macpherson (IV, 10), or could figure among the many quotations in *The Genius of Christianity* (IV, 2). Of the two types of ruins distinguished by Chateaubriand—the work "of time" and "of men" respectively—the ineluctable ruin of the solemn-admonitory seems to occur more often than the traumatic ruin of the venerable-regressive. The clearest example of the latter is the desecrated charterhouse in Paris, as Chateaubriand had seen it in 1792. But, as we read immediately after, "man is himself nothing but a fallen edifice, the remains of sin and death; [. . .] everything in him is nothing but ruins."[145] Or, elsewhere, "[man] is a building fallen and rebuilt with its own ruins," a sustained metaphor of the contradictions incurred by original sin.[146] This concept is used to generalize the historical criminality responsible for the second type of ruins. In fact, regardless of both types, the entire sepulchral obsession that pervades images, themes, and metaphors is rationalized theologically.[147] We have scrutinized Chateaubriand's interested dehistoricization of the events of the revolution: using no less interested theses, he could return much further back in history—even to before the Fall. It is a fallacy, it seems to me, to maintain that if God had not created the world at the same time both old and young, the grandeur inseparable from antiquity would have been missing in nature.[148] What matters most is that this lack of grandeur applies to history and to its monuments, until they have become immemorially ancient:

a monument is not venerable until a long past history has, so to speak, impressed itself beneath its vaults all blackened by the centuries. This is why there is nothing wonderful in a temple which one has seen erected, the echoes and domes of which have formed under our eyes.[149]

This intuition was too widespread among the Romantics not to be secular as well, and Victor Hugo raises it as an objection in a poem on the Arc de Triomphe, completed only months before in 1837.[150] In a short chapter of the *Genius of Christianity*—one of its most beautiful—Gothic churches merge with nature more seamlessly to the degree that they imitate her, having been modeled on the trunks and shadow, on the mystery and sounds of the forests of Gaul.[151] In the *Letter to M. de Fontanes on the Roman Campagna* (*Lettre à M. de Fontanes sur la campagne romaine*), the ruins of aqueducts and graves in turn "resemble the indigenous plants and forests of an earth composed of the dust of the dead and the debris of empires."[152] In the *Travels to Jerusalem and the Holy Land,* the pyramids are admired and defended against those who demand a "physical utility" in monuments; in their "moral utility," once again metahistory replaces history, and the permanence of a colossal funeral luxury bears witness to a past civilization: "What does it matter . . . whether these buildings were amphitheaters or sepulchers? Everything is a tomb in the country of a people that is no more."[153]

As for the wonderful pages on the castle of Combourg in Chateaubriand's *Memoirs from Beyond the Tomb,* they were the first to offer me, twenty-five years ago, the matter for some observations which are today included in this book (I, 1). It was in a book on themes of childhood memory: the prerevolutionary historicization of those themes seemed to be a novelty in relation to the model of individual memory derived from Rousseau, but also in relation to the emphasis on the absolute precariousness of human existence which still can be heard throughout the *Memoirs.* Before all else—and not only in this case—it was a matter of recognizing the venerable-regressive as an alternative to the reminiscent-affective and the solemn-admonitory. Another future category was implicated by the slide towards the sinister-terrifying; and it is with regard to the sinister-terrifying that I have again taken up the theme of the vastness of spaces in the residences of the old, dominant classes, spaces which in the eyes of the new classes seemed wasteful and terrifying (IV, 22). Chateaubriand's perspective towards Combourg is certainly not the estranged one of the new class, and yet he lacks the indifferent nonchalance of the old one. His family became impoverished and the castle was reacquired: with the immensity of this castle as the background, his childhood memories are characterized by the indelible daily life of the family and by unfillable spatial voids and dispersions —as I showed in my earlier study.[154]

After the castle came the convent (cf. IV, 11): the convent where George Sand spent three years of her adolescence in a boarding-school, an experience she recounted in the *Story of My Life* (*Histoire de ma vie*). The superabundance of space in these buildings is the result of incoherent, age-old enlargements and additions, and of the inherent impracticality of female life in the convent. In tracing this impracticality back implicitly to the *ancien régime*, Sand is much more critical, though genially so, than the nostalgic Chateaubriand; behind her sinister-terrifying lurks playfully the exhilaration of the schoolgirls, who chase down in cellars and garrets a secret worthy of a dark, Gothic novel.[155] Similar images and constants reappear in the first chapter of Nievo's *The Castle of Fratta* (*Confessioni di un Italiano*): architectural irrationality as a metaphor or metonymy of the irrationality of the former feudal regime; the irony with which this is regarded by an author from the party opposed to conservation; and the tenderness of childhood memory mixed with irony. The Castle of Fratta was bizarre in the irregularity of its "edges, corners, niches, and protuberances"; it had courtyards that mirrored the façades with their "internal disorder," and a kitchen "with an indefinite number of sides varying in size."[156] Rooms which are either too cavernous or too narrow, absurd connections between buildings of different styles, corridors or staircases that lead nowhere, uneven floors and steps between adjoining rooms: such elements constitute the building theme — to which we will return — belonging to the venerable-regressive even more than to the sinister-terrifying.[157] This theme's precise historical valence seems to be longer-lasting in proportion to the historical belatedness of countries or regions. At the end of the century, we come upon it again in Federico De Roberto's *The Viceroys* (*I Viceré*).[158] And, as we shall see, we also find it in some great southern Italian novels of the twentieth century.

It is but a short step from directing irony at images from the old world to challenging its values. The ideological substance of the venerable-regressive makes it the category most susceptible to refusal (IV, 11); and one of the shortest of our periodizations confines its codified recurrences to a period of roughly eighty years. These years witnessed, along with our historical turning point, a revolution and a restoration in France and Europe. We are concerned here with the building theme, and the word "restoration" has both a political and an architectural meaning; ever since Galileo, Descartes, and Voltaire, the metaphor of the crumbling or demolished building, propped up or rebuilt, had been used to express the progressive destruction and renewal of ideologies.[159] But if Chateaubriand succeeded in producing an accepted venerable-regressive in his writings before the Bourbon Restoration, the Restoration itself inspired writings in which the exemplariness of these same monumental images was refused. Using the Voltairean pamphlet as his weapon, Paul-Louis Courier, a literary enemy of the regime, justifies the "black bands" who speculated on the destruction of abbeys and castles for the benefit of small landowners: and what of the memories? They are memories only of superstitious ignorance or criminal license; the old Gothic stones are not profaned when they are used to build houses, bridges, and workshops for industrious people—they are purified.[160] Stendhal subjects the Gothic mode under the Restoration (and even in the medieval period) to a partisan and discerning sociology of art. In the medieval churches, the Gothic style inspired a "fear of hell"; now it is admired, instrumentally, by a class that "fears the return of '93."[161] In *Lamiel,* a preacher explodes firecrackers in the darkness of a Gothic church while he is describing hell, and a duchess has her feudal tower rebuilt with the same stones for the edification of the local Jacobins.[162]

I am again drawing from one of my essays of over twenty years ago: on the only chapter in *The Red and the Black (Le Rouge et le Noir)* in which Julien Sorel—as deeply adverse to the Restoration as Stendhal himself—accepts the pomp of the venerable-regressive, but so fleetingly that it amounts to a variant of refusal. Aside from the element of ambition in such a reversal, the young man is momentarily moved when he suddenly enters an immense and gloomy Gothic hall, whose "melancholy magnificence" is degraded by the rough masonry brickwork that blocks the ogival windows.[163] In this image I recognized the same contradiction which makes the whole chapter swarm with tiny symbols, and which Stendhal recognized as essential and fatal to the regime: it cannot valorize antiquity without making recent repairs to what has been ravaged by time; it cannot fight the recent on its own ground without squandering the charisma of the ancient.[164] A more general contradiction of the bourgeois age emerges from the contradiction of a highly particularized political transition: earlier, I connected it to the universal ambivalence towards time, which both wears out and ennobles (I, 6). It is as if in the Romantic conception of time, born of the new age, it were impossible to dissociate what is ennobled from what is worn down: even without the intimations of irrationality in old buildings, even without the spells cast by a terrifying narrative. This contradiction appears even in the literature of countries where there was no revolution, and where the repercussions of the French Revolution were scarcely felt. The castle in which Pushkin depicts a bored *Eugene Onegin* is "venerable," and "built / As castles should be built": "Excellent strong and comfortable / In the taste of sensible antiquity"; nonetheless, "All this today is antiquated, / I really don't know why."[165] In Mickiewicz's *Pan Tadeusz,* the Horeszkos' castle is in a state of only slight disrepair. But the aged vassal provokes a fight among the nobles by making the rusty wheels screech, and the chaffinch chirp on the pendulum, of one of the two chiming clocks which he winds each evening; they are "queer old fellows, long at odds with the sun, often indicating noon at sunset."[166]

After the generations who preserved a living memory of the *ancien régime* passed away, those generations disappeared who were able to cultivate its images with access to the first-hand testimony of an oral tradition — as in grandma's days (II, 4, 9). I would set the lower limit of the category — and not only for French literature — around 1848, a symbolic year not just on account of the death of Chateaubriand. In considering any examples after this date as isolated occurrences, I would make only one exception — for a thematic strand in which, however, the venerable-regressive was soon contaminated by other categories. We have already seen the continuity between the venerable-regressive and another category of correspondingly short duration — the prestigious-ornamental. It occurs through a transposition of ideological into aesthetic exemplariness, materially present in the decorative artifact (IV, 35, 37). But on analogous premises of the increasing emptiness of ideology and of a compensatory aestheticization, writers soon began to yearn for, idealize, and stylize the departed *ancien régime* as a moment of the historical past. This is the tradition that would lead to the *Fêtes galantes,* and which began with texts by Hugo, Gautier, and others (the example drawn from Pushkin [II, 9] showed French influence as well), much richer in the images we are concerned with than Verlaine's collection. The contamination was destined to be with the reminiscent-affective, for reasons we shall see later — drawn, for the last time, from another of my essays dating back more than twenty years. The thematic complex we are considering was also, however, liable to be contaminated by the threadbare-grotesque; we already saw it in Gautier's *Captain Fracasse* (V, 5). In fact, it extends the range of the *ancien régime* back over two centuries of Bourbon rule. In addition to the predilection the theme has for the licentious and outworn graces of the ages of Louis XV and Louis XVI, it is attracted not by the central stability of the age of Louis XIV, but — at the other extreme — by the picturesque unruliness of the age of Louis XIII.

Thus, during the first years of the reign of Louis Philippe, Gautier sets two fantastic tales in the time of the Regency or of Louis XV,[167] while his novel *Mademoiselle de Maupin* conjures a castle in the style of Henry IV or Louis XIII as an easily imagined setting for love.[168] "It is under Louis XIII," Nerval says of the castle brought back to life in the verses of his *Fantasy (Fantaisie),* but he fuses collective and individual time in dating a memory two centuries earlier.[169] Inspired by these lines, and expanding upon them in his *Past (Passé),* Hugo restores to the castle and the park their historical remoteness: where the couple of the present remembers ancient loves. I quote from the beginning of the poem:

It was a great castle of the time of Louis XIII.
The sunset reddened this forgotten palace.

. . . .

Under our eyes stretched, ancient felled glory,
One of those parks where the grass floods the walks,
Where, in a corner, half covered with ivy,
On a grey pedestal, Winter, dismal statue,
Warms himself with a marble fire under his hand.

Oh woe! The great basin slept, solitary lake.
A greenish Neptune grew moldy in the water.

. . . .

The tritons seemed to be shutting their eyes;
And, in the shadow, his stone jaws half-opened,
A bored old cave yawned at the end of the wood.

In the two final lines, I cannot say whether these images of the past condense
into the reminiscent-affective or dissolve into the solemn-admonitory:

Oh vanished times! Oh eclipsed splendors!
Oh suns descended behind the horizon![170]

Among the late nineteenth-century texts which can be linked with this thematic strand in its eighteenth-century meaning, Zola's *Abbé Mouret's Transgression* (*La Faute de l'abbé Mouret*) is an anomaly — and I mention it for this
very reason. A pavilion and park in the style of Louis XV, with their lascivious,
half-faded paintings and sunken marble women disfigured by the waves, play
host to the erotic initiation of the young priest. But the culture of which they
are the remains (and of which they preserve a library) belongs to the Enlightenment; their exemplariness, far from being regressive, harmonizes with solar
nature set loose in the wild in free abandon.[171]

In the isolated occurrences we have yet to consider, the historical values
either differ from those underlying the reaction against the rise of the bourgeoisie, between the eighteenth and nineteenth centuries, or, as in our most
recent examples, have different functions. In Hawthorne, an American Puritan version of the refused venerable-regressive projects an atavistic feeling of
guilt onto antiquated, cursed buildings (as Faulkner will later do [V, 3]): *The
House of the Seven Gables* takes its title from a building finished shortly after
the founding of the first colonial settlements in New England.[172] In *The Scarlet
Letter,* the narrator allegedly discovers the manuscript containing the story he
retells in the old Custom House of Salem, where he works as a surveyor, and
which serves as the title of the preface explaining the circumstances of the
discovery. Yet if the details of this discovery tend toward the Gothic (anticipat-

ing the dismal atmosphere of the story), a condescending irony nevertheless lingers in the rickety building, which is governed by a gerontocracy of ex–navy captains: a sleepy *ancien régime* of the New World.[173] But in the preface to *The Marble Faun*, the Italian setting is justified as an alternative to the country "where there is no shadow, no antiquity, no mystery, no picturesque and gloomy evil."[174] And the ambivalence of the images of Rome is tantamount to the contaminations which pull the category in different directions: insofar as it is refused, it leans towards the sinister-terrifying of the plot of a Gothic novel set in the Catholic south of Europe (IV, 22, 24) — as well as towards the worn-realistic of a decadent filth, "an inherited and inalienable curse."[175] On the other hand, insofar as it is accepted, or even idolized, by the three artists visiting the city, the venerable-regressive anticipates its coming resolution into the prestigious-ornamental. Here, the aestheticization of ruins (V, 4) delights in descriptions so exemplary they almost seem to have been lifted straight from a guidebook. There are too many of them, however, in proportion to the symbolic narrative thinness of the conflict between repressive Puritanism and pagan temptation.

In Flaubert's *The Temptation of St. Anthony*, the procession of bygone divinities is intended to make the saint doubt the unique truth of Christianity. Some complain of animal profanations even fouler than those St. Jerome described in a passage quoted earlier. Thus Isis, the domestic Roman Lares, and Jehovah himself cry out, respectively:

> Egypt! Egypt! The shoulders of your great immobile gods are whitened by the excrements of birds . . .

> But the forefathers of painted wax, locked up behind us, slowly become covered in mold. [. . .] under the teeth of rats our wooden bodies crumble.

> The jackal whines among the sepulchers; my temple is destroyed, my people dispersed![176]

Let us now return to nineteenth-century class divisions with Hardy's novel *Jude the Obscure*. The young orphan, an avid reader, judges a countryside deprived by furrows "of all history beyond that of the few recent months" to be ugly;[177] his ideal is the Gothic town of colleges and studies. When he arrives there, he does not yet know that what will exclude him, as if from a privilege, is that very excess of noble history which makes the alleys untraveled and the stones rotten:

> Down obscure alleys, apparently never trodden now by the foot of man, and whose very existence seemed to be forgotten, there would jut into the path porticoes, oriels, doorways of enriched and florid middle-age design, their

extinct air being accentuated by the rottenness of the stones. It seemed impossible that modern thought could house itself in such decrepit and superseded chambers.[178]

Halfway between working-class status and high culture is the occupation of restoring old buildings — buildings which were also prosaic when they were new: "They had done nothing but wait; and had become poetic." Something impossible for most men, Jude thinks:[179] as impossible as social advancement will prove to be for him. The "Christminster buns" he will end up cooking and selling, with windows, towers, and battlements made out of cake, savor less of the pretentious-fictitious than of an unattainable venerable-regressive degraded by faithfulness.[180]

The scenario of Gabriele D'Annunzio's *The Torch under the Bushel* (*La Fiaccola sotto il moggio*) calls for a house into which "all the ages" are crammed, from the Normans to the Bourbons; and "all is ancient, worn, corroded, cracked, covered in dust, doomed to perish."[181] The insistence on our thematic complex opens up the venerable-regressive to the most contaminations possible — as in the fragments we saw in V, 3. But here, despite many beautiful lines, the conventionality is neither intentional nor lapidary: "Do you wish / That I should count everything / What is stained, what has faded, / What is wrenched, curved, flaked, / Drenched, what drips or rots?"[182] To the four or five categories which come to mind, we should add the precious-potential for a treasure, the sinister-terrifying for a ghost, and the magic-superstitious for a deer-bone flute.[183] In a passage from Carlo Dossi, the love felt for the family furniture ("although worm-eaten, hollow, and falling to pieces") would seem to be expressed through individual memory, since it is written in the first person and precedes the real or fantastic series of *Loves* (*Amori*). But then we read that it is not "a part of my former life" so much as "part of the life of those who gave me blood and name," who seem to be "materially lingering" in the objects of the house. The narrator describes the physical intimacy between these objects and his more or less distant female ancestors from the *ancien régime*: a nun "three hundred years earlier one of my aunts" and a crucifix; his great-great-great-great-grandmother and a fan "with pink fleshy cherubs" and "ladies in farthingales and wigged courtiers"; his great-grandmother and a cup, drinking from which is like giving her "a kiss across a century"; and finally his grandmother and a damask chair, in which he saw her sitting with his own eyes, and from which she could have told him of the cruelties of the French Revolution.[184] Between the nineteenth and twentieth centuries, the feeling of tradition or of family decline now has haut-bourgeois rather than aristocratic references. Thomas Mann invests this feeling in one object, not in *Buddenbrooks*, but in

The Magic Mountain (*Der Zauberberg*), when Hans Castorp remembers how he used to have his austere, conservative, Protestant Hanseatic grandfather show him "the baptismal cup." The cup, which didn't match the much older silver saucer, would be taken out of the cupboard. The child's perspective on its other contents makes for the originality of a topical list of "things out of use and for that very reason attractive." But the cup had been used to baptize four generations before Hans, his father, and his grandfather; and perhaps the boy asked to see it just to hear the ancestral prefix (*Ur-*) repeated four times — a sepulchral sound that gave him a sense of communion with their sunken lives and let him breathe in the cold, musty smell of church.[185]

Isaak Babel's *The Road* (1932) takes place during the time of catastrophe for another *ancien régime*. In 1918, in St. Petersburg, the revolutionary commissars are settled in the favorite residence of the penultimate czar and czarina: after a bath, the Jewish narrator wraps himself in an enormous dressing gown which belonged to Alexander III — for all that, rather greasy and patched up. Here the refused venerable-regressive is the historical nemesis. At the beginning of the story, the traveler has escaped from a massacre that continues the pogroms of the czarist autocracy; and towards the end there is an allusion to the imminent massacre of the imperial family. But Babel's concision makes room for an alien reminiscent-affective and the solemn-admonitory evoked by the enormous upheaval of fortunes. Both emerge from the violation of the intimacy of the dead or deposed rulers:

> We passed the rest of the night going through Nicholas II's toys, his drums and locomotives, his christening shirt, and his notebooks with their childish scribbles. Pictures of grand dukes who had died in infancy, locks of their hair, the diaries of the Danish Princess Dagmar, the letters of her sister, the Queen of England, breathing perfume and decay, crumbling in our fingers.[186]

The protagonist of George Orwell's *Nineteen Eighty-Four* works in the Ministry of Truth, where the past is "controlled" — that is to say, canceled and brought up to date — and where destruction devices, functioning as wastepaper baskets, are called "memory holes."[187] The origin of the protagonist's transgression is his search for the elusive records of more than fifty years earlier.[188] In an album from that era, whose paper is soft and yellowed, he commences a diary at the risk of his life; he returns to the dirty antique shop where the owner offers him — again in the form of a list — only scraps, rarely of any beauty. A bedroom upstairs awakens in him an "ancestral memory" of peace and private calm,[189] and it becomes his meeting place with his accomplice and lover. But it is not true that the ubiquitous telescreen is not there: having accidentally confessed his horror of rats, he will have chosen the instrument of his future moral annihilation.[190] If the venerable-regressive is that on which progress and revolutions turned their backs, it was left to the dystopian nightmare to reinvent it as a refuge and a trap of hope.

7

The worn-realistic belongs so essentially to the nineteenth century that I am not inclined to recognize any isolated occurrences either before or afterwards. Before the nineteenth century, for several hundred years, the threadbare-grotesque seems never to have combined sufficient seriousness and everydayness to adumbrate its transformation; afterwards, in the twentieth century, the tradition always seems sufficiently continuous to permit us to speak of codified recurrences. Thus, within the course of one century, with further possible offshoots in the next, the massive quantity of major examples has yielded me by far the most imposing of the twelve categories. Beyond what I have cited, there are an incalculable number of passages of a minimal substance; and the outlines of a codification, both thematic and formal, are so clear that we must wonder why it has not attracted any attention before — and should welcome any future investigations into the subject. With so many relatively contemporary texts among our examples, this time the most instructive order of presentation will not be chronological. However, let us begin with the historical novel, the literary genre which had precedence in the first decades of the nineteenth century, beyond the imaginary precedence of its subjects. For reasons we have already mentioned (IV, 12), too great an infusion of the worn-realistic does not suit this genre.[191] And yet, the category's preconceptions are able to impose themselves — as in *The Betrothed* — in the twelfth century of the genre's most popular work: Scott's *Ivanhoe*. The castles of Torquilstone and Coningsburgh are ancient but not ruined. Still, in the best rooms at Torquilstone, the drapery accordingly sags, torn and discolored; and at the beginning of the novel, the description of the Druidic ruins follows a description of the swineherd's coat, made from the skin of an animal which is so worn down that it can no longer be identified.[192]

It would be anachronistic to use the word "déclassement" for the Norman feudal lords and their Saxon servants. But, as I said earlier, this word is the meeting place for the two implications by which the second adjective in "worn-realistic" is justified: first, the typical power of constituting reality through literary innovation; and, second, the typical signs of an unstable social reality, a new phenomenon in itself (II, 9; IV, 13). It was inevitable that nineteenth-century narrative would need to narrate its own century, in order to reflect in images the ambivalence of time which wears down and ennobles, and which may have worn out or ennobled either already too much or not yet enough (I, 6).[193] Let us let the texts speak for themselves; perhaps an assembly of texts that would be "surprised to find themselves together" — as George Sand remarked of certain objects set aside by old spinsters and nuns.[194] Here are two passages, from an unfinished novel by Stendhal, and a tale of the fantastic by Gautier:

> Everything was wonderful, expensive, but too new. In the hall a screen of blue velvet, decorated with its golden studs and slightly worn, would have said to passersby: "It was not only yesterday that we became rich . . . ," but a Grandet thinks of making a speculation on screens, and not of what they may say to passers-by in the hall.[195]

> What I liked about the luxury of this house was that nothing here seemed recent. The paintings, the gold, the damask, the brocade, were dull without being faded and did not irritate the eyes with the shrill glitter of newness. One felt that that richness was immemorial and that it had always been thus.[196]

In both cases, the bourgeois need for time that ennobles or that has ennobled is opposed and complementary to the danger of time that wears out and de-classes. In neither case do we have the worn-realistic: that which in the one case is postulated in the conditional as a corrective measure for the "too new," that which in the other is distanced from the shrillness of the new "without being faded" — both come quite close to the exemplariness of the semipositive category. Paradoxically, we also have the opposite of the worn-realistic when even what is worn out becomes exemplary. If we leap to another century (and take as given the ideology according to which the bourgeoisie and all its proprieties must be overthrown), we see this paradox in a poem of Brecht, which attributes the ennoblement of artifacts to their use:

> Of all handmade things the dearest
> To me are the used ones.
> The bruised copper containers with flattened edges,
> The knives and forks, the wooden handles of which
> Are worn by many hands: these forms
> Seemed to me the most noble.
>
> . . . .
>
> Entered into the use of many,
> Often altered, they improve their appearance and become precious
> Because often put to the test.[197]

The worn-realistic in theory begins with the déclassement of the previous ruling class. There are two conditions: first, that the disarray of aristocratic castles and palaces be no longer represented at a historical distance, but in the present day; and, second, that they be not exemplary in the mode of the venerable-regressive. Balzac's *The Chouans* (*Les Chouans*), the first published novel of *The Human Comedy* (*La Comédie humaine*), takes place in 1799 — thirty years earlier, halfway between history and the present day. The counter-revolutionary civil war has devastated the Breton manor of La Vivetière: the morbid description turns it into a "great ghost," "an empty and gloomy carcass," and gives it "all the appearance of a skeleton."[198] In Barbey d'Aurevilly's *A Married Priest* (*Un Prêtre marié*), the sacrilegious protagonist has bought the castle which the lords of his peasant childhood have lost, and seems to take pleasure in seeing its ruin:

> The dilapidation was frightful. The lacerated tapestries hung from the length of the wainscot like flags that seemed to be weeping over their defeat. The mirrors encrusted with dust and ignobly stained by flies showed greenish and false reflections from their cobwebs. The ceilings were flaking.[199]

In these cases, the loss of functionality is restrictive rather than extensive. It does not simply affect luxury or prestige or decorum — it compromises use, healthiness, and habitability (cf. IV, 5 to IV, 13). Incompatible with the status of a ruling class, such a restrictive sense is only found in extreme cases in the representations of bourgeois conditions. It is reserved for the two social extremes where the bourgeoisie either profits by the déclassement of others, or fears its own déclassement as a kind of relapse: the impoverishment of the aristocracy, and the poverty of the proletariat. The decline of ancient dwellings naturally has blander, and gradually less bland, variants, even when they have remained in the families' possession and have not been bought by someone lower in the social order.[200]

In Giovanni Verga's *Mastro-don Gesualdo*, the positive representation of the character who has just come into wealth corresponds to an alien or ironic representation of the noble family his daughter marries into. The Traos are in need of money to settle a debt "with six hundred years' interest" with the King of Spain, on the basis of "heaps of scrap paper and parchments."[201] While only a few lines embody Gesualdo's prosperity in "new furniture,"[202] their palace generates images throughout the novel. Terse hints diffuse these images, which are concentrated in two descriptions separated by many pages; here is the longer one:

> Whoever wanted could enter through the shattered front door. The courtyard was narrow, filled with stones and rubble. Along a small path in between nettles one reached the toothless staircase, tottering, also suffocated by weeds. At the top of this the falling door was barely shut by a rusty latch; and immediately upon entering one was hit by a waft of humid and heavy air, a

cellar-like stench of mold which rose from the floor decorated with the coat of arms, covered with broken crockery and scraps, rained from the unplastered vault, came in thick from the corridor as black as a dungeon, from the dark rooms which might be perceived in long succession, abandoned and naked, because of the bars of light which filtered through the unhinged windows.[203]

In Melville's *Benito Cereno* likewise, the description of the current state and archaic form of a ship superimposes dirt and decay on an outdated Spanish shape: seen from Melville's America rather than Verga's Sicily. Any narrative purposes cannot diminish the symbolically historical range of this marine worn-realistic. Here is one sentence: "Battered and mouldy, the castellated forecastle seemed some ancient turret, long ago taken by assault, and then left to decay."[204] In his *Asiatic Tales* (*Nouvelles asiatiques*), Gobineau, for his part, looks to an exotic continent whose history is even more ancient than Europe's, but which has reverted to barbarism — a continent where what is wasted, insofar as it is venerable-regressive, is made level with the negative category: "Unluckily a part of the arcades had collapsed, others were chipped, but ruins are an essential feature of all Asiatic arrangements."[205]

It is the bourgeois condition that is most vulnerable to every insufficiency of dignity or prestige, if not of luxury. Failing to bring things up to date undermines immediately the credit of a class that establishes it in the present, even when it pretends to draw it from the past. In Balzac, a Napoleonic baron may once have been a banker like d'Aldrigger, rather than a military man like Hulot. When d'Aldrigger dies in *The Firm of Nucingen* (*La Maison Nucingen*), we read that "the furniture of the mansion, which totaled ten years of age, could not be *renovated*"; and then (concerning a visitor): "never could the green damask with white ornaments appear to this young man either withered, or old, or stained, or fit to be *replaced*."[206] In diachronic terms, if one face of the Janus-faced class is turned towards indigence or splendor in the past, the other is turned towards splendor or indigence, respectively, in the future. The simultaneity of wealth and poverty is more abnormal, and usually attends those who are living in, or rather from, systematic dissipation: *A Harlot High and Low* (*Splendeurs et misères des courtisanes*). The list describing Esther's room includes "filthy broken clogs and pretty little shoes, lace boots a queen would envy, cracked common porcelain plates." And it is summed up thus: "this was the collection of lugubrious and joyous, miserable and rich things which hit the eye."[207] Among Zola's novels — whose explorations of society, section by section, never included one of the aristocracy — *Pot-Bouille* is the novel of the petit bourgeoisie. A physical atmosphere corresponds to the apparent moral respectability of the house: "a great air of cold cleanliness," "the dead calm of a bourgeois living room," "sweetness which smelled slightly stale."[208] But in the less comfortable living quarters, the coexistence of ostentation and privation is no longer detached from respectable mediocrity, as it is in Balzac. The kitchen betrays this coexistence: "the melancholy emptiness and the false luxury of families in which low-quality meat is bought in order to be able to put flowers on the table."[209]

No nineteenth-century novel would be able to tell the story of family neurosis, with all its peculiar rhythms and compulsory roles, as well as Alberto Moravia's *Time of Indifference* (*Gli indifferenti*). The desolate-disconnected here enters in more than one subjective description of the surroundings;[210] but the threat of déclassement which hangs over them belongs to the tradition of the worn-realistic. The haut-bourgeois widow is about to lose her mortgaged villa, in which her daughter's bedroom is still decorated as it was in her childhood, with dolls now "ragged and neglected,"[211] and at the bottom of the untended garden the "gardener's house" is filled with broken junk inside its bare walls.[212] Her less-distinguished friend has a light and youthful boudoir, in which only a second look betrays the scattered marks of the worn-realistic;[213] on the other hand, the worn-realistic dominates the son's journey and fantasies, in an almost intentional assumption of déclassement, when he goes to shoot the lover of the three women.[214] Only this lover, who will take possession of the villa and who embodies the most vulgar stratum of society, owns a house in which the useful and the new prevail.[215] The bourgeoisie renews its families and its people in the same periodic fashion in which it ought to bring its houses and furniture up to date; nor does its literature ignore, in the words of Marx's *Manifesto*,[216] that it "cannot exist without constantly revolutionizing the instruments of production," and in general without revolutionizing its technological inventions—as we have already seen (II, 9, 14). In *Madame Bovary*, a large, decaying room, used for a variety of purposes, is full of "disused farming implements, alongside a quantity of other dusty things of which it was impossible to guess the use."[217] In Turgenev's *Fathers and Sons*, where the conflict centers on scientific progressivism, the nihilist's father was once a doctor: at the end of the list of old things in his study, professional or otherwise, "in one corner stood a broken electric machine."[218]

All exchange comes to a standstill with the theme of avarice: poverty in wealth and waste in thrift, the true oxymoron of the bourgeois worn-realistic. By saving, the misers of the threadbare-grotesque only produced the emptiness of privation and inactivity (IV, 8, 9; V, 5), while Gogol's miser literally accumulates useless objects (II, 8). In *Capital*, Marx finds an only slightly less-demented parody of the accumulation of wealth in the popular prejudice that confuses capitalist production with hoarding, and in a note he cites Balzac's *Gobseck* as an example. Marx acknowledges that the author "represents the old usurer . . . as in his second childhood,"[219] when he talks and behaves according to an "illogical instinct" whose effects will soon be discovered:

In the room next to the one in which Gobseck had passed away, one could find some rotten pies, a multitude of edibles of all kinds, and also fish and shellfish which had become moldy, the different stenches of which almost succeeded in asphyxiating me. Everywhere worms and insects swarmed. These recently received gifts were mixed with boxes of every shape, tea chests, packages of coffee.

As the liquidator of the former colonial settlers of Haiti, the old man received many gifts, and the list is extended by the imminent arrival of "a whole bazaar of colonial victuals," as well as precious European goods.[220] This is almost a precious-potential only partially returned to nature; while, after a miser is murdered in *The Country Parson* (*Le Curé de village*), the dissolution is complete and the worn-realistic is extreme. The list describing his house as "naked, dilapidated, cold, and sinister" — that is, "the absurdities" of his fear of spending — is summed up by a "pile of rags which lived only inasmuch as they were upheld by the spirit of their owner, and which, once he was dead, fell into tatters, into dust, into chemical dissolution, into ruin, into I don't know what nameless thing."[221] The house of Dickens's miser in *Our Mutual Friend* is bare of everything, even of any "experience of human life": "This old house had wasted more from desuetude than it would have wasted from use, twenty years for one."[222] If, in Thackeray's *Vanity Fair,* parsimony is part of the rustic character of the elderly baronet, who initially passes himself off as the porter (just as Gogol's Plyushkin does for the housekeeper), his country park falls into ruin before his son inherits it.[223] In Mikhail Saltykov-Shchedrin's *The Golovlyov Family,* in the world of the small Russian gentry, the theme is as tyrannical as the mother and son who personify it — with tragic consequences for their immediate family. The filthiness of their victims' rooms and clothes is described more than the filthiness of their own.[224] One of these victims, another son, says of them: "There's masses of fresh food, but she won't touch it until all the old, rotten stuff's been eaten!" (needless to say, by the servants).[225]

Sloth, less *a priori* repellent than avarice, makes the protagonist responsible for the state of the house in Ivan Goncharov's *Oblomov.* This is a long novel where our category is most central and ubiquitous; more than ever, I can only quote from it very sparingly. At first sight, the room where for eight chapters Oblomov is almost always lying in bed, or in an armchair, or on a sofa, appears to be decorated in excellent taste, but on closer inspection it is so slovenly as to make one think it devoid of human life:

> Dust-covered cobwebs were festooned round the pictures on the walls; instead of reflecting the objects in the room, the mirrors were more like tablets which might be used for writing memoranda in the dust.

It is true there were two or three open books and a newspaper on the bookstands, an inkwell with pens on the bureau; but the open pages had turned yellow and were covered with dust — it was clear that they had been left like that for a long, long time; the newspaper bore last year's date, and if one were to dip a pen in the inkwell, a startled fly was as likely as not to come buzzing out of it.[226]

The comparison of mirrors to tablets reveals the recurring streaks of the threadbare-grotesque — especially in the comic dialogues with the servant. If the mirrors and other dusty surfaces confront Zakhar with his sloth,[227] the principal reflection — as is also the case with Sancho and Leporello — is between servant and master. Oblomov only blames himself when he scolds Zakhar about his deficient cleaning, and gets a reply which might have come from his own lips: "Sweep it [the dirt] up to-day and there'll be plenty of it to-morrow."[228] If Zakhar were to work harder, he would break more things, since he was not brought up among the narrow confines of city living rooms, but in the calm, open spaces of the countryside.[229] That is, for the same reason that Oblomov — ill at ease in the city — is immobilized in passivity: his "dream" is a long chapter of flashbacks and reminiscences of childhood, in the patriarchal shadow of a family of the country aristocracy. "They [the stairs] haven't fallen down, though they have stood there for sixteen years without any repairs," his father used to say of a rickety staircase, and Oblomov in St. Petersburg praises the ceiling where "the plaster is bulging — but it hasn't come down yet."[230]

Lust, a third deadly sin, makes the father in Dostoevsky's *The Brothers Karamazov* say, in a nonphysical sense: "I intend to carry on with my filthy kind of life to the end."[231] His house, welcoming despite its old furniture and infestation by mice — with "all sorts of box-rooms, hidden passages, and un-expected staircases" — is prefigured as the house of the crime only because of its excessive emptiness.[232] By contiguity or by association, more marked images surround his bastard son and servant Smerdyakov: the "tumble-down little house" in the neighboring garden, and the "old tumble-down green summer-house," which "for some reason" will seem to Alyosha "more de-crepit and dilapidated than the day before"; the "deserted lane at the back of the houses," "empty and uninhabited," where Dmitri jumps over the wall at night; the very room where Ivan comes to talk with his brother, which swarms with cockroaches "in great numbers, so that there was a continual rustling from them."[233] On the margins of the privilege which alleviates the materiality of existence, it is but a short step from the servants' quarters to the remote spaces of the closets, the attics, and the back stairs. Domestic outposts of the sewer (II, 11), functional of the nonfunctional and nonfunctional of the func-tional, such places are symbolic in themselves: they lend themselves less to the objectivity of the worn-realistic than to the categories where time is subjectively perceived.[234] In *The Double,* Golyadkin breaks into the house where he has been refused entrance through the back stairs, and hides "in the midst of rubbish, litter, and odds and ends of all sorts." When he returns to his own house, he is already chasing his double up the stairs: "At every turning there were heaped up masses of refuse from the flats."[235]

Of the five descriptions of rooms in *Crime and Punishment,* only the old usurer's appears to be clean.[236] The ragged poverty of the others, including a hotel room, is declared before or after the description itself; their very function as personal, defined, and practicable residences is diminished either by the position of a passageway, or by the low, narrow ceiling, or by the irregularity of the walls.[237] The student, the clerk, the landowner, and the prostitute are not proletarian, just as Ilyushechka's destitute family in *The Brothers Karamazov* is not.[238] But with the full-fledged entrance into narrative of the proletarian condition — no less subject to déclassement than that of the bourgeoisie — an essential restriction of the worn-realistic clearly emerges: the images of the category are scarce when déclassement does not enter into the theme. That is, when work and misery do *not* sink into beggary or criminality — even when they attempt, instead, rebellion. I am referring to the working-class and peasant novels of Zola, *Germinal* and *The Earth* (*La Terre*), and to Verga's *The House by the Medlar Tree* (*I Malavoglia*) despite the fates of Lia and 'Ntoni — I am not counting Gerhart Hauptmann's *The Weavers* (*Die Weber*) because it is a play. In Zola's *L'Assommoir,* the first famous images of the exterior of a large working-class building are also crude but not abject. Inside, the living quarters of the galvanizer and the washerwoman are respectable, as her shop, in its earlier days, had been;[239] but here is how it has ended up:

> Naturally, to the extent that sloth and misery entered, filthiness entered as well. One would have no longer recognized the pretty blue shop, the color of the sky, which once was Gervaise's pride. The wood and glass of the windows, which no one had remembered to wash, remained spattered with the dirt of carriages from top to bottom. Above the tables, on the brass rod three grey rags were spread, left by clients who had died in hospital. And inside it was even more shabby: the dampness of the linen dried close to the ceiling had unglued the paper; the pompadour chintz displayed tatters which hung like cobwebs heavy with dust; the machinery, broken, smashed with a poker, collapsed in its corner into a junk dealer's bits and pieces of old cast iron; the desk seemed to have been used as a table by a whole garrison, stained with coffee, wine, sticky with jam, greasy from Monday's guzzling.[240]

A relationship between misery and vice runs throughout the low worn-realistic, a relationship which neither Zola's denunciation nor Dostoevsky's pity can exclude. It is not necessarily moralistic or reactionary, as we see clearly in a story like Chekhov's *The Peasants:* the brief images which, at the beginning, evoke the declaration that "this was real poverty, and no mistake," are already equivalent, in the rebuttal of the accusation, to the final reflections on the vices of people who "seemed to live worse than beasts."[241] If, among the great writers, Dickens is the most consistently orthodox in attributing a clean poverty to virtue and a dirty one to vice, in his texts he dwells only fleetingly on this first condition and makes the second swarm with irrepressible vitality.[242] *Oliver Twist* precedes *L'Assommoir* by forty years, but is set in the murky, subproletarian underworld: the adjectives "dirty" and "filthy," superlatives such as "poorest class" or "lowest order," the crumbling or fallen houses, and the sterile-noxious of slime and mice recur throughout six descriptions.[243] In *Les Misérables,* a wall separates "noble poverty" from the "dejected, dirty, fetid, infected, dark, sordid" hovel.[244] La Masure Gorbeau, which encompasses both, is the first example of a hidden constant throughout the novel: the secluded, solitary, and antifunctional place in the center of Paris. One reaches it only by chance — or else by climbing over a wall, crawling through a hole, or sliding under a grating. One disappears within the enigmatic cloister of a convent, or within a gigantic brick elephant, or through the underground metropolitan sewer: Hugo is thus giving, with his hallucinatory worn-realistic, a negative contribution to the modern poetical discovery of the metropolis.[245]

Flaubert's neutral worn-realistic, scattered throughout the account of Frédéric's arrival at the suburbs of Paris in *Sentimental Education,*[246] becomes traumatic when we reach the neighborhood from which the June barricades have not yet been removed. Public violence has torn open private life: "One glimpsed the interior of chambers with their wallpaper all torn; certain delicate things had been preserved, at times."[247] The documentation of the category stretches from private interiors to public buildings, and I gave an explanation for this earlier. It also extends to the hospital, the school, the church, the office, the police station, the prison, etc.;[248] for the same reasons, locations abound which are subject to the interference of the two dimensions: intended by private citizens for the general public (IV, 13). Whether it is the shop, the law office, or the boarding house, whether goods are offered for sale, legal matters are settled, or the home is substituted for, Balzac and Dickens alone offer a demoralizing array of examples. In places of commerce, in Balzac, the coexistence of splendor and misery lies in their very contrast with the quality of the product or the size of the profits: a lodging above a printer's shop reveals "the cynical simplicity of commercial avarice";[249] "in an infected hovel" on the first floor, and "among the most dirty rubbish" on the second floor, "the most beautiful suspenders" and "the most elegant cardboards" are manufactured.[250] The

Galeries-de-Bois in Paris were "that sinister heap of mud, those windows encrusted by rain and dust, [etc. (the sentence develops the provisional character of the huts), where between 1789 and 1830] immense transactions took place."[251] In Dickens there is the storehouse, the second-hand clothes shop, the shop of stolen goods, the pawnshop, the antique shop.[252] In Hugo's *The Toilers of the Sea* (*Les Travailleurs de la mer*), an underworld hovel has its own shop, with a list of bizarre objects worthy of the threadbare-grotesque: "a Chinese parasol made of ox membrane and decorated with figures, with holes here and there and impossible to open or close," "a snuff box with a portrait of Marie-Antoinette, and an odd volume of Boisbertrand's Algebra."[253] Finally, Conrad begins *The Secret Agent* with a shop that is a sham.[254] In fact, it is a double sham: the terrorist for whom it is supposed to be a cover is in reality a spy for the London police.[255] The list of things in the window is counterfeit rather than ambiguous — compared to the sign advertising "stationery and newspapers."[256] Various recapitulations throughout the novel summarize the store's offerings: "wares of disreputable rubbish," "shadows of nondescript things," "doubtful wares," "shady wares," "secret wares."[257]

Balzac makes an observation about a lawyer's office which he generalizes at first to include sacristies and second-hand shops, and then to include the gambling house, the courtroom, the lottery, and the brothel. Negligence is understandable in a place where everyone goes and no one remains behind, where there is "no personal interest" that would make anyone "care about the elegance" of the place.[258] Echoing this observation, Dickens opposes "business" to "comfort" in two different law offices, with comfort coming off much the worse.[259] We have already seen a boarding house described by Dickens (V, 5), and the interior of the Pension Vauquer in Balzac's *Père Goriot* is a paradigmatic page for the themes and forms of the category.[260] The seriousness with which the humble subject-matter is taken up changes the scorn into an inverted exaltation, and absorbs what in Gogol, Goncharov, or Dickens would have been left as threadbare-grotesque: a prankster could write his name with his finger in the grease on the waxed cloth, and the hemp mats "slip away from under your feet without slipping away for good." The insufficiency of petit bourgeois decorum, which is here "economical, concentrated, worn poverty,"[261] instead largely relies on a more modern contamination. That is, a contamination between the worn-realistic and a precocious pretentious-fictitious,[262] in which objects are condemned on economic rather than on cultural grounds: from the scenes from Fénelon's *Telemachus* (*Télémaque*) on the walls to the "execrable engravings which take away your appetite," from the porcelain set "which is to be found everywhere nowadays" to the pendulum in "bluish marble in the worst taste." The dining room outdoes the sitting room in its "dull horrors," and here, in the second and longest of two canonical lists, there is a dense concentration of the pure worn-realistic. There follows a formal *a priori* parallel to the list — the sequence of pseudo-plethoric and anthropomorphic adjectives — with a figure of preterition: too long a description *would be necessary* to explain "how this furniture was old, cracked, rotten, trembling, chewed up, maimed, asquint, invalid, dying."[263]

As is clear from the preceding text, thematic topoi are both mixed odors and faded colors. The first (tangential to an inquiry into images) yields here "*boarding-house odor,*" that is, an odor of déclassement: the "smell of service, of the pantry, of the hospice." The second has already been pointed out in Balzac (IV, 5). It yields the "half-vanished golden threads" of the porcelain, and the living room "once painted a color that is now undistinguishable," in whose corners dirt traces out bizarre patterns.[264] These same processes reveal a passage of time together with nature's revenge against culture (IV, 28). At its most extreme, the worn-realistic decomposes into the sterile-noxious.[265] The topos of colors marks a visible stage of this decomposition, which, although still superficial, is already metamorphic. I conclude this section with a miniature anthology that documents it, as is necessary at least this once, from some authors already quoted up to the twentieth century:

> The tapestry . . . was tarnished and faded under the effects of the sun . . . (Scott, 1819).[266]

> . . . tapestry representing La Fontaine's fables; but one must have known it to recognize the subject, so difficult to perceive were the faded colors and the figures riddled with patches (Balzac, 1833).[267]

> . . . the baize . . . had long since lost all claim to its original hue of green and had gradually grown grey with dust and age, except where all traces of its natural colour were obliterated by ink stains (Dickens, 1837).[268]

> . . . his uniform was not green but of some mealy orange (Gogol, 1842).[269]

> Faded by the sun, the air, and the rain, the colors of these rags had become so uncertain that a painter would have had to make an effort to identify them by their correct names (Gautier, 1863).[270]

> . . . the shabby wallpaper was so dusty and tattered that while it was still possible to guess its color (yellow), the pattern was no longer discernable (Dostoevsky, 1866).[271]

> All the hues had turned to a dirty gray, in this closet rotten with dust and damp (Zola, 1867).[272]

> A great sofa occupied almost all of the wall at the end of the room; certainly it had once been of green rep, but the material, scratched, worn, patched, now bore, under large satins, a grayish color (Eça de Queiroz, 1877).[273]

The somber greenish colored paper on the walls has been smoked a dismal dirty gray ... (Gertrude Stein, 1909).[274]

The walls of my room were papered in red, but the green pattern in the shape of a heart had faded and covered the paper now like seedy pencil squiggles, of surprising regularity (Böll, 1953).[275]

8

In the case of the reminiscent-affective I also do not see any codified recurrences before the historical turning point, and I have found isolated occurrences before it that are even more exceptional and doubtful than those of the venerable-regressive. It was beyond the powers even of a Virgil or a Shakespeare to recognize in objects a passage of time individually perceived, and to present them with a moving complacence. In Book III of the *Aeneid,* Helenus and Andromache have rebuilt a "miniature Troy" in Epirus, where the monuments and rivers are named in imitation or simulation of their Trojan originals.[276] In precisely the same way, if the comparison is legitimate, Werther has had a frock coat made identical to the one he remembers (IV, 15). But the scope of the memories of the Trojan exiles extends well beyond the individual mind; while, at the end of Book IV, Aeneas's weapons and clothes, and the wedding bed, have an exclusively individual scope, without bearing any signs of the passage of time. As she asks that they be set on the suicidal pyre (whose pretext is magical), Dido declares that "it is right to abolish all memories of the abominable one": the denial of the reminiscent-affective. And yet, on the verge of dying, she stops "for a moment" to look at them as familiar things, weeps, and addresses "the sweet remains."[277] In *Richard II,* the Duke of Gloucester's widow is about to send for her brother-in-law asking him to visit her in her castle, and immediately she thinks better of it; what else would the visitor see:

> But empty lodgings and unfurnish'd walls,
> Unpeopled offices, untrodden stones?

That it is not worth the trouble because sorrow "dwells everywhere" is another indirect denial of the physicality of the reminiscent-affective.[278] The duke had been murdered by the order of the protagonist, the king, and it is Richard's tone that such verses adumbrate: deposed before he is eliminated, he will pity himself with elegiac complacence.[279]

The modern sense of memory was to develop from pre-Romantic individualism, one of whose premises was the weakening of religious concepts. In the case of childhood memory, I again refer to my previous book (V, 6; and cf. IV, 15): with Rousseau, the pathos which infused the earliest stages of human life came from its final ones; it came as a loan from aging and death, and was taken away from the expectation of an afterlife.[280] The reminiscent-affective was emerging at the expense of the solemn-admonitory. But we cannot speak of the reminiscent-affective for those few sublime paragraphs in the *Confessions*, since there is a dearth of images. However, they interest us because they prefigure a crossroads which will continue to divide, or rather to impede or let pass, the images of the category. Just as Jean-Jacques refrains from recovering by external means the half-forgotten words of a childhood song, so does he miss the chance to go and see whether a walnut tree associated with a memorable prank still exists.[281] The problem is the survival of the objects of memory outside memory itself: in both cases, he solves it, consciously or presumptively, by denying any interest in an enduring exterior reality and reserving his emotion for the interior spontaneous fact. Remembrance with the eyes shut versus a sentimental pilgrimage — or versus the cherishing of relics. These will remain the two possible ways, and from our point of view they are not equally fertile: in objects remembered without material mediations, the passage of time is necessarily annulled. Proust, who will one day theorize the first way as involuntary memory, will condemn the second as vain idolatry.

Rousseau was the great pioneer of both, having reinvented the memory of love in *The New Eloïse* (*La Nouvelle Héloïse*) even before childhood memory in the *Confessions*. In the famous visit that the former lovers Julie and Saint-Preux make to Meillerie, that journey to memorable places which, according to Lucan, Caesar made at Troy (V, 4) becomes a private one with a bourgeois sensibility — both with regard to their subjectivities and to the objects that greet them. As he comes upon a place unexpectedly, moreover, Saint-Preux has an experience of involuntary memory.[282] But not even in the presence of the place does Rousseau make visible any traces of the passage of time; it is only from the abolition of time that he takes satisfaction — just as Proust will one day do. The reminiscent-affective indeed began with Werther and René — or almost, rather, with Chateaubriand, given the thin substance of images in Goethe (IV, 15, 14). It was the pages of both Goethe and Chateaubriand that codified the sentimental pilgrimage, still recognizable after 150 years (IV, 18); and, in both, the novelty of the childhood memory was grafted onto a love story, whose pathos literature had always endorsed. The danger of arbitrarily indulging in the particularity of the sensorial, which all our categories dared to do in the decades of the historical turning point, was greater for the individual than for the collective imagination. In order of appearance, the venerable-regressive preceded the reminiscent-affective, and they both preceded the worn-realistic: the same risk was higher for the negative categories than for the semipositive ones, and only more than fifty years later would the desolate-disconnected make its appearance. Suspended between an immaterial — if not transcendent — path, and an immanent one suspected of fetishism, the reminiscent-affective remains the most elusive of all the categories.

On a miniature scale, the limits of the worthless or of the sickening were all the more marked: I have found nothing of sufficient pertinence or significance until the middle of the nineteenth century,[283] with one precocious exception. Only a German author like Jean Paul, not long after Rousseau, and midway between Werther and the Romantics, was able to invent the reminiscent-affective in such dimensions. It was almost as though, through an oblique transformation, he extracted it from the threadbare-grotesque: on the thin line between humor and its inseparable counterpart, sentimentalism, and in the endless discursive game typical of his style. His first truly original character, Wutz the modest schoolteacher, would not live such a docile, contented life in his narrow privacy if he did not methodically devote one hour each day to remembering different days of his childhood.[284] During his life, he himself rewrites in private the books he does not have the money to buy; at the time of his death, he hopes that his last moments will not be unfitting "for an author." On his bed there is "a whole assortment of goods," and he contemplates them for hours:

> On the bed cover there was a green taffeta baby's bonnet, with its only ribbon torn, a child's whip covered with worn golden sequins, a tin finger-ring, a box containing tiny booklets in 1280 format, a grandfather clock, a dirty exercise book, and a finger-long perch for finches. These were the ruins and surviving things of his childhood which he had frittered away in play. The museum of his *Greek antiquities* had always been under the stairs — since in a house which is the planting tub and the greenhouse of a single genealogical tree, things remain in their places undisturbed for fifty years; and as ever since his childhood it had been a fundamental law with him to put away all his toys in historical order, and since the whole year through no one except himself would look under the stairs: for these reasons on the day of preparation before the day of his death he could arrange around himself those urns of an already dead life and take pleasure in the past, since he was no longer able to take pleasure in the future.

The playful mitigates the pathetic by applying the archaeological language of the collective categories to a childhood reminiscent-affective. Using what the dying man has told him, the narrator then expands upon the "systematic catalogue of those gadgets and toys."[285]

Following Jean Paul, it was also a German author who, before the middle of the century, developed from the collective categories an intimate one of smaller dimensions. In Adalbert Stifter's *My Great-Grandfather's Portfolio*

(*Die Mappe meines Urgrossvaters*),[286] the pretext of the stories is not in itself original: the discovery of a manuscript during a pilgrimage to the house where he was born.[287] But the chapter is entitled *Antiques* (*Die Altertümer*),[288] and in introducing the great-grandfather it establishes the images and their poetics within the succession of generations. Each generation smiles at its ancestors' possessions, and replaces them; each generation believes that it will be made eternal through the provision of new things, which will proceed along "the road to destruction and oblivion."[289] Between the illusion of functionality and the final annihilation, it is as if the semipositivity of the reminiscent-affective achieves a kind of truce, reconciling forgetfulness and survival.[290] The "poetry of rubbish" is the "sad and sweet" poetry, stamped with everyday life, of that which lasts longer than human bones; of that which comforts the individual's solitude, which is the last and first element of long, unknown chains.[291] The attraction of "old" things, which redeems the range of its disparaging synonyms,[292] principally illuminates childhood memories. It is particularized by four or five lists, defunctionalizing pluralities (I, 1) not of words but of sentences;[293] enigma after enigma for the child, a "terrifying, intimate joy."[294] These two adjectives condense another contamination of categories.[295] And yet the decline of the supernatural, which hovered over the doctor of olden times, is the only exception to the quiet continuity of four generations.[296]

In France, even down to the 1830s, neither established Romanticism nor advances in descriptive capacities promoted the category as much as we might have expected. In Sainte-Beuve's novel *Volupté*, the visit to the places of childhood and youth is directly inspired by *René*, with two connected variations. The uncle's bourgeois house and garden replace a castle: on the outside bland signs of absence, on the inside scrupulous, silent conservation.[297] Hugo's poem *Olympio's Sadness* (*Tristesse d'Olympio*) is a visit to places of love. Whether they are unchanged or transformed, these places reveal nature's indifference to her human guests: the only ravage of time introduces the most admired line of the poem, with the peace and lassitude of the countryside in the evening. It is the deterioration of the wayside post, which in the dark has had many collisions with:

> The great groaning wagons returning at night.[298]

A decade earlier, Alphonse de Lamartine, in his *Milly or the Native Land* (*Milly ou la Terre natale*) drew a comparison which Saint-Preux had not drawn: the places "still full of the feasts of our soul" are as important as those which commemorate the splendors of an empire; his small fief is, for him, as large as Thebes or Palmyra. The poem's theme is the other face of a pilgrimage — the relationship between the persistence of memory and the permanence of property, a relationship enlivened when property is endangered (cf. IV, 15). The possible arrival of an unknown and hateful buyer compounds the threat of ivy and weeds; but, according to the curse that is now pronounced, utter natural ruin is a hundred times better than alienation.[299] Property and pilgrimage are sublimated quite differently in *The Vineyard and the House* (*La Vigne et la Maison*), the poetic masterpiece Lamartine will write in his old age, as a survivor of his own earlier literary fame. It is in the form of a dialogue: the "I" relives the past, sweetly confusing it with the present, while the Soul mourns the past, projecting it into a transcendental future. In the imaginary visit to the house, the "I" recognizes what is still there, the Soul sees who is no longer there and things that have changed. Only the Soul speaks of the streaks left by the rain on the façade or the swallows' nests inside: "Their chirruping on the flagstones / Covered by floating down / Is the only voice of these halls / Full of the silence of time."[300] But absence is the hope of restitution, the hearth to return to is elsewhere:

> In the unchangeable breast that will contain our souls
> Will we not be reunited with all that we have loved
> At the hearth where nobody is absent?[301]

The pre-Romantic model is still soberly recognizable in the only passage which, in all of *War and Peace,* offers any images of relevance to us. Among all the greatest authors, Tolstoy is certainly the least inclined towards any category of such images. Like Werther and René, Prince Andrei does not intentionally visit the paternal property where he was born and spent his childhood. He approaches it with his regiment, and "though there was nothing for him to do at Bald Hills, Prince Andrei with a characteristic desire to foment his own grief decided that he must ride there." The traumatic motivation of the images is the war before which his relatives have fled:

> No one was at the stone entrance-gates of the drive and the door stood open. Grass had already begun to grow on the garden paths, and horses and calves were straying in the English park. Prince Andrew rode up to the hot-house; some of the glass panes were broken, and of the trees in tubs some were overturned and others dried up.[302]

But when the large modern city replaces the countryside, the reminiscent-affective becomes even more precarious than it is made by expropriation or even by war. Dickens shows this at the end of *The Old Curiosity Shop*. Faithful to Nell's memory, Kit brings his children to London, to the site of the old house, where there is now a smooth road:

> At first he would draw with his stick a square upon the ground to show them where it used to stand. But, he soon became uncertain of the spot, and

could only say it was thereabouts, he thought, and these alterations were confusing.[303]

At its core, this is the theme of Baudelaire's *The Swan* (*Le Cygne*), although his passage through a new neighborhood evokes two other associated themes: first, Virgil's Andromache, with her fictitious remnants. What is now seen "in spirit," and had already had a "sketchy" and "confused" outline, will be described as unmovable in his melancholy and ponderous in his memory:

> Old Paris is no more (the shape of a town
> Changes faster, alas! than the heart of a mortal man);
>
> I now only see in spirit all those encampments of hovels,
> Those piles of rough-hewn capitals and pillars,
> The weeds, the great blocks greenish with the water of puddles,
> And, shining in the window-panes, confused bric-à-brac.
>
> . . . .
>
> Paris changes! But nothing in my melancholy
> Has moved! New palaces, scaffolding, blocks,
> Old suburbs, everything for me becomes allegory,
> And my dear memories are heavier than rocks.[304]

From the house, the countryside, or the neighborhood, let us return to smaller dimensions: to the room, to bric-à-brac, and to the furniture with its drawers which is contained by the one and contains the other. In Nerval's *Sylvie,* a nostalgia for the *ancien régime* — which contaminates the category with the venerable-regressive (V, 6) — intervenes, although every historical referent has been personalized, as if by a prenatal memory. The mediator is an uncle who lived "in the next-to-last years of the eighteenth century, in the way it was necessary to live to know them well": with his portraits, medallions, notes, and ribbons.[305] In the dreamlike, spur-of-the-moment nocturnal visit to the villages of the past, there is also a pilgrimage to his house.[306] Another mediator is Sylvie's aunt, or, more precisely, her aunt's wedding clothes. There is a delightful scene in which the young lady dresses up in "a corset of yellowed tulles, and withered ribbons," and the young narrator "as a groom of the past century," both having rummaged through the fragrant drawers glittering with cheap old tinsel.[307] But in Nerval, as we have seen, the overlapping of different periods can dissolve our constants along with time itself (V, 2). The figure of Time dominates a Renaissance pendulum clock that has not been wound for two centuries: "it is not in order to know the time that I bought that clock in Touraine."[308] In *Aurélia,* epochs and countries are condensed into a reliquary of journeys to the Orient (enclosed in a trinket box which belonged to the woman), and into the antique and exotic furniture which sums up a life of wandering and which fills up — like Faust's — the room in the clinic.[309]

I said earlier that I would have to draw again on one of my previous papers — dealing with *Winter Shiver* (*Frisson d'hiver*), a prose poem by Mallarmé. It is a masterpiece in which images of old furniture and evocations of the late eighteenth century found both their most original and their most exemplary motivations. There is a third category underlying the contamination between the reminiscent-affective and the venerable-regressive, thanks to the enigmatic shadow evoked at the windows of the room; I cannot, unfortunately, reproduce the text here, and I refer the reader to my earlier analysis.[310] What is indispensable is a certain relationship between memory and history, mediated by furnishings which have lasted longer than a human life span. Since childhood time is incommensurable with adult time, periods of centuries (as with Poe's ship, II, 15) are used to translate its length and distance; while the oblivion of the remotest personal events is translated into the unknowable origin of the object.[311] By disguising itself in the collective past, the individual past reanimates it, and the immanent paths of memory are dematerialized in Mallarmé by the transcendence of a ghost. In a less extraordinary text, Maupassant's short story *Old Objects* (*Vieux objets*), the two paths correspond to the modes of remembrance an old provincial lady describes in a letter to a Parisian friend: one, in front of the fireplace, occurs entirely in the mind. The other "is by far the better." It consists in going up to the storage room, where previously insignificant objects have assumed the meaning of ancient, unexpected witnesses — unless, having come from the grandparents or from who knows where, they no longer speak to living people.[312] In the meantime, the negative category had sprung from Baudelaire's chests and closets (II, 2; IV, 16). It may be surprising that, before Cros, it was Rimbaud in his sonnet *The Sideboard* (*Le Buffet*) who transposed them into an affectionate key. Here, the medley of old stuff is fragrant:

> It is there that one would find the medallions, the locks
> Of white or blond hair, the portraits, the dried flowers
> The scent of which mixes with the scents of the fruits.[313]

Between the nineteenth and twentieth centuries, during that last twilight season when it was not in danger of being reversed by the desolate-disconnected,[314] the reminiscent-affective concealed itself behind metalinguistic filters: allusive irony, affected naïveté. One could no longer — even though one wished to — reminisce and lament with the candor of one's romantically bourgeois grandparents. It is as if the complacence in melancholy had been passed on from custom to literature:

> Handsome building, sad abandoned!
> Big-bellied railings, twisted, worn!

> Silence! Suite of dead rooms!
> Smell of shadow! Smell of past!
> Smell of desolate abandon!

This is Guido Gozzano's *Miss Felicita* (*La signorina Felicita*), where the rubbish in the attic enjoys an even better fate than the kitsch in the living room (II, 4). As in Stifter, a poetics reclaims it, not despite its execrable taste, but because of its beauty:

> Rested beauty of the attic
> Where the century-old waste sleeps!
>
> . . . .
>
> Mousetraps, mattresses, crockery,
> Lanterns, baskets, furniture: rejected
> Rubbish, so dear to my Muse![315]

From the French model of Jammes, I choose a sentimental pilgrimage with a slender narrative plot, rather than an interior.[316] The "I" searching for the country house of his long-dead ancestors returns further back into the past than the reach of his own individual memory. The collective oblivion creates difficulties for him; he has an aversion, like Werther, to the new; he infuses the scene with decadent connotations, with no scruples of unreality; and he will come upon a door, a staircase, and an interior as decrepit as everything else on his way:

> It was midday by the old steeple, quite ruined,
> close to a tower as old as the past
>
> . . . .
>
> And I passed before the worm-eaten portals
> Of abandoned gardens where, through large railings,
> One saw, close to houses with no more families,
> Pink hollyhocks in the blue grass
> Near doors blocked by the old dust
> Like the doors of the coffins in cemeteries.[317]

Memory in the presence of objects and in their absence is united in a modern Greek poem by Cavafy. A room, once the site of homosexual love, like the rest of the house, has now been rented to commercial offices. Here, the recognition of the furniture can only occur through pure memories. He offers a tender surmise on the present state of absent things:

> The poor objects must still be somewhere around.[318]

We know what kind of memory, in Proust, serves as both the starting point and the end point of a narrative and theoretical summa. Insofar as involuntary memory is the only experience and knowledge outside of Time, the man who willfully searches for the past "in identical and consequently dead forms" is making a mistake.[319] Proust's criticism of the category is continuous and para-digmatic. The first of the seven novels closes with a melancholy version—on the vain futility of trying to localize in real space the regret for the Bois de Boulogne of another time.[320] Further on, explicitly and in passing, we read:

> Poets claim that we may find for a moment what we once were just by reenter-ing a certain house, a certain garden where we lived when we were young. These are deeply hazardous pilgrimages in consequence of which one achieves as many disappointments as successes. Fixed places, contemporaneous with different years—it is better to find them within ourselves.[321]

The demystification of the pilgrimage takes place shortly before the Narrator's final illuminations. La Vivonne, whose spring he believed as a child to be as otherworldly as the entrance into Hell, now appears to him "scanty and ugly," and the spring itself "a kind of square washing trough where bubbles rose"; the ends of mythically opposed walks reveal themselves to him as connected and close to one another.[322] Immediately after Time is regained, as he leafs through a copy of his favorite childhood novel, the Narrator gradually ampli-fies the aesthetic asceticism which—as we shall see—a young Proust had turned against the prestigious-ornamental. Not only would he refuse to collect other original editions, other period bindings, beside the ones he actually used in his early reading; but, even if he still owned one of them, he would never look at it, for fear of locking it into the present and silencing its childhood appeal.[323]

The crisis of the reminiscent-affective follows upon the crisis of the bour-geois conscience. Already in Tolstoy's late *Resurrection*, Nekhlifudov, observ-ing the seasonal house cleaning, "was surprised at the great number of things there were, all quite useless"; it is one of the moments that lead up to his decision to bequeath his land to the peasants. Further on, an antique high chair reminds him of his mother's bedroom. "He was suddenly filled with regret at the thought of the house that would tumble to ruin, the garden that would run wild"—a moment of moral wavering.[324] Walter Benjamin, in the tones of a moralizing progressivist, denounces the memento as a "secularized relic," deriving from dead experience rather than from the dead body, the deposit and inventory of the alienated man's past.[325] One chapter of Joyce's *Ulysses* is written in the question-and-answer form of a catechism. Some of these questions focus on the objects contained in two drawers of Bloom's desk. They are mostly bearers of some memory, and yet they are conflated—in their everydayness—with letters and legal papers of the present, disavowed among the measures and figures in the exhaustive aridity of the list's description and information.[326]

In the twentieth century, the semipositive category may be refused as an inauthentic moment even in antithesis to the authenticity of the negative one: this is the case in Sartre, or in Montale (IV, 17, 19). The reminiscent-affective may be salvaged by renouncing the physical correspondence between objects and memory, as does the desolate-disconnected (IV, 16), or else by renouncing contact with them in the present, following the path marked out from Rousseau to Proust.[327] In Babel's *Red Cavalry,* the "dense melancholy of memories," in Poland, torments the revolutionary Jew on the eve of the Sabbath: "Oh the rotted Talmuds of my childhood!" Still, it leads him to visit a Dickensian second-hand shop.[328] Bruno Schulz, the Polish Jewish writer, describes the *Cinnamon Shops* which were sometimes open late into the night as a childhood attraction, with their "dimly lit . . . dark and solemn" interiors smelling of a long list of rare goods.[329] And even *The Safe* (*A' casciaforte*) of a Neapolitan song popularized by Roberto Murolo is metaphorical, and its lists are not without elements of the threadbare-grotesque (as initially in Jean Paul). The safe is even more of a necessity than clothes and food, since it protects certain relics and keepsakes. But it is not easy to obtain one: "to what safe-maker can I describe it?"[330] The category can also be saved if it claims that a humble property of memory and affection cannot be reduced to money. In Böll's *Group Portrait with Lady* (*Gruppenbild mit Dame*), A. (the author) demands that the damage to his jacket be calculated using a different standard than that of insurance, since "an old thing is dearer than a new one," since its pockets held memories and odds and ends, and because "in the end one is a Western man and the *lacrimae rerum* have been seared into him."[331]

9

The periodization of the desolate-disconnected, and of some other categories, begins after the historical turning point. We may be tempted to speak of a second, more rapid historical turning point in the proliferation of images: focused on 1848 rather than 1789, at the final, rather than the initial, stage of the rise of the bourgeoisie. The few anterior isolated occurrences I am able to produce already fall within the Romantic era. Along with dysphoric memory, they foreshadow two other connected innovations in relation to the semipositive category: the alternative between memory's objects and its processes; and the alternative between the memory-related and the metaphorical, subjectively perceived (IV, 16). In Byron's *Manfred,* the countless days and nights, identical as grains of sand on the seashore, are a metaphor of his own past:

> . . . and one desert,
> Barren and cold, on which the wild waves break,
> But nothing rests, save carcasses and wrecks,
> Rocks, and the salt-surf weeds of bitterness.[332]

The Mephistopheles of Nikolaus Lenau's *Faust* takes pleasure, devil-like, in bad memory among men. He explains why with a comparison. In an old tower corroded by stormy weather, vultures have their nests:

> Thus corrodes the loud life storm,
> Thus corrodes the silent death worm,
> Even the aging edifice of memory:
> And if out of the broken joint there falls
> A piece of thought, intention, pain, joy,
> The birds of prey from hell, the passions,
> Often fly in with lightning speed
> And nest and breed in the crack.[333]

Even before Baudelaire, there were sporadic occurrences of that subjective metaphorical process which makes the protagonist of Georg Büchner's comedy *Leonce and Lena* lament: "My head is an empty ballroom, a few withered roses and creased ribbons on the floor, cracked violins in the corner."[334] With Baudelaire, the process becomes integral and absolute. In the lines we have already analyzed from *The Flowers of Evil,* the desolate-disconnected which is thereby inaugurated coincides with the "I" itself: the "I" *is like,* the "I" *is,* certain images (IV, 16; II, 2). In the prose poem *The Double Room* (*La Chambre double*), the indolent, lulling, and synaesthetic dream which makes the first sight of the room blissful culminates in the vanishing of time. Its real aspect, after trauma has knocked on the door, is not as an object of memory so much as all the horror of memory imposed by a resurrected Time:

> Oh horror! I remember, I remember! Yes! This hovel, this dwelling of eternal boredom, is truly mine. Here is my stupid, dusty, chipped furniture; the hearth without flame or ember, soiled with spit; the sad windows where the rain has drawn troughs in the dirt; the manuscripts, erased or incomplete; the calendar where the pencil has underlined the sinister dates![335]

In the objects of a personal and direct memory, repugnant rather than pleasurable, the relationship between the reminiscent-affective and the permanence of property is inverted (IV, 15; V, 8). The objects are prey to expropriation, dispersion, and dismantlement; they yield images with such themes as auction, removal, and demolition.[336] Of the two passages I have quoted from Flaubert's *Sentimental Education,* one evokes the solemn-admonitory for an unprofaned royal court, and the other represents the profanation of private life as worn-realistic (V, 4, 7). In the novel's account of the people's invasion of the Tuileries on February 24, 1848, this profanation is emphasized — without any trace of the venerable-regressive, which is not fitting for the fall of the "bourgeois" monarchy. And the novel ends, or almost ends, with the auction of Mme Arnoux's belongings, which exposes and pulls apart Frédéric's "I" in his amorous recollections:

> and the parceling out of these relics, in which he confusedly rediscovered the shape of her limbs, seemed like an atrocity to him, as if he had seen ravens tearing her corpse to pieces. [. . .] And thus, one after the other, there disappeared the large blue carpet sprinkled with camellias, which her pretty feet brushed in coming towards him, the small upholstered easy chair where he used always to sit facing her when they were alone; the two screens of the hearth, the ivory of which had been softened by contact with her hands [. . .]. It was as if parts of his heart were leaving with the things . . . [337]

An auction that implies an analogous relationship between man and woman, and then Andrea Sperelli's visit to the rooms not yet entirely despoiled, are the final incidents of D'Annunzio's *Pleasure* (*Il Piacere*).[338]

In Arthur Schnitzler's short story *Flight into Darkness* (*Flucht in die Finster-nis*), it is not love but madness that lies at the third corner of a triangle together with man and things. Images are scarce in a ubiquitous net of metaphoric correspondences; objects tremble uncertainly in the processes of a troubled memory. The house which the protagonist had quit, before leaving for a vacation on the advice of a doctor, is only recalled in a parapraxis upon his return; his parents' house, an "extremely ancient, now vanished, building in the center of town," will be remembered by that brother on whom he has focused his paranoia.[339] It is as if both places were related to their status as temporary dwellings as his identity was to a mental situation that puts it to the test. The search for a new apartment is turned upside down into a fragmentary and frustrated sentimental pilgrimage;[340] the hotel has also been chosen according to his memories, which connect it to a friend who died as a madman. In the phases in which his recognition of the place occurs, either as better or as worse than he remembers it,[341] the theme of ephemeral relief is introduced, a theme which will recur with clinical regularity. He succeeds in lending "an appearance of familiarity" to the room with the help of small things from his own luggage; but a nearby mirror is about to confront him with the deformation of his face:

> Then he proceeded to the bathroom, which — it was easy to see — only in accordance with the unwillingly recognized demands of a new age, had been converted from an unused attic to its current use. A yellowish lamp stuck into

the ceiling spread a feeble light in the windowless room, and the oblong mirror, which hung on the wall in a smooth, old golden frame, was cracked from top to bottom.[342]

In a discontinuous autobiographical text like Michel Leiris' *Manhood* (*L'Age d'Homme*), the festive hall at the Palais du Trocadéro forms an apt background for the memories which used to terrify the child amidst the public. "A funereal place if there ever was one," it was already comparable to the rooms of a morgue or an auction house. After its demolition, it metamorphoses through a series of alternative catastrophic metaphors, until it brushes up against the solemn-admonitory and is redeemed by its beauty:

> . . . this hall always sent a shiver down my spine, with its air at once miserable and official, like a morgue, a registry office, an auction house full of re-possessed furniture. The last glimpse I had of it was when it was being destroyed, and the vast space covered in rubble, deprived of its floor and armchairs (which laid bare its metal framework) conferred on it an air of a parliament after a revolution or an earthquake, of an old stranded carcass, steamer or sea monster; then, after the whole interior had been destroyed and the very dome had sunk, it became a Roman ruin, a circus in the wall of which Moorish windows had been cut and, in an adjoining room, the statue of Fame toppled to the ground like a slaughtered animal and, at the top, tattered drapery where the wind was engulfed. All made-up as a crumbling arena, one could say that at that moment Trocadéro theater was really beautiful.[343]

In a text halfway between memoir and narrative like Salvatore Satta's *Day of Judgment* (*Il Giorno del giudizio*), in the hinterland of a Sardinia threatened by progress, a dead priest's room has not been opened for twenty years (cf. IV, 15). It was God whom his sister had tried to lock in there, together with her brother's objects. When she reenters it, the bed, now a nesting place for mice and food for worms, crumbles at her first touch, "without even a squeak"; only a few threads are all that is left of the breviary and the hat, "witnesses to a past which might have never been."[344]

In Heinrich Böll's novel *A Clown's Opinions* (*Ansichten eines Clowns*), the step beyond the disintegration of objects occurs in an absence neither more nor less cruel than presence, and with no traces of the metaphorical. The rebel son of a good family is finally abandoned by his lover, who is beguiled by Catholic orthodoxy. He finds nothing belonging to her in the bathroom or in the closet, and thus rediscovers, without knowing what he would have preferred, "the deathly sentimentality which is inherent in things." As a child, he had understood "how terrible are the things left behind by someone leaving or dying," and, when his sister dies because of her Nazi fanaticism, he throws her things out of the window and sets them on fire.[345] Let us now move towards the metaphorical alternative to the memory-related—not outside of the memory-related altogether, but, finally, outside of direct memory itself—with an episode from Nathalie Sarraute's *Martereau*. On a rainy afternoon, the first-person narrator is driving an aunt and uncle to visit some property in the country they want to buy. In his account, the project seems to be more wishful, and its renunciation more unstable, insofar as the atmosphere of the old house seems to draw him into an almost transindividual memory:

> Doors open, still more doors give onto other rooms, boudoirs, smoking rooms, cupboards, secret cabinets . . . our own appurtenances are extended, we spread in all directions . . .
>
> It is doubtlessly this smell, of dampness, of moldiness, in this great abandoned house, in these slightly dilapidated rooms . . . I know not what vague exhalation . . . cold remains of other lives . . . this was already insinuating into me while I was spreading in all directions . . . [346]

In Guillaume Apollinaire's *The Musician of Saint-Merry* (*Le Musicien de Saint-Merry*), the house into which the musician disappears, along with his entranced throng of women, is a place of a far remoter transindividual memory. So remote that it becomes connected, *déclassé* as it is—but inhabited by magic—with images of the monarchical centuries of some other categories (V, 6, 8):

> The stranger halted one moment before a house for sale
> An abandoned house
> With broken windows
> It is a dwelling of the sixteenth century
> The courtyard is used to park delivery vans
> It is there that the musician entered.[347]

Giovanni Raboni's *Reclamation* (*Risanamento*) begins: "Of all this / Nothing is left."[348] The memory of the neighborhoods that have vanished is not entirely personal, as it was for Baudelaire (who, more desolate and more disconnected, is echoed in other poems a century later).[349] It is mediated by his father, to whom he submits both a question and an answer which would absolve things by discounting their importance:

> But what
> They have done, destroying houses,
> Destroying neighborhoods, here and elsewhere,
> What is its use? Evil was not
> In there, in the staircases, in the courtyards,

On the landings, at most there was damp there
That would make you ill. If my father
Were alive, I would ask him too: do you think
It is useful? is it the right way? It seems to me that evil
Is never in things, I would tell him.

"One is not miserable without feeling: a ruined house is not miserable," Pascal noted at the beginning of a hundred-year period that was austere in its use of images.[350] In the quatrains of Cros' *Dilapidation* (*Délabrement*), on the other hand, the "I" is compared to a house; if the reminiscent-affective of another of his sonnets has given us the first example in this book (II, 1; IV, 16), the last line of the first tercet provides an epigraph for the negative category:

Like an empty apartment with dirty floors,
With naked walls, flayed by the nails of pictures,
From where the furniture has been removed, the curtains,
Where the ground is covered with hay and rags

. . . .

That the rain and the wind from the open window
May cover with acrid mold and green moss
All these remains, horror of beloved memories!
. . . .[351]

The identification of the self with a hall appears again in the sole, fragmented composition of Coelho Pacheco, one of the heteronyms of the great, multi-faceted Portuguese poet Fernando Pessoa. In the first variant of this identification, the "I" extracts — "from the recess" of ancient panoplies — a "secret of the soul." In the second, the hall itself becomes for him "the structure of a soul." In the third, he enters the hall "with excessive coherence," and there finds himself to be "like anyone else":

But the wooden floor is concave and the doors don't shut
The sadness of the crucified panels in the doorways
Is a crooked sadness made of silence
From the grated windows the daylight enters
Which benumbs the glass of the panels and gathers in corners clots of
    blackness
At times cold winds sweep the long corridors
But there is a smell of old and peeling paint in the corners of the hall
And everything is painful in this mansion of old rubbish.[352]

In Gottfried Benn's last poem, written shortly before his death, his identification with more than one great author in the German language is inspired by a review of those final furnishings which were "for a short time a miserable home" to them. Beds, sofas, white cushions of their deaths:

All old stuff now or already no longer there,
Undeterminable, unsubstantial,
In painless eternal dissolution.[353]

In Pablo Neruda's surrealist language, before a communist poetics reduced it to clarity,[354] the metaphorical image stands both for the objects and for the processes of memory. Thus, in *Melancholy in the Families* (*Melancolía en las familias*), we have "an abandoned dining room,"[355] or, in *Ode with a Lamentation* (*Oda con un lamento*), the things which at its end "are there," but only "there" in the soul:

Because there is a dark room and a broken candelabra,
A few crooked chairs waiting for winter,
And a dead dove, with a number.[356]

Without a title like *The Destroyed Road* (*La calle destruida*), we would not be able to recognize the theme of demolition in lines even more densely figurative:

Over the towns
A tongue of putrid dust advances
Breaking rings, eroding paint,
Making the black chairs scream voicelessly.

Everything is covered by a deathly flavor
Of regression and dampness and wound.[357]

When modern hermeticism conceals and seems to suppress the zero degree of every metaphor, and the referent of every memory, not only does the distinction between the memory-related and the metaphorical waver, but so does the very distinction between functional and nonfunctional itself (IV, 17, 19; V, 2). This explains the absence from this book of many great authors—from the mature Mallarmé and Rimbaud to the twentieth-century lyric poets of, for example, Spain. And this despite the fact that modern poetry rarely avoided extending to the "refuse of the vile life" the privilege described by D'Annunzio:

here is a fragment of a tool, a scrap of cast iron, a crooked nail, an empty zinc box, a measure of twine, a splinter, a shaving.
Everything speaks to me, everything is a sign for me who can read. [. . .] The lines expressed by the casual encounter of objects invent a hermetic writing.[358]

It is in narrative, rather, that a desolate-disconnected is produced without any relation to memory, and even only implicitly metaphorical (IV, 17). A character's "I" may, for its part, project onto objects—if not himself, like the poetic "I"—a kind of meaning. It is this meaning which makes them into subjective symbols, and which synthesizes the world in a subjective allegory.

Already in the worn-realistic of an author like Dostoevsky, a similar temptation is often latent. And it would seem unnecessary to choose a different
category for the protagonist of *Notes from the Underground:* with his clothes
that are "old, worn, and threadbare," and "a huge yellow stain" on his pants,
the "American cloth sofa . . . with the stuffing sticking out of it," the "tattered
old dressing gown."[359] And yet, we also read that he considers himself "a
mouse and not a man," and it is he himself who takes the "stinking, disgusting,
subterranean hole" as a metaphor[360] — hence the title and the first subtitle of
the book. Writing about his "unfurnished self-contained flat," he confesses: "it
was my shell, the case into which I hid from humanity."[361] And it is also the
protagonist who dedicates the novel to the snow in its second subtitle, *Apropos of the Wet Snow:* "almost wet snow, yellow, dirty."[362] He associates
underground and snow in his memory of a coffin which is brought out of the
one and into the other: "There was such filth everywhere — litter, bits of shell
— an evil smell"; he will assail Liza with these images.[363]

The protagonist of Fyodor Sologub's novel *The Little Demon,* narrated in
the third person, is no less lonely and evil. In his hallucinatory persecution
mania, Peredonov suffers from what he sees or sees what makes him suffer:

> The attorney's house itself only strengthened and gave definite form to his
> feeling of oppression and fear. Indeed, it had an evil, angry look. The high
> roof seemed to frown over the windows, forcing them down on to the ground.
> The weatherboards and roof had once been painted a bright, cheerful colour,
> but time and the elements had turned them a dreary grey. The huge, heavy
> iron gates, higher than the house itself and apparently built to resist attackers,
> were kept constantly locked.[364]

Narrative dissolves myths and classical texts while rewriting them in Jules
Laforgue's *Moral Tales* (*Moralités légendaires*), and the quandary of his Hamlet is not the rottenness of the world, but the fact that he himself is rotten with
literature. His tower "stands like a leprous forgotten sentinel" at the bottom of
a park that is "the sewer where the detritus of the conservatories, the withered
bouquets of ephemeral galas are thrown";[365] and on the shore of a stagnant
bend of the Sund, from which a chorus of raucous toads rises:

> And the last eddies of industrious boats scarcely perturbed — certainly no
> more than the constant downpours — the skin disease of that corner of ripe
> water, oxidized by a drivel of gall scattered (like liquid malachite), poulticed
> here and there by groups of flat leaves . . .

The descriptive efflorescence continues too long for it to avoid declaring itself
the reflection of an "I": "This is why (except for storms) this corner of water is
properly the mirror of the unfortunate prince Hamlet . . ."[366]

Once the twentieth century is fully under way, the metaphorical projection does not need to be made explicit. In *Journey to the End of the Night* (*Voyage au bout de la nuit*), Céline's first-person narrative rages on, enough to distinguish the desolate-disconnected from the ex–worn-realistic, and to identify the nauseating place with the character — when Bardamu goes to consult a doctor more prestigious than himself:

> There still wasn't anyone in these laboratories, [. . .] nothing but upset things in great disorder, small corpses of gutted animals, cigarette butts, chipped gas burners, cages and glass jars containing mice in process of suffocating, retorts, bladders scattered around, broken stools, books and dust, again and always cigarette butts, their smell and that of a urinal dominating.[367]

At the beginning of Faulkner's *Light in August,* also narrated in the third person, the fate of a secluded woodworking factory is not seen through the eyes of any particular character. And yet, the desolation and disconnection render its fate subjective; they are enough to humanize what, of the broken tools and overwhelmed nature, is consigned to an oblivion worthy of the solemn-admonitory:

> But some of the machinery would be left, since new pieces could always be bought on the installment plan — gaunt, staring, motionless wheels rising from mounds of brick rubble and ragged weeds with a quality profoundly astonishing, and gutted boilers lifting their rusting and unsmoking stacks with an air stubborn, baffled and bemused upon a stump-pocked scene of profound and peaceful desolation, unplowed, untilled, gutting slowly into red and choked ravines beneath the long quiet rains of autumn and the galloping fury of vernal equinoxes. Then the hamlet which at its best day had borne no name listed on Post-office Department annals would not now even be remembered by the hookwormridden heirs-at-large who pulled the buildings down and burned them in cook-stoves and winter grates.[368]

On the threshold of the *nouveau roman*, in Alain Robbe-Grillet's *The Erasers* (*Les Gommes*), floating relics in a canal are reunited by chance. In the space of a few pages, they will try — in vain — to connect themselves into some brief pattern — a grotesque face, a voracious monster, a map of America. Washed up at the feet of the onlooker, they reflect nothing but indecipherability, and are not metaphors of anything:

> He looks at the oily water splashing at his feet in a corner nook of the quay; there a number of wrecks had assembled: a piece of wood stained with tar, two old corks of the ordinary kind, a fragment of an orange peel, and more tenuous crumbs, half-decomposed, more difficult to identify.[369]

On the other hand, the unreal thing called "Odradek" in *The Cares of a Family Man* (*Die Sorge des Hausvaters*) is opened to a class of meanings that is not undefined, although, as usual in Kafka, it is virtually infinite. The pieces of thread from the spool of which it is made are "torn, old, knotted one to the other but also tangled together . . . of the most various kinds and colors." Thus it has an origin, a past, which is displaced onto the absurd: the idea that "it had previously had some functional shape and was now simply broken" is belied by the absence of visible additions or fractures, by its "nonsensical but in its way finished" appearance.[370]

The symbolic vocation which separates domestic places of storage within the worn-realistic (V, 7) — treated tenderly in the semipositive category (V, 8) — marks the opening of Elsa Morante's novel *House of Liars* (*Menzogna e sortilegio*). Elisa's bedroom is reached through a closet which is almost blocked by its "rejected things," "resembling a barricade"; the window looks onto a backyard whose towering walls stop the sun from ever entering, and "between the stones covered in litter, some faded weed grows."[371] Hundreds of pages later we will learn that her parents' bedroom looked onto a "barren mountain all covered with broken earthenware and glass" — according to legend, "the gigantic, extremely ancient accumulation," along the centuries, of the city's litter and waste.[372] But the extreme case of the identification of a subject with rubbish is so metaphorical that it becomes literal: the subject's reincarnation as a living piece of refuse. It is Kafka's *The Metamorphosis*. In the sinister-terrifying — of which we ought to think of the story as telling in its own way — the supernatural often stands on the base of the worn-realistic (IV, 22). Here the humanity of the cockroach's point of view blurs the objectivity of the category. If Gregor's presence as an insect leads to objects piling up in the room, his bestial adaptations and desperate utilitarianism will alter their meaning:

> They had gotten used to putting things which might not be put elsewhere in that room, and there were many such things [. . .] which certainly might not be sold, but which one still didn't want to throw away. All these ended up in Gregor's room. Just like the ash can and trash can from the kitchen. Whatever was only for the moment unusable, the maid, who was always in a hurry, simply threw into Gregor's room.[373]

In Bruno Schulz's writings, too, the supernatural relies on the naturalism of a paradoxical desolate-disconnected, with a dash of lugubrious humor. The efflorescence of metaphors in a stylistic sense — the most important difference from Kafka — is rooted in the same soil as the themes of neglected spaces and animal metamorphoses: "a fantastic fermentation of matter."[374] The father, who occasionally becomes not only a cockroach, but also a fly, a shellfish, etc.,[375] knows all of its secrets. Thus he disappears for hours or days among closets and junk, "as if he were feverishly searching for something"; he remains "in permanent contact with the unseen world of mouseholes, dark corners, chimney vents, and dusty spaces under the floor"; or he gets up in the middle of lunch to go "tiptoe to the door of the adjoining room, and peer through the keyhole with the utmost caution."[376] The premise of his story of a vegetative, solitary, and ephemeral mirage is that:

> . . . in old apartments there are rooms which are sometimes forgotten. Unvisited for months on end, they wilt neglected between the old walls, and it happens that they close in on themselves, become overgrown with bricks and, lost once and for all to our memory, forfeit their only claim to existence. The doors, leading to them from some backstair landing, have been overlooked by people living in the apartment for so long that they merge with the wall, grow into it, and all trace of them is obliterated in a complicated design of lines and cracks.[377]

Before Schulz, Kafka was influenced by Alfred Kubin's "fantastic novel" *The Other Side* (*Die andere Seite*). A man who has founded a Kingdom of the Dream, in a region of Central Asia, detests "all that is progress"; he orders the acquisition of valuable antiquities, and also, one by one, useless old trinkets.[378] People only wear their parents' or grandparents' antiquated clothes.[379] It often happens that old cheese rinds are reclaimed, that coffins are delivered that have not been ordered, or that atrocious scenes are witnessed by the light of a match if one enters storehouses and cellars.[380] Everything succumbs to the aggressions of an American billionaire, to wild animals of the jungle, and to a morbid disintegration of matter.[381] It is not easy to determine how many categories are contaminated in the novel, as in so many other great works of the twentieth century. Thus I reserve a discussion of them for the next chapter, where I can treat each one at greater length than is possible here.

10

The magic-superstitious is the category with the oldest origin (II, 13; IV, 21). It would be possible to document it with Greek texts of the Homeric and Attic ages, if I had less rigorously distinguished the nonfunctionality required by the category: linking it to the death of animal bodies — an element prevailing over all those connotations of the strange, or of the noxious, which tune deathly instruments to mortal intentions. The bloodless sacrifice of vegetation thus remains outside the boundaries of pertinence which Greek literature never crossed, not even during the Alexandrian period. Hermes gives a plant

— difficult for men to pull up, but not for the gods — to the hero of the *Odyssey* to counteract Circe's spells;[382] in a fragment of a lost tragedy of Sophocles, Medea cuts up plants and roots;[383] in Euripides' tragedy, she barely names the poisons she will spread over the wedding gifts;[384] and, in the poem of Apollonius of Rhodes, she has made a potion with the juice of a flower sprung from the blood of Prometheus.[385] By the third century B.C., on the basis of a model dating back in turn to the fifth century B.C., a model was proposed which Latin antiquity and the European Renaissance would only coarsen and make more dire. The fifth-century one is a mime by Sophron of Syracuse, of which less than twenty lines survive;[386] that of the third century is Theocritus's second idyll, *The Spell*, about disappointed love. In the latter's prototype for future, similar lists, which has the singsong rhythm of a magical spell, a squashed salamander is added to flour, laurel, wax, bran, etc.[387] The passage conforms to ritual practices, attested to by papyrus texts on magic; later on it will, in turn, be subject to literary imitation: an archaically technical version of the alternative between previous reality or previous literature (III, 3). I will not deal here with ritual practices other than in a negative sense — in the cases that are clearly independent of them. Nor am I concerned with the various ends for which the materials provide the means: from love spells and the remedies for impotence to homicidal vengeance, from rejuvenation and invulnerability to necromancy.

The most ancient Latin list, from a poet of the early first century B.C., Laevius, has been passed down to us by the author of the latest list, Apuleius. It comes, not in his novel, but in the forensic oration *De magia*. I observe, however, that he quotes other poets as well — especially Homer and Virgil — as competent authorities in the field of magic, as he defends himself against the charge of sorcery.[388] In Eclogue VIII, Virgil had Latinized Theocritus's idyll in a classic imitation, before making love magic the pretext for Dido's suicide in book IV of the *Aeneid* (cf. V, 8).[389] But, in the same period, it was the young Horace rather than the young Virgil who was the first to innovate upon Greek ingredients. In Epode V, along with blood, he introduces a literarily pleasurable cascade of horrors, which exceeds, in its fearsomeness, the representation of the practical ritual — although it fits the case at hand. The youth who begins the text by imploring and ends it by cursing, is about to be buried up to his neck by Canidia and her fellow witches. He will die of hunger while looking at food; his extracted marrow and desiccated liver will yield a love potion to curb the infidelity of her old libertine lover:

> Canidia, her hair entwined with
> Short vipers and her head unkempt,

> Orders that wild figs be torn from tombs,
> Orders that funereal cypresses
> And eggs dyed with the foul blood of a frog
> And the feathers of a nocturnal screech owl
> And weeds which Iolcos and Hiberia
> Rich in poison, provide,
> And bones torn from the mouth of a hungry bitch
> Should burn on flames of Colchis.[390]

At the height of the next generation of urban and imperial literature, the distance between literature and magic was settled once and for all. Ever since historical times the one had inherited the prehistoric role of the other: art, sublimating magic, had split this inheritance with religion. It played the role of an institution which socially enhances the fantastic liberties of human thought and language (cf. I, 3) — the powers and the illusions of "symmetric logic."[391] The inoffensive workshop, now in service, would not stop borrowing whatever it needed from the old and dark arsenal, which had been marginalized for centuries, but not at all abandoned; and it borrowed with an awareness of regression wavering between terror and amusement.

In Tibullus and Propertius, the magical commonplaces abandon the ritual and the list and enter into the figures of an erotic rhetoric. Succumbing to his nemesis, Tibullus would drink for her a mixture of the poisons of Circe and Medea, the discharge of mares in heat and "a thousand other herbs";[392] while in Cynthia's jealousy, as related to Propertius by the servant, the category's macabre animal corporality may be found in her own sepulchral surroundings:

> portents of a swollen poisonous toad attract her
> and the gathered bones of desiccated snakes,
> and the feathers of a screech owl found among fallen tombs
> with the woolen belt which girdled the funeral coffin.[393]

Ritual and lists are not lacking in Ovid's *Metamorphoses* and in his *Fasti*. In accord with the latter's antiquarian intention and Roman folklore, the sacrifice to the goddess Tacita is made with domestic items: grains of incense in a rat hole, black fava beans and wine, a fish head and a bronze needle — as well as enchanted threads and lead.[394] But in the former poem, where mythology becomes encyclopedic entertainment, the most pleasurable credulity is nourished by what is less credible. Medea has gathered weeds for nine days and nights in Thessaly and elsewhere, flying in her chariot from valleys to mountains, from rivers to lakes, all of them famous;[395] and yet, in the list, the vegetable ingredients of the potion take up only two lines out of more than ten. After three lines of exotic or esoteric mineral corporality, it is animal corporality that touches upon the improbable together with the fearsome. In the final synthesis, unnamed things are added in hyperbolic numbers:

> there she cooks roots cut in the valley of Hemonia,
> and seeds and flowers and black juices.
> She mixes stones sought from the remotest East
> And sands washed by the tides of the Ocean;
> She adds dew gathered on the night of a full moon
> And foul wings with the flesh of the screech owl
> And the guts of a shape-shifting wolf who changes
> His bestial aspect into a human one; nor was the scaly
> Skin of a small water snake from the Cinyphius lacking,
> Nor the liver of an aged deer, to which she adds
> The beak and head of a crow nine centuries old.
> Since with these and a thousand other nameless things
> The barbarian prepared her plan which was greater than any mortal's.[396]

The poetic elaboration of magical techniques and recipes, when it does not draw them from an expertise whose outlines are familiar, may thus relegate them to legendary distant lands or surround them with an impending horror. Between the two directions, and not only chronologically, the tragic Seneca of *Medea* is much closer to the intense tone of Lucan than to the relaxed tone of Ovid: his inflated rhetoric of outdoing will be in large part responsible for his popularity during the modern Baroque era (cf. IV, 29). Thematic outdoing, quantitative expansion, and the competitive emulation of earlier literary models all converge. In the nurse's report, the witch begins by overcoming herself through what she herself fears:

> She exposes all her wealth, and whatever for a long time
> She herself feared she draws out, and reveals all
> The throng of evils, arcane, secret, concealed things.[397]

The evocation of snakes and the assortment of poisonous weeds extend over twenty-five and twenty-six lines, respectively; "Obscene birds: / The heart of the doleful owl, and of the raucous screech owl / The bowels torn from her alive" are thrown into the mixture at the end. Appearing just as they are summoned, the reptiles (like the weeds, from all over the world) are not only mythological but astrological as well. Indeed, Medea has said: "Now, now is the time / To do something greater then a vulgar trick." When she enters, she will only list mythical antonomastic body constituents, like the blood of Nessus or the feathers of the Harpies.[398] If the *Satyricon* is nearly contemporary with Seneca's tragedy, we can measure a crucial difference they represent by considering the aphrodisiacs Enotea offers to enhance Encolpius's virility —

goose liver, a leather phallus, and plants.[399] This is the difference between literary and everyday magic — or, more precisely, between tragic and comic magic. In Tacitus's *Annals,* when Germanicus's mortal disease discloses itself, "unearthed remains of human bodies," "half-burned ashes smeared with rotten blood" are discovered, along with magical curses against him.[400] Finally, technical caution is not in doubt in Apuleius's *The Golden Ass,* where magic colors the surroundings and drives the plot forward. For an earthly aim like Panfila's sexual predilection for handsome young boys, the means is the more disturbing but less extravagant cadaverous corporality, that of a human. On the other hand, when we read of the ritual, we already know that its effect will be grotesque (the resurrection of the flasks made of goat-skins):

> First of all she prepares the usual apparatus in the dismal shop, full of every kind of aroma and sheets written in incomprehensible letters and the wrecks of unhappy ships with the numerous limbs of corpses already mourned, and even buried; here noses and fingers, there on nails the flesh of men who had been hanged, elsewhere the preserved blood of slaughtered men and mutilated skulls snatched from the jaws of beasts.[401]

After the medieval period, the topoi of this Latin corpus were the favored objects of faithful imitation — Boccaccio, in the *Filocolo,* translates Ovid's list almost word for word.[402] In Sannazzaro's *Arcadia* the repertory of spells does not differ too widely between an old witch and a priest deeply learned in occult natural science. The witch uses the "poison of mares in love, the blood of the viper, the brain of rabid bears and the hairs from the end of the wolf's tail"; the priest swallows "the warm and palpitating heart of a blind mole," places on his tongue "the eye of an Indian tortoise," and knows the power of the tooth, snout, and obscene parts of the hyena, etc.[403] A character with the strength of Celestina (IV, 23) was necessary to restore the gusto of her craft to this commonplace tradition, even as she continued it and without removing its belief in the supernatural. The unorthodox face of the supernatural that concerns this category did not remain unscathed by critical irony in the literature of the Italian Renaissance; both a renewed religiosity and the very slackening of orthodox religiosity militated against it. Already, in the *Decameron,* a burlesque spell is offered to the enamored Calandrino. In order that he might conquer a woman by touching her with "writing," Bruno prescribes "a small amount of unborn paper and a live bat and three grains of incense and a blessed candle, and leave it to me."[404] In two passages from Folengo's *Baldus* there is no shortage of lists, which are composed more or less conventionally of unconventional objects. A misogynous tirade takes witches to be the last diabolical permutation of courtesans, bawds, and beguines; then Baldus finds them again as they are in the underwater court of the sorceress-goddess Gel-fora. The second list is lengthened by sacred things that are profaned. The first, making exceedingly explicit the tendency towards the metaliterary and the threadbare-grotesque that is implicit in macaronic language, passes beyond oddities to impossibilities: chicken's milk, horsefly's honey.[405]

Whenever an effect lacking mystery or fear is released in a smile or laughter, we may speak at our pleasure either of a refused magic-superstitious or of a contamination with the threadbare-grotesque. Even before *The Necromancer* of Ariosto's comedy is revealed as an itinerant charlatan (by his own words and those of his servant), his classical portents are comically misinterpreted — either literally or figuratively. The enumeration of the tools he needs to perform a spell is mingled with budget expenses and suggestions of ways to save money which dissipate its aura, while the *lectio facilior* of his ignorant counterpart debases the pentacle (*pentacolo*) into pots (*pentole*) or feathers (*pennacchi*).[406] In Aretino's *The Courtesan* (*La Cortigiana*), the procuress Aloigia is the heir of her "teacher," who was burned as a poisoner. The list of what she inherits (in an early edition, undramatically given in one single block) is broken into various exchanges:

> "Alembics to distill the weeds gathered with the new moon, waters to remove freckles, unguents to remove blemishes, a phial of lovers' tears, oil to resuscitate . . . I'd rather not say what." "Say it, madwoman." "The flesh." "What flesh?" "The flesh of the . . . you understand me?" "Of the girdle?" "Yes."

> "She leaves me unborn paper, the rope of the unjustly hanged, powder to kill the jealous, spells to drive people mad, prayers to induce sleep and recipes to restore young: she leaves me a trapped spirit." "Where?" "In a chamber-pot."

The old woman was popular and respected, a conscientious observer of fasts. The third elegiac praise, included between these two, is that "she would go like a dragon over the gallows to take out the eyes of the hanged, and like a paladin through the cemeteries to remove the fingernails from the dead at the beautiful hour of midnight." One thinks of Celestina, but here the dialogue's roguish comedy is crasser, lighter, and more candid.[407]

It was after the Reformation that, at the roots of the belief in magic, the element of immemorial superstition could give way to the Christian fear of the devil. According to the Huguenots, during the religious wars in France, the Catholic and Italian queen mother was in league with the devil. Agrippa d'Aubigné's great polemical poem, *Les Tragiques,* appropriates this charge and among his possible models only Lucan and his Erichtho reached the heights of the abomination that needed to be expressed. Whoever, like Catherine de' Medici, "wallows in horrid cemeteries at night," "idolizes Satan and his theology," and acts "as the purveyor of Hell" can act more directly on diabolical spirits than by means of things that can be listed:

> In vain, Queen, you have filled a shop
> With drugs of the magic profession and practice;
> In vain do you store in the skulls of the dead
> Black pitch, camphor to make your perfumes;
> In vain do you burn in them cypress and mandrake,
> The hemlock, the rue, and the white hellebore,
> The head of a red cat, the skin of a cerastes,
> The gall of a screech owl, the tongue of a raven,
> The blood of the bat and the milk
> Of the she-wolf taken at the moment when she finds
> Her den robbed and its fruit removed,
> The navel freshly cut from an aborted child,
> The heart of an old toad, the liver of a dipsas,
> The eyes of a basilisk, the tooth of a sick dog
> And the foam he produces in contemplating the waves,
> The tail of the fish which is an anchor for the fishermen
> Against which in vain wind and sail are tried,
> The virgin parchment, the palate of the owl:
> So many strange means you search for in vain,
> You have readier ones in your fatal hand.[408]

We have already seen in Régnier how Baroque exuberance was to contaminate the threadbare-grotesque with the magic-superstitious (IV, 8), and we have seen in *Macbeth* what kind of credibility it granted to the category itself (IV, 23). An equally famous passage by Shakespeare falls just outside its borders. The Queen Mab speech in *Romeo and Juliet* is the most poetic elaboration we possess, in miniature, of the topoi of impossible things, or *adynata*. These have always been related, in literature, to magic, which makes rivers flow backwards to their sources and the moon fall from the sky: Mab ties "elf-locks" into knots with dirty horses' hair, and is called a hag.[409] In the flying carousel of witches in Grimmelshausen's *Simplicissimus,* the animals, or their parts, which are played like musical instruments, become *adynata* that almost inspire horror.[410] But it was also in the Baroque age, that is, in the same age of a renewal of rationality, that the category, with its irrationality, lost ground. Unlike in Sannazzaro, theatrical and narrative pastoral relieved themselves of its burden: not only where magic is absent (Tasso, Guarini, Sidney), but also where it is benevolent (Montemayor) or deceptive (d'Urfé).[411] The good sorcerer in Corneille's *The Theatrical Illusion* disparages the ceremonies of the novices and has nothing but a cave and a wand, while the list running through his *Médée* condenses the mythological-antonomastic one of Seneca.[412] In Honorat de Bueil de Racan's *The Pastorals* (*Les Bergeries*), the most important thing about the sorcerer is his dwelling-place: "An old castle, / Now the frightful dwelling of goblins."[413] The same holds true in Cyrano de Bergerac's letter *For the Sorcerers* (*Pour les Sorciers*). A "mysteriously clad" old man, not without a "half-dead bat" hanging above his heart, appears to him. After performing astonishing marvels, he guides him:

> through hovels, under the frightful ruins of an old uninhabited castle, where the centuries for a thousand years had been working at sending the rooms into the cellars.

Then the old man reveals his identity, claims responsibility for numberless events predicated on superstition, and disappears.[414] But the Baroque writer and rationalist thinker Cyrano follows with a letter *Against Sorcerers* (*Contre les Sorciers*) — skepticism has the last word.[415] We are now in the middle of the seventeenth century. Images of castles have appeared in some of the latest codified recurrences of the semipositive category; one and a half centuries later, the same images will become available to the negative category.

At the time of the historical turning point and of the Gothic novel, the magic-superstitious is no more than an accessory of the sinister-terrifying (IV, 24) — occasional and contracted, although still vaguely codified. In Matthew Gregory Lewis's *The Monk*, rituals and implements twice appear from the point of view of characters who share the reader's passive expectation of the supernatural. When Matilda conjures Lucifer, we know nothing of the active expectation; when it is the Wandering Jew who exorcizes the Bloody Nun, we do not know to whom the active expectation belongs. The syntheses of brief lists are appropriate for dimly perceived or unknown objects. In one case, "round about this he placed various reliques, sculls, thighbones, &c."; in the other:

> she took various articles from the basket, the nature and name of most of which were unknown to the friar: but among the few which he distinguished he particularly observed three human fingers, and an agnus dei which she broke in pieces.[416]

In a fantastic oriental tale as original as William Beckford's *Vathek*, the points of contact with the *genre noir* are turned on their heads, and become black humor. The austerity of the queen, the caliph's mother, has only one exception: a sensual, perversely macabre and mephitic greed. For an infernal sacrifice, she raises pharaonic mummies from wells accessible only to them; she also draws "monstrous treasures" from her collection, which includes "the oil of the most poisonous snakes, the rhinoceros horns, and wood with the most suffocating odor, felled by magicians in the interior of the Indies; not to mention thousands of other horrible rarities . . ."[417]

Formulas of synthesis and figures of reticence coincide. In her kitchen, the witch of Goethe's *Faust* "draws a circle and places wonderful things within it" (stage direction);[418] E. T. A. Hoffmann is no less laconic in *The Golden Pot* (*Der goldene Topf*), where in the old woman's hovel "unknown strange tools lay in disorder on the floor,"[419] and in *The Sandman* (*Der Sandmann*) — where, in the scene between the father and the lawyer which the boy secretly witnesses, "all kinds of strange tools were scattered around."[420] Byron's *Manfred* will only say of his own activities that he drew "from withered bones, and skulls, and heap'd up dust, / Conclusions most forbidden."[421] Grillparzer's *Medea* places "various tools" (from a stage direction) in a chest that will be buried, and, in addition to the major objects, mentions "still more herbs, more than one stone of dark power"; when it is dug up, the container will be intuitively grasped as a fearful synthesis: "a small chest, black, with strange foreign markings."[422] In Weber's *The Free Hunter* (*Der Freischütz*), with a libretto by Friedrich Kind, melodrama brings onto the stage a true list, recited rhythmically over an orchestral pianissimo:

> Here firstly the lead. — A little crushed glass from broken church windows; here it is. — Some quicksilver! — Three bullets that have already hit! — The right eye of a she-owl! — The left one of a lynx! Probatum est![423]

Long before the passage by Maturin, dating from the same years, which we have already considered (IV, 24), during the Baroque age a theme had already appeared on the horizon in which the decline of the magical-superstitious category was inherent: the interchangeability, regressive or progressive, between magic and science. It was able to have results in the field of images that were opposed to the nonfunctional, and we shall find it again in the last chapter of this book.

We also find this theme in some nineteenth-century texts that remain within the category — although, by now, only as isolated occurrences. Hugo describes the cell of the priest — a sorcerer and a lover — in a tower in *The Hunchback of Notre-Dame* (*Notre-Dame de Paris*). It is compared to Faust's cell (by way of Rembrandt) in the instruments and carcasses piled up there for his magic; it is full of dust because of the long neglect due to the distraction caused by his love.[424] If, in the historical novel, magic foreshadows science, at the end of the century the science fiction novel lends an aura of magic to ultramodern machinery. In Auguste Villiers de l'Isle-Adam's *The Future Eve* (*L'Ève future*), Edison's own machines loom in a twilight; a list calls them unknown, enormous, or enigmatic. They are seen later by other eyes: "the laboratory appeared, positively, as a magic place; here, the natural could be no other than the extraordinary."[425] Other discontinuous occurrences have to do with the persistence, in scientific civilizations, of a practice all the more inextinguishable as it becomes more and more anachronistic. Historical backwardness is equivalent to the spatial or exotic periphery, as in the two passages from Mérimée (II, 13), but also to the social or folkloric periphery. In the town of Salem at the end of the seventeenth century, in a short story by Hawthorne, we are brought back to the obsession of the American Puritans with witchcraft. We do not learn whether *Young Goodman Brown* is awake or asleep when he goes to that forest by night where people gather around the devil; and a list such as the following is not the strangest of all the exchanges between his first companions: " 'when I was all anointed with the juice of smallage, and cinquefoil, and wolf's-bane' — 'Mingled with fine wheat and the fat of a new-born babe' [. . .]. — 'Ah, your worship knows the recipe.' "[426] In Hugo's *The Toilers of the Sea*, superstition envelops a house by the sea on the island of Guernsey. The "incautious nocturnal passersby who believed they had seen something" hang on their walls "rats without paws, bats without wings, carcasses of dead beasts, toads squashed between the pages of a Bible, sprigs of yellow lupin, strange ex-votos" out of expiatory caution.[427] But it is in cosmopolitan Paris, in a short story by Maupassant, that we find the sixth floor of a fortune-teller with her "strange things."[428]

In Hemingway's *For Whom the Bell Tolls,* the American intellectual fighting in the Spanish war is taught how to smell the unmistakable odor emitted by someone close to death: slaughterhouses and brothels, blood and sperm are all parts of it. Dead flowers first in a trash bin, then in an abandoned sack — which also smells of damp earth and nighttime prostitution.[429] But the superhuman conjecture in Bulgakov's *The Master and Margarita* does not have to do with folklore or exoticism, nor does it unfold in a geographically peripheral region. The devil returns, and creates havoc, in the middle of the bureaucratic positivism and the orthodox irreligiosity of Stalin's Moscow. The supernatural is the return of the repressed, a fiercely entertaining regression and aggression; it returns at the expense of a progressivism devolved into repression that is presumed to be invulnerable. The denial of every preconception of its deniers, the supernatural appears in the guise of a sumptuous feudal (and ecclesiastical) past more Western, furthermore, than Russian. Here is the interior, seen through the eyes of a dumbfounded barman, where the self-styled master of black magic has settled with his acolytes:

> Streaming through the large stained-glass windows [. . .] was an extraordinary light, similar to the light in a church. Wood was burning in the huge old-

fashioned fireplace despite the hot spring day. Yet it was not the least hot in the room; in fact, quite the opposite. A cellar-like dampness enveloped the man entering the room. [. . .] There was a table that made the God-fearing bartender shudder when he saw it: the table was covered with a brocaded altar-cloth. On the altar-cloth numerous bottles were arranged — potbellied, dusty, and mouldy. Amidst the bottles a plate gleamed, and it was immediately obvious that the plate was made of pure gold. By the fireplace a short red-headed man with a knife in his belt was roasting pieces of meat skewered on a long steel sword.[430]

This is a contamination with a remote venerable-regressive, but also, to be sure, with the sinister-terrifying, in the shiver of dampness and mold. The guests at the great sabbath ball, all of them great criminals in their lifetime, arrive by dropping down through an immense chimney in their gallows or coffins, as mutilated skeletons or decomposed cadavers; when they hit the ground, they rise up, suddenly made whole, wearing tail coats.[431] It is black humor that purges the reader of those awful passive expectations which belong to the philistines of the regime, and which terrify a few innocents. The two title characters are the beneficiaries and accomplices of active expectations. When one of the acolytes finally poisons them, taking "a moldy jug out of a piece of dark funeral brocade," it is so that their way towards immortal euphoria may be paved.[432] Literature takes revenge upon reality by summoning magic back to its hereditary fantastic role.

What about the superstitious alternative rather than magic, white rather than black (IV, 22, 23) — what about relics? In the abstract, the availability of images relative to this theme is beyond doubt. Concretely, it seems to disappear into the impossible. In the very few texts I have found, the substance tends either to remain below the minimum, or to develop alongside the topoi of impossible things. The relics of Friar Cipolla in Boccaccio are not obsolete, but are rather whimsically created to fool the people's credulity. They are ethereal *adynata* that reify the incorporeal or the intangible or the unattainable: the finger of the Holy Ghost, the rays of the Star of Bethlehem, the sweat of St. Michael in a vial.[433] Two centuries later, the critical potential of such a light-hearted and uninhibited caricature erupts as the reforming scorn of Calvin's *Treatise on Relics* (*Traité des reliques*). For instance, a vase of the burned flesh of Saint Laurence, vials of his blood or fat, and coals are venerated here and there; one could assemble two whole bodies from the bones that are displayed in France alone.[434] The impossible is sacrilegious imposture. In D'Annunzio's *The Flame* (*Il Fuoco*), in a Viennese museum, there are more images of reliquaries and gems than relics themselves: "Exiled things, become profane, no longer prayed to, no longer adored."[435] In more recent literary history, the artificial origins and the demystification of relics play a role in the story, although they form hardly any images, in some novels set in a European or American Catholic South: Tomasi di Lampedusa's *The Leopard* (*Il Gattopardo*) and García Márquez's *The Autumn of the Patriarch* (*El Otoño del Patriarca*).[436]

11

The Enlightenment, which interposes an interval of a century between the rarefied magic-superstitious and the concrete sinister-terrifying (IV, 24), is a necessary condition for the latter just as it is for the venerable-regressive or the reminiscent-affective. Chronologically asymmetrical to the semipositive category, the negative one has only scanty and isolated occurrences before the historical turning point — as if the force of religion had left more room for alternative black hopes than for fears not encompassed by its own vision of hell. In antiquity, Virgil once again gives us a unique moment. Dido's sorrow, which precipitates her death, is projected onto traditional premonitions and fears: the owl's nocturnal lamentations on the roof, a dream of people chased by the Furies. But no tradition had ever sanctioned the dream in which solitude, wandering, and the desert form an image of anguish from the empty space itself:

> And always to be abandoned
> Alone with herself, always it seems to her that she goes unaccompanied
> Down a long road, and searches for the Tyrians in a deserted land. . . .[437]

In the centuries of imperial Rome, stories are related about houses haunted by ghosts. One is recounted with conviction in a letter of Pliny the Younger; in Lucian's dialogue, *The Lover of Lies,* another is told through the voice of one of the credulous believers, who is contrasted with the skeptic. In both texts cause and effect are inverted with respect to the modern form of the theme. The building does not become frightful because uninhabited, but uninhabited because frightful: "thus it was tumbling down and the roof was dilapidated, and there was no one who had the courage to enter it," we read in Lucian.[438] In Ronsard's hymn *The Demons* (*Les Daimons*), steeped in medieval and Renaissance demonology, science sustains an active rather than a passive attitude towards such places, without being tempted by the magical. The places are what interest us: of the evil demons, "Some habitually dwell in ruined mansions, / Or in the secluded places of great cities / In some corner on a side"; others trouble inhabited houses at night, and in the morning nothing seems to have been broken or moved.[439]

As we have seen, the castle first appears at the beginning of the seventeenth century (V, 10). In Marc-Antoine Girard de Saint-Amant's *Solitude* (*La Solitude*), it is not out of place among the wild and horrible objects relished as occasions precisely for solitary pleasure: the Baroque accommodation of extremes (IV, 29) redeems melancholy as lively curiosity. Fear is pleasurable, and in the verses I refrain from quoting here a skeleton and a ghost are motivated by a pastoral story:

> How I love to see the decadence
> Of these old ruined castles
> Against which rebellious years
> Have deployed their insolence!
> Sorcerers hold their Sabbath there;
> Goblin demons retire there,
> Who for malicious frolic
> Deceive our senses and torment us;
> There do snakes and owls
> Nest in a thousand holes.
>
> . . . .
>
> The floor of the highest story
> Has collapsed to the cellar,
> Which the snail and the toad
> Sully with their poison and spittle.[440]

The Baroque extremism of the nauseating and the macabre aims, on the other hand, to plumb the depths of terror, beginning with the comparative-hyperbolic paradoxes of Shakespeare's Juliet. She is prepared to do anything rather than marry a man she does not love:

> Or shut me nightly in a charnel-house
> O'er-cover'd quite with dead men's rattling bones,
> With reeky shanks, and yellow chapless skulls;
> Or bid me go into a new-made grave
> And hide me with a dead man in his shroud.[441]

Friar Lawrence's stratagem takes the figure literally; and beforehand, in the monologue in which she hesitates before drinking the potion, the young girl finds herself directly confronted with the place where the cadaverous imagery is closest to being real:

> The horrible conceit of death and night,
> Together with the terror of the place,
> As in a vault, an ancient receptacle,
> Where, for these many hundred years, the bones
> Of all my buried ancestors were pack'd.[442]

As many centuries old as a castle, the crypt does not provoke any descriptions, nor does the sinister-terrifying yet avail itself of categories of the passage of time. The all too natural horror of death overcomes the legendary super-natural, the rumor that down there "at some hours in the night spirits resort," the danger of suffocating "In the vault / To whose foul mouth no healthsome air breathes in," the "loathsome smells," the putrefaction of the man killed shortly before. Suicidal madness, the other risk Juliet envisions, would make material use of the bones of her ancestors as a game or a tool.[443] In the monologue Romeo delivers over Juliet's presumed corpse, the eroticization of death today seems close to a pre-Romantic inversion of values: the desire never to leave the dark place again, which is transfigured into a "palace" — and even the worms become "chambermaids."[444]

But until the historical turning point, the category can hardly take effect except at its most concrete and sensory thematic pole, or at its most abstract and vacant one — that is, either as the corpse itself or as pure space. The necromantic governor of the island of Glubbdubdrib, in the third voyage of Swift's *Gulliver's Travels,* has two columns of guards, and the utopian account leaves little doubt where they have been summoned from: "armed and dressed after a very antick manner, and something in their countenance that made my flesh creep with a horror I cannot express."[445] I cannot neglect to mention an erudite essay like Charles de Saint-Évremond's late seventeenth-century *Dissertation on the Word "Vast"* (*Dissertation sur le mot de vaste*), which in some parts anticipates Freud's study of the uncanny, and in others exactly the unity of the subject of this book. "*Vastitas,* excessive greatness"; "There is something frightful about the sight of a vast house; vast apartments have never made anyone desire to live there"; "*Vastus quasi vastatus,* vast is almost the same as wasted, ruined."[446] In Prévost's novels, two widowers create for themselves secluded spaces artificially protected from sunlight, with few objects on display or in disarray. Black externalizations of the mourning and melancholy they serve to cultivate; secularizations of monastic retreat and contemplation, a burial of the living — guiltless intimations of the spaces of Sade.[447]

At the historical turning point, the passage from nights to tombs and ruins, and then to castles and to convents that are too vast, to the first ruined interiors presented seriously, would take place as though by thematic contagion or by a transitive property. The beginning of Edward Young's *Night Thoughts* (V, 4) confronts the horror of silence and darkness: no objects are discerned there; the poet prepares to redeem their negativity in a supreme meditation. Yet it always remains an instance of the solemn-admonitory, whose solitary Protestant religiosity may best be cultivated in the blind, mute hour of the night:

> Silence, how dead! and darkness, how profound!
> Nor eye, nor list'ning ear, an object finds;
> Creation sleeps. 'Tis as the gen'ral pulse
> Of life stood still, and nature made a pause;
> An awful pause! prophetic of her end.[448]

More than half a century later, in the first of Novalis's *Hymns to the Night* (*Hymnen an die Nacht*), the "I" turns away with an analogous movement away from light and the world. If the nocturnal negative profits from the inversion of values, what is about to burst forth from it are "distances of memory, desires of youth, dreams of childhood": it is now the age of the reminiscent-affective. Once again, we are amidst nothing more than the shadows of images:

> I turn downwards to the holy, inexpressible, mysterious Night. Far away lies the world — is sunken into a dark hole — its place is wasted and lonely.[449]

Without a cosmic or intimate metaphysics, the night remained a time unprotected from the supernatural of the new category, a time consonant with equally unprotected places. Like so many of the pre-Romantic themes — in a century of incomparable progress in socialization, technologies, and ease of living — it was a "return of the surmounted."[450] Giuseppe Parini's *The Day* (*Il Giorno*) is a good example, regardless of its otherwise permanent satiric irony: in the solemn opening with the adverb "Once . . ." and the use of the imperfect, after three lines of the poem on "Night." Today brightly lit and worldly, it was once terrifying for our rude ancestors:

> A terrible,
> Gigantic shadow was seen to rise
> Up over houses and over the high towers
> With ancient skulls scattered at their feet.
>
> . . . .
>
> And the rumor is still that pale ghosts
> Along the walls of the deserted roofs
> Let out a long shrill lament,
> Which from afar through the vast darkness
> Dogs would answer, howling.[451]

1772: Jacques Cazotte's *The Devil in Love* (*Le Diable amoureux*) is the first French narrative text where we can recognize one among those literary genres that will privilege the images of the category. In the meantime, the evocation of Beelzebub occurs amidst the ruins of Portici. The solemn-admonitory preceding it disorients the imagination, and reserves for the senses an impenetrable darkness:

These remains of the most august monuments, fallen, broken, scattered, covered with thorns, bring unusual ideas to my imagination. "See, I said, the
power of time over the works of the pride and industry of man." We advanced
among the ruins, and finally we reached, almost feeling our way through this
rubble, a place so dark, that no exterior light could penetrate it.[452]

In the France of the 1780s and 1790s, the novels of the Marquis de Sade are,
clandestinely, contemporary with the English Gothic novel.[453] Their paradoxical and antisocial Enlightenment preconceptions exclude the supernatural;
and this fact would seem to exclude them from our interest here. But when the
novelty of their images graduates or refines effects of fear, Sade's novels veer
into a supernatural order which fear must communicate with, at the regressive
and infantile extremity of the unknown. Free from any signs of the passage of
time, Sade's images, rather than occupying space, articulate and widen it. In
this space, an insurmountable isolation is a condition for cruel pleasures themselves, and not only for their physical impunity. The Castle of Silling in the
Black Forest, where *The 120 Days of Sodom* (*Les 120 Journées de Sodome*)
are celebrated, is protected — as if in concentric circles — by an impassable
road, a mountain, and a ravine. Three hundred stairs underground, it has a
torture chamber: "And there, what peace! To what extent mustn't the scoun-
drel have been *reassured* whom crime led there together with a victim!"[454] The
reassurance of the torturers is the other face of the victims' fear, which is
muffled still more by the snow that covers the valley.[455] In one of the stories,
the point of view, although not that of the victim herself, belongs to her guide
in the palace of a necrophilic duke:

> Through meanderings and corridors, as somber as they were immense, we
> finally reached a gloomy apartment, lit only by six candles placed on the
> ground around a mattress of black satin; the whole chamber was decked out
> for mourning, and we were frightened when we entered it.[456]

In the third and final version of Sade's novel, *The New Justine, or the
Misfortunes of Virtue* (*La Nouvelle Justine ou Les Malheurs de la vertu*), a
third-person narrator has replaced the first-person narrator. What has not
changed is the perspective of the victim who, through various narrative transitions, gradually discovers from the outside the places and devices of sadism.
Passive expectation, with its slow, anguished increments, is worth far more, as
literature, than the active practice of monotonous pornography and of the
verbose ideology of perversion. The arrival at the convent of Sainte-Marie-
des-Bois is an archetype of suspense; Justine notices a bell tower in the distance, makes inquiries about it, tries in vain to find someone to escort her
there, loses sight of it, and realizes she has underestimated how far away it is.

"All the while no human trace appears before her eyes: not a house, and her only road is a path covered in brambles, which appear to be useful only to wild beasts." The convent's distance from the town foreshadows the surprises it harbors within;[457] if the topography is patterned after Silling's inaccessibility, the description is now a peroration against the hope of escaping it. A masked door; a long, dark, twisting, narrow descending passageway; cellars; dungeons with mice, lizards, toads, and snakes; thick forest camouflage above — and a cemetery where the victims lie unburied, with "soft and flexible earth" and a skull, where the escape finally succeeds.[458] The Count de Gernande's castle is only isolated by a large park and high walls: "But this large building was well short of having as many people in it as it appeared to be built for"; "after having passed through a long row of apartments, as somber and as solitary as the rest of the castle. . . ."[459] Elevation isolates the castle of the forger Roland (matched in depth by his cave of represented and actual atrocities, below many doors and a steep descent after the stairs):

> when she finally perceived a castle perched on the peak of a mountain, on the edge of a frightful precipice into which it seemed ready to sink. No road appeared to lead to it; the one they were on, frequented only by goats and covered everywhere with stones, nonetheless reached that terrifying lair, far more like a thieves' refuge than the dwelling place of honest people.[460]

1764: the first tale to be subtitled *A Gothic Story*, with an extremity of southern Italy in its title, was Horace Walpole's *The Castle of Otranto*. One memorable moment is the escape of the young girl who is being pursued downward through the underground passages between the castle and the cathedral:

> An awful silence reigned throughout those subterranean regions, except now and then some blasts of wind that shook the doors she had passed, and which grating on the rusty hinges reechoed through that long labyrinth of darkness.

Darkness and space, silence and sounds, transform into an innovation that scarcity of images which would in itself have been conservative. The young girl thinks she hears a footstep or a sigh; a door is opened but then shut again; the wind blows out her lamp; the rays of the moon shine through the ruined roof; a stone stairway descends into a dark chasm.[461]

1777: Clara Reeve's *The Old English Baron* borrowed Walpole's subtitle,[462] halfway between him and Radcliffe.

As a test, the young Edmund must spend the night in the haunted apartment of a castle: its key is hard to find "among a parcel of old rusty keys in a lumber room." Left alone, he surveys the room:

the furniture, by long neglect, was decayed and dropping to pieces; the bed was devoured by the moths, and occupied by the rats, who had built their nests there with impunity for many generations. The bedding was very damp, for the rain had forced its way through the ceiling.

The description briefly extends to an adjacent room, "the furniture of which was in the same tattered condition."[463] This is the first time, if I am not mistaken, that a deteriorating interior is presented seriously with elements of such tangible baseness — in other words, without the threadbare-grotesque. It would be the most precocious instance of the worn-realistic were it not for the context, whose unequivocal effect of disquieting expectation makes it an instance of the sinister-terrifying. It makes sense historically, at the moment when terror was considered a variant of the sublime; it alone was thus capable of endowing a moth- and mice-ridden bed with the same gravitas as the ruins of Portici. Like these ruins themselves, the images that would deserve the hybrid name of "sinister-realistic"(cf. II, 9) prepare the way for the supernatural through a sense of the passage of time, which is equivalent to a more or less perceptible stench of death (IV, 22).

Walpole's novel claimed to be the translation of a narrative more ancient than its Gothic print.[464] But, once again, Clara Reeve was the first to have embodied the antiquity of the Gothic story itself in a manuscript from which the story is drawn; even when she merely wants to shorten the narrative, the characters "are effaced by time and damp."[465] In the codified recurrences of the category, the overabundance of time may be interchanged or combined with the overabundance of space. Both empty expanses hint at the truth Gautier formulated with the following words: "so quickly things made for man and from which man is absent acquire a supernatural air!"[466] Ann Radcliffe's second major novel, *The Italian,* is closer to Sade in its expectation of fear in which illusions of the supernatural are not made explicit. The coach which leads to the prisons of the Inquisition passes by the monuments of ancient Rome, and here too an overabundance of time summons the solemn-admonitory; through a derelict suburb, along immense walls that no light pierces through, one reaches the point where a space — glimpsed, perceived, heard, smelled — becomes overabundant as well.[467] In the same Catholic, monastic setting, in Lewis's *The Monk,* a similar space shrinks into a suffocating one where the woman is buried alive. The horror becomes contaminated with the disgust of the sterile-noxious, and the Baroque and surrealist (or expressionist) extremes meet, in the passage where the novel — later translated freely by Artaud — outdoes Shakespeare: in the sensations of the toad on the woman's breast, the lizard in her hair, the putrid worms between her fingers.[468]

The exhumation of a corpse closes an exceptional novel, whose singular power needed a century to be recognized, and where the demonic infects Calvinism rather than Catholicism, James Hogg's *The Private Memoirs and Confessions of a Justified Sinner*. The dryness of the final chronicle, however, fits squarely with the absence of the category's images in two earlier narrations: only the little book containing the second, found in a tomb, is "damp, rotten and yellow."[469] The manuscript in which the first story of *Melmoth the Wanderer* was read (IV, 24) is also "discoloured, obliterated, and mutilated," with "mouldy and crumbling" pages.[470] But here the sinister-terrifying begins to do without ruins or dungeons and castles or convents: it overlaps with the worn-realistic in an old miser's house, whose interior and exterior squalor are both described. The portrait of the ancestor who never died is thrown together with "a great deal of decayed and useless lumber, such as might be supposed to be heaped up to rot in a miser's closet."[471] Maturin already goes beyond the parodic reactions which the fashionable mode had provoked. There is, for one, the conventional caricature of Thomas Love Peacock's *Nightmare Abbey,* a manor in "a highly picturesque state of semi-dilapidation" the heir to which builds "models of cells and recesses, sliding panels and secret passages, that would have baffled the skill of the Parisian police."[472] For another, there is Jane Austen's delightful narrative caricature in *Northanger Abbey,* where the very young reader of novels has a power of elaborating the real into the mysterious worthy of Don Quixote himself, and once she is disillusioned her lover lectures her by appealing less to absolute verisimilitude than to an enlightened, English modernity.[473]

With Hoffmann, as we have seen (IV, 25), a sinister-terrifying unconfined to remote places enters the code. It is contiguous to normal time and space, barely concealed or directly exposed within the modern urban expanse: as at the end of the century in Stevenson (II, 14), and in Stoker, who had led us to oppose a centripetal movement to a centrifugal one in the places of the supernatural (IV, 26). The title of another short story of the German master announces this feature: in *The Deserted House* (*Das öde Haus*), the exterior is not unremarkable, as it was in the house of Gluck the knight; and the interior will be seen and described more fleetingly. Right away it stands out as an enigma among the sumptuous buildings of the busy street, with its badly repaired roof, the paper stuck in the windows, and the colorless walls. The door without a bell, handle, or keyhole is a particular object symbolizing a fracture in spatial contiguity.[474] Poe, on the other hand, so often a great prophet of future themes, continues the centrifugal tradition through the originality of the nightmare vision that serves as a variant of it. In the first phase of *The Fall of the House of Usher,* the place is said to be unreachable in less than a day's journey; the day and the road foreshadow its oppressiveness. There is "a mystery all insoluble" in the contemplation of the house, "an atmosphere peculiar" to it and its surroundings—and to its interior, with the "profuse, comfortless, antique, and tattered" furniture.[475] This atmosphere arises from an intersection, implicit or reasoned, between incompatible logical categories: inanimate things which can be neither living nor dead are presented as animate insofar as they are alive and dead at the same time. At the end of the story, the supernatural lies in the inexplicable coincidences between the sounds evoked in a reading and their distant echoes, not in the fact itself that the buried woman rises from her coffin.[476] But all the images of the house as a living corpse anticipate, rather than prepare the way for, the supernatural, as, elsewhere in Poe, the ship does (II, 15; and cf. IV, 31).[477] The house's stones, to which the insane proprietor attributes feeling and influence,[478] express a sinister contradiction in their state of conservation:

> The discoloration of ages had been great. Minute *fungi* overspread the whole exterior, hanging in a fine tangled web-work from the eaves. Yet all this was apart from any extraordinary dilapidation. No portion of the masonry had fallen; and there appeared to be a wild inconsistency between its still perfect adaptation of parts, and the crumbling condition of the individual stones. In this there was much that reminded me of the specious totality of old woodwork which has rotten for long years in some neglected vault, with no disturbance from the breath of the external air.[479]

That the swinging balance between belief and criticism is the typical form of the nineteenth-century supernatural (II, 9) is true only if this balance is measured independently of strictly narrative resolutions, either in the marvelous or in the verisimilar sense: that is, if it is enough that doubt be thematized. On what side of this oscillation—when there are any—are the images of the category? On both sides, as is necessary in a compromise-formation: they can both contribute to the belief accorded the supernatural in a suitable space-time, and they can oppose suggestion or hallucination as critical alternatives to the supernatural. Maupassant's short story *Apparition,* despite ending with proof of the substance of the ghost, thematizes doubt. A page before the ambience I am quoting, we have been told of the extreme state of abandon of the outside of the castle; a few lines later, it proves impossible to let any light through the rusted windows:

> The apartment was so dark that I could distinguish nothing in it at first. I stopped, struck by the moldy and sickening smell of the uninhabited and condemned places, dead rooms. Then, gradually, my eyes became accustomed to the darkness and I saw quite clearly a large room in disorder.[480]

The Head of Hair (*La Chevelure*) is an impure example, or rather it would be one, if the sinister-terrifying were not by nature a parasitic category. It is contaminated with the prestigious-ornamental, and, less obviously, with the reminiscent-affective: the passion for collecting antiques strays into imaginary necrophilia and madness. An Italian piece of furniture of the seventeenth century may be bought and placed in one's room. But the drawer in which the fatal fetish lies is a hiding place: dead time can only survive in a minuscule, neglected space.[481] Technological progress, after all, can also create repressed spaces, using no other dead times or supernatural features than a fearful presentiment or an awareness of crime. In Zola's *La Bête humaine,* they emanate from a house placed slantwise, in a garden cut into by the railway. The place is rendered desolate and remote by a long tunnel on the one side and a badly maintained path running alongside the tracks on the other.[482]

Past the threshold of the twentieth century, the only supernatural in Conrad's short story *The Inn of the Two Witches: A Find* is nothing more than an impending mysterious death. The subtitle points to the traditional mediation that opens up the depths of time: a manuscript, buried under books bought in London "in a street which no longer exists, from a second-hand book-seller in the last stage of decay."[483] But the suspicious backwardness of coastal Spain for an Englishman in 1813 is only secondarily entrusted to images of temporal categories. There is something of the worn-realistic in the clothes of the natives, the trash in the empty rooms of the inn, the dust on the floor of the room of death.[484] And there is a hint of venerable-regressive in the bed itself with its enormous canopy, where an archbishop has slept and which appears worthy of him, as there is in the heavy armchairs "like the spoils of a grandee's palace."[485] But, excluding any witches' brew in a pot that smells delicious,[486] what is primary here are indirect and empty images of space: "the spot seemed the most lonely corner of the earth and as if accursed in its uninhabited desolate barrenness"; "the desert solitudes he had been traversing for the last six hours — the oppressive sense of an uninhabited world."[487] A seemingly agoraphobic space, which leads to the claustrophobia of the archbishop's bed. In her short story *Afterward,* Edith Wharton used a disconcerting innovation, playing between space and time, to emulate Henry James's masterpiece ghost story *The Turn of the Screw* (IV, 26). The house deep in an English county acquired by an American couple has a dense European aura of the past, and they romantically, "perversely" longed for its unmodern discomfort.[488] As for the ghost, he would be recognizable only long *after* having been seen: the man who comes to fulfill the legend is not of the place; he avenges wrongs committed overseas and has been dead for one day. And yet it is the house that holds his secret,[489] that has made possible — how can we doubt it? — his coming.

James himself, in an unfinished novel, had conceived of a house within which time would become space or space time. If the American Ralph Pendrel has inherited a house in London dating ca. 1710, it is thanks to what is generally recognized as the "sense" that is most of all his own, *The Sense of the Past*.[490] An unknown relative of the English branch of the family had written him a posthumous letter. He was grateful for never having — other than in one of his booklets — "seen the love of old things, of the scrutable, palpable past"; "felt an ear for stilled voices, as precious as they are faint, as seizable, truly, as they are fine."[491] The house reveals itself to Ralph as a mysterious, familiar concordance of antiquity and habitability, untouched by any deterioration.[492] It is enchanting to feel separated from the rainy London outside, "much more by time than by space"; just as the house is his own, where in the evenings he wanders alone, so too is the time he sinks into "his time."[493] The nocturnal vigil fulfills a prior consciousness of having hesitated before frightening implications.[494] The coming to life of the portrait of a young man becomes an exchange of identities beyond time: when Ralph returns to confine himself in his house, after having confided what is happening to only one other person, he leaves 1910 and relives that life again in 1820. We thus see an identification between James's two great themes, the spectral and the intercontinental. American historical memory rediscovers a ghostly actuality on English soil — unless it is the English historical memory that does so through the hypersensitivity of the man who has returned from America.[495]

Gustav Meyrinck, the author of *The Golem* (*Der Golem*), was the illegitimate son of a nobleman and a Jewish mother. He drew nightmares from that historical memory which only the Jews, along with the nobility, preserve in a direct line in the modern world. His houses in the ghetto of Prague reflect, as in a distorting mirror, the architectural irrationality of the old feudal world (V, 6). With a "sinister and dilapidated" aspect, they have grown over the centuries "without thought" and without any regard for one another, "like weeds which burst out from the soil": "there a half crooked cornered house with a façade that bends inward, next to it another: sticking out like an eyetooth."[496] Behind the façades and down various secret stairs, the Jewish recesses and closets of Kafka or Schulz (V, 9) are expanded in long passageways and underground chambers worthy of the Gothic tradition. At the center of the dream-like plot is a doorless room with a grated window, the legendary retreat of the Golem; the protagonist who has made it into a symbol arrives there, spends the night, and escapes wearing the medieval clothes that were moldering in the emptiness of a corner.[497] The story opens with the "dead worthless things" of a second-hand shop owner who, if some passerby asks about their price, frightens him off by muttering incomprehensibly under his harelip.[498] It ends with the "urban renewal" of the ghetto, in whose rubble[499] mysteries and horrors would be swept away together with memory. The codified recurrences in this novel, written in 1915, are certainly among the latest examples of any literary quality. In the twentieth century, the sinister-terrifying has not survived (aside from a few exceptions) as anything other than a product designed for consumption; or it has passed into another language altogether with the images of the cinema.

12

If it is possible to speak of codified recurrences for the precious-potential, its constants of subject-matter are formalized in long-lived topoi rather than in literary genres. The patterns and degrees of such a formalization make it preferable here to present it, rather than in an approximately unified chronological order, in two successive series — according to the status of the "resource" that the category defines in the imaginary reality of the texts: according to whether the value of this resource lies on a literal-factual plane or on a metaphoric-symbolic one. Insofar as the two planes can be distinguished, on the first, material value for the most part corresponds to wealth, and hence often to power; on the second, to the immateriality of cultural or moral values. However, wealth and power do not always figure as morally — or even materially — beneficial or innocuous. The insistence on their harmful effects, in other words, is the occurrence of a refused precious-potential, a refusal not to be confused, as for every other semipositive category, with a commutation into its corresponding negative category. It is true here that both phenomena, as they intimately alternate or coexist, seem to return us more than ever to the ambivalence of ambivalences: feces, which Freud identified at the origin of the ambivalence of gold and money. The ambivalence is reproduced both by the peculiar reversibility between the precious-potential and the sterile-noxious (IV, 31), and by the frequent inversion of hidden value into an ill-omened, negative one. Marx, for his part, counts their aesthetic properties among the reasons that gold and silver are universally taken up as money: "They appear, so to speak, as solidified light raised from a subterranean world."[500]

Two lines from the Book of Isaiah are the biblical archetype of beneficial promise. They were written two centuries after the prophet (cf. IV, 28), since the Eternal One addresses Cyrus, King of Persia, and, so that He may be recognized, gives many assurances of omnipotence: "and I will give you hidden treasures; and the riches of the secrets of the Ark."[501] Aeschylus's Prometheus is proud of having been the first to reveal "The goods / Hidden within the earth to men, / Bronze, iron, silver, and gold."[502] Horace, however, establishes the classical paradigm of a desire for gold that is the transgression par excellence of a moral rule of measure; the treasure is better neglected, therefore, than harmful: "Undiscovered gold and thus better placed / When the earth conceals it."[503] The Earth is the mother of the Gods, who fight for primacy in Ronsard's *Hymn to Gold* (*Hymne de l'Or*). And it is she who wins the contest, defeating Neptune by revealing the unknown and unnamed metal in her bowels:

> The Earth their mother stung by sorrow
> That over her another should carry this honor,
> Opened her large breast, and through the clefts
> Of her skin, showed them the mines of shining GOLD . . .
>
> .   .   .   .
>
> Forthwith the stunned Gods confessed
> That she was the richest, and with flatteries urged her
> To give them a little of that radiant thing
> Which her womb concealed, to decorate the Skies,
> (They did not name it, because unlike now
> GOLD, being unknown, was not yet named)[504]

Horace disparaged gold, contradictorily but not by chance, in the context of Roman imperialism.[505] Modern imperialism, on the other hand, wrapped in the banner of Christianity, does not suffer from any contradictions in the Portuguese national poem it inspires: Camões' *The Lusiads* (*Os Lusíadas*). The wealth of foreign lands suffices as another justification for the war that should unite the Europeans against the infidels who have captured the divine Sepulcher. In the breath of an octave, the line before this justification turns an entire continent — a metonymy for an unbounded container — into a precious-potential:

> In Lydia, Assyria, golden threads are wrought;
> Africa conceals in itself shining veins.
> Thus at least let such wealth move you,
> Since the Holy House cannot.[506]

Elsewhere, similar projections cover a more circumscribed region of Africa, or an island of the Persian Gulf, or India:

> To this unknown Hemisphere is born
> The metal for which people most sweat.[507]

> Look at the Isle of Bahrein, whose bottom
> Is decorated by its rich pearls, which imitate
> The color of Dawn.[508]

> Know that you are in India, where a varied
> People spreads, rich and prosperous
> With shining gold and fine precious stones.[509]

The desire for wealth is inseparable from the allure of an exotic just inside of, or just beyond, the borders of the fabulous and the unknown. Like distant kingdoms, the depths of the sea and the routes across it function as images of the category, since they are still wild and inviolate. It is no matter that Bacchus discovers the first by sinking down into Neptune's palace, or that Vasco da Gama navigates his ship through the second:

> He discovers the undiscovered sea beds
> Where the sands are of fine silver . . .[510]

> Over seas never plowed by other bark,
> To kingdoms so remote and secluded.[511]

When Luís de Góngora refers to the same navigation, in his *First Solitude* (*Soledad primera*), he addresses not Vasco, but Greed: this is the case throughout the entire recapitulation of the ocean voyages, which the poet contrasts with an ideal rustic peace evoked by an old man who has lost his son at sea. The virtual anti-imperialism, unlike that which we found in the classical moralism of Horace, does not mean the precious and the potential cannot be caressed:

> The kingdoms of Dawn you finally kissed,
> Whose purple breasts are spotless pearls,
>   Whose secret mines
> Today keep for you their most precious gem.[512]

The ambivalence tilts more towards the negative twenty lines earlier, where the uncharted Pacific Ocean offers up both pearls and "murderous metals."[513] In Góngora's *Polyphemus and Galatea* (*Polifemo y Galatea*), a shipwreck washes up on shore "Sabaean spices, in cases, / And the riches of Cambay, in chests": their deterioration from oriental delights into "Scylla's trophy," and into the miserable booty of harpies, has something of punishment about it, and almost of the solemn-admonitory.[514] In Calderón de la Barca's famous *auto sacramental*, God himself as the Author convenes *The Great Stage of the World* (*El gran teatro del mundo*) for a dramatic recital of human life. Among the allegorical roles he assigns, the most pleasurable is the most dangerous for the soul: only the Rich Man will go to Hell, and the World who distributes the stage props gives him jewels. The adjectival rhetoric of his words insinuates one mortal sin before almost all the others—avarice:

> My entrails for you
> I will break in pieces;
> I will draw out of my womb
> All the silver and gold
> Which, as miserly treasure,
> So secretly I enclosed.[515]

Christopher Marlowe's *Doctor Faustus* will also go to Hell, as the legend requires. In his yearning for hedonistic omnipotence that tempts him to command the spirits, the desire for wealth comes first. Both Faustus and his two masters in magic express it with a verbal magnificence that rivals the oceans, continents, and abysmal depths of the Spanish and Portuguese examples:

> I'll have them fly to India for gold,
> Ransack the ocean for orient pearl.

> The spirits tell me they can dry the sea,
> And fetch the treasure of all foreign wracks.
> Yea, all the wealth that our forefathers hid
> Within the massy entrails of the earth.[516]

From the lyric to the fairytale, from the exotic to the dream-narrative, the worst of the sterile-noxious — ordure, rotting — can be reversed through verbal fantasy into their resplendent opposites. Ariel's second song in *The Tempest* speaks of the bottom of the sea after a shipwreck, as in the first example I drew from Shakespeare (IV, 27). The "sea-change" of bones into corals and eyes into pearls, of cadaverous corporality into "something rich and strange," magically denies the terrestrial negative of putrefaction; it also redeems in a sublimated continuity the presumed death of the father.[517] In a fairytale by Basile, the prince who has been turned into a snake must pave a park with precious stones to win the king's daughter. He performs the impossible feat without any difficulty, but not without following an implicit rule of conversion between opposites. At his request, his peasant foster-father collects and disseminates fragments of domestic containers, enumerated in a threadbare-grotesque list complete with "brims of chamber pots."[518] We may as well mention the travels of Sinbad the sailor, taking the *Arabian Nights* as a classic not of the Arab medieval period, but, in its translation by Galland, of the early French eighteenth century. The metamorphoses coalesce into the simultaneous presence of opposites. The valley of the second journey is strewn with surprisingly large diamonds, and snakes just as large; in the fourth journey, the cave in which the dead are buried along with their living spouses swarms with rotting remains, and with the jewels stripped from them; in the sixth journey, along the coast of an island, the remains of many shipwrecks pile up into a countless number of horrible bones, and into another of merchandise and precious stones.[519]

In the great Catholic and Protestant epics, *Jerusalem Delivered* and *Paradise Lost,* we can compare two passages on the basis of the precious-potential. It is as if the acceptance or refusal of the category corresponded to a theological alternative regarding nature, where the Creator has enclosed reserves either of providential good or of predestined evil. The space is intercontinental before it is telescopic, expanded by geographical and later by scientific discoveries. In Tasso, the future landing on the other side of the Atlantic is prophesied to the knights who seek Rinaldo in the Fortunate Isles (the Canaries).[520] The wise old man with whom they stop to meet possesses a secret dwelling — symbolic of his knowledge — in caverns hidden beneath a river. Next to the center of all the waters of the globe, myriad lights shine forth in the unseen womb of the earth:

> And they observe all around the rich river
> The shore painted with precious stones,
> From where, as if lit by many torches,
> That place shines and the horror of darkness is conquered.
> Here with a bluish light sparkle
> Celestial sapphire and hyacinth,
> Carbuncle flames and firm diamond
> Shines, and beautiful emerald laughs in mirth.[521]

In Milton a place of evil is presented, or evil is presented as a place, in an infinite space that exists already before the fall of the rebellious angels. In the first two books, it is inexhaustibly signified by narration and speeches, as well as by images: "A universe of death, which God by curse / Created evil, for evil only good."[522] The metaphysical condescends, and the moralistic soars, to the level of the mythological. In that lower realm, brigades of renegade spirits extract materials from a sulfurous hill to build — in one hour — a Pandemonium that surpasses Babylon and Egypt in its magnificence; their leader is Mammon, at whose urging future men:

> Ransacked the centre, and with impious hands
> Rifled the bowels of their mother Earth
> For treasures better hid. Soon had his crew
> Opened into the hill a spacious wound
> And digged out ribs of gold. Let none admire
> That riches grow in Hell; that soil may best
> Deserve the precious bane.[523]

In this world, the demonization of buried treasure is sanctioned by legends in which ghosts guard the spot where it is hidden. In one page from Grimmelshausen's *Simplicissimus,* the images of precious-potential and enrichment triumph over the sinister-terrifying rather than the sterile-noxious: we are never told what a balky and trembling horse has seen in the cellar of a ruined house. Simplicius would not have noticed that the beast's terror focused on one particular corner of the wall if he had not been familiar with these legends; they prove to be true in spite of the peasants' version, whose fantastic character subtracts as little from them as the traces of time do from the treasure.[524]

After the historical turning point, wealth and power in relation to the exploitation of nature had unprecedented reach and consequences, and the precious-potential found room in the poetry, and ideology, of more than one grand work of synthesis. In the first act of the second part of *Faust,* the Empire is in a state of chaos and the Emperor is short of money. Goethe has Mephistopheles make a suggestion: "But wisdom knows how to extract the deepest thing. / In the veins of mountains, in the foundations of walls / Gold minted and unminted is to be found."[525] When the devil clarifies his meaning, gold that is still raw in nature yields to that which is once again raw — historical gold, so to speak. That is, to all the treasures, from the barbarian invasions onwards, which have been preserved and hidden in the soil — and the soil belongs to the Emperor.[526] An introverted German substitute for colonial resources, drawn not from the distance of adventure but from the depth of the past. During the masquerade — which includes a prodigal Plutus, and "rock surgeons" or gold-dowsing gnomes[527] — a signature is extracted from the Emperor: it is paper money. "This note is worth a thousand crowns. / Its security, as a safe pledge, is / Uncounted buried goods in imperial land."[528] The legally flawless solution is in fact a diabolical invention: the general optimism with which it is welcomed gives rise to satirical scenes. And yet this satire is not enough for us to speak of a refusal of this precious-potential of dubious paper value. For Faust, it has the allure of the immeasurable as well as of the depths: "The excess of treasures which, *rigid,* / Awaits in the deep soil of your lands, / Lies unused. The widest thought / Is for such riches the most meager limit."[529] Mephistopheles' enticement, with the peasant's unexpected discoveries and the expert's risky excavations, already touched upon the category's metaphorical width. I could shift a maxim like the following into the next series, the metaphorical-symbolic: "In darkness mysteries are at home," and the Emperor's answer: "If something is valuable, it must come to light."[530]

In the last act of Shelley's *Prometheus Unbound,* the world is regenerated after the fall of Jove's tyranny and of the shackles that bind the liberating hero. Penetrating the abyss, mobile rays — from the forehead of one of the many cosmic personifications of the drama — reveal in passing "the secrets of the earth's deep heart": I do not reproduce here fifty or so wonderful lines. In the succession of images, only the first represent the value and power of raw, fertile nature, mines, caves, and springs (with echoes of Shakespeare, cf. IV, 27). What follows are the "Melancholy ruins / Of cycles that have been annulled," and despite their antiquity they bear witness to the regime of oppressive violence only recently abolished: pieces of ships, instruments of war and trophies, means of destruction themselves destroyed; cities of inhuman people, with monstrous skeletons and works crushed into annihilation; anatomies of primordial winged beasts, scaly, twisting, or colossal, that roamed everywhere before the flood overwhelmed them. Since the denial of the negativity of all of this is more than half-positive, such a refused paleontological venerable-regressive is the equivalent of a buried precious-potential.[531]

The category has a central importance, with the widest gap between original purity and harmful effects, in Wagner's *The Ring of the Nibelung* (*Der Ring des Nibelungen*). It is not enough to verify its images in the verbal language of the tetralogy. To be sure, words do dictate the contents of the vast story, but they do not narrate it in the full formal sense. It falls to the semantic power of music to concretize the category's images in the first scene of the prologue — called precisely *Das Rheingold*. This scene inaugurates the mature art of Wagner as well as an epoch of the modern orchestra. The anterior eternity of gold in nature's bosom, at the bottom of the river, only endures for one last moment. In the score, that is, for fifty-five bars: the calm metallic sound of the horns beneath the liquid sound of the violins, a crescendo of harps and the luminous entrance of the trumpet (behind which two clashes of the cymbals and triangle shine through), culminating in the orchestral fortissimo which envelops, foam-like, the vocal trio of the Rhinemaidens.[532] On the other hand, the enslaving and alienating powers of the cursed ring, forged when the gold was stolen, generate obsessive rhythms or harmonic and timbral deformities throughout three of the four operas. Rather than an intact or perverted precious-potential,[533] the words form images of a peculiar venerable-regressive: a vegetal venerable-regressive, since it is natural and prehistorical. The golden fruits that preserve the Gods' youthfulness immediately wither when Freia, who cultivates them, is captured.[534] The sacred forest has slowly withered, wounded by the tearing of a branch, which Wotan had made into a lance, the origin of pacts and writing.[535]

In Villiers de l'Isle-Adam's *Axel*, an immense German treasure, concealed by the father from the Napoleonic armies, is a fitting object of renunciation for the idealistic suicide of the son. The ambitions which the symbolist drama fails to live up to can be measured by the theme's precedents: the gold of the Nibelung, but also of Faust.[536] I have less to quote of any importance from the nineteenth-century novel than from the theater, thanks to its myths and symbols. In Scott's *Ivanhoe*, the aged Jew figuratively bewails the goods he stole from a ship during a storm: "I robed the seething billows in my choice silks — perfumed their briny foam with myrrh and aloes — enriched their caverns with gold and silver work!"[537] In Dumas' *The Count of Monte Cristo* (*Le Comte de Monte-Cristo*), it is the century-old treasure of a cardinal poisoned by the Borgia Pope that endows the hero, besides wealth, with the prodigious powers of the avenger. But in seizing control of the treasure he is not only guided by the ingenuity — smiled upon by chance (with no need here to cite Poe as a source, IV, 31) — of the learned abbot who has taught him during his imprisonment.[538] Dumas' contribution is that luck which grants all wishes, characterizes the serial novel, and produces a background of wild, luminous euphoria to the discovery of the treasure on the uninhabited island of the Tuscan archipelago.[539] The plot of Dickens's *Our Mutual Friend* turns on the inheritance of a miser who has made his fortune as a garbage contractor. "Coal-dust, vegetable-dust, bone-dust, crockery-dust, rough dust, and sifted dust"[540] were all mixed together in the piles in his courtyard; the rumors that treasures are hidden within them prolong the mirages and maneuvering until the novel's villains are finally disappointed: "No valuables turned up"[541] — a nonexistent precious-potential, as well as being harmful and inseparable from its contrary. Money is connected with dung in the episode where the "Lives and Anecdotes of Misers" are read aloud: one placed a deposit in the dung heap of the stable, just as others used a jar of pickles in a watch case, in a mousetrap, etc.[542] Hugo's *Les Misérables* makes this closeness literal in the Paris sewers (cf. II, 11; V, 7), where exploration reveals the mud to be full of "precious objects, jewels of gold and silver, gems, coins."[543]

In its deputed exotic and colonial space, by now unbounded, the category is consigned to moral ambiguity by colonialism, just as exoticism consigns it to be reversed into its opposite. In Stevenson's *Treasure Island,* which expands into a novel the short story by Poe that could have borne the same title, the setting moves from the American coast to the South Seas, and the ingenious deciphering unfolds as a dangerous adventure. The boy narrator feels a repulsion for the island when he first sees it, and the doctor picks up the scent of rot and disease: "It was plainly a damp, feverish, unhealthy spot."[544] The wreck of the ship on the shore is a sad sight, wrapped in dripping sea-weed and its deck covered in flowers.[545] But the stagnant value of the treasure is not scorned, as it is by Robinson Crusoe (IV, 30), because its use is suspended: it is the prize of a conscious hunt from one hemisphere to the other. Prefigured by the hoard of a pirate,[546] marked by a victim's skeleton, as in Poe,[547] and (also as in Poe) consisting of countless and various ingots and coins,[548] the treasure is discovered by a collaboration between former pirates and private citizens whom chance has made its legitimate heirs. And, as with Crusoe, the treasure's origin inspires a reflective horror in the latter, but certainly not a renunciation:

> How many [lives] it had cost in the amassing, what blood and sorrow, what
> good ships scuttled on the deep, what brave men walking the plank blindfold,
> what shot of cannon, what shame and lies and cruelty, perhaps no man alive
> could tell.[549]

The clear Victorian conscience begins to fare badly with Conrad's *Nostromo*. The South American silver mine's profits were exactly balanced by its
cost in the bones of Indian laborers; its abandonment to tropical nature makes
the images of the most concrete passage of the novel sterile-noxious.[550]
Charles Gould, an idealist who grew up with family piety towards the abandoned silver mine, brings it back into use,[551] and he identifies the peace of the
republic with his own and foreign profit, while corruption and cruelty disgrace
the revolutionary independence fighters. But the cargo that the brave sailor
Nostromo takes to an uninhabited island for safety fulfills the precious-
potential of the legend told by the poor: cursed treasures in the barren peninsula, guarded by two living-dead men.[552] The moral reversal of the man of the
people falls short of becoming ideological, and the ingratitude of the rich does
not assuage his feeling of guilt for having appropriated the unknown treasure.
When he wants to confess, on the verge of his death, the response is: "No one
misses it now. Let it be lost for ever."[553] A metonymy of a metonymy, the
estimation of lost value stands in relation to the mine as the mine does to the
wild continent, which represents the true precious-potential.

Later, in André Malraux's *The Royal Way* (*La Voie royale*), an adventure
endows the object of its quest with more than financial and aesthetic value. In
a region between Cambodia and Siam that has been reclaimed by the forest,
there are temples from the centuries of our medieval period. Their value consists in their transportable contents: statues and bas-reliefs to be sawn off from
a slender rock façade. These remains barely emerge from the ground, immersed in the "world of a submarine abyss," whose vegetation resists the
attack of archaeological conjectures and manual operations; amphibians, insects, and worms, immobile or fleeing, live on the ancient, rotting stone. The
pleasure of the result, welcome and gratuitous, has conquered a solemn-
admonitory which the extreme conspiracy of time and space pushes towards
the inhuman:

> More than those dead stones barely animated by the passage of frogs which
> had never seen a man, more than this temple crushed by so decisive an aban-
> don, more than the clandestine violence of vegetable life, something inhuman
> weighed down upon the rubble and the voracious plants, fixed like terrified
> beings in an anxiety which protected — with the strength of a corpse — the
> figures whose age-long gestures reigned over a court of millipedes and ruin-
> dwelling beasts.[554]

We still have to traverse the second series of texts, where the precious-potential works on a metaphorical or symbolic plane, and hints materially at nonmaterial values. The topos that urges the discovery of whatever might possibly yield an advantage has both classical and biblical origins, especially in the Gospels, with the command not to hide one's light under a bushel.[555] Concealment may, on the contrary, be advantageous and praiseworthy: in this sense as well, the category alternates between the beneficial and the malevolent, is either accepted or refused. It may be independent of images, but the images which it uses are near to being topoi. The flower stands for virginity in an epithalamium by Catullus, where, in contrast to the male chorus, the female chorus upholds it as a value:

> As a secluded flower is born in a closed garden,
> Unknown to the herds, by no plow touched,
> And is lulled by the breeze, fortified by the sun, fed by the rain.[556]

Dante wrote *The Banquet* (*Il Convivio*) in the vernacular, not in Latin:

> Because no thing is useful, except insofar as it is used, nor is its goodness potential, which is not perfectly in being; just as gold, pearls and other buried treasures . . . ; because those in the hand of the miser are in a lower place than the earth where the treasure is buried.[557]

For Boccaccio, who endows Cisti, a humble baker, with the "highest soul," nature and fortune often behave like mortals:

> who, uncertain of future events, for their circumstances they bury their dearest things in the vilest places of their houses, as being the less suspect, and hence in greatest need they draw them out, the vile place having more safely preserved them than a beautiful chamber would have.[558]

In *Athalie* the royal child, secretly rescued from the massacre and raised in the shadow of the Temple of Jerusalem, is a spiritual treasure substituting for David's gold, which is said to have been hidden there.[559] For Racine's sobriety in the use of metaphors, a daring comparison is not necessary:

> Thus in a secret valley,
> On the edge of a pure stream,
> Protected from the north wind, grows
> A young lily, love of nature.[560]

In Manzoni's last, unfinished sacred hymn, *All Saints* (*Ognissanti*), the asocial value of solitary sainthood seems doubtful to the eyes of the world: "To what avail the miserly / Treasures of solitary virtue." The answer exhorts us to ask God, metaphorically, why he allows the "silent" flower to grow in inhospitable lands:

which opens before Him alone
the magnificence of his colored veil,
which spreads to the deserts of the sky
the fragrance of its cup, and dies.[561]

It is a good that Goethe's *Torquato Tasso,* refraining from scattering his desire about, retires into himself in order to worship Leonora d'Este:

Thus does man search in the wide sand of the sea
In vain for a pearl, which hidden,
closed in its silent shell, rests.[562]

In Da Ponte's *Memoirs,* it is an evil that in Vienna Mozart should remain:

unknown and obscure, like a precious stone which, buried in the bowels of the earth, conceals the brilliant virtue of its splendor.[563]

In *Ill-Fortune* (*Le Guignon*), Baudelaire has shifted Gray's metaphors (IV, 27), with all of their ambivalence, from the dead of the countryside to the fate of the poet. Between mourning and consolation, between outward failure and secluded purity:

— Many a jewel sleeps shrouded
In darkness and oblivion,
Far beyond the spade and the sounding line;

Many a flower sheds with regret
Its scent as sweet as a secret
Within deep solitudes.[564]

Without any regret, the reserves which Mallarmé's *Herodias* invokes as accomplices of her virginity imply the solitary destiny of poetry:

You know it, gardens of amethysts, buried
Endlessly within dazzled wise depths,
Unknown gold, preserving your ancient light
Under the somber sleep of a primal earth. . . .[565]

For Woolf's *Orlando,* the hidden and tenacious mental associations that burden every single thing with something else are an embarrassment; and the very metaphor used to express them will seem inadequate and superfluous:

like the lump of glass which, after a year at the bottom of the sea, is grown about with bones and dragon-flies, and coins and the tresses of drowned women.[566]

Proust, on the other hand, knows how to take up the comparison of the flower again without making it banal — as a figure for the isolated and hidden spontaneity with which kindness would be spread among men:

> In the furthermost corners, the loneliest spot, one wonders in seeing her bloom on her own, like a poppy in a secluded valley, the same as those in the rest of the world, though it has never seen them, and has never known anything but the wind which at times makes its red solitary hood shiver.[567]

We must finally identify a metaphorical or symbolic precious-potential contained not within the short span of a rhetorical figure, but, at varying lengths, in the course of a narration. In the third episode of Joyce's *Ulysses,* Stephen wanders along a beach in the morning, and, in accordance with the Homeric frame of reference, battles with Proteus: that is, with the primitive metamorphosis which matter and objects eroded by the sea represent for him, and which may be fixed and subdued by language. It is not an easy phenomenon to pinpoint with a quotation. Here is the moment of erosion:

> His boots trod again a damp crackling mast, razorshells, squeaking pebbles, that on the unnumbered pebbles beats, wood sieved by the shipworm, lost Armada.[568]

In a fantasy towards the end of the chapter, the corresponding moment of recovery makes use of Shakespeare's "sea change" and of a line from Milton.[569] But even earlier:

> Signatures of all things I am here to read, seaspawn and seawrack, the nearing tide, that rusty boot . . .[570]

> These heavy sands are language tide and winds have silted here. And there, the stoneheaps of dead builders, a warren of weasel rats. Hide gold there. Try it. You have some.[571]

Even in contexts which are not natural but cultural, lost and recovered things seem to be connected with the category; it symbolizes poetry itself in both the examples with which I conclude this section. In Breton's *Nadja,* the precious-potential is the flea market: "I go there often, looking for those objects which one cannot find anywhere else, outmoded, fragmented, unusable, almost incomprehensible, in fact perverted in the sense that I mean and that I like" (cf. II, 12). Here he finds an edition of the complete works of Rimbaud "lost among a tiny exhibition of rags, yellowed photographs of the past century, worthless books and metal spoons."[572] In Gadda's *Mechanics* (*La Meccanica*), the list of useless things contained "in a box of shaved and grimy wood, with partitions" would only be further proof of his flair for the threadbare-grotesque (IV, 38; V, 5). But the joy of patiently rummaging through the box is compared to the joy of a young poet "when he skims and rummages through old poets for their young, budding words."[573]

13

The sterile-noxious is the category whose unity is less grounded in literature, beyond constants of subject-matter, and its documented examples are the most intermittent. Earlier I pointed out its biblical and classical origins: biblical for the images of cultural corporality reabsorbed by nature, that is, "once again raw" (IV, 28); and classical for the images of natural corporality untouched by culture, that is, "still raw" (IV, 29). In the first case I explained why the sterile-noxious is so often contaminated with all six of the categories for which the passage of time is crucial. Given the explanation's importance for the argument of this book, it bears repeating here: "there is no revenge of nature against culture in which we may not perceive the passage of time, nor is there a perception of the passage of time without the revenge of nature against culture." For this reason, a history of the sterile-noxious of reabsorption or of return would be almost indistinguishable from a history of its contaminations. Before the historical turning point, contamination occurred above all with the solemn-admonitory; afterwards, above all with other negative categories—including the sinister-terrifying. According to Benjamin Constant, things built by man for his use fail to converse with him in a congenial language, as nature does—until, that is, their utility is annihilated by time: "destruction, in passing over them, puts them again in contact with nature. Modern edifices are silent, but ruins speak."[574]

On the other hand, in the case where nature is either still or always raw, and destined to remain raw forever, the images rarely venture beyond the boundary of what is unrelated to man. The topoi that formalized the category in antiquity, and up until the historical turning point, establish some of these images at the limit: their brevity and predictability themselves neutralize a repellent strangeness. If, as I have said (IV, 29), the *locus horridus* was a topos in Latin literature, and its archetype was the infernal landscape, a position was assigned to the edge of the world in more than a supernatural and subterranean sense. Both a geographical and a cultural border divided the world into the civilized and the barbarian before it did so into the known and the fabulous. The Italy of Virgil's famous eulogy in the *Georgics* has crops and herds and mines and temperate seasons, as well as lineages and cities. But it is defined just as much by what animals it has *not* had or does *not* have now: in myth, fire-breathing bulls and the seed of dragon's teeth; in the present, tigers and fierce lions, snakes that drag and coil their immense rings.[575] In the *Eclogues,* if sterile or noxious flora grow in place of crops and flowers, it means that the gods of the countryside are sharing in a human mourning:

In the furrows to which we often entrusted large grains of barley,
Are born the barren darnel and sterile oats;
Instead of the tender violet, instead of the purple narcissus
The thistle springs and the hawthorn with sharp prickles.[576]

With only a single epithet, Horace is able to give prominence to the names of places far from the center of the Empire, and often not safely secured at its frontiers. Thus he makes use, and tempers the fear, of the nonfamiliar by drawing rhetorical figures from it: antonomasia, hyperbole. Let the example of an ode that is throughout a modest challenge to the eccentric and the exotic suffice. The innocent man defends himself only with his virtue:

If he has to travel through the boiling
Syrtes, or through the inhospitable
Caucasus, or in those places which the fabulous
Hydaspes licks.[577]

Once, a wolf—a monster that "not even the land of Juba generates, barren / Nurse of lions"—fled before the unarmed poet. And he would continue loving the sweet Lalage, even if he were exiled under harsh extremes of climate which stifle vegetation or habitation, and which are so extreme as to do without geographical denominations:

Put me where in the lazy field
No plant is refreshed in the summer air,
That side of the earth by the vapors and hurtful
Jove distressed:
Place me under the chariot of the too close
Sun in a land without dwellings. . . .[578]

In a later period, Lucan devotes more than half a book of his poem to recounting how the army of the Republic crossed the Libyan desert:

We enter the sterile lands and the burnt regions of the earth,
Where Titan [the sun] is excessive and water springs scarce,
And the dry fields swarm with deadly snakes.[579]

Cato speaks as a commander, and he measures the love of virtue and fatherland by the hardships of the test: "The snake, thirst, the heat of the sand / Are sweets to virtue"; "Only Libya can prove with its profusion of evils, / How men ought to flee."[580] Here as well, to be sure, we have antonomasia and hyperbole with moral implications. But the human boundary to be crossed is spatial before all else: "We move through a land beyond which / To the south none other was given by the gods to mortals."[581] The subject matter is developed and emphasized, rather than merely hinted at. Instead of Horace's brief epithet, the Syrtes receive a long description of forty-five lines: "Thus has nature evilly abandoned and devoted to no use / This part of herself."[582] Whereas two lines of Virgil describe kinds of reptiles absolutely foreign to Italy, here they are accounted for mythologically and characterized zoologically in two hundred lines, which go on to tell how they tormented the Roman soldiers to death.[583]

Dante makes one of the pits in the Eighth Circle of Hell outdo even Libya, borrowing the names of the snakes from Lucan.[584] Earlier, taking from Seneca the anaphoric negations of fruitful vegetation, he simply appropriated the pagan hell for his own:

> We set off into a wood
> Unmarked by any path.
> No green leaf, but of a dark hue;
> No straight boughs, but knotty and contorted;
> No fruits were there, but poisoned twigs.[585]

Compared with Latin literature, Italian literature raises the art of combining topoi and sources to a higher power. It would seem laughable to consider the "deserted fields" where Petrarch's love-induced solitude takes shelter as sterile-noxious; and yet the "human vestiges" from which he flees,[586] along with Dante's absence of "any path," is echoed in a third poet. Ariosto's uninhabited places are not margins but scattered voids, within a decentralized, medieval geography rather than the concentric model of the ancient world:

> For six days I went morning and night
> Over mounds and slopes horrid and strange,
> Where there was no road, nor *any path,*
> Nor even signs of *human vestiges;*
> Then I reached a valley, untilled and wild,
> Surrounded by ravines and fearful dens.[587]

A taste for density of evocation again condenses Lucan's Africa and reptiles into two lines, through a figure of *adynaton,* in which compassion is demanded even from the nonhuman:

> Neither the squalid serpents,
> Nor the blinded tiger fired with greater rage,
> Nor that which from Atlantis to the red shores
> Wanders poisonous over the hot sand. . . .[588]

could escape feeling pity for Angelica, tied to a rock and offered up as food for the sea monster. Augmented by Ariosto, the same topos returns in Tasso, and no less synthetically. But it returns with a nonfigurative sense since what is considered here is the diverse host of animals standing guard at the foot of Armida's magic mountain:

> Whatever monstrous and fierce
> Wanders between the Nile and the end of the Atlas Mountains
> Seems gathered here, and as many beasts
> As Hercynia has within itself, as the Hyrcanian forests.[589]

With his enchanted forest, Tasso in his turn reanimates the infernal origins of the sterile-noxious. He does so, however, not in the next world or at the edges of this world, but "not far from the Christian tents," six miles from Jerusalem.[590] The proximity of the place, whose shadow is unnatural by day and supernatural by night, is well suited to convey that complicity with evil and attraction to remorse which establish in the poem a morbid moral modernity. In the description of the forest, the category's images, within the space of two octaves, prepare the theme that will occupy Canto XIII; if the theme included nonanthropomorphic imagery, it would be sinister-terrifying. As we have seen (IV, 29), Marino outdoes Tasso's own outdoing in his recasting of the poem. I had taken up this example precisely because the Baroque amplification of sources clears a space for the category, which is elsewhere marginal and compressed (not unlike what occurred with Lucan in antiquity). But the sterile-noxious can also be compressed into two or three lines and confined within a metaphor in another way: when, as a figure for moral evil—as Tasso used it—the category translates this evil into a violent nausea triggered by sex—as Shakespeare sometimes does. Seen through Hamlet's neurosis, the world is no more than an obscene luxuriance of vegetation:

> Fie on't! O fie! 'tis an unweeded garden
> That grows to seed; things rank and gross in nature
> Possess it merely.[591]

For Othello, the nightmare of jealousy transforms the ultimate intimacy, where love is the source of life, into "A cistern for foul toads / To knot and gender in"; Desdemona proclaims her innocence:

> O! ay; as summer flies are in the shambles,
> That quicken even with blowing.[592]

The dinner that the stone guest offers to Tirso's *Burlador* consists of infernal antonomasias and hyperboles: scorpions and vipers, stewed thistle thorns and gall and vinegar.[593] Góngora offers an elliptical contamination with the solemn-admonitory: "Those which the trees barely allow / To be towers today"; he then inverts the semipositive and negative roles, giving to vegetation the task of ennobling the fallen stones:

They lie now, and their naked stones
Are clothed by pitiful ivy:
Because to ruin and disasters
Time knows how to add green flatteries[594]

Still another echo: between late antiquity and the extreme ramifications of
Renaissance imitation in an already pre-Romantic eighteenth century. In the
meantime, the borders of the known world had expanded beyond measure.
Nevertheless, the reflections upon the known world, with which Philosophy
moderates Ambition in Boethius's *Consolation of Philosophy,* reappear in the
more amplified images of Young's *Night Thoughts* (V, 4, 11):

A part how small of the terraqueous globe
Is tenanted by man! the rest a waste,
Rocks, deserts, frozen seas, and burning sands:
Wild haunts of monsters, poisons, stings, and death
Such is earth's melancholy map![595]

It does not seem possible to follow this series of recurrences, all the more
codified because more tenuous, with anything but random, isolated occurrences up to the historical turning point. The distinction more likely to help us
identify particular constants considers the position of the sterile-noxious with
respect to inhabited space: either internal or external; either detached and
distant, or contiguous, underlying, interpenetrating. The barrenness of the sea
drove Faust to repel it from a European coast (IV, 32). In Coleridge's *The Rime
of the Ancient Mariner,* the nightmare of water that does not quench one's
thirst breeds rottenness and monsters because the fabulous aspect of the ballad
concerns maritime discoveries: "We were the first that ever burst / Into that
silent sea"; the ocean is the Pacific (as we read in the prose gloss in margin) and
the latitude is the equator:

Water, water, every where,
And all the boards did shrink;
Water, water, every where,
And not a drop to drink.
The very deep did rot: O Christ!
That ever this should be!
Yea, slimy things did crawl with legs
Upon the slimy sea.[596]

In Mickiewicz's *Pan Tadeusz,* "the deep abysses of the Lithuanian forests"
have not yet been explored. Although these are not very far from the castle, the
noble hunters know only their edges. "Only rumor or fable knows what goes
on within them," and the popular belief in a kingdom of animals reigning at

their center is reported with detailed relish. Before this, however, both in the text and in the topography, the category is tinged with the sinister and the magical; the last insidious zone to be penetrated is related to hell:

> little lakes, half overgrown with grass, so deep that men cannot find their bottom; in them it is very probable that devils dwell. The water of those wells is iridescent, spotted with a bloody rust, and from within continually raises a steam that breathes forth a nasty odour, from which the trees around lose their bark and leaves; bald, dwarfed, wormlike, and sick, hanging their branches knotted together with moss, and with humped trunks bearded with filthy fungi, they sit around the water, like a group of witches warming themselves around a kettle in which they are boiling a corpse.[597]

In the Indian Ocean, in Melville's *Moby Dick,* Captain Ahab apostrophizes the enormous head of the first sperm whale his crew has killed and decapitated; the inaccessible, at once desired and feared, lies at the bottom of an unsounded vertical abyss — not in a space horizontally remote. It is no longer fable or legend, but the immense implications of science and history which now inspire the fantasy:

> speak, mighty head, and tell us the secret thing that is in thee. Of all divers, thou hast dived the deepest. That head upon which the upper sun now gleams, has moved amid this world's foundations. Where unrecorded names and navies rust, and untold hopes and anchors rot; where in her murderous hold this frigate earth is ballasted with bones of millions of the drowned; there, in that awful waterland, there was thy most familiar home. Thou hast been where bell or diver never went. . . .[598]

Whether at home or overseas, the fabulous and the legendary were constituted by a relationship, a mediation between the known and the unknown. Once the colonial conquest of much of the world had taken place, in Conrad's *Heart of Darkness* they are extinguished in the immediate and the unrelated: the horror of the unknown survives behind the squalor that makes the known absurd. The few visible signs of colonization seem senseless: the bombardment of the jungle from the sea, or the work being done on a railroad in the jungle and the metal wrecks it leaves behind.[599] In the countermovement of the sterile-noxious, culture is quickly reabsorbed by nature: "Still I passed through several abandoned villages. There's something pathetically childish in the ruins of grass walls."[600] Only the dried human heads, mistaken for decorations on the poles of a ruined fence,[601] equate the inhumanity of the white men with that of the natives and the environment. As in Mann (IV, 32), there is a symbolic overdetermination of nature; but here, the thousand-year repression of the sterile-noxious of the purely foreign yields at last to moral disquietude. What the comparisons translate is an absolute threat:

Going up that river was like travelling back to the earliest beginnings of the world, when vegetation rioted on the earth and the big-trees were kings. An empty stream, a great silence, an impenetrable forest. The air was warm, thick, heavy, sluggish. There was no joy in the brilliance of sunshine [. . .] till you thought yourself bewitched and cut off for ever from everything you had known once — somewhere — far away — in another existence perhaps. There were moments when one's past came back to one, as it will sometimes when you have not a moment to spare to yourself; but it came in the shape of an unrestful and noisy dream, remembered with wonder amongst the over-whelming realities of this strange world of plants, and water, and silence. And this stillness of life did not in the least resemble a peace. It was the stillness of an implacable force brooding over an inscrutable intention. It looked at you with a vengeful aspect.[602]

In other equally isolated occurrences, as I have said, the images of the category thrive at close quarters rather than at a great distance: they penetrate into the corners, they thicken at the frontiers, they mine the foundations. The Marquis de Custine visits Nicholas I's Russia, making observations with piti-less insight. In the origins of St. Petersburg he sees the proudest triumph of autocracy — and the most costly in human lives. From its artificiality, opposed to nature, he deduces a precariousness which may remind us of the biblical prophet:

If this capital without roots in history or in the soil should be forgotten by the sovereign for a single day; if a new policy should lead the thoughts of the master elsewhere, the granite hidden underwater would crumble, the inun-dated lowlands return to their natural state, and the legitimate guests of solitude again take possession of their dwellings.[603]

In Zola's cycle, *Les Rougon-Macquart,* the correspondence between the novels and their social contexts ties dozens of descriptions to backgrounds of the division of labor. The first novel, *The Fortune of the Rougons (La Fortune des Rougon),* is not yet so specialized; and the description with which it begins prefaces the whole cycle with the biological universal of death, resistant to social utility, luxuriant in its natural reproduction of life. It is the ground of an abandoned cemetery on the outskirts of the imaginary Provençal town: having been replaced because it was filled to excess, it has remained correspondingly fertile. The fruits of the monstrous pear trees seem repugnant to the house-wives. No buyers can be found for the land, which belongs to the town: too many bones have resurfaced, which were profaned by pranks and carried in cartloads down the road. The municipality must resign itself to renting it out as a lumberyard, but gypsies choose to live there as well. The reuse is limited in time and space; the area again becomes sinister in the evening, especially in winter; on one strip of land at the edge, the power of vegetation and the breath of the ancient cemetery endure.[604] There, among the tombstones and the bone fragments, the adolescent idyll of Silvère and Miette will blossom; there, with his execution, politics will give death the last word.[605] The tragedy of another adolescent idyll, which gives a tale by Gottfried Keller its title — *A Village Romeo and Juliet* (*Romeo und Julia auf dem Dorfe*) — springs from a barren strip of ground in the middle of the Swiss countryside. Between two cultivated fields there lies a third, which for many years has been covered in weeds, and with the stones the owners of the other two have thrown into it from both sides — until "all the stones in the world seemed to be gathered there."[606] Their fight for possession of the space in between brings both the well-to-do farmers to financial ruin; the worn-realistic is a sign of their déclassement. The sterile-noxious is situated even beyond this, or before the social order.[607] The heir, who possesses no written deeds to the land, survives in the community of vagabonds who live in the forests: he reveals himself to the lovers, the children of the two enemies, on top of the fatal mound of stones, where he leads them as he is trying to take them with him.[608] In their choice, instead, of double suicide in the river, nature remains a deadly alternative to society, which cannot sublimate its brutality without leaving gaps.

In the plays of Maurice Maeterlinck, displacement into legend and a feigned medieval onomastics only evoke the upper classes of the fin de siècle: ennobled and isolated, they fulfilled modern destinies in those castles. Historical regimes are no longer the referents of the building theme which we recognize there (V, 6). In *Alladine and Palomides,* we are lost among blind corridors and staircases, among windows and doors; the last door opens onto a pond.[609] In *Pelleas and Melisande,* the dead water stagnates beneath the castle, which is built over enormous subterranean caverns — no one knows where they lead. From there below wafts an odor of death; it would be high time to pay attention to the cracks in the pillars of the vaults, so that the castle should not be swallowed up one night. The symbol does not lean towards the solemn-admonitory (as with Woolf's island, II, 10), but towards a moral projection of the sterile-noxious, more general or vague than the impending adultery and fratricide.[610] The category's reversibility into a precious-potential of treasures and nocturnal or solar splendors, emphasized in one drama after another, has the same kind of meaning: both when it occurs after intervening scenes, and when it occurs in direct succession.[611]

However, in literature, symbolic processes are hardly the monopoly of the symbolist age. It is thanks to these processes, in Roth's *Radetzky March* (*Radetzkymarsch*), that certain images acquire their meaning — in this case, of a historical and political variety — and gather contaminations typical of the twentieth-century novel. The Habsburg monarchy's northeastern border was with the Russian Empire. In the prejudices of the protagonist's old father, whose adopted city is Vienna, it was a region:

> on the edges of which it was likely that one could already hear the Siberian wind howling. There, bears and wolves, and even worse monsters such as fleas and lice, threatened the civilized Austrian. The Ruthenian peasants sacrificed to heathen gods, and the Jews cruelly raged against all that others possessed.[612]

The authorial voice describes the region as among the most singular, a center of trade between two worlds, often illicit, always haphazard and clandestine: lists of goods, ultramiscellaneous or wretched to the point of uselessness; traffic in deserters and prostitutes to other continents.[613] Count Chojnicki, the great landowner with high family connections, wastes his time with alchemical experiments in a crumbling hunting pavilion. It is his task, as it were, to interpret the relationship between the frontier and the state: the threat of disintegration is refracted from the one to the other in his prophetic defeatism.[614] The sterile-noxious, which is the only appropriate category for the landscape, becomes decomposition in the open air in the field next to a factory of bristle workers:

> The men of this region were marsh-born. The marshes stretched uncannily over the whole territory, on both sides of the main road, with frogs, fever bacilli, and poisonous weeds . . .[615]

> The factory was an old dilapidated building [. . .] surrounded by a vast untilled area, where for innumerable years dung had been unloaded, dead cats and rats were left to rot, tin containers rusted, broken earthenware pots lay next to tattered shoes.[616]

In Faulkner's *The Sound and the Fury,* the category sanctions a marginalization of race and class: the cabins of the black families. The sterile-noxious substitutes vegetation with a mishmash of artifacts, reduces it to wilderness, and desiccates it, as though it were only nourished by a smell:

> They [small cabins] were set in small grassless plots littered with broken things, bricks, planks, crockery, things of a once utilitarian value. What growth there was consisted of rank weeds and the trees were mulberries and locusts and sycamores — trees that partook also of the foul desiccation which surrounded the houses; trees whose very burgeoning seemed to be the sad and stubborn remnant of September, as if even spring had passed them by, leaving them to feed upon the rich and unmistakable smell of negroes in which they grew.[617]

In Sartre's *Nausea* the obsession with nature is metaphysical, in proportion to the assurance with which the bourgeois have established themselves in the physical world (IV, 17). It is against them, rather than against himself, that Roquentin directs his fantasies of vegetation encamped outside cities and about to assail them, or of matter which erupts in atrocious excrescences and effervescences.[618] At its limit of improbability, the negative category would deny functionality and punish a positivism whose unproblematic arrogance is the true scandal:

> They have never seen anything else but the tamed water that runs from faucets, but the light which gushes forth from the bulbs when one presses the switch, but the half-cast, bastard trees which are held up by forked supports. They have the proof, a hundred times a day, that everything is done through mechanisms, that the world obeys fixed and unchangeable laws. [. . .] Nonetheless, great vague nature has slipped within their town, and has infiltrated everywhere, their houses, their offices, themselves [. . .] I *see* it myself, this nature, I *see* it.[619]

In Italo Calvino's *Invisible Cities* (*Le città invisibili*), three of the many cities Marco Polo describes to Kublai Khan are represented as split, according to that reversibility in which the category participates: split in a Janus-faced, vertical, or horizontal sense.[620] Moriana "consists only in a right side and a wrong side, like a piece of paper, with a figure on one side and one on the other that can neither detach themselves nor look at each other." Beersheba is aware of having a celestial and an infernal projection: it refuses to acknowledge that the latter is meticulously planned and the former is generously anal. Leonia measures its opulence "by the things that every day are thrown away to make space for the new," and that mingle outside with the rubbish heaps of other cities. The positive face of Moriana has matter that belongs to the precious-potential, and so too, especially, does the celestial projection of Beersheba, whose inhabitants "accumulate noble metals and rare stones"; while the daily renewal of Leonia shines with nothing but the efficiency of consumption. In all three cases the negative face is the clutter and removal of repressed matter, a sterile-noxious contiguous to the city that has produced it. Remnants of manufactured things bring several lists close to the worn-realistic or the threadbare-grotesque: on the hidden face of Moriana, in the fecal projections of Beersheba (both the one presumed to be in Hell, and the other hovering in the sky), among the mounds of detritus, whose landslides pose a grave threat to Leonia. In the last two cases, the city is challenged by sewage (II, 11), the modern world by an apotheosis of defecation and by the hypertrophy of rubbish.

We can also register a sterile-noxious of cadaverous horror and animal disgust, contaminated for the most part with the sinister-terrifying (V, 11). Only long before the historical turning point could the dismembering of the body be exhibited with a fable-like, dry tone. In Matteo Maria Boiardo's *Roland Enamored* (*Orlando innamorato*):

> Here he sees an arm, there half a head,
> There a hand bitten off.
> All around the forest is full
> Of legs or truncated shoulders
> And lacerated limbs and strange pieces,
> As if pulled from the mouths of dogs and wolves.[621]

The extreme expressionist violence of a poem like Gottfried Benn's *Beautiful Youth* (*Schöne Jugend*) lies in the displacement of compassion from nonliving human corporality to nonhuman living corporality, from the drowned girl in the morgue to the brood of mice. Repugnant by virtue of these mice alone, the corpse matters only as a shelter and pasture for them. And their young age is hardly enough, usually, to secure our identification with these creatures, not even an ironic one:

> They survived on liver and kidneys,
> They drank the cold blood and had
> Here spent a beautiful youth.
> And beautiful and quick their death came as well:
> They were thrown all together in the water.
> Ah, how the little snouts squeaked![622]

14

The beginning of both of the last categories, like the desolate-disconnected, must be placed after the historical turning point, with a second, minor historical turning point at 1848. I have spoken of the prestigious-ornamental's continuity with the venerable-regressive, a kind of distillation of its exemplariness from the ideological to the aesthetic (IV, 35, 37; V, 6). The residues of primary functionality which the images of the category would presuppose are as a rule decorative; and in the secondary refunctionalization — that is, in the up-to-dateness of decoration — they are nearly always reabsorbed to the point of no longer being noticed. As a result, the prestigious-ornamental is the most difficult category to document and has the briefest periodization, taking the symbolic year of 1914 as its lower limit. In the decades of the fin de siècle and the belle époque, however, I believe that the documented examples might be much more abundant than the ones I am about to provide, if I were to extend the inquiry to minor authors and forgotten texts — or rather, if this book were fed on research, rather than composed like an essay. Confining ourselves to the greatest authors, we find an example in Balzac which eludes the sphere of nonfunctionality itself, and which forces us to consider the category premature in 1839. In *Lost Illusions,* the low-ranking — although millionaire — banker loves the Greek style. He has scattered examples of it throughout his apartment, drawing patiently from the Empire taste, and the grace of antiquity he has diffused there is frail but elegant.[623] We may say that in so doing he has neither defunctionalized nor decontextualized any materials or models.

Things are different in *Ligeia,* written in 1838 — Poe is again a precursor, if more confusingly here than elsewhere. The gratuitous luxury with which the widower decorates the interior of an abbey for his unloved bride displays itself in an excessive variety of elements. Solemn carvings from Egypt; an immense piece of Venetian glass; a pierced roof with a "semi-Gothic, semi-Druidical" design; a censer in Saracen style; candelabra of oriental shape; a bed of Indian pattern; sarcophagi from the tombs of Luxor; arabesques in the tapestries woven with gold; phantasmagorias inspired by the "superstition of the Norman" or by the "guilty slumbers of the monk."[624] Is this the voluntary or involuntary triumph of kitsch? In more or less the same way as some pages from Balzac I summarized earlier (IV, 34), it may seem such to our negative value judgment; but in the text it is only presented as an extremely refined and perverse fantasy. If the excuse of commodification does not hold for a private interior, as in Balzac, the excuses of an "impending madness" and an enslavement in the "fetters of opium" do not put any distance between the author and the "I." An alibi pushed even farther towards the fantastic, hypnotic, and oneiric would end by dragging the images beyond the field which concerns us, and make the opposition between the functional and the nonfunctional waver on its basis in reality (V, 2). This is what happens in the visionary exoticism and in the euphoria of perfection of certain poems and prose-poems of Baudelaire,[625] beyond the prestigious-ornamental, and well beyond any precedent set by Baudelaire's much-admired Poe.

If the category's brief duration allowed us to distinguish any codified recurrences, I would point out the earliest ones in Flaubert's *Sentimental Education* — two times out of three in the house of Dambreuse. Here is part of the description of the evening of the reception:

> . . . the buffet resembled the high altar of a cathedral, or a jewelry exhibition, so many were the plates, covers, place settings, and spoons of silver or gold plate, in the middle of faceted crystals, which cast iridescent glimmers above the meats. The three other drawing rooms overflowed with objets d'art: landscapes by masters on the walls, ivory and porcelain on the edges of tables, chinoiseries on the sideboards; lacquered screens were displayed in front of windows, camellia tufts climbed up mantelpieces. . . .[626]

The reader may have recognized in the first lines a variation of the later ones that open the description of the room in *A Simple Heart* (II, 7): a place that "looked like both a chapel and a bazaar, containing as it did so many . . . objects and . . . things." Here the chapel is magnified into a cathedral, the bazaar is refined into an exhibition, the comparison of private with public denounces an extroverted pomp rather than an extravagant introversion. Yet it is always an excess — like the copiousness of lists, like the verb "overflowed with": an excess which neither involves decontextualizations nor attracts any irony (as in the examples of IV, 35 and II, 5), but rather lends grandeur to the act of decoration. M. Dambreuse has a unique but significant trait in common with Huysmans' des Esseintes. He is a nobleman who has severed himself from his class, in order to take part in every regime in the course of a half-century;[627] his opportunism conforms to the industrial age, just as paradoxically des Esseintes' aestheticism does (IV, 37). The other two Parisian interiors we can compare in the novel are the boudoirs of a high-class kept woman, Rosanette, and of Mme Dambreuse. The social disparity makes no difference in the respective presentations of overabundant frills and decorations, which follow a scheme we are familiar with (II, 13): synthesis — "a whole collection of curiosities," "every kind of object"; a more or less detailed list; a synthetic summation which makes explicit the agreement — fundamental to the category — of the objects with one another, and then with their contextual background: "and all this blended," etc.; "all these things, however, were harmonized," etc.[628]

It is no great exaggeration to suppose that the nucleus of the prestigious-ornamental can be reduced to Huysmans' novel and its immediate reception. Works famous in their own right play a role in this reception, but they water down that share of the heroic spirit which the coherence of des Esseintes' contradictions retains. In place of physical and nervous defects, there is a supernatural element in Wilde's *The Picture of Dorian Gray;* in place of solitary confinement, there is a lush and dissipated eroticism in D'Annunzio's *Pleasure.* In Wilde's novel Huysmans' work has a precise function, and is the subject of an entire chapter. Dorian Gray has taken it as a material object of the imitation he draws from it, and has had nine copies rebound in different colors, each suited to a different mood and fantasy. The ensuing account of this imitation is a free, digressive, and popularizing recapitulation. It boasts a richly peculiar and sonorously pleasurable vocabulary, and touches upon some other categories: the magic-superstitious through the legendary effects of jewels, the solemn-admonitory through the effects of time on things and fabrics — which hearken back to the novel's fundamental theme of the transience of youth.[629] In D'Annunzio, Andrea Sperelli's identification with his own house makes him converge with des Esseintes in two passages where he is alone, but occupied with the memory or the expectation of women. The first time, from a vulgate of symbolist correspondences we are brought to "I would almost say the erotic essence," "I would almost say the aphrodisiac virtuality" of objects: "This delicate actor could not comprehend the comedy of love without its scenery."[630] The second time, the anticipated possession is of a pure and chaste woman. Only then do we learn how the bedroom is decorated, from a lexically meticulous description that will follow this introduction:

> . . . and that room appeared to him the place most deserving of welcoming such a pleasure, because it would have made the singular taste of profanation and sacrilege — which in his opinion the secret act should possess — more acute.
>
> The room was religious, like a chapel. Almost every ecclesiastical cloth he possessed and almost every tapestry with a sacred subject was gathered here.[631]

The choices made in Huysmans between hereditary ownership and theological doubt become here cultural spice for the physical act. In fact, many pages before, we found a candid and unproblematic indication of how quickly the French character's inimitability was to be inflated and trivialized:

> That year, in Rome, the love for bibelots and for bric-à-brac had become excessive; every drawing room of the nobility and of the haut-bourgeoisie was cluttered with "curiosities"; each lady cut the fabric for the cushions of her sofa from a chasuble or a pluvial and placed her roses in an apothecary's vase from Umbria or in a cup of chalcedony.[632]

We may situate James's *The Spoils of Poynton* in the wake of the same model only as an intimate and severe Protestant version of it, which dramatizes the relationships of aesthetic value to ethical value and to duration. Collecting antiquarian wonders in the house of Poynton had cost Mrs. Gereth a life of utter self-denial. Her young friend Fleda, through whose eyes the story is narrated, recognizes in her a passion that is "absolutely unselfish — she cared nothing for mere possession."[633] Although filled with memories for her, the objects do not represent a true reminiscent-affective: they do not relate to any circumstances but those of their adventurous discovery.[634] The two women begin their friendship in a shared disgust for the pretentious-fictitious of the Brigstocks' house. Its ugliness, "fundamental and systematic," seemingly expresses an "abnormal nature": with slightly more concrete images, given James's economy in this respect (IV, 26; V, 3), than he uses for the prestigious-ornamental.[635] Good taste seems to be, like grace, predestined, unaccounted for by Fleda's origins in a poor family, in which the father collects harmless scraps and the sister's house is worse than modest.[636] And yet she is the daughter-in-law Mrs. Gereth would prefer, since she herself is excluded from her husband's inheritance, and she knows that Poynton will be lost if her culturally ignorant son marries the vulgar Mona Brigstock. Mrs. Gereth's ideal of "completeness and perfection" tells her that even the "cynical unity" of Mona's house would be better than a mixture of the two houses.[637] The elect and the damned in both an aesthetic and an ethical sense seem to coincide, and the elect have found their calling in defeat: Fleda's renunciatory scruples, Mona's punctilious overbearingness, and the weakness of the handsome Owen Gereth all converge. At the wrong moment, Mrs. Gereth herself restores the treasures she had moved, hazarding an ethical compromise in seizing them and an aesthetic compromise in choosing "chopped limbs" in a "happy whole." Thus Poynton is reduced to the "spoils" of the title,[638] long before their loss and the (perhaps superfluous) fire at the conclusion. Fleda is moved by the furnishings of an alternative house inherited from an unmarried aunt, which Mrs. Gereth disdains. For her, the memory of those who have been disappointed reclaims its rights in the "little melancholy, tender, tell-tale things"; while Mrs. Gereth can only arrive at the "ultimate vanity of all things."[639]

All that remains of any importance are several examples of a refused prestigious-ornamental in the greatest authors. In the same year that *Against Nature* was published, Tolstoy began his story *The Death of Ivan Ilyich*. The incompatible dimensions of worldliness and sickness inadvertently collide through objects. While giving instructions to an upholsterer for his new apartment, the protagonist falls off a ladder, and neither he nor the reader suspects the fate of which his contusion will be the first sign. But the author immediately corrects the character's illusions with regard to furniture and furnishings. The appeals court counselor Ivan has chosen them with a preference for antiques, "which he considered particularly *comme il faut,*" and "which gave a particularly aristocratic character to the whole place"; to him and his relatives, for whom his vanity intends it, the result seems magnificent and original. But a few lines lay bare the imitation lying within this originality, and, within the imitation, the undesired resemblances instead of the desired ones:

> In reality it was just what is usually seen in the houses of people of moderate means who want to appear rich, and therefore succeed only in resembling others like themselves: there were damasks, dark wood, plants, rugs, and dull and polished bronzes — all the things people of a certain class have in order to resemble people of another class.[640]

In Mallarmé's prose there breathes a singular sense of modern reality — which the stereotype of the pure poet makes us habitually neglect; and which in one case goes beyond even the refusal of the category, pushing towards a disenchanted, prescient normalization. The journalistic occasion was an international exposition in London in 1871–72.[641] The attempt to fuse art with industry is "that of the whole modern age"; industry, with its "hasty and economical" procedures, is in charge of the "popular multiplication" of objects "once made beautiful exclusively by their rarity," of wonders "for many years buried in a few hereditary residences."[642] The apparent optimism of the tone does not disguise the problems, but tries to overturn them with the claim that the word "authentic" is about to lose value.[643] One can only hearken back to the reigns of the last century, thanks to the subsequent end of stylistic inventiveness,[644] and one can simulate materially, to perfection, the passage of time which cannot be erased from cultural consciousness: "ornaments that are pallid enough, and gilding that is faded enough, for the inherent charm of new things not to damage the superannuated reminiscences which these perpetuated styles evoke."[645]

The reservations which Proust began to formulate about the prestigious-ornamental are the same that will make *Remembrance of Things Past* (*À la Recherche du temps perdu*) a vast criticism of the reminiscent-affective (V, 8). Already, before having identified an immaterial experience that eludes the metamorphoses of time, he has begun to harbor a mistrust towards the material fetish: it is unable to preserve any substance, whether more or less intimate, in time. The theme occurs twice, although unrefined, in *Jean Santeuil*, that great, posthumously published work of Proust's youth. The palace of the wealthy Mme Desroches has not been organically furnished, as it had once been, according to the tastes and needs of the dwellers there; the arbitrary choice between a Renaissance or Empire style, Louis XIV or XV or XVI, tells us nothing about the past of the person who chooses it or the past which it preserves as a museum.[646] In the palace of the Duke d'Étampes, the concentration of anachronistic comforts in a drawing room is more nobly authentic:

> For the objects which were once loved for themselves, are later loved as symbols of the past and diverted then from their primitive meaning, just as in poetic language the words taken as images are no longer understood in their primitive meaning. Thus, on the table with golden goat's feet, an inkstand was not used to write in that room where no one wrote, but to evoke the time when this luxurious life was a familiar one.

But it is not so simple to de- and refunctionalize: if we imagine the time when the old life, to which reuse now turns, was living, or how one day the current life that enjoys it will be dead,[647] the leaps in time evoke a dampened solemn-admonitory. Closer in time to Proust's masterpiece, in a critical discussion which does not develop any images, a text on Ruskin defines and rejects "idolatry." It is an aestheticizing fetishism of objects consecrated by contact with artists, or by coinciding with elements of works of art; more than in Ruskin's writings, Proust has an easier time illustrating it in the acts and sayings of Count Robert de Montesquiou.[648] The Count was the man who, a

quarter of a century before lending Proust the character traits for M. de
Charlus, had lent them to Huysmans for the character of des Esseintes. In
Remembrance of Things Past, the fetishism of the prestigious-ornamental is so
transcended as to be transfigured into the fiery idealism of the only morally
untouchable character, the only one who is loved without reservation: the
grandmother. The narrator's irony remains tender and admiring when confronted with the zeal with which she pursues the intellectual edification of
others — against the vulgarity of the useful, and heedless of the small disasters
worthy of the threadbare-grotesque:

> Even when she had to give a so-called useful present to someone, when she
> had to give an armchair, some cutlery, a walking stick, she would look for
> "ancient" ones, as if their useful character having been effaced by their long
> obsolescence, they appeared more inclined to tell us of the lives of men of past
> times rather than serve the needs of our times. [. . .] At home it was impossi-
> ble to count [. . .] the number of armchairs offered by her to young fiancées or
> old married couples which, at the first attempt made to use them, had imme-
> diately collapsed under the weight of one of the recipients. But my grand-
> mother would have thought it miserly to be too concerned about the solidity
> of woodwork where it was still possible to distinguish a gallantry, a smile, or
> sometimes a beautiful imagination of the past.[649]

After the First World War, I can only speak of isolated occurrences, which a
story may set shortly after it, as in Roth (II, 5), or shortly before it, as when
Musil practically liquidated the category (IV, 38). In 1921, Proust wrote a
preface to Paul Morand's three literary portraits of women, entitled, significantly, *Fancy Goods (Tendres stocks).* The passion of Morand's Clarisse for all
kinds of small objects makes for crowded surfaces and crammed drawers,
until it forces the temporary exile of the whole collection into the attic; it
ranges from antique sales and luxury auctions to second-hand shops and flea
markets. Of the half-dozen short lists in just over six pages, the modest and the
useless predominate, "even to screws, door handles, nails, old coins." It is
especially the love for the false, for the counterfeit object, that makes us think
of the negative category; as do the "thousands of objects aimed at other uses
than their presumed ones," such as "telescope-penholders," etc. But the culture of the London lady is not at all inferior to that of the author who addresses her formally as *vous.* She exhibits a refined mania which does without
any occasions for the reminiscent-affective, which finds excuses in an indifferent bad faith, and redistributes her choices with capricious generosity. Her
prestigious-ornamental is by now so shrewd that it can stretch, pleasurably,
well beyond the limits of the ancient, the expensive, and the rare.[650] In closing,

I should mention Walter Benjamin's inexorable ideological strictness concerning the playful labor of the collector: he subjects himself to "the Sisyphian task of divesting things of their character as commodities"; he dreams of a "world that is not just distant and long gone but also better," in which men remain unprovided with what is necessary but "things are freed from the drudgery of being useful."[651] It is as though the Marxist critique of commodity fetishism,[652] with a political rather than an aesthetic asceticism, were superimposed on the Proustian critique of what I might call anticommodity fetishism.

15

In the nineteenth century, the production of literature with an effect of kitsch preceded the kitsch that was represented in literature (IV, 34; V, 14). The two phenomena must not be confused; and this sweeps away any isolated occurrences of the pretentious-fictitious before the upper limit of 1848. The great exception forces us to leap back in time almost two millennia, and certainly does not constitute a traditional precedent from antiquity, but rather a case that has always been problematic. I am referring to the so-called *Trimalchio's Feast* (*Cena Trimalchionis*): the longest and best-known fragment of Petronius's *Satyricon,* whose singularity comes at the price of uncertainties about the author, the date of composition, the literary genre, and textual lacunae. For every reader, as for every philologist armed with extraliterary knowledge, the bad taste of the display of magnificence in the house of the nouveau riche Trimalchio is beyond dispute. The formal criterion on which the example's pertinence for us depends supports this judgment: a divergence of levels and points of view within the text. Encolpius, the narrator, and his companions Asciltus and Giton look down upon the master of the house and his court, as does the author, and their laughter, which on many occasions they can hardly stifle, mirrors the reader's.[653] The opulence of the spectacle excludes the threadbare-grotesque. On the other hand, it promotes garish decontextualizations, which can be compared at close range with the modern results of the category.

Although Trimalchio sends for mushroom seeds from India,[654] we would wait in vain for the eclectic consequences of an imperial cosmopolitanism. His naïve evocations — to use the terms of the semantic tree — produce idle, contrived artifices, and his ideal of distinction and power lies somewhere between the mechanical and the theatrical: he has gifts for his guests lowered from the ceiling of the dining hall, devises complicated word games for a lottery, and is proud of his cook because he knows how to make anything into something else.[655] It is in the culinary surprises and metamorphoses that the pretentious-fictitious runs wild. Let us ignore the dynamism of each apparition: peacock's eggs made of flour, with a garden warbler for a chick;[656] dishes each corresponding to a zodiacal sign in a table display;[657] a winged, Pegasus-like hare;[658] thrushes flying out from a hole cut in a boar's flank;[659] sausages pouring out of a slit in a pig's belly;[660] pies and fruits bursting with saffron when they are touched;[661] oysters and mussels bursting out of cracked amphorae.[662] Underlying all this is a vulgar carpe diem, a boorish anxiety for pleasure and waste, all the more shameless as it ignores its denial of death. If the skeleton on the table — in this case silver and flexible[663] — had passed from Egypt to become part of Roman custom, I would also propose for the category of the pretentious-fictitious Trimalchio's lachrymose and public instructions for his funeral monument, complete with his measurements and sculptured figures, among them a broken urn.[664] Perhaps Flaubert, who enjoyed the *Satyricon*, remembered all this for Emma's tomb, and perhaps also for the edible arabesques of the wedding cake (IV, 36).

A fantastical tale by Gautier of 1840, *The Mummy's Foot* (*Le Pied de Momie*), begins with a description of an antique dealer's shop, where "all centuries and countries seemed to have met by appointment." It is a brief imitation of the description in *The Wild Ass's Skin*, but no longer with Balzac's exalted tone (IV, 34). In fact, it is preceded by a suspicion about the authenticity of the merchandise, and by a scornful dating of the proliferation of similar shops: "since it became fashionable to buy ancient furniture and the lowliest stockbroker feels obliged to have his *Medieval Chamber*."[665] The dream in which a pharaoh's daughter, who has been dead for thirty centuries, comes to retrieve her foot, which was bought as a paperweight, is recounted light-heartedly. And yet it literalizes the kind of metonymic evocation through which the whole emerges from a part, an entire subterranean Egypt from only a single embalmed limb; and in the final surprise, on awakening, it touches on the supernatural.[666] We have reached it after setting off, through realistic counterweight, from the vicinity of the pretentious-fictitious. The category is still not unmistakably present in a passage from *The Ring and the Book*, which Robert Browning, Flaubert's elder, finished publishing in the same year as *Sentimental Education*. The dramatic poem narrates, in many monologues and just as many different versions, a bloody event that happened in Rome in 1698. The author begins with the discovery of his source, an old yellow book with an account of a trial, which caught his eye in a market on a piazza in Florence. The list of rubbish varies the connotations of the ravages of time with those of mediocrity, of the surrogate, and of the false. Thus the irony of the commentary upon them yields something different from the threadbare-grotesque, but through a contamination it anticipates the solemn-admonitory:

of the terrible experiences lived in the past only that printed testimony endures, lost in the fatuous hodgepodge — where a harmless inauthenticity is both expected and circumscribed:

> 'Mongst odds and ends of ravage, picture-frames
> White through the worn gilt, mirror-sconces chipped,
> Bronze angel-heads once knobs attached to chests,
> (Handled when ancient dames chose forth brocade)
> Modern chalk drawings, studies from the nude,
> Samples of stone, jet, breccia, porphyry
> Polished and rough, sundry amazing busts
> In baked earth (broken, Providence be praised!)
> A wreck of tapestry, proudly-purposed web
> When reds and blues were indeed red and blue,
> Now offered as a mat to save bare feet
> (Since carpets constitute a cruel cost)
> Treading the chill scagliola bedward: then
> A pile of brown-etched prints, two *crazie* each,
> Stopped by a conch a-top from fluttering forth . . .
> .   .   .   .
> From these . . . Oh, with a Lionard going cheap
> if it should prove, as promised, that Joconde
> Whereof a copy contents the Louvre! — these
> I picked this book from.[667]

Dickens, who always remained a master of the threadbare-grotesque (IV, 13; V, 5), already makes use of an unmistakable pretentious-fictitious in a list in *Little Dorrit* (1855–57). A version the less modern, to be sure, inasmuch as what unites the disparate things is a goal related to commerce or collection; but by now the innocence of the private collection is no longer protected from industrial malice:

> There were antiquities from Central Italy, made by the best modern houses in that department of industry; bits of mummy from Egypt (and perhaps Birmingham); model gondolas from Venice; model villages from Switzerland; morsels of tessellated pavement from Herculaneum and Pompeii, like petrified minced veal; ashes out of tombs, and lava out of Vesuvius; Spanish fans, Spezzian straw hats, Moorish slippers, Tuscan hair-pins, Carrara sculpture, Trasteverini scarves, Genoese velvets and filigree, Neapolitan coral, Roman cameos, Geneva jewellery, Arab lanterns, rosaries blest all round by the Pope himself, and an infinite variety of lumber.[668]

For no other category is the emergence of codified recurrences so tied to a single author as this one is to Flaubert. If in Balzac the pretentious-fictitious sprang up contaminated with the worn-realistic (V, 7), in Flaubert it tends to replace the worn-realistic as what constitutes reality: cultural inauthenticity rather than social instability, decontextualization rather than déclassement. They are no less inevitable, and not much less naïve, even if we move from the province to the capital, or if we climb the class hierarchy. In *Sentimental Education,* the public ballroom L'Alhambra, which I have already mentioned (IV, 38), was opened in the Champs Élysées; the four adjectives that refer to different cultures are not designed to clash, but are rather blended into an obvious compound:

> Two parallel *Moorish* galleries stretched on the right and the left. Facing was the wall of a house, which occupied one whole end, and the fourth side (where the restaurant was) represented a *Gothic* cloister with colored stained-glass windows. A kind of *Chinese* roofing covered the platform where the musicians played; the floor was covered everywhere with asphalt, and *Venetian* lanterns hanging from poles formed, from a distance, a crown of multi-colored fire over the quadrilles.[669]

The brevity of a list camouflages the jumble in the house of Pellerin, the indecisive and eloquent painter (and Frédéric, in a single verb, indulges in a pseudo-experience):

> The things surrounding him reinforced the power of his word: one saw a death's head on a prayer stool, a few yataghans, a monk's robe; Frédéric wore it.[670]

The jumble is neutralized in the equal dryness of another list, in the cemetery where Dambreuse is taken. I quote, after the first sentence, those in which the intuition of a funerary kitsch best transports the representation of kitsch into literature:

> The tombs rose in the middle of trees, broken columns, pyramids, temples, dolmens, obelisks, Etruscan crypts with bronze doors. One perceived, in some of them, a kind of funerary boudoir, with rustic armchairs and foldable chairs. [. . .] plaster statuettes: small boys and maidens or small angels suspended in the air by a copper string: many even have a zinc roof overhead.[671]

In *Bouvard and Pécuchet (Bouvard et Pécuchet)*, unremitting decontextualization, a constant of the descriptions and in some sense of the plots, at once propels and hinders the novel's story, which takes something of the form of a heterogeneous list. In their encyclopedic impulse, the two retired clerks are not satisfied with retracing this or that totality from conventional metonymies. Science after science and practice after practice, it is as if their fickle dilettantism aspired to cover the totality of totalities, driven onward by periodic failure. Can their failure, their accidental choices, their elementary doubts, be

blamed on their mediocrity or is it due to the disintegration of modern knowledge and experience? Perhaps the weakness of Flaubert's great unfinished
work is this double, ambiguous motivation between characters as subjects and
the world as object: the former are too small or too big, the latter is simplified
or complicated accordingly. The pretentious-fictitious of the images has to do
with this dilemma. When the two men, disappointed by agriculture, take up
gardening, here is the classification of genres they have read about in a treatise:

> First of all there is the melancholy and Romantic genre, which distinguishes
> itself by evergreens, ruins, tombs, and "an ex-voto to the Virgin, pointing to
> the place where a gentleman has fallen under the sword of an assassin." The
> terrible genre is composed by hanging rocks, broken trees, burned-down
> cabins, the exotic genre by the planting of Peruvian cereus "to give birth to
> memories in a settler or a traveler." The grave genre must offer, like Ermenon-
> ville, a temple to philosophy. Obelisks and triumphal arches characterize the
> majestic genre, moss and caves the mysterious genre, a lake the dreamy genre.
> There is even the fantastic genre, the most beautiful specimen of which was
> lately to be seen in a garden in Wurtemberg—since there one met in succes-
> sion a wild boar, a hermit, several tombs, and a boat which detached itself
> alone from the shore, to lead you into a boudoir, where jets of water streamed
> over you as you lay on the sofa.

Starting from such premises, whatever gaucheness they add to their plan and
its execution can hardly be thought to make things worse.[672] The result is no
more or less kitsch than when they act on their own, as in the description
(which I cannot quote in full) of the indescribable museum they set up in their
house, as archaeologists and antiquarians.[673] Heterogeneity sneaks in where
one would least expect it. The poor condition of a Renaissance chest proves its
authenticity, but the stereotypical subjects of the panels are partly classical,
partly biblical;[674] in a list of fertilizers, a Belgian and a Swiss preparation mix
in with guano, carefully preserved excrement, and carrion—all of which
draws from Bouvard's enthusiasm the canonical Freudian inversion *avant la
lettre:* "But this is gold! It is gold!"[675] A list of books and objects already
foreshadows interdisciplinary and international disorder in Pécuchet's house
in Paris,[676] before the inheritance which takes the pair's leisurely studies into
the provinces.

   The province, the petite bourgeoisie, and personal mediocrity are large
enough pastures for the inauthentic cultural experience to roam; or is it rather,
without the degree affecting the quality, the modern world—in its entirety?
The dilemma raised by Flaubert's entire oeuvre, but unresolved by his last
novel, persists throughout the subsequent success of the pretentious-fictitious.
In this sense, its implications may be either restrictive or extensive, guardedly

optimistic or utterly pessimistic. Compared to the great founder, the less extremist school, as is usually the case, prevailed. In *Pierre and Jean (Pierre et Jean)*, written by Flaubert's own disciple Maupassant, we are in Le Havre. Of the dining room decorated by a married couple in their apartment, we are told that less provincial eyes and hands could have achieved different results:

> This room with bamboo furniture, grotesque figures, Chinese vases, gold-sequined silks, transparent curtains where glass pearls seemed like drops of water, fans nailed to the walls to hold the cloths, with its screens, its sabers, its masks, its cranes made with real feathers, all its minute trinkets in porcelain, wood, paper, ivory, mother of pearl and bronze, had the pretentious and mannered aspect which unskilled hands and ignorant eyes give to those things which require most tact, taste and artistic education. Nonetheless it was the most admired room.[677]

The same holds true in the Andalusian province of Federico García Lorca's *Doña Rosita the Spinster (Doña Rosita la soltera)*, whose second act takes place in 1900. The caricatured progressivism that dates Rosita's birthday presents also attunes them, by contrast, to the static, remote setting. From the professor of economics she receives "an Eiffel Tower of mother of pearl on two doves bearing in their beaks the wheel of industry," which she prefers to a "small silver cannon through whose hole you could see the Virgin of Lurdes, or Lourdes" etc., "because in better taste."[678] The motherly maid's gift, a Louis XV thermometer case, surpasses the gift of her spinster friends, a barometer:

> In the middle of the velvet there is a fountain made with real snails, and above the fountain there is a kiosk in metal wire with green roses: the water of the basin is a cluster of azure sequins and the actual fountain is the thermometer itself. The puddles all around are painted in oils and on top a nightingale, all embroidered in golden thread, is drinking. I wanted it to have a string and sing, but it was not possible.[679]

In the New Zealand evoked in the stories of Katherine Mansfield, the seaside shopkeeper in *At the Bay* invites a maid for tea; she shows her dozens of new photographs, soon to be enlarged to a life-size scale, as she prefers them. The "style" of montage which frames her is the same as that of the etchings which thrilled Emma Bovary, when she too pulled back the tissue covering. Technology has vulgarized it, lowering its quality and widening its circle of customers:

> Mrs. Stubbs sat in an arm-chair, leaning very much to one side. There was a look of mild astonishment on her large face, and well there might be. For though the arm-chair stood on a carpet, to the left of it, miraculously skirting the carpet board, there was a dashing water-fall. On her right stood a Grecian

pillar with a giant fern-tree on either side of it, and in the background towered
a gaunt mountain, pale with snow. — "It's a nice style, isn't it?" shouted Mrs.
Stubbs.[680]

Drohobycz was a small town in Austro-Hungarian Galicia at the time of
Bruno Schulz's childhood. His fiction renders the newness of the industrial
neighborhood surreal, as if it were artificial and ephemeral, on the margins of
an ancient local stability. In the Street of Crocodiles, nonexperience is presented as experience, save for the metamorphoses of the shops and disillusion-
ments of the clients. The images of architectural "pseudo-Americanism" are a
prelude to would-be depravities, intoxicating frustrations:

> a rich but empty and colourless vegetation of pretentious vulgarity. One could
> see there cheap jerrybuilt houses with grotesque façades, covered with a mon-
> strous stucco of cracked plaster. The old, shaky suburban houses had large,
> hastily constructed portals grafted on to them which only on close inspection
> revealed themselves as miserable imitations of metropolitan splendour.[681]

The judgments explicitly spell out that superiority of the author which
defines the category. In the southern Italy of Elsa Morante's *House of Liars,*
the shamelessness of the decorative taste is owed to prostitution; it is contaminated with the worn-realistic in the house of Elisa's future adoptive mother.
Elisa, as narrator, is here more aware than her past self: "to my puerile lack of
experience that dwelling appeared elegant and sumptuous."[682] At the beginning of the novel, on the other hand, the judgment conforms to the retrospective role of narrator which Elisa is about to assume:

> I will spare myself the description of this exhibition of bad taste and shame;
> this crowded furniture, swollen and cheap imitations of the most various
> styles; and the loud and dirty upholstery, the cushions, the pretentious figu-
> rines and the second-hand finds; the photographs touched up in watercolors,
> and black with dust, often accompanied by trivial inscriptions.[683]

In Albert Cohen's *Belle du Seigneur,* a comic bitterness punishes Madame
Deume for the hypocritical, indomitable earnestness with which she performs
her mix of sanctimony and snobbery. It informs the plethora of objects and the
clutter in the description of her bedroom — six sentences where several lists
stretch out with no verb. Disparate origins and conventional insignificance
have, by now and for some time, become a topos in more than just a literary
sense. En masse, and with the exception of some extreme cases, they conform
to a custom in which everything is in its place because everything is out of
place, in which obsolete objects are merely the displayed portion of customary ones:

> Above the chimney, a pendulum clock in gilt bronze, topped by a flag-bearing soldier dying for his country; a bridal crown under a glass globe; some evergreens; a small bust of Napoleon, an Italian mandolin player in clay; a Chinese peasant sticking out his tongue; a blue velvet casket encrusted with shells, a souvenir from Mont Saint-Michel; a small Belgian flag; a small vehicle in spun glass; a porcelain geisha; a marquis in false Dresden china; a small metallic slipper, stuffed with velvet for a pincushion; a large pebble, a souvenir of Ostend. [. . .] On the walls, an enormous heart in carved wood, scattered with small hearts containing photographs [. . .]; Japanese fans; a Spanish shawl; a Westminster chime; biblical verses either in poker-work, or in phosphorescent paint, or embroidered in feather-stitch.[684]

The implications of the images in Woolf's *Orlando* are no longer of marginal and deteriorated places, or classes, or people, but of a generation's repudiation of an entire epoch — an epoch more imposing than Gozzano's 1850 (II, 4). The protagonist, who lives her thirty-six years across five centuries, has a vision in St. James's Park in the nineteenth century. In a mirage produced by the sun, Victorian kitsch is monumentalized as an obscene and strident accumulation of things; it does not lie in the individual metonymies, but in the sum of them. In turn, this kitsch represents the whole, rather than a part, of the century which generated it. It gives the pretense of lasting forever, we read immediately after, but with the new century it will disappear without a trace:

> a pyramid, hecatomb, or trophy (for it had something of a banquet-table air) — a conglomeration at any rate of the most heterogeneous and ill-assorted objects, piled higgledy-piggledy in a vast mound where the statue of Queen Victoria now stands! Draped about a vast cross of fretted and floriated gold were widow's weeds and bridal veils; hooked on to other excrescences were crystal palaces, bassinettes, military helmets, memorial wreaths, trousers, whiskers, wedding cakes, cannon, Christmas trees, telescopes, extinct monsters, globes, maps, elephants, and mathematical instruments — [. . .]. The incongruity of the objects, the association of the fully clothed and the partly draped, the garishness of the different colours and their plaid-like juxtapositions afflicted Orlando with the most profound dismay. She had never, in all her life, seen anything at once so indecent, so hideous, and so monumental.[685]

Accusing a country — that is, a national character — of kitsch is even more restrictive than chronologically imputing it to a period in time. In Jean Giraudoux's *Siegfried,* the argument over the identity of the amnesiac war veteran never veers from a cultured and pacifist neutrality between France and Germany as fatherlands. The Secession style of the scenery of the second act shows how common it is in Germany for proverbs to be embroidered onto cushions; or worse, for Nordic mythology and zoology to be defunctionalized in everyday functions. The French philologist who explains all this tries in vain to justify it:

> Look: you take a match from this squirrel, you strike it on the back of Wotan, and you light the cigarette you have taken from that swan's belly. You flick the ash into this Valkyrie and throw the butt into the bear. . . . This circle of legendary animals or heroes, which the Germans like to set going for each of their most banal functions, is life, after all.[686]

To my knowledge, Gadda is the writer in whom the reach of the pretentious-fictitious becomes most extensive and pessimistic. I have already explained how, in Gadda's pluralism of cultures and styles, Flaubert's vision of modernity seems to be brought up to date; and how his comic disposition nevertheless destines the category to a continual contamination with the threadbare-grotesque (IV, 38). This latter category is dominant in the prose of *Clutter at Porta Ludovica* (*Carabattole a Porta Ludovica*). The Saturday afternoon fair in Milan is the incoherent outlet of an essential avarice unworthy to be called reminiscent-affective: "that instinct to preserve, to retain, not to give up a button: in any case not to incur a loss, to use in any way, and to the last obtainable penny" the things one already possesses (cf. V, 5); "a wish — but also an economy and a calculating certainty — to succeed in merging the threadbare with the useful, the part with the whole." The first image is a "frame in fake mahogany, girdled with golden peppers, with the portrait of the first wife of the uncle of the ex–brother-in-law of our father!" Later on, delays and absences presuppose a passage of time; here I give one list to stand in for the rest: "pear-shaped enema bulbs dating from 1912, stools with strawless seats, charcoal hand warmers, phonograph horns in Liberty style, of course without the pho-nograph." A "bronze hunting dog 'pointing' at the cheese-graters" produces the same effect of contiguity we saw in Balzac's shop (IV, 34). While the mention of "wreck," "beach," and "shipwreck" touches on the precious-potential (cf. V, 12), the sentence that lowers the whole to the pretentious-fictitious is the same one that exalts it as an epiphany of a historical totality: "Oh! the clothing of human civilization is, after all, made of bathtubs and potato peelers, of brass castors and cuckoo clocks that go 'croak-croak,' if they croak at all."[687]

The institutional form of kitsch as pseudo-experience is advertising — an interested promise, a shameless guarantee, an untrustworthy sample. It is too ubiquitous and obsessive in our daily lives — in reality — to infuse a large body of texts, insofar as today's literature is averse to realistic duplication. The representations I will quote, in this chapter and the next, date for the most part to the first half of the twentieth century. In Moravia's *Time of Indifference,* the son and brother, who with his lack of moral identity best embodies the title, sees this presumed identity symbolized by a mannequin in an advertisement. The character's projection onto the mannequin does not prevent an objective analysis of the mode in which it functions:

> painted in vivid colors, cut out from cardboard, depicted according to a model more human than fantastic, it had an immovable, stupid and laughing expression, and large brown eyes full of candid and unquenchable trust; it wore an elegant dressing gown, it had obviously just got out of bed, and without ever tiring, without ever stopping smiling, with a demonstrative gesture, it stropped the blade of a razor again and again on a strip of leather; sharpening it. There could be no connection between the banal action it was executing and the happy satisfaction of its pink face, but precisely in this absurdity lay the effectiveness of the advertisement; that disproportionate happiness did not want to call attention to the imbecility of the man, but to the good quality of the razor; it did not want to show all the advantage of possessing modest intelligence but that of shaving with a good blade.[688]

Funerary kitsch, which had not escaped Flaubert, is a sufficient theme for Waugh's *The Loved One*. There it aspires to the perfect neutralization — almost to the point of euphoria — of another's death, even if it is violent. For this purpose, descriptions of procedures are worth more than single images — such as the dickeys, or the shrouds that cover only the front, worn by the corpses, and the "allegorical, infantile or erotic" statues of the tombs.[689] In the neighborhood of the funeral parlor, we again see that specific American pretentious-fictitious which tries to emulate the models of the Old World (IV, 37): "This perfect replica of an old English Manor," built out of iron to withstand earthquakes and nuclear bombs, represents a first degree of imitation. "This seat is made of authentic old Scotch stone from the highlands of Aberdeen" represents a second. "This is more than a replica, it is a reconstruction," clearly cleansed of the ravages of time, suggests still another;[690] and the voice of the public address system, when it is switched on, declares: "You are standing in the Church of St. Peter-without-the-walls, Oxford, one of England's oldest and most venerable places of worship. Here . . ."[691] In contrast to what happens in the film studios, the difficulty is not in understanding that the façades which seem solid are actually made of plaster and cardboard; it is in believing that the steel-framed manor house has its three dimensions and that there is nothing temporary about it.[692]

For the woman who delivers a monologue while half-buried at center stage, in Beckett's *Happy Days,* deciphering the writing on the handle of a toothbrush is a time-consuming, gradual, and intermittent task: "fully guaranteed . . . genuine pure . . . hog's bristles." This should be sufficient reason for us to consider it in connection with advertising and the pretentious-fictitious.[693]

The shopping bag lying next to her is not reminiscent-affective, even though it was given to her one day by the other maimed human character on stage;[694] the objects she draws from it offer her alternative resources less fragmented than her communications with him. Or, than her discussion of him, to which the objects serve as a strict counterpoint, precisely from the moment when reading the toothbrush requires first spectacles, then a handkerchief to clean both the spectacles and the toothbrush — and finally a magnifying glass. "There is of course the bag," "there will always be the bag."[695] The objects taken out are put back in, one by one, or as "unidentifiable odds and ends."[696] If one of them is broken outside the bag, tomorrow it will be found intact inside, "to help me through the day."[697] The woman doubts she would be able to "enumerate its contents" exhaustively: "The depths in particular, who knows what treasures. What comforts."[698] She believes that the things produce small noises, that they have a life, she wonders what she would do without them, since she has been abandoned by words.[699] To the small extent to which the criterion of functionality does not waver, as if in a dream (V, 2), objects remain the only presumed source of utility and the only human context; but they mark and fill the time of the very condition in which everything has been revealed as useless, of a metaphysical decontextualization more humorous than sinister.

VI

Some Twentieth-Century Novels

I

The fragmentary quotations of which we have had our fill were necessary in an essay concerned with thematic constants: our task was to present these in chapter II, to classify them in chapter IV, and to document them in chapter V. I have quoted in their entirety, or nearly in their entirety, not much more or less than half a dozen poetic texts. On the other hand, texts of every genre have not always been commented upon exclusively as the bearers of certain images: if the images sometimes appeared central and dominant in a work, they often entered into a close relationship with thematic components of other kinds. And at times we could perceive their significant, if not decisive, position in the structure of the work, and in the relationships between part and part and between part and whole. Let us return to some examples drawn from the novel, where the phenomenon is less straightforward than within the confines of a poem or a short story: I have hinted at the abundant centrality of images in *Oblomov,* their hidden pervasiveness in *Les Misérables* (V, 7); I have outlined their structural importance in *Madame Bovary* (IV, 36), *Against Nature* (IV, 37), and *The Spoils of Poynton* (V, 14). But it is in twentieth-century novels that I have been concerned with sounding in greater depth their relationship with other thematic elements—thus in *The Great Gatsby* (IV, 37),

Nausea (IV, 17), and *Acquainted with Grief* (IV, 38); succinctly, at least, in *Time of Indifference* (V, 7), *The Master and Margarita* (V, 10), and *Nineteen Eighty-Four* (V, 6). In *To the Lighthouse* (II, 10), we had glimpsed a different phenomenon, the contaminations of categories — which elsewhere become more unpredictable alterations. Now, throughout the series of twentieth-century novels I have chosen to analyze in this chapter, the images' power of structuration and a crisis of the system of categories seem connected: is the semantic tree perhaps a summa of nineteenth-century classificatory hypotheses? The periodization of the categories has three of the twelve start from the second half of the nineteenth century, four from the late eighteenth century, and the rest, of earlier origins, last up until the present day. On the one hand, the continuous modern renewal enriches and complicates the entire tradition; on the other hand, it increases the need to explain the images through textual connections. But an analysis is possible only thanks to the very categories which its results will then alter and compromise.

2

The Lost Domain (*Le Grand Meaulnes*), published in 1913 by Alain-Fournier (Henri Fournier, 1886–1914), presupposes a contamination already familiar to us: between the venerable-regressive and the reminiscent-affective, under the aegis of a nostalgic idealization of the *ancien régime* (V, 6, 8). It makes little difference that the only date before the 1890s of the narration is 1830, carrying an explicit reference to the grandmothers of sixty years before. As well as being the date of a silk waistcoat (the first eccentric image),[1] it is also understood to be the date of *Hernani*: the prearranged call which will tear the groom away on the eve of his marriage is a romantic reminiscence of Hernani's horn.[2] The determination of the historical category becomes secondary, as is the social outcome, an ancient family's demise. The characters are no more than adolescents: François Seurel, the first-person narrator, when the story takes place; Augustin Meaulnes, the friend who witnesses by chance a strange party in a mysterious mansion; Yvonne de Galais, and her brother Frantz for whose uncelebrated wedding the party had been planned with a privileged role for the children. The party and the mansion occupy a space and time separate from that of the adults. The route to the estate remains untraceable, since Meaulnes has fallen asleep in the coach both on the way there and on the way back; his gradual disorientation, up until his arrival at the surprising destination, unfolds along a road wandering through space, which he hopes to enter again but will not be able to.[3] The antiquity of the mansion (certainly antedating 1830) postulates that time which stretches back further than the individual

past, and which as we know can translate the incommensurable time of childhood (II, 15; V, 8). Thus the boy, right after he has spotted "the spire of a gray
tower" in the distance, is astonished by the exciting certainty which invades
him: "So much joy," he said to himself, "because I am approaching this old
dovecot, full of owls and drafts!"[4]

As though the coach whose mare has strayed and abandoned him had
metamorphosed, he climbs to a window by leaping from one to another of the
old carriages that fill the courtyard. He sleeps once more the sleep of a
seventeen-year-old in an alcove which, like the rest of the room, is cluttered
with peculiar objects: "He lifted the curtain at the end and discovered a great
low bed, covered with old gilt books, lutes with broken cords, and candelabras
scattered here and there."[5] What the protagonist of the late symbolist novel is
realizing as an enchantment remotivates the contamination of categories beyond narrative reasons, and before he himself discovers them. Their young age
makes him, or Frantz, unusual subjects for the reminiscent-affective: the childlike happiness which the party and mansion symbolize is represented as lost
and sought after even before it has been lived. The chivalric loyalty corresponding to feudal images will come at a high price within the plot, but the
present succumbs *a priori* within the caprice which artificially brings the past
back to life, and which makes times intersect. The preparations made for the
small party salvage some scraps from abandon and ruin; distant collective
memories are personalized, the current occasion is dematerialized, halfway
between the playful and the ghostly. That the *ancien régime* signifies childhood
becomes both literal and metalinguistic:

> Upon a heavy dressing table of cracked marble, they had laid out what was
> necessary to transform any boy into a dandy [. . .]. But the waxing of the
> wood flooring had been forgotten; and Meaulnes could feel sand and plaster
> slipping under his soles. Again he had the impression of being in a house long
> abandoned . . .[6]

> Everything seemed to be old and ruined. The openings at the bottom of the
> stairs were empty, the doors having been removed long before; no one had
> even replaced the glass of the windows, which formed black holes in the wall.
> And yet all these buildings had a mysterious festive air.[7]

We even have a hint of the architectural irrationality of the *ancien régime* (V,
6): "there were stables built in an amusing disorder . . ."[8] But the images of our
repertory enter into a secret textual homology with other ones. There "shone a
December sun, clear and glacial" on the midday solitude of the boy's arrival;[9]
the next morning, he finds himself "as though transported into a spring day,"
under the sun of the first days of April.[10] Strangely, a sun which is to the frozen

season as the precarious feast is to its derelict background: "Strange morning! Strange pleasure party! It was cold despite the winter sun"; "But suddenly a chilling gust of wind came to remind the strange party's guests of winter."[11] When the estate so long sought after is identified by simple chance as the Sablonnières, almost everything has been destroyed and sold.[12] The last part of the novel resolves the mysteries, disappoints expectations, and dissolves childhood; in its prosaic melancholy, the reminiscent-affective retreats into more ordinary forms. Within the houses and shops of bourgeois uncles, as in the Sablonnières, memories and photographs, drawers and wardrobes, etc., are lavishly present.[13] But from the beginning the college of Sainte-Agathe, in a wintry light of the countryside, foreshadows a domestic version of the building theme peculiar to the venerable-regressive: with its "rooms full of dusty straw," the house had seemed to François' mother so "ill-built" that she had counted "all the openings that would have had to be condemned" to make it habitable.[14] Among the "immense gloomy garrets of the first floor" and "the abandoned rooms of substitute teachers," Meaulnes finds where to lose himself as soon as he arrives. He discovers a sun or a moon from the charred fireworks of the Fourteenth of July: residues of festivity.[15] The latent ubiquity of the principal images, connecting the college and the estate in the novel's uncertain topography,[16] has been established early enough for the reader not to notice it.

3

If I now turn to *Arturo's Island* (*L'isola di Arturo*), published in 1957 by Elsa Morante (1918–85), the transition does not lack a literary-historical pretext (as in II, 2): Alain-Fournier's novel was certainly one of her models. But in Procida (less the real island than an imaginary one), the feudal residue is not delimited as it is in the French province. The relationship of the monuments to the landscape is what relegates southern Italy to the regions passed over by progress, along the road from east to west and south to north: relationship that is desultory, complementary, degraded, permanent, and misunderstood.[17] Too many civilizations are layered in immeasurable chronologies, which blur many centuries or a half-century with a "circa," an "at least," a "more than," a "maybe."[18] Two buildings, opposed and assimilated to each other, emerge: one a former castle and the other a former friary: the Penitentiary, which dominates the island, and the house where the man who bequeathed it to Arturo's father only allowed young boys to enter. The venerable-regressive of both buildings ends up harboring wrongdoing, which in the Penitentiary is punished by the state, and in the house is private and indefinable. Nunziatina, the sixteen-year-old stepmother, initially mistakes one building for the other because the father has boasted of living in a castle.[19] But the author and the reader never enter the Penitentiary, and they do not even go near it before the final twist of the plot. In the immense solitary proportions of the Walled Ground (*Terra Murata*), which exhibits an anachronistic public majesty (cf. IV, 13), remote history and rudimentary nature meet. A "lugubrious and sacred fiefdom," a "funereal Olympus," and close by there are huts clustered "in a labyrinth of crossings, steeps, and slopes," or destroyed and left as tall ruins;[20] but also, on a cliff hanging over the sea, an "irregular and massive shape" like a "corroded mountain of tufa," "gigantic blind walls" like a "pile of natural rocks."[21] Arturo first sees it as an "abandoned manor house," a "fantastic ruin, inhabited only by snakes, owls, and swallows."[22] In our vocabulary, it is a contamination of the venerable-regressive and the sterile-noxious: the Mediterranean evocations remove the negativity of the latter category.

Just as the road to the prison-castle is a gallery "without other flooring than a thick layer of dust," so too in the House of the Lads (*Casa dei Guaglioni*) it is impossible to say "what material or color the floor was made of, which was hidden under a layer of hardened dust."[23] Here the profaned austerity of the venerable-regressive has emptied out the interior: the only remaining traces of the friary, its refectory converted into a hall of revelry, are a "holy water stoup in alabaster" and "the brothers' ancient hearth."[24] In the chests of drawers and closets, "the odors of who knows what defunct Bourbon bourgeoisie" are less ancient.[25] When the convivial owner dies, his remains are reclaimed and dispersed in a "kind of pillaging";[26] and the father maliciously takes advantage of the legends of ghosts, which one always expects in a castle, to intimidate Nunziatina.[27] The dilapidated state of the building might only have been suggested by metonymic touches of the worn-realistic, rust and faded colors, unsorted remnants, or dusty lamps.[28] But this same category is contaminated in its turn with a sterile-noxious fully redeemed—through the eyes of the boy, who says of himself:

> No one gave any thought to the disorder and dirt of our rooms, which to us seemed as natural as the vegetation of the untended garden between the walls of the house [. . .]. You could even find there, among other things, rotting around the grown carob tree, the carcasses of furniture covered with moss, broken crockery, demijohns, oars, wheels, etc. Between the stones and rubbish, plants with swollen, thorny leaves grew, sometimes as beautiful and mysterious as exotic plants.[29]

The thousand-year-old theme of the cursed animal invasion is softened into a fable-like and familiar euphoria (well short, however, of the oneiric suspension of the criterion of functionality, V, 2):

I believe that spiders, lizards, birds, and in general all nonhuman beings, must have considered our house an uninhabited tower of Barbarossa's era, or even a sea cliff. Along the external wall, from crevices and secret passages lizards sprouted as if from the earth; swallows by the thousands and wasps made their nests there. [. . .] Certainly there were at least a couple of owls who lived inside the house, although it was impossible for me to discover where [. . .]. In some of the house's abandoned rooms, the windows, out of forgetfulness, would remain open in all seasons. And it would happen upon entering one of these rooms suddenly, after an interval of months, that one would collide with a bat; or else hear the cries of mysterious nestlings in a chest, or between the rafters.[30]

It is but a short step from this sterile-noxious — even shorter than to the sighting of fantastic animal species[31] — to a precious-potential of raw island nature: fossil shells, underwater plants, starfish, sea urchins, and cockles.[32] Arturo will never again capture the odor he breathed in his house except "at the bottom of some boat, or in some cavern."[33]

His fantasy is too exalted by reading like Don Quixote's to confine itself to the love of his house and his island, not to imagine traveling around the world — the same travels which in his blind admiration he credits to his father. Even though half-German, the latter is also suffused with the ex-feudal Italian South, in the idle haughtiness which hides the misery of his homosexual obsession with adolescence. It is as though the father perversely, and the son literarily, inherit from on high the fascinations and illusions of their monumental landscape; while Nunziatina, a woman and one of the people, corresponds to the values of the southern venerable-regressive from below. Ignorance, prejudice, a horizon limited to Naples and its environs,[34] "respect for the Constituted Authority,"[35] do not deform her moral frankness which is secure in its intuition, her sweetness, generosity, and patience. She too (cf. II, 7) compensates for cultural inferiority, according to which the false or vulgar trinkets that she likes to receive as gifts, the small pictures of different Madonnas she is devoted to, should be defined as pretentious-fictitious;[36] and it is symbolic that for a long time she is the true inhabitant of the house, which to Arturo seems deserted when he glimpses its walls and windows from the sea or from a distance.[37] When his semi-incestuous love for her can no longer be repressed, the myth of the father quickly collapses into a seething disenchantment. The neglected contemporary political situation[38] overturns the timeless chronologies; the sad departure from the island is also a precocious intellectual's escape from his own country, less universally symbolic than the end of adolescence.

4

The Bear by William Faulkner (1897–1962) also begins with an adolescent's isolated ideals and with the power of wild nature, against the background of the American South. In its definitive version, it is the longest story in the collection *Go Down, Moses,* published in 1942 as a unified structure: the dispersion in which the author *immerses* chronology, genealogy, and information is just slightly greater than in his novels. An analysis of one of the seven stories cannot avoid organic references to the others. *The Bear* draws the education of Ike McCaslin from its predecessor, *The Old People.* He is initiated into the secret rituals of the forest and the hunt, as if these were sacred lore, by the old Sam Fathers, the son of an Indian chief and a mulatto slave. On the other hand Ike is the heir of the cotton plantation which his grandfather, one of the founding settlers, had bought from Sam's father and cleared from the forest. Two different orders of inherited values, from people of different blood, converge in him; at twenty-one he will choose to renounce his property, convinced that no one has a right to own the land. But the text posits such a tension between convictions and events, between right and destiny, between past and future, that values and countervalues are split and overturned. According to Ike, according to right and to the past, the forest is unconquered and vigorous; property is transient and culpable. According to the voice of the author, who knows the facts and the future, the days of the forest are numbered, while property remorselessly transforms the face of the earth.

In the terms of our categories, the illegitimacy of property produces an insufficient venerable-regressive; the undeniably primordial nature of the forest produces a justified sterile-noxious, a hidden alternative. Although the scarcity of images is no exception to Faulkner's rule (V, 3), their structured anomaly calls for consideration here. The venerable-regressive par excellence, buildings, come to Ike in tainted condition — both on his father's and on his mother's side. The one left to him by his grandfather is a "tremendous abortive edifice scarcely yet out of embryo, as if even old Carothers McCaslin had paused aghast at the concrete indication of his own vanity's boundless conceiving."[39] The estate of his maternal uncle should be called Warwick, claims his mother, like the one in England which he would have held as an earl; but the gateless entrance, the disappearance of the furniture, and the sooty mess in the hearth form part of a worn-realistic that tells of nobility's déclassement.[40] The property of the "freed" Fonsiba and her husband the pastor is a worn-realistic of the black working-class — the wooden building "which seemed in process of being flattened by the rain to a nameless and valueless rubble of dissolution in that roadless and even pathless waste of unfenced fallow and wilderness jungle."[41] Ike had inherited from his uncle a silver cup full of gold coins and sealed with wax. But once the old wastrel is dead, Ike, having come of age, only finds copper coins in the packet, along with a tin coffeepot and some IOUs.[42] Nonetheless, this inheritance is opposed, as a tangible "thing," to the pallid scrawls of writing.

These scrawls are contained in the ledgers that chronicle the property's history: commercial transactions, the selling and freeing of slaves. They are inseparable from the "commissary," that is, the office, shop, and storehouse, and hence from the list of provisions,[43] and when recent the ledgers are no less functional than these. After the Civil War, the books were filled up and replaced in quick succession, in "new and dustless" bindings;[44] the whole plantation had been subjected to the older ones, just as half the world was for a long time subjected to the city of Rome.[45] These "older ledgers, clumsy and archaic in size and shape," "the ledgers in their scarred cracked leather bindings" should be semipositive symbols.[46] Instead they bear witness to an original sin, not only against the earth, but also against the race that has been enslaved: the incest committed by the slavemaster grandfather who had fathered an illegitimate son with his own illegitimate daughter of mixed blood, whose mother had drowned herself. The writing has evil as its signified, and has too little or too much physical resistance as a signifier. The volumes are no more (in the tradition of the Gothic novel, V, 11) than "yellowed" pages, "old and frail," "faded" ink, characters, or blocks of entries.[47] Already in *The Old People,* the family possession seems to Ike "as trivial and without reality as the now faded and archaic script in the chancery book in Jefferson which allocated it to them."[48] The contrasting wrong is that the contents of the volume should still be, after many years, "fixed immutably, finished, unalterable, harmless."[49] The last adjective expresses inefficacy, and returns in a comparison with the events of the war: "This was chronicled in a harsher book."[50] The implicit, foreshadowed comparison, however, is with that quite different collection of signs which Ike reads in the forest, "bigger and older than any recorded documents."[51]

The "print" of the mutilated paw of the bear in the wet earth dissolves right in front of one's eyes;[52] the trunk torn by his claws crumbles and is quickly reabsorbed.[53] And yet such writing is more lasting because it is *not* unalterable, it is susceptible to conversion and reuse, it may be translated into "myriad life."[54] In that world where the passage of humans leaves neither "mark nor scar," exemplary values are preserved, bearing the aspect of the times of Sam's Indian ancestors;[55] Ike accepts them: "the wilderness the old bear ran in was his college."[56] But Old Ben would not have deserved his own name and myth had he not appeared as "an anachronism, indomitable and invincible out of an old dead time, a phantom," if he did not inhabit "that doomed wilderness whose edges were being constantly and punily gnawed at by men with plows and axes who feared it because it was wilderness."[57] In *The Old People* the boundary with the fields is sharp and sudden: at the end of *The Bear* the logging rights have been sold to a company, and a small train runs between two still impervious ramparts; in the story that follows, *Delta Autumn,* the hunting reserve must be reached by car through a land where "no scream of panther but instead the long hooting of locomotives"[58] is heard. The relationship between the inhuman and the human is inverted with respect to the traditional contamination between the sterile-noxious and the solemn-admonitory (IV, 28; V, 4). Now the aged Ike understands why he had not wanted to own that land: then there had been enough of it not to worry about arresting — at least within its boundaries — "what people called progress." Falling asleep with a vision of immortal prey[59] does not protect but rather absolves him from the reproach of his cousin in *The Bear,* who, reciting Keats, accuses him of wanting to freeze beauty and time.[60]

5

Let us now return to a European south with *The Leopard* of Giuseppe Tomasi di Lampedusa (1896–1957), published posthumously in 1958. Here the problem is not to renounce a property, but rather to defend its age-old legitimacy. The aristocracy's loss of its primacy in landownership, with the Risorgimento in Sicily, is entirely transcribed through a subjective experience. Although the authorial voice does not refrain from intervening or giving us information, in six of the novel's eight parts the consciousness and perspective are essentially of *one* character, Don Fabrizio Salina. As the bearer of authority, he is authoritarian only on the exterior, a skeptical conservative, who is dissected and pitied for an intimate passivity which a nineteenth-century author would only have been able to represent as a moral infirmity. The traditional literary rule that aims to keep images of aged things scarce in the historical novel (IV, 12; V, 7) seems for the most part still to be in force. Not, however, on the grounds of verisimilitude, as much as in view of an essential wish fulfillment: it begins by restoring the circumstances, and similarly the ambience of a particular time, to an integrity which precedes the crisis. Within the villa near Palermo or the palace in the country, property tempers and ennobles the devastating power of the sun shining outside. The euphoria of this effect of light is primary:[61] and it is not by chance that it acts as a counterpoint to the first anxieties about privilege.[62] In contrast to the many damaged statues and mold-covered fountains, in whose venerable-regressive we saw the *ancien régime* aestheticized (V, 6, 8), the Flora and the Amphitrite of the two gardens are intact.[63] "The promise of a pleasure which would never turn to pain emanated" from the jets of the latter: as he lies dying, the prince will consider "the sense of tradition and eternity expressed through stone and water" among the clearest profit items in the balance sheet of his life.[64] Even the "chipped pomp" of the family dinner, the "extremely fine patched table cloth" and surviving plates from the most varied sets,[65] only slightly compel us to speak of the worn-realistic.

The negative category, rather than the semipositive one, shows itself where the protection of the narrator ceases — beyond the private princely circle. In the court of Naples "one walked along interminable halls of magnificent architecture and sickening furniture (just like the Bourbon monarchy), one entered dirty little corners and ill-kept stairs."[66] The excessive number of convents in Palermo are "the despots of the view," "elephantine, pitch black"; still undamaged,[67] they seem predestined for antiquity and emptiness. There is already a "half-destroyed" villa of an illustrious family, where "the best-preserved apartment could barely serve as a pen for goats."[68] In the end, when it will be seen flourishing once again,[69] it will be thanks to the matrimonial and political compromise made by its heir — Tancredi Falconeri, who, by playing at disavowing legitimacy, renews privilege. Don Fabrizio has let his nephew have his own way, admiring his dexterity. In the only description of a house that does not belong to him, the prince is indignant over its owner's failure to renovate the furnishings dating back seventy years; but he changes nothing in his houses, and it comforts him that one finds everything in the same state as it was fifty years ago.[70] The gold in someone else's ballroom, faded and no longer glaring, inspires in him painful associations with the color of his own fields, "begging for clemency under the tyranny of the sun."[71] The sterile-noxious of excessive heat and light, of the lack of water and vegetation, is exalted and merciful in such Baroque humanizations of the landscape.[72] In evoking the atmosphere of the lower classes, it works as a kind of alibi for the worn-realistic. Don Fabrizio grants himself this very alibi in his interview with the Piedmontese envoy: displacing the responsibility for civil backwardness from history to the climate.[73] The most consistent worn-realistic, a vision of the tragic little town at dawn, follows immediately after.[74]

The abnormality of the venerable-regressive compensates for the double exception it entails: to the tradition of the historical novel, but also to the unity of the perspective, since the category develops in the only absence of Don Fabrizio from the six parts in which he is otherwise present. It is the episode in which Tancredi and Angelica explore the palace of Donnafugata. One of its owner's sayings condenses its meaning:

they set off as though towards an unknown land, and it was indeed unknown because not even Don Fabrizio had ever set foot in many of those lost apartments, a fact which caused him no small pleasure, however, since he was accustomed to saying that a palace in which all the rooms were known was not worthy of being inhabited.[75]

It is not so much dusty abandon as their very overabundance that renders exemplary such a great number of rooms: far from suggesting the decadence of a great family's seat, they confirm its wealth. Thus the late and cultivated reprise of the subcategory of the *ancien régime* is remotivated, hearkens back from 1860 to "the dark pleasures in which the dying eighteenth century had delighted," and calls back to life "the powdered little devils" to the point of grazing the sinister in the tiny apartment, once the scene of unspecified sadistic practices.[76] Hyperbolic excess and disorientation favor the two lovers; but in a deeper sense Tancredi is displaying his class's immense past to the beautiful nouveau riche, and initiating her into it. It is here that their rapture is in danger of falling back, through an illicit consummation, into feudal licentiousness — while in their future marriage this rapture will fade.[77]

The moment when memories are personalized in a reminiscent-affective is death: when one is alone. Don Fabrizio's death is declassed, as if in retaliation, in the foul-smelling anonymous hotel from whose window he gazes at the "unreachable" house, "very far away." And he displaces his compassion (cf. II, 3) from himself onto things:

> . . . he thought again [. . .] of all these things which now seemed to him humble even though precious, [. . .] which were kept alive by him, which would soon fall, guiltless, into a limbo of abandon and oblivion; his heart dropped, he forgot his own agony while thinking of the imminent end of these poor beloved things.[78]

The last part of the novel is seemingly built on the double meaning of "relics," either the white magic-superstitious or the reminiscent-affective: both kinds, not having withstood an inspection, official or unannounced, are abandoned to the trash heap. The fraud and the catastrophic sifting of the holy relics (V, 10) enact a cultural decline on the part of the three spinsters. In the "hell of mummified memories" of Concetta's room, only the stuffed dog Bendicò is innocuous; when the portrait of the father is no more than "a few square centimeters of canvas," and the chests of her unused trousseau no more than "a few square meters of wood," it becomes the only keepsake where a desolate-disconnected survives. Despite the displacement into the dog's glass eyes of "the humble reproach of things that are discarded, that one wants to annul," the final act of the novel extinguishes it in insensibility: Bendicò is thrown out with the trash and ends as a heap of livid dust.[79] Concetta had a right to succeed not only to her father's domestic authority, but also to his consciousness and perspective; having been sacrificed a half-century earlier by his compromise with Tancredi, she is among those who have paid a historical price of which they are unaware.

6

As for a particular adolescent, so also for the history of a family: as we return to America — Latin America this time — we will confront images of a nature more primitive than the Mediterranean. In *One Hundred Years of Solitude* (1967) by Gabriel García Márquez, born in 1928, in the place of a single individual we have a unitary plurality of family memory: drawn out to the 'seventh generation, confirmed by the repetition of names, and translated by the impression of the great-great-great-great-grandmother that time "turns in a circle."[80] Still, this plurality does not diminish the force of the characters' individuation, any more than the hyperbolic surrealism detracts from the tale's credibility. Both characteristics have to do with the overwhelming power of nature: the individual becomes collective as if coalescing before her, the incredible becomes spontaneous as if it rose to her heights, within the confines of a human rationalization that has no time to stop being recent. The novel recounts the larger story of the attempts and the failure to connect an equatorial village with distant progress. In the first of four narrative phases, the family's founder, José Arcadio Buendía, exhibits the enthusiasm, the optimism, and the extravagance of a progressive Don Quixote: he finds applications for the novelties the gypsies bring to Macondo, retracing the path of the great inventions on the other side of the virgin forest. The results are no more than something of the precious-potential or magic-superstitious or venerable-regressive of late medieval Europe. In an alchemical laboratory he melts the gold of thirty doubloons into a burned concoction, then succeeds in isolating it again — only to be told by his son that it looks like "dog shit."[81] His idea is to extract gold from the earth using the power of a magnet: he digs up "a fifteenth-century suit of armor" containing "a calcified skeleton wearing around its neck a copper reliquary containing a lock of hair of a woman."[82] His expedition reaches a Spanish galleon stuck in the ground twelve kilometers from the sea, with the hull encrusted with moss and pilot fish, and within a flowery wood.[83]

In the second phase, with a less genial irony, the political approximation of progress is more cruelly illusory: the thirty-two civil wars between liberals and conservatives, instigated and lost by the melancholy Colonel Aureliano Buendía. In the third phase, progress comes to Macondo of its own accord. It consists of colonization by North American banana planters: the natives are subjected to both its well-being and its massacres, so that only a single Buendía will bear witness to a train filled with the corpses of the strikers. The first train arrived "eight months late," the movies, the phonograph, and the telephone have been welcomed as their gypsy forerunners had been. Technology does not surpass magic (cf. IV, 24; V, 10) except in the extremity of metaphysical doubt: "by now no one could know with absolute certainty where the limits of reality were."[84] The only character who is integrated, with superficial contrasts, into the Buendía family has the same affinity for abstracting from reality, and is as quixotic as the family's founder. In a venerable-ultraregressive sense, however: the category, more ironically refused and estranged than ever, conforms to the continent by exaggeration. Fernanda del Carpio had grown up "in a lugubrious city along the stone alleys of which, in fearful nights, the carriages of viceroys still hobbled."[85] She had been raised to be a queen, and was accustomed to answer the call of nature in a golden chamber pot; but from "the noble house paved with tombstones," now mortgaged, she only brings with her "the innumerable and unserviceable wrecks of a family catastrophe that was two centuries late in taking place."[86] The rest of the "family cemetery" is transferred to Macondo by her father's Christmas gifts to his grandchildren—with his own remains in a coffin as the last gift of all.[87] She finally carries out the rule she has imposed of dining with candelabra and silver cutlery while "sitting at a solitary head of the table at the far end of fifteen empty chairs";[88] she too surrenders to individual memory when she is near death (cf. VI, 5), wearing "the moldy queen's dress" in front of the mirror, converting "the regal vestments into a machine for recollections."[89]

The reminiscent-affective and the desolate-disconnected have a greater reach than the desiccated petals and butterflies,[90] dolls or moldy pianola rolls— thrown onto the fire or the rubbish pile.[91] Their contamination with the sterile-noxious derives almost from a transitive property: if memory is inherent to the condition called solitude, and if solitude is embedded within climatic and physical nature, the discrepancy between memory and nature is resolved. Putrescence, rubbish, and ashes are localized in the hearts of the characters through metaphor.[92] But the "replacement of external by psychic reality," a logical characteristic of the unconscious according to Freud,[93] moves from the metaphorical to the literal, that is, to narrative. The surrealist supernatural forms "symmetrical"[94] equations along the axes of the relationships of space, of time, between cause and effect, life and death. It is Melquíades' posthumous sorcery that makes his apartment shine, immune from dust and dirt until his "definitive death"; the colonel is the only one among the family to see the apartment turned into a dung heap, where a "livid flora" prospers and there lingers a "smell of putrid memories."[95] The sterile-noxious, always an objective sign of the passage of time (IV, 28; V, 13), is here a measure of time that is either subjectively suspended or unrestrained. Thus Rebeca's survival, forgotten by all, in a large house on the corner of the square:

> The joints weakened by rust, the doors barely suspended by mounds of cob-webs, the windows sealed by dampness, and the pavement broken by grass and wild flowers, in the cracks of which lizards and every kind of noxious animal nested, all seemed to confirm the version that there had been no human being there for at least half a century.

The intruder who has broken down the door bears a close resemblance to someone else, according to the widow dressed in clothes of the last century, who "through the fog of the dust saw him in the fog of past times."[96] Once she is dead, the walls and floors peel off and resist restoration with darnel and weeds.[97] The continuous exchange between the natural and the memorial permeates the novel. The men of the first expedition into the virgin forest feel "oppressed by their most ancient memories."[98] After the wars the colonel, ignoring the damage in the house, frees himself from the "insidious traps that nostalgia was laying for him"—even though he steps into one of them at the hour of his death.[99] Almost five years of rain, foreseen or provoked by the owner of the banana plantation, begin along with the fourth phase the regression of civilization. In defense of which, the only nonillusory force proves to be the industriousness of women; and Ursula, in her longevity, proves to be the reliable protagonist. Once she has died, once the humble, submissive mother Santa Sofía de la Piedad has surrendered as well, the battle against the leeches, frogs, snails, roaches, and carnivorous ants of the flood is lost—when the woodworm is "roaring," and the growth of wild weeds is a "hiss."[100] With an analogous "voracity," oblivion "rots" memories;[101] but the "biblical hurricane," which wipes out the city where the last-born of the humans shows an animal part, begins like a wind "full of the voices of the past, [. . .] of sighs of disillusions predating the most tenacious nostalgia."[102]

7

In contrast to the American and Italian novels we have just considered, the natives remain in the background in the Mexico of *Under the Volcano*, published in 1947 by Malcolm Lowry (1909–57). The national past, marked by the most memorable of racial collisions, weighs on them like an instinct: in the prudence of the old Amerindian women witnessing a bloody deed, pity and terror seem to be reconciled "through the various tragedies of Mexican history"; in the cheerfulness of the people in an arena, "Mexico laughed away its tragic history"—only to be bored instead.[103] But four foreigners are the observers, whose narrative perspectives alternate throughout the twelve chapters. There is an English consul who has resigned after the severing of diplomatic relations; his stepbrother, a former left-wing journalist; his wife, formerly a movie actress; and a French childhood friend, a former film director. Being cultured, they read that history through monuments which have accumulated in layers while remaining foreign to the landscape (cf. VI, 3). A small American drugstore in Quauhnahuac is around the corner from Cortés's palace; at Parián, a gloomy ancient capital, shops and inns take up the cells of a monastery; a castle is a beer factory in Maximilian of Austria's park; a church burnt during the revolution, with "an air of being damned," is full of pumpkins.[104] But at the beginning, the "desolate splendor" of a modern hotel, drained swimming pools, and playing fields invaded by weeds[105] all reflect a worldwide catastrophe rather than a Mexican one. The formal structure of the novel, in which the first chapter takes place on a day one year after the events recounted from the second to the twelfth chapter, turns on the greatest thematic ellipsis: between anticipation and retrospection, before 2 November 1939 and after 2 November 1938, war has broken out. One page after the transition from the opening in the author's voice to the character's point of view, the following sentences give us a key:

> What had happened just a year ago today seemed already to belong in a different age. One would have thought the horrors of the present would have swallowed it like a drop of water. It was not so. Though tragedy was in the process of becoming unreal and meaningless it seemed one was still permitted to remember the days when an individual life held some value and was not a mere misprint in a communiqué.[106]

Through the stream of not one but four consciousnesses, the infinitesimal proliferation of leitmotivs is not a repetition but a cyclical variation. In the fourth chapter, the ruins of Maximilian's palace are seen by Hugh and Yvonne together: with the dewy grass in the chapel, a lone pillar as a "meaningless mouldering emblem," and the birds perched on ruined towers and crumbling walls, the place appears "so reconciled to its own ruin no sadness touched it." Yvonne confines herself to saying that the history of the emperor and of Charlotte was "awfully tragic."[107] The same place seems "part of a nightmare" to Laruelle in chapter I—earlier in the text, but later in time: "The shattered evil-smelling chapel, overgrown with weeds, the crumbling walls, splashed with urine, on which scorpions lurked—wrecked entablature, sad archivolt, slippery stones covered with excreta."[108] Is it a difference in outlook or in date? Laruelle believes that, for the imperial couple, Mexico was an Eden "beginning to turn under their noses into a prison and smell like a brewery, their only majesty at last that of tragedy"; and the ghostly voice that he can almost hear in this spot is the Consul's[109] — of another man, that is, who when tragedy had not yet been made meaningless along with individual life, had not succeeded in squandering all nobility through an ignoble degradation. The word "tragedy" opens the first of the chapters told from the Consul's perspective, and sums up both the view of his garden and the voice of his alcohol-fueled remorse: "The tragedy, proclaimed [. . .] reviewed and interpreted. . . ." It is proclaimed by the overflowing or wilted vegetation, by the disaster into which neglect has thrown what at one time had been an earthly paradise — including "the bad melodrama of the broken chair" and the collapsed sofa-bed[110] — when the illusion of normality and order, brought on by his first drinks, is shattered by further ones: "Over his house, [. . .] the tragic wings of untenable responsibilities hovered."[111]

In this Mexico, nature does not become objective as the sterile-noxious, nor history as the venerable-regressive, because it is the all-encompassing hell of a metaphorical desolate-disconnected. The impending devaluation of the individual makes the individual the only, desperate reserve of a value of meaning which can be ascribed to things: the tragic Consul *is* not only his garden, and vice versa, nor *is* he the only one to be something else in turn. There is at least one avowed projection for each character, and for Laruelle this happens from the beginning of the first chapter:

> He passed a field where a faded blue Ford, a total wreck, had been pushed beneath a hedge on the slope: two bricks had been set under its front wheels against involuntary departure. What are you waiting for, he wanted to ask it, feeling a sort of kinship, an empathy, for those tatters of ancient hood flapping.[112]

Yvonne identifies herself and her husband in an enlarged photograph of a rock cracked in two pieces, on the brink of disintegration: "She was one of the rocks and she yearned to save the other."[113] Closer to the memory-related, Hugh personifies his guitars as awaiting him, each of their strings broken and the case a "soundless cave for spiders and steamflies."[114] The Consul wonders how many glasses and bottles he has "hidden himself" in; and whether perhaps "the solitary clue to his identity" may lie forever among the infinite number he has thrown away or broken.[115] The "phantoms of himself" which surround his final delirium, that is, the Nazi-sympathizing military police, his future killers, "and the ash and sputum on the filthy floor — did not each correspond [. . .] to some fraction of his being?"[116]

Thus images without the metaphor of an "I" may also be taken up subjectively, or even without an explicit metaphor.[117] The most comprehensive is the ravine that cleaves and runs through the entire landscape—grazing the Consul's garden as its fifth side: it reproduces itself in every hole,[118] every piece of trash is destined to end up there, every character stares at it in horror. In the gorge, Laruelle contemplates "finality . . . and cleavage,"[119] and the Consul "the frightful cleft, the eternal horror of opposites." His vision confuses mythology and scatology—tragedy and degradation: "its normal role of general Tartarus and gigantic jakes," "the cloacal Prometheus who doubtless inhabited it."[120] At the bottom of the gorge Hugh sees a dead dog among the refuse, which prefigures the end of the Consul himself,[121] a piece of human waste. Reclaiming his right to perdition from the senseless necessity of history, the Consul refers to history itself with the only metaphor of the novel that starts from an abstraction to find its concrete equivalent: "Like a *barranca*, a ravine, choked up with refuse . . ."[122]

8

While a dead dog is thrown down into the ravine after Lowry's protagonist at the end of his novel, *The Trial (Der Prozess)*, left incomplete in 1914–15 by Franz Kafka (1883–1924), ends with the dog-like death of Joseph K. The sinister-terrifying of the eighteenth and nineteenth centuries superimposed itself as a parasite, preferably on the worn-realistic (II, 9, 14; IV, 22; V, 11); Kafka's originality normalizes, beyond any precedent, this double compromise between verisimilitude and inverisimilitude, between the lowness of images and mystery. The "symmetrical" logic of his supernatural does not overwhelm ordinary rationality with hyperbolic and humorous euphoria, as Márquez's did (VI, 6). Rather it anesthetizes rationality along with the anguish that ought to spring from it, and does not impose itself as obvious without allowing reason some sort of resistance: emotions, reflections, plausible explanations, although they gradually become more passive and uncertain. What is harbored in those places where the poorest tenants toss "their useless trash" is discovered by K. as follows:

> The Examining Magistrate certainly would not be waiting and sitting in the attic. The wooden stairway revealed nothing, no matter how long one looked at it. Suddenly K. noticed a small card next to the entrance, and going up to it he read in a childish, unpracticed hand: "Access to the Court Chanceries." Were the Court Chanceries really here, in the attic of this tenement house?

A short step from the impossible embodied in an assertion to the true embodied in a question: the surprise is contained in the question mark; many sentences of reassuring rationalizations follow.[123] When he hears sighs behind the door of a storage closet in the bank, the secure seat of his respectability, K. freezes, "stupefied." Within, there are "unserviceable old printed forms, earthenware ink bottles, overturned and empty"; but also court officials. When he finds an "unchanged" spectacle the next evening, "he cannot control himself."[124] The suspension of time is greater than the invasion of space, precisely because the latter is more at risk than the former: the opposition between exterior and interior is specified in the opposition between the spatial and the mental, and is erased by an occult reversibility.

The house he must go to for a first hearing is in "an out-of-the-way suburban street, where K. had never been before."[125] K.'s uncle later takes him to see the lawyer and drives near the same suburb: the uncle gives no weight to the coincidence.[126] Later still, after learning that the painter lives "in quite an opposite suburb,"[127] K. is right to shrink back before what he sees beyond a small door in his studio:

> "What is this?" he asked the painter. "What are you surprised at?" the latter asked, surprised in his turn. "They are the Court Chanceries. Did you not know that the Court Chanceries were here? There are Court Chanceries in almost every attic, why should they be missing here?"[128]

The exterior sense of direction, or of location, is annulled by a contrasting sense of virtual ubiquity: more suitable for the fitful permanence of an interior force. Indeed, K. is frightened "especially of himself," of his "ignorance in legal matters"—a literal unpreparedness for a symmetrical space: for the accused not to let himself be taken by surprise would mean "not to look unsuspectingly to the right, when the judge stood near him on the left."[129] A shiver of modulation in a spatial sense spreads out when the lawyer, declaring by word and gesture that there is another person in his bedroom, appears to conjure him up. "And truly there in the corner something started to move"; if surprise has made K. rudely ask where, once he has made out the director of the Chancery by the light of the candle—and before the lawyer claims to explain—his inference amounts to a resigned acceptance: "He must not even have been breathing, to have remained so long unnoticed."[130] The objection he is not brave enough to express is a matter of institutional, if not of material, space, regarding the nonidentity of the court in the Palace of Justice with the one in the attic.[131]

A space expanded by unexpected capacities, and alternately compressed by oppressive narrowness: as though it were modeled on attics and closets, which are additions to the habitable, so shrunken as to be uninhabitable. Their symbolic value, which I identified as exceptions to the worn-realistic (V, 7, 9), would suggest a sinister-terrifying superimposed on the desolate-disconnected, if only hallucinatory objectivity were not different from metaphorical subjectivity. Outside of these places, the unmotivated stretches from the haphazard to the absurd: from the jumble of furniture in the oblong dining room in the boardinghouse, to the "side pulpit" in the cathedral, so small that it keeps the preacher immobilized and bent over.[132] Nearby or within the chanceries, the step behind the door of the attic, the only or many ways leading out of it, the tall, narrow, long, straight stairway at the painter's house may remind us of the irrationality of ancient buildings (V, 6, 11).[133] The lawyers are allotted a narrow, low-ceilinged room, with a tiny window too high up and a hole in the floor; the merchant who sleeps in the lawyer's house is assigned a low, windowless room taken up entirely by the small bed.[134] In the painter's miserable bedroom, where one can only take two steps in any direction, the paintings are kept under the bed, and behind the bed is the little door onto the chanceries.[135] K.'s repeated feeling of suffocation, vertigo, and inability to breathe the air[136] is a reaction to the widespread and traditional connotation of the worn-realistic — dirt. It is more or less justified, in "gray, tall rented houses, lived in by poor people,"[137] or around the painter's house:

> It was an even poorer area, the houses were even darker, the alleys full of dirt that wandered slowly over the melted snow. [. . .] down by the collapsed wall there was a hole, whence just as K. approached spurted a disgusting, yellow, fuming liquid, in front of which some rats sought refuge in the nearby canal.[138]

But nothing would justify the presence of the Court in such houses. The examining magistrate's notebook, stained and yellowed, is deformed by continuous leafing, and K. lifts it up "as if it disgusted him"; the books with half-torn covers, held together by string, have to be dusted; the accused men in the corridor, although they belong to the upper class, are "slovenly dressed"; a small window cannot be opened because of the sheer amount of soot that cascades out; the dust blown from the painter's canvases whirls in the air for some time.[139] "How dirty everything is here," K. says in the hearing room; "We're sinking in dirt!" he shouts, calling for the closet to be cleaned.[140] The only discovery of any other implicit meaning of these images and words is that, opening the judge's books, one finds obscene drawings and titles:[141] thus the reversibility of the oppositions takes the form of an equivalence between the physical and the moral. This meaning is more implicit insofar as the further logical reversibility within the moral sphere, between the accused and the judges, or even between innocence and guilt, is also implicit. Exteriorized in the claustrophobic space, the innocent man's feeling of guilt is confessed; materialized in the court's sordidness, his unclean conscience is projected.

9

No supernatural, but the unreconcilable logic of madness disturbs space in *Brothers (Fratelli)*, published in 1978 by Carmelo Samonà (1926–90). The narrator's seclusion with his ailing brother "in an old apartment in the heart of the city," which reeks of a déclassement from above, rests on a traumatic absoluteness, given the reticence about all that has come before. "From the time when, alone among my family, I agreed to assist my brother and to live with him in the large house . . ."[142] A house which is not only a background, but also an occasion and measure of the confrontation in which the unbridgeable distance between the brothers begins to diminish. By now it has become "nobly inadequate to its purposes," and within, "the measurements of the rooms and the necessities of life no longer coincide"; the two brothers are surrounded by an "air of imminent relocation." The emptiness of the house reflects the abdication of memory—which precludes any complacence or repugnance:

> Every so often, tools of uncertain use interrupt the sequence of empty spaces: velvets in semidarknesses, strange pieces of silver, miniatures in wood and ivory, braziers, tin suits of armor, porcelain. They are probably the residues of a family intimacy which it is difficult for us to refer to a precise time: today they only serve to distribute the surfaces, define and separate the routes.
>
> Sometimes we try to remember distant episodes through a single object: a mirror, for instance, an old brazier, a jug. But we don't succeed. [. . .] we cannot find things solid enough to serve as levers to reconstruct a past. For this reason with the few objects that remain we have a relationship deprived of emotional resonances; a relationship more of verification and orientation, I would say, than of memory.[143]

We are beyond the reminiscent-affective and almost beyond the desolate-disconnected: the functions to be fulfilled are more humble or more strange, and so is the antifunctional to be suffered. The *where* represents the greatest problem for the "most obvious needs," eating, sleeping, and passing the winter evenings, and it is "the very vastness of the apartment . . . which invites a variety of solutions." The two never stop exploring the house. They stop for a short while in "comfortable and appropriate" spots; moving beds and wardrobes, scattering old junk around, they occupy "the innumerable rooms" one by one, then they desert them again, huddling in the warmth of a few rooms around the kitchen.[144] Thus, the house's dimensions slip beyond any realistic control, and their hyperbolic reach remains the presupposition for thought, dialogue, and action. In the morning, the sick brother can "take up a place in a distant corner of the house," offering the challenge of a new search; his longest "absence" inside the house lasts three days and three nights.[145]

The two men's identities are reduced to a relationship "based on certain rules of proximity and distance," "in a continuous departing and reuniting of distances and voids." Illness, the "cause" of all these displacements, becomes the "consequence" of standing still;[146] not only does it reverberate in space, but it unfolds and lingers there. In the patient, it affects mostly "the activity of thought," but it always reveals itself "materially," and the "coincidence" between *being* and *being in a place* seems natural to him.[147] He acts as though, exposed to the opposed anxieties of agoraphobia or claustrophobia along the normal horizontal line, he wished to escape along an impossible vertical one: "any space can appear to him a desert in which he risks losing himself, or, vice versa, a prison too confined in which he gropes"; he fantasizes about "underground or flying houses," an *above* and *underneath* conquered by "tracing the lines of drop-offs or rises at certain points on the floor or in the air."[148] As in the sinister-terrifying, the uninhabited habitable encourages ghosts. Here playfulness placates these phantoms with inventive patience: a cure for the incurable, an animated refunctionalization of the house. Its nakedness, like a white screen, confronts a reality devoid of meaning. Thus its "disconnected vastness lets it recapture in spectacle what it has lost in economy of spaces and functions": through the transformation of rooms into flatlands, walls into ramparts, and corridors into rivers, through the camouflaging of old objects for fabulous uses.[149] The narrator dreams, for his part, of "limpid and soberly decorated houses, functional objects."[150] Among the distorted variations of books and histories which they both weave, the metamorphosis of the fairy into a whale might suggest a more profound contrast with the bare empty house: "a delicate and maternal whale, in whose belly-retreat, rich in food and fresh bluish waters, Pinocchio claimed to settle, probably forever."[151] But with the duet from *Don Carlos* (the hoary Philip II and the nonagenarian Grand Inquisitor), they prefer to evoke and abuse paternal authority—the "millennial hierarchy."[152]

The ailing brother resembles the father in his rare, faulty adjustments to the logic of "cause and effect," of "maximum profit at minimum expense,"[153] while a tortured grace always mitigates his spontaneity. The relationship is one-sided on both ends: the one exercises all the power and obligation, the other all the charm and contagion. The reader's identification does not heed the call of the irresponsible except out of compassion for the rational, which participates in it, and which has left behind a conniving optimism about education. A Timetable had been thought out on a map of the house: it strove to regulate hours, routes, and customs, to prevent anything unexpected and any variations; that nothing but "dusty remains of cartons with still legible inscriptions" came to light perhaps depended on a single error in calculation.[154] Illness, which uses books as objects, fears and despises the fixedness (cf. VI, 4) and authority of writing.[155] When some sheets of the daily accounts begin to be lost and are later discovered in disarray, violence between the two brothers is not far off[156] — reserved for the final return to the house: house and city, alternating in their days, follow one another in the two halves of the novel. For the sick brother, the outside world is nothing but "an immense expansion," nothing but "the inside-out and disarranged dress" of the apartment.[157] Just as while defecating he suffers "a dissipation of his own body," and wishes to "preserve intact and undamaged" a part of himself in his feces, so too going outside is "a painful expulsive mechanism."[158] Later, things change outdoors. Without any "perimeters of walls," in "an insidious, immensely plural geometry of relations,"[159] with the dispersal of the way to the gardens among ancient twisting byways, the roles become confused.[160] The haze of repression in which the narrator shrouds a third character — the "woman with the lame dog" — makes the language she speaks mostly mythical: unifying and "maternal," healer of the world's fractures[161] — the world that is reduced to food crumbs in the other's pockets, to "crusts and delicate clots, now dried up, of his excrement," to "bread crumbs, pebbles, blades of grass."[162]

10

Large houses and ghosts are remembered reality or the supernatural in the first novel of our series to be published (1910): *Notebooks of Malte Laurids Brigge* (*Die Aufzeichnungen des Malte Laurids Brigge*), by Rainer Maria Rilke (1875–1926). A young writer who keeps a diary while in Paris, poor and suffering from a severe nervous disorder, spent his childhood in Denmark as the son of a noble family. The diary form facilitates the elision of any information about his passage from one condition to the other, thus leaving the central theme of déclassement unexplained. A few years before 1914, the worn-realistic has abdicated (we have found it, in an untrustworthy form, only in Kafka, VI, 8); the very individualism which has stabilized the bourgeois system can no longer feel its destructive results except subjectively. Even though that *now,* which in one of Rilke's more beautiful lines — indispensable here — was the time of autumn:

> He who has no house now, will never build himself another.[163]

seems to become, or is on the verge of becoming, a historical *now* — fulfilling the poem in which a flag high above foreshadows a storm, while below "the windows do not tremble yet, and the dust is still heavy."[164] The "I" who in the novel soon remembers the house, "When I think of the house, where there is no one now . . . ," projects onto an indefinite subject the negative aspect of the relationship between the reminiscent-affective and property (IV, 15; V, 8):

It is very hard to imagine that all that is no more, that strange people live in the old long mansion. [. . .]

And one has no one and nothing and travels around the world with a trunk and a chest of books and practically without curiosity. What kind of a life is this really: without a house, without heirlooms, without dogs. If at least one had one's memories. But who has them? Were childhood there, it is as if buried.[165]

Malte writes that he should have lived, like Francis Jammes (poet of the reminiscent-affective, V, 8), in an inherited country house among only "quiet and sedentary things"; but it "went differently, God knows why." His old furniture rots in a barn where he "had" to put them, and he has no roof, and the rain gets into his eyes.[166] He calls "houses" the mansions which were despoiled on the same date: "The time has come when everything comes out of the houses, they can no longer keep anything."[167]

Apart from the author's biographical premises, Malte's aristocratic origin has a metaphorical or antonomastic value as a counterweight to his rejection. It is as though there were no half-measures: on one side stand the owners of the most sumptuous, spacious, lasting homes; on the other stands the human refuse of the capital where the poet lives in exile, who nod to and acknowledge him as one of their own, "scum, shells of men, which Destiny has spat out."[168] And rented rooms like his own: "full of previous renters," with an armchair that has "a certain gray-oily mold in its green cover, into which all heads seem to fit."[169] In his childhood memories, lost privilege never appears as a sense of stable and impersonal tradition (cf. VI, 5). The only episode that puts the child in contact with the past ends in an estranged terror: he draws eighteenth-century costumes and masks from the dark, gloomy closets of a corner room under the roof; he stands dressed up before the incredulous, or persuaded, or vindictive mirror; having shattered the trinkets on a little table (among which is a small bottle, cf. IV, 16) into fragments, he senses he is about to faint, and flees.[170] As for his relatives, they enjoy especially privileged and individually extravagant relationships with death, either passing away or beyond the grave. At the hospital for the poor in Paris, people die "mass-produced" deaths, and, in the sanatoriums, they die one of the deaths "laid down by the institute"; for his paternal grandfather's two-month agony, the long old mansion did not have enough rooms where he could be continually moved.[171] His father died in the "oppressive" room of a rented floor, with other people's windows facing his own, but the fear of being buried alive on account of which the doctors pierce his heart sprang from a deciphering of the last words of Christian IV.[172]

In memory, the maternal grandfather's castle disperses into fragmentary spaces, as if it had been dropped and shattered to pieces: the dinner hall "sucked" every other image into the shadow of its vault and corners, "without returning anything definite in their place."[173] The relative from another century who slowly crossed the hall, from the door in the mezzanine to the one that a young cousin closed behind her with a bow, had, according to the old man, a "perfect right" to be there.[174] The mother looked for springs and hidden compartments to find "something more" in the secretaire of her dead sister, whose visitation at teatime was seen only, but unmistakably, by the dog.[175] The ghost-mansion of the Schulins, who moved into its side wings after a fire, continues to exist for both the child and the mother, and they perceive objects and smells that used to belong to it.[176] Throughout, more often than the sinister-terrifying becomes memorial, the desolate-disconnected becomes ghostly as it anthropomorphizes objects and smells: "timid, fearful," "absent-minded, sleepy," "spoiled" objects are mentioned;[177] along with the street which smells "of iodoform, of frying potato grease, of anguish."[178] The most famous page is something like a description denied to us, since at the sight of the demolished house Malte says he immediately ran away, having "recognized" it. It differs from the nineteenth-century descriptions of the worn-realistic category also in the intricately detailed topos of colors (V, 7), because it is cruelly carried out from the point of view of life: with the horror of an everyday that is all the more inextinguishable as it is denuded and anatomically flayed. After the passage I quote, the familiar, carnal persistence of smells is analyzed at length:

> On the different floors, walls of rooms could be seen to which the tapestries were still fixed, and here and there the beginnings of the floor and the ceiling. Next to the walls of the rooms a dirty white space remained along the whole length, through which there crept, with unspeakably repellent movements, like those of a flaccid worm, almost digestive, the uncovered, rusty conduits of the water-closet pipes. Of the paths which the lighting gas had passed through, there remained gray, dusty traces along the edge of the ceilings, and here and there unexpectedly they bent right round and ran into the colored wall and into a hole that was a black and brutal gash. The most unforgettable thing, however, were the walls themselves. The tenacious life of these rooms had not let itself be annihilated. It was still there, holding on to the remaining nails, standing on the remains of floors no wider than a hand's breadth, creeping under the beginnings of corners where just a little internal space was left. One could see into what color, slowly, year after year, it had been transformed: blue into moldy green, green into gray, and yellow into old, stale, rotting white. But this life was also in the fresher parts which had been preserved behind mirrors, pictures, and wardrobes; because it had traced and retraced their contours and had been, together with cobwebs and dust, also in these hidden places now laid bare. And it was in every strip that had been scraped off, in the damp bubbles

on the bottom edges of the tapestries, it shook in the torn shreds, it seeped through the loathsome stains formed long before.[179]

11

A Parisian childhood and adolescence are narrated in *Death on Credit* (*Mort à crédit*), published in 1936 by Céline (Louis-Ferdinand Destouches, 1894–1961). For the first-person narrator, in the present tense of the opening pages, Paris has changed, as in the verses of Baudelaire (V, 8) — and a bus passes by impetuously among the ruins: "Soon there will be nothing but earthenware half-skyscrapers everywhere."[180] Throughout the entire novel, the theme is the battle for survival of defeated private individuals of the lower middle class within industrial society's pursuit of novelty. The reminiscent-affective, as a weariness of change, only announces itself at the beginning of the retrospective tale from the 1890s: "He who will change the crooked lamp-post at the corner of number 12 will cause me great sorrow."[181] If Céline's prose provides an exclamatory, repetitive, and hyperbolic outlet for aggression (cutting up passages into quotations is extremely difficult here), an exceptional tenderness preserves the character of the grandmother from this violence. But the business in which the mother, a failed fashion designer, assists her, halfway between the second-hand shop and the antique shop, is not spared: "the scrapings of time are sad . . . vile, dowdy"; "anything" is sold, as in a list that ends with "items of junk that no longer have names, and things which no one will ever know."[182] The merchants' familiarity with the objects is the other side of their decorative use. They eat in the kitchen, in a "display fit for a dirty museum," among "the unsalvageable, the unsellable, the unpresentable, the worst horrors"; they must even check under the furniture after the lady clients have left everything in disorder; so as not to lose any of their customers, they must pretend not to notice when one of them furtively swipes a handkerchief; they must lend out, for a private recital, a table that is "a Louis XV, the only one we were really sure about," and exhibit a bedside cupboard at a marketplace, putting sandwiches in it to "preserve, amongst the vegetables and the tripe, a flavor of Louis XV, despite everything."[183]

What the narrator's family should gain thanks to their professional competence, they lose because of their disinterestedness. This unbalance does not equate a prestigious-ornamental, appreciated by those who know what they are selling, with a pretentious-fictitious, reserved for those who have no idea what they are buying (cf. IV, 35, 36). Rather, it is the disgrace of the times that underlines the contrast; fashion no longer seems absurdly fickle,[184] but is now interpretable and irreversible:

> First, mother perfectly understood, and admitted it to herself with tears, that the taste for beautiful things was being lost [. . .]. No longer any refinement among the rich . . . No longer any delicacy . . . Nor any estimation for finely wrought things, for the pieces of work made entirely by hand . . . More than depraved infatuations for mechanical rubbish, embroidery that unravels, that melts and peels in the washing [. . .].
> It was true decadence for anyone who had known the "authentic."[185]

In the episode that follows, the youth finds a job: personal bad luck dogs him, turning him into the scapegoat — by no means meek — for the misfortunes of his family, or of his entire class. The goldsmith Gorloge's merchandise is frenetic kitsch, a half-century too late for the taste of the most precocious of avant-gardes, Romanticism:

> And then all this is to be bought? Who? My God! Who? Nothing was lacking in point of she-dragons, she-demons, imps, vampires . . . The whole formidable team of bogeymen . . . The insomnia of an entire world [. . .]. Articles like that, meant to terrify, were no longer in circulation. After the last Romantics people hid them away in fear . . . Maybe they were passed on in the family? . . . at the time they were inherited, but with plenty of precautions . . .[186]

In the subsequent episode, he is sent to boarding school in England. The site is magnificent;[187] but close by construction works for another school soon come into view, which is on a no less magnificent spot, and which will have "an open space for sports at least four times as big as ours"; essentially "an orgy of luxury" which makes the young boy think: "I understood something about competition!"[188] The losers suffer their fate on the margins of the comparison of the functionality of things. The students' defection to the other school is followed just as quickly by the removal of all the furniture: the grand piano last of all, dismantled so that it may be taken out. The foreign boarder and an idiot are the only ones who stay behind in the dormitory.[189] In Paris, the first buses are beginning to triumph over horses: "I certainly saw Progress coming . . . but I never found a place for me . . ."[190] He seeks in vain for a job with dying enterprises, wholesale dealers of chasubles and candelabra makers, "retailers of objects so sad that words failed you."[191]

Throughout the second half of the novel, he finds work wherever his ill fortune decrees: from presumably ancient goods he comes to a presumably recent technology, from the more or less authentic to the more or less advanced. Courtial des Pereires, a publicist and inventor, "never stopped producing, imagining, conceiving, resolving, pretending."[192] His style of speech — in which the authorial practice of redundancy finds its best justification — is as volcanic as his office is chaotic:

From the threshold of the shop up to the second-floor ceiling, every step, every raised surface, piece of furniture, chair, closet, above, below, there was nothing that was not buried under papers, booklets, unsold copies in disarray, a tragic medley, all cracked and peeled, the work of Courtial was all there, pell-mell, in pyramids, lying fallow [. . .]. One penetrated into it accidentally, feeling one's way a little . . . one sunk in filth, an ephemeral cesspool . . . within the trembling cliff . . . that would collapse all at once! All of a sudden the cataract! . . .[193]

The bankrupt grandeur of the character is that of a progressive Don Quixote, not among the pioneers (cf. VI, 6), but in a capital city; and in the field whose logic most rapidly changes the new into the old. A megalomaniac positivist passion and a "cult of certain progress" clash with the "rising danger of mass production," from which Courtial predicts the death of craftsmanship and the diminution of personality.[194] The vintage balloon, which he insists on still flying, has lost shreds of fabric in landing on tree tops, bell towers, and telegraph poles; it is symbolically patched up with pieces from the rubber skin of an archetype, until it crashes and explodes, with asphyxiating smells, into a marsh.[195] The "competition of airplanes" has delivered the fatal blow.[196] Equally ill starred is the "Polyvalent Villa," which can blend in organically with the landscape and is thus rescued from the destiny of the solemn-admonitory;[197] even less fortunate is the "Divers' Bell," the obsession of a rapacious priest, designed for the easy recovery of the precious-potential, underwater treasure, which abounds in seas around the globe, and not only along the Mexican coastline.[198] Finally, the "Wave Generator" is supposed to be able to grow gigantic potatoes with the help of radio waves. What results is an arrest of petty thieves and a proliferation of vermin: the suicide, his head blown to bits, ends up being wrapped in a salvaged piece from the "Archimedes," his first balloon.[199]

12

In *Lolita*, published in 1955 by Vladimir Nabokov (1899–1977), kitsch lends itself to an incomparable thematic itinerary. The absolute mirage of a perversion as passion, or of a passion as perversion, is placed under the aegis of Proust:[200] that which lets a man, thirty or forty years older, identify "nymphets" among girls between the ages of nine and fourteen. The narrative tactic is implicitly Proustian when the vision of Lolita strikes Humbert Humbert "without any warning,"[201] or when the letter he receives is actually from Lolita, who had disappeared three years before.[202] But she is a small, petulant character, not at all unknowable like Albertine; and after her transformation into a married and pregnant seventeen-year-old,[203] love and retrospective jealousy do not linger along the road to oblivion. They discharge themselves with stubborn arbitrariness in the murder of his former rival. This murder has something of a suicide about it—Quilty being a kind of impotent, more perverted double of Humbert.[204] It also turns the text into a first-person memoir, written in prison while Humbert awaits trial. Despite the grave circumstances of the trial, an unrepentant erotic euphoria is allied to an insolent scattering of comedy, humor, and jokes.[205] The cynicism of love laughs at everything; it smiles at itself. Thus the old threadbare-grotesque confirms its marginalization, or its transformation, in the modern age (V, 5). Nabokov has written that he needed an "exhilarating setting," and that nothing is more exhilarating than "philistine vulgarity":[206] in terms of images, that is, nothing fits better than the pretentious-fictitious. In the novel's asphalted America, we have no occasion to laugh at the frustrations of poverty, though we do so at the manipulations of desire. A common denominator may be intuited between kitsch and perverted passion: both, for their promises to deceive, must already have kept them at the moment deception begins.

In a classic erotic chain, with two deaths at its ends, neither of which is rendered tragically, Charlotte marries Humbert, who adores Lolita, who runs away with Quilty. If we want to make the protagonist pay for all the insults with which he protects himself from psychoanalysis, and to threaten him with a less stereotypical version of psychoanalysis than what the author conceived,[207] we may ask whether, after all, everything can be reduced to the following: Humbert adores Lolita, who adores kitsch—which is not a rival. Is it an obstacle, an aid, a mediated object of desire? Is it perhaps where their consciousnesses most diverge that an unconscious envy of a lost puerile naïveté most thrives? He had grown up in the bright and artificial world of his father's grand hotel on the Riviera; he does not find its equal among the American hotels, but he does find a color photograph of it.[208] The house of Lolita's mother, for its part, is "a white frame horror . . . dingy and old," its bathroom full of "limp wet things" hanging over the bathtub and "the question mark of a hair inside."[209] It is "a kind of horrible hybridization between the comedy of so-called 'functional modern furniture' and the tragedy of decrepit rockers and rickety lamp tables with dead lamps"[210]—which is to say, between the threadbare-grotesque and the pretentious-fictitious. As a wife, Charlotte takes it upon herself to improve the house, following a handbook called *Your Home Is You*.[211] The twelve-year-old's dreams are of the same mold, filtered through magazines and comics, from the squalid to the conventional. And Humbert goes mad for her mix "of tender dreamy childishness and a kind of eerie vulgarity, stemming from the snub-nosed cuteness of ads and magazine pictures";[212] the big stores where he buys clothes for her have "a touch of the mythological and the enchanted," they are "a rather eerie place."[213] She gives herself to the commercialized paradises as though to a faith, a duty, or as responding to a personal appeal:

> She believed, with a kind of celestial trust, any advertisement or advice [. . .]. If a roadside sign said VISIT OUR GIFT SHOP — we *had* to visit it, *had* to buy its Indian curios, dolls, copper jewelry, cactus candy. [. . .] She it was to whom ads were dedicated: the ideal consumer, the subject and object of every foul poster.[214]

In the "useless beauty" of the landscape along the sides of the freeway, she refuses to take an interest, to the point of rage.[215] She knows no other nature but a perverted culture; conversely, regarding sex, she believes that natural coitus is nonprocreative license.[216]

The hotel where this is consummated is the threshold of the pretentious-fictitious: in Room 342, where a catalogue of furniture doubled by mirrors is enough to evoke it; in the din of the elevator and the roars of flushing toilets at night which belie the old-fashioned, down-home atmosphere.[217] The entire time they spend living together as lovers takes place in the world of freeways, where the "Functional Motel" has, above and beyond its name, curtains to create "a morning illusion of Venice and sunshine when actually it was Pennsylvania and rain."[218] The variety of motels parades before us as a direct object of the triple, Flaubertian *nous connûmes* — which it is "regal entertainment" to transpose, from an evasive experience of travel, to an ironic knowledge of nothing.[219] The category's images characterize the destinations more than the nightly stops in the race up and down, across and back through the forty-eight states; Lolita needs a daily destination, although it nauseates her once they arrive there:

> The object in view might be anything — a lighthouse in Virginia, a natural cave in Arkansas converted to a café, a collection of guns and violins somewhere in Oklahoma, a replica of the Grotto of Lourdes in Louisiana, shabby photographs of the bonanza mining period in the local museum of a Rocky Mountains resort, anything whatsoever.[220]

A little later, a similar list stretches out for pages, which puts Nabokov alongside Gadda, though less bitter or more cheerful, as Flaubert's heir in the line of extensive decontextualization (IV, 38; V, 15). More than any single invention, their sheer number, heterogeneity and disorder create kitsch, with a counterpoint of sarcasm and puns that is more sparkling than ever. There is little use in quoting: "A zoo in Indiana where a large troop of monkeys lived on a concrete replica of Christopher Columbus' flagship."[221] The final balance sheet has the seriousness of the solemn-admonitory, because the vanity established is that of love itself. "We had been everywhere. We had really seen nothing"; there only remained "a collection of dog-eared maps, ruined tour-books, old tires," and Lolita's sobs every night.[222] When the motels on their route give way to old hotels, the adventure is finished,[223] and she will land, with her solid, deaf husband, in the drab surroundings of the worn-realistic, wiser than her mother's house.[224]

13

I have chosen the preceding eleven novels on the traditional presumption that they will *endure;* according to the twelfth, this very privilege would be worth very little: *everything* endures in a contemporary culture that destroys nothing and creates nothing. I am not burdened by a plot in reconstructing the paradigms of the images in *Life, a User's Manual* (*La Vie mode d'emploi*), published in 1978 by Georges Perec (1936–82). The plan of the novel is to represent all the lives enclosed in a large Parisian building: apartment by apartment, room by room, in spatial succession and temporal simultaneity. Its monumental, patient execution is mostly pleasurable within each sector, but it cannot be read effortlessly from start to finish. The ironic intelligence saves precisely the moment which has by now become hackneyed — long after Mallarmé had made it heroically all-enveloping in a sonnet, and Proust in an entire narrative: that moment in which the work mirrors itself or describes its own genesis. The painter Valène plans to paint the vertical cross-sections of the building, with his own character in the act of painting himself.[225] The laborious, abstract, and arbitrary project that occupies the idle, rich Bartlebooth aims to "exhaust" a "constituted fragment" of the world;[226] all the embryonic narratives ascribed to other characters bounce playfully between the banal and the bizarre. The predominating documentary impulse, parodying the faith in cognition that sustained the monumental cycles of Balzac or Zola, arranges facts as though in a reference book. Its all-inclusive form is the list: even when we count only lists of things, this novel has more of them than any other text I have quoted so far. It is true that these lists defunctionalize things, and that defunctionalized things constitute reality (I, 1; II, 9), but here the excess of lists, by a transitive property, amasses too much reality with the sole intention of reporting too little of it.

The narrative begins on the staircase of 11 rue Simon-Crubellier, an "old-fashioned place, of doubtful cleanliness," with the old elevator almost always out of order.[227] But in what follows the worn-realistic will be little more than a statistically necessary element of the lists.[228] It is replaced by the pretentious-fictitious, as we have already seen in Flaubert (V, 15): oscillating indifferently between the probable and the improbable, often appropriating the comedy of the former threadbare-grotesque into its own. In an antique dealer's back room, where clutter prevents a thorough inventory, "a supposed egg of a fossil dodo bird"[229] stands outside the code. An artisan offers plastic goods from Indonesia at least a half-century old: one could swear they are authentic, "at times even with the traces of false repairs."[230] The "kitsch objects" of one list are presented as meticulously functional,[231] and the typewriter in another has passed for "one of the most perfected objects ever conceived." And yet it has ended up in one of the eight cellars inspected one by one, not far from the magazine cover trumpeting the solution of "the most fantastic enigma of history": whether Louis XVII and l'Aiglon had met on the 8 August 1808 at Fiume.[232] That Napoleonic hats are mass-produced in Japan is stated in reference to a collection of *unica,* one-of-a-kind objects. There are those intended as such, like the "Octobasse," a "monstrous double bass": one player handles the bow sitting on a stool and the other handles the strings standing on a stepladder; and those that are accidental, like the chalk used in Einstein's memorable lecture — but also "Tarzan's first underwear."[233] After a dinner in a Chinese-Bulgarian restaurant between Pigalle and Montmartre, four cabarets offer in one night, for seventy-five francs, "all the *esprit gaulois* of Paris," Tangiers belly dances, a medieval atmosphere, and "a showplace of elegant depravity."[234] In a passage worthy of an anthology, two large hotel agencies work together to furnish their clients with unusual comforts: parks with, among other things, a gigantic aquarium, a museum of ancient art, a pyramid, a Gothic church, a Plaza de Toros. There are plans to include the ruins of a thirteenth-century Irish abbey within the perimeter of a hotel, and to transport Darius's palace from Persepolis and rebuild it in Huixtla (Mexico).[235]

Valène conceives the idea for his painting starting from less improbable architectural vicissitudes: beyond the "sad patrols of the movers and the undertakers," from the certainty that the house and the neighborhood will disappear. It is not only bombs, fire, or earthquakes that prohibit contrasting the fragility of the human condition with the invulnerability of stone. The representation of prophetic warnings in the style of advertising — a piece of irresistible literary bravura — is as modern as the opposite impulse was dated: "the same fever that, towards eighteen hundred fifty [. . .] caused these buildings to rise from the earth, will from now on unremittingly work towards their destruction." No date can detract from the metahistorical value of the demolition of the building, "restored to its raw materials," besides "tons and tons of rubble and dust."[236] Nor does the fact that Valène, "the oldest inhabitant of the building," cultivates the memory of things, no less than of people: his character is not individualized by the delicate *ubi sunt* he addresses to the vanished forms of cocoa boxes and packs of "thermogenetic cotton wool."[237] If the pretentious-fictitious functions as the dominant within the novel, the solemn-admonitory is the dominant of the dominant. With the novelty that transience is not taken for granted, as it had been in a world unaware of the modern idea of progress: it emerges, as a disenchantment, from the very consequences of progress which the idea of progress ignored. Thus the last and the first of our categories are contaminated. Irony pours the interchangeable vanity of experiences into the mass of the pretentious-fictitious; as the vanity of vanities, melancholy restores it to the somber magnificence of the solemn-admonitory:

> Now, in the small sitting-room, there remains what remains when nothing remains: flies, for instance, or flyers that students have slipped under every door in the building advertising a new toothpaste or offering a reduction of twenty five centimes for every three packets of detergent bought, [. . .] or else those insignificant things which trail along the floor or in the corners of closets and about which no one knows either how they got there or why they have remained: three withered wild flowers, limp stems at whose ends there languish filaments one might call calcified, an empty Coca-Cola bottle, a cake box, opened, still accompanied by its false raffia string on which the words "Delicacies of Louis XV, Confectioners since 1742" draw a beautiful oval surrounded by a garland flanked by four puffy cherubs, or, behind the door of the landing, a kind of clothes hanger in wrought iron with a mirror cracked into three pieces of unequal surface area which vaguely trace the shape of a Y in the frame of which there is still a postcard portraying a young athlete, clearly Japanese, holding in her extended arm a lit torch.[238]

VII

Praising and Disparaging the Functional

Would I ever have been able to collect, for the images of functional corporality in literature, such an imposing number of examples as I did for those of nonfunctional corporality? The question itself implies a certain partiality in favor of this book's assumption: the predilection of literature for one type of image rather than the other, its tendency to welcome with the first one a return of the repressed (I, 3, 4). That I did not happen to collect an equal number of examples of the other type of image — of the functional — may be thought to depend not only on a preconception such as underlies any specialized inquiry, but also on a theoretical one. Perhaps there would have been enough material to fill a separate book, or to make this one twice as long. The number of examples might confer even more authority, since the scrutiny of the texts was not intentional, organized, and exhaustive; and, in this final chapter, my reflections on a much scantier and more fortuitous series will possess only an interest that resonates through comparison with the more substantial one we have already considered. We can say immediately what principal conjecture synthesizes these reflections. The literary representation of functional things, compared to its opposite, seems to me much more closely tied to an attitude which is inclined to transcend representation itself — in an intellectual, moral, but also affective sense. An attitude that, when confronted with the practical and symbolic functionality of things, displays positive valuations and reactions, manifests pride and boasting, delight and enthusiasm. And this happens for many centuries before the appearance of the opposite alternative: the display of negative valuations and reactions, the manifestation of blame or diffidence, of irritation or scorn.

We may call this attitude evaluative, or *axiological,* with reference to cultural systems of values and countervalues. To be sure, as we have continuously had occasion to see, it never entirely fails to accompany the representation of nonfunctional things as well: negative for the solely negative imagery, partially positive for the semipositive. I would say rather that historically the proportion of representation and evaluation remains on average the same, in the cases of functional and nonfunctional corporality respectively, until the turning point between the eighteenth and nineteenth centuries. It is in this era that the sudden increase in frequency of the representation of the nonfunctional moves along with its emancipation from the axiological attitude; as for the functional, the greater innovation of the modern period takes nothing away from the permanence of that attitude. This innovation consists in a typical expression of "civilization's discontents" that is — as I have said — a possible axiological inversion, with protest as an alternative to exaltation. The representation of the nonfunctional and the protest against the functional are distinct literary phenomena, even though they are related and can be traced back to the same historical premises: within the phenomenon we have been concerned with until now, I have assumed a thematically indirect and genetically unintentional contradiction of social ideals and social realities, a return of the repressed intrinsic to literary discourse. By the other phenomenon, I mean a directly thematic and ideologically voluntary protest. But this is not to say that it is free of ambivalence; just as the first alternative (the exaltation of the functional) is also not free of it, though in the opposite sense, starting with the epoch in which it ceases to be the only possible axiological attitude.

2

In the *Odyssey* it is through the voice of Telemachus, that is, through the admiration of the character who looks on, that the interior of Menelaus's palace is evoked in its brilliant display of precious stones, and in astonishment compared to the court of Zeus. The interior of Alcinous's palace in the splendor of its sunlight or moonlight is described by the voice of the author; but the description begins with the hesitant Odysseus's pausing at the threshold, and ends with his entrance, "when he had admired all in his heart."[1] Admiration both for the preciousness of the materials and for the skill that has crafted them, without the functional being distinguished from the ornamental, efficiency from wealth, or civilization from luxury. In Book I of the *Aeneid,* the admiration in the description of Dido's palace, and the banquet lit by torches that "conquer the night," is no different; here, moreover, the hero has already had occasion to admire the rising, monumental city being built.[2] Again, in the joyful ending of the first Arthurian romance by Chrétien de Troyes, *Erec and Enide* (*Érec et Énide*), we see admiration in the account of the sumptuous court held by King Arthur to crown the two heroes. Among the wonderful objects prepared for this event are two identical thrones, a suit of clothes, two crowns, and a scepter.[3]

If we move from the beginnings of the so-called Matter of Brittany to the beginnings of the so-called Matter of France, that is to *The Song of Roland* (*Chanson de Roland*), the first appearance of Charlemagne in the poem gives us a variation in the background:

> Under a pine, next to a hawthorn,
> Was a throne of pure gold:
> There sits the king who rules sweet France.[4]

The throne is the product of an aristocratic culture, as in the preceding passages; but the pine and the hawthorn, propitious and joyous, belong to nature, and as such they identify the site in advance as regal. They lead us to extend our range of examples from culture to nature, and from interior to exterior spaces. We should also extend it from the hierarchical level of the royal palaces and their inhabitants to progressively lower levels: as far as the privilege of a moral and cultural, if not social, nobility, concedes it — a privilege which, from antiquity to the Middle Ages to the Renaissance, is also the condition of a positive relationship between men and things. One chapter in Curtius's book, "The Ideal Landscape,"[5] documents that such a relationship with a propitious and joyful nature has inspired an entire tradition of examples; his opening reference to the laudatory commonplaces of rhetoric leaves no doubts about what I call the axiological attitude. By exalting nature just as much as dwellings and furniture, poets exalt the characters worthy of enjoying them, or the situations and activities that deserve such accommodating and beautiful backdrops. In the paragraph that Curtius devotes to the commonplace of the *locus amoenus,*[6] this customary auspicious landscape seems to be associated with elevated intellectual activities — rather than stories of love: from the philosophical discourse of Phaedrus and Socrates in the shade of a plane tree and the singing of the cicadas on the shore of the Ilyssus in Plato's dialogue,[7] to the many examples of pastoral poetizing and singing.

The commonplace does not change when the background shines thanks to a verdant and flowering vegetation and an ornate and welcoming architecture, filled with other excellent manmade objects. This is the case of the various isolated villas which the noble, wise, and virtuous young ladies choose in the *Decameron* as the places to tell stories with their companions in time of plague; here is the first of them:

> This place was above a small mountain, from every side quite far from our roads, with various trees and plants all full of leafy branches pleasant to the eye; on top of which was a palace with a beautiful and large courtyard in the center, and with loggias and halls and rooms, each one beautiful and decorated with joyous paintings, surrounded by lawns and wonderful gardens and wells of the freshest water.[8]

In *Orlando Furioso,* waters and foliage contribute as much as cloths and jewels to making the city of Damascus into a paradise of spring colors and odors:

> Through the city two crystalline rivers
> Water through different courses
> An infinite number of gardens,
> Never devoid of flowers, of branches.
>
> . . . .
>
> All covered is the main street
> With clothes of different joyful colors
> And sweet-smelling grass, and the ground
> And walls with sylvan branches.
> Every door was decorated, every window,
> With the finest drapes and carpets,
> But even more with beautiful and well-adorned ladies
> With rich jewels and magnificent gowns.[9]

In *Jerusalem Delivered* the castle of Armida with its garden is an oasis that evil sorcery has placed within the sterile-noxious landscape of the Dead Sea (cf. IV, 29). This unsettles neither the purity of the commonplace, nor the naturalness of the imaginary place's enchantment, nor the happy affinity of culture and nature:

> The air is soft and the sky is clear, and joyous
> Are the trees and lawns and the waves pure and sweet,
> Where among the delightful myrtles
> A source rises and a rivulet spreads:
> Into the womb of the grasses fall quiet slumbers
> With a soft murmur of branches;

The birds sing; nor do I tell of the marbles and the gold,
Made wonderful by art and work.

Upon the grass where the shade is thickest
And close to the sound of clear waters
With sculpted vases she made the proud table ready
And rich with choice and costly food.
Here there was what every season yields,
What the earth gives or the sea sends,
What art dresses; and a hundred beautiful,
Careful maids served the banquet.[10]

In *Gargantua,* the construction and adornment of the Abbey of Thélème marshal an encomiastic encyclopedia of names: from the precious materials and techniques of shaping them, to the products to be used. The joyous humanistic activities which it will foster are no less exceedingly diverse. Nature is everywhere, because it is above all in the free hedonistic spontaneity prescribed for such activity; but there is also a pleasure garden, a well-planned orchard, a large park teeming with wild game.[11]

3

Between the Renaissance and the historical turning point stretches the era which in the first chapter (referring back to the last volume of a cycle of mine) I called that of alliance between literature and Enlightenment rationality (I, 7). First, running from the end of the sixteenth to the middle of the seventeenth century (if one accepts the periodization suggested in that book), the so-called literary Baroque must be understood in light of its contemporaneity with the new philosophy, science, and technology. And its formal explosion of metaphorical figurativeness, its thematic parade of unreal appearances, constitutes both a modernistic forward flight and an antilogical regression grounded in religion. Then, during the seventeenth and eighteenth centuries (according to the same periodization), through the season of so-called French classicism, whose influence spread to become a European model, and the critical explosion of the Enlightenment proper, there continues a poetics rigorously shy of metaphor and equivocation, myth and miracle.[12] From the perspective that interests us here, what characterizes the two centuries in question is the extinction of a commonplace like the *locus amoenus*: a place which ensured harmony between culture and nature, beyond the cases where both were present simultaneously, even in those cases where only one or the other favorably and functionally smiled upon man. The latent association was still natural; the first surge of cultural rationality, developing without interruption, marks its end, and once the two terms were separated they finally developed into opposites. From the Baroque age onwards, culture is only exalted in the artificiality of its progress: hence as non-nature, or even as an antinatural function. From the Enlightenment onwards, nature is only exalted in its intact and original health: hence as nonculture, in necessary opposition to cultural progress. It will thus be historically accurate to reserve the attribute "functional" for the objects of an exaltation of cultural progress itself; and to see in the exaltation of an inviolate nature the premise, if not the preliminary form, of the axiological inversion—a protest against the functional.

To illustrate these opposing moments, I can do no better than arrange a symbolic confrontation between two pages written one and a half centuries apart. Bringing these two pages together was suggested to me by chance, in the course of my reading. It is not by chance, however, that they bear the names of two such protagonists of the history of thought as Descartes and Rousseau; nor that they belong to nonfictional genres, the one epistolary, the other autobiographical, rather than to literature in a strong sense, to fictional genres. In both passages, very little is concretized as images of functional corporality; what matters is the precociousness of their respective axiological attitudes, positive and negative. In one, we find the philosopher happy to have discovered in urban civilization a comparable, or rather by now preferable, alternative to country solitude close to nature. In the other, we have the philosopher unhappy at no longer being able to find even in wild nature an alternative to his isolation among men—unreachable by their civilization. I quote here less than the essential from both pages. A retreat in the middle of Amsterdam, Descartes argues in 1631, is far more perfect than the most pleasant and tranquil retreats in a monastery or in the country; there one always runs the risk of being disturbed by the neighbors:

> . . . while in this great city where I am, there being no man, except me, who does not practice commerce, everyone is so attentive to his own profit, that I could dwell here all my life without ever being seen by anyone. I go walking every day in the midst of the confusion of a great crowd, with as much freedom and calm as you could do on your country paths, and I consider the men I see no more than I would the trees one meets in your forests, or the animals that feed there. The very noise of their errands interrupts my reveries no more than the sound of a brook. And if on occasion I reflect upon their actions, I receive the same pleasure that you would feel in seeing peasants cultivating your land; since I see that all their work serves to embellish the place of my dwelling, and to ensure that I lack for nothing. And if pleasure is to be felt in observing the fruit grow in your orchards, and taking stock of its

abundance, you should reflect that an equal amount is to be felt in observing ships put in here bearing in abundance all that the Indies produce, and all that is most rare in Europe. What other place could you choose in the rest of the world, where every commodity of life, and all desirable curiosities, are so easy to be found as they are here?[13]

In 1777, the aged Rousseau, alone and suffering from persecution mania, tells of a botanical expedition undertaken in the heights of the Swiss Jura (the lines I omit speak of the birds he hears calling and of the mountain plants he finds):

> I was alone, I penetrated the winding crannies of the mountain, and from wood to wood, from rock to rock I reached a dell so hidden that I had never in my life seen a wilder sight. Black firs intermingled with prodigious beeches of which many had fallen, so ancient they were, and intertwining with one another, blocked this dell with impenetrable barriers, some gaps left by this somber rampart offered nothing beyond but rocks that were cut off perpendicularly and horrible precipices which I did not dare look over except when lying on my belly. [. . .] and, more at ease, I started to daydream, thinking that I found myself in a refuge unknown to all the universe where persecutors would never discover me. A feeling of pride soon mixed with this reverie. I compared myself to those great voyagers who discovered a deserted island, and I said to myself with self-satisfaction: doubtless, I am the first mortal to have penetrated here; and I considered myself another Columbus. While I was swaggering to myself with this idea, I heard at a short distance a kind of clicking sound that I seemed to recognize; I listen: the same noise is repeated and multiplied. Surprised and curious, I get up and open a way through a thicket of bushes on the side where the noise came from, and in a valley twenty paces from the very spot which I believed myself to have been the first to reach, I see a stocking factory.
>
> I cannot express the confused and contradictory agitation that I felt in my heart at this discovery.[14]

When we read the page from Descartes today, the modernity of the facts seems prophetic. And yet it is all of a part with the almost irritating, incomprehensible outdatedness of the value judgment: that within the large city the individual is not "seen by anyone" since everybody is so preoccupied with making a profit, that he in his turn takes no more notice of other men than he would of trees or of animals — these are simply circumstances which ensure the individual an undisturbed peace and freedom. It raises not even a suspicion of anything inhuman and unnatural. Urban culture, with its comforts and abundance, seems instead to be benign as a substitute nature; the international and intercontinental contribution functionalizes, and thus humanizes, the globe. The modern capital city, which will one day — beginning with Balzac or

Baudelaire — be perceived with axiological ambivalence and with a powerful accent on the negative, is still at this stage an object of pure exaltation. In order to understand why, it is certainly necessary to read a few lines more, and to remember that the safety which the philosopher enjoyed as such in the commercial republic was anything but guaranteed in France. Necessary but not sufficient — if we are unable to restore historical fullness to the novelty, for us long emptied, of the exaltation and its object.

In precisely the same way, to understand Rousseau's disappointment at the sight of the stocking factory it is not enough to read a few more lines, or to remember his obsessions and his double isolation, as an Enlightenment thinker among the *bien-pensants,* and as a dissident among the *philosophes.* In the page from him, it may be difficult to restore historical fullness to the long-emptied novelty of an axiologically negative reaction — if not yet of a protest proper. Every other Enlightenment thinker in his place would not have failed to celebrate a victory of the functional, and with this of the human: a victory all the more triumphant insofar as the establishment of the functional in such a wild place was unexpected. Rousseau, in laughing at his own chastened vanity with which the emotional excursion ends, pities the defeat of nature while he demystifies as belated his fantasies of discovery.[15] His inauthentic wilderness experience was too involuntary not to remain very far from the future kitsch; but in the mixture of nature and industry, presented immediately after as exclusively Swiss, kitsch does not seem so very distant as an objective threat to the integrity of the landscape. Both Descartes' Holland and Rousseau's Switzerland, in short, betray more virtual modernity than the authors' subjective consciousnesses might know.

4

The second part of *Don Quixote* was published (1615) not many years before Descartes' letter was written. Arriving in Barcelona, Sancho Panza and his master behold the sea for the first time. They find it much more spacious than the marshes they had seen in La Mancha. But in the eyes of the gentleman and the peasant from Spain's interior, the novelty consists much less in the spectacle of nature than in the spectacle of galleys, sails, and flags — set to the tune of fanfares and artillery. Two chapters later, they are welcomed with military honors aboard the captain's galley. Upon the raising of the sail and weighing of the anchor, Sancho is astounded at the display of technical efficiency: the prison discipline of the rowers, the clamor of the ship setting off to sea. At this point we read:

When Sancho saw all those colored feet moving at once, for such he believed the oars to be, he said to himself: "these are truly enchanted things, and not those that my master says."[16]

Confronted with such novel perceptions, the character reacts just as he did to the sea: by comparing them with previous sights, referring the new to the known as much as possible. First in the authorial voice, then in the voice of Sancho's thoughts, he does this two consecutive times in different ways.

First, he conceives of the oars as "colored feet" (he had already imagined the masses of timber propelling themselves through the water as having feet): a naïve and estranged form of the ancient figure of *catachresis,* which resorts linguistically to the known in order to designate the new.[17] Second, he compares the seeming enchantment of what he sees with the presumed enchantments known all too well to the squire of Don Quixote. A comparison that is tied to the peculiar thematic complex of the novel; nevertheless, its logic is no less historically representative. If, by definition, every form of the supernatural can only partially be understood and perceived, then, similarly by definition, any technological efficiency complicated enough to elude the purview of the senses can be related to the supernatural. As in the modern era, so too in the archaic eras: when, in Greek, the word *tekhne* applied to magical abilities as well, before it was restricted to solely artisanal ones; or, in Latin, the secular and professional meaning of "profane" developed from its sacred and ritualistic sense; or, in the Romance languages, there was an etymological contamination between "mystery" and "mastery." Literary figurativeness climbs the slope that languages have already descended, moving from the periodic novelty of technological facts to the inescapable priority of supernatural hypotheses.

The figure or topos to which Sancho's comparison is closest seems to me what Curtius called "outdoing," documenting it with ancient and medieval examples.[18] If *x* is a predicate, and *y* is a person or thing that exemplifies it par excellence, it is not enough to say that another person or thing is "as *x* as *y*": one makes the hyperbole outdo the antonomasia by saying that it is "more *x* than *y*." Modernistic ever since late antiquity (*taceat superata vetustas,* Claudian wrote),[19] such a figure at once satisfied the ideological modernism and the figurative extremism of Baroque taste.[20] Sancho in fact goes even further than an outdoing: he does not make the comparison in terms of more or less, but of all or nothing. Not "the things I see are more inexplicable than the magic ones," or "are more magic than others," but simply "they are the true, the only magic ones." The preeminence of the new over the known is here able to succeed in supplantation because the disempowered supernatural is magic —

not religion. But in two short sentences Cervantes creates a brilliant synthesis, with more enduring traits than one would have imagined in its characterizing of the relationship between literature and the functional. The surprising sense of the new, the resort from the new to the known; the supernatural as the preferred term of comparison; catachresis and outdoing as its privileged rhetorical forms, the one born from a dearth of words and the other from an excess of experience, the one from perplexity and the other from superiority.

In 1784, when Vincenzo Monti celebrates the first aerial flight, literature's positive axiological attitude towards the triumphs of the functional has by now reached its peak. If the traits we analyzed in Cervantes are all recognizable in the ode *To M. de Montgolfier* (*Al signor di Montgolfier*), the style dignifies them: enthusiasm speaks with cultivated eloquence rather than with the common sense of the peasant. From the novelty of the flight over Paris, the initial past tense harkens back to the mythological, rather than Christian-magical, antiquity of Jason and his first sea voyage. The comparison soon produces an outdoing: "It defeated Argonautic marvels, / Your aerial course." The supernatural of pagan mythology was acceptable precisely because it had been rendered lifeless by convention. And yet, just as a dead etymology can become reanimated, myth has a flickering of rediscovered credibility. In light of a page of Lévi-Strauss I quoted earlier (III, 5), the classicizing Monti would ideally reunite the technical revolution of the eighteenth century to nothing less than the Neolithic revolution. The literal legitimacy of the outdoing is unusual — since sea voyages, regardless of the customs of millennia, are less portentous than aerial ones. On the other hand the rationalist poetic forbids the use of direct, and even more of specialized, words in the ode's elevated style: it demands noble periphrases which, referring to recent discoveries, are the equivalent of so many catachreses.

Readers were required to recognize everything that more convenient editions would later spell out in a footnote. I shall imitate that practice here, with glosses in brackets:

> Human daring, peaceful
> Safe philosophy,
> What force now, what limit
> Can measure your power?
> You stole the thunderbolt from the sky
> That defeated, before you
> With broken wings fell
> And grazed your heels   [*invention of the lightning rod*].
> Calculation arrested, guided
> By your daring thought,

```
The motion and orbits of the stars,
Olympus and the infinite            [discovery of universal gravitation].
The remotest stars revealed
Their unknown aspect
And timidly brought near
Their virgin flames                 [discoveries due to the telescope].
You dared to divide the rays of the sun,
To weigh this air
            [resolution of the solar spectrum, invention of the barometer].²¹
```

The revolutions of poetic language, not of science, which have intervened between Monti's day and our own, make it difficult for such periphrases to give us much pleasure today. In the age of neoclassical taste, they were neither riddles nor taboos, but the source of literary pleasure, as is the case with any poetic figure. It is not so much that periphrases were necessary because one could not call certain things by their names, but that calling them by their names would have represented an unpoetic alternative to periphrasis. The circumlocution displays the axiological space of enthusiasm: the same space disclosed by mythical comparison and outdoing.

We needed a text with an antiquated air in order to introduce us to the epoch since which, once or more than once in a generation, scientific and technological progress has renewed the life of humans, and made them grow old more quickly. Earlier literature exalted a functional that was acquired: one preexisting within the cultural heritage, made equal to a second nature by custom, when not in harmony with primal nature. Its later equivalent, brought up to date and less natural, will continue to be an object of representation, lending itself more to implicit praise than to the novelty of blame. But now the most interesting functional is not acquired, but rather, so to speak, in process of acquisition: it is surprising and experimental, projected into the future, open to curiosity and hope just as it is exposed to suspicion and fear. In the predilection shown by modern literature, I would say that it is precisely the first of the two—the acquired—that succumbs in the confrontation with the nonfunctional. When things function well, their functioning will be more evident than the things themselves: hence the frequent terseness and synthesis of enunciation with which they are described. A single example, from the greatest of those writers who rarely avail themselves of the nonfunctional: Tolstoy (cf. V, 8). In the 1805 of the historical novel *War and Peace*, a machine like the lathe (extremely old, albeit perfected) in the studio of Prince Bolkonsky attests to the old man's Rousseau-like training:

> The enormous study was full of things evidently in constant use. The large
> table covered with books and plans, the tall glassfronted bookcase with keys

in the locks, the high desk for writing while standing up, on which lay an open exercise-book, and the lathe with tools laid ready to hand and shavings scattered around, all indicated continuous, varied, and orderly activity.[22]

Until the end of the chapter I shall proceed with examples of a functional that is in process of acquisition; and if I only concern myself with those cases where we find at least one of the traits which convey Sancho Panza's astonishment, I will only be neglecting a few instances.

5

In a sonnet of 1843 by Giuseppe Gioacchino Belli, *The Steam Carriages* (*Le carrozze a vapore*), a commoner, no more educated than Sancho, pours out his thoughts about railways; rather than admiring, he is superstitiously outraged. A carriage that seems to fly is not a natural thing, nor can it be good, since it has not been adopted by the Pope, and therefore it can only be a diabolical, supernatural entity. Peering out from behind the character, the author disagrees with his regressive common sense, and hence approves of the progressive rationality that leaves him behind; literally, however, the author's reason grants words, logic, and sympathy to the character's misconception. A common technique of Enlightenment irony, here in a late example — with flavorful dialect in the original:

> How is it natural? Natural schmatural.
> Can it be a natural effect
> For a carriage to fly as if it had wings?
> Here there is a secret pact with the devil.
>
> So now a few buckets of water are better
> Than six horses, huh, don Pavolo?
> For me, I call it as I see it:
> This whole invention is a piece of work from Hell.[23]

But the polarity of functional and supernatural now lacks the polemical necessity which it had possessed in the eighteenth century — it coincides less straightforwardly with the polarity of progress and regression. I refer not to the history of ideas or of political, religious, or technological life; I am speaking of exaltation that is already not whole-hearted, of protest that is not yet without second thoughts, in literature. The novelty of the railroad anticipates the renewal whereby the French Romantics were making the noble style outdated. Victor Hugo himself, the protagonist of this renewal, in 1837 can only speak of that novelty in verse through a double periphrasis for the law of gravity and for the train that seems to deny its effects. The catachresis spans an entire quatrain:

Oh poets! The iron and ardent vapor
Wipe from the earth, while you are dreaming,
The age-old weight hanging from every object,
Which broke hard pavements under heavy wheels.[24]

In the last quatrain of the poem, the social and scientific progress thus far exalted is unexpectedly related to religion. Eclecticism is the only spirit of conservation that can ask itself, with secret fear, whether the relation is either/or:

But in the midst of this progress of which our age is proud,
Within this great refulgence of a dazzling century,
One thing, O Jesus, frightens me secretly,
It is the echo of your voice that weakens.[25]

General axiological doubt and particular linguistic insufficiency, distinct in Hugo, are united in several stanzas of Alfred de Vigny's *The Shepherd's House* (*La Maison du berger*), published in 1844. A primitive country vehicle announces the disinterested, slow journey of love — opposed to the new mode of travel, swift, noisy, and dangerous:

May God guide to its destination the thundering steam
On the rails of the roads that cross the mountains,
May an Angel stand upon the noise of its forge
When it goes underground and makes the bridges tremble
And, devouring the boilers with its teeth of fire,
Bores through cities and leaps over rivers
Faster than the deer in the heat of his bounding.

Yes, if the blue-eyed Angel will not watch over its journey,
And with the sword in his hand does not sweep down and defend it,
If he has not counted the beating of the lever, if he hears not
Every turn of the wheel in its triumphant course,
If he has not his eye on the waters and his hand on the embers,
To shatter to pieces the magic furnace
The pebble of a child will always be enough.[26]

Vigny writes "rails of the roads" (*le fer des chemins*), less humble than the straightforward "railroad" (*chemin de fer*). The only straightforward expressions used to define the railroad I would count are "the beating of the lever," "turn of the wheel"; more vaguely "boilers," "waters," and "embers." Within the ample periphrasis that expresses the danger, we may consider all the other expressions as catachreses, "thundering steam," "the noise of its forge," "teeth of fire," "magic furnace." In the three ensuing stanzas: "the iron bull, fuming, blowing, and bellowing," "the burning belly of the bull of Carthage," "bellowing dragon that a wise man has brought to birth," "wings of fire."[27] The catachresis's resort from the new to the known inevitably insists on antiquity,

mythology, and magic. This is confirmed, moreover, by the greater awkward-
ness of the natural comparisons: the outdoing whereby the train goes faster
than the deer, and then the parallel with the arrow, in a classical style. The
supernatural of God and the Angel, who must be vigilant with the attentive-
ness of a locomotive engineer, imparts an ideological irresoluteness and emotional dismay to the very needs that underlie the catachresis — to the necessity,
that is, of a mediation between the new and the known. This necessity is
conveyed later on in a list of urgent reasons to take the train: a dying mother or
friend, a military or scientific project of national importance.

Poetic language recovers all its enchantment, along with its self-assurance,
when it returns to the sweetness of contingent situations which innovation is on
the verge of destroying, or when it considers the frigidity of the uniform situation which evolution is about to establish. The disorder of the old-time journey,
innocently antifunctional, belongs to the past; the future belongs to the order of
the new time and space which functionality measures and constrains:

> Never again will we hear stamping on the road
> The lively foot of a horse on the burning cobbles;
> Adieu, slow journeys, distant noises that one hears,
> The laughter of the passersby, the slow turning of the wheel,
> The unexpected bends on varying slopes,
> A friend met, the hours forgotten,
> The hope of arriving late in a wild place.
>
> Distance and time are defeated. Science
> Traces around the earth a sad and straight road.
> The world is reduced by our experience
> And the equator is only too narrow a ring.
> Chance is no longer. Everyone will slip along his line
> Immobile in the single place which departure allots him,
> Immersed in a silent and cold calculation.[28]

6

It would be a mistake to expect metamorphoses of outdoing to become
more proud and optimistic (in comparison with the Baroque or neoclassical
figure) as the innovations of the times become more incommensurable. This
disproportion introduces into every comparison between new and known an
awareness of paradox, which is a root of ambivalence. When Baudelaire
writes in 1846 that the heroes of the *Iliad* only measure up to the ankles of
Balzac's characters, the judgment is anything but purely literary. But there is
nothing more ambivalent than the vindication he has it follow, a vindication of

values like "modern beauty," and the invisible diffusion of the marvelous in Parisian life.[29] In more hidden variants, outdoing is recognizable precisely because the supernatural is the losing term, set against the victorious one of capitalistic functionality. Here is how Balzac can represent the feverish shifts in the focus of attention on the Paris stock exchange: "At this hour when all interests are at stake, Moses, appearing with his two luminous horns, would barely receive the honor of a pun, and would be denied by people who are busy delaying payment on futures contracts."[30] Does the sentence express disapproval for the distracted unbelief of the speculators, or admiration for the enormity and the unpredictability of the modern whirl of investments? In the most paradoxical fashion, the context of *Melmoth Reconciled* (*Melmoth réconcilié,* 1835) confirms that compared to this state of affairs there is no room for miracles of any other kind. Balzac tries to redeem the conclusion of Maturin's novel (IV, 24) by saving the protagonist; but the original story poorly survives the new contrivance that the pact with the devil ends up precisely in the stock exchange, undersold and undervalued.

Such patent outdoing encourages me not to speak of the history of ideas, but to adduce figurative moments from well-known ideological writings. The recognition of the revolutionary role of the bourgeoisie in the *Communist Manifesto* (*Manifest der Kommunistischen Partei*) does not imply any ideological incoherence: the irreversibility of the changes provoked by this class is the very condition of an inescapably progressivist criticism like Marx's. But the ruthlessness of the critique does not exclude admiration for the grandeur of the change effected, and, axiologically, allows a conscious margin of ambivalence. The comparison between the new and the known, between the wonders of bourgeois activity and the greatest monuments in stone and the greatest migrations of ancient and medieval peoples, is historically necessary. And with this comparison an outdoing, a figure of admiration, also becomes necessary:

> It [the bourgeoisie] has been the first to show what man's activity can bring about. It has accomplished wonders surpassing Egyptian pyramids, Roman aqueducts, and Gothic cathedrals; it has conducted expeditions that dwarf all former migrations of peoples and crusades.[31]

In a posthumous text of 1857, the known which Marx compares to the new is not only ancient but supernatural as well — Greek mythology. The text concerns the problem of its survival, or rather its value as a model, which was preserved until modern times by an art which presupposed that mythology as a weltanschauung. Here as well there is no ideological incoherence; but the axiological ambivalence is at its peak — unless it is completely absent, keeping in mind that the last terms of the comparison are heterogeneous. On the one hand, the aesthetic superiority of Greek art is undisputed, just as is, on the other hand, the practical, technological superiority of modern reality. It is, however, the latter superiority which takes the form of an outdoing, to the detriment of the intermediary mythological term, since it constitutes an effective rather than a fantastic dominion over the forces of nature:

> Is the conception of nature and of social relations which underlies Greek imagination and therefore Greek mythology possible in the age of self-actors, railways, locomotives and the electric telegraph? What is Vulcan compared with Roberts & Co., Jupiter compared with the lightning rod and Hermes compared with the Crédit Mobilier? All mythology subdues, dominates and fashions the forces of nature in the imagination and through the imagination: it therefore disappears when real domination over these forces is established. What becomes of Fama beside Printing House Square?[32]

The recurrence of certain types of comparisons throughout the first book of *Capital* is not only indicative of Marx's humanistic culture, and of a habit of antonomastic allusions with a polemical and ironic purpose. Here the new consists in particular or general elements of the capitalist and colonialist system, while the known consists in various references to the supernatural: religious or magical, pagan or Christian, mythological or poetic. In rare cases, it consists of references to antiquity or literature without the supernatural. In most cases the known succumbs to the new in an explicit outdoing; we find actual verbs of outdoing in the first and third sentences I quote here:

> Dante would have found the worst horrors of his *Inferno* outstripped in this factory.

> This power of Asiatic and Egyptian kings, Etruscan theocrats, etc., has in modern society been transferred to the capitalist.

> The description of the workshops, more especially those of the London printers and tailors, surpasses the most loathsome fantasies of our romance writers.

> The law, finally, which always balances the relative surplus-population, or industrial reserve army, with the extent and energy of accumulation, this law chains the laborer to capital more firmly than the wedges of Vulcan did Prometheus to the rock.

> The Governor-General of the East India Company took part in this private traffic. His favorites received contracts under conditions whereby they, cleverer than the alchemists, made gold out of nothing.

> It [the colonial system] was "the strange God" who perched himself on the altar cheek by jowl with the old Gods of Europe, and one fine day with a shove and a kick threw them all into a heap.

At the same time when the burning of witches stopped in England, the hanging of banknote forgers started there.[33]

Faust—where we have already read lines that exalt the functional (IV, 11, 32)—was the model of a typically nineteenth-century relationship between legendary matter and present-day referents. A relationship which I would define as a remotivation: where a present-day fact is sufficiently problematic to become the signified of a legendary fact, and the legendary fact sufficiently mysterious to serve as signifier of the present-day fact. The difference between the treatise entitled *Capital* and the musical dramas known as *The Ring of the Nibelung* (cf. V, 12) is not only ideological. And yet the second title refers us through a mythical metaphor to the same reality which the first spells out: Romantic anticapitalism, questionable from the point of view of ideology, recounts history as antinature and represents aspects of that reality with unsurpassed horror. I refer to the subterranean scene in Nibelheim, to its nightmarish moments within the tragicomedy that is *Das Rheingold*. Wagner modernizes medieval Nordic sources, and has the ring yield for its creator Alberich the forced labor of his peers, the dwarves—smiths who are humiliated as miners. "Now the evil one forces us / To crawl through caverns, / For him alone / Always laboring / [. . .] / So we have to espy, / Find and dig, / Melt the booty, / Forge the casting, / Without peace or rest / To heap up the master's treasure."[34] In 1848, not coincidentally the date when the Wagnerian cycle was begun, the Marxist manifesto attributed to the bourgeoisie the total and unifying conquest of the world: "It has *accomplished wonders*," reads the text we quoted above. Wagner has his Wotan say that "Powerful *wonders* / Alberich *would have accomplished*"; and the dwarf himself says: "I think of *accomplishing wonders* one day: / With the treasure I shall win and make my possession / The whole world."[35]

Not without a threatening grandeur, here the functional figures as cursed. Literally cursed, in its causes and effects, thanks to the myth; and there is no more disquieting example of this myth's remotivation than the invisible omnipresence of Alberich: "For him you must labor, / Where you do not perceive him; / Where you do not notice him / Expect him to be"; "No one sees me / When he seeks me; / But I am everywhere, / Hidden to the eye."[36] This is an effect of a metamorphic helmet, enslaved to the ring as technology is to capital, which disguises itself regressively as magic. The helmet will only harm the characters who use it, even when in *Götterdämmerung* a prophetic abolition of distance (reserved for machines with names prefixed by *tele-*) will be added to its wondrous powers: "if you have a desire for the most distant place";[37] and worse, the distortion of appearance will thereby infiltrate the most intimate of emotional relationships. In the Nibelheim workshop, it is adulation as well which expresses outdoing: "I have seen much, / I have found strange things: / Yet have I never seen / Such wonders."[38] But the recourse from the new to the known is inverted in the hallucinatory and allegorical reference of the mythical supernatural to modernity. Perhaps it is not outlandish to identify the analogue of a verbal catachresis in the use of the orchestra: where timbral innovation depends on the unheard-of mobilization of the brass section (not to mention the eighteen offstage anvils), and points the imagination towards heavy metals — not of armor, but of machinery. What is all the more remarkable is that language, or song, is denied to the proletarian mass that is deformed into dwarfish proportions. Balzac had not found room for the working class in the *Human Comedy;* Wagner's stage direction grants his Nibelungs, outside of the score, only an inarticulate cry of terror.[39]

Outdoing in the name of progress may contain in itself the ambivalence of the oedipal rivalry, between the desire to destroy and the desire to succeed the father, between taking his place in order to diverge from him and taking his place in order to become him. In Walt Whitman's *Song of the Exposition,* recited in 1871 at the inauguration of the American Institute in New York, the ancient and the modern are transposed spatially into the opposition of the Old and New World; the invocation to the Muse has the sense and exhibits the language of an insouciant desecration, which does not spare the biblical any more than it does the classical:

> Come Muse migrate from Greece and Ionia,
> Cross out please those immensely overpaid accounts,
> That matter of Troy and Achilles' wrath, and Aeneas', Odysseus'
>   wanderings,
> Placard "Removed" and "To let" on the rocks of your snowy Parnassus,
> Repeat at Jerusalem, place the notice high on Jaffa's gate and on Mount
>   Moriah,
> The same on the walls of your German, French and Spanish castles, and
>   Italian collections,
> For know a better, fresher, busier sphere, a wide, untried domain awaits,
>   demands you.[40]

And the "dame of dames" crosses the ocean. A longer recapitulation of the Euro-Oriental mythical patrimony, which could not "detain" her, moves from the Egyptian tombs to the Carolingian and Arthurian Middle Ages; all of it a refused venerable-regressive, sent to the graveyard — or a solemn-admonitory yielding to a rotation of space rather than time:

> Jerusalem a handful of ashes blown by the wind, extinct . . .

In the new environment, the "illustrious emigrant" will be pleased to stay:

> By thud of machinery and shrill steam-whistle undismay'd,
> Bluff'd not a bit by drain-pipe, gasometers, artificial fertilizers . . .[41]

The "strata" of his anterior themes, concealed by the modern ones, will become their "foundations." The "cathedral" of industry will be more powerful and beautiful, proud and picturesque, than the monuments which embodied such qualities; but the fracture of outdoing, in the name of the identity of the human race, gives way to the continuity of the resort to the known. Without catachresis or metaphor, things are suggestively called by their own names in the verses on the exposition rooms that will display technological processes in action and lectures on nature and art. But the materials' change in shape will be seen to happen "as if by magic"; and the next paragraph moderates the outdoing into a recourse to the past: these are America's pyramids and obelisks, lighthouse of Alexandria, hanging gardens of Babylon, and temple of Olympia.[42] Like transferable titles of nobility, recourse and outdoing work on behalf of the ideals which are hoped to triumph: their substitutive myth's ascetic nakedness and utopian inadequacy have need of them. Technology and science, production and specialization, work and domesticity. In this text, the language of enthusiasm may well be the very rejuvenation of Monti's language; if today it too has an antiquated air, it is because we have learned that it is scarcely feasible for all the nine Muses:

> To teach the average man the glory of his daily walk and trade. . . .[43]

7

After the railroad and photography, during the positivist belle époque, the automobile and the telephone move from expositions into daily life and the airplane takes flight — to confine ourselves to the new functionalities which the discourse of Proust's seven novels mainly grapples with. Proust's poetics allowed him to present an absolute and hence lasting impression of the new by presupposing its relativity, its transitoriness menaced by habit. In the major thematic constants running through the depths of his work, habit — provided it is not reassurance countering an unknown that arouses anguish — is the indifference from which the unknown that arouses fascination stands out or in which it is extinguished. This ever-changing paradigm gives fixed form to the most varied contents, and certainly the unknown as a term comprehends more than technological innovations. But to confront them the only possible instrument is a poetics that has truth begin with metaphor:[44] worn down by indifferent habit, the literally correct word is worthless. It is as if one or more metaphors, in following or preceding that word, veering off towards the fascinating unknown, served the function of catachreses. A procedure, on the other hand, which is all the more indispensable as the things in question are more common: in the first and most famous passage to use this conception, this procedure catches the reader unawares, so that the feeling of a phenomenon as natural as rain becomes authentic, as though experienced for the first time.[45] For a cultural invention still relatively recent around 1900, the simplicity of the conventional recourse to the supernatural is eventually overwhelmed by the profusion and precision of Proust's mythological inventiveness:

> The telephone was at that time not in such common use as it is today. And yet habit takes so little time to divest of their mysteries the sacred forces with which we are in contact that, not having been connected immediately, the only thought I had was that it was truly long, truly inconvenient, and I almost intended to make a complaint: like all of us today, I found not quick enough for my tastes, in its brisk changes, that wonderful enchantment by which a few moments are enough to conjure up close to us, invisible yet present, the being we desired to speak with [. . .]. We need do nothing else for this miracle to take place but bring our lips to the magic mouthpiece and to call — at times a little too long, I admit — the Watchful Virgins whose voices we hear daily without ever seeing their faces, and who are our guardian angels in the vertiginous obscurity whose doors they jealously watch; the All-Powerful Ones who make the absent arise at our side, without our being permitted to perceive them; the Danaids of the invisible who ceaselessly empty, fill, and pass on to one another the urn of sounds; the ironical Furies who, when we murmured a confidence to a friend, with the hope that no one could hear us, call out to us cruelly: "I'm listening"; the perennially irritated maidservants of Mystery, the touchy priestesses of the Invisible, the Maidens of the Telephone![46]

After the intermediary voices, when the voice of a loved one is in question, the figural relationship is inverted and intensified. Metaphor and the supernatural have lent themselves to the novelty of the telephone; now it is the telephone that lends a heart-rending metaphor to the distance of those we love, rendered all the more palpable by the illusion of proximity; or to another supernatural distance, in which the mystery of technology foreshadows a definitive one:

> Quite often, listening in that way, without seeing her who talked to me from afar, it has seemed to me that this voice called from the depths from which one does not reascend, and I have known that anxiety which would clutch at me one day, when a voice would return thus (alone, and no longer linked to a body that I would never see again) to murmur into my ear words that I would have wanted to kiss at their passage over lips forever turned to dust.[47]

Proust does not fear the widest tonal range: from this last, he returns to the personification through metaphor of the instrument, whose receiver, hung up and then picked up, chatters on as endlessly as Pulcinella. Then he again considers the telephone as a metaphorical means instead of an end. The magic of the new functional leads to another new, and painful, discovery in the grandmother's voice: isolated from her face for the first time, sweetly changed, cracked by suffering. With the sudden cutting off of the telephone lines, and the unheard calls on both sides, the metaphor of loss is deepened. He calls to the grandmother in vain, like the abandoned Orpheus calling the name of his dead wife; finally, when it is no longer necessary to name them, mythology returns to flatter the maidens of the telephone with its transfigurations.[48] In the next novel, the airplane will be named only after the authentic feeling and the mythical comparison:

> I saw about fifty meters above me, in the sun, between two great shining steel wings which bore it away, a being whose figure, barely distinct, seemed to me to resemble that of a man. I was as moved as a Greek could have been who for the first time saw a demigod.[49]

In the same way, in Woolf's *Orlando* the moment of wonder before technological novelties is hyperbolized — that is to say, made verisimilar — by the fantastic inverisimilitude of the chronology (cf. V, 15). The protagonist reacts to electric lighting under Edward VII as one who was born (a man) in the sixteenth century; as one who had seen, after the reigns of Elizabeth I and James I, the eighteenth century of Queen Anne and the nineteenth century of Queen Victoria. At Orlando's disposal is a memory and habit neither short like individual ones, nor transient like the collective memory which is their sum, but as durable as the one and as long as the other. The midnight darkness in the outlying roads of London under James I has already been described:

> But it was [. . .] now, in the evening, that the change was most remarkable. Look at the lights in the houses! At a touch, a whole room was lit; hundreds of rooms were lit; and one was precisely the same as the other. One could see everything in the little square-shaped boxes; there was no privacy; none of those lingering old shadows and odd corners that there used to be; none of those women in aprons carrying wobbly lamps which they put down carefully on this table and on that. At a touch, the whole room was bright. And the sky was bright all night long; and the pavements were bright; everything was bright.[50]

In 1928, the "biography" has reached the year of its publication; but Orlando, reflecting on the present, can allow herself distant lived comparisons: differences, alas, from the ideal century which balanced specialized progress and the spread of Enlightenment; resemblances, on the other hand, to magical beliefs whose lot is always to be anterior, and always to return. What other recourse against that which, only because it is real, silences the simple question of how it can be possible?

> The very fabric of life now, she thought as she rose [in the lift], is magic. In the eighteenth century, we knew how everything was done; but here I rise through the air; I listen to voices in America; I see men flying — but how it's done, I can't even begin to wonder. So my belief in magic returns.[51]

It is not by chance that the new and the supernatural, for those narrators who renew the very dimension of time, do not exclude outdoing: an individual impression — even if it takes place over a fantastic span of times — and all the more absolute the more it is relative, is incommensurable with famous precedents. In the years immediately before and after the First World War, the traditional figure of scorn of tradition was instead prolonged by the intercontinental success of Whitman before it was by the historic avant-gardes. In the fourth of the *Five Great Odes* (*Cinq Grandes Odes*) of Paul Claudel (1907), the poet's resistance to the "Muse who is Grace" invents an alibi by singing the magnification of man "withdrawn from chance"; for whom planetary colonialism and visionary mechanization open up a "Triumphal Road." Here is one verse:

> I will do it with a poem that will no longer be the adventure of Ulysses among the Lestrygonians and the Cyclopes, but the knowledge of the earth . . .[52]

In *Song for Argentina* (*Canto a la Argentina*) by the Nicaraguan Rubén Darío (1910), an immense southern space awaits the exodus of flocks of humans from the distant ancient countries of Europe; the generous welcome muffles but does not spare comparisons in favor of the New World. The most prominent of these is reserved for the most humble of the emigrants or natives: "Caesars of labor / Multipliers of bread, / More powerful than Genghis Khan / or than Nebuchadnezzar." Among the mighty traffic of the city, the wagons full of iron and the rumbling, the metaphorical catachresis and the recourse to the legendary have more or less precise referents: "Speedy steel hippogryph, / Electric rosebushes, flowers / Of a thousand and one nights, pomp / Of Babylon."[53] In 1909 we reach the avant-gardes, with Marinetti's *Manifesto of Futurism* (*Manifesto del Futurismo*). More heedless than ever of its own precariousness in the past, continuous outdoing makes ever more excessive claims to sound unheard-of; the present of an oedipal abolition underestimates the banal future towards which it is rushing: either of appointments as academicians or of periodic, expected uproars. One wishes that today the most vulgarized example of the figure in our century were merely to have an outdated flavor, and not worse (namely, fascist) associations:

> A racing car with its hood decorated with large tubes like snakes with explosive breath . . . a roaring automobile, which seems to be propelled by a machine-gun, is more beautiful than the Winged Victory of Samothrace.

From the new of the machine, the metaphoric catachresis reverts to the natural known — since the cultural known must be condemned: "building sites set alight by violent electric moons"; "greedy stations, devouring smoking snakes"; "ample-bosomed locomotives, pawing the rails, like enormous steel horses bridled with tubes."[54]

Pessoa's *Triumphal Ode* (*Ode triunfal*), written under the heteronym of Álvaro de Campos (cf. V, 9), has a different poetic density, and in 1914 served as the manifesto of the Portuguese avant-garde. There is no lack of images, vocabulary, and enthusiasm for a mechanical modernity whose beauty was "entirely unknown to the ancients"; for all that makes "today different from yesterday."[55] What is lacking is any temptation to reify the precariousness of such difference, to remove the past and the future. Only the circulation of both is recognized in the present:

> I sing, and I sing the present, and also the past and the future,
> For the present is the whole of the past and the whole of the future
> And there are Plato and Virgil within the machines and the electric lights,
> Only because Virgil and Plato existed once and were humans,
> And pieces of the Alexander the Great of maybe the fiftieth century,
> Atoms that will have a fever for the brain of the Aeschylus of the hundredth
>   century
> Are running through these belts and these pistons and these wheels.[56]

The recourse to the known happens in the opposite way from outdoing: under the aegis of a kind of panchronicity which can be perceived in modernity, or of a pantheism which can be felt tangibly in the functional. It occurs in a natural, cultural, and supernatural field: engines are a "tropical nature," locomotives are a "flora" with the fragrance of oil and coal; traveling salesmen are the "knights-errant of Industry"; all modern things are the "new metallic and dynamic revelation of God."[57] Thus "a balance sheet is as natural as a tree" — preferably with falsified balances — "and a parliament as beautiful as a butterfly."[58] Modernity need not coincide with the functional alone; mechanized realities alternate with others denoting a rather chronic inefficiency — politics and its scandals, the mixed crowd of the city "that passes by and never passes," the shop windows with their "useless articles that everyone wants to buy," the amorality of the poor "untouchable by any progress."[59] A sprinkling of provincial melancholy, here and there worthy of reminding the Italian reader, allowing for all differences, of the exhibitionist and fleeting festive days of Leopardi. The feeling of being on a cultural and geographical periphery is latent, as it usually is under all the four or more names that the author alternates between; while he strengthens the excitement of modernity with ostentatious naïveté, he subtly dispels the naïve triumphalism which the title led us to fear.

A triumphalism more justifiable, because it has only just snatched from utopia its bloody revolutionary premise, returns ironically to that utopia par excellence which places only its premises in this world—religion. Mayakovsky's *150,000,000* (1919–20) pray to the Father imploring the literal human incarnation of the Son, and they take upon themselves the miracles of the Son to outdo the creation of the Father:

> We have come,
>   millions
>   of godless ones,
>   pagans,
>   atheists—
> beating
>   our heads,
>   through rusty iron
>   through the field—
>   we all
> devoutly
> will pray to the lord God.
> Come forth
>   not from the starry
>   tender bed
> iron god
>   fiery god,
> god not of Marses
>   Neptunes and Vegas
> god of flesh—
>   god-man!
> Not driven upwards
> grounded on the stars,
> earthly one
>   come forth
> among us,
>   appear!
> Not the one
>   "who dwelleth in the heavens."

Before everyone's eyes
today
we ourselves
will perform
        miracles.

. . . .

We go forth to a heroic deed
                        three times harder than god's
who created
        by giving things to emptiness.
But we
    creating the new, not only have to
dream things up,
                we have also to dynamite the old.[60]

In surrealism, the progressive claim to the wonders of the everyday, to the so-called irrational or in other words to "symmetric logic" (cf. II, 12 and V, 10), was a liberating moment: despite its futile aspects, playful when not superstitious, despite the anti-analytical misunderstandings within Breton's admiration for Freud. In a passage from Louis Aragon's *Paris Peasant* (1926), the collection of features which we have followed over three centuries is still recognizable in its entirety. But it has largely passed from rhetoric to ideology, from writing to thought: the supernatural does not so much serve as a term of comparison with the functional, as the functional perpetuates the supernatural by renewing it. Having delegated to machines the faculties of thought, man rediscovers terror and panic before an uncontrollable and unstoppable "thought of his own thought." This "magical domination" does not spring from the principle of utility; pride, which seems to translate Monti's neoclassical language into the surrealist tongue, leads to a further religious question: "Now that we have made lightning curl up at our feet like a kitten, and now that without trembling any more than the eagle we have counted the freckles on the face of the sun, to whom shall we bear the cult of worship?"[61] It is a question not of "puerility" as it was for Olympus or the Eucharist, but precisely of speed, that throughout the countryside only "deserted oratories, overturned calvaries" are to be seen. The acceleration of time, incompatible with the folds of the virgins' robes, has its own suitable gods; metaphor transforms them at length — as in Proust — before naming them:

They are great red gods, great yellow gods, great green gods [. . .]. A strange statuary presides over the birth of these simulacra. Almost never before had men been satisfied with such a barbarous appearance of destiny and strength. Nameless sculptors who have raised these metallic ghosts did not know they were submitting to a tradition as alive as the one giving churches the shape of crosses. These idols have a kinship between them that makes them formidable. Painted in many colors with English words and words of new creation, with a single long and supple arm, a luminous head without a face, a single foot, and a belly with a wheel bearing numbers, gas stations sometimes have the allure of the divinities of Egypt or of those of the cannibal tribes that worship only war. Oh Texaco motor oil, Eco, Shell, great inscriptions declaring human potential! Soon we will cross ourselves before your fountains, and the youngest among us will die for having looked up to their nymphs of naphtha.[62]

8

The Wagnerian scene of Nibelheim, up until now the least ambivalent example of protest (VII, 6), was also the one where the recourse to the past takes the most ambiguous form. The new, which falls back onto the known, fully drawing on Nordic myth for subterranean dwarves and a cursed ring, is available *a posteriori*. The known, which rebounds towards the new, forcing us to recognize modern referents like the workshop and capital, is available *a priori*. When the future takes the place of the past, and an incredible invention takes the place of a mythical tradition, the result is a relationship between the fantastic and the functional which is typical of the science fiction of protest. The founding novel of this last genre, succeeding to Verne's positivist optimism, is H. G. Wells's *The Time Machine* (1895): the "time traveler" finds two different species descended from man in the world of the year 802701, and the inferior one has developed from the industrial tendency to confine workers under the surface of the earth[63] — like Wagner's Nibelungs. In the A.F. (the year of the Ford era) 631 in Aldous Huxley's *Brave New World* (1932), and in a much worse way in Orwell's *Nineteen Eighty-Four* (1949, cf. V, 6), the only relations with the past and its culture are destructive erasure and repressive falsification. Kafka is too unique for us to consider a short story like *In the Penal Settlement* (*In der Strafkolonie*, 1914) within the genre of science fiction of protest: the punitive fanaticism of the perfected torture device was the invention of a dead commander, it is on the verge of yielding to the innovative humanitarianism of the current commander, and its only hope of recovery is in a prophecy of resurrection. Orwell's novel was written just after World War II, but after the extermination camps and the atomic bomb it is not only the exaltation of the functional that becomes unlikely to appear in literature. A fantastic and tragic protest, foresighted and horrified, has become unlikely as well: reality has reduced it to silence, has outstripped it.

Comic protest, proportioned not to mass murder but to the steady flow of subtle violence, certainly clings to life more stubbornly. We already encountered it as something frequently inseparable from the pretentious-fictitious, kitsch, and advertising, particularly in Gadda (IV, 38; V, 15). The continuation of the passage I quoted from *Acquainted with Grief* rages against the "functional twentieth century," harping on the discomfort of toilets. Thanks to their comfort, in a state of happy indecency, an ironic exaltation of the functional reaches its peak in the unfinished short story *The House* (*La casa*), written in 1935–36. I mention it because it provided me with the latest example of outdoing in terms of date—one that is obviously light-hearted, and supreme within a classification that is not imaginary and mythical, but numerical and scientific:

> . . . a firm earthquake-proof structure absolutely "inébranlable" and Mercalli would have to add many numbers to his tragic scale, if he wanted to classify the unknown earthquakes capable of making my house tremble.[64]

Absent the irony, this would be the same language used by advertisements, in which perpetual outdoing constitutes sales promotion and lust for acquisition: with or without the support of catachresis, of its neologisms and Anglicisms. Here is where the history of the rhetorical combination that was synthesized in Cervantes comes to its end. In short, it was the history of utilitarian progress— from the demystification of the supernatural to the mystification of the quotidian. We now understand better the limits, which I already suggested (V, 15), on literary representation of advertising. Advertising itself ought in theory to hand down its own literary or artistic masterpieces to the future; the problem is to understand why the entertainment and flattery of the masses should seem to be so much less suited to this outcome than were the entertainment and flattery of princes and the elite in the past. Let us turn to a less distant past for the best examples of how utilitarian progressivism has in fact nourished masterpieces at its own expense.

The chemist Homais in *Madame Bovary,* whose advanced ideas turn his admired Voltaire and Rousseau into cretins, eclipses all French precursors and successors: from the July Monarchy until late positivism, popular like Henri Monnier's M. Prudhomme, or sophisticated like Villiers de l'Isle-Adam's Tribulat Bonhomet. The latter author's reactionary penetration already goes beyond mimesis into caricature, aligning itself with a comic rather than tragic protest, albeit fantastic in its own way. *The Celestial Bill-Posting* (*L'Affichage céleste,* 1873) as a story is a trick: an emphatic voice in an advertising style has the floor from start to finish. While it mimics Faust in deploring the surviving sterility of nature (IV, 32), it hardly preserves the memory of a heroic precariousness in the intention of surmounting it. Rather than the challenge accepted ahead of time by the practical spirit, what seems praiseworthy and moral is the compensation offered, always belatedly, to the spirit of gain:

> What is the use [. . .] of these azure vaults that serve no purpose but to sustain the morbid imagination of the last dreamers? Would it not be a deed that would acquire legitimate rights to public gratitude, and, let's say it (why not?) to the admiration of Posterity, to convert these sterile spaces into a truly and fruitfully instructive spectacle, to make this immense expanse valuable and, finally, to produce a good revenue from these indefinite and transparent Solognes?
> [. . .]
> At first, the very thing appears to border on the Impossible and almost on Insanity. To clear the sky for cultivation, to put a value on the stars, exploit the dusk and dawn, organize the evening, to turn to account the firmament unproductive till today, what a dream! What a thorny task, bristling with difficulties! But, strengthened by the Spirit of Progress, to what problems could Man not manage to find the solution?[65]

There is no outdoing between the new of the advertisement projected into the sky, and the known — mythological rather than astronomical — of the most famous constellation. As fiction, the new rather outdoes any real novelty; the old rhetorical projection of astonishment is shaped to the visual projection imagined in the stars:

> Would it not be enough to make even the Great Bear wonder, if suddenly, between its sublime paws, there should rise this disquieting announcement: *Are corsets necessary, yes or no?*[66]

Villiers appears in Breton's *Anthology of Black Humor* (*Anthologie de l'humour noir*). In the case of other writers, who are even more congenial to the surrealists, the distortion of mimesis into caricature contests the bourgeoisie's realistic assurance in its habits of thought. In a literature we may define as presurrealist, between 1868 and 1914, there survives, if I may say so, in retrospect the best of what surrealism produced. It is unusual objects that mediate the relationship of the world and Père Ubu, the plump Macbeth of the marionettes in Jarry's *Ubu roi* (1896), whose physical and financial appetites lay bare, according to the author, the anarchic nature of the bourgeoisie.[67] Objects enter into the character's speech after he has assumed power, and they have names that nonsensically distort the functionality suggested by the normal indirect object after the French preposition *à* (in the sense of *for*). The function is immediately understood to be aggressive in "knife for face," in "scissors for ears";[68] or, also immediately, to be possessive in "cabman for phynance" [*sic*], "horse for phynance," or "hook for finance";[69] or aggressive because possessive, as in "saber for finance," "pistol for phynance."[70] Likewise in the regicide's entire apparatus of enrichment:

Bring me the chest for Nobles and the hook for Nobles and the knife for Nobles and the book for Nobles! then, let in the Nobles.[71]

If the use of a "helmet for finance" is already more doubtful, and a "rod for physics" is halfway between the senseless and the phallic,[72] the combinations of other elements with the antifunctional excremental make one's head spin. The excremental, in fact, is the subject of Ubu's favorite interjection — *merdre!* [*sic*]. What is the use of a "saber for shit," of a "hook for shit," of "scissors for shit"? How can one manage to fight a battle with weapons "as good for shit as for phynance and for physics"?[73] Catachresis once provided the missing word for the new thing, but here it is the thing which the new absurdity of words lacks. Words are assembled with automatic freedom into combinations of variants: as if, since there are scissors for ears and sabers and hooks for finance, both cannot fail to have a version for shit. Pointlessly outdoing a lexicon of practicality, bombastically or obscenely, the expressions have the air of corresponding to situations with well-equipped practical precision.

The novels of Raymond Roussel may be admired or considered unreadable, owing to the preestablished counterbalance between two opposing defects. Banality and extravagance, the tedium of the conventional and the strain of the complicated, have an equal share in the two so-called aspects of form and content. In *Locus Solus* (1914), the park of the scientist Canterel provides spectacles which are as complicated and gratuitous in their origin as the prose describing them is official in its pace and predictable in its phrasing. The reanimated corpses inside a giant glass cage, who enact in the kitsch of repetition the salient moments of their lives, have been treated with *vitalium* and *resurrectina*: perfectly respectable neologisms, whose chemical composition and anatomic application are described in the explanatory style used to publicize scientific discoveries.[74] The anarchic soul and the bureaucratic soul of the bourgeoisie, unaware of each other in Jarry's or Roussel's truculent or frigid fantasies, interpenetrated in Lautréamont's archetypal and encyclopedic presurrealism. *Maldoror* (*Les Chants de Maldoror,* 1868–69) would be no more than a chaotic compilation of late Romantic themes were it not for the dazzling plurality of voices, not only within songs and stanzas, but even within pages and sentences. There is this minimal distinction to begin with: together with the voice of an evildoer or vampire the voice of a functionary or schoolteacher makes itself heard. It seems to me that the first voice has been given a hearing much more often than the second — or rather, than all the others that can be distinguished, than the perverse effect which their counterpoint has of denying authenticity to all of them.

The most celebrated sentence uses four consecutive comparisons to conjure the beauty of a sixteen-year-old English boy dangerously lusted after by Maldoror. It begins from the known: if not because the human body is nature, then because the figure of comparison is a culture of Homeric antiquity, and pederastic sadism is a Romantic legend in Goethe's ballad *Erlkönig*, to which the text has already parodically referred.[75] The sentence then veers into the new:

> He is as beautiful as the retractability of the claws of predatory birds; or even, as the uncertainty of the muscular movements in the wounds in the soft parts of the posterior cervical region; or rather, like that perpetual mousetrap, always reset by the trapped animal, which is the only thing capable of capturing rodents indefinitely, and of working even when concealed under straw; and above all, as the chance encounter on a dissection table of a sewing machine and an umbrella![76]

The first two comparisons take up as models of beauty, but in the form of abstract concepts, animal or human physiological properties; the third is a perfected domestic tool ill-suited for idealization; the fourth is an improbable contact between utilitarian objects of discordant uses. One of the meanings of the nonsense is that beauty is no longer measured by the natural or the literary, but by the scientifically or practically useful, by its language and peculiarities. The only outdoing is that incomparable things are compared, and the only catachresis is that a specialist jargon is adopted; in at least one word, "working *even* when concealed," the rhetoric of advertising peeks through.

The last text in this book is by the same author, Cros, from whom I drew the first text in an imitation of the workings of chance (II, 1). This time the choice of one of his dramatic monologues, *Times of Yore* (*Autrefois*), is not accidental. That olden time promised by the title as an object of discourse has ceased to guarantee the existence of the known, since all that exists belongs by right to the new — that is to say, to the time of inventions. Here there is no outdoing of the past; the past is annulled. New words are not invented, but, through a lack of invention, those that would allow the past to be spoken of are renounced:

> A long time ago — but a long time isn't enough to give you an idea . . . And yet, how to explain better?
>
> A long, long, long time ago; long, long time indeed.
>
> Well, one day . . . no, there were no days, or nights, so once, but there wasn't . . . Yes, once, how else would you say? Well, he got it into his head (no, there was no head), in the idea . . . yes, that's right, in the idea of doing something.
>
> He wanted to drink. But drink what? There was no vermouth, no madeira, no white wine, no red wine, no Dréher beer, no cider, no water! The fact is, you don't think it was necessary to invent all that, that it hadn't been done yet, that progress has marched. Oh! progress![77]

The impossibility of drinking, in the absence even of water, is repeated along with the intentions of eating, singing, dancing, sleeping — there was no night; loving — there were no women; dying — a question either of suicide, or of sanitation. The elemental nature of the actions successively attempted justifies the repetitiveness of their abandonment, the contradictions between a necessary progress and its petty setbacks amuse the listeners on the surface. But the contradictions are profoundly grave: if the things to be done did not yet exist, how could the subject have any notion of them? If he had no notion of them, how could he have the intention of doing them? And if he had no intention, is the impossible tale itself a succession of lies?

> So he wanted nothing! (*Plaintive*). Is there any more unhappy situation! . . . (*Reconsidering*). No, don't cry! There was no situation, no unhappiness. Happiness, unhappiness, that's all modern!

> The end of the story? But there was no end. No end had been invented. Ending is an invention, a progress! Oh! progress! progress![78]

The logic of such an ending, more imperious than the stuttering beginning, recedes stealthily to silence it: surely not even the beginning, a long time ago, had been invented. The silence lurking behind the monologue, an immense rest after fleeting words, as for Hamlet, comes from the other extremity of the metaphysical silence of death. It is the silence of and about origins, greater than the silence about the beginning of language itself, a silence as inviolable in 1878 as it is today. The trumpeting of progress echoes and expires against this distant backdrop, in the fullest sense obsolete.

Notes

Quotations are cited both to pages in the editions used, and also, for the convenience of readers who may not have access to these editions, to the parts of works where the quoted passages occur, such as chapters of novels and acts and scenes of plays.

Where passages quoted form part of a longer whole of which the reader should be aware, the pages of the longer passage are given in parentheses after the pages of the actual quotation.

In quoted passages, omissions of one of two words are indicated by dots in the usual way; longer omissions are indicated by dots within brackets.

Places of publication are omitted for editions by the following publishers: Everyman's Library (London and New York), Oxford University Press (Oxford and New York), Penguin (Harmondsworth), and Princeton University Press (Princeton, N.J.).

Chapter I. What This Book Is About

1. L. Spitzer, "Enumerative Style and Its Significance in Whitman, Rilke, Werfel," *Modern Language Quarterly* 3 (1942): 171–204.

2. Even as an essay and not an exhaustive study, the book could not have been based on a satisfactory apparatus of references to previous studies: rather than being merely poor in secondary bibliography, my footnotes will nearly always dispense with it. On the one hand, too many and too varied texts and areas are touched upon to be able to scour relevant bibliographies with the kind of completeness required in monographs. On the other hand, the thread that connects so many quotations was too individual to allow any

hope for the existence of directly useful studies — with very few exceptions. Between too much and not enough, it is obvious that the studies that were in fact consulted were numerous, even leaving out of account those that I assimilated long before beginning to write: many debts will be clearly recognizable between the lines to specialists. But what was useful to me as both information and guideline would have been for the reader nothing more than a series of discontinuous and often either narrowly academic or sectorial references.

3. These books appeared in 1971, 1973, 1979, and 1982 respectively; they were later organized in three volumes, under the general title of *Letteratura, ragione e represso:* I. *Due letture freudiane: Fedra e il Misantropo* (Turin: Einaudi, 1990); II. *Per una teoria freudiana della letteratura* (Turin: Einaudi, 2000); III. *Illuminismo, barocco e retorica freudiana* (Turin: Einaudi, 1997). The first essay in I, and most of II, were translated into English as *Toward a Freudian Theory of Literature, With an Analysis of Racine's "Phèdre"* (Baltimore: Johns Hopkins University Press, 1978).

4. Cf. Orlando, *Toward a Freudian Theory of Literature, With an Analysis of Racine's "Phèdre"* (Baltimore: Johns Hopkins University Press, 1978), 15: I explained there, why I chose to use the terms "repression" and "repressed" not in "a narrow or technical sense, in accordance with the strict usage of Freud's English translators," but in a wider sense "which no longer makes necessary the exclusion of particular contents from the conscious level," so that these terms may also refer "to the prohibition by which some contents are officially censured in a society."

5. Cf. Ibid., 191–99; Orlando, *Illuminismo, barocco e retorica freudiana* (Turin: Einaudi, 1997), 4–9.

6. *Introductory Lectures on Psycho-Analysis,* XXIII: S. Freud, *The Standard Edition of the Complete Psychological Works,* vol. 16 (London: Hogarth, 1953), 372.

7. *Anti-Dühring,* in K. Marx and F. Engels, *Collected Works,* vol. 25 (London: Lawrence and Wishart; New York: International Publishers; Moscow: Progress Publishers, 1986), 16.

8. *Capital,* pt. I, chap. 1, sec. 1: K. Marx, *Capital: A Critical Analysis of Capitalist Production, London 1887. Text* (Berlin: Dietz, 1990), 29; and cf. *A Contribution to the Critique of Political Economy,* K. Marx and F. Engels, *Collected Works,* vol. 29 (London: Lawrence and Wishart; New York: International Publishers; Moscow: Progress Publishers, 1986), 29:269.

9. *Civilization and its Discontents:* S. Freud, *The Standard Edition of the Complete Psychological Works,* vol. 21 (London: Hogarth, 1961), 99–100 n. 1.

Chapter II. First, Confused Examples

1. Ch. Cros and T. Corbière, *Oeuvres complètes* (Paris: Bibliothèque de la Pléiade, 1970), 47. Almahs are female oriental singers and dancers.

2. Baudelaire, *Oeuvres complètes,* vol. 1 (Paris: Bibliothèque de la Pléiade, 1975), 73.

3. J. L. Borges, *Obra poética, 1923–1977* (Buenos Aires: Alianza-Emecé, 1981), 335.

4. G. Gozzano, *Poesie e prose* (Milan: Garzanti, 1966), 144.

5. Chap. XVII: J. Roth, *Werke in drei Bänden,* vol. 2 (Cologne and Berlin: Kiepenheuer and Witsch, 1956), 428–29. Ulrich von Hutten, knight and humanist, supported the beginnings of the Lutheran Reformation.

6. Ibid., 424, 428.

7. A. von Arnim, *Isabella von Ägypten* (Zurich: Manesse, 1958), 70–71.

8. Chap. IV: Flaubert, *Oeuvres*, vol. 2 (Paris: Bibliothèque de la Pléiade, 1952), 617.

9. Ibid., 611.

10. Ibid., 622.

11. Part I, chap. 6: N. Gogol, *Dead Souls,* trans. R. Pevear and L. Volokhonsky (New York: Pantheon Books, 1996), 115–16.

12. Ibid., 117.

13. E. Auerbach, *Mimesis: The Representation of Reality in Western Literature* (Princeton University Press, 1968), 480–81, and chap. 19 passim.

14. Ibid., 491, and chap. 8 passim.

15. Chap. 3: *The Queen of Spades:* A. Pushkin, *The Collected Stories,* trans. P. Debreczeny (New York: Knopf, 1999), 272–73.

16. Ibid., 265.

17. Section 5 of the poem: Gozzano, *Poesie e prose,* 149.

18. Part I, chap. 5: V. Woolf, *To the Lighthouse* (Everyman's Library, 1957), 30–31.

19. Cf. the description of the house's attics, used as the children's rooms, in the form of a list: "and [the sun] lit up bats, flannels, straw hats, ink-pots, paint-pots, beetles, and the skulls of small birds, while it drew from the long frilled strips of seaweeds pinned to the wall a smell of salt and weeds, which was in the towels too, gritty with sand from bathing" (ibid., 9).

20. Ibid., 18; cf. a passage regarding the husband, 51–52.

21. Part II, chap. II: ibid., 146.

22. Ibid., 149–50.

23. Ibid., 156–59.

24. Part II, chap. IX: ibid., 159–60. Cf. the anticipation of the theme, 153.

25. Ibid., 160–61. There immediately follows the work of repair: 161–64.

26. V. Hugo, *Oeuvres poétiques*, vol. 2 (Paris: Bibliothèque de la Pléiade, 1967), 189–91.

27. VI: A. Breton, *Oeuvres complètes*, vol. 2 (Paris: Bibliothèque de la Pléiade, 1992), 769.

28. A. Breton, *Oeuvres complètes,* vol. 1 (Paris: Bibliothèque de la Pléiade, 1988), 314–15.

29. Chap. XII: P. Mérimée, *Théâtre de Clara Gazul. Romans et nouvelles* (Paris: Bibliothèque de la Pléiade, 1978), 349.

30. Chap. II: ibid., 952.

31. R. L. Stevenson, *Dr. Jekyll and Mr. Hyde, The Merry Men and Other Tales,* (Everyman's Library, 1968), 4.

32. Ibid., 7, 14, 22, 34, 35, 39, 43.

33. E. A. Poe, *Poetry and Tales* (New York: Library of America, 1984), 196; and cf. 319–20.

34. Ibid., 194, 196, 197.

35. Ibid., 195–96.

Chapter III. Making Decisions in Order to Proceed

1. Fontenelle, *Préface sur l'utilité des mathématiques,* in *Antike und Moderne in der Literaturdiskussion des 18. Jahrhunderts* (Berlin: Akademie-Verlag, 1966), 208.

2. B. Croce, *Guide to Aesthetics*, trans. P. Romanell (Indianapolis: Bobbs-Merrill, 1965), 79.

3. Cf. G. Genette, *Figures II* (Paris: Seuil, 1966), 94, 100.

4. E. R. Curtius, *European Literature and the Latin Middle Ages*, trans. W. Trask (Princeton University Press, 1953).

5. M. Praz, *The Romantic Agony*, trans. A. Davidson (1933; Oxford University Press, 1970).

6. Cf. Orlando, *Toward a Freudian Theory of Literature, With an Analysis of Racine's "Phèdre"* (Baltimore: Johns Hopkins University Press, 1978), 28.

7. I translate from C. Lévi-Strauss, *Race et histoire* (Paris: Denoël, 1987), 62–63.

8. Cf. Orlando, *Toward a Freudian Theory*, 179–86.

9. Ibid., 146–51; and cf. L. Hjelmslev, *Prolegomena to a Theory of Language* (Baltimore: Waverley Press, 1953), 31–32.

10. Ibid., 32, 36.

Chapter IV. A Tree Neither Genealogical Nor Botanical

1. *Epistulae ad familiares*, IV, 5: *M. Tulli Ciceronis Epistulae*, vol. 1 (Oxford University Press, 1982), 111–12.

2. Part IV, Book II, Chap. IX: Chateaubriand, *Essai sur les révolutions. Génie du christianisme* (Paris: Bibliothèque de la Pléiade, 1978), 939.

3. Ibid., 937.

4. Cf. ibid., 1845–46, 1846–47. More explicit, albeit more general, references to the Revolution's violation of the tombs were made three chapters earlier, 933.

5. Ibid., 938.

6. Auerbach, *Mimesis: The Representation of Reality in Western Literature* (Princeton University Press, 1968), 454–58.

7. Chateaubriand, *Génie*, 938–39.

8. P. Scarron, *Poésies diverses* (Paris: Didier, 1947), 496–97. For Castiglione, see below, note 26; and cf. Lope de Vega, *Obras poéticas* (Barcelona: Planeta, 1983), 1367–68.

9. Scarron, *Poésies diverses*, 496: variant in lines 3–6.

10. XXXIV, oct. 76, lines 2–8, in the context of octaves 75–81: L. Ariosto, *Tutte le opere*, vol. 1 (Milan: Mondadori, 1964), 901–3.

11. Lines 11–22: *M. Val. Martialis Epigrammata* (Oxford University Press, 1929), unpaginated.

12. Line 8, ibid.

13. X, 4, line 10; cf. VIII, 3 and IX, 50, ibid.

14. H. de Balzac, *La Comédie humaine*, vol. 7 (Paris: Bibliothèque de la Pléiade, 1977), 55, 451.

15. Ibid., 58.

16. Ibid., 72–73.

17. *The Old Maid* (*La Vieille fille*): H. de Balzac, *La Comédie humaine*, vol. 4 (Paris: Bibliothèque de la Pléiade, 1976), 830; and cf. Auerbach, *Mimesis*, 477–78.

18. A. Jarry, *Oeuvres complètes*, vol. 1 (Paris: Bibliothèque de la Pléiade, 1972), 497.

19. P. Bracciolini, *Historiae de varietate fortunae* (Paris: Coustelier, 1723; facsimile in *Opera omnia,* Turin: Bottega d'Erasmo, 1966, vol. 2), 6–7.

20. Ibid., 5, 7.

21. Ibid., 9 (8–25, 25–39).

22. Ibid., 1–2, 34–36, 37.

23. To Guarino Veronese, December 15, 1416: *Prosatori latini del Quattrocento* (Milan and Naples: Ricciardi, 1952), 244–45.

24. *Le Testament, Ballade des dames du temps jadis* (*Ballade of the Ladies of Yore*), in *Poètes et romanciers du Moyen Age* (Paris: Bibliothèque de la Pléiade, 1952), 1153–54; J. Manrique, *Coplas por la muerte de su padre* (*Stanzas on His Father's Death*), *Poesía* (Madrid: Cátedra, 1979), 153.

25. Lines 6063–88, 6115–17: *Le Roman de la Rose,* vol. 1 (Paris: Champion, 1970), 186–88.

26. In *Lirici del Cinquecento* (Turin: Utet, 1976), 191. Cf. Du Bellay, in *Poètes du XVIe siècle* (Paris: Bibliothèque de la Pléiade, 1953), 421.

27. Cf. F. Petrarca, *Rime, Trionfi e Poesie latine* (Milan and Naples: Ricciardi, 1951), 3 (I, lines 9–14), 378 (CCXCII, line 8), 406 (CCCXX, line 14).

28. D. Diderot, *Oeuvres esthétiques* (Paris: Garnier, 1959), 641.

29. Ibid., 643–44.

30. Ibid., 644–45.

31. XLVIII: F. Berni, *Rime* (Turin: Einaudi, 1969), 108–9 (106–16).

32. Ibid., 110.

33. Ibid.

34. Cf. lines 139–41; 22, 126; 145–50; 151–52, 157–60, 172, 178–88, 212–13, 220–25.

35. M. Régnier, *Oeuvres complètes* (Paris: Les Belles Lettres, 1954), 100, 103–4.

36. Ibid., 101–2. Blue- or second-water is lye-wash; May-butter is an ointment for wounds.

37. Cf. F. Berni, *Rime,* 115, lines 202–4.

38. F. de Quevedo, *La Vida del Buscón llamado don Pablos* (Salamanca: Universidad de Salamanca, 1965), 15–20, 91–93, 132, 135–46.

39. Ibid., 32–47.

40. Ibid., 142.

41. Book I, chap. III: ibid., 34.

42. Book I, chap. III: ibid., 45–46.

43. Ibid., 157–58.

44. *The Poems of Ossian,* 2 vols. (Edinburgh: Constable and Co., 1805), 1:320–22.

45. Ibid., 520.

46. Ibid., 476.

47. Ibid., 241.

48. Cf. *The Songs of Selma,* ibid., 451–53 (and the *Nocturnal Song of a Wandering Shepherd of Asia*); *Dar-thula,* ibid., 377–80 (and *The Sorrows of Young Werther,* Book II). There is a similar apostrophe to the sun in *Carthon:* ibid., 342–46.

49. Ibid., 311, 313; ibid., 2:297, 335. Cf. *Berrathon,* ibid., 1:570–78. This very formula will be translated into Russian at the beginning of the first canto, and at the end of

the last, in Pushkin's poem *Ruslan and Ludmila;* it will also be repeated in the original English, at the conclusion of Lermontov's poem *Freedom's Last Son.*

50. Cf. *The Poems of Ossian,* 2:327–28, 341–42.

51. Ibid., 327–28.

52. *Temora,* Book III: ibid., 110; *Fingal,* Book III: ibid., 1:113. Cf. *Fingal,* Book I: ibid., 17; *Cath-Loda:* ibid., 2:317–18.

53. Ibid., 1:358; 2:190.

54. Ibid., 1:51. Cf. the ending of *The War of Caros,* ibid., 249–50.

55. J. W. von Goethe, *Faust* (Wiesbaden: Insel, 1959), 149.

56. Lines 398–409: ibid., 150.

57. Ibid., 151.

58. Lines 656–59: ibid., 157. In *Faust* part II, the same stage direction gives the title to the first scene of act II, and the room is "unchanged" — except that the windows are dustier, there are more spiders' webs, etc., as Mephistopheles points out. He is pleased by what Faust disliked: swarms of insects emerge from the old fur that he has shaken, they greet him in unison, and he sends them back to the jars, parchments, broken vases, and skulls' eye-holes, playing on the double meaning of the word *Grillen* ("crickets" and "whims") that are forever at home "in such medley and musty life" (ibid., 344–45).

59. Lines 668–69, 674–75: ibid., 158.

60. Lines 676–79: ibid.

61. Lines 682–85: ibid.

62. Line 582: ibid., 155. All the quoted imagery is enhanced by contrast (however the evocations of the Macrocosm and of the Spirit of the Earth are interpreted) by the grandiose metaphoric imagery summoned by them. In it "operating nature," opposing an inoperative culture, shows itself as an infinite universal functionality: "How celestial powers rise and descend / And hand each other golden buckets!" (lines 441, 449–50: ibid., 151); "So do I work at the whirling loom of time / And weave the living clothing of divinity" (lines 508–9: ibid., 153).

63. A. de Musset, *Poésies complètes* (Paris: Bibliothèque de la Pléiade, 1957), 276, 277, 280–87, 289.

64. Ibid., 283–84.

65. Ibid., 285–87.

66. Ibid., 273–74.

67. For the uncanny as a typically post-Enlightenment, Romantic element (including this same example from Musset), cf. Orlando, *Illuminismo, barocco e retorica freudiana* (Turin: Einaudi, 1997), 15–17, 23–26.

68. Chap. III: A. Manzoni, *Tutte le opere,* vol. 2, bks. 1–3 (Milan: Mondadori, 1954), 2/1:44.

69. Ibid., 375.

70. Ibid., 45.

71. Ibid., 78.

72. Ibid., 125.

73. Ibid., 76; and cf. Manzoni, *Tutte le opere,* 2/2:42, and 2/3:80.

74. Manzoni, *Tutte le opere,* 2/1:190.

75. Ibid., 295. My emphasis.

76. Ibid., 477–78.

77. Ibid., 521–22.

78. Ibid., 579–80.

79. Auerbach, *Mimesis*, 491–92.

80. Chap. L: Ch. Dickens, *The Personal History of David Copperfield* (Oxford University Press, 1948), 716–17.

81. Chap. I: *The Oxford Chekhov*, trans. R. Hingley, vol. 6: *Stories 1892–1893* (Oxford University Press, 1971), 121.

82. G. Genette, *Narrative Discourse* (Oxford: Blackwell, 1980), 235–37.

83. *The Oxford Chekhov*, 6:130.

84. Ibid., 138.

85. Chateaubriand, *Génie*, 714–16.

86. Chateaubriand, *René*, in *Oeuvres romanesques et voyages*, vol. 1 (Paris: Bibliothèque de la Pléiade, 1969), 119–30.

87. Ibid., 136–37.

88. F. de Chateaubriand, *Mémoires d'Outre-Tombe*, vol. 1 (Paris: Bordas, 1989), 236.

89. Chateaubriand, *Les Natchez*, in *Oeuvres romanesques et voyages*, 1:437–38; *René*, ibid., 117–18; *Atala*, ibid., 36. The return to beloved places that are found devastated is a recurrent theme in *Les Natchez*: ibid., 301–2, 510–11, more generically pp. 437 and 465.

90. Book II: J. W. von Goethe, *Die Leiden des jungen Werthers* (Frankfurt am Main: Insel, 1973), 98–99.

91. Ibid., 98.

92. Cf. F. Orlando, "La Découverte du souvenir d'enfance au Premier Livre des 'Confessions,'" *Annales de la Société Jean-Jacques Rousseau* (1968): 156–57, 159–61.

93. Goethe, *Die Leiden*, 107.

94. Chap. L: W. M. Thackeray, *Vanity Fair* (Everyman's Library, 1970), 499–500.

95. Chap. LXI: ibid., 619–20.

96. Baudelaire, *Oeuvres complètes*, vol. 1 (Paris: Bibliothèque de la Pléiade, 1975), 47–48. Compare lines 3–4 to the line of Régnier: a precise proof of Baudelaire's reminiscence, ibid., 353–54 (*Mademoiselle Bistouri*).

97. T. S. Eliot, *Collected Poems* (London: Faber & Faber, 1936), 24–26. In the course of the third fragment, a quotation that began eleven lines earlier is closed.

98. In *The Waste Land* alone, cf. lines 20–30 (with the famous "A heap of broken images," "fear in a handful of dust"); 104 ("withered stumps of time"); 173–79 ("The river bears no empty bottles, sandwich papers, / Silk handkerchiefs, cardboard boxes, cigarette ends"); 187–95 ("Bones cast in a little low dry garret, / Rattled by the rat's foot only)"; 266–67 ("The river sweats / Oil and tar"); 292 ("Trams and dusty trees"); 381–89 ("There is the empty chapel, only the wind's home. / It has no windows, and the door swings"); cf. ibid., 59–84.

99. J.-P. Sartre, *Oeuvres romanesques* (Paris: Bibliothèque de la Pléiade, 1981), 15.

100. Ibid., 15–16.

101. Ibid., 79.

102. Ibid., 16.

103. Ibid., 52–53.

104. Ibid., 31–34.

105. O. V. de L.-Milosz, *Poésies*, vol. 2 (Paris: Silvaire, 1960), 133–35. The collection is *La Confession de Lemuel.*

106. As an example of the thinness of a nonetheless metaphorical, and not memory-related, example of the desolate-disconnected, I would point to some lines of *Notizie dall'Amiata* (*News from Mount Amiata*) in *Le Occasioni* (*Occasions*): E. Montale, *L'opera in versi* (Turin: Einaudi, 1980), 181–83; and inversely—that is, poetry in the strongest sense in the last published collection—a few lines of *Sul lago d'Orta* (*On Lake Orta*), 567.

107. *I nuovi iconografi* (*The New Iconographers*): ibid., 483; *Per finire* (*To Conclude*), 508 (from which the quotation is taken). On the "importance" of himself, cf. the second section of *Piccolo diario* (*Short Diary*), 793.

108. Ibid., 566.

109. The same with which the reminiscent-affective is contaminated—accepted, and bowing to the solemn-admonitory—by the "villas of the South Americans" in *Dov'era il tennis . . .* (*Where the Tennis Court was . . .* , one of the two prose pieces in *La Bufera* [*Storm*]): ibid., 215–16.

110. *La verità* (*The Truth*): ibid., 582. Cf. the sewer image, and the poetics grafted onto it, in an untitled text in *Satura II*, 388.

111. *Il repertorio* (*The Repertoire*): ibid., 393; and an analogous metaphor in *Quel che più conta* (*What Counts Most*), 475.

112. Ibid., 299.

113. *Poichè la vita fugge* (*Since Life Flies*): ibid., 701.

114. Ibid., p. 426: I am leaving out five lines. The "wooden bulldog" had already appeared in *Ballata scritta in una clinica* (*Ballad Written in a Clinic*), 210. Elsewhere, objects more laconically replace the subject: "What remained of the father was a mustache iron and maybe / An Evangelical bible" (*Lettera a Bobi* [*Letter to Bobi*], 454); "Of relics for you / That I don't know: calendars, cases, vials, and creams" (*La Belle Dame Sans Merci*, 344); an obvious relic is the old photograph (*Nel '38* [*In '38*], 699; *Quartetto* [*Quartet*], 700). Such promising titles as *The Lumber Rooms* (*I ripostigli*), 616, and *The Hiding Places II* (*I nascondigli II*), 683, are extraneous to our themes.

115. Montale, *L'opera in versi*, 310: I have omitted two lines. "Encrusted up to my neck" can be connected to "encrusted up to my hair" (*Dormiveglia* [*Dozing*], 615) and to "entangled up to my neck" (*La buccia della Terra . . .* [*The Rind of the Earth . . .*], 651). The brother's pieces of music are "Now buried in trunks or gone / To the pulp mill" in *Xenia I 13*, 293. Cf. the "Cabinet / That I have saved from clean-ups and floods" in *Retrocededendo* [*Moving Backwards*], 428.

116. VI, line 423: *M. Annaei Lucani De Bello Civili Libri X* (Stuttgart and Leipzig: Teubner, 1997, 148, and cf. line 615 (155).

117. Lines 420, 423: ibid., 148.

118. Lines 434–506, 507–69: ibid., 148–51.

119. Lines 511–12, 572–73: ibid., 151, 154.

120. Lines 440–41, 446, 527–28, 730–49: ibid., 149, 152.

121. Lines 461ff.: ibid., 149–50.

122. Line 434: ibid., 148.

123. Lines 492–99, 651–53: ibid., 151, 156.

124. Lines 436–37: ibid., 148.

125. Lines 509, 577–78: ibid., 151, 154.

126. Lines 637–51: ibid., 156.

127. Lines 670–84: ibid., 157.

128. Lines 529–69: ibid., 152–53.

129. Book 2, chap. 2: A. Radcliffe, *The Mysteries of Udolpho* (Oxford University Press, 1966), 178–79.

130. Book 2, chap. 5: ibid., 232.

131. Book 3, chap. 11: ibid., 479.

132. Ibid., 190, and cf. 177.

133. Ibid., 229–30, 465.

134. Ibid., 474.

135. Ibid., 343–48.

136. Ibid., 458. Cf. M. Bloch, *Feudal Society*, trans. L. A. Manyon (London: Routledge & Kegan Paul, 1961), 302.

137. Radcliffe, *The Mysteries*, 231–33.

138. Ibid., 258.

139. Ibid., 308–9.

140. Cf. especially act I, sc. 3, lines 39–43: W. Shakespeare, *Tragedies* (Oxford University Press, 1912), 558.

141. Ibid., 597.

142. Ibid., 555.

143. Ibid., act IV, sc. 1: 593–94.

144. Ibid., 595.

145. Ibid., 594.

146. F. de Rojas, *La Celestina* (Madrid: Cátedra, 1991), 103.

147. Act I: ibid., 110.

148. Ibid., 181, and cf. (in the five additional acts) passages related to the bravo Centurio's house, 314, and to the servant Sosia's clothes, 318–19.

149. Act I: ibid., 111.

150. Act I: ibid., 112.

151. Ibid., 111, 113.

152. Act III: ibid., 146–47. May-water (*agua de mayo*) is an aphrodisiac.

153. Act VII: ibid., 196.

154. Ibid., 147–48.

155. Ibid., 113.

156. Ibid., 153–54, 162, 171.

157. Act IV: ibid., 164.

158. Cf. Orlando, *Toward a Freudian Theory of Literature, With an Analysis of Racine's "Phèdre"* (Baltimore: Johns Hopkins University Press, 1978), 196–98; *Illuminismo*, 15–17.

159. Ch. R. Maturin, *Melmoth the Wanderer* (Lincoln: University of Nebraska Press, 1966), 223–36; allowing for the specifics of the case, it nevertheless seems impossible not to apply the Freudian concept of denial to the note on p. 233 (chap. 17).

160. Ibid., 7–8.

161. Ibid., 19–20, 379.

162. Ibid., 297, 300–2.

163. Chap. XIII: ibid., 201–2.

164. Ibid., 203–5.

165. Ibid., 206–8.

166. Ibid., 205, 207, 406.

167. E. T. A. Hoffmann, *Sämtliche poetischen Werke,* vol. 1: *Phantasiestücke* (Berlin and Darmstadt: Tempel, 1963), 23.

168. Ibid.

169. Ibid., 17–18.

170. Ibid., 24.

171. Ibid., 18, 20, 27.

172. Ibid., 25.

173. Ibid., 27.

174. Preface to *The Aspern Papers, The Turn of the Screw, The Liars, The Two Faces:* H. James, *Literary Criticism. French Writers. Other European Writers. The Prefaces to the New York Edition* (New York: Library of America, 1984), 1181–89; H. James, *Complete Stories: 1892–1898* (New York: Library of America, 1996), 635, and cf. 731.

175. *Three Essays on Sexuality, II:* S. Freud, *The Standard Edition of the Complete Psychological Works,* vol. 7 (London: Hogarth, 1953), 191.

176. Starting point of the well-known debate: E. Wilson, *The Ambiguity of Henry James,* in *The Triple Thinkers* (Penguin, 1962), 102–50, esp. 102–9, 141–43.

177. James, *Complete Stories: 1892–1898,* 639.

178. Chap. I: ibid., 645–46.

179. Ibid., 636, 641.

180. Chap. III: ibid., 653.

181. Ibid., 655.

182. Chap. X: ibid., 687.

183. Ibid., 693.

184. B. Stoker, *Dracula* (Oxford University Press, 1983), 240–41, 319.

185. Ibid., 14–53 (in particular 14–16, 19, 26, 34, 35, 46–48).

186. Ibid., 315, 319, 320–21, 340.

187. Ibid., 36.

188. Ibid., 241.

189. Chap. II: ibid., 23–24.

190. Ibid., 250 (249–539).

191. Ibid., 297, and cf. 228, 264–65, 299–301.

192. Ibid., 196–97, 200.

193. Ibid., 292, 321.

194. Ibid., 186, and cf. 191–92 for developments concerning Charcot and hypnosis.

195. Ibid., 238.

196. Ibid., 164 (cf. earlier 5, 28, 33); 130; 209–10.

197. Ibid., 242, 274, 291–92, 298, 300–301.

198. Ibid., 313.

199. Ibid., 241.

200. *Communicating Vessels:* A. Breton, *Oeuvres complètes*, vol. 2 (Paris: Bibliothèque de la Pléiade, 1992), 120, 129–33, and illustration p. 121.

201. Stoker, *Dracula*, 31.

202. Ibid., 300–301.

203. Ibid., 12–13, 21–22; 47.

204. Act I, sc. IV: W. Shakespeare, *Histories and Poems* (Oxford University Press, 1912), 762.

205. T. Gray, *Poems, Letters and Essays* (Everyman's Library, 1963), 28–29.

206. Ibid., 30.

207. Ibid., 31–32.

208. *Biblia Sacra juxta Vulgatam Clementinam* (Rome, Tournai, and Paris: Desclée et Socii, 1947), 866.

209. Ibid., 897–98.

210. Cf. Is. XV:6, ibid., 869, against Moab; Is. XIX:5–7, 873, against Egypt.

211. Ibid., 1037. Cf. Is. XIV:22–23, 868, against Babylon; Is. XVII:2, 871, against Damascus; Jer. XLIX:33, 1020, against the "Arabs" (Kedar). More complex are the examples in Zeph. II:9 and 13–15, 1208–9, against Moab, Ammon, and Assyria; Jer. L:39–40, 1033, against Babylon. Curses of uninhabitability without mention of animals, Jer. LI:43, 1037, against Babylon; Ez. XXXV:3–4, 7, 9, 14–15, 1113, against Edom.

212. Cf. Is. XIII:19; Jer. L:40; Zeph. II:9.

213. Jer. IX:10–11, ibid., 969; and cf. Is. XVII:10, 885; Is. XXXII:13–14, 894.

214. Is. XXXV:7, 9, ibid., 898.

215. The two lines following those quoted emphasize the idea that the land is eternally theirs: Is. XXXIV:16–17; "none of them shall be missing; one shall not seek the other."

216. XVIII, oct. 85–101: G. B. Marino, *L'Adone*, 2 vols. (Milan: Mondadori, 1976), 1:1102–6; XVIII, oct. 232–41: 1139–41. The comment by G. Pozzi refers to Giovanni Tarcagnota's *Adone* (1550), ibid., 2:645, 648–49; but the first source was a little ode by pseudo-Theocritus, *On the Dead Adonis*, in *Bucolici Graeci* (Oxford University Press, 1952), 166–7.

217. XVII, oct. 50, XVIII, oct. 43: Marino, *L'Adone*, 1:1043, 1091.

218. XVIII, oct. 67–69: ibid., 1097–98.

219. X, lines 710–16; VIII, lines 334–37: P. Ovidii Nasonis *Metamorphoses* (Leipzig: Teubner, 1977), 252, 185.

220. XIV, oct. 92: L. Ariosto, *Tutte le opere*, vol. 1 (Milan: Mondadori, 1964), 312.

221. Cf. *Jerusalem Delivered*, XIII, oct. 3, lines 5–8, and *Jerusalem Conquered*, VI, oct. 116, lines 1–3: T. Tasso, *Poesie* (Milan and Naples: Ricciardi, 1964), 321, 551.

222. Cf. *Jerusalem Delivered*, VII, oct. 28; X, oct. 61; *Jerusalem Conquered*, VI, oct. 115–20: ibid., 170, 264, 551. Here also "malign air," "barren soil," "unprosperous fields," "tepid waters," "horrible swamp," "unblessed ancient shores," "unfruitful bank," "sulfurous scorched strand." G. Pozzi's commentary (cf. Marino, *L'Adone*, 2:645) mentions Ovid as a source, rather than Tasso's lesser-known poem.

223. Cf. Book VI of the *Aeneid*, lines 268–330 (in particular lines 296–97, 323, 327): P. Vergili Maronis *Opera* (Oxford University Press, 1969), 235–37; and Seneca's tale of Theseus returning from hell in *The Madness of Hercules* (*Hercules furens*), lines 662–827

(in particular lines 686–89, 698–706): *L. Annaei Senecae Tragoediae* (Oxford University Press, 1986), 26–31.

224. D. Defoe, *Robinson Crusoe* (Everyman's Library, 1956), 38–39, 41–44, 48–49, 62–64, 139–41.

225. Ibid., 43, 63.

226. Ibid., 39.

227. Ibid., 43–44.

228. Ibid., 45–46; 130–31, where no mention is made of the money (and thus I interpret the later "I lugg'd this money home to my cave" etc., 141, as a reference to the first, rather than to the second deposit).

229. Ibid., 95–96, and cf. 94–95.

230. Tim. I, III:8: *turpe lucrum.*

231. Defoe, *Robinson Crusoe,* 120–21, 134, 151.

232. Ibid., 139–41.

233. Ibid., 142.

234. Ibid., 202 (confirming the supposition of note 228).

235. Ibid., 207.

236. E. A. Poe, *Poetry and Tales* (New York: Library of America, 1984), 560.

237. Ibid., 570.

238. Ibid., 562, 565–66, 567–68, 575, 585.

239. Ibid., 575; cf. 585–86.

240. Ibid., 578.

241. Ibid., 563, 583, 585, 593–94, 573.

242. Ibid., 572–73.

243. Ibid., 577–78, 583; and cf. M. Bonaparte, *The Life and Works of Edgar Allan Poe,* trans. J. Rodker (London: Hogarth, 1971).

244. Ibid., 562, 581, 586; 582; 592.

245. Ibid., 579–80.

246. Ibid., 595–96.

247. Bonaparte, *Life and Works,* 366.

248. Goethe, *Faust,* 453–54.

249. Ibid., 455, 457.

250. Lines 10212–21: ibid., 457–58.

251. Ibid., 457.

252. Ibid., 460–82.

253. Ibid., 487–89, 492–93.

254. Ibid., 499.

255. Chap. I: T. Mann, *Erzählungen* (Oldenburg: Fischer, 1959), 447.

256. Ibid., 449, 457.

257. Ibid., 474.

258. Ibid., 472, 480.

259. *Three Essays on Sexuality,* 1:144 n. 1 (the first paragraph is an addition of 1909); *Leonardo da Vinci and a Memory of his Childhood*: S. Freud, *The Standard Edition of the Complete Psychological Works,* vol. 11 (London: Hogarth, 1957), 98–101.

260. Mann, *Erzählungen,* 493–94, 496–97, 498.

261. Ibid., 472, 479, 483, 503.

262. Ibid., 480.

263. Chap. III: ibid., 480–81.

264. Ibid., 458, 459; 500, 502, 520; 523.

265. Ibid., 499, 501, 508, 509, 517, 519, 521.

266. Ibid., 500–501, 514–15.

267. The second of the three is less relevant: ibid., 502–3.

268. Chap. V: ibid., 520–21.

269. Chap. V: ibid., 512.

270. Chap. III: W. Scott, *The Antiquary* (Everyman's Library, 1975), 31–32 (cf. 321–22, the sentence about the "museum").

271. Ibid., 24.

272. Ibid., 33.

273. The irregular building of Monkbarns (28, 331), and the romantic ruins of Saint-Ruth (152–53 et passim), as well as the gloomy Catholic castle of Glenallan (259, 261, 263), are little developed in this direction.

274. Ibid., 156–57; 202–3; 214; 224–25, 395.

275. Ibid., 85–96.

276. Ibid., 142; and cf. p. 173, where he criticizes the architecture of the reign of James I.

277. H. de Balzac, *La Comédie humaine*, vol. 10 (Paris: Bibliothèque de la Pléiade, 1969), 69.

278. Ibid., 70–71, 72–73.

279. Ibid., 74–77.

280. Ibid., 79, 237. It is relevant to my argument that it is possible to trace in the Hoffmannesque antiquarian of *The Wild Ass's Skin* a prototype of the character of Gobseck — in whom capitalism takes on a human form.

281. Ibid., 69.

282. A. France, *Oeuvres*, 4 vols. (Paris: Bibliothèque de la Pléiade, 1984–94), 2:736–37.

283. Chap. IV: ibid., 738.

284. Ibid., 770; *L'Anneau d'améthyste* (*The Amethyst Ring*), XXVI: France, *Oeuvres*, 3:167 (163–68).

285. France, *Oeuvres,* 2:732.

286. *Le Mannequin d'osier* (*The Wicker Dummy*): ibid., 974–79; *L'Anneau d'améthyste* (*The Amethyst Ring*): France, *Oeuvres,* 3:149.

287. Part I, chap. IV: Flaubert, *Oeuvres*, vol. 1 (Paris: Bibliothèque de la Pléiade, 1951), 351.

288. Ibid., 357–59.

289. Part I, chap. VI: ibid., 359–60.

290. Ibid., 379.

291. Ibid., 504.

292. Ibid., 509.

293. Ibid., 641. We should consider also the image of the trumpets of fame, cut out from a perfumery advertisement, in the poverty-stricken house of the nurse (409); and the perfectly useless construction of half-moons and spheres which the tax collector Binet is finishing on a lathe when Emma visits him (604).

294. J.-K. Huysmans, *À rebours* (Paris: Fasquelle, 1955), 31–32, 261–62; 35–36.

295. Ibid., 32–33, 54–55, 266–68.

296. Ibid., 43.

297. Ibid., 122–29, 77–79; 51–53.

298. Ibid., 44–45.

299. Ibid., 181–82.

300. Ibid., 109–17.

301. Ibid., 40.

302. Ibid., 71–75, 82.

303. F. Scott Fitzgerald, *The Great Gatsby* (Penguin, 1950), 11.

304. Ibid., 95, 97.

305. Ibid., 187.

306. Ibid., 67.

307. Chap. III: ibid., 51–52.

308. Ibid., 98.

309. Ibid., 179–80. Cf. B. Franklin, *Autobiography* (Everyman's Library, 1964), 74–79.

310. Fitzgerald, *The Great Gatsby,* 174, 179.

311. Ibid., 154–55.

312. Ibid., 85.

313. Ibid., 88, 96–99.

314. Ibid., 117.

315. Ibid., 153.

316. Ibid., 12–14; though this applies less to the house Tom owns in New York for his mistress: 34–35.

317. Ibid., 126.

318. Ibid., 160, and in the context, "his ancestral home."

319. Ibid., 181–82 (and cf. also, for this character, ibid., 60–61).

320. Ibid., 29, 166 (and cf. 30, 32, 128, 130).

321. R. Musil, *Der Mann ohne Eigenschaften* (Reinbek bei Hamburg: Rowohlt, 1952), 11–12.

322. Ibid., 32–35 (the name comes from the official Austro-Hungarian abbreviation for the two adjectives "imperial-royal" or *kaiserlich-königlich: k.-k.*).

323. Ibid., 90–91.

324. Ibid., 190–91.

325. Ibid., 16–18.

326. Ibid., 14–15.

327. Ibid., 18–19.

328. Ibid., 13–14; cf. pp. 277–79, where the discomfort and inequalities of the mansions and palaces which have remained in the possession of the nobility are distinguished from the rational comforts introduced in others by the new bourgeois owners.

329. Ibid., 19.

330. Ibid., 19–20.

331. See, for instance, F. Nietzsche, *Beyond Good and Evil*, trans. R. J. Hollingdale (Penguin, 1972), 152–54 nn. 223, 224.

332. Musil, *Der Mann ohne Eigenschaften*, 20–21; cf. 30, where Ulrich's residence, glimpsed at by night by Bonadea, appears to her "unexpectedly beautiful."

333. Ibid., 128, 129–33.

334. Part I, chap. I: C. E. Gadda, *Romanzi e Racconti*, vol. 1 (Milan: Garzanti, 1988), 584–85; and earlier, 580. Pastrufacio is the capital of Maradagál. Sommaruga and Coppedè were architects working in Milan in the first years of the nineteenth century, Alessi is a Milanese architect of the sixteenth century. "PLM" are the initials of the Paris-Lyon-Méditerranée railroad.

335. Ibid., 673, 633.

336. Ibid., 746–47.

337. Ibid., 615, 639, 712; and cf. 640–43, 712.

338. Ibid., 722, 713; 631 and passim; 639.

339. Ibid., 619.

340. Ibid., 686–88.

341. From the point of view of Gonzalo: "All excuses are good, to the villa, to the villa!" (ibid., 659); of the swindling night guard: "Pull money out of the walls, in the villa. From all villas!" (669); of the mother: "all that was born from the Villa, or from the Villa-Idea . . ." (706); of the father: "For my children, the villa . . . ," "for the future the villa, the villa" (728–29). Or, for everyone, from the author's point of view: "The head of the library . . . who, it goes without saying, owned a villa . . ." (606); "The embrace of the villa — of each person's own villa, of course . . ." (624).

342. *Adalgisa:* ibid., 404 n. 4; Flaubert, *Oeuvres*, vol. 2 (Paris: Bibliothèque de la Pléiade, 1952), 102.

343. Gadda, *Romanzi e Racconti*, 1:404 nn. 1, 3.

344. Ibid., 740. Cf., in *Cinema* (*The Philosophers' Madonna* [*La Madonna dei filosofi*]), the Corso Garibaldi "winding and covered in peanut shells, flattened cigarette butts, spit of every *color and consistency* . . ." (ibid., 59: my emphasis).

Chapter V. Twelve Categories Not to Be Too Sharply Distinguished

1. G. Leopardi, *Tutte le opere: Le poesie e le prose*, 3 vols. (Milan: Mondadori, 1940), 1:76–77. In the *Zibaldone di pensieri*, 57 (2 vols. [Milan: Garzanti, 1991], 1:78, and cf. 3:499n), the same letter of Werther I discussed above (9 May 1772) is cited with approval.

2. V, oct. 10, lines 4–8: L. Ariosto, *Tutte le opere*, vol. 1 (Milan: Mondadori, 1964), 83. I could also mention, within the same line of reasoning, the "rotten houses," "broken house," "old walls," "broken hostel," where the Maganzesi are hiding and where Marfisa hunts them out in the third of the *Five Cantos*, oct. 102, 109, 111; L. Ariosto, *Cinque canti* (Turin: Einaudi, 1977), 91, 93.

3. II, 7: G. Boccaccio, *Tutte le opere*, vol. 4 (Milan: Mondadori, 1976), 170 (169–71).

4. Part II, chap. LV: M. de Cervantes, *Segunda parte del Ingenioso Caballero Don Quijote de la Mancha*, vol. 2 (Madrid: Cátedra, 1977), 439 [439–43].

5. Act IV, sc. VI: Corneille, *Oeuvres complètes*, vol. 1 (Paris: Bibliothèque de la Pléiade, 1980), 667.

6. X, oct. 29, lines 1–4: Tasso, *Poesie* (Milan and Naples: Ricciardi, 1964), 255 (255–57).

7. VI *Giuseppe Caponsacchi*, lines 515–17: R. Browning, *The Ring and the Book* (Everyman's Library, 1968), 215.

8. Chap. V: I. Svevo, *Romanzi* (Milan: Mondadori, 1985), 749–50.

9. The direct source of the four lines quoted is Boccaccio, *Decameron*, IV, 1 (*Tutte le opere*, 4:356), where the cave, so long unused "that almost no one remembered its existence," possesses a full narrative functionality for the loves of Ghismonda and Guiscardo; so do the expressions "secret steps" and, further on (360), "most secret way." If there is a minimal degree of lingering, it tends towards the sense of the sterile-noxious: Tasso not only increases it, but has also oriented it in a different direction.

10. V, 18: La Fontaine, *Oeuvres complètes*, vol. 1 (Paris: Bibliothèque de la Pléiade, 1991), 200–201.

11. VIII, 22: ibid., 332.

12. XI, 9: ibid., 443.

13. Leopardi, *Tutte le opere: Le poesie e le prose*, 1:44–45.

14. P. B. Shelley, *Poems*, vol. 1 (Everyman's Library, 1953), 330.

15. J. Keats, *Poetical Works* (Oxford University Press, 1956), 209.

16. Part I, chap. IV: G. de Nerval, *Oeuvres complètes*, vol. 3 (Paris: Bibliothèque de la Pléiade, 1993), 703.

17. II, line 363: *P. Vergili Maronis Opera* (Oxford University Press, 1969), 138. Cf. line 290, where Hector speaks in his dream: "Troy falls from its great height" (ibid., 136).

18. Act I, sc. II, lines 201–2: Racine, *Oeuvres complètes*, vol. 1 (Paris: Bibliothèque de la Pléiade, 1999), 204. Cf. lines 185–86: "Until at the foot of Troy's smoking walls / The bloody winners divided their prey" (ibid.).

19. Chap. XXXIII: C. R. Maturin, *Melmoth the Wanderer* (Lincoln: University of Nebraska Press, 1966), 383.

20. Chap. VII: M. Lowry, *Under the Volcano* (Penguin, 1963), 205.

21. Chap. V: V. Woolf, *Orlando: A Biography* (London: Hogarth, 1970), 226.

22. G. García Márquez, *Cien años de soledad* (Buenos Aires: Editorial Sudamericana, 1969), 97.

23. L. Aragon, *Le Paysan de Paris* (Paris: Gallimard, 1926), 17.

24. LIII, À M. de Neuilly: Ch. de Brosses, *Lettres familières écrites d'Italie en 1739 et 1740*, vol. 2 (Paris: Éditions d'aujourd'hui, 1977), 399.

25. Book VIII, chap. IV: H. Fielding, *The History of Tom Jones*, vol. 1 (Everyman's Library, 1963), 329–30.

26. Saint-Simon, *Mémoires*, vol. 8 (Paris: Bibliothèque de la Pléiade, 1988), 87–88.

27. Auerbach, *Mimesis: The Representation of Reality in Western Literature* (Princeton University Press, 1968), 414–33.

28. Saint-Simon, *Mémoires*, 8:85–86.

29. Ibid., 86–87.

30. Part VII: Chateaubriand, *Itinéraire de Paris à Jérusalem et de Jérusalem à Paris*, in *Oeuvres romanesques et voyages*, vol. 2 (Paris: Bibliothèque de la Pléiade, 1969), 1213.

31. Jornada III: Tirso de Molina, *El Burlador de Sevilla y Convidado de piedra* (Madrid: Estudios, 1989), 279.

32. Ibid., 280.

33. Cf. Th. Fontane, *Effi Briest* (Frankfurt am Main: Insel, 1977), 65–66, 71, 74–76, 85–98, 101–5, 119–21, 157–60, 205–6, 219, 247–48.

34. Here images of decadence abound, and may be differentiated by our categories: worn-realistic (W. Faulkner, *Sartoris* [New York: New American Library, 1964], 88–89, 94–95, 99–100, 120–22, 182, 227); reminiscent-affective (62–64, 85–88, 178–79, 242); desolate-disconnected, and similar lists of small objects (44, 77–78, 222, 276); magic-superstitious (107).

35. Cf. W. Faulkner, *Light in August* (Penguin, 1971), 29, 37, 42, 170–74, 174–81, 192–213; *Absalom, Absalom!* (Penguin, 1975), 6, 12, 31–33, 109–10, 175–77, 299–308.

36. We could go back to the first half of the second millennium B.C., with the Egyptian *Song of the Harper* from the tomb of King Antef: "They that built houses, / Their places are no more; / What has been done with them? / [. . .] / Their walls have crumbled / Their places are no more, / As if they had never been" (cf. M. Lichtheim, "The Songs of the Harpers," *Journal of Near Eastern Studies* 4 [1945]: 192). The theme of *ubi sunt* has allowed a scholar to compare a passage in Aeschylus's *Persian Women* with passages from a Babylonian text and from the Second Book of Kings—where only persons however, not buildings, are named (M. L. West, *The East Face of Helicon: West Asiatic Elements in Greek Poetry and Myth* [Oxford University Press, 1999], 552–53). We cannot go back any further than the last centuries of the second millennium, with the Assyrian-Babylonian dialogue (whether pessimistic or farcical) in which the master does not want to choose and the slave produces arguments for and against; in the following lines, the issue is why one should not perform generous acts: "Go up on to the ancient ruin heaps and walk about; / See the skulls of high and low. / Which is the malefactor, and which is the benefactor?" (W. G. Lambert, *Babylonian Wisdom Literature* [Oxford University Press, 1967], 148–49); we cannot know, the editor declares on p. 140, whether the first line quotes the beginning and end of the *Epic of Gilgamesh*—where the mention of great walls, however, does not at all entail the theme of transience.

37. Lines 818–20: *Aeschyli Septem quae supersunt Tragoediae* (Oxford University Press, 1955), 239.

38. Lines 108–9; 1317, 1319, 1322: *Euripidis Fabulae*, vol. 2 (Oxford University Press, 1981), 185, 229.

39. Book IX, nos. 104, 101, 103: *The Greek Anthology*, vol. 3 (London: Heinemann; Cambridge, Mass.: Harvard University Press, 1917), 52, 54. No. 28: 16; no. 151: 78; no. 62: 32.

40. II, lines 1144–45: *Lucreti De Rerum Natura Libri Sex* (Oxford University Press, 1922), unpaginated; II, lines 1173–74; V, lines 306–8.

41. IV, 10, lines 27–30: Propertius, *Elegies* (Cambridge, Mass.: Harvard University Press, 1990), 436.

42. *Life of Marius,* 40: *Plutarchi Vitae Parallelae*, vol. 3, fasc. 1 (Leipzig: Teubner, 1971), 253. The source, Velleius Paterculus (II, 19), is even more concise, too much so to be of any interest to us: C. *Vellei Paterculi ex Historiae Romanae Libris Duobus quae supersunt* (Leipzig: Teubner, 1933), 34–35.

43. IX, lines 964–69: M. *Annaei Lucani De Bello Civili Libri X* (Stuttgart and Leipzig: Teubner, 1997), 260; and cf. lines 961–63, 970–86 (260–61).

44. *Of His Return* (*De reditu suo*), Book I, lines 27, 47–164 (specifically, lines 95–104): *Minor Latin Poets,* vol. 2 (London: Heinemann; Cambridge, Mass.: Harvard University Press, 1935), 766, 768–76. One century later, Ennodius will praise Theodoric for

having made Rome young again by "cutting away the rotting limbs of its old-age": *Magni Felicis Ennodi Opera,* Monumenta Germaniae historica. Auctores antiquissimi, vol. VII (Berlin: Weidmann, 1885), 210.

45. Book I, lines 227–28 (Castrum Novum): *Minor Latin Poets,* 2:782; lines 285–86 ff. (Cosa), 788; lines 401–14 (Populonia), 798–800.

46. *Sancti Ambrosii Opera, Pars X, Epistulae et Acta,* 1, *Epistularum Libri I–VI* (Vienna: Hoelder-Pichler-Tempsky, 1968), 67–68 [VIII (*Maur.* 39), 3].

47. *Of the Destruction of Thuringia (De excidio Thoringiae),* lines 1–20: *Venanti Fortunati Opera Poetica,* Monumenta Germaniae historica. Auctores antiquissimi, vol. 4, part 1 (Berlin: Weidmann, 1881), 271.

48. See *Anglo-Saxon Poetry* (Everyman's Library, 1954, 84): I have used this modern English translation. My emphasis.

49. Cf. L. Mittner, *Storia della letteratura tedesca,* vol. 1 (Turin: Einaudi, 1977), 67–72.

50. *Beowulf* (Manchester University Press, 1997), 164–65.

51. XXX, lines 2101–14: banquet, harps, tales of far-off times, ibid., 134–35; XXIV, lines 2455–59: "a deserted wine-hall, a windswept resting-place bereft of joy," "no sound of harp, mirth in the courts, as once there was": 150–53.

52. XXXII, lines 2231–65: ibid., 140–43.

53. *Dum simulacra mihi:* cf. *The Oxford Book of Medieval Latin Verse* (1959), 221–22.

54. Ibid., 220–21.

55. *Purg.* XII, lines 61–63: Dante Alighieri, *La Divina Commedia* (Milan and Naples: Ricciardi, 1957), 532.

56. *Epistulae ad familiares,* VI, 2: F. Petrarca, *Le Familiari,* vol. 2 (Florence: Sansoni, 1934), 55–60.

57. *Rerum vulgarium fragmenta,* LIII, lines 29–35: Petrarca, *Rime, Trionfi e Poesie latine* (Milan and Naples: Ricciardi, 1951), 77. In the *Triumphus Temporis* (*The Triumph of Time*), a beautiful tercet lacks images to which we might apply the purest interpretation of the category: "Your greatness and your pomp will pass, / Seignories pass and kingdoms pass: / Everything is interrupted by mortal time" (ibid., 552).

58. From *Commentarii Rerum Memorabilium* (*The Book of Memoirs*): *Prosatori latini del Quattrocento* (Milan and Naples: Ricciardi, 1952), 680–83.

59. *Ad Ruinas Cumarum, Urbis Vetustissimae* (*Before the Ruins of Cumae, Ancient City*): *Poeti latini del Quattrocento* (Milan and Naples: Ricciardi, 1964), 1138–39.

60. F. Colonna, *Hypnerotomachia Poliphili,* vol. 1 (Padua: Antenore, 1980), 14–15 (and 15–50), 229–30.

61. II, lines 299–303: Petrarca, *Rime, Trionfi,* 626–27.

62. *About Rome* (*De Roma*): this text, and important variations drawn from later anthologies, can be found in R. Mortier, *La poétique des ruines en France: Ses origines, ses variations de la Renaissance à Victor Hugo* (Geneva: Droz, 1974), 47–48 (on the fortune of the epigram, 46–55). Cf. J. Du Bellay, in *Poètes du XVIe siècle* (Paris: Bibliothèque de la Pléiade, 1953), 419–20; E. Spenser, *Poetical Works* (Oxford University Press, 1957), 509; F. de Quevedo, *Obras completas: Poesía original,* vol. 1 (Barcelona: Planeta, 1963), 258–59 (*To Rome Buried by Her Ruins* [*A Roma sepultada en sus ruinas*]).

63. *Poètes du XVI Siècle,* 419–20. In the rest of the collection, the range of our category almost coincides with the variety of "disappointment": cf. the sonnets *Who will wish to see* (*Qui voudra voir,* with a necromantic comparison), 420; *Sacred hills* (*Sacrés coteaux;* cf. IV, 6, note 26), 421; *Pale spirits* (*Pâles Esprits*), 424; *That I have not yet* (*Que n'ai-je encore,* containing the verse "the stony bones of these ancient walls"), 428; *You who of Rome* (*Toi qui de Rome*), 429; *Who has sometimes seen* (*Qui a vu quelquefois,* containing the oxymoron "old dusty honor"), ibid. And in the *Regrets: If I go up to the Palace* (*Si je monte au Palais,* for the last tercet), 477; *Wherever I look* (*Où que je tourne l'oeil*), 488; *Ronsard, I have seen the pride* (*Ronsard, j'ai vu l'orgueil,* quatrains), 516–17.

64. Du Bellay, *La Deffence et l'Illustration de la Langue françoyse* (Paris: Didier, 1948), 113.

65. Spenser, *Poetical Works,* 471–73 (the short poem occupies pages 471–78; the title of the collection is: *Complaints: Containing Sundrie Small Poems of the World Vanitie*).

66. XV, oct. 20, lines 1–6: Tasso, *Poesie,* 370. The precedent is an octave from Boiardo's *Orlando innamorato* (Book II, canto XXVII, oct. 45) where Brandimarte lands near Carthage — which was almost Rome's equal: "You see nothing of her now, except dryness, / Pomp and civilization are lost; / And the great triumphs and superb haughtiness / Have been taken away by fortune, and the name barely survives": M. M. Boiardo, *Orlando innamorato, Amorum Libri,* vol. 2 (Turin: Utet, 1966), 436.

67. Act V, sc. III: J. Webster and J. Ford, *Selected Plays* (Everyman's Library, 1961), 176.

68. M. de Montaigne, *Journal de Voyage en Italie* (Paris: Les Belles Lettres, 1946), 211–13.

69. À Monseigneur le Cardinal de la Valette, 3 June 1623: G. de Balzac, *Lettres* (Paris: Banqueteau, 1634), 21–22.

70. Part III, chap. 1: Bossuet: *Discourse on Universal History* (*Discours sur l'Histoire Universelle*), in *Oeuvres* (Paris: Bibliothèque de la Pléiade, 1961), 952.

71. Chap. IX: Voltaire, *Romans et contes* (Paris: Bibliothèque de la Pléiade, 1979), 395–96.

72. XLV, À M. de Quintin: De Brosses, *Lettres familières,* 2:215.

73. Ibid., 216.

74. Night IX: E. Young, *The Poetical Works,* vol. 1 (London: Bell and Daldy, n.d.), 227–28.

75. W. Goethe, *Poetische Werke,* vol. 1, *Gedichte* (Stuttgart: Cotta, n.d.), 379–86. In the anonymous *Bonaventura's Wakes* (*Nachtwachen von Bonaventura,* 1805) what is refused is not the solemn-admonitory, nor even the venerable-regressive, as the exemplariness of the ancient world: but rather the new public and learned institution which will if anything concern the prestigious-ornamental — the museum. The refunctionalization of the remains of the past — not meditative nor ideological but cultural and aesthetic — is simply a profanation. And a Romantic irony of protest and renunciation leaves it to the threadbare-grotesque: the statues that represented supreme human beauty are reduced to "cripples without arms or legs, some of them deprived of heads"; they were exhumed from Herculaneum and the bed of the Tiber as "corpses and torsos." "An invalid asylum for immortal gods and heroes . . ." They can only be admired at the expense of nature (there is even someone who kisses the perfect backside of a Venus); the

choice would be either to adore these remains or to bury them again (Wake XIII: Bona-ventura, *Nachtwachen* [Stuttgart: Reclam, 1964], 108, 109–10 [107–11]). On the other hand, the sentences Hegel devotes to the "ruins of an ancient sovereignty" sound like a retrospective sanction of the entire tradition, in the *Lectures on the Philosophy of History* (Introduction, III c: G. W. F. Hegel, *Vorlesungen über die Philosophie der Geschichte* [Stuttgart: Reclam, 1961], 129).

76. *Invocation:* Volney, *Oeuvres,* vol. 1 (Paris: Fayard, 1989), 169–70.

77. Chap. I: ibid., 172–73; chap. II: 175–79.

78. Vol. V, chap. III: L. Sterne, *Tristram Shandy* (London and Glasgow: Collins, 1955), 272–74, with a complete translation and an amusing misunderstanding of Uncle Toby's: within the entire context, the parodic imitation of the solemn-admonitory does not corre-spond, of course, to the threadbare-grotesque.

79. Book IV: Chateaubriand, *Oeuvres romanesques et voyages,* 2:158–59.

80. Canto IV, stanzas 44–46: G. Byron, *The Poetical Works* (Oxford University Press, 1959), 233 and 888n. Throughout this poem, I can provide continuous examples of the transformation of the solemn-admonitory into the venerable-regressive: cf. I, 7 (181); I, 23 (184); II, 6 (195); II, 11–15 (196–97); II, 53 (202); II, 86 (207); III, 46–47 (215–16); III, 65 (219); IV, 1–19 (227–30); IV, 25–26 (230–31); IV, 78–82 (237–38); IV, 104–10 (241–42). The long lingering on the Colosseum, IV, 128–45 (244–46), returns in *Man-fred,* act III, sc. IV, lines 8–41 (ibid., 404–5).

81. XVI, I: V. Hugo, *La Légende des siècles. La Fin de Satan. Dieu* (Paris: Bibliothèque de la Pléiade, 1962), 272 (268–76). Hugo the traveler's mournful antiquarian curiosities eventually reach to the category, within the ruins of the castle of Falkenburg; Letter XX, V. Hugo, *Le Rhin,* vol. 1 (Paris: Imprimerie Nationale, 1985), 276–77, 283–84.

82. Part III, chap. I: Flaubert, *Oeuvres,* vol. 2 (Paris: Bibliothèque de la Pléiade, 1952), 353–54.

83. Chap. XXXI: E. Wharton, *The Age of Innocence* (Penguin, 1985), 258; and cf. 260, 286–87.

84. Borges, *Obra poética. 1923–1977* (Buenos Aires: Alianza-Emecé, 1981), 383–84 (in *The Tiger's Gold* [*El oro de los tigres*], 1972), 426–27 and 459 (in *The Deep Rose* [*La Rosa profunda*], 1975).

85. *Diario del '72* (*1972 Diary*): Montale, *L'opera in versi,* 477. The *toriada* is the corrida: the *chime emanates,* as has been stated, from the entrance of Escamillo in *Carmen.*

86. Lines 383–84, 414–36, 453–55, 458–60, 466–70: *Aristophanis Comoediae* (Ox-ford University Press, 1906), 17, 19, 20.

87. Lines 82–84, 87: *T. Macci Plauti Comoediae* (Oxford University Press, 1904), 1:101.

88. *Metamorphoses,* VIII, lines 660–63: *P. Ovidii Nasonis Metamorphoses* (Leipzig: Teubner, 1977), 196. In his rewriting, La Fontaine employs greater irony (*Philémon et Baucis,* XII, 25, lines 61–68: La Fontaine, *Oeuvres complètes,* 1:504–5).

89. XCV, 8; CXXXV, 3–4; CXXXVI, 1–3: Pétrone, *Le Satiricon* (Paris: Les Belles Lettres, 1962), 100, 166, 167–68.

90. XXIII, 5: ibid., 20.

91. IX, 49 (and cf. VIII, 28): *M. Val. Martialis Epigrammata* (Oxford University Press, 1929), unpaginated.

92. There is almost what amounts to a double exception, both to the symbolic charge of the images, and to the prejudice that low images are nonserious, in a celebrated passage by Chrétien de Troyes. This is the episode of the Castle of Worst Adventure in *The Knight with the Lion,* where Yvain finds three hundred maidens weaving golden and silken cloth, in a wage-earning oppression which translates the textile industry of the twelfth century into the fairytale-like. A medieval worn-realistic? The clothes worn by the maidens, however, are of a piece with the human image of delicate necks and faces pale through hunger and poverty: "And at their breasts and elbows / Their clothes were torn, / And the shirts on their backs unclean" (lines 5195–97, in the context of lines 5182–85 and following: Chrétien de Troyes, *Le Chevalier au Lion* [*Yvain*] (Paris: Champion, 1982), 158 ff. As for the poverty of the protagonist's clothes in *Érec and Énide,* which is desired by the father's lower-noble pride, it is indeed described in more detail in seven lines (402–8); but the ensuing thirty lines on her beauty (411–41) form an overwhelming and symbolically extreme balance (as do, between brief reprises of the first image in lines 1548–50 and 1625–30, the forty verses on the magnificent attire the queen later gives her at court): Chrétien de Troyes, *Érec et Énide* (Paris: Champion, 1981), 13–14, 16–17, and 48–50.

93. CXXXVI: *Poètes et romanciers du Moyen Age* (Paris: Bibliothèque de la Pléiade, 1952), 1182 (cf. *Le Lais,* XVIII: ibid., 1139) and 1185.

94. *Decameron,* VI, 10: Boccaccio, *Tutte le opere,* 4:568–69. The proverbially huge cauldron of Altopascio was the center piece of a soup-kitchen.

95. XXV, lines 159–61, 175–78, 260–67: T. Folengo, *Baldus* (Turin: Einaudi, 1989), 852–53, 858–59.

96. Chap. I: F. Rabelais, *Oeuvres complètes* (Paris: Bibliothèque de la Pléiade, 1994), 10.

97. LVII and XIX: F. Berni, *Rime* (Turin: Einaudi, 1969), 159–60, 54.

98. Tractado II: *Lazarillo de Tormes* (Madrid: Cátedra, 1987), 47–48, 54–62.

99. Ibid., 63–64.

100. Tractado III: ibid., 74–75.

101. Ibid., 96–97.

102. Book I, chap. 1: H. J. Ch. von Grimmelshausen, *Der abenteuerliche Simplicissimus Teutsch* (Stuttgart: Reclam, 1961), 47–49. The weaver is Arachne, her thread is the spider's web; the material is paper, and there is a pun on St. Nicolas: *Niklaus = Nichtglas,* "no glass."

103. Book III, chap. XXIV: ibid., 363–65.

104. *Continuatio,* chap. XI: ibid., 626–36. Simplicius's attire, upon his return from his hermitage in the forest (98–99), is painted, and the portrait is stored among rarities and antiquities: 105–6.

105. M. de Cervantes, *El Ingenioso Hidalgo Don Quijote de la Mancha,* vol. 1 (Madrid, Cátedra, 1977), 85: *adarga* is an oval shield of leather.

106. Part I, chap. I: ibid., 89.

107. G. Galilei, *Scritti letterari* (Florence: Le Monnier, 1970), 502–3; cf. Orlando, *Illuminismo, barocco e retorica freudiana* (Turin: Einaudi, 1997), 67–68, 89–91.

108. *Romeo and Juliet,* act V, sc. I, lines 42–48: W. Shakespeare, *Tragedies* (Oxford University Press, 1912), 375.

109. *The Seven Little Doves* (*Li sette palommielle*), IV, 8: G. Basile, *Lo cunto de li cunti* (Milan: Garzanti, 1986), 800–803. Time is an old man with a very worn cloak "patched up with sewn cards with the names of this and that," who quickly chews whatever is at hand, "even the plaster of the walls"; his mother's hand "smells of mold and tastes moldy": 802–5.

110. Book I, 23–24: D. Bartoli, *La Cina* (Milan: Bompiani, 1975), 74–75.

111. Cf. Orlando, *Illuminismo*, 75–77, and chap. III passim (65–127).

112. VII, XIII, LVIII: Saint-Amant, *Oeuvres*, vol. 3 (Paris: Didier, 1969), 6, 11, 44 (1–78).

113. Book II: *Romanciers du XVIIᵉ siècle* (Paris: Bibliothèque de la Pléiade, 1958), 1063–66. Cf. also 953–54: chamber, furniture, and library of a miserly and foolish lawyer.

114. Act II, sc. I: Molière, *Oeuvres complètes*, vol. 2 (Paris: Bibliothèque de la Pléiade, 1971), 533–35 (the financial operation is explained by the editor in a note, 1388).

115. Canto V: Boileau, *Oeuvres complètes* (Paris: Bibliothèque de la Pléiade, 1966), 70–71, 216–17.

116. Letter CXLII: Montesquieu, *Oeuvres complètes*, vol. 1 (Paris: Bibliothèque de la Pléiade, 1956), 349.

117. D. Diderot, *Le Neveu de Rameau* (Geneva: Droz, 1963), 29, 95.

118. Act II, sc. II: C. Goldoni, *Tutte le opere* (Milan: Mondadori, 1960), 7:654–56.

119. Like the manuscript of the peace treaties between Sparta and Athens in Demosthenes' own handwriting (act II, sc. IX-X), and cf. Harlequin's caricatures (sc. XII); but also petrified fish and mummies from Aleppo (act III, sc. I–III: C. Goldoni, *Tutte le opere*, vol. 2 [Milan: Mondadori, 1973], 927–30, 933, 942–45).

120. Swift, *Poetical Works* (Oxford University Press, 1967), 476–80. In *A Beautiful Young Nymph Going to Bed* it is a prostitute who is disgustingly stripped, or rather taken to pieces: 517–19; and cf., for the excremental female associations, the theme and the last line of *Cassinus and Peter: A Tragical Elegy*: 528–31.

121. W. Scott, *The Bride of Lammermoor* (Everyman's Library, 1964), 81, 85, 90, 119, 122, 162 (the tower); 85; 123–29, 129–40, 256–69; cf. 333 (Caleb's end).

122. Let one example stand in for all: the parlor of the Peacock Inn (cf. Dickens, *The Posthumous Papers of the Pickwick Club* [Oxford University Press, 1948], 175–76 [chap. XIV]).

123. Chap. VIII: Ch. Dickens, *Martin Chuzzlewit* (Oxford University Press, 1951), 124, 127–31.

124. N. Gogol, *The Collected Tales* (New York: Pantheon Books, 1998), 397 (the uniform of Akaki Akakevich), 400 (the overcoat), 402–3 (the latter's worn state in the dialogue with the tailor, and the snuffbox of the tailor with its paper patch).

125. Chap. I: Th. Gautier, *Le Capitaine Fracasse* (Paris: Garnier, 1961), 5, 8, 9. The Castle of Sigognac is mentioned again while it is being abandoned: 46 and 52; and then the narrative returns to it at the end, finding it first in a worse condition: 458–62, and then happily restored: 490–95. By contrast, there is another well-functioning and prosperous castle: 85–90; and a deserted one, but not in ruins: 372–73, the background of nocturnal fears: 375–81, 391. We should add the threadbare-grotesque of the ancient titles of nobility, 225; of the clothing: 12, 14–15, 95, including a *poète crotté* worthy of

Saint-Amant: 295–96; of a swordsman's hovel: 303–6, with a list worthy of Régnier (cf. IV, 8).

126. Trilussa, *Tutte le poesie* (Milan: Mondadori, 1975), 129. The close connection between dialect and burlesque always tips Trilussa's obsolete objects towards the threadbare-grotesque, even when it is contaminated with the reminiscent-affective (*Memories of a chest of drawers* [*Ricordi di un comò*], 555–56), with the desolate-disconnected (*Demolition* [*Demolizzione*], 726), or with the solemn-admonitory (*Attic* [*Soffitta*], 853).

127. Chap. IX: Gadda, *Romanzi e racconti*, vol. 2 (Milan: Garzanti, 1989), 226.

128. Act II, sc. III; act III, sc. I: W. H. Auden and Ch. Kallman, *The Rake's Progress* (London: Boosey and Hawkes, 1951), 30–37, 40–42. I also mention, in the libretto by Giuseppe Adami for Puccini's *The Cloak* (*Il Tabarro*), the "strange objects" collected in her bag by Frugola (G. Puccini, *Il Tabarro, Suor Angelica, Gianni Schicchi* [Milan: Ricordi, 1918], 14–15).

129. XXI, lines 393–95; XXII, lines 184–86: *Homeri Opera*, vol. 4, *Odysseae Libros XIII–XXIV continens* (Oxford University Press, 1919), 161–62, 170; cf. XVI, lines 288–90, XIX, lines 7–9 (67, 112), and for Ulysses' bed, XVI, lines 34–35 (58). Perhaps the beggar's costume with which Athena transforms Ulysses (XIII, lines 434–38; XVII, lines 197–98: 16, 81) and the poor clothing of Laertes (XXIV, lines 227–31: 202–3) may be read, though more indirectly, from the same perspective; we should otherwise call it a worn-realistic of the Hellenic archaic age.

130. Lines 1010–13, and cf. 997–1004: *Aeschyli Tragoediae*, 319.

131. *Georgicae*, I, lines 493–97: *Vergili Opera*, 44–45.

132. VII, lines 391–99: *Lucani De Bello Civili*, 176–77.

133. *Annales*, I, 60–62: *Cornelii Taciti Annalium Ab Excessu Divi Augusti Libri* (Oxford University Press, 1906), 35–36.

134. *Annales*, II, 53–54, 59–61: ibid., 74–75, 78–79.

135. *Pharsalia*, VII, lines 397–99 (see note 132).

136. II, 6, lines 35–36: Propertius, *Elegies*, 138.

137. *Epistulae*, CVII: St. Jerome, *Select Letters* (Cambridge, Mass.: Harvard University Press; London: Heinemann, 1980), 340–42. Two centuries earlier, Clement of Alexandria had placed more stress on Christian exhortation than on the decay of the sites of pagan religion: "The old oak, venerated by desert sands, and the oracle which has here rotted together with the oak itself, let them be abandoned to the myths of the past" (Clement of Alexandria, *The Exhortation to the Greeks. The Rich Man's Salvation* [Cambridge, Mass.: Harvard University Press; London: Heinemann, 1960], 26).

138. *Liber I Machabaeorum*, IV, 38–40: *Biblia Sacra juxta Vulgatam Clementinam* (Rome, Tournai, and Paris: Desclée et Socii, 1947), 1236.

139. Lines 1–5: *Poema de mio Cid* (Madrid: Castalia, 1978), 75. In the *Filocolo* by Boccaccio (IV, 1), Florio recognizes in Tuscany a venerable-regressive more ancient than his own Roman paganism: a temple of "unknown strange gods." At its core, the reverent gesture is already humanistic which, in order to sacrifice to these gods, has him "remove the grass and branches and bushes, which through long disuse have grown over the ancient altar, and similarly clean and decorate the figures of the gods with new ornaments with a pious hand" (Boccaccio, *Tutte le opere, vol. 1* [Milan: Mondadori, 1967], 359–60).

140. Act I, lines 419–22, and act II, line 1060: Lope de Vega, *El mejor alcalde, el rey* (Madrid: Cátedra, 1993), 77 and 104. The one may say "that I am something, or was," the other "I am a gentleman, / Although poor: the ways of fortune," lines 578, 1361–62: ibid., 83, 114. Cf. the "ill-built little house" of the father, lines 202–4: ibid., 68.

141. Cf. lines 387–90: ibid., 76. *The Tellos of Meneses* (*Los Tellos de Menéses*) are, in León, "peasants / Although Goths," and even of the "blood of Rodrigo the Goth"; their coats of arms "do not fear time, nor are they conquered by oblivion": *Comedias escogidas de Frey Lope Felix de Vega Carpio* (Madrid: Atlas, 1946), 533, 525, 538, and cf. p. 517. The only pertinent object in the two parts of the drama does not sound threadbare-grotesque: the pants which Tello the Elder would like to dig out from old chests and wear, and which date back to the marriage of his grandfather: ibid., 546.

142. The region was considered a Spanish Boeotia. The dating is between 750 and 1470; *Obras de Lope de Vega*, vol. XXIV: *Crónicas y leyendas dramáticas de España* (Madrid: B.A.E., 1968), 396–97. Perhaps for the glory of the Catholic kings, unifiers of the faith on the peninsula (377), Lope claims anachronistically that the survivors had never been converted, and reserves a final baptism for them.

143. Act I: ibid., 358–61. The climax of the text is the long series of questions, worthy of a noble savage, which the old barbarian addresses to the captured lady: 371–73.

144. Act III: ibid., 396.

145. Part III, book V, chap. III: Chateaubriand, *Essai sur les révolutions. Génie du christianisme* (Paris: Bibliothèque de la Pléiade, 1978), 881–83. Cf., in *Memoirs from Beyond the Tomb,* the monastery of the Cordeliers transformed into a revolutionary club (book IX, chap. 3: Chateaubriand, *Mémoires d'Outre-Tombe*, vol. 1 [Paris: Bordas, 1989], 484–85). And cf. the church set on fire during the Spanish War in *Days of Hope* (*L'Espoir*): A. Malraux, *Oeuvres complètes*, vol. 2 (Paris: Bibliothèque de la Pléiade, 1996), 149–50.

146. Chateaubriand, *Génie,* 535.

147. The main thematic references are to the chapters on Christian architecture (part III, book I, chaps. 6–8: ibid. 797–802), on ruins (part III, book V, chaps. 3–5: 881–87), and on graves (part IV, book II, chaps. 1–9: 926–39). I add some shorter passages: the uninhabited stars, perhaps because of sin, "resplendent solitudes" (537); the mysterious American ruins (546–47); birds' eggs and human tombs (570–71); migratory birds and great ruins (572–73); the typical sounds of cloisters, temples, cemeteries, and crypts (788); the laboratories of atheistic natural scientists as schools of Death (818).

148. Ibid., 555–56.

149. Part III, book I, chap. VIII: ibid., 800–1.

150. *À l'Arc de Triomphe:* V. Hugo, *Oeuvres poétiques*, vol. 1 (Paris: Bibliothèque de la Pléiade, 1964), 936–48 (specifically pp. 937–38, 942–43; reversal of the theme: 943–45).

151. Chateaubriand, *Génie,* 801–2.

152. Chateaubriand, *Oeuvres romanesques et voyages,* 2:1477.

153. Ibid., 1142–44.

154. F. Orlando, *Infanzia, memoria e storia da Rousseau ai romantici* (Padua: Liviana, 1966), 79–105. I referred particularly to pp. 83–86, 92–103; the most pertinent quotations are from Chateaubriand, *Mémoires d'Outre-tombe,* 1, 168–69 (book I, chap. 7), 209–12 (book III, chap. 1), 212–14 (book III, chap. 2).

155. Orlando, *Infanzia, memoria e storia;* I referred to pp. 205–10; the most pertinent

quotations are from G. Sand, *Histoire de ma vie,* part III, chap. XI: *Oeuvres auto-biographiques,* vol. 1 (Paris: Bibliothèque de la Pléiade, 1970), 870–73, 886–90.

156. Chap. I: I. Nievo, *Le confessioni di un Italiano* (Padua: Marsilio, 1990), 6. I had shown the persistence of a vocabulary of discordance and interference in the picture Nievo paints of the local jurisdictions in the Friuli region of that era: 17–24 (reminiscent of Manzoni's edicts, that is, projection of the *ancien régime* in seventeenth-century, Spanish garb); even in the symbolic nose of the Chancellor, "aquiline, pug-nosed, hooked, and flat at the same time," "a Gordian knot of several noses aborted together," 9: cf. Orlando, *Infanzia, memoria e storia,* 206–7. Later on in the chronology of the novel, from the Napoleonic period to 1848, the Castle of Fratta truly becomes venerable-regressive à la Chateaubriand: it becomes antifunctional not only in its construction, but in its being destined to desolation and demolition, consigned to the reminiscent-affective of pilgrimages (Nievo, *Le confessioni,* 673–74, 725–27, 746, 848–49, 883–84). On Byron in Venice: "Poets are like the sparrows who willingly make their nests among the ruins" (817).

157. As an American of the Romantic generation, Poe is able to render the theme sinister without any historical implications: in the boarding school of *William Wilson* one is never certain what floor one is on, steps leading from one room to another are never missing, and five years are not enough to find out exactly where one's dormitory is (E. A. Poe, *Poetry and Tales* [New York: The Library of America, 1984], 339–40, 346).

158. Part I, chaps. III, V, part II, chap. VII: F. De Roberto, *Romanzi, novelle e saggi* (Milan: Mondadori, 1993), 501, 559, 851.

159. Orlando, *Illuminismo,* 217–18 (with quotations).

160. *Letters to the Editor of the "Censeur"* (*Lettres au rédacteur du "Censeur"*), V: P.-L. Courier, *Oeuvres complètes* (Paris: Bibliothèque de la Pléiade, 1951), 20–21 (18–22).

161. *Memoirs of a Tourist* (*Mémoires d'un touriste*): Stendhal, *Voyages en France* (Paris: Bibliothèque de la Pléiade, 1992), 312 (and cf. 15, 178 second note, 476), 149.

162. Chaps. II, V: Stendhal, *Romans,* vol. 2 (Paris: Bibliothèque de la Pléiade, 1952), 884–86, 928–31.

163. Part I, chap. XVIII: ibid., 314. At a later date, after the publication of the novel, the author himself confessed that he was susceptible to evocations of the Gothic, under certain conditions: cf. *Voyages en France,* 150, 192–93.

164. Cf. *Il recente e l'antico nel cap. I, 18 di "Le Rouge et le Noir,"* in Orlando, *Le costanti e le varianti* (Bologna: Il Mulino, 1983), 135–62; specifically 135–36, 152–55, and for other examples of Gothic architecture in the novel, 155–56.

165. Chap. II, stanzas 1–3: A. Pushkin, *Eugene Onegin,* trans. V. Nabokov, vol. 1 (London: Routledge and Kegan Paul, 1976), 125–26.

166. Books II, V: A. Mickiewicz, *Pan Tadeusz,* trans. G. R. Noyes (London and Toronto: Dent and Dutton, 1930), 42, 142–43; cf. 149, and the old house of Matyasz Dobrzynski, covered with plants and animals and scarred by gunshots and saber cuts, 168–70.

167. *The Coffee Pot* [*La Cafetière*], of 1831: Th. Gautier, *Récits fantastiques* (Paris: Flammarion, 1981), 56; *Omphale, A Rococo History* [*Omphale, histoire rococo*], of 1834: ibid., 103–4 (for the interior, since the exterior is degraded to the point of being worn-realistic). Two passages from Musset's short stories are of a later date. The Louis

XV bathroom in *Margot,* of 1838: A. de Musset, *Oeuvres complètes en prose* (Paris: Bibliothèque de la Pléiade, 1960), 538; Versailles during the reign of Louis XV in *The Beauty Mark (La Mouche),* of 1853: ibid., 664–65, 666–67, 676 (and cf. the poem *On Three Steps of Pink Marble [Sur trois marches de marbre rose]*: Musset, *Poésies complètes* (Paris: Bibliothèque de la Pléiade, 1957), 454–59).

168. Chaps. I, IX: Th. Gautier, *Mademoiselle de Maupin* (Paris: Garnier, 1955), 55–6, 186–87. Cf. another castle whose architectural disorder returns us to the theme dealt with immediately before: 119–21; statues, stairs, broken and moss-grown vases: 206–78.

169. G. de Nerval, *Oeuvres complètes,* vol. 1 (Paris: Bibliothèque de la Pléiade, 1989), 339. The image of the castle, dating this time to Henri IV, reappears twenty years later in *Sylvie* (chap. II): Nerval, *Oeuvres complètes,* 3:541.

170. Hugo, *Oeuvres poétiques,* 1:970–71 (in *The Inner Voices [Les Voix intérieures]*): the poem is of 1835. Cf. *The Statue (La Statue)* of 1837 (in *The Rays and the Shadows [Les Rayons et les ombres]*), ibid., 1105–8.

171. É. Zola, *Les Rougon-Macquart,* vol. 1 (Paris: Bibliothèque de la Pléiade, 1960), 1248, 1251, 1316, 1354–56, 1394–96 for the interior; 1346–47, 1351–52 for the exterior, and 1358 with lizards on the ruins of the burnt castle. The luxuriant vegetation of the Paradou passes beyond natural healthiness towards the sterile-noxious: 1252–53, 1327–30, 1345–47, 1351, and cf. 1404–5. The orthodox instances of the venerable-regressive are less interesting in *The Dream (Le Rêve)*: É. Zola, *Les Rougon-Macquart,* vol. 4 (Paris: Bibliothèque de la Pléiade, 1966), 826–27, 849, 859–64.

172. Chap. XVII: "What we call real estate — the solid ground to build a house on — is the broad foundation on which nearly all the guilt of this world rests. A man will commit almost any wrong [. . .] only to build a great, gloomy, dark chambered mansion, for himself to die in, and for his posterity to be miserable in": N. Hawthorne, *The House of the Seven Gables* (Everyman's Library, 1977), 254. Cf. specifically 1–2, 6–8, 23–25, 130, 252; developments towards the sinister-terrifying: 16–17, 267–72.

173. "The Custom-House": N. Hawthorne, *The Scarlet Letter* (Oxford University Press, 1990), 7, 12–16 (3–44). The author is tied to the place where his ancestors in the seventeenth century had been pioneers and judges of bloodthirsty austerity, by "a kind of domestic familiarity with the past" (8–10); the preface moves closer towards it as if through a series of containers. In the town that has declined commercially there is the decrepit dock, at the head of the dock the custom-house surrounded by grass, on the first floor the squalid office (4–7); on the second floor, an excessively large room whose walls were never plastered, where there are a number of barrels with bundles of official documents, which the floor is also covered with; these documents are "never more to be glanced at by human eyes" (28–29). One rainy day, poking through the names of sunken or rotten ships and merchants' names, by now illegible on their tombstones, the officer-writer has the feeling that he is bringing a treasure to light: wrapped in parchment, the papers of an eighteenth-century surveyor (whose skeleton and wig he knew to have been recently exhumed); among these papers there is a ragged piece of scarlet cloth in the shape of the letter A, and a dingy roll of foolscap sheets containing an exposition of the facts (29–33).

174. N. Hawthorne, *The Marble Faun* (New York: New American Library, 1980), vi;

"Romance and poetry, like ivy, lichens, and wall-flowers, need Ruin to make them grow," ibid. In a terrifying American short story of the end of the century, *The Death of Halpin Frayser* by Ambrose Bierce, we read of an abandoned country school: "It was ruined, but not a ruin — a typical Californian substitute for what are known to guide-bookers abroad as 'monuments of the past' " (*The Best of Ambrose Bierce* [Secaucus, N.J.: The Citadel Press, 1946], 199).

175. Hawthorne, *The Marble Faun*, 279–80; cf. further worn-realistic, 34–35, 136. The city where every stone bears some criminal imprint (no less than the macabre cemetery of the Capuchins, 144–45) belongs to the Gothic tradition: 296–97; it is possible to construct buildings that are almost immortal, but not to stop them from ageing "moldy, unhealthy, lugubrious, full of stenches of death, specters and stains of murders": 219–20. Rome is like a corpse and time is her gravedigger, 113; it is impossible to leave her without being physically and morally nauseated, only to return to her with familiar intimacy: 235–36; culture and climate would lead us to believe her ruins are much closer to us in time than the walls of an English abbey or castle: 124–25. The Italian Middle Ages are also represented by a "tower in the Apennines": 157–59; it has hundreds of rooms: 161–62; rotting frescoes: 165–66; abandoned prisons and owls: 185–86.

176. V: Flaubert, *Oeuvres*, vol. 1 (Paris: Bibliothèque de la Pléiade, 1951), 159, 173, 175.

177. Th. Hardy, *Jude the Obscure* (London: Macmillan, 1966), 18.

178. Part II, chap. I: ibid., 85–86.

179. Ibid., 90–91.

180. Ibid., 323.

181. G. D'Annunzio, *Tragedie, sogni e misteri*, vol. 1 (Milan: Mondadori, 1940), 937.

182. Act I, sc. II: ibid., 965. The theme of the home is constant: 938–42, 960–61, 989–90 (the parchments), 1040–41; the character of Gigliola is assimilated to things: 951, 1052. A countertheme is the nostalgia for a healthy environment: 991–92.

183. Ibid., 964–65, 1043–44, 1019–21.

184. C. Dossi, *Loves (Amori)*, (Milan: Adelphi, 1987), 23–25.

185. Chap. II: Th. Mann, *Der Zauberberg* (Berlin-Frankfurt am Main: Fischer, 1956), 21–22.

186. I. Babel, *The Complete Works*, trans. P. Constantine (New York and London: Norton, 2002), 663–65 (659–66). Dagmar was the name of Alexander III's wife and the mother of Nicholas II before she was called Maria Fyodorovna. Cf. the first very short version of 1922, *An Evening with the Empress*, ibid., 110 (109–11). In Pasternak's novel, in the middle of the Revolution a broken old *carillon* starts playing "its complicated minuet" again, suddenly and with traumatic effects (chap. VI, 11: B. Pasternak, *Doctor Zhivago*, trans. M. Hayward and M. Harari [London: Collins and Harvill, 1958], 182).

187. G. Orwell, *Nineteen Eighty-Four* (Penguin, 1954), 31, 33–36; and cf. 66–67, 199–200.

188. Ibid., 6–7, 29, 63, 73–77; and cf. 145 (the toast to "the past").

189. Ibid., 9, 78–83, 123–24. The shop participates in that worn-realistic which, scattered everywhere (7, 20–21, 51, etc.), characterizes the working-class neighborhoods (69).

190. Ibid., 112–15, 118–19, 177–80, 227–31.

191. Hugo's *The Hunchback of Notre-Dame* takes place in 1482: although the cathedral was built between 1163 and 1250, the author does not make the mistake of representing it as marked by time. Only in parentheses does he wonder if a tower was the same one which is visible *today* (1831) in its degraded state; and jokes about it with the same threadbare-grotesque used for the clothing of the poor poet and the miserly king, and for a procuress's apartment (V. Hugo, *Notre-Dame de Paris, 1482. Les Travailleurs de la mer* [Paris: Bibliothèque de la Pléiade, 1975], 250, 253, 426, 291). Thus the only contemporary worn-realistic is the sinister scaffold at the end of the novel — "which dated from 1328" (499).

192. W. Scott, *Ivanhoe* (Everyman's Library, 1962), 199–201, 412–13; 213–14; 28. There is a passage in which the historical novelist abstains from giving the names of five knights, for reasons of, and with images belonging to the solemn-admonitory: 94–95.

193. This ambivalence is formulated in quantitative terms, that is in terms of dosage, as I myself do in this book, in the masterpiece of modern Catalan narrative: *Bearn,* by Llorenç Villalonga (1961). Don Toni, the aristocratic intellectual protagonist from Majorca, at the sight of the ruins asserts that Rome is "too old. The same thing happens with wine, to be good it has to be old, it has to have the dregs in it. But take care that it does not have too much, take care not to overstep the 'mark.' Rome has overstepped it long ago"; part II, chap. X (L. Villalonga, *Bearn* [Barcelona: Club, 1961], 202–3).

194. G. Sand, *Oeuvres autobiographiques,* 1:872, and see above, note 155.

195. *Lucien Leuwen,* part II, chap. XLVIII: Stendhal, *Romans,* vol. 1 (Paris: Bibliothèque de la Pléiade, 1952), 1168. Cf. the way in which Dickens, in *Our Mutual Friend,* ridicules the members and the house of the nouveau-riche Veneering family with the adjectives "new" and "bran-new": "all things were in a state of high varnish and polish"; the style of the Podsnaps is different: "everything was made to look as heavy as it could, and to take up as much room as possible" (Ch. Dickens, *Our Mutual Friend* [Oxford University Press, 1952], 6, 131).

196. *Spirite,* chap. IX: Th. Gautier, *Spirite* (Paris: Nizet, 1970), 131–32. Cf. at the end of *Capitaine Fracasse,* the mixture of ancient silver with the new so that the recovered luxury "should not look too recent" (Gautier, *Le Capitaine Fracasse,* 495). But in the eyes of a prince from Catania in De Roberto's *The Viceroys,* indeed, in contrast to the luxury of the nouveaux-riches "the age of the furniture and of the liveries was like an added title of nobility" (part II, chap. VII: De Roberto, *Romanzi, novelle e saggi,* 852).

197. B. Brecht, *Gedichte und Lieder* (Berlin and Frankfurt am Main: Suhrkamp, 1981), 46. Brecht dignifies the worn-humble and worn-useful into a venerable without the regressive; according to the implications of the same ideology, that which is irreparably worn yields to hope as a refused venerable-regressive in a poem by Fortini, *The Eaves* (*La gronda*). It is not the irrationality of an entire building that is taken as a silenced metaphor of bourgeois society, but only the marginal space of a corner. Its structure of rotten wood — as the following stanza predicts — will one day collapse if a mere swallow perches on it: "I discover from the window the corner of the eaves, / In an old house, which is of corroded wood / And bent by layers of tiles. Swallows perch there / Sometimes. Here and there, on the roof, on the hinges / And along the pipes, pools of tar, mortar / Of miserable repairs. But the wind and the snow / If they wear out the lead of the gutter, the rotten rafter / They do not yet break it" (F. Fortini, *Una sola volta per sempre: Poesie 1938–1973* [Turin: Einaudi, 1978], 238).

198. Chap. II: Balzac, *La Comédie humaine*, vol. 8 (Paris: Bibliothèque de la Pléiade, 1977), 1026–27, and cf. 1030–31. We have a unique case in the wonderful tale which Balzac placed at the end of *Another Study of a Woman* (*Autre Étude de femme*: Balzac, *La Comédie humaine*, vol. 3 [Paris: Bibliothèque de la Pléiade, 1976], 710–29). The Grande Bretèche was a feudal residence, which the opening dwells upon in proportion to its dimensions, its dilapidation, and its mystery: it is obvious, and insufficient, that the images may be read no longer as worn-realistic, but as a rampant sterile-noxious of vegetation and animals. The interpretive uncertainty does not derive from a contamination of categories so much as from an "immense enigma," and moves hand in hand with the revelation of the "secret," or at least of the "caprice," which that ruin encloses or betrays (710–12). We learn that the will of the proprietress, a countess, has ordered that no one should enter the house, or repair it, until fifty years after her death (717); the atrocious revenge which the husband had carried out between those walls is traced back in time, letting us understand that the countess in her turn had avenged herself, as it were, on places and things. Only then may the sterile-noxious of curse and destruction become open to characterization (IV, 28). Just as the sumptuous exemplarity of aristocratic waste becomes *retrospectively* recognizable in the enormous holocaust of material goods, in "this kind of monumentalized sorrow" (712): along with this exemplariness, it is especially the venerable-regressive, refused, though not without admiration, which we recognize as well. The entire backstory confirms this, from the glacial vastness of the castle in which the countess is on the verge of death (715–17), to the unbreakable reticence and imperative munificence with which the conjugal drama is acted out (pp. 725–29). As the landlady says of the count: "When one's a noble, you know . . ." (719).

199. Chap. III: Barbey d'Aurevilly, *Oeuvres romanesques complètes*, vol. 1 (Paris: Bibliothèque de la Pléiade, 1964), 911, and the following paragraph.

200. For the first instance cf., in an order that goes from best preserved to worst preserved, A. Fogazzaro, *A Little Ancient World* (*Piccolo mondo antico* [Milan: Garzanti, 1989]), 105–6; L. Capuana, *The Marquis of Roccaverdina* (*Il marchese di Roccaverdina* [Milan: Garzanti, 1974]), 16–17; I. S. Turgenev, *A Nest of Gentlefolk and Other Stories*, trans. J. Coulson (Oxford University Press, 1959), 71–72, 73–74; B. Perez Galdós, *Tristana* (*Novelas y miscelanea*, vol. 3 [Madrid: Aguilar, 1973]), 359. In the Russian countryside of Turgenev, a decade before the abolition of serfdom, the gradation of decay of the landowners' dwellings ranges from neglected and outdated arrangements to bare wooden ruins which have reverted to wilderness: cf. I. Turgenev, *Sketches from a Hunter's Album*, trans. R. Freeborn (Penguin, 1990), 186–87 (*Two Landowners*), 294–95 (*Hamlet of the Shchigrovsky District*), 324–15 (*Chertopkhanov and Nedopyuskin*), 45–46 (*Raspberry Water*), 233 (*Singers*), 62 (*My Neighbour Radilov*). For the second case, France, *Le Mannequin d'osier* (*Oeuvres*, 2:908–9); D'Annunzio, *The Flame* (*Il Fuoco: Prose di romanzi*, vol. 2 [Milan: Mondadori, 1989]), 378–79.

201. G. Verga, *Tutti i romanzi*, vol. 3 (Florence: Sansoni, 1983), 424.

202. Ibid., 427.

203. Part III, chap. I: ibid., 519–20. The "unhinged windows" also appear in the other description, 341, and "toothless" applies as well to the cornice which first serves to introduce the building with the initial fire: 340–42; "shattered front door" recurs, 472, and the same attribute is used for an altar, 500. On 342 and 473, we find again a "dismantled building"; 477, "black flags, pierced and eaten by mice, with the Trao coat of

arms." The refusal to sell the house and the gradual closing of the rooms are laughed about by others, 346–47. Similar images and vocabulary for other aristocrats: the theater and small palace of the Rubieras, 348–49, 353; the stair of the *cavalier* Peperito, 408; the rooms of the Marquis of Limoli, 599; the only worn-realistic which is not reserved for the nobles is for the itinerant players, 495.

204. H. Melville, *Billy Budd, Sailor and Other Stories* (Penguin, 1970), 219–21, and cf. 251–53. The *Pequod*, the noble and melancholy ship decorated with whaling trophies in *Moby Dick,* is not only battered by time and by the sea, but is of an antiquated design (chap. XVI): H. Melville, *Moby Dick* (Oxford University Press, 1991), 70–71.

205. *Histoire de Gambèr-Aly:* A.-J. de Gobineau, *Nouvelles asiatiques* (Paris: Garnier, 1965), 148.

206. Balzac, *La Comédie humaine*, vol. 6 (Paris: Bibliothèque de la Pléiade, 1977), 361–62. My emphasis.

207. Ibid., 449–50. Similar to the room of a young, ambitious man like Rastignac: "The opulence and the poverty coupled spontaneously in the bed, on the walls, everywhere," in *The Wild Ass's Skin* (*La Peau de chagrin*, Balzac, *La Comédie humaine*, vol. 10 [Paris: Bibliothèque de la Pléiade, 1969], 193–94). In the luxurious disorder of the bedchamber of the Countess of Restaud, there is already "poverty, concealed underneath," in *Gobseck* (Balzac, *La Comédie humaine,* vol. 2 [Paris: Bibliothèque de la Pléiade, 1976], 972–73).

208. Chaps. I, VI: É. Zola, *Les Rougon-Macquart*, vol. 3 (Paris: Bibliothèque de la Pléiade, 1964), 4, 6–7, 110; cf. the corridor of the servants, 101. It is on the stairs, at night, that the silence of virtue is most imposing: 20, 292.

209. Chap. II: ibid., 27; and 54: "a luxury of flowers, of superb and costly roses, covered the mediocrity of the butter and the ancient dust of the biscuits . . ."

210. A. Moravia, *Gli indifferenti. Le ambizioni sbagliate* (Milan: Bompiani, 1967), 53 (the corridor in which "habit and boredom lay in ambush," as seen from Carla's viewpoint); 250 (her own room), etc.

211. Ibid., 71–72.

212. Ibid., 119–23.

213. Ibid., 78; cf. 75–76, 281, 294.

214. Ibid., 301–3, 304–5.

215. Ibid., 138, 196; cf. 204, 207.

216. *The Communist Manifesto:* K. Marx and F. Engels, *Collected Works*, vol. 6 (London: Lawrence and Wishart; New York: International Publishers; Moscow: Progress Publishers, 1986), 487.

217. Part I, chap. V: Flaubert, *Oeuvres,* 1:354.

218. Chap. XX: I. Turgenev, *Fathers and Sons,* trans. R. Freeborn (Oxford University Press, 1998), 137–38.

219. Part VII, chap. 24, sect. 2: K. Marx, *Capital: A Critical Analysis of Capitalist Production, London 1887. Text* (Berlin: Dietz, 1990), 510 n. 32.

220. Balzac, *La Comédie Humaine,* 2:1011–12; cf. 1009–10.

221. Chap. II: Balzac, *La Comédie humaine*, vol. 9 (Paris: Bibliothèque de la Pléiade, 1978), 684. The worn-realistic in the house of Balzac's most celebrated miser, Eugénie Grandet's father, is much more moderate: cf. Balzac, *La Comédie humaine,* 3:1039–41,

1069–70, 1071, 1074. Of the one-eyed miser in *Lost Illusions* (*Les Illusions perdues*) cf. the clothes, Balzac, *La Comédie humaine*, vol. 5 (Paris: Bibliothèque de la Pléiade, 1977), 507–8.

222. Book I, chap. XV: Dickens, *Our Mutual Friend*, 183–84.

223. W. M. Thackeray, *Vanity Fair* (Everyman's Library, 1970), 64, 65, 398; cf. by contrast 441.

224. M. Saltykov-Shchedrin, *The Golovlyov Family*, trans. R. Wilks (Penguin, 1988), 26, 35, in particular 64; 167, 240; passim.

225. Ibid., 59, and cf. 58.

226. Part I, chap. I: I. Goncharov, *Oblomov*, trans. D. Magarshack (Penguin, 1954), 15.

227. Ibid., 94.

228. Ibid., 19–22. Faced with the idea of moving, the positions are inverted and Oblomov takes upon himself all the pessimism and fear, cf. 90–93.

229. Ibid., 75–76.

230. Ibid., 127, 41. The uncollapsed part of the hanging gallery surrounding the house at Oblomovka survived, shored up with old scraps, 111, 126–27; in one of the villages, for generations a small cottage leaned on the edge of a precipice, 107. For Oblomov's parents the roots of sloth had been thrift, 128–29; for the son, it is the ideal of an overwhelmingly sheltered life, 376. Oblomov does not long survive the recovery of this kind of life, through his marriage with a modest housewife; but it produces a description in which order and domestic cleanliness herald the triumph of functionality: 461–62.

231. F. Dostoyevsky, *The Brothers Karamazov*, trans. D. Magarshack, 2 vols. (Penguin, 1958), 1:201.

232. Ibid., description of the whole, 105; of the dining room, 142. The night of the death he "kept walking from one room to another," 323; "He kept pacing up and down his empty rooms," 330; after his death, the children will not want to live "in their father's empty house," 2, 707. Rooms "entirely empty and not lived in," alongside pomp and gloom, are also to be found in the house of the merchant Samsonov, ibid., 433–34. Another well-known house of crime, sinister more than worn, and described less than evoked (cf. V, 3) appears in F. Dostoyevsky, *The Idiot*, trans. D. Magarshack (Penguin, 1958), 235–36, 238, 250, 254, 444–46, 642–43, 645, 649–52.

233. Dostoyevsky, *The Brothers Karamazov*, 1:117, 118, 260; 2:459; 2:719. The relationship between Smerdyakov and the inhabitants of the hut allows Alyosha to overhear him in conversation in the garden; and later, for him to be welcomed into the other hut where the dialogues with Ivan take place. Dmitri jumps over the wall in the very spot he knows the illegitimate son's mother had once done.

234. Exceptions, albeit heterogeneous: Capuana, *Il marchese di Roccaverdina*, 56; Sartre, *The Reprieve* (*Le Sursis*, J.-P. Sartre, *Oeuvres romanesques* [Paris: Bibliothèque de la Pléiade, 1981], 834); the stage scenery in act II of De Filippo, *The Voices Within* (*Le voci di dentro* [Turin: Einaudi, 1971], 29). The throwing of rubbish into the courtyard, which remains anonymous despite the investigations of the landlady, is a transgression in H. Böll, *A Clown's Opinions* (*Ansichten eines Clowns* [Munich: dtv, 1967], 158).

235. Chaps. IV, V: F. Dostoyevsky, *The Double*, trans. C. Garnett (New York: Dover, 1997), 25 (the words are repeated almost immediately, and later, 123), 38.

236. F. Dostoevsky, *Crime and Punishment*, trans. R. Pevear and L. Volokhonsky (New York: Vintage, 1993), 7–8.

237. Ibid., 24–25 ("the poorest of rooms": Marmeladov); 27–28 ("a tiny closet . . . , of a most pathetic appearance": Raskolnikov, and cf. 424); 315 ("The poverty was evident": Sonya); 503 (in a hotel: Svidrigailov).

238. The whole episode is marked by the category: the clothes of the child: Dostoyevsky, *The Brothers Karamazov*, 1:208; his father's house: 229–30; the church where his funeral is held: 2:906; his little boots after his death: 2:909. The brief but intense vision of the *izbas* under the rain, in a crucial moment of the main plot: 2:586; and also the dirty sheet of paper of Dmitri's letter: 726.

239. É. Zola, *Les Rougon-Macquart*, vol. 2 (Paris: Bibliothèque de la Pléiade, 1961), 413–16, 497; cf. the previous lodging: 464–66. On the other hand, at the beginning, Gervaise and Lantier's furnished room is miserable, as though it were a premonition: 375–76.

240. Chap. IX: ibid., 643–44, continuing with Gervaise, who by now is wallowing in filth; and cf. the final bareness of the rooms, aside from the unsellable rubbish and cobwebs (a hint of the threadbare-grotesque in free indirect discourse, all on the part of the character): 750–51.

241. *The Oxford Chekhov*, vol. 8: *Stories 1895–1897*, trans. R. Hingley (Oxford University Press, 1965), 195, 197; 221.

242. Of the first, we have a perfect short example in *The Old Curiosity Shop* (Oxford University Press, 1970), 78, and cf. 119–20; of the second (to confine ourselves to the same novel), repulsive images, and I would dare say the moralizing of the sterile-noxious, accompany the character Quilp and his wharf: 29, 43, 162, and cf. 503–10. In Balzac's *Lost Illusions,* immediately after a description of a room which refers to a previous description, the comparison is explicit: "How great a difference between this cynical disorder and the clean, decent poverty of d'Arthez?"; the later description, however, is almost twice as long as the earlier one (the subject is young authors and journalists): Balzac, *La Comédie humaine*, 5:312, 349–50.

243. Dickens, *Oliver Twist* (Oxford University Press, 1949), 35, 55, 128–29, 184, 277–78, 381–82; in the third, fifth, and sixth instances there are references to declassing of places ("it had belonged to better people"; "it had . . . furnished employment . . ."; "thirty or forty years ago . . . it was a thriving place").

244. Part III, book VIII, chap. VI: V. Hugo, *Les Misérables* (Paris: Bibliothèque de la Pléiade, 1951), 759–61.

245. Too beautiful and too long to be quoted in fragments, even in a note. La Masure Gorbeau: ibid., 445–47, 448–51, and in the subsequent narrative developments: 796–97, 800–801. The convent of Petit-Picpus: 476–77, 479–81 (what the images prepare here, save for the thematic constant, turn it into a kind of refused venerable-regressive). The Napoleonic elephant of Gavroche: 974–75, 978–79. The sewers of Paris: 1281–1300, specifically 1291–94. Some less noticeable, but all the more interesting, variants of the constant: the house which Jean Valjean rents in rue Plumet: 895–97, 902–3; the Bâtiment-Neuf of the jail, and the demolished house of rue du Roi-de-Sicile: 988–89, 992–93; finally, even the out-of-the-way grave in Père-Lachaise, 1486.

246. Flaubert, *Oeuvres*, 2:133–34.

247. Part III, chap. I: ibid., 365–66. See also the rubbish on the bridge of a boat, 36; the poverty of a restaurant, 55; the remains of a park and pavilion, 281. An instance of the worn-realistic with politically traumatic allusions, in the twentieth century: one of the last hiding places of the priest persecuted by anti-religious violence in Mexico is the banana house emptied of everything, "except the useless or the broken," in G. Greene, *The Power and the Glory* (Penguin, 1991), 142–45.

248. Cf., as relatively casual examples, the school-room in Dickens, *David Copperfield*, 77–78; the university in Chekhov, *A Dreary Story* (*The Oxford Chekhov*, vol. 5: *Stories 1889–1891*, trans. R. Hingley [Oxford University Press, 1970], 37–38); the country church, and the church in the old cemetery with equally old houses (and not without the solemn-admonitory), in Dickens, *The Old Curiosity Shop* (129, 348, 385–86, 397–98); the church and parish priest's house in Saltykov-Shchedrin, *The Golovlyov Family* (166, 190–91); the seminary in Stendhal, *The Red and the Black* (*Romans*, 1:376); the tax office in A. Strindberg, *The Red Room*, trans. E. Sprigge (London: Dent, 1967), 7–8; the police office in Stendhal, *The Charterhouse of Parma* (*Romans*, 2:200), in Dostoevsky, *Crime and Punishment* (94–95, 526), and in R. Musil, *Der Mann ohne Eigenschaften* (Reinbek bei Hamburg: Rowohlt, 1952), 158; the prison blocks in L. Tolstoy, *Resurrection*, trans. L. Maude (New York: Grosset and Dunlap, 1927), 119, 200, 205; the slaughterhouse in Zola, *L'Assommoir* (*Les Rougon-Macquart*, 2:768), and in Chekhov, *My Life* (*The Oxford Chekhov*, 8:149–50). Even in D'Annunzio's poetry the images of the port can only be ascribed to our category, even if they are endorsed by a poetics like the following: "nothing—was alien to me" (*Maia, Laus Vitae*, V, lines 127–51): G. D'Annunzio, *Versi d'amore e di gloria* (Milan: Mondadori, 1984), 45–46, and cf. 14; and by patriotic and warlike implications: *Merope, La canzone dei trofei*, lines 64–78 (ibid., 671).

249. *Lost Illusions:* Balzac, *La Comédie humaine*, 5:129–30.

250. *Greatness and Decline of César Birotteau* (*Histoire de la grandeur et de la décadence de César Birotteau*): Balzac, *La Comédie humaine*, 6:257–58.

251. *Lost Illusions:* Balzac, *La Comédie humaine*, 5:357. Cf. the moneylender's shop in *A Harlot's Progress:* Balzac, *La Comédie humaine*, 6:571. And cf. the shops of the Passage du Pont-Neuf, among which is the one where the action starts, at the beginning of *Thérèse Raquin* by Zola (Paris: Fasquelle, 1954), 15–18.

252. Cf. Dickens, *David Copperfield*, 154, 183–84; *Oliver Twist*, 184 (see above note 243); *Our Mutual Friend*, 352; *The Old Curiosity Shop*, 4–5, 13–14, and cf. 107, 217 (not devoid of latent sinister-terrifying).

253. Part I, book V, chap. VI: Hugo, *Notre-Dame de Paris*, 740.

254. Chap. I: J. Conrad, *The Secret Agent* (Penguin, 1975), 13–14.

255. The defenders of the law and the revolutionaries are made to converge here in their absurd delinquency by the whole plot, even if the professor had not identified the policemen with the terrorists, and the narrator had not identified them with housebreakers (ibid., 64, 82).

256. Cf. ibid., 38.

257. Ibid., 40, 127, 160, 174, 209, 213; and yet the shop has financial value: 52, 192, 221. The meeting between the chief inspector and the perfect anarchist, in a dark alley, takes place in front of another shop. It is a real one selling furniture, and is more sur-

rounded and marked by the worn-realistic, not without metaphors, 74 — as are the places where the subversives meet and live: 58, 59, 241, 242.

258. *Colonel Chabert* (*Le Colonel Chabert*): Balzac, *La Comédie humaine*, 3:313–15.

259. Dickens, *The Posthumous Papers of the Pickwick Club*, 427–29, and *Martin Chuzzlewit*, 175–76. A peculiar professional studio, which belongs to the category despite the fact that the workplace is the dining room, is that of the medium in Gertrude Stein's *Three Lives* (New York: Vintage, 1936), 59.

260. *Père Goriot*: Balzac, *La Comédie humaine*, 3:52–54 (159, the room of Goriot himself in the boarding house).

261. Ibid.

262. A few years apart, the same contaminations, with the threadbare-grotesque and the pretentious-fictitious respectively, differentiate two other law offices in Dickens and Balzac: cf. Dickens, *The Old Curiosity Shop*, 244 (and 260, 272); *Le Cousin Pons*, in Balzac, *La Comédie humaine*, vol. 7 (Paris: Bibliothèque de la Pléiade, 1977), 634–35.

263. *Père Goriot*: Balzac, *La Comédie humaine*, 3:52–54.

264. Ibid.; cf. the Paris hotel room in *Lost Illusions*, Balzac, *La Comédie humaine*, 5:257; the inns and the theater in Saltykov-Shchedrin, *The Golovlyov Family*, 273; the tavern in J.-K. Huysmans, *Down There* (*Là-Bas* [Paris: Plon, 1908], 267); the small room rented for adultery, and for the Bovary-style mortification of Luisa, in Eça de Queiroz, *Cousin Basilio* (*O primo Basílio* [Oporto: Lello e Irmão, n.d.], 233–5); the rented room, fundamental to the plot, in H. Böll, *And Never Said a Single Word* (*Und sagte kein einziges Wort* [Munich: dtv, 1980], 33–34, 54–55).

265. A perfectly explicit example, although serene and devoid of repugnance, in Pasternak, *Doctor Zhivago*, 141: "two rows of discarded wooden coaches. The rain had washed them clean of paint, and worms and damp had rotted them from inside, so that now they were reverting to their original kinship with the wood of the forest, which started just beyond the rolling stock, with its lichen, its birches, and the towering clouds above it" (chap. V, 10).

266. Chap. XXIII: Scott, *Ivanhoe*, 213–14.

267. *Eugénie Grandet*: Balzac, *La Comédie humaine*, 3:1040. Further down: "ribbons of golden wood, on which the flies had so licentiously frolicked that the gilding was a problem . . ."

268. Chap. XXXI: Dickens, *The Posthumous Papers of the Pickwick Club*, 427.

269. Gogol, *The Overcoat*, in *The Collected Tales*, 397.

270. Gautier, *Le Capitaine Fracasse*, 95. Cf. 12: "A kind of livery with faded galloons, and of a color which a professional painter would have had to make an effort to define"; and, more decisively threadbare-grotesque, for a pair of trousers: "Strong probabilities would lead one to believe that they had been red, but this important point was not absolutely proved . . ."

271. Part VI, chap. VI: Dostoevsky, *Crime and Punishment*, 503.

272. Chap. I: Zola, *Thérèse Raquin*, 18.

273. Eça de Queiroz, *O primo Basílio*, 256.

274. *The Good Anna*, part II: G. Stein, *Three Lives*, 59.

275. Chap. VII: H. Böll, *Und sagte kein einziges Wort*, 54–55. Further below, the topos that has opened the description concludes it, with the impossibility of recognizing the bears woven into the wool of the blankets.

276. III, lines 300–5, 333–36, 349–51: *Vergili Opera,* 162–64.

277. IV, lines 494–98, 648–51: ibid., 191, 196.

278. Act I, sc. II: W. Shakespeare, *Histories and Poems* (Oxford University Press, 1912), 96.

279. Just two of the many famous lines, in which renunciation is more tangible: "All pomp and majesty I do forswear; / My manors, rents, revenues, I forgo," ibid., 145. Another line tends towards the solemn-admonitory: "Let's talk of graves, of worms and epitaphs," 129 (and its echo will be heard, although in the mouth of a hypocrite, in Tourneur's *The Revenger's Tragedy:* "Talk to me my Lords, / Of sepulchres, and mighty emperor's bones, / That's thought for me": *Jacobean Tragedies* (Oxford University Press, 1969), 148.

280. Cf. IV, 15, note 92.

281. Book I: J.-J. Rousseau, *Oeuvres complètes,* vol. 1 (Paris: Bibliothèque de la Pléiade, 1959), 11–12, 24 (21–24): commented in Orlando, "La Découverte du souvenir d'enfance au Premier Livre des 'Confessions,' " *Annales de la Société Jean-Jacques Rousseau* (1968): 157–58, 169–71.

282. Part IV, chap. XVII; part V, chap. IX: J.-J. Rousseau, *Oeuvres complètes,* vol. 2 (Paris: Bibliothèque de la Pléiade, 1961), 517–19, 615. For involuntary memory cf. also Rousseau, *Oeuvres complètes,* 1:226 (and a passage from Alfieri's *Autobiography* [*Vita*] in V. Alfieri, *Vita, rime e satire* [Turin: Utet, 1978], 72: commented in Orlando, "La Découverte du souvenir d'enfance," 171–72).

283. For instance: in Sterne's *A Sentimental Journey,* the snuff box, a gift from the good old monk, is kept religiously — in its literal meaning — but does not appear to be worn; the love letters in La Fleur's pocketbook do, however, but they do not constitute memories (L. Sterne, *A Sentimental Journey through France and Italy* [Oxford University Press, 1928], 34, 85). In *A Journey Round my Room* by Xavier de Maistre (1794), with a promising title and theme, the serious lingering on distant letters and the playful lingering on the dried rose do not generate any substantial images (X. de Maistre, *Voyage autour de ma chambre* [Paris: Flammarion, n.d.], 70–71, 72–73). *The Flower* withered among the pages of a book, in a poem by Pushkin (1828), summons not memories but melancholy questions about the unknown (this poem is *not* included in A. Pushkin, *The Poems, Prose and Plays,* trans. A. Yarmolinsky [New York: The Modern Library, 1964]). Poetry, papers, letters, and memories of love are contained in the many drawers of a secretaire, in J. Janin, *The Dead Donkey and the Guillotined Woman* (*L'Âne mort et la femme guillotinée* [Paris: Flammarion, 1973], 71–74).

284. *Life of the Contented Little Schoolteacher Maria Wutz from Auenthal:* Jean Paul, *Leben des Vergnügten Schulmeisterlein Maria Wutz in Auenthal,* in *Werke,* vol. I:1 (Munich: Hanser, 1960], 423–25.

285. Ibid., 454–57. In a supplementary text: "Such things should always be laid away, and all the flowers of joy, although withered, should be pasted into an herbarium; not even old tail coats, polonaises, and frock coats (the other clothes are less characteristic) should be given away or auctioned off, but they should be hung as the husks of consumed hours, empty cocoons of departed joys, bills of payment or dead hand, devolved upon the memory of the departed years" (*The Passing Bell, or Seven Last Words to the Reader of the Biography and Idylls* [*Ausläuten oder Sieben Letzte Worte an die Leser der Lebensbeschreibung und der Idylle*]): ibid., 462. Other old toys in the garret and in a closet, his

own and those of his dead brother, stir the feelings, in sickness and in health, of another parish priest and teacher, the protagonist of the novel *Life of Quintus Fixlein:* cf. *Leben des Quintus Fixlein,* in Jean Paul, *Werke,* vol. 4 (Munich: Hanser, 1962), 84–86, 182.

286. Published in four versions: I select the second (1847, *Studien III*), although the fourth is very interesting (1867, posthumous: cf. A. Stifter, *Die Mappe meines Urgrossvaters. Schilderungen. Briefe* [Munich: Winkler, 1986], 9–29).

287. A. Stifter, *Die Mappe meines Urgrossvaters* (Stuttgart: Reclam, 1988), 16–17, 18–24.

288. In the first version (1841) *The Antiques (Die Antiken)*. All quotations are drawn from this chapter I (7–25).

289. Ibid., 7, 11, 16, 25.

290. Some explicit passages: "In the darkness of the chest, dear mamma used to keep many rarities, which had no other use than to lie there forever" (ibid., 10); "In every house there are objects which are not thrown away because a part of our heart is attached to them, but which are usually put away in drawers and never glanced at again" (ibid., 19, and cf. the same forgetfulness: 21, 22, 23).

291. Ibid., 12–13.

292. Confining myself to nouns, and distributing English synonyms with the same measure of arbitrariness which has been used throughout this book: *Trödel* = trinkets (ibid., 9), *Kram* = rubbish (9, 23), *Altertümliches* = old stuff (9), *Schutt* = scraps (9), *Kehricht* = trash (12), *Wegwurf* = refuse (12), *Plunder* = gimcrack (12), *Trümmer* = smithereens (13, 17), *Wust* = waste (17), *Reste* = leftovers (17). The semipositive range is less wide: *Reliquien* = relics (10), *Gedenksachen* = keepsakes (11), *Denkmale* = monuments (13).

293. The list from the deep fog of infancy, ibid., 9; from the unexplored background behind the carriages: 9–10; from the chest of rarities and from the chest of clothes: 10–11; from the furniture and upholstery of the great-grandfather by candlelight, 14. Separately, the list of scrap paper from which his diary resurfaces: 19–21. The adult who revisits the house will experience the disillusionment of reduced dimensions, deterioration, and (cf. IV, 15) change: 17–18.

294. Ibid., 8.

295. "At that time there would have been many more old things, if as children we had been able to overcome the terror of the numerous uneven corners which still remained, and in which since eternity lumber had taken refuge": cf. following passage, ibid., 9–10, and the other major turn towards the sinister-terrifying, 14–15.

296. Ibid., 15; if we do not take into account a diminished reverence for the reliquary of clothes, 10.

297. Chap. XXIV: Sainte-Beuve, *Volupté* (Paris: Fasquelle, 1928), 348–49 (cf. Orlando, *Infanzia, memoria e storia,* 227–29). In a contemporary poem by Pushkin—as also for Werther—the places where he was exiled for two years, in a family estate, appear unchanged after ten years, or transformed but not in decline: *I visited again,* cf. Pushkin, *The Poems, Prose and Plays,* 83.

298. Hugo, *Oeuvres poétiques,* 1:1095 (1093–98, in *Les Rayons et les ombres*).

299. Lamartine, *Oeuvres poétiques complètes* (Paris: Bibliothèque de la Pléiade, 1963), 395–96, 397–98 (392–99; cf. Orlando, *Infanzia, memoria e storia,* 161–63).

300. Ibid., 1486–87, 1488–89 (1484–94).

301. Ibid., 1493. It is only in an opera with the regressive power of Wagner's *Tristan und Isolde* that there is a return to the places of childhood in which memory is transcended along a different axis: in depth and backwards in time, rather than upwards. At the beginning of the last act, Kurwenal has brought the wounded and unconscious Tristan back to the Nordic seaside castle of Kareol in Brittany: the scenery "gives the impression of the absence of the owners, ill kept, damaged here and there and covered with weeds"—a medieval Combourg, if the Arthurian legend does not preclude an echo of Chateaubriand (IV, 14; V, 6). But the squire wonders in vain: "do you not recognize the castle—of the fathers?" The sleep from which Tristan emerges leaves him with no memory but a reign of Night, anterior even to the most familiar of daytime appearances; this reign is metaphysical through the warm physicality of a nostalgia for the womb, while the "empty and deserted" sea and the mortal bleeding of the wound repeat the birth trauma (R. Wagner, *Tristan und Isolde* [Stuttgart: Reclam, 1958], 59–63, 73).

302. Book 3, part II, chap. 5: L. Tolstoy, *War and Peace*, trans. L. and A. Maude, vol. 2 (New York and Toronto: Knopf, 1992), 2381–82. In Verga, *Mastro-don Gesualdo*, Isabella hastens to the place in the country of her recently lost love: Verga: *Tutti i romanzi*, 3:543–44. In *Monsieur Bergeret in Paris* (*Monsieur Bergeret à Paris*) by Anatole France, the direction of the pilgrimage is inverted: the protagonist and his sister, coming from the province, recover their childhood memories in a hundred-year-old apartment in the capital (France, *Oeuvres*, 3:208–10).

303. Dickens, *The Old Curiosity Shop*, 555.

304. Baudelaire, *Oeuvres complètes*, vol. 1 (Paris: Bibliothèque de la Pléiade, 1975), 85–87.

305. Chap. I: Nerval, *Oeuvres complètes*, 3:538.

306. Chap. IX: ibid., 556: undoubtedly a reminiscence of the uncle's house in Sainte-Beuve (see above, note 297, and cf. Orlando, *Infanzia, memoria e storia*, 229–32).

307. Chap. VI: Nerval, *Oeuvres complètes*, 3:550–51.

308. Chap. III: ibid., 543–44.

309. Part II, chaps. II, VI: ibid., 726, 742–43.

310. Cf. S. Mallarmé, *Oeuvres complètes*, vol. 1 (Paris: Bibliothèque de la Pléiade, 1998), 415–16; and "Le due facce dei simboli in un poema in prosa di Mallarmé (lettura di 'Frisson d'hiver,' " in Orlando, *Le costanti e le varianti* (the analysis extends to six other texts by Mallarmé, in some of which the appearance of the old furniture is proportionate to the density of language).

311. Cf. ibid., 338.

312. Maupassant, *Contes et Nouvelles*, vol. 1 (Paris: Bibliothèque de la Pléiade, 1974), 398–401. The story repeats, at times word for word, chap. XII of the novel *A Life* (*Une Vie*) (Maupassant, *Romans* [Paris: Bibliothèque de la Pléiade, 1987], 169–71). In the libretto by H. Meilhac and L. Halévy for Offenbach's *Parisian Life,* there is a pleasing conventional formulation in which youthful erotic fetishism is the premise of the reminiscent-affective of old age; the sentimental irony of the operetta extends both of these to the lower extremities, from women's hands to feet, since the verse belongs to a rondeau which a glovemaker sings to a shoemaker. Here are the last lines (modified when they are set to music): "Oh rapture of an icy heart! / These boots are our past / And this is how, sirs, /

Feeling / Makes everything sacred, boot or glove!" (Offenbach, *La Vie parisienne* [Score for voice and piano; Paris: Heugel, 1866], 85–90). Regarding Rodolphe's reminiscent-affective in *Madame Bovary,* cf. IV, 36, note 292.

313. A. Rimbaud, *Oeuvres complètes* (Paris: Bibliothèque de la Pléiade, 1972), 34–35.

314. I am not thinking, of course, of a linear chronology. In the last pages of *The Maias* by Eça de Queiroz, Carlos's visit with his friend Ega to the palace which is the background of family memories develops as a slow and gradual sentimental pilgrimage (Eça de Queiroz, *Os Maias: Episódios de vida romántica* [Oporto: Lello e Irmâo, 1945], 459–63); but Maria's things, stuffed into a lidless hatbox, are "mixed as if in a promiscuity of rubbish"; and in the grandfather's study, the emotion is cut short by the exasperating surprise of the sneezes caused by the scattering of pepper (pp. 461–62). In Rodenbach's *Bruges-la-Morte,* a widower has chosen the gloomiest of towns to live out his grief— where, however, his only memories are those which construct a sanctuary in his own house; the images are less overabundant than we might have expected, amidst meteorological and acoustic evocations: G. Rodenbach, *Bruges-la-Morte* (Brussels: Labor, 1986), 21–22, 53–54 for the house, 25–28, 32–33 for the town, and passim. The "Grandparents' house" is very affectionately presented in Pirandello, *Notebooks of Serafino Gubbio* (*Quaderni di Serafino Gubbio operatore*), a novel which appeared in 1915 with the title *Shoot!* (*Si gira . . .* ; L. Pirandello, *Tutti i Romanzi,* vol. 2 [Milan: Mondadori, 1973], 540–41); ten years earlier the mother's house in *The Late Mattia Pascal* (*Il fu Mattia Pascal,* ibid, 1 [1973]:327) is more oppressive.

315. G. Gozzano, *Poesie e prose* (Milan: Garzanti, 1966), 127, 131–32 (126–43); in the attic there are hints—in both cases ironic—of the sinister-terrifying with the portrait of the cursed marchioness, and of the solemn-admonitory with Tasso's effigy.

316. *From the Angelus of the Morning to the Angelus of the Evening:* F. Jammes, *De l'Angelus de l'aube à l'Angelus du soir* (Paris: Gallimard, 1971): cf. *Silence . . . ,* 28–29; *The Dining-Room* (*La Salle à manger*), 62–63; *Old House* (*Vieille maison*), 72–73.

317. *I went to visit* (*J'ai été visiter*): ibid., 83 (82–85).

318. *Afternoon Sun:* Cavafy, *The Complete Poems,* trans. R. Dalven (New York: Harcourt, Brace & World, 1961), 99.

319. M. Proust, *À la recherche du temps perdu,* vol. 1 (Paris: Bibliothèque de la Pléiade, 1987), 117: I take this expression from the celebrated passage which draws a comparison between Louis XIV and Aunt Léonie.

320. *Swann's Way* (*Du côté de chez Swann*), III: ibid., 414–20, and particularly the last two sentences.

321. *The Guermantes Way* (*Le Côté de Guermantes*), I: Proust, *À la recherche du temps perdu,* vol. 2 (Paris: Bibliothèque de la Pléiade, 1988), 390.

322. *Albertine Gone* (*Albertine disparue*), IV: Proust, *À la recherche du temps perdu,* vol. 4 (Paris: Bibliothèque de la Pléiade, 1989), 266–68.

323. *Time regained* (*Le Temps retrouvé*): ibid., 465–66 (461–66).

324. Part I, chap. XLV; part II, chap. I: Tolstoy, *Resurrection,* 173, 299.

325. *Central Park:* W. Benjamin, *Selected Writings,* vol. 4: *(1938–40),* (Cambridge, Mass.: Harvard University Press, 2003), 182.

326. J. Joyce, *Ulysses* (London: The Bodley Head, 1960), 848–50, 852–53. In the first drawer are listed "fading photographs," "a butt of red partly liquified sealing wax," "an

old sandglass," "an infantile epistle" of Milly, "a cameo brooch" of Bloom's mother, "a pink ribbon which had festooned an Easter egg in the year 1899," "a 1d. adhesive stamp, lavender, of the reign of Queen Victoria," etc. In the second drawer: "An indistinct daguerreotype" of the father and grandfather; "An ancient hagadah book" of Jewish Passover worship.

327. A sentimental pilgrimage to the boarding school of adolescence ends *Fermina Márquez* by Valéry Larbaud; but the plot is concluded by an object hurled — after many others — in an abandoned and closed classroom worthy of the negative category, a dead room "devoted to fearful gods" (Valéry Larbaud, *Oeuvres* [Paris: Bibliothèque de la Pléiade, 1958], 392–3, 385–6).

328. I. Babel, *The Collected Stories*, trans. W. Morison (Penguin, 1961), 60 (*Gedali:* 60–63).

329. B. Schulz, *The Street of Crocodiles*, trans. Wieniewska (London: Pan Books, 1980), 56 (56–65).

330. The poem is by Alfonso Mangione, the music by Nicola Valente (1928). It is a text difficult to find except in records: it is worthwhile reproducing it here, in one of the (various) strophic arrangements: "1. I am looking for a safe, / And guess to do what? / I have no stocks, I have no income / I don't have clothes to cover my back! / But I need a safe / I surely must have it! / I have to keep all the letters / That my Rosina wrote to me / A miniature picture / Of Aunt Sophia, God rest her soul, / A lock of hair, / A coral horn, / The beak of the parrot / Which we lost in '23." "2. I'm looking for a safe, / But to what safe-maker can I describe it? / Certain relics, certain keepsakes, / If you keep them outside might disappear! / St. Casimir the Martyr / Get me this safe! / I have to keep all the letters / That my Rosina wrote to me, / A twelve-lire bill / Issued by the bank, / The handle of a bucket, / The splinter of a mirror, / The rind of an old cheese / And an orange-colored jacket . . ." "3. These are memories that in a safe / And there alone, must be kept . . . / When they take away my bread / I stand it quietly without kicking . . . / Yes, I know, life is tragic, / But they must give me the safe! / I have to keep all the letters / That my Rosina wrote to me, / The wick of a candle / Stuck in the candlestick, / A doll from Miccio, / A lens in its case, / And the tail of a rocking horse / Which reminds me of the best age" (*Napoletana*, VIII, Durium ms AI 7706). Miccio was a store patronized by well-to-do Neapolitans at the beginning of the twentieth century.

331. Chap. IX: H. Böll, *Gruppenbild mit Dame* (Munich: dtv, 1974), 318–21.

332. Act II, sc. I: Byron, *The Poetical Works,* 395 (cf. *Titus Andronicus*, act III, sc. 1, lines 94–98: Shakespeare, *Tragedies*, 255).

333. *Faust:* N. Lenau, *Werke* (Hamburg: Hoffmann und Campe, 1966), 303–4.

334. Act I: G. Büchner, *Gesammelte Werke* (Munich: Golmann, 1959), 117. In *The Death of Danton (Dantons Tod)*, the condemned man says to himself: tomorrow you will be "a broken fiddle"; "an empty bottle"; "a holed pair of trousers; you will be thrown into the wardrobe and the moths will eat you" (ibid., 68).

335. Baudelaire, *Oeuvres complètes*, 1:281 (280–82). Cf. with the memories in *Le Flacon* the lines 2–4 of *The Digging Skeleton (Le Squelette laboureur)*: on the dusty quays of the Seine, "cadaverous" books sleep like mummies (ibid., 93).

336. In the "large and dismal house" put up for auction and then demolished at the end of *Great Expectations* (Ch. Dickens, *Great Expectations* [Oxford University Press,

1999], 55, 507, 516–18), the horrors of repugnant memory had been so mysterious, enduring, and eccentric that I wonder whether Dickens had known Balzac's Grande Bretèche: cf. above, note 198. A rich, spoiled young girl, abandoned by her fiancé on the day of her wedding, Miss Havisham stopped the clocks at the hour when she had received the fatal letter; she has grown old, shut up within the darkness of the mansion she has left to decay, wandering about in the festive hall that has turned into a den of cobwebs, mice, and roaches (59–62, 64–5, 68–9, 85–6, 90–1). Although the author's own threadbare-grotesque plays with these vermin (V, 5), although her father was no more than a country gentleman, a brewer of beer (191), two points recall Balzac: the excess of the price a victim of the upper classes pays for a private quarrel, as though avenging oneself at length upon things; and the enigmatic gradualism with which the first-person narrator moves from the incomprehensible to its explanation (more mixed here, to be sure, with melodramatic suspense). But if both examples are powerfully impure, here the centrality of the desolate-disconnected emerges in the old woman's assimilation of her "I" to that "heap of decay," the rotten wedding cake: "It and I have worn away together" (95–96).

337. Invasion of the Tuileries (part III, chap. I): Flaubert, *Oeuvres*, 2:320–21, for instance: "In the chamber of the queen, a woman was shining her ribbons with pomade ..."; "An obscene curiosity made them rummage through all the closets, all the recesses, to open all the drawers ..." Auction (part III, chap. V): ibid., 443–44 (list of things in the court of the auction house, 442). In the second sentence here quoted, the syntactic relation between the things and the recollections is similar to that of a famous sentence in *Madame Bovary*: between the limbs of the dying woman, and their past sinful employment (Flaubert, *Oeuvres*, 1:622).

338. Book IV, chap. III: D'Annunzio, *Prose di romanzi*, vol. 1 (Milan: Mondadori, 1988), 1:354–58.

339. A. Schnitzler, *Casanovas Heimfahrt und andere Erzählungen* (Frankfurt am Main: Fischer, 1978), 130, 188.

340. Ibid., 135. Cf. the images of moving out, which Paula experiences serenely, 169–70; of a house not yet ready to live in, which the couple rents, 175.

341. Ibid., 130, 132; cf. 140 and 200 for the recognition of another place.

342. Chap. III: ibid., 130–31. Cf. 145, for a feeling of missing his own objects in the office; 147, 200–1, two other backgrounds of comfortable rooms, but in a hotel.

343. Chap. V: M. Leiris, *L'Âge d'homme* (Paris: Gallimard, 1946), 118 (117–22).

344. Chap. XVIII: S. Satta, *Il giorno del giudizio* (Milan: Adelphi, 1990), 257–58 (cf. 162–70, 241–57).

345. Chap. XXIII: Böll, *Ansichten eines Clowns*, 230, 232–33; 233–35.

346. N. Sarraute, *Oeuvres complètes* (Paris: Bibliothèque de la Pléiade, 1996), 240 (239–41).

347. Apollinaire, *Oeuvres poétiques* (Paris: Bibliothèque de la Pléiade, 1959), 190 (188–91).

348. G. Raboni, *Tutte le poesie (1951–1998)* (Milan: Garzanti, 2000), 41.

349. Cf., for *Le Cygne*, V, 8; and cf. the first *Spleen* with *Song* (*Canzone*): "When it rains they are truly disgusting / The windows covered with grease, the heater / Sending smoke in the corners and in the kitchen / The salt getting stuck together, The wax cloth / getting sticky"; the second *Spleen* with *Serenade* (*Serenata*): "with this dream / Of low

corridors, faded, with many doors / Dimmed by chloride and cupboards / Full of register books, medicines, stuffed eagles" (ibid., 35, 105–6; cf. Baudelaire, *Oeuvres complètes*, 1:72–73).

350. Br. 399: B. Pascal, *Pensées* (Paris: Garnier, 1964), 171.

351. Ch. Cros and T. Corbière, *Oeuvres complètes* (Paris: Bibliothèque de la Pléiade, 1970), 135.

352. *Beyond Another Ocean* (*Para além doutro oceano*): F. Pessoa, *Obra poética* (Rio de Janeiro: Aguilar, 1972), 425–26, 426, 430.

353. *There Can Be No Mourning* (*Kann keine Trauer sein*): G. Benn, *Gedichte in der Fassung der Erstdrucke* (Frankfurt am Main: Fischer, 1982), 476.

354. In *Navigations and Returns* (*Navegaciones y regresos*), fourth volume of the *Elementary Odes* (*Odas elementales*), Neruda sings an *Ode to Things* (*Oda a las cosas*) in which the love of things, both cosmic and materialist, does not forget that "Everything bears / In the handles, in the outline, / The imprint of fingers / Of a remote hand / Lost / In the most forgotten forgetfulness"; one *Ode to Broken Things* (*Oda a las cosas rotas*), in which all those produced by life "grinding / glass, wearing out fabrics, / making shards, / mincing / shapes" are treasures which should be dropped in a bag into the sea, which would refashion them: P. Neruda, *Navegaciones y regresos* (Buenos Aires: Losada, 1971), 43 (41–44), 49 (48–50).

355. P. Neruda, *Residencia en la tierra (1925–1935)* (Buenos Aires: Losada, 1958), 92–93.

356. Ibid., 101–2.

357. Ibid., 89–91.

358. *A Hundred and Hundred and Hundred and Hundred Pages of the Secret Book of Gabriele D'Annunzio, Tempted to Die* (*Cento e cento e cento e cento pagine del libro segreto di Gabriele D'Annunzio tentato di morire*), in G. D'Annunzio, *Il venturiero senza ventura . . .*, in *Prose di ricerca . . .*, vol. 2 (Milan: Mondadori, 1950), 849–50.

359. F. Dostoevsky, *The Best Short Stories*, trans. D. Magarshack (New York: The Modern Library, 2001), 156 (and 161), 193, 205; cf. the disorder of the "small, narrow, low-ceilinged room," 172.

360. Ibid., 102, 103.

361. Ibid., 197.

362. Ibid., 130 (also 157, 167, 170–71, 190, 210–11).

363. Ibid., 173–75; 187 ("Your grave will be full of slush and dirt and wet snow"; "They will fill in your grave with wet blue clay"; "Dirt and mud, dirt and mud . . .").

364. Chap. IX: F. Sologub, *The Little Demon*, trans. R. Wilks (Penguin, 1994), 77. Note the topos of colors (V, 7).

365. *Hamlet or the Consequences of Filial Piety* (*Hamlet ou les suites de la piété filiale*): J. Laforgue, *Moralités légendaires* (n.p.: Mercure de France, 1964), 13 (11–61).

366. Ibid., 13–15.

367. Céline, *Voyage au bout de la nuit. Mort à credit* (Paris: Bibliothèque de la Pléiade, 1962), 276; an emphasis upon the vivisected animals and the stench of their corpses: 276–78 ("the endless cooking of vegetable scrapings, asphyxiated guinea-pigs and other uncertain putrescences").

368. Chap. I: Faulkner, *Light in August*, 6.

369. Chap. II: A. Robbe-Grillet, *Les Gommes* (Paris: Les Éditions de Minuit, 1953), 26 and cf. 37.

370. F. Kafka, *Die Erzählungen* (Frankfurt am Main: Fischer, 1961), 144–45.

371. *Introducing the Story of my Family* (*Introduzione alla storia della mia famiglia*), chap. II: E. Morante, *Menzogna e sortilegio* (Turin: Einaudi, 1962), 16.

372. Part IV, chap. VI: ibid., 429. Her father's native town apparently partly consisted of the ruins left by an earthquake thirty years earlier: from the sterile-noxious to the sinister-terrifying, ibid., 319–20, 332.

373. Chap. III: Kafka, *Die Erzählungen,* 80–81, and cf. 78–79.

374. *Treatise on Tailors' Dummies, Conclusion:* Schulz, *The Street of Crocodiles,* 42.

375. *Cockroaches:* ibid., 78; *Dead Season:* B. Schulz, *Sanatorium under the Sign of the Hourglass,* trans. C. Wieniewska (New York: Walker and Co., 1978), 104–5; *Father's Last Escape:* ibid., 174–78.

376. *Visitation:* Schulz, *The Street of Crocodiles,* 24–25; *Cinnamon Shops:* ibid., 56–57.

377. *Treatise on Tailors' Dummies, Conclusion:* ibid., 43. Cf. 19 (*Visitation*), where the absurd hyperbole precedes the supernatural: because of the similarity of the "dark houses with empty blind façades," if one entered the wrong house, it was possible to become lost "in a real labyrinth of unfamiliar apartments and balconies, and unexpected doors opening on to strange empty courtyards"; and only to remember the paternal staircase "many days later."

378. A. Kubin, *Die andere Seite: Ein phantastischer Roman* (Munich: Spangenberg, 1975), 9, 18–19, 74.

379. Ibid., 57.

380. Ibid., 85, 96–98.

381. Concerning the latter, cf. ibid., 187, 190, 195–96.

382. X, lines 290–92, 302–6: *Homeri Opera,* vol. 3: *Odysseae Libros I–XII continens* (Oxford University Press, 1917), 178.

383. Pearson, fr. 534, *The Herb-Gatherers* or *The Sorcerers: The Fragments of Sophocles,* vol. 2 (Cambridge University Press, 1917), 172–75.

384. *Medea,* line 789: *Euripidis Fabulae,* vol. 1 (Oxford University Press, 1984), 127.

385. III, lines 843–66: *Apollonii Rhodii Argonautica* (Oxford University Press, 1961), 146.

386. Cf. A. S. F. Gow, *Theocritus,* vol. 2 (Cambridge University Press, 1950), 34.

387. II, lines 17–63: *Bucolici Graeci* (Oxford University Press, 1952), 10–12.

388. *Pro se de magia liber (Apologia),* XXX–XXXI: *Apulei Platonici Madaurensis Opera quae supersunt,* vol. 2, fasc. 1 (Leipzig: Teubner, 1972), 34–36. Concerning the fragment from Laevius, cf. also *Fragmenta Poetarum Latinorum Epicorum et Lyricorum* (Leipzig: Teubner, 1982), 25.

389. *Buc.* VIII, lines 64–104: *Vergili Opera,* 22–23; *Aen.* IV, lines 512–16: ibid., 192.

390. V, lines 15–24: *Q. Horati Flacci Opera* (Oxford University Press, 1901), 116.

391. I refer to that fundamental continuation of Freud's theory, the volume by I. Matte Blanco, *The Unconscious as Infinite Sets: Essay in Bi-Logic* (London: Duckworth, 1975): see specifically chap. III (35–60), and cf. Orlando, *Illuminismo,* 7, 22–23, 115–17, 134–37.

392. *Elegies,* II, 4, lines 55–60: *Tibulli Aliorumque Carminum Libri Tres* (Oxford University Press, 1915), 39–40.

393. *Elegies,* III, 6, lines 27–30: Propertius, *Elegies, 272.*

394. II, lines 571–80: *P. Ovidii Nasonis Fastorum Libri Sex* (Leipzig: Teubner, 1978), 43–44.

395. VII, lines 218–36: *Ovidii Metamorphoses,* 153–54.

396. VII, lines 264–76: ibid., 155.

397. Lines 677–79: *L. Annaei Senecae Tragoediae* (Oxford University Press, 1986), 149.

398. Lines 732–34, 692–93, 773–84 specifically (in the context of lines 670–739 spoken by the nurse, and lines 740–844 by Medea): ibid., 149–55.

399. CXXXVII, 10–CXXXVIII, 2: Pétrone, *Le Satiricon,* 171–72.

400. *Annales,* II, 69: *Taciti Annalium Libri,* 83.

401. Book III, XVII 4–5: *Apulei Platonici Madaurensis Metamorphoseon Libri XI* (Leipzig: Teubner, 1931), 65; and cf. book II, XXXII; book III, IX 7–9, XVI–XVIII: 51–52, 58–59, 63–66.

402. IV, [31], 33: Boccaccio, *Tutte le opere,* 1:401–2.

403. Prosa IX: I. Sannazzaro, *Opere* (Turin: Utet, 1952), 137, 140–41; once again the expected objects recur in the magical practice of old Enareto, in Prosa X (157–59). Cf. lines 46–48 in the tercets which conclude Prosa VI (102); and cf. Boiardo's poem, book I, canto V, ott. 17: Boiardo, *Orlando innamorato,* vol. 1 (Turin: Utet, 1966), 280.

404. IX, 5: Boccaccio, *Tutte le opere,* 4:813. "Unborn paper" = paper made from the skin of an unborn animal.

405. XVI, lines 605–26; XXIII, lines 444–64: Folengo, *Baldus,* 546–48, 784–86.

406. Act I, sc. III; act II, sc. I and II; act III, sc. IV: Ariosto, *Tutte le opere* vol. 4: *Commedie* (Milan: Mondadori, 1974), 463–67, 473–74 and 477–78, 499–502. In the first edition, the enumeration preceded the portents, and the charlatanism was exposed even later (cf. 375–78, 381–85, 387–88 and 391–92).

407. Act II, sc. VII: P. Aretino, *Teatro* (Milan: Mondadori, 1971), 130–33; and cf. 690–92. For "unborn paper" see above, note 404.

408. Book I, *Miseries (Misères),* lines 902, 913, 952, 921–40: A. d'Aubigné, *Oeuvres* (Paris: Bibliothèque de la Pléiade, 1969), 42–43.

409. Act I, sc. IV: Shakespeare, *Tragedies,* 317–18.

410. Book II, chap. XVII: Grimmelshausen, *Der abenteuerliche Simplicissimus,* 201–3.

411. J. de Montemayor, *La Diana* (Paris: Bouret, 1937), 147ff., 206ff., and passim (books IV, V); D'Urfé, *L'Astrée* (Geneva: Slatkine, 1966), 157ff. (book V, *History of Climanthe's Deception* [*Histoire de la tromperie de Climanthe*]).

412. Corneille, *Oeuvres complètes,* 1:617, 621; 573.

413. *Théâtre du XVII siècle* (Paris: Bibliothèque de la Pléiade, 1972), 1:306, and cf. 315, 319.

414. Cyrano de Bergerac, *Oeuvres complètes* (Paris: Belin, 1977), 57–59 (57–61). The list of the objects belonging to the astrologer and sorcerer, who keeps the Lame Devil imprisoned in a flask in his attic, is rather spare: both in the Spanish original (1641) by Vélez de Guevara, and in the French reworking (1707) by Lesage (L. Vélez de Guevara, *El*

Diablo Cojuelo [Madrid: Castalia, 1988], 67: tranco I; Lesage, *Le Diable boiteux* [Paris and The Hague: Mouton, 1970], 85–86: chap. I).

415. Cf. Cyrano de Bergerac, *Oeuvres complètes,* 62–67.

416. Book II, chap. IV; book III, chap. VII: M. G. Lewis, *The Monk* (New York: Grove, 1959), 180, 272–73.

417. W. Beckford, *Vathek* (Paris: Flammarion, 1981), 78. For the perverted tastes of Carathis (a caricature of a Puritan mother in her rigid atrociousness), of her blind and mute negresses and her camel, cf. 78–81, 86, 124–26, 128.

418. Goethe, *Faust* (Wiesbaden: Insel, 1959), 213.

419. E. T. A. Hoffmann, *Sämtliche poetischen Werke,* vol. 1: *Phantasiestücke* (Berlin and Darmstadt: Tempel, 1963), 210.

420. Ibid., 614.

421. Act II, sc. II: Byron, *The Poetical Works,* 396–97.

422. Acts I and IV: Grillparzer, *Werke,* vol. 2 (Salzburg and Stuttgart: Bergland Buch, 1958), 257, 308.

423. Act II, no. 10, bars 261–63: C. M. von Weber, *Der Freischütz* (Stuttgart: Reclam, 1956), 45 and cf. the full score, Eulenburg, 242.

424. Book VII, chap. IV: Hugo, *Notre-Dame de Paris,* 263–66.

425. Book I, chap. I; book II, chap. I: Villiers de l'Isle-Adam, *Oeuvres complètes,* vol. 1 (Paris: Bibliothèque de la Pléiade, 1986), 768, 822.

426. N. Hawthorne, *Young Goodman Brown and Other Tales* (Oxford University Press, 1991), 115 (111–24).

427. Part I, book V, chap. IV: Hugo, *Notre-Dame de Paris,* 720.

428. *Misti:* Maupassant, *Contes et nouvelles* 1:1156 (1153–58).

429. Chap. XIX: E. Hemingway, *For Whom the Bell Tolls* (Penguin, 1958), 244–46.

430. Chap. XVIII: M. Bulgakov, *The Master and Margarita*, trans. D. Burgin and K. Tiernan O' Connor (Dana Point: Ardis, 1995), 172. The hall is also cluttered with swords and capes, ibid.; cf. the other interior in which Margarita is granted access to Woland's presence, 216, and the latter's indecent clothes, 217, 232, 234. A literal religious venerable-regressive is illuminated by the moon, in the corner "where amidst the dust and cobwebs hung a forgotten icon," 42.

431. Ibid., 226–27.

432. Ibid., 312.

433. *Decameron*, VI, 10: Boccaccio, *Tutte le opere,* 4:572–73.

434. J. Calvin, *Avertissement contre l'astrologie–Traité des reliques* (Paris: Colin, 1962), 86.

435. Part I: D'Annunzio, *Prose di romanzi,* 2:376.

436. G. Tomasi di Lampedusa, *Opere* (Milan: Mondadori, 1995), 241–42, 255–56 (part VIII); G. García Márquez, *El Otoño del Patriarca* (Barcelona: Plaza & Janez, 1975), 156–58 (137–61).

437. IV, lines 466–68 (452–73): *Vergili Opera,* 190.

438. Ep. VII, 27: *C. Plini Caecili Secundi Epistularum Libri Decem* (Oxford University Press, 1963), 220–22; *Philopseudes,* 31, 12–13: *Luciani Opera,* vol. 2 (Oxford University Press, 1974), 194.

439. Lines 231–50: Ronsard, *Oeuvres complètes*, vol. 8 (Paris: Didier, 1963), 127–28 (115–39).

440. Saint-Amant, *Oeuvres* (Paris: Didier, 1971), 39–42 (33–48).

441. *Romeo and Juliet,* act IV, sc. I: Shakespeare, *Tragedies,* 364–65.

442. Act IV, sc. III: ibid., 368.

443. Ibid., 368–69. Parasitic upon the sterile-noxious (and not without buried gold), the sinister-terrifying "at dead time of the night" would also lead to madness or to death in those lines of *Titus Andronicus* which are more powerful than any scenery: "barren detested vale," "abhorred pit" suited for murder (act II, sc. III, lines 92–104: Shakespeare, *Tragedies,* 245, but also sc. I, line 128, 242, and sc. III passim, 243–50).

444. Ibid., 380.

445. Part III, chap. VII: J. Swift, *Gulliver's Travels* (Everyman's Library, 1954), 207.

446. Saint-Évremond, *Oeuvres en prose,* vol. 3 (Paris: Didier, 1966), 380–81 (375–417).

447. Cf. *Memories and Adventures of a Man of Quality Who Has Retired from the World (Mémoires et aventures d'un homme de qualité qui s'est retiré du monde),* book V, where the deceased wife's possessions are a reminiscent-affective exposed to perpetual adoration (and the gloomy underground episode among the ruins of Tusculum, which precedes the bereavement, already smacks of the Gothic); *The Dean of Coleraine (Le Doyen de Killerine),* part VI, book XI, where the survivor of a faithless woman who committed suicide takes refuge in an abbey: *Oeuvres de Prévost,* vol. 1 (Presses Universitaires de Grenoble, 1978), 1:97 (and 93–95); 3 [1978]:337. In *The Life and Entertaining Adventures of Mr. Cleveland (Le Philosophe Anglais ou Histoire de Monsieur Cleveland),* book I, the shelter offered to Cromwell's young, illegitimate son exempts the immense caverns of a natural dungeon at the center of a mountain from sinister or noxious connotations: *Oeuvres de Prévost,* vol. 2 (Presses Universitaires de Grenoble, 1977), 29, 36, 40.

448. Night I: Young, *The Poetical Works,* 1:2.

449. Novalis, *Werke in einem Band* (Munich and Vienna: Hanser, 1982), 149, and cf. the first verse edition, 148 (147–51).

450. Cf. IV, 24, note 158. In Goethe's *Wilhelm Meister's Apprenticeship,* at the end of the century, the words of Philine's song will be: "Do not sing with mournful accent / The solitude of the Night; / No, she is, o sweet beauties, / Made for companionship": book V, chap. X: W. Goethe, *Wilhelm Meisters Lehrjahre,* vol. 2 (Munich: dtv, 1962), 36.

451. *La Notte,* lines 10–13, 24–28: Parini, *Il Giorno* (Milan: Rusconi, 1984), 325–26. It is well known that Foscolo recalls this passage, speaking of Parini, in *On Sepulchres (Dei Sepolcri),* lines 78–86, with sinister images in a masterpiece of sepulchral poetry; if we cannot speak of the venerable-regressive in their case, it is only because representations corresponding to the interpretation are missing (V, 1): U. Foscolo, *Opere,* vol. I: *Poesie e tragedie* (Turin: Einaudi-Gallimard, 1994), 25.

452. J. Cazotte, *Le Diable amoureux* (Paris: Flammarion, 1979), 57.

453. In his *Idea on the Novel (Idée sur les romans)* prefixed to *The Crimes of Love (Les Crimes de l'amour)* in 1801, Sade speaks not of this literary contemporaneity, but of the contemporaneity of the English literary genre and the "revolutionary upheavals which affected the whole of Europe." This genre is the "indispensable fruit" of the age: at a time when the reality of misfortunes outstripped the imagination of fiction, in order to interest the reader one had to "call hell to one's aid": Marquis de Sade, *Oeuvres complètes,* vol. 10 (Paris: Au Cercle du Livre précieux, 1966), 15.

454. *Introduction:* Marquis de Sade, *Oeuvres complètes*, vol. 13 (Paris: Au Cercle du Livre précieux, 1967), 44–45, 48–49.

455. Ibid., 207.

456. Part I, Journée XXIX: ibid., 328.

457. Chap. VII: Marquis de Sade, *Oeuvres Complètes*, vol. 6 (Paris: Au Cercle du Livre précieux, 1966), 301–4. Cf. the 1787 version, vol. 14 (1967), 388–90, and that of 1791, vol. 3 (1966), 158–60; in this 1797 version, the arrival at M. De Bandole's castle, situated in the wilderness, still comes first, but it is brief, 6:282.

458. Chaps. IX and XII: ibid., 353–56 (cf. 309–10); and Marquis de Sade, *Oeuvres Complètes*, vol. 7 (Paris: Au Cercle du Livre précieux, 1966), 85–88. 1791, 3:177–79 (cf. 163), and 222–25.

459. Chap. XIII: Sade, *Oeuvres Complètes,* 7:121–22, 133. 1791, 3:228–29, 236.

460. Chap. XVIII: Sade, *Oeuvres Complètes,* 7:299 (and cf. 305–6). 1791, 3:267–68 (and cf. 273–74). Here, see also the 1787 version, 14:426–27, with two interesting variations: the declaration of the young girl's aversion to "all isolated places"; the supernatural, rather than the criminal, is used to introduce the castle: "giving rather the idea of a dwelling place of ghosts, than that of people made for society . . ." That there may be an echo of this castle in the one belonging to Manzoni's Unnamed (A. Manzoni, *Tutte le opere,* vol. 2, bk. 1 [Milan: Mondadori, 1954], 338–39) is confirmed on the next page, when Don Rodrigo is "led through a labyrinth of dark corridors" (340).

461. Chap. I: H. Walpole, *The Castle of Otranto* (Oxford University Press, 1969), 25–27 (cf. a labyrinth of caves, once the dwelling place of hermits and now presumed to be inhabited by evil spirits, 71–72).

462. But the title, in the first edition, was *The Champion of Virtue.*

463. C. Reeve, *The Old English Baron: A Gothic Story* (Oxford University Press, 1977), 41–42.

464. Preface to the first edition: Walpole, *The Castle of Otranto,* 3.

465. Reeve, *The Old English Baron,* 27.

466. Gautier, *Le Capitaine Fracasse,* 8.

467. Book II, chap. VI: A. Radcliffe, *The Italian* (Oxford University Press, 1968), 195–97, and 201, 309–11, 325–26. Cf. the solitary house on the shores of the Adriatic, 209–12, 232; the villa destroyed by the earthquake, 260–65; the doors of the city in ruin, 273.

468. Book III, chap. XI: Lewis, *The Monk,* 395–96, and earlier 384–85, 390. Nocturnal vision of a partially ruined castle, 165–66. In the great tissue of decamerons written in French by the Polish writer Potocki, *Manuscript Found in Saragossa,* the narrator's awakening under a gallows between two corpses will remain unexplained from Day 2 to Day 66: "I lay on pieces of rope, wrecks of wheels, remains of human carcasses, and on the frightful rags which putrefaction had torn from them" (J. Potocki, *Manuscrit trouvé à Saragosse* [Paris: Corti, 1989], 23 and cf. 631).

469. J. Hogg, *The Private Memoirs and Confessions of a Justified Sinner* (Oxford University Press, 1981), 243–45, 249–53.

470. Book I, chap. III: Maturin, *Melmoth,* 21–44. The state of the manuscript on many occasions makes it impossible to decipher, precisely when moral horror reaches its peak: 23, 24, 25, 29, 33, 34, 41, 44 (only on p. 43 does a moral censure have authority without the contribution of physical causes).

471. Book I, chap. I: ibid., 13; descriptions on pp. 6–7, 19. The house is of a higher rank on p. 24; in the tradition the ruins of the monastery, cemetery, and chapel (cf. IV, 24, note 162); well beyond the quotidian are the ruins of Sheeva's pagoda: 212–13, 243, 245, 246.

472. Chap. I, II: T. L. Peacock, *Nightmare Abbey. Crotchet Castle* (Penguin, 1986), 39–48; and cf. respectively 42, 46, 49; 47, 92, 114.

473. Chap. XXIV: J. Austen, *Northanger Abbey. Persuasion* (Everyman's Library, 1966), 163: "Remember the country and the age in which we live. Remember that we are English, that we are Christians. [. . .] does our education prepare us for such atrocities? Do our laws connive at them? Could they be perpetrated without being known, in a country like this . . . ?" In at least two passages Catherine's fantasies are actualized in backgrounds worthy of the Gothic novel: 68, 112–13. In Thackeray's *Vanity Fair,* the too vast and dark interiors of the houses of the Crawleys, both in town and in the country, suggest ghosts and the very memory of Udolpho to Rebecca (Thackeray, *Vanity Fair,* 67–72). On the effect of the reading of these novels in the *Histoire de ma vie* by George Sand, see above, note 155. A suggestive example of the fondness for similar settings in France is the Spanish castle in the ghost story *Inès de Las Sierras* (1837): cf. Nodier, *Contes* (Paris: Garnier, 1961), 673–79 (660–717).

474. Hoffmann, *Sämtliche poetischen Werke*, vol. 1: *Phantasiestücke,* 735–36; for the interior, 743, 753 (also here, as in *Ritter Gluck,* "antiquated splendor": "in altertümlicher [instead of "verjährter"] Pracht," cf. ibid., 25.

475. Poe, *Poetry and Tales,* 317–21.

476. Ibid., 332–35.

477. Cf. IV, 31, note 243.

478. Poe, *Poetry and Tales,* 327–28.

479. Ibid., 319–20.

480. Maupassant, *Contes et nouvelles,* 1:782–84 (780–87).

481. Maupassant, *Contes et nouvelles*, vol. 2 (Paris: Bibliothèque de la Pléiade, 1979), 108–10 (107–13). In another short story told by a madman, *Qui sait? (Who knows?),* the attachment to antique furniture costs him their visible escape from the house and mysterious return. The commercialization of the prestigious-ornamental seems to be an abuse in a list (ending with a tabernacle "from which God had moved out") of objects "which survived their natural possessors, their century, their time, their fashions to be bought, as curiosities, by new generations": ibid., 1232 (1225–37).

482. Chap. II: Zola, *Les Rougon-Macquart,* 4:1025–26; cf. 1009, 1037, 1133, 1134–35, 1188, 1275–76, 1299.

483. J. Conrad, *Within the Tides* (Penguin, 1978), 119–20.

484. Ibid., 123 (the little man's hat), 124 (the youth's jacket), 136 (the girl's stockings); 136, 138, 140.

485. Ibid., 137; cf. earlier 134, later 143–44.

486. Ibid., 132.

487. Ibid., 125, 130–31 and passim.

488. E. Wharton, *The Ghost Stories* (New York: Scribner, 1973), 48, 49–50.

489. Ibid., 51, 52, 71–72.

490. Book I: H. James, *The Sense of the Past* (London: Collins, 1917), 32–33. Begun in

1899–1900, the novel was taken up again in 1914–15 but cut short by James's fatal illness.

491. Book II: ibid., 41–42. From the place he is about to take possession of, he wants "the very tick of the old stopped clocks," "the hour of the day at which this and that had happened"; he even expects—analogously with the privilege that I earlier ascribed to literature (I, 2)—"evidence of a sort for which there had never been documents enough, or for which documents mainly, however multiplied, would never *be* enough" (book II: ibid., 48).

492. Book II: ibid., 64–67; which is to say that the sinister-terrifying is preparing to become parasitic less on the categories of time (cf. IV, 26) than on the prestigious-ornamental, and less on the prestigious-ornamental than on the functional. The knocker of the high door behind which Ralph disappears at the end of book III is "an engine huge, heavy, ancient, brazen, polished"; the vestibule has marble tiles where, following the topos (V, 7), "the white was worn nearly to yellow and the black nearly to blue" (61–62). But inside the house objects are only "smoothed with service" (65); the signs of the passage of time are reduced to the recurrence of the adjective *old,* and to "however tarnished" as a predicate of "glass" (66). Ralph is not interested in knowing whether the objects are original or have been collected in modern times, whether they are genuine rarities or a fortuitous mix (67–68).

493. Book II: ibid., 64, 65.

494. Book II: ibid., 57.

495. It is certainly not surprising, as it appears to an American woman, that Ralph has guessed the sorcery of particular places and old objects or surfaces "in *this* place, which denies the old at every turn and contains so few such objects or surfaces" (book I, ibid., 34). The sign of Europe, in Europe, hovers before him by contrast on the dock, on the train, on the omnibus (book II: ibid., 58). The house itself seems to reveal to him "an inimitable reserve in respect to the modern world," to have halted on the threshold of the nineteenth century "with a kind of disgust" (46). The outside appears to him in its modern grayness (51), but the rooms provide relief and gratitude "for their luck," thanks to "all they had escaped knowing, all that, in the vulgarest of ages, they had succeeded in not inheriting" (66).

496. G. Meyrinck, *Der Golem* (Frankfurt am Main and Berlin: Ullstein, 1990), 32.

497. Ibid., 50, 57–58, 103–9, 114 (the dress dates to the seventeenth century on p. 191).

498. Ibid., 12, 14–16; cf. 34, rain and rust; 110, "dead things" also in the doorless room; 266, a reminiscent-affective among "small worthless old stuff."

499. Ibid., 258–61. Cf. the other legend, that of the "wall of the last streetlamp" (with its alchemical vision and its millenary precious-potential): 186, 191–92.

500. *A Contribution to the Critique of Political Economy:* K. Marx and F. Engels, *Collected Works,* vol. 29 (London: Lawrence and Wishart; New York: International Publishers; Moscow: Progress Publishers, 1986), 386. The rarity of diamonds in the earth's crust makes them the ideal matter to exemplify the directly proportional relationship between labor time and value: cf. Marx, *Capital,* 33–34 (part I, chap. 1, section 1).

501. Is. XLIV 3: *Biblia Sacra,* 915.

502. *Prometheus Bound,* lines 500–3: *Aeschyli Tragoediae,* 122.

503. *Carm.*, III, III, 49–50: *Horati Opera,* 57. Cf. *Sat.*, I, I, 41–42, and *Carm.* II, II, 1–4: ibid., 134, 34. For the topos, cf. *Ovidii Metamorphoses,* 5–6 (book I, lines 137–42); *Anicii Manlii Severini Boethii Philosophiae Consolatio* (Turnhout: Brepols, 1957), 29 (II 5, lines 26–30); Spenser, *Poetical Works,* 101 (*Faerie Queene*, II, VII, oct. 17).

504. Lines 267–94: Ronsard, *Oeuvres complètes,* 8:191–92. The praise of gold does not open the poet to the charge of avarice, because whoever keeps and cherishes "some moldy treasure in a rusty chest" loses the favor of the Muses: lines 27–32, 181.

505. Cf. lines 42–48, 53–56 of the quoted ode (*Horati Opera* 57).

506. VII, oct. 11, lines 5–8: Camões, *Obra completa* (Rio de Janeiro: Aguilar, 1963), 165.

507. X, oct. 93, lines 5–6: ibid., 250.

508. X, oct. 102, lines 5–7: ibid., p. 252.

509. VII, oct. 31, lines 5–7: ibid., 169. Vasco da Gama in his turn celebrates the riches of Portugal to the king of Calcutta, VII, oct. 61: 176.

510. VI, oct. 9, lines 1–2: ibid., 141.

511. VII, oct. 30, lines 7–8: ibid., 169.

512. Lines 447–60: L. de Góngora y Argote, *Obras completas* (Madrid: Aguilar, 1956), 646.

513. Lines 430–34: ibid., 645.

514. Lines. 433–36, 441–48: ibid., 631.

515. Lines 523–28: Calderón de la Barca, *El gran teatro del mundo. El gran mercado del mundo* (Madrid: Cátedra, 1987), 56–57 (and cf. lines 865–82, avarice; lines 529–30 and 739–51, the other sins: 67–68, 57, 63–64).

516. *The Tragical History of Doctor Faustus,* act I, sc. I: Chr. Marlowe, *The Complete Plays* (Penguin, 1986), 268, 270. *The Jew of Malta* appears "in his counting house, with heaps of gold before him"; that for his frenzied, perfidious cupidity the accumulation of "infinite riches in a little room" is real, does not take away from the verbal magnificence of the satisfaction expressed; lines 19–38, ibid., 349 (cf. lines 68–70, and, for the ghostly attraction of the treasures, lines 24–27; ibid., 400, 368). *Tamburlaine the Great,* in his turn, whose verbal magnificence soars higher as his frenetic and inexhaustible ambition becomes greater, can imagine that the kings of India will dig their mines to please him (part I, lines 263–65: ibid., 149).

517. Act I, sc. II: W. Shakespeare, *Comedies* (Oxford University Press, 1911), 22–23.

518. *The Snake (Lo Serpe),* II, 5: Basile, *Lo cunto de li cunti,* 340.

519. Cf. *Les Mille et une Nuits: Contes arabes traduits par Galland,* vol. 1 (Paris: Garnier, 1960), 1:186–88, 204–6, 214–16. In the most renowned nineteenth-century fairytale, Andersen's little mermaid — seeking the witch of the sea behind the abyss of the Maelstrom — does not see anything which may be called semipositive in the depths of the sea. Among white skeletons, and another mermaid suffocated by polyps, there are only "ships' rudders and sea-chests": H. Andersen, *Fairy Tales,* trans. L. W. Kingsland (Oxford University Press, 1997), 74.

520. XV, oct. 24–32: Tasso, *Poesie,* 371–74.

521. XIV, oct. 39, and cf. oct. 35–41, 48: ibid., 352–54, 355–56.

522. II, lines 622–23: Milton, *The English Poems* (Oxford University Press, 1946), 149.

523. I, lines 670–722: ibid., 130–31. The predicate of the treasures is a reminiscence of

that of the *melius situm* gold in Horace, see above, note 503. Cf. the sulfur and niter unearthed in the sky by the rebellious angels, to feed a diabolical artillery (VI, lines 472–91, 509–20: ibid., 242–43).

524. Book III, chap. XII: Grimmelshausen, *Simplicissimus,* 312–16. In the episode of the Mummelsee, the king of the elves allows Simplicius to see the bed of the Pacific, with pearls and precious stones of other proportions (book V, chap. XVI: 531). In the added sixth part, a story of treasure and ghosts does not contribute many images (*Continuatio,* chaps. XV-XVI: 655, 657–58).

525. Lines 4892–94: Goethe, *Faust,* 293.

526. Ibid., 294.

527. Ibid., 318–19, 322, 324.

528. Lines 6058–60: ibid., 328–29.

529. Lines 6111–14ff.: ibid., 330.

530. Lines 5032, 5034: ibid., 296–97. Mythological hints of hoarded gold, and of sunken treasures, may also be found in the *Classical Walpurgis Night* of act II: 361, 375, 389.

531. Shelley, *Poems,* vol. 2 (Everyman's Library, 1953), 210–11. The spirit of the earth lies sleeping within a multiple traveling orb, and the rays shine forth from a star on its brow, 209. There was some precious-potential among Prometheus's gifts to humanity: "And gems and poisons, and all subtlest forms / Hidden beneath the mountains and the waves" (act II, sc. IV: 183). Since it refers to a revenge planned by the tyrant Jove on the eve of his downfall, I would consider the beautiful comparison which shows how this revenge would fall into the void as venerable-regressive: "As rainy wind through the abandoned gate / Of a fallen palace" (act I: 154).

532. R. Wagner, *Das Rheingold,* orchestra score (London: Eulenburg, n.d.), 105–25 (from the indication *Gleichmässig ruhig im Zeitmass* to the entrance of Alberich's voice).

533. The most representative synthetic passage is where Loge informs the Gods: "It is a trinket / In the depth of water, / For the joy of laughing maidens: / But, if into a round / Ring it is forged, / It helps a man to supreme power, / Conquers the world for him": R. Wagner, *Das Rheingold* (Stuttgart: Reclam, 1958), 38 (sc. II).

534. Ibid., 43.

535. *Götterdämmerung,* Prologue: R. Wagner, *Götterdämmerung* (Stuttgart: Reclam, 1958), 12.

536. Villiers de L'Isle-Adam, *Oeuvres complètes* (Paris: Bibliothèque de la Pléiade, 1986), 2:582–88, 599–602, 610–18, 653–54. The reminiscence of *Faust* (which is not mentioned among the others by the editor, 1412–13) seems precise to me in the sentence: "the underground belongs to the State" (618); cf. "The earth is the Emperor's": Goethe, *Faust,* 294 (line 4938).

537. Chap. X: Scott, *Ivanhoe,* 115. Scott develops a reminiscence of Shakespeare's *Merchant of Venice*: "Would scatter all her [my vessel's] spices on the stream, / Enrobe the roaring waters with my silks" (Shakespeare, *Comedies,* 594).

538. Chap. XVIII: Dumas, *Le Comte de Monte-Cristo* (Paris: Bibliothèque de la Pléiade, 1981), 190–203, and cf. earlier 86–87, 131, 134–39, later 205, 208.

539. Chap. XXIV: ibid., 249–58, and cf. earlier 235–36, 239–45, later 259, 261–62. A surreal, exotic precious-potential, of artisanal design and marine maturation, would be worth quoting, in chap. LXII: cf. 771.

540. Book I, chap. II: Dickens, *Our Mutual Friend,* 13.

541. Part I, chap. VII: ibid., 84–85; later 185, 213, 299–304, 478, 480, 487–90, 497–98, 502; finally, 779. In the happy ending, for good Mrs. Boffin, it is as if the money of the old man had again started to shine in the sun "after a long, long rust in the dark": 778.

542. Ibid., 481–84; cf. 466–67, 473–74.

543. Part V, book II, chap. IV: Hugo, *Les Misérables,* 1292.

544. R. L. Stevenson, *Treasure Island* (London and Glasgow: Collins, 1953), 106, 107, 125, 147.

545. Ibid., 186.

546. Ibid., 48–49 (the contents of Billy Bones's chest), 242 (reference).

547. Ibid., 226–27 (I am referring, in *The Gold-Bug,* both to the place-marking skull and to the two buried skeletons, cf. IV, 31, notes 241, 243).

548. Stevenson, *Treasure Island,* 242–43.

549. Part VI, chap. XXXIII: ibid., 240.

550. Part I, chap. VI: J. Conrad, *Nostromo* (Penguin, 1963), 55, 56–57.

551. Ibid., 61, 97, 180.

552. Part I, chap. I: ibid., 17–19; and cf. the references to the legend, all spoken or thought by Nostromo: 215, 217, 221, 379, 431, 435. The only references in the authorial voice, 412, follow the solitary death—caused by the treasure—of Martin Decoud, who weighs himself down with four ingots to sink into the sea.

553. Part III, chap. XIII: ibid., 457–58.

554. Part II, chap. II: A. Malraux, *Oeuvres complètes,* vol. 1 (Paris: Bibliothèque de la Pléiade, 1989), 425 (423–32); cf. 374, 377, 391–92, 396, 416, 418–20.

555. Matt. V:15. We see the dictate turned upside down in a passage by Schopenhauer. If we could contemplate all the great individuals and events whose development was hindered by chance or by error, "we would shiver and weep over the lost treasures of whole ages of the world"; but we would be wrong, because the source of the Will is inexhaustible, and in the world of its appearances there is neither real loss nor real gain (*The World as Will and Idea,* Book III, 35: A. Schopenhauer, *Die Welt als Wille und Vorstellung,* vol. 1 [Zurich: Diogenes, 1977], 237–38).

556. LXII, lines 39–41: *C. Valerii Catulli Carmina* (Oxford University Press, 1958), 52.

557. Tractate I, chap. IX: Dante Alighieri, *Tutte le opere* (Florence: Sansoni, 1965), 118.

558. *Decameron,* VI, 2: Boccaccio, *Tutte le opere,* 4:538.

559. Racine, *Oeuvres complètes,* 1:1018 (act I, sc. I, lines 48–560), 1075–77 (act V, sc. II, lines 1584–93, 1649–54), 1080 (sc. V, lines 1715, 1727), 1083 (sc. VI, line 1778).

560. Act II, sc. IX, lines 778–85: ibid., 1046.

561. A. Manzoni, *Tutte le opere,* vol. 1 (Milan: Mondadori, 1957), 255–57 (variations of these lines: 258–59).

562. Act II, sc. I: J. W. Goethe, *Weimarer Dramen,* vol. 1 (Munich: dtv, 1975), 162. Pearls are the good at the bottom of the sea which also has its evil in the self-revealing parallel which the lyrical "I" makes in Heine's *The Book of Songs:* "My heart much resembles the sea, / Has storms and ebbs and flows, / And many a beautiful pearl / Rests in its depth" (*The Return Home* [*Die Heimkehr*], VIII: H. Heine, *Buch der Lieder* [Munich: dtv, 1983], 112).

563. L. Da Ponte, *Memorie. Libretti mozartiani* (Milan: Garzanti, 1976), 104. In Balzac's *The Lily of the Valley* (*Le Lys dans la vallée*), the images almost go no farther than the title (Balzac, *La Comédie Humaine*, 9:987); it is in *Louis Lambert* that the mystical intellectual compares himself, and is compared, to an unknown flower: Balzac, *La Comédie humaine*, vol. 11 (Paris: Bibliothèque de la Pléiade, 1980), 652–92.

564. Baudelaire, *Oeuvres complètes*, 1:17. Cf. *Baudelaire e il "valore dormente"* (*lettura di "Le Guignon"*), in Orlando, *Le costanti e le varianti*, 295–307. In *Benediction* (*Bénédiction*), the first poem of *Les Fleurs du Mal*, "the lost jewels of ancient Palmira / The unknown metals, the pearls of the sea" will not be enough for the compensatory diadem which God prepares for the poet (Baudelaire, *Oeuvres complètes*, 1:9). In *Satan's Litanies* (*Les Litanies de Satan*), the devil is aware of sleeping valuables: "You who know in which corner of the envious earth / The jealous God has hidden the precious stones, / [. . .] / You whose clear eye knows the deep arsenals / Where the people of metal sleep buried . . ." (124).

565. S. Mallarmé, *Oeuvres complètes*, 1:21 (17–22). In the supreme evanescence of Mallarmé's last sonnet, *To Nothing But the Urge to Travel* (*Au seul souci de voyager*), a spectral Vasco da Gama is greeted: his journey is not towards, but "beyond" a "splendid and turbid" India. What the monotonous cry of a bird around his topsail announces, without changing his course, is "A useless deposit / Night, desperation and precious stones." The uselessness of the precious-potential is no longer that in which the value of poetry is affirmed, but that of all to which poetry denies value, in the metaphysical "smile" with which Vasco moves onward (ibid., 40–41).

566. Chap. II: Woolf, *Orlando*, 93–94. The following example from Aragon, *The Holy Week*, is even closer to reversion into the opposite category: "The rest will be nothing but the dirt of men which the Atlantic may well roll endlessly over, on the shores of Portugal or elsewhere, with the remains of the great depths, the pierced shells, the seaweed and the debris of distant wrecks" (L. Aragon, *La Semaine sainte* [Paris: Gallimard, 1958], 433; chap. XIII).

567. *Within a Budding Grove*, II: Proust, *À la recherche* . . . , 2:100. This passage abbreviates, reduces to its quintessential form, an earlier one: M. Proust, *Jean Santeuil* (Paris: Bibliothèque de la Pléiade, 1971), 470–71.

568. Joyce, *Ulysses*, 50. The unconnected relative clause is the slightly inaccurate mental quotation of a line from *King Lear*, act IV, sc. VI, line 22.

569. Ibid., 63. See above, note 517. Line 167 of *Lycidas*, "Sunk though he be beneath the watery floor," is close to the category (like other wonderful lines of the poem, 155–59, 164, 172, 174–75) through the imagery of death by drowning and transcendental survival (Milton, *The English Poems*, 38–39).

570. Joyce, *Ulysses*, 45. *De signatura rerum* (*The Seal of Things*) is the title of a work by Jakob Böhme.

571. Ibid., 55–56.

572. Breton, *Oeuvres complètes*, vol. 1 (Paris: Bibliothèque de la Pléiade, 1988), 676.

573. Gadda, *Romanzi e racconti*, 2:531. In Malraux's *Days of Hope*, revolution and civil war alter cultural contexts by bringing them close to nature once again: objects of small or great value are recovered, piled up, and thrown out of houses, respectively because of the opening of the pawn shops, requisitions, and demolitions (Malraux, *Oeuvres complètes*, 2:40–43; 118, 122, 385; 298, 431–32).

574. B. Constant, *On the Thirty Years War. On Schiller's Tragedy, Wallenstein and on German Theater* (*De la guerre des Trente Ans. De la tragédie de Wallstein, par Schiller, et du théatre allemand*), in *Oeuvres* (Paris: Bibliothèque de la Pléiade, 1957), 900.

575. II, lines 140–42, 151–54 (136–76): *Vergili Opera,* 50–51.

576. V, lines 36–39, and cf. 34–35: ibid., 13. Close imitation in Sannazzaro, *L'Arcadia,* Prose V, in *Opere,* 91.

577. *Carm.,* I, XXII, lines 5–8: *Horati Opera,* 20.

578. Lines 15–16, 16–22: ibid. See above, note 505.

579. IX, lines 382–84: *Lucani De Bello Civili,* 239.

580. IX, lines 402–3, 405–6: ibid., 240.

581. IX, lines 605–6: ibid., 247. Cf. IX, lines 435–37, 696–97 (241, 250).

582. IX, lines 310–11 (303–47): ibid., 236 (236–38).

583. IX, lines 619–99, 700–33, 734–838: ibid., 248–56.

584. *Inf.* XXIV, lines 82–91: Dante, *La Divina Commedia,* 277–79.

585. *Inf.* XIII, lines 1–9: ibid., 148. Cf. lines 698–700 of Seneca's *The Madness of Hercules,* and cf. IV, 29, note 223.

586. XXXV, lines 1–4: Petrarca, *Rime, Trionfi,* 51.

587. II, oct. 41: Ariosto, *Tutte le opere,* 1:32 (and cf. VIII, oct. 19; ibid., 151). Italics are mine. The landscape has become traumatically strange, horrid, and deserted in Luigi Tansillo's sonnets inspired by the volcanic eruption of 1538 at the Campi Flegrei: that the place was one of the entrances to hell in the classical imagination renders the search through the uninhabited space, driven by amorous desperation, even more extreme. The images here too (cf. IV, 6) arise from the series of vocatives: "Strange cliffs, hard mountains, tall shuddering / Ruins, and stones uncovered and naked under the sky ... / [...] / Proud horror, silent forests, and many / Black grassy caves opened in cracked rocks: / Abandoned, sterile deserts / Where wandering beasts fear to go ..." (*Lirici del Cinquecento* [Turin: Utet, 1976], 521–22; cf. the other sonnet, 518, and the octave which turns the theme towards the solemn-admonitory, 522).

588. VIII, oct. 67: Ariosto, *Tutte le opere,* 1:163.

589. XV, oct. 51: Tasso, *Poesie,* 379.

590. XIII, oct. 2–3 (later 4–49): ibid., 321 (pp. 321–34). Cf. III, oct. 56, lines 7–8: ibid., 74.

591. *Hamlet,* act I, sc. II, lines 133–37: Shakespeare, *Tragedies,* 637.

592. *Othello,* act IV, sc. II, lines 56–66: ibid., 917–18.

593. Jornada III: Tirso de Molina, *El Burlador de Sevilla,* 283–85.

594. *Soledad primera,* lines 212–13, 218–21: Góngora, *Obras completas,* 639.

595. Night I: Young, *The Poetical Works,* 1:10; cf. *Boethii Philosophiae Consolatio,* 32 (II, 7, 4–5, prose).

596. Part II, lines 105–6, 119–26: S. T. Coleridge, *Poems* (Oxford University Press, 1960), 190–91 (186–209).

597. Book IV: Mickiewicz, *Pan Tadeusz,* 105–6 (105–7).

598. Chap. LXX: Melville, *Moby Dick,* 319. We have another extremity to which the novel's theme pushes the imagination in a prehistoric chronology—or rather, before the time which "began with man": "I obtain dim, shuddering glimpses into those Polar eternities; when wedged bastions of ice pressed hard upon what are now the Tropics; and in all the 25,000 miles of this world's circumference, not an inhabitable hand's breadth of

land was visible. Then the whole world was the whale's . . . ," 467–68 (chap. CIV). On the surface and in the present, instead, the grandeur of the Pacific Ocean produces euphoria, ibid., 492–93, 499–501.

599. Conrad, *Youth: A Narrative. Heart of Darkness. The End of the Tether* (Everyman's Library, 1971), 61–62, 63–64. The absurd, which is also linguistic, turns the precious-potential of ivory, which the natives sometimes bury, into a "fossil," 115–16.

600. Chap. I: ibid., 70–71.

601. Ibid., 121, 130–31.

602. Chap. II: ibid., 92–93; and cf. 86.

603. *Russia in 1839* (*La Russie en 1839*), Pétersbourg, 12 juillet 1839, au soir: Marquis de Custine, *Lettres de Russie* (Paris: Gallimard, 1975), 104.

604. Chap. I: Zola, *Les Rougon-Macquart*, 1:5–9.

605. Ibid., 9–17, 187 (the small door and the old key of the grandmother, cf. 44–45), 192–98, 206–9; 309–15.

606. G. Keller, *Die Leute von Seldwyla* (Frankfurt am Main: Insel, 1987), 83 (71–150); cf. 71–72, 79–80, and after Manz's purchase of the field and the reduction of Marti's usurpation to a small triangular plot of land, on the stones of which "a forest of nettle and thistle" blooms again: 82–83, 85.

607. Worn-realistic of the furnishings which the Manzes transport to the town, of the apartments where they live and keep a tavern, of the wife's clothes: ibid., 90, 91, 92; of the hundred-year-old villa degraded into a tavern, where the poorest people dance on feast days: 137–38. But the description of the field in front of Marti's house, at its end, strays into the sterile-noxious: it is now almost the same as that "field without an owner from which all misfortune originated," 101–3, and with narrative displacement from one place to the other, 104–5.

608. Ibid., 105–6, 145.

609. Act I: M. Maeterlinck, *Théatre*, vol. 2 (Geneva: Slatkine, 1979), 122–23.

610. Act III, sc. III: ibid., 55–57.

611. With intervening scenes: in *Pelleas*, cf. the one cited with act II, sc. III (ibid., 38); in *Alladine,* with act IV (152, 154–55, 157–58) where the opposite conversion later occurs (159). In direct succession: in *Princess Maleine* (*La Princesse Maleine*), ibid., 1:23–25; in *Ariadne and Bluebeard* (*Ariane et Barbe-bleu*): 152–56. The castle of *The Death of Tintagiles* (*La Mort de Tintagiles*) is gloomy, with no conversion, ibid., 3 (1979): 207.

612. Part II, chap. XI: J. Roth, *Werke in drei Bänden*, vol. 1 (Cologne and Berlin: Kiepenheuer und Witsch, 1956), 142.

613. Ibid., 117–19, 155.

614. Ibid., 124–27, 146–51 (list of alchemical and chemical instruments, 149).

615. Part II, chap. IX: ibid., 119.

616. Part II, chap. XII: ibid., 163.

617. "April Eight, 1928": W. Faulkner, *The Sound and the Fury* (Penguin, 1970), 258.

618. Sartre, *Oeuvres romanesques*, 184, 187–89.

619. Ibid., 186–87.

620. I. Calvino, *Le città invisibili* (Turin: Einaudi, 1984), 111, 117–18, 119–21. The following quotations and references are to be distributed according to the three names of the cities.

621. Book III, canto III, oct. 50, lines 3–8: Boiardo, *Orlando innamorato*, 2:543.

622. G. Benn, *Gedichte in der Fassung der Erstdrucke*, 22.

623. Balzac, *La Comédie humaine*, 5:505–6.

624. Poe, *Poetry and Tales*, 269–71. The mixture receives less emphasis in the Venetian palace of a short story published three years earlier, *The Assignation;* it is described thus: "Little attention had been paid to the *decora* of what is technically called *keeping*, or to the proprieties of nationality" (204–5).

625. For instance, the *Invitation to Travel* (*Invitation au voyage*), both in verse, and in prose; *The Double Room* (from which I have already quoted the subsequent rupture, V, 9): Baudelaire, *Oeuvres complètes*, 1:53–54, 301–3, 280–82.

626. Part II, chap. II: Flaubert, *Oeuvres*, 2:188.

627. Ibid., 50, 408.

628. Part II, chap. VI; part III, chap III: ibid., 288, 395.

629. Chap. XI: O. Wilde, *The Works* (London and Glasgow: Collins, 1952), 102–15: I refer particularly to pp. 102, 108, 109, and cf. 106 for the scents, 106–7 for strange musical instruments, 107–9 for jewels, 109–10 for embroidery and upholstery, 110 for ecclesiastical clothes. Dorian has already said: "I love beautiful things that one can touch and handle. Old brocades, green bronzes, lacquer-work, carved ivories, exquisite surroundings, luxury, pomp, there is much to be got from all these" (91).

630. Book I, chap. I: D'Annunzio, *Prose di romanzi*, 1:16–18.

631. Book III, chap. I: ibid., 232–33.

632. Book I, chap. III: ibid., 67; and cf. 63–70, the entire scene of a first auction (for the second, which closes the novel, see above, note 338), and an object like the death's head–clock: 68–69. Lord Heathfield's library, 319–24, is a pornographic-sadistic variation on the library in *Against Nature*. Some moments when the prestigious-ornamental merges with the venerable-regressive idealizing the *ancien régime*: 167 and 291, eighteenth-century music and jewels, respectively.

633. Chap. XVIII: H. James, *The Spoils of Poynton* (Penguin, 1978), 153; cf. 12 (the patience of a collector and money), 20 ("things," which are the whole world for her), 54 (the "deep morality" she aspires to), 105 (the suitable background for her image), 166 (her greatness). Thus for Fleda the final loss of the objects is a "gain to memory and love," which makes her a participant in a "religion," and the objects themselves cannot be reduced to personal possessions: 169–70.

634. Poynton is "the record of a life," ibid., 18, and cf. 13, 24–25; if its silence is "charged with memories," that "everything" that is in the air is "every history of every find, every circumstance of every struggle," 43. The most clearly identified object is rendered almost precious-potential, since it was acquired "by an odd and romantic chance — a clue followed through mazes of secrecy till the treasure was at last unearthed," 54 (Mrs. Gereth is called a "treasure-hunter" on p. 18).

635. Chap. I: ibid., 7–8 (already on p. 5, the pair "ugliness and stupidity"; 14, Mona's "taint" is almost indecent to mention); and cf. 26, the kitsch in the winter garden at Waterbath. On the side of the semipositive category, fleeting imagery on pp. 19, 43, 52; 57, "the sweetest Louis Seize [. . .] — old chastened, figured, faded, France."

636. The father's collection is listed as old calendars, matchboxes, cheap ashtrays, etc., ibid., 104 (but insofar as it certainly constitutes a precedent, he may be mistaken in

believing that his daughters have "not inherited" his taste): 105, 110, 113; and cf. the tea set, 112. For the sister's house cf. 128, 129, 139, 169, and with Mrs. Gereth visiting: 171–72.

637. Ibid., 38, and cf. 15–16, 25.

638. Ibid, 57: according to Fleda it is the "wrong" which turns the objects "to ugliness"; or which lessens the quality of the age of Louis XVI, 76. But the glimpse, in a flash, of the "great gaps" at Poynton, 52, is consistent with the certainty that there was nothing to be rejected there, while, at Ricks' house, the too cluttered objects are "too much like a minuet danced on a hearth-rug," 53–54. The first occurrence of "the spoils" is on p. 63.

639. Chap. XXI: ibid., 178–81, and cf. 40 for the first impression produced on both women by Ricks' house. On p. 172 the words concerning Mrs. Gereth; she assimilates things and persons while writing to Fleda: "with nothing else but my four walls, you'll at any rate be a bit of furniture," 177.

640. Chap. III: L. Tolstoy, *Collected Shorter Fiction*, trans. L. and A. Maude and N. G. Cooper, vol. 2 (New York and Toronto: Knopf, 2001), 2:131–32.

641. *Letters on the London International Exposition, (Lettres sur l'Exposition Internationale de Londres)*: S. Mallarmé, *Oeuvres complètes*, vol. 2 (Paris: Bibliothèque de la Pléiade, 2003), 365–79; *London International Expositions (Expositions Internationales de Londres)*: ibid., 382–88. A more extensive analysis and quotations can be found in my paper "Le due facce dei simboli" (see above, note 310), 331–36.

642. Mallarmé, *Oeuvres complètes*, 2, converging passages: pp. 366 and 385.

643. Ibid., converging passages: pp. 374 and 386.

644. Ibid., 367; and cf. 385.

645. Ibid., 366; and cf. 377.

646. M. Proust, *Jean Santeuil* (Paris: Bibliothèque de la Pléiade, 1971), 434–36.

647. *Worldly Figures: The Duke d'Étampes (Figures mondaines: Le Duc d'Étampes)*: ibid., 723–25.

648. *John Ruskin*: Proust, *Contre Sainte-Beuve* (Paris: Bibliothèque de la Pléiade, 1971), 129–38, and particularly 135–37.

649. *Swann's Way*, I, I: Proust, *À la recherche . . .*, 1:39–40. In the hotel at Doncières, an eighteenth-century building, the narrator is spared the suffering hostility he feels for unfamiliar rooms, thanks to an "excess of luxury, useless to a modern hotel, and which, excluded from any practical purpose, had acquired a kind of life in its inactivity"; thus, the irrationality of *ancien regime* buildings becomes enjoyable: "corridors which retraced their own steps, the pointless comings and goings of which crossed continuously, vestibules as long as galleries and as decorated as drawing rooms," "innumerable small rooms which, quite unmindful of symmetry, ran around it, stunned, escaping in disorder up to the garden . . ." (*The Guermantes' Way*, I: Proust, *À la recherche . . .*, 2:381–83). The room in *Days of Reading (Journées de lecture)* was beautiful because it was "full of things which could not serve any purpose and which timidly disguised, to the point of making their use extremely difficult, those which served some purpose" (Proust, *Contre Saint-Beuve*, 164–66).

650. *Clarisse*: P. Morand, *Nouvelles complètes* (Paris: Bibliothèque de la Pléiade, 1992), 19–22 (13–28). In the first pages of Natalie Sarraute's *The Planetarium (Le Planétarium)*, a female consciousness, leaving no room for the voice or vision of the

author, suffers the single and dual problem of realizing the prestigious-ornamental and avoiding the pretentious-fictitious: for her own house, she reproduces a small oval door of a cathedral cloister, to replace a door in bad taste, and then has the handle and metallic plaque removed because of their vulgarity (N. Sarraute, *Oeuvres complètes,* 341–50, 354–56).

651. W. Benjamin, *The Arcades Project,* trans. H. Eiland and K. McLaughlin (Cambridge, Mass.: Harvard University Press, 1999), 19.

652. Part I, chap. 1, section 4: Marx, *Capital,* 61–73.

653. Cf. XXXII, 1; XXXVI, 4; XLVII, 7; LVI, 10; LVII, 1; LVIII, 1: Pétrone, *Le Satiricon:* 28, 32, 45, 54, 55. In the last two passages, where first Asciltus's, then Giton's irrepressible laughter causes the wrath of a freedman of Trimalchio, his protests make their feeling of superiority explicit: "Maybe you do not like the elegances of my master? Certainly you are more magnificent, and used to giving better banquets" (54).

654. XXXVIII, 4: ibid., 33.

655. LX, 1–4; LVI, 7–9; LXX, 2: ibid., 58, 53–54, 69.

656. XXXIII, 3–8: ibid., 28–29.

657. XXXV, 1–4: ibid., 31.

658. XXXVI, 1–2: ibid., 32.

659. XL: ibid., 36–37.

660. XLIX: ibid., 46–47.

661. LX, 4–6: ibid., 58–59.

662. LXX, 4–6: ibid., 70.

663. XXXIV, 8–10: ibid., 30–31.

664. LXXI, 5–11: ibid., 71–72.

665. Gautier, *Récits fantastiques,* 179–81.

666. Ibid., 181–93.

667. I, lines 53–75: Browning, *The Ring and the Book,* 2–3. Notice the topos of color (V, 7) in the tenth quoted line. Cf. I, lines 661–78: 16–17.

668. Part I, chap. XVI: Ch. Dickens, *Little Dorrit* (Oxford University Press, 1963), 192–93.

669. Part I, chap. V: Flaubert, *Oeuvres,* 2:102. My emphasis. The literary descendants of this building, or of this Flaubertian archetype of a stylistically hybrid building, do not seem to be limited to Gadda. Specifically, I have found in Gozzano's story *The Diva's Sandals* (*I sandali della diva*), "a villa of atrocious taste: Anglo-Swiss-Chinese taste" (in Gozzano, *Poesie e prose,* 547; cf. 549–50, 552–53, for more of the pretentious-fictitious contaminated with the reminiscent-affective, as in the lines commented upon in II, 4); in Tournier's novel *Erlkönig,* the *Jagdhaus* of William II, "which had elements of the Chinese pagoda and the Swiss chalet," and cf. the context (M. Tournier, *Le Roi des Aulnes* [Paris: Gallimard, 1970], 211).

670. Part I, chap. IV: Flaubert, *Oeuvres,* 2:69.

671. Part III, chap. IV: ibid., 412. It is moral disgust, not yet the sense of kitsch, which leads to the contrast between the town cemetery and the purity of the country cemetery in a poem by Pushkin (1836): *When, lost in thought . . . ,* cf. Pushkin, *The Poems, Prose and Plays,* 87.

672. Chap. II: G. Flaubert, *Bouvard et Pécuchet* (Naples and Paris: Istituto Univer-

sitario Orientale–Nizet, 1964), 310–11; and cf. 311–13, 315–17. Rousseau's first tomb was in Ermenonville.

673. Ibid., 363–64.

674. Ibid., 361.

675. Ibid., 301–2.

676. Ibid., 275.

677. Chap. VII: Maupassant, *Romans,* 798.

678. Act II: F. García Lorca, *Obras completas* (Madrid: Aguilar, 1957), 1287 (1261–1348).

679. Act II: ibid., 1292–93; cf. 1302.

680. K. Mansfield, *34 Short Stories* (London and Glasgow: Collins, 1972), 135–36 (114–48).

681. Schulz, *The Street of Crocodiles,* 67 (66–74).

682. Part V, chap. 11: Morante, *Menzogna e sortilegio,* 470–71.

683. *Introduzione alla storia della mia famiglia,* chap. I: ibid., 12. In the fake letters of the cousin, the liberties taken with geography and history transform the globe into a single metropolis (part VI, chap. IV: ibid., 592–93).

684. Part II, chap. XVI: A. Cohen, *Belle du Seigneur* (Paris: Bibliothèque de la Pléiade, 1988), 157–58.

685. Chap. V: Woolf, *Orlando,* 209–10; cf. 267. In Lawrence's *Lady Chatterley's Lover* ([Penguin, 1961], 154), the chest of Japanese lacquer is from the same epoch; within it toiletries, equipment for writing, sewing, and first aid, fit together "like a puzzle"—nonfunctional of the functional: "The thing was wonderfully made and contrived, excellent craftsmanship of the Victorian order. But somehow it was monstrous . . ."

686. Act II, sc. I: J. Giraudoux, *Théatre complet* (Paris: Bibliothèque de la Pléiade, 1982), 24. In the previous narrative version, *Siegfried and the Man from Limoges (Siegfried et le Limousin),* there is a corresponding passage with other imagery: J. Giraudoux, *Oeuvres romanesques complètes,* vol. 1 (Paris: Bibliothèque de la Pléiade, 1990), 678–79.

687. In *Towards the Charterhouse (Verso la Certosa):* C. E. Gadda, *Saggi Giornali Favole,* vol. 1 (Milan: Garzanti, 1991), 309–12 (previous version with slight variations, *The Years [Gli Anni],* ibid., 231–34). Milan itself is elevated to the capital of the pretentious-fictitious of buildings in two prose works from *The Wonders of Italy (Le meraviglie d'Italia): Map of Milan—Nobility of Buildings (Pianta di Milano—Decoro dei Palazzi),* ibid., 57–60, and *Booklet (Libello),* 87–96 (a few lines, or the two paragraphs, concerning the roofs of the city would be sufficient: 58, 93).

688. Chap. XIII: Moravia, *Gli indifferenti,* 277–79; cf. for the word "mannequin" with thematic value: 42, 145, 333.

689. E. Waugh, *The Loved One* (Penguin, 1951), 41–65.

690. Ibid., 35, 98, 63–64.

691. Ibid., 63.

692. Ibid., 35.

693. S. Beckett, *The Complete Dramatic Works* (London: Faber and Faber, 1990), 138–40, 143; only on this last page is the sentence entirely reconstructed. The satisfaction of the "addition to one's knowledge, however trifling" that each day brings, tells us

precisely that the advertising universe never provides any addition. Cf. 144, 158–59; and the reading of a medicine label, promising "instant improvement": 141.

694. Ibid., 160. The trash cans in which the grandparents live in *Endgame* produce on stage a surreal metaphoric desolate-disconnected (ibid., 96, 98, and passim).

695. Ibid., 148; cf. 151, 160, 162.

696. Ibid., 146, 157–58; 154–55.

697. Ibid., 154.

698. Ibid., 151.

699. Ibid., 162.

Chapter VI. Some Twentieth-Century Novels

1. Alain-Fournier, *Le Grand Meaulnes* (Paris: Émile-Paul, 1913), 41–42: a piece of clothing "such as the young men who danced with our grandmothers, in the balls of the 1830s, must have worn" (part I, chap. 7).

2. Cf. ibid., 141 (II, 4), 252–53 (III, 7–8), 320 (III, 16); and V. Hugo, *Théatre complet*, vol. 1 (Paris: Bibliothèque de la Pléiade, 1963), 1251–52, 1301–6 (*Hernani*, act III, sc. 7; act V, scenes 3–5).

3. Alain-Fournier, *Le Grand Meaulnes*: 30 (I, 5), 48–62 (I, 8–10), 109 (I, 17); 36 (I, 6), 43, 46–47 (I, 7), 124–25 (II, 2), 139 (II, 4), 148 (II, 5), 157–58 (II, 7), 164–69 (II, 9).

4. Ibid., 64 (I, 11). An immediate association with the preparation for the large summer feasts at La Ferté where the young boy had been brought up: 64–65 (I, 11).

5. Ibid., 66–68 (I, 11). Again the carriages: 105–7, 110 (I, 17) (and Yvonne's, 207 [III, 2]).

6. Ibid., 73–74 (I, 13). And young men's attire "of a long time ago," "of the beginning of the century," stored not within the furniture of the place, but in a pile of cardboard boxes.

7. Ibid., 74–75 (I, 13).

8. Ibid., p. 87 (I, 15). And cf. later the identification of the ruins as a "maze of edifices," 199 (III, 1), of the demolished dwelling as "so strange and complicated," 241 (III, 6). Here there are more images of abandon and destruction, 88–89 (I, 15), of rust, 97 (I, 16).

9. Ibid., 63 (I, 11).

10. Ibid., 86 (I, 15).

11. Ibid., 90–91 (I, 15).

12. Ibid., 198–200 (III, 1); and cf. 205 (III, 2), 229 (III, 4), 241–42 (III, 6), 251–52 (III, 7), 270–74 (III, 10).

13. Ibid., 202–4 (III,2), 215–17 (III, 3), 290–91 (III, 12), 294–95 (III, 13). Cf. the barren courtyard of Meaulnes' house: 223–24 (III, 4), and the suburban sadness of Valentine's, 318 (III, 16).

14. Ibid., 1–3 (I, 1); later on it will be said that the boys are well acquainted with "the meanders and passages of the great dwelling," 116 (II, 1).

15. Ibid., 7–9 (I, 1); the nocturnal background for the great revelations of Augustin to François is a large garret, where they can feel the penetrating "silence of the three attics," 40 (I, 7). Frantz, during his brief stay in school, distracts the class by distributing "strange treasures," "precious objects": 127–29, 135 (II, 4).

16. Meaulnes' unauthorized departure is from a farm that "is a great feudal building": ibid., 23 (I, 4); he spends the night in a "dark building," an "abandoned sheep-fold," where "a smell of mold" prevails, 61 (I, 10). In Sainte-Agathe, at night, the boys are first drawn by ambush into a "maze of little alleys and dead-ends," then "into a wide space from which the way out was blocked by the courtyard of a long-abandoned farm": 121–22 (II, 2).

17. All the more so as Procida was an island of "poor fishermen and peasants, and its rare *palaces* were all, inevitably, either convents, or churches, or fortresses, or prisons": E. Morante, *L'isola di Arturo* (Turin: Einaudi, 1957), 16–17 (chap. 1).

18. Ibid., "imperial gardens," 12; "during and after the wars of the past century," 17; "Bourbon bourgeoisie," 21; "Barbarossa's age," 22 (I); "Turkish corsairs," 311 (VII); "Spanish seventeenth century," 324 (VIII); "centuries old," 12; "For approximately two hundred years," 14; "nearly half a century ago," 17; "at least three centuries ago," 16; "For more than two centuries," 16 (I); "maybe for the last fifty years," 325 (VIII).

19. Ibid., 77 (II); and cf. "another Castle," 299 (VII). This can be seen from the house, 15 (I).

20. Ibid., 37 (I), 304, 306–9, 311–12 (VII).

21. Ibid., 304, 312 (VII).

22. Ibid., 15 (I); and cf. 245 (V).

23. Ibid., 309 (VII), 22 (I).

24. Ibid., 24 (I), 325 (VIII).

25. Ibid., 21 (I).

26. Ibid., 25 (I).

27. Ibid., 90, 95–96, 122–23 (II), 153 (III), 211–12 (IV).

28. Ibid., 16, 21–22, 24 (I), 92 (II) (light bulb), 238 (V) (pistol), 324–25, 332 (sofa), 353 (VIII).

29. Ibid., 20 (I); cf. 136 (III): "our house . . . with its historical dirt and its natural disorder . . ."

30. Ibid., 22–23 (I).

31. Ibid., 23 (I); cf. 15 (I), the "turquoise lizard."

32. Ibid., 22, 39 (I), 204 (IV). Cf. 126 (II), the transfiguration of winter as a "magnificent fiefdom": and in its great night, the transfiguration of the house into a den, of the island into a forest with its hidden summer animals.

33. Ibid., 22 (I). The comparison between the house and a cave is derogatory for Nunziatina's mother, but not for Arturo: 210–11 (IV); the worn-realistic in a real cave, 360 (VIII).

34. Ibid., 100–103 (II).

35. That does not forbid a feeling of compassion for the poor imprisoned youths: ibid., 77–78 (II).

36. Ibid., 84 (II), 160 (III); 92–94 (II). Much less naïve, but vaguely in the same sense, the mention of the house's furniture with an illusory feminine reference, 17 (I).

37. Ibid., 170 (III), 197 (IV), 296 (VI).

38. Ibid., 329, 367–68 (VIII). The Munich Agreement of 1938.

39. W. Faulkner, *Go Down, Moses and Other Stories* (Penguin, 1960), 200 (IV). According to Faulkner's leitmotiv-like practice, the building is characterized with the

same and different words on 200 above, and on 229–30 (IV). To the incompleteness of the building there corresponds the false authority of the twin sons, who shut the blacks in it at sunset, only to let them out the other side during the night.

40. Ibid., 230–31, 232 (IV) (and the "broken shutter-less window," 231); cf. in *Was*, 10–11, 13–14 (II).

41. Ibid., 211 (211–14) (IV). Another instance of an African-American worn-realistic: the clothes of Sam Fathers, 156 (I); in *The Fire and the Hearth*: 59 (chap. 1, 3), 76–77 (II, 2), 81 (II, 3); in *Go Down, Moses* (which gives the title to the collection): 281, 285 (II).

42. Ibid., 229, 230, 232, 233–34 (IV). In *The Fire and the Hearth*, the precious-potential is culpable and doomed to failure: the black cousin Lucas Beauchamp ends up renouncing the search for buried treasures: 35–36 (I, 1), 63–64 (I, 4), 67–68, 68–69 (II, 1), 72, 78 (II, 2), 84 (III, 1), 100 (III, 2), 105–6 (III, 3).

43. Ibid., 194–95 (IV); cf., in *The Fire and the Hearth*: 66 (II, 1), 80 (II, 3).

44. Ibid., 223–24 (IV).

45. Ibid., 196 (IV).

46. Ibid., 195, 199 (IV); reprise of the leitmotiv, 204 (IV).

47. Ibid., 195, 199, 206, 207, 220, 228 (IV).

48. Ibid., 132 (I).

49. Ibid., 204 (IV).

50. Ibid., 220–21 (IV).

51. Ibid., 145 (I).

52. Ibid., 152, 158 (I).

53. Ibid., 156 (I).

54. Ibid., 250 (I). Cf. the recycling of death in the earth: 249–50 (V), and, in *The Old People*, 144 (III). Another form of writing incomprehensible to whites is, in *Pantaloon in Black*, the one that marks the disorderly tombs with insignificant scraps, "but actually of a profound meaning," 107 (I).

55. Ibid., 154 (I).

56. Ibid., 160 (II).

57. Ibid., 147 (I); reprise of the leitmotiv, 148.

58. Ibid., 257; cf. 136 (I); 240–41, 243–46 (V); 253, 256–59.

59. Ibid., 267–68.

60. Ibid., 226 (IV): the poem is *Ode on a Grecian Urn*. In *The Fire and the Hearth*, Lucas's criticism is that Ike has "turned apostate to his name and lineage" by renouncing the land, 36 (I, 1) (and that the cousin — contrary to what is narrated in *The Bear* — was able to "take the land from the true heir," from him, 40).

61. In his beautiful *Memories of Childhood* (*Ricordi d'infanzia*), the writing of which (1955) interrupted the drafting of the novel, the love for the patrician home destroyed by bombing is concentrated within this same effect of light: G. Tomasi di Lampedusa, *Opere* (Milan: Mondadori, 1995), 345–48, especially 353–54. It also appears in the first datable memory, 339.

62. Tomasi di Lampedusa, *Opere*, 40 (part I): "The house was serene, light and ornate; most importantly it was his"; ibid. (I): "The rooms of the administration were still deserted, silently lit by the sun through the closed shutters"; 49 (I): "down, around the villa, the luminous silence was deep, extremely lordly"; 69 (II): "Everything was perfectly tidy:

the pictures in their heavy frames were dusted, the gilt of the ancient bindings shone their discreet fire, the high sun made the gray marble surrounding every door resplendent"; 71 (II): "he passed through the hall of tapestries, by the blue one, by the yellow one; the lowered shutters filtered the light, in his study the Boulle clock ticked softly. 'What peace, my God, what peace!' "

63. Ibid., 22–23 (I), 77 (II).

64. Ibid., 233 (VII).

65. Ibid., 29 (I).

66. Ibid., 26 (I).

67. Ibid., 34, 35 (I); equally unharmed are the female convents on 85–86 and 88–91 (II).

68. Ibid., 32 (I), 128 (III).

69. Ibid., 243 (VIII).

70. Ibid., 206 (VI) and 69 (II). Never insensible to a literal, dynastic loyalty to the past, Don Fabrizio sums up, in his own contradictions, all the characters of his kind: he mistreats his son and scolds his wife for their scandalized reaction to Tancredi (54–55 [I], 100–2 [III]); he vacillates in looking down on his reactionary brother-in-law and on Ferdinand II himself (25, 28, 55 [I]; 46–47 [I], 108–9 [III]); he suffers for the lesson in loyalty he receives from Don Ciccio Tumeo (113–14 [III]). We will return to the daughter Concetta later on.

71. Ibid., 209 (VI). Cf. 221 (VI): "The light of dawn filtered in through the joints of the shutters, plebeian . . ."

72. Ibid., 44 (I): "the sides of the Monte Pellegrino burnt, burrowed and eternal like poverty"; 57 (II): "desperate cliffs that sorghum and broom could not console"; 103–4 (III): "rounded top over rounded top, discomforted and irrational"; 225 (VII): "the deceitful smile of the Strait, immediately gainsaid by the burnt Peloro hills . . ."

73. Ibid., pp. 172–73 (IV).

74. Ibid., 177–78 (IV). Cf. the boats, 35 (I), the biscuits, 109 (III); nothing in the house of Father Pirrone, 182 (V).

75. Ibid., 150–51: almost everything could be quoted: 148–54 (IV); 161 (IV): "this house is as big as our Duomo!" Cavriaghi says. The palace had been introduced on 68 (II); it is possible to trace a hidden thematic foreshadowing of the episode, including the ignorance of the owner, in the presentation of the prince's desk on 42 (I).

76. Ibid., 148, 153 (the carillons), 153–54 (IV).

77. Ibid., 150–51 (IV): "Tancredi wanted Angelica to know the whole palace"; 156–57 (IV), and cf. 97, 119–20 (III). The cultivated, seventy-year-old Angelica will set the castles of the Loire against "the Baroque disquietude of the palace of Donnafugata for which she felt an inexplicable aversion": 247–48 (VIII).

78. Ibid., 229 (VII), and cf. 228–29 (VII).

79. Ibid., 244–45, 256–57 (VIII).

80. G. García Márquez, *Cien años de soledad* (Buenos Aires: Editorial Sudamericana, 1969), 169 (X), 192 (XI), 253 (XV), 285 (XVII); Pilar Ternera has an analogous impression, 333 (XIX).

81. Ibid., 13–14 (I), 32 (II); the experimentation continues: 36, 37, 38 (II), 39 (III).

82. Ibid., 9–10 (I).

83. Ibid., 18 (I): a reference to Stevenson, cf. V, 12, note 545. Only the antiquated raft of José Arcadio Segundo will succeed in navigating the river up to Macondo: 169–70 (X). What the first José Arcadio encountered sailing around the world is also archaic: "a sea dragon in whose belly the helmet, buckles, and arms of a crusader were found," "the ghost of Victor Hugo's corsair ship, with its sails torn by the winds of death, the masts eroded by sea roaches," 84 (V): this is the legend mentioned above in II, 15; and Hugo's poem referred to is *The Peasants on the Sea Shore* (*Les Paysans aux bords de la mer*), III, in *The Legend of the Centuries* (*La Légende des Siècles*, XXVII). Aureliano Babilonia reaches adolescence "without knowing anything of his own time, but with the fundamental notions of a medieval man," 301 (XVIII). The plaster St. Joseph, filled with gold coins, is a precious-potential of miraculous unearthing and malevolent effect, which will cost the last José Arcadio his life: 168 (X), 209–10 (XII), 278–79 (XVI), 314, 317 (XVIII).

84. Ibid., 193–95 (XI-XII).

85. Ibid., 178–79 (XI).

86. Ibid., 179–81 (XI).

87. Ibid., 185–86 (XI).

88. Ibid., 183 (XI), 305 (XVIII), and cf. 179 (XI).

89. Ibid., 308 (XVIII).

90. Ibid., 63, 65 ("fresh lilies") (IV), 80 (V), 99 (VI).

91. Ibid., 222 (XIII), and cf. 121 (VII), 150 (IX), 225 (XIII); p. 236 (XIV).

92. Aureliano seeks, and cannot find, "the place where his affections had putrefied" in his heart, 152 (IX). In Rebeca's heart, solitude "had reduced to ashes the sleepy mounds of nostalgic rubbish," 190 (XI). Fernanda's heart of "compressed ashes . . . crumbled at the first attacks of nostalgia," 308 (XVIII).

93. *The Unconscious:* S. Freud, *The Standard Edition of the Complete Psychological Works*, vol. 14 (London: Hogarth, 1957), 187.

94. Cf. V, 10, note 391.

95. Marquez, *Cien años de soledad*, 160–61 (X), 209 (XII), 224 (XIII), 301–2 (XVIII); and cf. pp. 68 (IV), 262, 264–65 (XV) (the young officer, a stranger to the family, sees in the same way as the colonel had done), 284–85 (XVII), 304 (XVIII).

96. Ibid., 189–90 (XI); and cf. pp. 119 (VII), 139 (VIII).

97. Ibid., 139 (VIII), 292 (XVII).

98. Ibid., 17–18 (I); the crossing of this "enchanted region," and the discovery of the galleon, are mentioned periodically (pp. 129 [VIII], 169 [X], 199 [XII], 250 [XV], 280 [XVI], 323 [XIX]). The crossing of the plateau by Aureliano Segundo is translated throughout into metaphors of inward experience, 181 (XI).

99. Ibid., 151 (IX), 220 (XIII).

100. Ibid., 268, 280 (XVI), 283–84 (XVII), 303–4 (XVIII), 345, 346 (XX), and passim. For the functional activity of Ursula against the sterile-noxious, cf. pp. 15 (I), 157 (IX), 284 (XVII); Amaranta Ursula continues it: 293 (XVII), 318 (XIX). Santa Sofía de la Piedad leaves when the ants enter the house, 304 (XVIII).

101. Ibid., 292 (XVII); in one of the visions of Macondo in ruins, "the inhabitants felled by memories," 324 (XIX).

102. Ibid., 350 (XX).

103. M. Lowry, *Under the Volcano* (Penguin, 1963), 251 (chap. VIII); 256, 259 (IX).

104. Ibid., 58 (II), 119, 116 (IV), 242 (VIII). The ruins of a Greek temple: 331–32 (XI).

105. Ibid., 9–11 (I).

106. Ibid., 11 (I).

107. Ibid., 127 (IV); cf., for the park and annexes, 115–16 (IV).

108. Ibid., 20 (I).

109. Ibid., 20–21 (I).

110. Ibid., 70–71, 72–73 (III). Cf. 69 (II), the hingeless gate, tossed to the ground and half-hidden. Both the expression "wreck" and the Edenic parallel are Yvonne's: 78 (III), 101–2 (IV). When the time comes to move towards death, the Consul will say that he has made up his "melodramatic little mind, what's left of it," 315 (X).

111. Ibid., 133 (V); and cf. 131–32 (V). On p. 92 (III): "Vague images of grief and tragedy flickered in his mind . . ."

112. Ibid., 19 (I).

113. Ibid., 59–60 (II); cf. 339–40 (XII).

114. Ibid., 158–59 (VI).

115. Ibid., 294 (X).

116. Ibid., 362 (XII).

117. For the first hypothesis: ibid., 15 (I) (plow in mute supplication); 287 (X) (springboard like a forgotten victim); 327 (XI) (restaurant that is a death and a ghost). For the second hypothesis: 23 (I) (antediluvian remains and abandoned lighthouse); 50 (II) (sea wrecks); 244 (VIII) (refuse under a stone cross); 281 (IX) (greenhouse filled with weeds); 318 (XI) (abandoned plows and cars); 339 and 352–53 (XI) (dead scorpion). Referring directly to the protagonist: the British Consulate, squalid and closed, 223 (VII); the menu, stained and bent, on which he has written chaotically: 329, 330–31 (XI).

118. Ibid., 21 (I), 62 (II), in the road that leads to the Consul's villa; p. 70, in his garden. The previous slope is "little better than a rubbish heap with smoldering debris," 59.

119. Ibid., 21 (I). And he calls Quauhnahuac, where on every side the abyss lies in ambush: "dormitory for vultures and city Moloch!"

120. Ibid., 134 (V).

121. Ibid., 236 (VIII), and cf. 375–76 (XII). A fourth vision, 104 (IV), is of Hugh together with Yvonne; as is an olfactory presentiment: "Rotting vegetation lay about them, and there was a smell of decay; the *barranca* couldn't be far off," 322 (XI).

122. Ibid., 311 (X).

123. F. Kafka, *Der Prozess* (Frankfurt am Main: Fischer, 1958), 76 (chap. III).

124. Ibid., 103, 111 (V).

125. Ibid., 44–45 (II).

126. Ibid., 121 (VI).

127. Ibid., 169 (VII).

128. Ibid., 197 (VII).

129. Ibid., 197–98 (VII).

130. Ibid., 127–28 (VI). Cf. the passage in Hoffmann, IV, 25, note 169.

131. Ibid., 127 (VI). K.'s execution will take place in an open but deserted space, outside the city but, strangely, too close to it as well: "So quickly did they come out of the city, which in that direction fitted almost without transition to the fields. A small stone quarry, abandoned and deserted, was close to a house still entirely belonging to the city," 270 (X).

132. Ibid., 98 (IV), 248 (IX) (and cf. 253 [IX]).

133. Ibid., 80, 83–84 (III), 170–71 (VII). The two golden buttons of the court ushers seem torn "from an old officer's coat," 77 (III); the clerks are dressed "very badly and unfashionably," 88 (III).

134. Ibid., 140 (VII), 218–19 (VIII) (and cf. 233 [VIII]).

135. Ibid., 174, 187–88, 195–96 (VII).

136. In the room of the first hearing his sight is clouded by a smoky and dusty atmosphere, ibid., 53, 59–60, 61 (II); in the attic the unbreathable air makes him sick: 85–86 (III) (while the other clerks, accustomed to it, feel ill in the relatively fresh air of the stairs, 92 [III]); the air is inexplicably, increasingly dense on the stairs and in the painter's room, and worse in the adjoining chanceries: 170, 178–79, 186–87, 194, 198 (VII); and cf. 209 (VIII).

137. Ibid., 47 (II).

138. Ibid., 169 (VII).

139. Ibid., 54, 56 (II); 67; 80; 86 (III); 196 (VII).

140. Ibid., 67 (III), 111 (V).

141. Ibid., 67 (III).

142. C. Samonà, *"Fratelli" e tutta l'opera narrativa* (Milan: Mondadori, 2002), 9 (chap. II). Cf. 5 (I): "Ever since, my father being dead, my elder brothers have left one at a time"; 6 (I): "still damp stains of removed pictures, traces, perceived only by us, emptied of decent furniture"; "The furniture would diminish in number from year to year [...] as a result of sales and departures . . ."

143. Ibid., 5–6 (I).

144. Ibid., 7 (I).

145. Ibid., 27 (VII), 86–88 (XX). For his part, the narrator can gently threaten to hide in a "secret room and . . . remain there for ever," 29 (VII); one of his last illusions is "that of being invited to a decisive congress that is about to be held in some distant room of the apartment," 92 (XXI).

146. Ibid., 7–8 (I).

147. Ibid., 9 (II), 50–60 (XV).

148. Ibid., 12–13 (III), and cf. 77–78 (XIX).

149. Ibid., 15 (III), 20 (IV).

150. Ibid., 10 (II); cf. pp. 42–43 (X), and for the exterior (vicious circles or straight lines) 77–78 (XIX).

151. Ibid., 19 (IV). A parallel confirmation: the sentence mentioned in the previous note ends with a third direct object: "wide grassy gardens *rich in* centenary trees," 10 (II) (my emphasis).

152. Ibid., 18, 20 (IV), and cf. 87 (XX). Samonà, a Hispanist, knew that the historical infante Don Carlos — very different from Schiller's and Verdi's character — died demented at twenty-three: the allusion overdetermines the quotation from the libretto bearing his name. The literary digressions treat badly another aged father, Geppetto: 18–19 (IV).

153. Ibid., 24, 25–26 (VI).

154. Ibid., 36–37, 39 (IX). A more flexible compromise is represented by the "oblique timetables, deviating and yet perfect, competing with those of calendars and clocks," 42 (X). Outdoors, and with an even readier renunciation: "If I could fix my brother's escapes

into a compulsory scheme, if I could myself count them and plot them beforehand . . . ,"
74 (XVIII).

155. Ibid., 19–20 (IV), 37–39 (IX).

156. Ibid., 82–83, up to 84–86 (XX) (but cf. also 40–42 [X]).

157. Ibid., 45 (XI). Visions and noises from outdoors, hitherto inaccessible and out of
focus, had preceded the description of the house, 5 (I).

158. Ibid., 32–33 (VIII), 44–46 (XI).

159. Ibid., 47 (XII).

160. Ibid., 48–51 (XII–XIII). On the sides of the straight avenue "risen from a demolition of the old town," it is the old town itself that attracts the sick brother with its
"mysterious curves, narrow nooks, grayness," 49 (XII).

161. Ibid., 64–66 (XVI). The woman possesses the city-space as well: "guide or cox-
swain of our routes: expert, then, of roads, houses, markets, short cuts, small squares,
alleys, crossings and unusual meeting places," 72 (XVII). Metaphorical parallels between
the sick brother and a dog are repeated, 14 (III), 28, 29 (VII), 34 (VIII), 56 (XIV), before
the narrator asks him jokingly: "and if you were the lame dog?" 61 (XV); all the more
terrifying are the uncertainties of memory concerning the killing of the animal, and the
loss of the page which told of it: 67–68 (XVI), 82 (XX).

162. Ibid., 33 (VIII), 84 (XX); he prefers "small stones, pebbles, notebooks, food
remains, slender grass blades, even books," 58 (XV), to money; and cf. the series of gift
objects that the woman sends through him, among which are shells, pendants, and sea
stones, 70 (XVII). The texts and tales "reduced to narrative poultices" are "like toys
attacked and dismembered in their most obvious mechanisms," 17 (IV). The idea of
trauma (impossible to locate, between psyches and cells) enters into the characterization
of his language: "lucid fragments of a speech that has lost its compactness in consequence
of a distant, terrifying explosion"; "the connections have been broken, the meanings
inverted and perverted, but luminous splinters of that ancient linguistic treasure still rise
to the lips," 21 (V).

163. *Autumn Day (Herbsttag)*, in *The Book of Pictures:* R. M. Rilke, *Das Buch der
Bilder* (Frankfurt am Main: Insel, 1976), 37–38.

164. *Foreboding (Vorgefühl):* ibid., 42.

165. R. M. Rilke, *Die Aufzeichnungen des Malte Laurids Brigge* (Frankfurt am Main:
Insel, 1982), 14–19. He mentions fleetingly that the houses of his two grandparents have
passed into other hands: 25, 92, 124.

166. Ibid., 38–39.

167. Ibid., 107.

168. Ibid., 36–37.

169. Ibid., 44–45; he has no one to save him from kneeling for a quarter of an hour,
trying to stop smoke from pouring out of the heater. As a foreshadowing of exile, among
his childhood memories there is a collision one evening with a gigantic man whose hostile
face and fist he catches sight of: he transforms the road into that of "a foreign city, a city
where nothing is forgiven": 176–77.

170. Ibid., 84–90.

171. Ibid., 13, 14–18. The grandmother had been indignant that her daughter-in-law,
dying before her, had claimed precedence: 100–101.

172. Ibid., 124–25, 125–28, 129–30. The dead man's features are "tidied, like the furniture in a guest room from which someone had departed," 125; the narrow rooms "seemed to be offended like all rented apartments where someone has died," 129. The paper on which the testimony about the king had been copied has been "for a long time folded, undone, broken along the edges," 129.

173. Ibid., 25–26.

174. Ibid., 31–33; cf. 33–35, and 93–97 for the children's search for the picture of the deceased, in the gallery or in the attic. The grandfather calls a woman who has been dead for a century and a half "our little one," 30; dictating his memories, he sees the character he was speaking of materialize, 123.

175. Ibid., 73–74, 74–76. The souls of those who have worked out her enthralling lace designs, according to the mother, will not have gone to heaven, but into the lace itself: 110–12.

176. Ibid., 110–17. The remotest memory is that of an extremely thin hand which one night stretched towards the child's from a wall under the table: 77–80.

177. Ibid., 14–15; cf. 110 (a remnant of lace among broken toys), 141 and 144–47 (the sound of a tin lid, and things which are driven to imitate men by human maladjustment), 148–49 (the placing of a bookmark between pages), 184 (the emptiness of a jewel box).

178. Ibid., 9; cf. 88 (the dark and turbid essence of the broken bottle), 129 (the "persuasive" scent of a letter of the father), 167 (the rooms when schoolchildren wake up, "full of a coldness that smells of gray").

179. Ibid., 41–43.

180. Céline, *Voyage au bout de la nuit. Mort à crédit* (Paris: Bibliothèque de la Pléiade, 1962), 506–7.

181. Ibid., 516. The uninterrupted analepsis begins with the character of the ancient Aunt Armide: "In the shadow, behind Aunt Armide, behind her armchair, there was all that is finished," relatives and literary characters and politicians and the imperfect subjunctive, 533–35. The project for the electrification or demolition of the passage des Bérésinas is, on the other hand, a promise that does not come true, 766–67.

182. Ibid., 541–42. The dirt of the passage, a true sterile-noxious of the city, matches the sadness of the profession, 557; the father is forced, "the worst humiliation for a man of his education," to scrape excrement from the ground in front of the shop, 562, 563. The exposition of 1882, whose remains stand to the hubbub of the past in a miserable relationship worthy of the solemn-admonitory, had only served to "annoy the small merchants," 565.

183. Ibid., 543; 542, 551–52; 570–73, 591. The father's rages tear trinkets to pieces, 553; there are trinkets and jewels in the nightmares of the sick child, 577; the mother mourns the dead grandmother when she sees the goods, 595. After her death, the merchandise in the shop has become "fake, and miserly, and pitiful," 588.

184. Ibid., 746–47, letter of the father: "A variation, a brutal leap, absolutely unexpected in the course of fashion, has reduced our hopes to nothing [. . .]. Without any warning sign, the favor of the clientele has resolutely turned away, has literally started escaping from these articles, for other vogues, other whims . . ."

185. Ibid., 760–61. As early as Zola's *The Ladies' Paradise* (*Au Bonheur des dames*), of 1883, the department store that offers everything crushes the small, specialized mer-

chants who resemble artisans: É. Zola, *Les Rougon-Macquart*, vol. 3 (Paris: Bibliothèque de la Pléiade, 1964), 409, 410–11, and cf. 393, 403, 405–15, 470, 588, 591, 597, 599, 734, 755, 762.

186. Céline, *Voyage au bout de la nuit. Mort à crédit*, 648–49. The worst things in the grandmother's shop, by comparison, were roses; and cf. the shop with chinoiserie, where Ferdinand makes a sale, 656.

187. Ibid., 707.

188. Ibid., 731–33.

189. Ibid., 737; 743, 744–45, 751, 752.

190. Ibid., 181–82.

191. Ibid., 788.

192. Ibid., 818.

193. Ibid., 828; and cf. the *bureau tunisien*, 839.

194. Ibid., 851–52.

195. Ibid., 818, 863–64, 865, 887–88, 889–90.

196. Ibid., 888; from the heart of Brittany, they write to Courtial: "Sir, with your equipment, you belong in the Museums": 899–900.

197. Ibid., 852–55; Courtial's booklet read: "Haughty manor houses! Ornaments of our fields, what have you ended in? Dust . . ." The worst hovels he sees from the height of his flights seem to him to be clumsy copies of his project.

198. Ibid., 918–21 and passim until 935ff.

199. Ibid., 953–54, 989–91, 1000–4, 1007–10, 1037–38; Courtial's wife, who still respects him only as an aeronaut, and obstinately denies that the last balloon has crashed (893, 899, 903), has saved the remains of the first from the office attacked by a furious mob: 964–65. Like the sweet Nora Merrywin of the English boarding school, she continues the line of the grandmother's protective and courageous femininity (cf. for instance 980–81).

200. V. Nabokov, *Lolita* (Penguin, 1980), 251–52 (part II, chap. 25): this is the most explicit passage, but cf. the references to Proust, 16 (I, 5), 77 (I, 18), 262 (II, 27) (and the literal quotations from another classic French story of unrequited love, *Carmen* by Mérimée: 276, 278 [II, 19]).

201. Ibid., 39 (I, 10).

202. Ibid., 264 (II, 27). The belated, hypothetical reassessment of her intelligence, the remorse for the lack of genuine communication, are Proustian: 282–83 (II, 32), and cf. p. 149 (II, 1).

203. Ibid., 267–68, 275–76 (II, 29).

204. Pavor Manor, the "festive and ramshackle castle" of Quilty, mirrors for Humbert his own state of drunkenness, ibid., 291–92; Quilty is wearing a dressing gown similar to one of Humbert's, 293; during the struggle, bodies, verbs, and pronouns are mixed, 297; he wants to turn the house and the copyright over to him: 299–300 (II, 35); "I was all covered with Quilty, after the murder," 304 (II, 36). Another, uglier double is Godin, whose pederastic predilection for a tender age is doubly perverse (cf. his "orientally furnished den," 179 [II, 6]).

205. According to this tripartite division of Freud (cf. *Jokes and their Relation to the Unconscious*: S. Freud, *The Standard Edition of the Complete Psychological Works*, vol.

8 [London: Hogarth, 1960], passim), I would say broadly that comic superiority is directed toward the kitsch and the surroundings; humorous self-denial comes at the expense of the memoirist himself; while the jokes, crackling everywhere, serve both aggressive and erotic tendencies — endlessly manipulating the names of Humbert and Lolita.

206. Ibid., 313 (*On a Book Entitled "Lolita"*).

207. Ibid., 34–35 (I, 9), 284 (II, 32) and passim (for instance pp. 53 [I, 11], 125 [I, 28], 272 [II, 29]; and 312 [*On a Book* . . .]).

208. Ibid., 10 (I, 2); 145 (II, 1), 153 (II, 2) (seaside associations, and the memory of the young girl he loved at the time, dance delightfully around the image of Lolita).

209. Ibid., 36–39 (I, 10).

210. Ibid., 38.

211. Ibid., 77–78 (I, 18).

212. Ibid., 44 (I, 11).

213. Ibid., 108 (I, 25). Cf. the list of gifts he buys for her after having revealed her mother's death, 141 (I, 33); the memory effect of a neon sign, 280 (II, 30).

214. Ibid., 146 (II, 1).

215. Ibid., 150 (II, 1).

216. Ibid., 133 (I, 29).

217. Ibid., 118 (I, 27) (the only details mentioned: "a Tuscan rose chenille spread," "two frilled, pink-shaded night-lamps"); 129–30, 131–32 (I, 29). Cf. the "seasick murals," 121 (I, 27).

218. Ibid., 143 (II, 1).

219. Ibid., 143–45 (II, 1). The reprise, with a transposition to the first person plural, is of the famous beginning of the penultimate chapter of *Sentimental Education:* "He traveled. / He learned . . ." (Flaubert, *Oeuvres,* vol. 2 [Paris: Bibliothèque de la Pléiade, 1952], 448).

220. Ibid., 149 (II, 1).

221. Ibid., 156, from 152–56 (II, 2).

222. Ibid., 173 (II, 3). Cf. the tourist guide already "atrociously crippled," "battered," 152 (II, 1).

223. Ibid., 208–9 (II, 16). To avoid going out of his mind, Humbert anonymously gives the reminiscent-affective of all that remains to him of Lolita, "wanton treasures," to an orphanage, 253 (II, 25).

224. Ibid., 267 (II, 28). A "dilapidated . . . farmhouse," a "scarecrow of a house," where she had been forced to spend a summer, had terrified Lolita: 146–47 (II, 1).

225. G. Perec, *La Vie mode d'emploi. Romans* (Paris: Hachette, 1978), 168 (part II, chap. 28), 290–91 (III, 51), 602 (*Epilogue*), and passim.

226. Ibid., 156–58 (II, 26) and passim.

227. Ibid., 20 (I, 1); the stairway as a place where class distinctions are marked will be taken up again, 275–80 (III, 49).

228. As an example, ibid., 306–7 (III, 52); out of lists: 46 (I, 7), 132 (II, 23).

229. Ibid., 138–40 (II, 24); codified items (cf. above IV, 34; V, 15) the Japanese painted scroll placed on the Louis XVI desk, the Dutch-Venetian-Chinese lampshades.

230. Ibid., 318–19 (III, 54).

231. Ibid., 62–63 (I, 11).

232. Ibid., 204 (pp. 203–5) (II, 33). Even when they are not tidied and clean (201–3 [II, 33], 427–28 [IV, 72]) the other cellars are in any case described by lists in which the mixed and casual, rather than the broken and the dirty, are dominant: 403, 404–5 (IV, 67), 452–53 (IV, 76), 554, 556–57 (V, 91). The same thing occurs in the "attempt at an inventory" of things that have been found on the stairs over the years: 406–7 (IV, 68).

233. Ibid., 117 (II, 22). (The "Octobasse" was really invented in the nineteenth century.) We even have a list of relics of the Passion, geographically dispersed, 119 (II, 22); and a list of black magic, with parodically conservative elements such as "hangman's nails," "hyena's kidney stones," "sheep's shoulder blades," "dead donkeys' heads": 193–94 (II, 31).

234. Ibid., 591 (VI, 98).

235. Ibid., 520, 521, 523 (517–23) (V, 87). An overabundance of cultural mementoes is spread evenly throughout the whole book. Nevertheless, in an eight-story building and in six hundred pages, it is no small thing that there are references to Victor Hugo (88 [I, 17]), Napoleon (200 [II, 32]), Mme de La Fayette and Henrietta of England (281 [III, 49]), Sade and Louis XVI (492), Racine the younger (492 [IV, 83]); not counting a living pupil of Schönberg (39 [I, 6]).

236. Ibid., 168–72 (II, 28). Cf. the hallucinatory and quasi-science-fictional imagination of Valène, musing on the catastrophic destruction of the building: 281–82 (III, 49), and on its supposed gradual and endless underground extent: 444–47 (IV, 74).

237. Ibid., 89–91 (I, 17); right from the start he is the one who preserves, who remembers: 35 (I, 4), 36 (I, 5), 48 (I, 8), 75 (I, 13). A silent love is attributed to him, he preserves individual relics of it, and he suppresses them; but the page that contains all of this ends with an abandoned room, where dust and sadness transcend or elude the reminiscent-affective in the sense I am about to identify: 313–14 (III, 53).

238. Ibid., 49 (I, 8) (the pastry cake box is certainly the same one that will be found on the stairs, 406 [IV, 68]). Cf. the final paragraph of a very detailed description of a drawing-room the day after a party, 176 (173–76) (II, 29).

Chapter VII. Praising and Disparaging the Functional

1. IV, lines 71–75; VII, lines 81–135: *Homeri Opera,* vol. 3: *Odysseae Libros I–XII continens* (Oxford University Press, 1917): 55–56, 116–18.

2. I, lines 637–42, 723–27; 421–29: *P. Vergili Maronis Opera* (Oxford University Press, 1969), 123, 125; 116.

3. Chrétien de Troyes, *Érec et Énide* (Paris: Champion, 1981), 202–9: specifically lines 6651–64, 6742–47, 6774–91, 6808–19 (cf. V, 5, note 92). The *Song of the Nibelung* exalts every kind of craft: one example from among the first mentioned is the armor and riding equipment of Siegfried and his companions (III, str. 71–74: *Das Nibelungenlied* [Stuttgart: Reclam, 1997], 28).

4. VIII, lines 114–16: *La Chanson de Roland* (Milan and Naples: Ricciardi, 1971), 20.

5. E. R. Curtius, *European Literature and the Latin Middle Ages,* trans. W. Trask (Princeton University Press, 1953), 183–202 (only the "epic landscape," 200–202, comes close to being a hostile nature).

6. Ibid., 195–200.

7. *Phaedrus*, 229a–b, 230b: *Platonis Opera*, vol. 2 (Oxford University Press, 1901), 225–26, 227; and cf. Curtius, *European Literature*, 187.

8. I, *Introduction:* G. Boccaccio, *Tutte le Opere*, vol. 4 (Milan: Mondadori, 1976), 26, and cf. earlier 22–23; cf. at greater length 235–38 (III, introd.).

9. XVII, oct. 19–20: L. Ariosto, *Tutte le opere*, vol. 1 (Milan: Mondadori, 1964), 377–78.

10. X, oct. 63–64: T. Tasso, *Poesie* (Milan and Naples: Ricciardi, 1964), 264–65.

11. Chaps. LIII, LV–LVII: F. Rabelais, *Oeuvres complètes* (Paris: Bibliothèque de la Pléiade, 1994), 155; and 149–51, 154–60, passim.

12. Orlando, *Illuminismo, barocco e retorica freudiana* (Turin: Einaudi, 1997), 65–87, 87–127.

13. Letter to Guez de Balzac of 5 May 1631: Descartes, *Oeuvres et lettres* (Paris: Bibliothèque de la Pléiade, 1953), 941–43.

14. *The Reveries of a Solitary Walker, VIIth Walk* (*Les Rêveries du promeneur solitaire, VII Promenade*): J.-J. Rousseau, *Oeuvres complètes*, vol. 1 (Paris: Bibliothèque de la Pléiade, 1959), 1070–72.

15. Cf. in Book IV of *The Confessions,* renouncing a visit to the supposed pastoral places where *L'Astrée* is set, after having learned that ironworking was prospering there, ibid., 164.

16. Part II, chap. LXIII: M. de Cervantes, *Segunda parte del Ingenioso Caballero Don Quijote de la Mancha*, vol. 2 (Madrid: Cátedra, 1977), 508, and cf. 491.

17. Concerning the verbal formulations of estrangement, an essential element of a pre-Enlightenment culture contemporary with that of the Baroque, cf. Orlando, *Illuminismo,* 137–42, 150–63.

18. Curtius, *European Literature*, 162–65 (the German word employed is *Überbietung*).

19. *Against Rufinus* (*Contra Rufinum*), book I, line 283 and context; mentioned by Curtius, ibid.

20. Cf. Orlando, *Illuminismo*, 77–78.

21. Lines 23–24, 113–30: V. Monti, *Poesie* (Turin: Utet, 1969), 97, 101–2.

22. Book 1, part I, chap. 22: L. Tolstoy, *War and Peace*, trans. L. and A. Maude, vol. 1 (New York and Toronto: Knopf, 1992), 110.

23. G. G. Belli, *I sonetti*, vol. 4 (Milan: Feltrinelli, 1965), 2097.

24. *The Voices Inside* (*Les Voix intérieures*), I: V. Hugo, *Oeuvres poétiques*, vol. 1 (Paris: Bibliothèque de la Pléiade, 1964), 924 (923–24).

25. Ibid.

26. A. de Vigny, *Oeuvres complètes*, vol. 1 (Paris: Bibliothèque de la Pléiade, 1986), 121–22.

27. Ibid.

28. Ibid.

29. *Salon de 1846:* Baudelaire, *Oeuvres complètes*, vol. 2 (Paris: Bibliothèque de la Pléiade, 1976), 493–96.

30. Balzac, *La Comédie humaine*, vol. 10 (Paris: Bibliothèque de la Pléiade, 1969), 385.

31. *The Communist Manifesto:* K. Marx and F. Engels, *Collected Works*, vol. 6 (Lon-

don: Lawrence and Wishart; New York: International Publishers; Moscow: Progress Publishers, 1986), 487.

32. *Introduction to the Outlines of the Critique of Political Economy* (rough draft of 1857): K. Marx and F. Engels, *Collected Works* (see note 31), 28 [1986]: 47. In keeping with the German original, I have substituted "Greek mythology" for "Greek art" in the citation. Further down: "Is Achilles possible when powder and shot have been invented? And is the *Iliad* possible at all when the printing press and even the printing machine exist?"

33. Marx, *Capital: A Critical Analysis of Capitalist Production, London 1887. Text* (Berlin: Dietz, 1990), 213 (Part III, chap. 10, sect. 3), 288 (IV, 13), 406 (IV, 15, 8, c), 559 (VII, 25, 4), 652, 653 (VIII, 31). The original German verbs of outdoing in the first and third sentences quoted are "übertroffen" and "überbietet," respectively (Marx and Engels, *Werke,* vol. 23 [Berlin: Dietz, 1962], 261, 488–89]; for the last sentence quoted (lacking in the English translation of 1887, cf. 655), I refer to the German text: ibid., 783 (VIII, 31). The expression in quotation marks, in the sixth of the seven passages, inverts a parallel drawn by Diderot's most famous character: this was how the European God, according to a Jesuitical tactic, had supplanted the idols of the colonized countries (Diderot, *Le Neveu de Rameau* [Geneva: Droz, 1963], 82).

34. Sc. III: Wagner, *Das Rheingold* (text) (Stuttgart: Reclam, 1958), 48.

35. Ibid., 51–53.

36. Ibid., 47, 54–55.

37. Act 1, sc. II: Wagner, *Götterdämmerung* (Stuttgart: Reclam, 1958), 25.

38. Wagner, *Das Rheingold,* 55.

39. Ibid., 51; and cf. *Das Rheingold* (score) (London: Eulenburg, n.d), 435.

40. Lines 15–21: Walt Whitman, *Leaves of Grass* (Everyman's Library, 1947), 166–67 (166–74). Jaffa was the port of Jerusalem, and Solomon's Temple stood upon Mount Moriah. A late epigram of Goethe's already directed optimistic envy *To the United States* (*Den Vereinigten Staaten*), and irony for the venerable-regressive towards the European continent: "America, it goes better with you / Than with our continent, the old one, / You have no ruined castles, / Nor any basalt" (W. Goethe, *Poetische Werke,* vol. 1: *Gedichte* [Stuttgart: Cotta, n.d.], 1125).

41. Lines 44 (39–53), 56–57: Whitman, *Leaves of Grass,* 167–68.

42. Lines 36–37, 73–79, 66–68, 95–110, 111–13: ibid., 167–70.

43. Cf. line 140: ibid., 171.

44. Cf. M. Proust, *À la recherche du temps perdu,* vol. 4 (Paris: Bibliothèque de la Pléiade, 1989), 468.

45. Cf. ibid., vol. 1 (Paris: Bibliothèque de la Pléiade, 1987), 100.

46. *The Guermantes Way,* I: ibid., vol. 2 (Paris: Bibliothèque de la Pléiade, 1988), 431–32.

47. Ibid., 432.

48. Ibid., 432–35. The same mythology for the telephone, more briefly, in an episode of *The Captive* (*La Prisonnière*): M. Proust, *À la recherche du temps perdu,* vol. 3 (Paris: Bibliothèque de la Pléiade, 1988), 606–9.

49. *The Cities of the Plain,* II, 3: ibid., 417. Cf. airplanes and valkyries during the war, Proust, *À la recherche . . . ,* 4:337, 338; and the brief mythologizing of the bicycles, *À la recherche . . . ,* 3:675, 678 (the "mythological wheel" of Albertine's bicycle, 4:70).

50. Chap. VI: Woolf, *Orlando: A Biography* (London: Hogarth, 1970), 267; and cf. 55.

51. Ibid., 270.

52. P. Claudel, *Oeuvre poétique* (Paris: Bibliothèque de la Pléiade, 1957), 267 (263–77). Cf. *Richard Wagner: Reverie of a French Poet* (*Richard Wagner: Rêverie d'un poète français*): "All the positive work of the nineteenth century is for the artists, as if it had never been. Examine how few of them have been interested in the present, sympathetic towards what was changing and transforming under their eyes, towards the innovations that the railroad, for instance, brought with it. This is something that only economists and socialists attempted to speak of, as well as they could in their jargon, and no one understood (except Whitman) those brothers who have been placed at our disposal all over the planet" (Claudel, *Oeuvres en prose* [Paris: Bibliothèque de la Pléiade, 1965], 865–66).

53. R. Darío, *Poesías completas* (Madrid: Aguilar, 1968), 807, 808 (797–824).

54. F. T. Marinetti, *Teoria e invenzione futurista* (Milan: Mondadori, 1983), 10–11.

55. F. Pessoa, *Obra poética* (Rio de Janeiro: Aguilar, 1972), 306, 308 (306–11).

56. Ibid., 306. Cf., at the other end of the ode: "Eia the whole past within the present! / Eia all the future already within us! Eia!" 311; the sea is the same sea as when Plato talked with Aristotle, 308–9.

57. Ibid., 306–8. There is even a metaphysical moment, in parentheses, concerning the mystery of the world and that we all must die, 310.

58. Ibid., 308.

59. Ibid., 307; 307 and 309; 308; 309–10.

60. For the translation of Mayakovsky's lines I am indebted to the kindness of Professor Michael Wachtel, of Princeton University.

61. *The Feeling of Nature on the Buttes-Chaumont* (*Le Sentiment de la nature aux Buttes-Chaumont*), chap. II: L. Aragon, *Le paysan de Paris* (Paris: Gallimard, 1948), 144–46.

62. Ibid.

63. Chap. V: H. G. Wells, *The Time Machine* (Everyman's Library, 1978), 54–57.

64. Gadda, *Romanzi e racconti*, vol. 2 (Milan: Garzanti, 1989), 1120–24 (1107–32).

65. In *Cruel Tales* (*Contes cruels*): Villiers de l'Isle-Adam, *Oeuvres complètes*, vol. 1 (Paris: Bibliothèque de la Pléiade, 1986), 577–80. Sologne, at the center of France, is a sandy and marshy region.

66. Ibid.

67. A. Jarry, *Oeuvres complètes*, vol. 1 (Paris: Bibliothèque de la Pléiade, 1972), 467.

68. Ibid., 377.

69. Ibid., 373; 378, 384, 392, 393, 395; 377, 384.

70. Ibid., 369, 373, 376; 382.

71. Act III, sc. II: ibid., 370.

72. Ibid., 380, 382, 384. For the second object, cf. note on pp. 1160–61. The farcical spelling of the word *phynance* is justified by an analogy with the word *physique*.

73. Ibid., 377, 384; 377, 382; 380; 381. The alterations of pronunciation or spelling (*oneilles, phynances, merdre*) are untranslatable.

74. Chap. IV: R. Roussel, *Locus Solus* ([Montreuil]: Pauvert, 1965), 143–45 (113–219).

75. I, 11: Lautréamont and G. Nouveau, *Oeuvres complètes* (Paris: Bibliothèque de la Pléiade, 1970), 64–69.

76. VI, [3]: ibid., 224–25.

77. Ch. Cros and T. Corbière, *Oeuvres complètes* (Paris: Bibliothèque de la Pléiade, 1970), 297.

78. Ibid., 297–98.

Index of Subjects

Bold type indicates extended discussion of a subject.

Ancien régime. See Reminiscent-affective; Venerable-regressive

Avarice, miser, characters of, 30–33, 77, 95–97, 110, 230, 237, 255–256, 259, 299, 305, 310, 312, 340, 455

Categories of images: unified subject of the inquiry, 3–4, 11, 12, 17, 175, 183, 294; classifying: 8, 58, 62–63, 83, 84, 193, 206, 343–344; semipositive or negative categories, primary and secondary functionality, 8–11, 13–14, 61, 84, 101, 115, 158, 172, 325; refused, 101, 102 (*see also under individual categories*); periodizations, 218–219, 344; isolated occurrences and codified recurrences of, 218, 228; contamination between, pure or impure examples, 79, 81–82, 94–95, 98–99, 104, 111, 115, 120, 123, 162–163, 165, 173, 189,

192, 204, 213–215, 217–218, 223–225, 279, 246, 249, 260, 265, 267, 268, 281, 286, 287, 301, 315, 318, 322, 324, 333, 338, 340, 344–45, 347, 351, 355–356, 374, 429, 435, 463; commutation between, 73–76, 79, 172, 175, 192, 226, 230, 303; transformation between, 83–84, 123, 148, 160, 219, 227, 237–238, 370

Collections. *See* Museums, collections

Commodities and nonfunctionality (in images), 9, 15–16, 18–19, 26, 28, 180–181, 184–188, 191, 235, 239–240, 250, 259–260, 301, 302, 307, 314, 323, 331–334, 340, 367–368, 370–371, 373; anticommodities, 15–16, 18–19, 40, 51, 56, 186, 337

Culture and nature (in images). *See* nature and culture

Desolate-disconnected, 10, 19–20, 119–128, 130–135, 162, 229, 255, 263–264, 268, 271–281, 325, 353–356,

Index of Names and Texts

Bold type indicates extended discussion of a text.

437; *Notes from the Underground*,
278, 447
Doyle, A. Conan, 157
Dreyfus, A., 187
Du Barry, Mme, 184–185
Du Bellay, J., 225; *Defense and Illustration of the French Language (La Deffence et l'Illustration de la Langue françoyse)*, 224, 425; *New comer, who search for Rome . . .* , 224, 424; *Regrets*, 425; *Rome's Antiquities*, 87, 411, 425
Du Bos, Ch., 133
Du Cange, Ch. Du Fresne, 195
Dumas, A., *The Count of Monte Cristo*, 310, 456

Eça de Queirós, J. M. de, *Cousin Basilio*, 261, 440; *The Maias*, 444
Edison, Th., 289
Edward IV (of England), 158
Edward VII (of England), 395
Einstein, A., 373
Eliot, T. S., *Rhapsody on a Windy Night*, 123–125, 129, 413; *The Waste Land*, 125, 413
Elisabeth I (of England), 395
Engels, F., 14; *Anti-Dühring*, 14, 408
Ennodius (Magnus Felix), *Panegyric Addressed to the Much Merciful King Theodoric (Panegyricus dictus clementissimo regi Theodorico)*, 423
Epicure, 220
Euripides, *Medea*, 282, 448; *Telephos*, 229; *The Trojan Women*, 219, 423

Faulkner, W., 218, 247; *Absalom, Absalom!*, 218, 423; *The Bear* (in Go down, Moses), 349–351, 466–467; *Light in August*, 218, 279, 423, 447; *Sartoris*, 218, 423; *The Sound and the Fury*, 323, 460
Fénelon, F. de Salignac de La Mothe-, *The Adventures of Telemachus, Son of Ulysses (Les Aventures de Télémaque, fils d'Ulysse)*, 260

Ferdinand II (of Naples), 468
Fielding, H., *The History of Tom Jones, a Foundling*, 215, 237, 422
Fitzgerald, F. Scott, *The Great Gatsby*, 196–199, 343, 420
Flaubert, G., 200, 204, 333, 334, 336, 340, 371, 372; *Bouvard and Pécuchet*, 335, 463–464; *Madame Bovary*, 189–192, 255, 333, 337, 343, 401, 419, 436, 444, 446; *Sentimental Education*, 191, 228, 259, 272–273, 326, 333, 335, 371, 421, 426, 438–439, 446, 461, 463, 475; *A Simple Heart*, 27–29, 30, 42, 180, 203, 327, 409; *The Temptation of St. Anthony*, 189, 248, 433
Fogazzaro, A., *Small Ancient World*, 435
Folengo, T., *Baldus*, 231–232, 285, 427, 449
Fontane, Th., *Effi Briest*, 217, 422
Fontanes, L. de, 243
Fontenelle, B. le Bovier de, *Foreword on the Utility of Mathematics*, VI, 47, 409
Ford, H., 400, 425
Fortini, F., *The Eaves*, 434
Foscolo, U., *On Sepulchers*, 451
France, A., *The Amethyst Ring*, 419; *The Elm-Tree on the Mall*, 186–189, 191–192, 192, 195, 419; *Monsieur Bergeret in Paris*, 443; *The Wicker Dummy*, 419, 435
Franklin, B., *Autobiography*, 197, 420
Franz Joseph I (Emperor of Austria), 199
Frederick I (called Barbarossa, Emperor), 348, 466
Freud, S., 5–10, 52, 56, 58, 60, 157, 202, 399, 448; *Character and Anal Eroticism*, 12, 303, 336; *Civilization and Its Discontents*, 16, 408; *Introductory Lectures on Psycho-Analysis*, 12–14, 16, 408; *Jokes and Their Relation to the Unconscious*, 474–475; *Negation*, 415; *Leonardo da Vinci and a Memory of his Childhood*, 178, 418; *Three Essays on Sexuality*, 153, 178, 416,